THE ENVIRONMENTAL FUTURE

THE
ENVIRONMENTAL
FUTURE

*Proceedings of the first International Conference
on Environmental Future, held in Finland from
27 June to 3 July 1971*

edited by

NICHOLAS POLUNIN

BOOKS
10 East 53d St., New York 10022
(a division of Harper & Row Publishers, Inc.)

First published 1972 by
THE MACMILLAN PRESS LTD
London and Basingstoke
Associated companies in New York Toronto
Melbourne Dublin Johannesburg and Madras
Published in the U.S.A. 1972 by
HARPER & ROW PUBLISHERS, INC.
BARNES & NOBLE IMPORT DIVISION

06–4956261

Printed in Great Britain

Foreword

Finland is resolutely striving to improve the mutual understanding between the different political and cultural systems. The protection of the environment is a suitable field for this purpose, because there are plenty of mutual interests regardless of the stage of development or structure of the area, and because it is vital for all of us; it is a part of the peace policy. Consequently, it seemed natural for us to support the proposal, coming originally from Professor Nicholas Polunin, that we should act as host country for an international conference on the future of the environment which seemed urgently needed.

Admittedly there are many conferences—including rather many on various aspects of the environment—but mostly they deal with the past and present, and so we found particular merit in the idea of having one looking as far as possible into the future. This idea emerged from the 'Environmental Congress' held by the Jyväskylä Arts Festival in July 1970, was furthered by some of my governmental colleagues, and was also favoured by the Finnish National Commission for UNESCO. Consequently, I was pleased to lend my support and advocate that of my government in every possible way.

To my regret I was unable in the end to attend the Conference in person; but I received favourable reports about its progress and general usefulness, as was to be expected from its widely distinguished membership. It was encouraging to note that this first conference of its kind voted unanimously at its conclusion to continue with further such attempts and under the same leadership at intervals of a few years henceforth—which would seem most important in view of the need that politicians and the world's governments are feeling increasingly for guidance in environmental matters.

I deeply hope that we shall rapidly achieve concrete results and all together be able to do more for rational development *and* the environment—for positive change of human existence and the quality of life on earth.

I should like to express my sincere gratitude to the members of the steering and organizing committees and to all others who contributed to the success of the Conference. I also hope that these proceedings will be a useful contribution for the coming United Nations Conference on the Human Environment and for enlightened reading throughout the world.

AHTI KARJALAINEN
Formerly *Prime Minister of Finland*
and Chairman of the Finnish Organizing Committee
Helsinki, 10 January 1972

Contents

Preface

In July 1970 the Jyväskylä Arts Festival held what was called an 'Environmental Congress', to which I was invited as guest speaker. During this lively if mainly local gathering I realized that a conference of far wider scope and clientele would be valuable—especially if it could look into future possibilities of action rather than merely bemoan the present deteriorating situation.

After a good deal of informal discussion, the following resolution was proposed and passed unanimously at the final plenary session:

> 'The Environmental Congress held during 6–11 July 1970 at Jyväskylä, Finland, alarmed at the accelerating changes towards widespread environmental degradation which are threatening the health and very survival of the biosphere and human life as we know them, and realizing that very much more will have to be done to counter these tendencies as human population increases still further, recommends to the appropriate authorities the organization of a high-level International Conference on Environmental Futurology in which leading specialists of global outlook shall prognosticate what in their expert view is most likely to happen and can be done to avoid further catastrophes to man and nature—the results of their deliberations and discussions to be published in dignified book form in good time for the United Nations Conference on the Human Environment to be held in Stockholm in June 1972.'

The idea behind this was that the UN Conference on the Human Environment, being a high-level governmental one, would consist of previously-agreed 'set-pieces', and give little or no opportunity for free expression of views by scientific or other specialists. It consequently seemed important to collect these more enlightened views with special regard to the future, and to make them generally available for consideration by the participants of the UN Conference and by others thereafter.

Among the most active supporters and developers of this theme, which we then called 'Environmental Futurology', were Mr Pentti Sillantaus, Chairman of the Jyväskylä Arts Festival and member of the Finnish Parliament, Mr Hannu Halinen, Secretary-General of the Festival, and Professor Kauko Sipponen, at that time Secretary of State in the Prime Minister's office. It was largely through their energetic help that it was tentatively decided to hold such a global conference on the future of the environment in connection with the Jyväskylä Arts Festival in June–July 1971, although final confirmation had to await the passage of the Finnish national budget which was delayed until early in that year. The sponsors were to be (and ultimately were) the Government of Finland (providing the greatest financial support), the Finnish National Commission for UNESCO (later, UNESCO headquarters also provided valuable backing), and the Jyväskylä Arts Festival.

The Prime Minister of Finland, H.E. Dr Ahti Karjalainen, took on the Chairmanship of the Finnish Organizing Committee*, with Professor Sipponen as Vice-Chairman, and I was made Chairman of the International Steering Committee*, which soon decided on the programme and chose the desired principal participants. H.E. Urho Kekkonen, President of Finland, graciously agreed to be Festival Patron, and Sir Julian Huxley, who was most helpful with wise counsel throughout, served as Conference Scientific Patron. The name of the occasion was changed to the more dignified form of 'International Conference on Environmental Future', and I myself was designated editor of the proceedings.

As was stated in the outline programme, 'The object of the Conference is to bring together, for free discussion in a stimulating atmosphere, as complete a range of leading experts as possible, covering between them all the main aspects of environmental study and implications. Their chief tasks will be (*a*) to give specialist accounts of the global situation in their fields, (*b*) to prognosticate what in their considered opinion is most likely to happen in the foreseeable future, and (*c*) to suggest what can and should be done to alleviate environmental degradation and to avoid concomitant catastrophes to Man and Nature.' Thus in spite of its high-level sponsorship and membership, the Conference was conceived as, and always remained, a private occasion preserving full freedom of speech and expression.

Taking the subject of the environment in the widest sense, we divided it arbitrarily into seventeen sections which would correspond to as many conference sessions extending over five days, and invited outstanding 'keynote' speakers and chairmen/discussion leaders for them. In spite of the shortness of time for organizing, we managed to bring together what was widely remarked on as an impressive group of scientific and other specialist leaders and delegates, actually exceeding our optimum number of participants. Indeed it seemed that if such a gathering could not see far into the environmental future, no other one was likely to be able to do so.

Besides principal speakers and chairmen or discussion leaders of sessions, we had a category of what we called 'roving eminents'—people of eminence who, without being responsible for a particular paper or session, were specially invited and encouraged to take part in the discussions. We also invited certain chosen international organizations to send delegates and nations to send qualified observers†. As Finland was host country, a number of her national or other organizations and institutions were encouraged to send observers, those which did so being listed separately, together with their attending representatives, on pp. 644–6.

The Conference started with transport from Helsinki on the morning of Sunday 27 June when the 'State Luncheon' outside the capital city was addressed by the Finnish Minister of Foreign Trade, H.E. Olavi Mattila, who was also the Minister responsible for Environmental Matters and has since become Foreign Minister. The other speakers on this sunlit inaugural

---

* The composition of these committees is indicated in Appendix II on page 647; each held a series of meetings in its home base of Helsinki and Geneva, respectively.

† All such 'official' participants are listed in Appendix I (pp. 639 *et seq.*).

occasion were Professor Sipponen and myself. Deputizing for the Prime
Minister who was unavoidably absent—prime ministers are apt to have
rather numerous and peremptory calls on their time—Minister Mattila
welcomed the delegates on behalf of the Government of Finland. 'We are',
he said, 'especially happy that there are representatives from very many
nations here' and 'from many international organizations that are responsible to a very great extent for the planning and practical implementation of
protection and development work, and for research associated with environmental issues'; he emphasized that these 'issues are not local [but]
concern all nations—the human community as a whole'. Conveying 'the
good wishes of the Government to this Conference'—which I subsequently
thanked them for supporting so well—Minister Mattila stressed that they
had 'not sought to limit its planning. The purpose has been to ensure a
certain functional framework and . . . to provide the conditions for the
production of very diversified information. This will probably lead, I hope,
to deeper study of the aims and means of environmental protection.' He
further pointed out: 'That the Conference now beginning is basically a
conference of scientists is also very important. It emphasizes the role of
ecology and will give the decision-makers knowledge that they sorely need.
. . . I wish to emphasize, too, that the participants in this Conference are
chiefly [attending as] private individuals, and this will help to create a
climate for the free exchange of opinions and discussion . . . rich in ideas. I
venture to believe in the success of this Conference. However, this will
require vigorous free discussion both at the actual conference meetings and
outside them. I urge you to engage in such debate, and hope that the
Conference will be able to add to our knowledge also of planning and
decision-making at the practical level for solutions to environmental problems and more organized international cooperation.'

As the topics announced for the Conference were often extremely wide,
some speakers naturally preferred to concentrate on limited aspects of the
major theme indicated by the title of the session: in such cases, attempts
were made to have the discussion, or contributed notes or papers, fill in
gaps and round off the major theme—at least so far as time and space
allowed. The keynote papers were mostly presented as spoken résumés which
did not always follow exactly the written versions; this will explain some
apparent discrepancies or incongruities in the discussions.

To keep this book within reasonable bounds, there had to be drastic
compression or deletion of much of what was said and of some of what was
written—especially when extraneous or repetitious. In other cases items were
combined. Any really substantial change from what was actually said
(apart from total deletion) in the published version of the discussions is
indicated in square brackets, while some additional papers or shorter contributions are included at the ends of discussions. Except in one case of an
additional paper of which the author was present, and another which was
added subsequently, the additions were contributed by persons who had been
invited but were unable to attend the actual Conference, and, needless to
say, were not considered in the discussions. This procedure was intended to
improve coverage, particularly by 'filling in' topics to which, for one reason

or another, sessions could not be devoted—including human population as a general theme and three others which are dealt with in the final chapter, namely education, documentation, and legislation.

These 'extended' proceedings were edited as a matter of urgency both for the United Nations Conference on the Human Environment—to whose secretariat they were 'fed' during editing in Geneva—and for Macmillan, the chosen publishers. In this and with expert typing the help of Mrs Dorothy Oliveau is gratefully acknowledged, as is that of my former secretary Miss Janet Taylor and her successor Mrs Avis Hoekemeijer; their diligent support was especially needed in view of the fact that, although during our Conference at Jyväskylä the main problems of language were solved by simultaneous interpretation between English, Finnish, and Russian, the difficulties of transcription from the recording tapes proved rather much for local typists and so two more were flown in from Helsinki. Even then matters got so behindhand that many speakers did not receive their scripts for correction—especially in the second half of the Conference. Finally, instead of being sent out individually to the speakers concerned, all the later scripts were shipped to me together and mislaid for some weeks in transit, whereupon the time lost could only be made up by my working on the spot with what I had, relying on authors' proof-correction as the main stage of checking in many cases.

As indicated on the penultimate full page of the text, at its final plenary session the Conference voted unanimously to continue with further such events at from two- to four-year intervals in the future: consequently we will go on striving to justify our title retained for this book. Although our Finnish friends pioneered in sponsoring the first such conference, with their Prime Minister signing the personal invitations and those to chosen international organizations, they are accustomed to the principle of rotation, and feel that they should 'hand on the torch' to one of the other 'neutral' countries that are now being considered as possible hosts to the next International Conference on Environmental Future.

NICHOLAS POLUNIN
15 chemin F. Lehmann,
1218 Grand-Saconnex,
Geneva, Switzerland,
14 January 1972.

I

INTRODUCTION: BACKGROUND AND HISTORY

Keynote Paper

Future Environments: A Reflective View of the Background

by

FRANK FRASER DARLING*

Vice-President of IUCN and of the Conservation Foundation;
Shefford-Woodlands House, Newbury, Berkshire, England

INTRODUCTION

This Conference is to be about the global environment in the future, which implies that we are not entirely satisfied with it in the present and that we have some inkling of what it was like in the past. The geologists have told us the story of the aeons before there was life, of the spread and recessions of oceans, of the appearance of life, and the rise and fall of great forests in the days long before man came. The palaeontologists have mapped for us the development of living organisms in the past as manifested in the fossil record. The early history of man is still obscure, but we have some notion

* Read by Professor Vero C. Wynne-Edwards, Regius Professor of Natural History in the University of Aberdeen, Scotland, and Chairman of the Natural Environment Research Council of the United Kingdom, in the enforced absence of Sir Frank Fraser Darling through illness.—Ed.

of his activities as a hunter and fire-raiser—positive environment-influencing activities, but probably very slow-acting ones, conducted with complete unconcern for, and lack of knowledge of, any influence of change.

The archaeologist, especially in the last fifty years, has uncovered long-past cultures and has enabled us to see what artifacts were made and of what material, so that we can infer with greater accuracy what influences early man was having on the face of the planet. We have been getting more and more data leading us to be able to understand something of early man's imagination and his conceptions of beauty. Finally, literacy and our ability to decipher early writings have helped enormously our orientation. The thought of past cultures is comprehensible to us in terms of environment.

Love of beauty, natural and contrived, is a characteristic of the human being and we can scarcely question the statement that art is an emanation of nature. Decoration copies natural forms, and if there is some abstraction it is but an expression of cultivation, of subtler suggestion. I have the feeling that in earlier days mankind made space in the wilderness for palace and hovel, but without any thought of an almost moral nature that he was pushing back the wilderness, or that the wilderness was something derogatory to be pushed back. That attitude must have come with a monotheism in which the deity was identified especially with man, and that nature was outside—right outside. Not all cultures took such a view, but there did seem to be an eclectic attitude of borrowing such doctrines as appeared most pleasing. The Chinese created gardens of cunningly contrived natures for private delectation; the Persians walled away the desert or arid steppe to create a *paradiso* within, of running water and flowers. Here was a most cultivated notion of environment for those who could enjoy it.

On a slightly different plane, Kublai Khan established hunting parks where animals could be hunted in more certain profusion than in the wild; Norman kings in England reserved 'forests'—the archaic term for wild wastes—for their special hunting, and the barons reserved 'chases' of the same order. Environment as something contrived or reserved was to do largely with leisure. Gardens were in the same category, satisfying the aesthetic sense. The French had their architectural sensitivity satisfied in the arrangement and control of living plants on a large scale; the English were rather less ordered, and were known for the '*jardin intime*', which the French would copy in some corner of their own.

The eighteenth-century English developed the 'park', which had existed near great houses outside the actual gardens as a remnant of the wilderness; but now it had to be contrived and embellished by the creation of a lake. The landscape architecture of Repton and Capability Brown still survives and is appreciated. The venison was doubtless a valuable addition to the table, but the aesthetic delight in a herd of deer was probably becoming of greater importance. The Royal Parks of London were opened to the populace, who certainly enjoyed them. Today they are treasured by the general public as lungs for the great city—places that give greenness, where you can walk, ride, or just sit during a lunch-hour.

ENVIRONMENT AND TOWNS

Town planning is not new by any means; indeed, classical antiquity seems to have been well ahead of ages that followed. If we take the view that modern times began with the Renaissance, we have beautiful examples, as in Sienna, of cities built to a plan and not just proliferating. The Spanish in the New World built on a much more sensitive environmental basis than the later North American towns which were pushing westward. The pity is that the Spanish sensitivity did not extend to nature, and the puritanically-based North American civilization felt almost that there was divine reward in exploiting forest, prairie, and tundra. Yet the New England town commons evidenced a desire for an orderly and pleasant environment at an early stage. The city of Washington was planned by le Notre and presented an ecologically sound piece of landscape architecture; but commercialism and what I always think of as surface tension has pulled people in at a much faster rate than cultivated men such as Jefferson could ever have imagined. New York, Rome, and London can also be areas of declining quality of environment for the same reason.

You will see that a pleasance of environment is a tenuous thing, some-times sought by an individual for his personal pleasure, sometimes dimly discerned as a public good, sometimes actively imagined and sought by the few for the good of the many. When, in the thirteenth century, a man was hanged in London for burning dirty sea-coal, there was evidently a general consensus of opinion that the city should not be a smoke-laden hollow. But the urbanization which I have likened to surface tension was too much for London, and it was not until the later 1950s that control of air pollution became positive—so that now, less than twenty years after the last great 'London particular', London enjoys 50 per cent more sunshine than in the early 1950s. Here is a big step in the direction of constant, active, public concern for the environment. Equally, the dirty River Thames is much cleaner than it was fifty years ago, despite the vastly increased human population living on its banks. The point is that civic sense has had its impact in addition to some personal desire which might be only selfish. At the same time, the more widely the personal desire for the pleasant environ-ment can be felt and expressed, the more likely are we to get civic action.

GLOBAL CONSIDERATIONS

In this very slight résumé of interest in the environment, ranging from the largely selfish wish to the unfolding public desire for the general good, I have dealt only with the very small and immediate. Concern for the global environment is something very new: it could scarcely have risen in an earlier day when nature was dominant rather than man, when man was relatively few and when scientific knowledge was scanty. Could man possibly have had the foresight, say in the seventeenth century, to have set out to order development to prevent the disasters which have happened since? I do not think so. I think it much more likely that we have had to make all the mistakes we have in begetting a plethora of people and now persuading ourselves that our industrial expansion and exploitation of resources and land are absolutely necessary in order to feed the people, before we could understand our predicament, gain the scientific knowledge to apprehend the damage that has been done, and humbly apply ourselves as a world population to this new concept of the global environment.

Awareness is not yet general, for there are still many pleasant environments left in our world, and through selfishness and apathy there is still a good deal of resistance to any modification of an earlier unbridled exploitation. Nevertheless, planned obsolescence as a desirable commercial principle for industrial nations has taken a severe knock. What an immense difference there is today from the world dream of the expanding economy which was accepted less than twenty years ago!

We are gathered here in Jyväskylä by the invitation and hospitality of the highest governmental and other authorities of Finland to look into the environmental future. This is a country of great natural beauty of water, forests, and tundra, which has contributed notably to civilization in architecture, music, design, and technical skills. The fact that Finland calls this Conference is no arrogance of contentment with her own state, but an expression of enquiring humility in a world in which we are all inevitably closer together than we were in the past. The world's problems are our own, those of each of us. We have come here to make some analysis and synthesis in the light of our growing comprehension of, and apprehension about, global problems. Next year the world will be coming to Stockholm at the ministerial level for the United Nations Conference on the Human Environment. It is our duty this week to add to understanding of the global environmental future by producing a volume of work which we can place before our ministerial colleagues at Stockholm and which we can hope may lighten their labours.

The broad subject of the global environment is a fit one for some philosophical contemplation. Except for the great climatic changes that have taken place at intervals of thousands of years, the most powerful agent of change is man, acting either directly or sometimes indirectly and unintentionally. If the estimate is broadly true that the world population was around 250 millions only two thousand years ago, and that the rate of increase was even then quite slow, man had already had a remarkable influence in Asia and Europe in changing the face of the earth. The smelting of metal had a profound effect because the only fuel was that immediately derived from vegetation, namely wood. The bared landscape of Anatolia and the metallurgical cunning of the early Levantines are not unrelated. The bared landscapes of the loess hills of China and that country's pre-eminence in producing durable pots and intricate bronze castings from an early time are not fortuitous. These two industrial processes—of smelting and alloying on one hand and of the production of hard impervious pottery on the other— showed remarkable empirical chemical skill, and we know that man's ability to make himself comfortable by buffering the environment was well developed from very early times.

Yet the rise of human population seems to have been a very slow one. Why? It is easy enough to say 'disease' in a large and all-embracing way, but if we could take ourselves back reliably we might find that killing disease except of very young infants was not so great until urbanization subjected people to mass infections. Density-dependence of diseases must have been an important factor in promoting them until urban populations acquired some limited immunities, whereafter such populations could grow. At the same time we must remember what a violent creature man is: we know in our own time that war is horrible, but it does not kill enough people to reduce the world population significantly. Nevertheless, there have been periods of violence beyond the normal casualties of war, reaching to sheer extermination of communities.

The history of the heartland of Asia is quite staggering in this connection: the Chinese probably numbered a hundred millions when the Mongol scourge fell, and after a century or less, the population was only sixty millions—a 40 per cent reduction—and all natural increase was negated. The southern and westward surges of the Mongols were equally devastating, wiping out large cities—except for skilled artisans who were moved elsewhere as a matter of policy. The Mongols were but one example of searing, exterminating hordes in a violent world. Population was kept down, yet such is reproductive potential in this unique species of long gestation that new pressures were created within remarkably few years. The general trend of human population was relentlessly upwards.

DEVELOPMENTS IN EUROPE

It seems that after the mediaeval period, say around A.D. 1500, there began a steady increase in European population. Perhaps this was possible because there was a real rise in the standard of living. We were yet a long way from the mechanization of the Industrial Revolution, which depended upon harnessing steam; but an appreciable amount of labour-saving engineering had already been thought out in essentials, and had been applied to such power as was available—principally from water. The mill dam was not an elaborate storage of power, and its effectiveness depended on the longest radius possible for the mill wheel relative to the water that was being shot down from the lade. Only on the fringes of Europe, as in the Outer Hebrides of Scotland, did women still grind corn by hand in a quern.

Water mills were also geared to give power to saw the trunks of trees into planks and to produce a draught of air for a blast furnace. If you read Defoe's Travels through the North of England in the early eighteenth century (Defoe, 1724–27), you realize that Britain was all ready for steam, and steam to be generated on fossil fuel; for a large part of the natural timber had gone, having been burnt for all manner of reasons. What is called the Black Country had repeated the mistakes of China—burnt the wood to produce porcelain for home consumption and export.

HUMAN POPULATION PRESSURES

I suppose the depression of poverty exercises some depression of population, but not much. In our modern day we are convinced that poverty and unbridled population increase go together. We hold it to be an axiom that a rising standard of living is the best depressant of the birth-rate. This may not be quite true either, but in general it is, if the ethos changes as well. However, poverty also changes in style, and that of today is not so searing physically as it must have been five hundred years ago. Psychologically, perhaps, it is worse now.

The immense, almost exponential, rise in human population in the world has taken place in less than two hundred years, synchronously with the Industrial Revolution. Large areas of the world may not have become industrialized, but because industrial countries needed to sell, the fact is that their products spread world-wide very quickly. I read the other day that aniline dyes from Germany were in common use by the oasis peoples of Chinese Turkestan—a remote enough region—by 1875. In general, where the physical work-load was lifted ever so little, the standard of living rose and the death-rate fell.

Medicine, or rather the application of it, is sometimes blamed for the rise of populations in habitats which cannot sustain the increased numbers of mouths; but this is surely the most cock-eyed way of looking at things. What person with the power to relieve suffering will let a child die? The trouble is that a wide gap or cultural lag exists which does not bring about a balance of birth-rate with death-rate. Evangelism and personal satisfaction in the power to relieve suffering—so often an expression of vanity—should be attended by an equal propaganda on the ethics of responsibility. We did not attend to this side of life-saving soon enough; nor are we being much more than mealy-mouthed about it now, and our great question is, 'Are we too late?' Some think yes and some think no, and some think Science will find a way. A fast-declining number think God will find a way. His remedies can scarcely be expected to be kind ones if believers and non-believers continue in that kind of complacency.

We come back to the plain fact that science and technology and the access to fossil fuels made possible the proliferation of mankind to such an extent that not only was life made easier for the many though not for all, but there has also come about an awareness that many parts of the environment have deteriorated—not only in physical aspects but in social ones as well. Some towns have become behavioural sinks—to use Calhoun's term—and we simply do not know how to get that kind of an aggregation of human beings turned around and headed in the direction of being human beings. It is quite false to use the simile that people are living like beasts, for our growing knowledge of animal behaviour shows us that beasts do not live like that unless they, too, have been degraded to live in broiler houses and intensive pens—like human beings in slums, ghettos, barrios, and the like. What troubles me is that I do not think we see clearly enough the dreadful vortex we are in; for it is a vortex in which our circular motion is getting narrower in diameter, trying to catch up, as it were, with the increasing population, the pace of which grows faster the deeper we get!

FURTHER REFLECTIONS

I have been called a doom-watch man, which is a pity because I am still human enough to have an active delight in life and appreciation of the planet's beauty. Also, the ordinary human being is not a pessimist through and through, but a blend of fear and hope. These emotions in intellectual terms mean that man, having the power of foresight, can understand the probable consequences of his actions, and if these have been antipathetical to his survival, he can make a move towards their correction; also, even if it is not optimism, he can admit that what he foresees could be fallible but that it is worthwhile trying to move aright. There is only one end to defeatism: suicide.

The gloomy environmental picture painted in terms of swarming population and pollution of air, water, and land, is offset by the sheer beauty of much of our world and of the human spirit. The more aware we are of our environment—of the scientific laws which guide the physiology of the biosphere—and of our own social psychology, the greater does the challenge of our survival appear to us, and possibly the more we can relish the challenge. Mind you, in the ecological, conservational, and environmental fields, there are too many Don Quixotes full of false idealism and prone to tilt at windmills; and, please remember, there is a great mass of Sancho Panzas who say we have never had it so good and who are willing to sacrifice the eternal to the expedient. Can we move the Sancho Panzas?

The Sancho Panzas have a great deal of power. They constitute the mass of voters. They do not need to be active in their negative attitudes—just supine and without thought for posterity. The glimmerings of questions about the infinite quality of global resources arose in the second half of the nineteenth century with the publication of *Man and Nature; or, Physical Geography as Modified by Human Action* by George Perkins Marsh in 1864. This book has been called by Lewis Mumford (1931) 'the fountainhead of the conservation movement'. Marsh (1864) described in global terms what was happening to forests, water, soil, and wildlife; he was a scholar and ultimately a professional diplomat, not a biologist, and he would certainly not have heard the word 'ecology' when he wrote. Scholarly minds, not retreating to the cloister but maintaining a vivid, physical contact with the earth, are probably our continuing greatest need in guiding land-use policies. Malthus's work (*cf.* 1817) on population had been published first in 1798, yet Marsh did not mention this book in his *Man and Nature*, which seems strange to us now; but we have the advantage of hindsight.

A few of us linked the philosophies of Malthus and Marsh in the 1930s, but this was looked upon as mere intellectual speculation. The impact was made by William Vogt in 1948 with *Road to Survival*. This sardonic, biting book did what Vogt intended: wake up the world to the fact that the scriptural injunction to increase and multiply was out of date, and that human multiplication could be the greatest threat to human survival. Reaction to the book was often vitriolic and angry, but there was also some sympathetic response. Vogt had been Chief of the Conservation Branch of the Organization of American States and had worked in Central and South America. He lost his job; but the population problem has remained to the fore in world thinking.

It illustrates the barrier of language that the Russian, Alexander Woeikof, Professor of Geography at St Petersburg, should have worked through the

latter part of the nineteenth century and produced his paper on the influence
of man on the earth in 1901 without reference to Marsh; equally, Woeikof's
paper was translated into French and German but not into English. His emphasis on what was happening to the surface of the earth as a result of wrong
practices would have been directly applicable, especially in the United States
a generation earlier; but even Marsh had not got through to his own
countrymen by then. Woeikof did think in terms of population, but on the
whole considered matters rather optimistically—there seemed to be so much
room in those days, and indeed still is in his native land. Nathaniel Shaler,
Professor of Geology at Harvard, had also thought about resources, practices,
and the future, in the book which he published in 1905. His concern with
population found its expression largely in antipathy to the spread of towns,
rather than in numbers of people on the earth. Shaler's views about urban
expansion have been common in the twentieth century without their being
related organically with environmental thinking. This is another instance of
how an intellectual climate has to develop in its own time.

NATIONAL PARKS AND RESERVES

I have remarked that perhaps the world has to get into trouble before
widespread thinking in terms of conservation or even self-preservation can
arise. The United States had got to this stage by A.D. 1900, though Marsh,
Shaler, and Thoreau (1854), had blazed the trail. Aesthetically striking, and
profound in its consequences, had been the event the centenary of which we
commemorate in 1972—the establishment of the Yellowstone National Park.
The idea of national parks as inviolable reservations of environment has
caught on—as can be gathered from the substantial volume from the International Union for Conservation of Nature and Natural Resources which
lists and briefly describes the world's national parks and equivalent reserves
(IUCN, 1971).

The struggle for national parks in the United States, and the awakening of
public opinion to the devastation which had taken place through a bald
exploitative economy of forest felling, overgrazing, and killing of wildlife,
worked together in developing the skills of conservation. Theodore Roosevelt
was no St Francis of Assisi, but he did realize what was happening and threw
his presidential weight into the movement. Gifford Pinchot, as a wealthy
independent man, became Chief of the new Forest Service. Stephen Mather
subsequently moulded the National Park Service into a *corps élite*, and
clarified what had been a rather sloppy administration of national parks.
A White House Conference on Conservation was convened in 1908.

These ideas were slow to get around other parts of the world: for example,
Great Britain did not understand the word in Roosevelt's sense of 'conser-
vation through wise use' until the late 1940s, and when the International
Union was established at Fontainebleau in 1948, the European nations
rejected the word Conservation and made the Union for the *Protection* of
Nature. 'Conservation' was substituted in the name at the 1956 General
Assembly in Edinburgh. Meanwhile, many European nations had developed
their agriculture and forestry slowly through the centuries, and had arrived

at a broadly wise and careful use of the land. Consequently, the impacts of misuse had not struck them as hard as they are doing now.

Conservation became an interpretation of ecology in action, and was applied in the United States on a broad front—soil, water, forests, and wildlife. Once more disaster had its place, for the Dust-Bowl of 1934 stimulated some magnificent work—and not only in the scientific and technical fields, for the hearts of men had been touched and encouraged to literary expression. *Deserts on the March* by Paul Sears (1935) is an excellent example. As a quaternary botanist of international reputation, Sears had felt a constant social involvement with the fate of the planet's covering.

In fact, there began to emerge an ethic of conservation, of care for the earth. No one was clearer-sighted in this field nor more felicitous in expression than Aldo Leopold (1949) who, after serving in the United States Forest Service, had become Professor of Wildlife Management in the University of Wisconsin. Thirty-five years ago it was quite difficult to impress the notion of responsibility on a nation of unbridled private enterprise where soil and what grew in it were there to be exploited to the quickest commercial advantage. Happily, the status and influence of Aldo Leopold have grown since his premature death in 1948.

Vogt's *Road to Survival* was matched in influence by another book published in the same year. This was the late Fairfield Osborn's *Our Plundered Planet* (1948). Here again, population was linked with what we were doing to the planet through the course of history, so that we were given a larger view and a more personal involvement. Osborn was no professional biologist, but inherited a biological concern and a deep love of animals. His book was the ideal simple introduction to the historical and social horizons of environmental study. It was quickly taken up elsewhere in the world and was translated into sixteen languages. Fairfield Osborn also established the Conservation Foundation in 1948, which body has had wide international interests and commitments, and has been remarkable, in what has become a rather emotional field, for its scientific integrity and impartiality of approach. The Conservation Foundation has had a steadying effect over the years, as well as an enlarging one.

The decade of the 1950s was one of consolidation, of the application of critical standards of ecology to conservation; it was also remarkable for the Wenner-Gren Conference on 'The Role of Man in Changing the Face of the Earth', held at Princeton. A group of seventy-five scholars mostly of international repute, covering between them a wide range of disciplines, talked for a week, and the ultimate volume appeared in 1956 (Thomas, 1956). Each new crop of students in what have come to be called the earth sciences uses this book; it has become fundamental, and must have had much to do with the development of the attitudes of the decade of the 1960s, which turned the world mind to concern with the environment. This was something larger than conservation, being an integration of thinking towards acceptance of the fact that man is the dominant mammal on the face of the earth, and that the environmental future is in man's hands—as indeed is his very survival.

EMERGING ENVIRONMENTAL POLICY

I have sketched an unsure groping by man towards a constructive human ecology attended by an emergent ethic of responsibility. The twin problems of population and pollution are now to the fore in general awareness, and we know that the human population is going to increase considerably before it can level out and, hopefully, gently decline. The developed West has certain standards of general well-being which it has not yet really reached: let that be well remembered. The saying goes that there are no votes in sewage, but I could make another aphorism that there is a lot of violence in inadequate sewerage. It is quite amazing that civilized nations can concentrate on the vote-catching line of building houses and yet depend on a century-old sewerage system to cope with the increasing wastes. The recent strike in Britain of waste-disposal workers showed how near the edge we were running. There was some spillage of sewage into the River Thames, but the weather was kind in that an unusually dry spell eased the pressures of storm water and afterwards a sharp wet spell scoured the river in a most helpful manner.

Conservation and ecology have taken on a new and significant dimension in that the human being is no longer a thing apart from the rest of the biosphere. We are of it and in it in no uncertain way. Those of us who are of the West have a tremendous responsibility for the whole world, in that it is our technology which is often crucial. We are asked for technological help in development, and it is for us to see that such schemes are not ecological disasters; and yet we have to show that, by denying some short-sighted schemes, we are not trying to withhold from the underdeveloped world the debatable benefits which we enjoy. It also needs to be said by someone who can speak without fear that it is idle talk to suggest that we can in any short or foreseeable future extend to the underdeveloped world these same debatable high standards of living that we enjoy. They cannot be so extended without environmental crisis, because 20 per cent of the world's population is using much more than half of all the available planetary resources. We are a very expensive kind of culture in our present world. Rather is it for us of the West at this juncture humbly to enquire how we can avoid polluting the biosphere, how we can prevent waste, and how we can keep the resource-base recharged.

The natural cycles of conversion are models that we should attempt to copy and emulate in our own technologies. The age of planned obsolescence is morally dead and gone, and the sooner the motor-car manufacturers give up their dithering with annual styles, the more they will help to allay a truly bourgeois style of building artificial status-symbols. The need is for economies in extravagant production and the employment of more personal art. The present 'trendy' painting by the owners of motor-cars a few years old is not to be despised. The car is still running and outwardly it is individual.

Finally, technology is not some whipping-horse. We could not endure today without it, and it is technology that is going to pull us out of our difficulties—technology directed to our environmental problems.

The term integration had its day twenty years ago. We were all busy integrating; we were not quite sure what. Now, if we are not too shy to use the word, I think we are much more aware of its desirable meaning. The future global environment is everyone's concern, and all the skills man has can find a place in trying to fashion the environment in deference to the laws of nature. I, as a naturalist fond of wild places, took a long time to see that man's integration with nature in building a sewage farm could be a beautiful thing in itself. A developed agriculture practising rotation cropping, using the nitrogen cycle and leguminous plants, is also beautiful in itself, as well as producing the pleasing landscape of a settled agriculture.

Because many of our technologies take us away from processes which we have come to discover in nature, new and hurtful architectures have come into our lives; the landscape architect inspired by ecology has a fresh and continuing function of integration in our world. When a marine architect or airplane designer produces a new craft, it is beautiful because it has to function in fast movement. The new vessels grow even more beautiful as they move faster. Land-based industry has to grow out of the tradition of the extended backyard operation, to take its place as something which does not pollute or produce psychosomatic depression.

We cannot all talk the same language in describing our skills, but I believe the time is coming when we can all talk together with interest because as men of good will we are seeking the same goal of a habitable and satisfying environment which need not be stereotyped. Whatever degree of extremity we may have reached, there is no cause for defeatism, for the mind of man is still young.

REFERENCES

DEFOE, Daniel (1724–27). *A Tour Thro' the Whole Island of Great Britain, Divided into Circuits or Journeys* ... G. Strahan, London: 3 vols, maps (or later editions).

IUCN (1971). *United Nations List of National Parks and Equivalent Reserves.* Hayez, Brussels: 601 pp., illustr.

LEOPOLD, Aldo (1949). *A Sand County Almanac, and Sketches Here and There.* Oxford University Press, New York: xiii + 226 pp., illustr.

MALTHUS, Thomas R. (1817). *An Essay on the Principle of Population* ... (5th edn). J. Murray, London: 3 vols (or other editions).

MARSH, George P. (1864). *Man and Nature; or, Physical Geography as Modified by Human Action.* C. Scribner, New York, and Sampson Low, London: xix + 577 pp. (Edition edited by David Lowenthal. Belknap Press and Harvard University Press, Cambridge, Mass.: xxix + 472 pp., 1965.)

MUMFORD, Lewis (1931). *The Brown Decades; A Study of the Arts in America, 1865–1895.* Harcourt, Brace, New York: xii + 266 pp., illustr.

OSBORN, Fairfield (1948). *Our Plundered Planet.* Little, Brown, Boston: xiv + 217 pp.

SEARS, Paul B. (1935). *Deserts on the March.* University of Oklahoma Press, Norman, Oklahoma: vi + 231 pp., illustr. (or 1947 edn of xi + 178 pp.).

SHALER, Nathaniel S. (1905). *Man and the Earth.* Fox, Duffield, New York: vi + 240 pp.

THOMAS, WILLIAM L., Jr (Ed.) (1956). *Man's Role in Changing the Face of the Earth.* University of Chicago Press, Chicago: xxxviii + 1193 pp., illustr.

THOREAU, Henry D. (1854). *Walden: or, Life in the Woods.* Ticknor & Fields, Boston: 357 pp.

VOGT, William (1948). *Road to Survival.* W. Sloane Associates, New York: xvi + 335 pp., illustr.

WOEIKOF, Alexander (1901). De l'influence de l'homme sur la terre. *Annales de Géographie,* **10**, pp. 97–114, 193–215.

DISCUSSION

Periäinen (Chairman)

Sir Frank Fraser Darling presents in his paper the history of man's influence on nature, with a survey of what man has done to nature. In so doing he immediately raises the twin problems of our world of today: the problems of population and pollution. Yet according to him we can, through constructive thinking and responsible use of technology, pull ourselves out of our difficulties in these respects.

In his paper, in which he attempts and I think largely succeeds in covering the entire field, Sir Frank speaks mainly about the relationship between man and nature. Nor have we any difficulty in agreeing with what he has said. But, as a background for a conference on the environmental future, we should not underestimate the problems existing and to be foreseen in the relationships between man and man-made environments, as well as between natural and man-made environments.

Man has created and produced his own environment, which we call the technological environment or technosphere—meaning everything that man has artificially done or produced in material form—including machines, houses, cities, and urban agglomerations, etc. The technological environment is especially manifest in urban areas, and its influence on man can be seen in the continuously increasing number and magnitude of individual and social disorders: criminality, human aggressiveness, drugs, mental disorders, and anxiety, alienation, and fear. Thus there is mental and social as well as physical pollution.

Perhaps the most important reasons for this situation are two. Firstly, there is still considerable lack of knowledge about the interaction between man and the technological environment; we seem to have far more exact knowledge about nature and its structures than about the human mind and our own behaviour in the environment.

Secondly, we have had migration into the urban areas—that is, population increase with resulting lack of space and amenities. This seems to be today's situation, but the problems of the future have the same root: in some thirty years the world's population will double itself. From the viewpoint of nature, this means conservation and protection from men, but from the viewpoint of the technological environment it means creating and producing in thirty years as many houses, urban agglomerations, and other technological elements, as exist now—plus the extra ones needed to raise the standards of living.

We have nature, we shall get the people, and we are unable to deny, or not produce, the technological environment. We are responsible both for nature and for the technological environment. But first of all, we are responsible for man himself—for his physical, mental, and social, well-being. So, the question should be posed in this way: from the point of view of man, what is the functional task and significance of the total environment in the future as well as today?

One possibility for finding some answer to this question is to examine the evolution of man as a human being from the primeval wild state to the technological version of today. On this I am no expert, and most of you know well the history of that evolution. So I won't attempt to go into details but merely ask where and when man—or, more exactly, western man—has taken the wrong path, making the wrong decisions in the history of creating the environmental situation with which we are now confronted? For it should be noted that technology, as a means for satisfying some needs and fulfilling some goals, is not inimical to nature; but the values and goals of man can be and all too often are!

On the other hand, thinking of one individual man, we know that his development from birth to the attainment of a complete personality depends on two things: first, on his genetic inheritance which defines the confines or limits of all his potential possibilities, and secondly, on his interaction with the environment, on which depends how much of his genetic inheritance he can use. From the point of view of the physical, mental, and social development of the individual man, all the main categories of the environment—natural, social, and technological—are of a decisive importance.

It is possible to conclude that the function of biologically clean or cleansed nature is a basic condition for the satisfactory life and even survival of man, the man-made technological environment being a reflection of his needs and goals—a means for man's mental development and new extensions. Thus human society is responsible not only for the balance of nature and for the technological environment but also for the well-being and happiness of man.

The crisis in which we now are may be a useful crisis, as Fraser Darling says. For we are forced by it to take at last both nature and our environment very seriously. We should also look back into our history and try to answer the question of where we have gone wrong, striving meanwhile to learn from past mistakes and to do better in our decisions for the future.

Wynne-Edwards

One of the most important things in Fraser Darling's paper was the statement that the population of adults in the world will continue to grow for some time; and at the same time we are conscious of the rapid increase in use of the irreplaceable resources. Yet we must have wealth in order to solve the problems of today. The greatest problem, in my view, that faces the conservationist is to find out how to come to an economic plateau—how to stop the increasingly rapid growth of the resource use, and yet maintain a sufficient wealth to cope with the difficult environmental problems that have already developed.

Kaprio

I was very happy to hear, listed in this introduction, some of the problems concerning man as the centre of development in relationship to nature, and you, Mr Chairman, continuing in the same line. In the World Health Organization we have been slowly exposed to changing attitudes—most of all, to the importance of the environment on one hand and to the population question on the other. I have been serving for about fifteen years now in

WHO, which, of course, has UN Special Fund support in both of these fields of action, and I would like to mention one additional aspect which I think is very important for all of you. This is the rise of expectation in the 'third world.'

It has often been said that the people of the West—or perhaps of certain parts of the northern hemisphere plus Australia and a few other regions—are using half of the resources of the world. To convince the rest of the world, namely those less-advanced countries, that they have to arrest their technological development, after all that we have said in the United Nations, will be extremely difficult. Also we can see, in contemplating the population problem, how this was considered until the 1960s as a kind of white man's trick to stop the development of the third world. Only after censuses in 1960 and 1961 did several big countries, especially in south-east Asia, realize that they really were overburdened by their rapid population increases and consequently start to request the United Nations for support in solving their population problems.

So we, who already have a relatively high standard of living and are in a strong position, will have to be very tactful with the others; yet at the same time there is need for leadership from the third world if we are to solve many of the problems on a global scale. There is also a need for change from the paternalistic attitude of both the socialist and developed capitalist countries in the northern hemisphere, who are apt to say what they think should be done without taking into consideration the often differing viewpoints of others. Already there are signs of change: I'm just back from Morocco where I had the honour to be present when the work on a big dam was started. This dam will guarantee water for the cities of Casablanca and Rabat. In a few years' time there will be the water needed—but only for about eighteen years, as the population is growing so rapidly that by about 1990 there will again not be enough water. This is now well known to the government and will influence their population control policy.

Personally I feel that, in the environment, the most significant factor is the growth of world population. But how are we going to change things in the future? There can only be a very complicated way ahead. Yet such conferences as this one are extremely useful, because they help to get the whole world behind our thinking and to prepare the rich countries for sharing more completely than they are sharing now. There is need for much more money and effort to be invested both in solving our own pollution problems and for helping to share the results with the whole world.

Johnson

I think it will certainly be important for this Conference to focus on the pressures and effects of human population. Surely we all know the figures: the first thousand million not until 1830, the second by 1930, the third between 1930 and 1960, while the present total is some 3.6 thousand millions. The United Nations Population Division gives different projections of the future. If we take one projection, that is based on the constant fertility assumption, which means maintaining 1965 levels of fertility, we can foresee having a world of over 8 thousand million people soon after the end of this millennium. However, there is a very great danger in talking about a population problem as though it was the problem of the developing world and not of the developed world. I think an environment conference should focus strongly on the 'population problem' of the developed countries in so far as these populations, multiplied by affluence and by the precise technology 'mix' which we have at the moment, give us just as much impact in the global environmental sense as do the undeveloped countries.

To me this seems a political matter as well as a real scientific point. From time to time I have been involved with the work of another conference which is being prepared for at the moment—the United Nations Conference on the Human Environment, which will be held in Stockholm in 1972. I see very real hostility developing among the so-called less-developed countries to the stress and the emphasis which is being placed on the environment by the rich countries. They see it, among other things, as a trick to divert attention away from what they consider more pressing problems to do with raising their standards of living. If you add an emphasis on population which once more is aimed at 'them' rather than at our own population, I think you would compound an already delicate situation. I therefore believe it is both scientifically correct and politically correct that, when we in this Conference talk about population, we should talk about it very much in a global sense, thinking of the developed countries' apparently low rates of population growth as being as important as the undeveloped countries' high rates.

Fosberg

I would like to agree completely with the immediately preceding speaker except that I would like to change one word. He spoke about the *developed* world and *developed* nations. Now I would like to present the terms *overdeveloped* world and *overdeveloped* nations to be used instead.

Laird

Professor Wynne-Edwards put his finger on a statement of major importance in Sir Frank Fraser Darling's paper: 'we know that the human population is going to increase considerably before it can level out and, hopefully, gently decline'. I'd like to endorse his remarks while highlighting another of the sentiments expressed in his paper, by quoting 'what person with the power to relieve suffering will let a child die?' Now earlier in Sir Frank's paper it was stated that 'killing disease except of very young infants was not so great until urbanization subjected people to mass infections'. This is true enough for certain communicable and some vector-borne diseases. It is less applicable, though, to some other very important vector-borne entities such as jungle yellow fever and other zoonoses, and also to malaria, which has often killed very large numbers of people far from urban concentrations. I would hope that during our Conference this fact is borne in mind; for the reason that certain pesticides currently causing much concern (largely because of their misuse in what were just referred to as overdeveloped areas) are still of crucial importance to the well-being, and often the very survival, of large numbers of people in less fortunate parts of the world. This question, I submit, merits our most thoughtful attention.

Hashimoto

I would like to speak from the standpoint of Japan, because I'm the only delegate from Japan. We have already had discussions on the problems of environment from the standpoint of the human population question. But we should be careful how we handle these discussions. Who produces man's environmental problems? It is largely the developed countries, whose people have industrial and political potential. They produce pesticides and sell them to underdeveloped countries. In developing countries pesticides have considerable merit but they also bring disadvantages: that is one key point.

A second point: some countries have not much financial wealth but are quite rich in natural resources, while some countries are quite rich in environmental capacity but not in productive capacity. Some countries, again, are quite rich in terms of population, but are still poor in potentials of consumption and production. How can we reconcile these complicated problems between developing and developed countries?

A third problem which we should not overlook is the rural problem, because we are being heavily oriented in urbanized environments. For example, in the case of pesticides, rural people are occupationally exposed to them in addition to being exposed through food, air, and water, that are all polluted by pesticides. Ecology of the rural population must be kept in mind. On the other hand, because of the population distribution, epidemiological data are difficult to gain towards significant interpretation of health effects on rural populations. In Japan, it was in rural areas that environmental health disasters such as Minamata disease and Itai-itai disease practically had to happen—not in urban areas. The reason for this is that people eat and drink in the same place for life-long terms, and that leads to a kind of intoxication.

A fourth point is that instead of eschatology, we should know how to handle an uncertainty—especially a probable risk. There are many probable risks in uncertain situations, but a worrying point is that we don't have a proper orientation in an established risk-spectrum as part of the background of policy decision.

Goldman

There seems to me a certain area of unrealism about the discussion so far as it relates to underdeveloped countries. I think it is important for us to recognize that the developing countries want the things that we currently have in the developed countries, and I think it is wrong for us to say or to believe that we can stop either the population or their economic growth simply by saying that they are following a mistaken policy. Before we can do that, and before we can even think about it, we should consider what we have to do in our own countries. If, for example, the countries of Asia were to develop in the manner in which the United States and much of western Europe have developed, or the Soviet Union seems to be developing, we could expect in China alone some 350 million automobiles. It is not unrealistic to expect this, if we assume that the rate they would like to achieve will be the same kind of rate that we have in the USA. For example, the Soviet Union have announced that they are going to increase their automobile production. If you look at Japan, which is after all an Asian country, you see automobile production already rising rapidly. So I think that we have to recognize that these countries want these goods, are going to obtain them, and before we can ask them to stop we shall have to put our own houses in order. One of the speakers mentioned that pesticides, which are so dangerous in the West or in the northern hemisphere, are very important in the southern hemisphere. Some people in the southern hemisphere have said that demands in the USA for stopping production of DDT amount to genocide. So before we can do anything I think we have to recognize that the problem comes back home. And I think perhaps we'll find that the major issue at this Conference will relate to the question of the North *versus* South and the rich *versus* those who want to be rich.

Kuenen

It should be considered essential that we don't mix up concepts. One of the questions which we are currently discussing is that of population growth, the other being the extent of pollution per head of the population. It is quite obvious that population growth can be stopped. And it's quite obvious that pollution per head of the population is at present a problem of the technologically developed nations and should not spread throughout the world. There is no question of stopping economic development of the under-developed nations. It is only a question of trying to increase their well-being without increasing unduly the pollution per head of the population. In the previous discussions I feel these two aspects have tended to get mixed up. As regards the efforts of WHO, we should be quite clear that what we want to achieve is not to let children die, but to prevent them from being born. We are grateful to the medical profession for saving life; we wish it would also be concerned with keeping the quality of life at a reasonable level by preventing the populations of the world from growing indefinitely.

Polunin

Mr Chairman: Before you close this, our initial session, which I feel has not lost in interest through wandering from its allotted task, I would like to make an announcement on behalf of two of our expected colleagues. They are Academician Aleksandr Ivanovich Oparin, the former Biological Secretary and a Member of the Presidium of the Academy of Sciences of the USSR, and Academician Aleksandr Pavlovich Vinogradov, currently Vice-President of the Academy of Sciences of the USSR. Both are in their middle seventies but still actively directing major institutes of the Academy— circumstances which naturally combine to make it difficult for them to travel much. The last thing I heard on behalf of Academician Vinogradov was in a cable from Assistant Vice-President Goedekian saying 'due illness Academician Vinogradov cannot inform you definitely participation International Conference Finland/stop/hope cable you nearest future'. Not hearing further I had hoped that he would be with us here now, but to our great regret when the Soviet Delegation arrived in Helsinki the day before yesterday it was without him, and without much hope of his being able to come. They were also without Academician Oparin, though assuring us that he was fully expected to follow with his wife at any moment. I have been in close touch with him by frequent letter, etc., until a matter of days ago, when he still fully expected to come, and he has prepared for us a paper provisionally entitled 'the possibility of appearance and existence of life outside of the earth'—meaning, of course, any form of life that does not have to be maintained artificially outside the biosphere. As biologists among you will know, Academician Oparin is the great biochemist student of the origin of life, and so, even though hopes are now dwindling of his coming here and presenting his paper personally, I feel we should include it as part of our Conference's (extended) proceedings where they deal with the general background [murmurs of approval and no further discussion of this subject]. For there can scarcely be any question that, with the virtual impossibility of maintaining fully effective quarantine, any discovery by man of anything elsewhere in the universe or beyond which could possibly be considered a form of life, might have the most profound effect on the biosphere and its environmental future. [Academician Oparin's paper follows.]

The Possibility of Life outside Earth's Biosphere

by

ALEKSANDR IVANOVICH OPARIN

Director, A. N. Bakh Institute of Biochemistry,
Academy of Sciences of the USSR, Leninsky Prospekt 33,
Moscow B–71, USSR.

INTRODUCTION

To the man of science of some 100–200 years ago, the world appeared as some kind of grandiose mechanism that had been created by the laws of conservation of mass and energy. In this mechanism, everything remained unchanging and all phenomena occurred according to closed cycles, permanently returning to their original positions. Because of this, it seemed that everything in the world could be easily calculated and predicted, much as we predict the course of day and night or winter and summer—phenomena of which the bases lie in the revolution of the earth or its orbiting around the sun.

However, that belief in the unchangeability of all reality now yields its place in the minds of people to another principle, which had already been proclaimed by the great dialectic of ancient Greece, Heraclitos: 'Everything is in flux'. And indeed we do live in a world which is constantly changing, undergoing evolution. This process of development has a progressive character and causes the appearance of all new, more complex, multiform and strongly differentiated forms of reality.

Development cannot proceed simultaneously and in the same manner everywhere, as circumstances vary. In different areas of the universe, and on different cosmic bodies, evolutionary development is occurring through various pathways and at various rates. Because of this we should not present it schematically as a single, straight line, but rather as a fan spread out into various pathways, the separate branches of which could lead to very complex and perfect forms of organization and motion of matter.

We know nothing as yet about many of these forms; in some cases we do not even suspect their existence. But our special attention is attracted to the pathway of evolutionary development of carbonaceous compounds, since it was this that led us here on the earth to the origin of life and ultimately to human society.

At the present time we only know life from one single example, that of our planet earth. From this we must derive our opinions of other possible forms of biological organization. Because of this, the earth and the events which occurred on it should serve as a model for our current views of life in the universe.

LIFE SEEMINGLY INEVITABLE

As long as it was believed that life on the earth resulted from some sort of extremely rare 'lucky chance', this belief could not give us any help towards considering the existence of life outside of this planet—apart, perhaps, from the calculation of the probability of such an event, though such calculation could hardly give us any real satisfaction. However, today we have every reason to view the origin of terrestrial life not as a 'lucky happenstance' but as a phenomenon entirely regulated by natural laws and an inalienable and integral part of the general evolutionary development of our planet.

The search for life outside of the earth is only a part of the more general question posed to science as to the origin of life in the universe. The study of the conception of life on earth becomes an investigation of only one example of an event which must surely have occurred in the universe a countless number of times. Therefore, the elucidation of the question of how life appeared on earth must undoubtedly result in strong arguments in favour of the existence of life elsewhere in the universe.

THREE STAGES OF EVOLUTION

Taking a general view of the whole pathway of evolution of carbonaceous compounds either outside of the earth or, especially, on its surface, we find we can separate it into three principal stages: abiogenic, biological, and social (Oparin, 1964).

It is very important to realize that this evolutionary process proceeded and is proceeding at ever-increasing rates. Schematically it can be represented as a curve that is steeply concave upwards; and at certain points of the curve (after the origin of life and the appearance of human beings) the acceleration of development becomes especially pronounced.

Abiotic Stage
Abiogenic evolution of carbonaceous compounds was accomplished even long before the appearance of our solar system, and its duration can be

estimated, probably, in ten of thousands of millions of years. After the origin of life, a new order of biochemical transformations—metabolism—appeared, and the progress of the organic world began to proceed at much faster rates. To accomplish these extremely important events, the evolution of this world has needed only hundreds or even tens of millions of years. The biological evolution of man lasted about one million years or somewhat more, while the social transformations have been realized in thousands of years, centuries, or, at the present time, in even shorter periods.

Such acceleration of development during the transition from one stage of evolution to another, involves a very important principle that, after the appearance of new forms of organization of motion, the old ones are to some extent pushed into the background. Certainly, they remain represented in the newly appearing material objects; but the rates of development peculiar to the old forms are relatively low, and so they play only a very limited role in further progress, the further fate of new natural bodies being determined mainly by their own special properties.

Recent radioastronomical investigations have demonstrated the presence and sometimes even abundance of such compounds as water, ammonia, hydrogen cyanide, cyanoacetylene, formaldehyde, formamide*, and carbon oxide, in intergalaxial and interstellar space (Snyder & Buhl, 1969, 1970; Snyder et al., 1969; Turner, 1970; Wilson et al., 1970; Zuckerman et al., 1970; Marsden, 1971). Chemical evolution of these compounds, proceeding under a wide variety of conditions, may easily lead to the formation of biologically important substances, such as amino-acids and purine and pyrimidine bases and their various polymers.

This was proved by many modelling experiments which to some degree reproduced the known conditions of Mars and other planets, as well as the environment that was supposed to occur on the primitive, still lifeless earth. Several authors demonstrated, in these experiments, that organic substances are formed under the influence of different energy-sources (electrical discharge, heat, short-wave ultra-violet radioactive decay, etc.), with different relative concentration of initial components, and under different reaction conditions (Proc. Third Internat. Conf. on the Origin of Life, 1971).

Nevertheless, the principal set of the substances formed is very uniform in various experiments. For example, in the course of modelling of abiogenic syntheses, it is mainly the amino-acids occurring in present-day organisms that are formed.

Very interesting and evident results in this direction have recently been obtained in the NASA Ames Research Center, after analysis of the Murchison meteorite which had fallen in Australia (Kvenvolden et al., 1971). The bulk of amino-acid material found in it consisted of components of present-day proteins: glycine, alanine, valine, proline, and glutamic acid. But besides these were found traces of twelve other amino-acids that are not peculiar to proteins but are known to be formed in abiogenic syntheses. The presence

* See the note on 'Complex Organic Molecules in Outer Space' by Professors G. W. Swenson, Jr, & W. H. Flygare (Biological Conservation, 4(1), p. 60, 1971) who, however, emphasize that this presence should not be construed as having any significance in connection with the origin of life.—Ed.

of these suggests that amino-acids have not appeared in the Murchison meteorite after terrestrial contamination, but have been synthesized in the meteorite itself.

The conditions of the synthesis certainly must have differed from those that we observe on earth, and yet in this case the same amino-acids were formed as in the earth's biosphere; in the meteorite, however, they were present in the racemized state (i.e., with equal amounts of D and L optical isomers).

It has recently been shown that at further transformations, during poly-merization of amino-acids, peptides are formed in which the pattern of neighbouring amino-acids is very close to that in present-day proteins (Steinman & Cole, 1967). We may also point to the fact that, after either thermal or photochemical syntheses of purines and pyrimidines, adenine prevails quantitatively among the products. This can be readily explained by its intramolecular structure (Pullman, 1971).

Thus, at this initial stage of evolution of carbonaceous compounds, the process was governed mainly by the laws of chemistry—by the intramolecular structure of the substances going through the evolution (Kenyon & Stein-man, 1969).

Certainly, the further fate of the abiogenically formed organic materials might be basically different on different cosmic bodies. In some cases they could even undergo a complete degradation. This, it seems likely, occurs on the unprotected lunar surface, where organic substances from the meteor-ites that have fallen onto it are decomposed by solar wind. On the contrary, in other cases, the organic substances might be buried for a long time in the form of high molecular but extremely stable compounds that are not cap-able of further evolution—such as meteorite bitumens.

Here on the earth the evolution of the organic substances had to proceed in the environment of various 'subvital areas'—on the surface and in the depths of the oceans and in their littorals, in some shallow freshwater pools, in any drying puddles, in water droplets moistening 'soil' particles, etc. Certainly this environment will have influenced somewhat the rate and direction of the evolution of organic substances under the given local conditions, but, at the same time, the intramolecular properties of the sub-stances evolving were of principal importance.

Biotic Stage

The situation changed drastically after the transition from the abiotic stage of evolution to the biological one. At this most important stage the forming influences of environment acquired a decisive role in the further development.

It is peculiar to life that it is not simply dispersed through space in the manner of abiogenically-formed substances in the 'primordial soup'. It manifests itself through discrete systems that are spatially separated from the exterior environment but also interact with the latter in the manner of open systems.

Only on the basis of the specific thermodynamics of this class of systems could there appear the capability of counteracting the increase of entropy—

the feature inherent in living organisms in contrast to the inorganic world. For this to happen it was necessary first of all for the appearance of some kind of phase relations in the originally homogenous solution, and the formation of some spatially separated, integral multimolecular systems which could oppose themselves to the external environment and retain, at the same time, a permanent interaction with it.

The appearance of such multiphase systems is widely distributed in nature and we frequently observe it in laboratory experiments. Without doubt this process occurred on the surface of the lifeless earth on a grandiose scale, and numerous laboratory experiments have demonstrated that it does not depend upon the pre-existence of the strictly-determined intramolecular organization of the polymers responsible for systems formation. In particular, our modelling experiments showed that even simple mixing of the solutions of the polymers with random or monotonous structure, readily causes the formation of phase-separated complexes and coacervate drops.

These are isolated from the surrounding solution by a clearly-defined surface but are capable of selective uptake of various substances from the environment and of transferring to it the products of reactions occurring within the drops. As a result of this, the drops can exist for a long time and their stability bears not a fully static but a stationary character. Incorporation of various accelerants of chemical processes—catalysts—into the drops allowed us to demonstrate in the simplest manner a modelling of metabolism.

With the proper ratio between the rates of chemical reactions occurring in the drops, they increased before our eyes in volume and mass (Oparin, 1968). The drops having more perfect internal organization and better adaptation to the environment, grew more rapidly and had less chance to undergo decomposition and disappear as individual structures.

This was demonstrated in our modelling experiments when two kinds of drops were present and growing in the same solution. Some of them contained more complex and perfect combinations of catalysts than did others. It was obvious that the more perfect drops were growing rapidly whereas growth of the less perfect ones was strongly retarded; after a short time they stopped growing and sometimes went into degradation (Oparin et al., 1968).

Thus, these experiments demonstrate to us the elements of a new law—the beginning of prebiological natural selection of 'protobionts' or 'probionts', the forerunners of living organisms which formerly appeared on the earth's surface (Oparin, 1971b).

The laws of chemistry and thermodynamic potentials permitted the formation of a great number and variety of these systems (Prigogine, 1955). Most of them, in their chemical composition and character of intermolecular linkages, as well as in their structure, were basically different from contemporary organisms, including the most primitive ones. But, since all systems not fitting the environment were destroyed by natural selection, most of the 'probionts' disappeared from the earth's surface, never to return, and their role in evolution came to nothing. Only the systems that were gradually drawing nearer to biological forms could survive for further evolution. Accordingly, on the basis of interaction with the environment and through natural selection—originally showing itself in the direct Darwinian sense but later complicated owing to the origin of the genetic code— there could arise an exceptionally high adaptiveness, or 'purposiveness', of organization of both whole living systems and their integral parts (molecules, organoides, and organs), that is characteristic of all the living world from top to bottom, including the most primitive organisms (Oparin, 1971*a*).

Thus, at the outset of the second stage of evolution of carbonaceous compounds at the origin of life, new biological laws were added to the initially existing chemical ones.

From that moment the conditions of the surrounding environment and, corresponding to them, the internal organization of integral living systems, began to play a decisive role in evolution. Frequently, our notions concerning the possibility of life outside the earth's biosphere are based on the question of whether such terrestrial organisms as are known to us may survive under the conditions of another cosmic body. But such an approach is a very narrow one. The actual forms in which life manifests itself are the derivatives of the environment under which they appear and develop. An environment moulds the organism by creating very perfect and complex systems of adaptation.

If no life had existed on our planet outside the oceans, and no plants and animals had existed on the dry land, on the basis of theory it would have been extremely difficult to assume the latter possibility. From the point of view of a jellyfish, life on the dry land would seem to be complete nonsense. Such strictly terrestrial forms of life could appear only thanks to the complicated process of adaptation of dry-land organisms to water metabolism outside the hydrosphere.

However, life is not only the product of a surrounding environment, but changes this environment by itself. When studying the sphere of the earth's surface occupied now by living organisms, the so-called biosphere, we can see a gigantic remaking produced here by life at all periods of its existence— in spite of the fact that the mass of living matter is rather small, if compared with the total mass of abiogenic material in this zone.

These great changes have resulted from the appearance, in the process of development of life, of a new and more advanced form of organization and motion of matter: biological metabolism. This biological metabolism favours the rapid transfer of chemical elements and the formation of new compounds—all the processes that Vernadsky (1960) termed the geochemical energy of life when connecting this concept with the rate of growth and multiplication of organisms.

As a result of the vital activities of microorganisms, plants, and animals, radical changes in the primary atmosphere, hydrosphere, and upper layers of the lithosphere, took place. Their physical properties, as well as chemical composition, changed. Thus, for instance, we have every reason to believe that the primary atmosphere of the earth was a reducing one, devoid of free oxygen, and that O_2 in the present-day atmosphere has arisen almost completely from the biological activity of photosynthesis.

Green organisms—mainly unicellular phytoplanktonic organisms of the hydrosphere—are the principal transformers of solar light energy. Organisms also play a leading role in the formation of soil and sedimentary rocks of the lithosphere. It may be calculated that at least 10^{12} to 10^{13} metric tons of calcium are participating in the continuous turnover that is going on in living matter; that is an appreciable part of all the calcium present in the earth's crust, which contains about 7.10^{17} tons of this element (cf. Vernadsky, 1960).

Social Stage

Currently and very widely, the processes of formation of sedimentary rocks and the general influence of life in the surrounding environment are manifesting themselves before our eyes. However, the beginning of the third stage of evolution—the appearance of human society—exerted a qualitatively new influence on the development of the biosphere. 'When a living being endowed with intellect appeared on the earth', wrote Vernadsky (1940), 'our planet entered the new stage of its history. Biosphere turned into noosphere.'

As a result of the productive and scientific activities of human society, deep and far-reaching changes of the biosphere occur. A powerful intrusion of noosphere into the biosphere transforms the latter at an exceptionally high rate and on a colossal scale.

Sometimes the magnitude of geochemical processes which accompany human industrial activity even exceeds that of the natural ones. Thus, for example, the mass of rocks extracted from the entrails of the earth during recent decades is comparable with the natural geological phenomena that have occurred during enormous intervals of time. The carbon of coal and oil formerly disappeared from biogeochemical turnover and was buried for many millions of years. But now it is again introduced by man into this turnover, appreciably enriching the troposphere with carbon dioxide. Man creates artificial zones of concentration of living matter and radically changes the biological aspects of a largely man-made biosphere of plants, animals, and microorganisms. Unfortunately, in some cases these changes of natural conditions are not favourable for man himself, and will need the urgent and deliberate interference of all human society to remedy.

In spite of the still relatively small biomass of all mankind, the noosphere develops very rapidly owing to the fact that human society is a new form of existence, developing at extremely high rates. We even sometimes hear that the progress of mankind involves the very rapid individual biological improvement of man, and that in the near future human beings will strongly excel the present-day ones in their physical and mental development. We know, however, that the biological nature of human beings who lived thousands of years ago hardly differed significantly from the present-day living ones, and that the mental abilities of ancient men of wisdom were by no means inferior to our own. For centuries the high road of human progress passed not through the biological improvement of mankind but through advancement of his social life.

Certainly, biological laws retain their power over man, who doubtless develops like all other organisms under the subordination of these laws. Yet significant changing of his biological organization needs time-intervals that are much longer than those which are needed for radical changes in human society.

E.F.—2*

It is characteristic of the social stage of development that it makes progress not only on the basis of transfer of genetic 'information' from one generation to the next, but also on the much more perfect fundamentals which are specific only to human society. A man does not create everything anew each time from the whole complex of his individual knowledge, but mainly receives it in already-prepared form as a result of the social labours of preceding generations. He grasps this knowledge through words, images, and writings. This is intelligible for human beings, as only they have this last signal system which is a qualitatively new characteristic of man.

Thus, the knowledge we possess and are applying so effectively in our practical activity is the fruit of social labour, and the result of the development of human society. The social form of development is much more perfect than the biological one, moreover developing at an incomparably faster rate as we have already noted. Thus decades and even centuries are inadequate for radical biological modification of man, as of other organisms. But in this time-span human beings have acquired an unprecedented power over surrounding nature. We can move on the ground faster than any fallow-deer, travel in the water better than any fish, and fly in the air incomparably faster and farther than any bird. But this is not because of wings or fins and gills appearing in the human organism: it is his social, not biological, progress that allows man an unprecedented dominance over the living world.

In particular, we observe this in the field of overcoming distances and in the appearance of advanced ways of information transfer. Computer techniques have promoted almost incredibly the intellectual abilities of the human being. But in many other respects, in particular in problems of food and nutrition, man is still standing at a relatively low stage of development. It is this fact which causes widespread misgivings—that the rapid increase in human population will lead to the spreading of hunger and increasing environmental degradation. Yet I have no doubt that in the future human society, basing its activities on social development, will overcome these problems.

SUMMARY AND CONCLUSION

To summarize we may say that the first, abiotic stage of evolutionary development of carbonaceous compounds is widely spread in the universe. It obviously proceeded and is proceeding on many celestial bodies, because the development at this stage is determined mainly by general chemical properties of substances passing through evolution. The question is, how far has this process gone on any given cosmic object?

In contrast to the first stage, the second stage—the appearance and development of life—has strongly depended upon environmental conditions that may radically differ on various cosmic bodies. This stage of evolution, in order to proceed along a similar pathway to that followed on the earth, had to occur under planetary conditions that were fairly closely comparable with our terrestrial ones.

The development of life might thus proceed on other cosmic bodies in a different manner and at a different rate from that occurring on the earth. In some circumstances its rate could even overtake the terrestrial processes and lead to the appearance of other, very complicated and perfect forms of organization and motion. But these forms would not necessarily be similar to those of our human society.

With my current conviction that, given suitable conditions, the emergence of life and organic evolution have been virtually inevitable, it seems to me that there could well be some form of life on any other cosmic body where conditions allow it. But whether such cosmic bodies actually exist we do not yet know. At present it seems unlikely that there is any suitable planet in our own solar system apart from the earth; but elsewhere, in another galaxy or universe, would be another matter—an entirely open question.

REFERENCES

KENYON, D. H. & STEINMAN, G. (1969). *Biochemical Predestination.* McGraw-Hill, New York: viii + 332 pp., illustr.

KVENVOLDEN, K. A., LAWLESS, J.G. & PONNAMPERUMA, C. (1971). Non-protein amino-acids in the Murchison meteorite. *Proc. Nat. Acad. Sci., USA,* **68**(2), pp. 486–90.

MARSDEN, B. G. (1971). *International Astronomical Union Circular,* No. 2319.

OPARIN, A. I. (1964). *The Chemical Origin of Life* (transl. from the Russian by Ann Synge). Charles C Thomas, Springfield, Illinois: xxvii + 124 pp., 22 figs.

OPARIN, A. I. (1968). *Genesis and Evolutionary Development of Life.* Academic Press, New York: vii + 203 pp., illustr.

OPARIN, A. I., SEREBROVSKAYA, K. B. & VASILEVA, N. V. (1968). Modelling of pre-biological selection of over-molecular systems (coacervate drops). *Dokl. Acad. Nauk SSSR,* **181**(3), pp. 744–6.

OPARIN, A. I. (1971a). Modern aspects of the problem of the origin of life. *Scientia,* Milano, Annus LXV, Ser. vii, pp. 195–206.

OPARIN, A. I. (1971b). Coacerbate drops as models of prebiological systems. Pp. 1–78 and 10 figs. in *Prebiotic and Biochemical Evolution* (Ed. A. P. Kimball & J. Oró). North-Holland, Amsterdam-London: x + 296 pp., illustr.

PRIGOGINE, I. (1955), *An Introduction to the Thermodynamics of Irreversible Processes.* Charles C Thomas, Springfield, Illinois: 115 pp.

PROC. THIRD INTERNAT. CONF. ON THE ORIGIN OF LIFE (1971). *Molecular Evolution.* I. Chemical evolution and the origin of life (Ed. R. Buvet & C. Ponnamperuma), North-Holland, Amsterdam: xi + 560 pp.

PULLMAN, B. (1971). Electronic factors in biochemical evolution. In *Exobiology* (Ed. C. Ponnamperuma). North-Holland, Amsterdam: 485 pp.

SNYDER, L. E. & BUHL, D. (1969). Water-vapor clouds in the interstellar medium. *Astrophys. J.,* **155**(2), pp. 65–70, illustr.

SNYDER, L. E., BUHL, D., ZUCKERMAN, B. & PALMER, P. (1969). Microwave detection of interstellar formaldehyde. *Physical Rev. Letters,* **22**(13), pp. 679–81, 2 figs.

SNYDER, L. E. & BUHL, D. (1970). *International Astronomical Union Circular,* No. 2251.

STEINMAN, G. & COLE, M. N. (1967). Synthesis of biologically pertinent peptides under possible primordial conditions. *Proc. Nat. Acad. Sci., USA,* **58**, pp. 735–42.

TURNER, B. (1970). *International Astronomical Union Circular,* No. 2268.

VERNADSKY, V. I. (1940). [*Biogeochimitscheskie Oscherki.*—in Russian only.] Acad. Sci. USSR, Moscow-Leningrad, p. 185.

VERNADSKY, V. I. (1960). [*Izbrannuie sochineniya.*—in Russian.] Akademiya Nauk SSSR., Moskva: Tom IV, pt. 2, 651 pp., Tom V, 422 pp.

WILSON, R. W., JEFFERTS, K. B. & PENZIAS, A. A. (1970). Carbon monoxide in the Orion nebulae. *Astrophys. J.,* **161**(2), pp. 43–50, illustr.

ZUCKERMAN, B., BUHL, D., PALMER, P. & SNYDER, L. E. (1970). Observations of inter-stellar formaldehyde. *Astrophys. J.,* **160**, pp. 485–506, illustr.

2

THE BIOSPHERE TODAY

Keynote Paper

The Biosphere Today

by

NICHOLAS POLUNIN

Editor of Biological Conservation *and of* Plant Science Monographs,
15 Chemin F.-Lehmann, 1218 Grand-Saconnex,
Geneva, Switzerland

INTRODUCTION

Wondering recently in London how to present this enormous subject to an enlightened but very mixed audience, I strolled out into St James's and then through Green and Hyde Parks. The grass was still short and the trees were bare, but here and there fine clumps of daffodils and flashes of crocuses were in full bloom, and the 'lakes' were alive with all manner of waterfowl. In quiet corners I met more blackbirds than one generally sees in a long walk in the country—not to mention the hordes of pigeons and sparrows. Some early-flowering *Prunus* trees added a delicate tinge of pink. The entire prospect was delightful in early spring, though almost entirely artificial: not at all typical of the biosphere, but an impressive display of what man has created—and can do even better—when the will, knowledge, and money, are available. Given these last three prerequisites, it is also a portent of what we may expect to see more and more of in future, as human population burgeons and great cities multiply, extend, and ultimately coalesce.

So far as we yet know, the biosphere—the 'envelope' of our planet earth in which life can exist normally, that is, without the costly apparatus of space-ships, etc.—is the only such phenomenon in the universe. Extending from the bottoms of the oceans and lakes and the deepest depths of the earth's outer crust to which living roots and microorganisms penetrate, right up to the highest levels of the atmosphere (at least 10,000 metres) to which spores and other living bodies occur naturally, it supports the virtual entirety of vital activity—including man's. Until relatively recent times the biosphere had been widely thought of as practically unalterable or at least inviolable; but now we know that it is changing in many ways, being in fact quite alarmingly fragile.

Different aspects of this fragility will be emphasized and discussed in this Conference by leading authorities in pursuing our main theme of prognosti-cating what is likely to happen in the future as far as they can foresee it, and in suggesting what can and should be done to alleviate environmental degradation and avoid concomitant catastrophes to man and nature. In this there are clearly two extremes among the possibilities, namely what is to be expected and should be done if present trends continue unabated, and what may be hoped for if man takes a firm hold of himself and effectively curbs his ecologically less desirable activities. Probably something between these ex-tremes can be most confidently expected with the widespread modern awakening to what is happening and with environmental education getting under way. Yet man's lustful habits are notoriously difficult to change.

Not being, I hope, one to rush in 'where angels fear to tread', or to pit my meagre knowledge against experts in their fields, my task is nevertheless to paint a broad picture of the current but ever-changing situation of and in the biosphere. For in spite of earlier suppositions it is ever-changing, and not merely inevitably in the manner and because of life itself, but in definite and often highly undesirable directions which tend to be irreversible. Apart from some entirely natural phenonema such as the release of radiation (Russell, 1969) and of compounds of mercury (Harriss, 1971) and lead (Goldberg, 1970) from the earth, most of the undesirable trends are due to man's activity since he became the heavy-handed superdominant of the world.

MAIN COMPONENTS OF THE BIOSPHERE

Probably because the entities with which they deal are so complex, biologists have acquired a propensity for classifying or at least categorizing whatever they deal with. In this context they are apt to look on the biosphere as being made up of the hydrosphere (whether marine or freshwater), the relatively thin biogeosphere (whether aerial or sub-aquatic, and including the pedosphere or soil layer where there is one), and the atmosphere (so far as it actually supports life). We all know something of the composition and significance of these three components, and I need not dwell on them; let us, however, consider them briefly from the standpoint of interchangeability, for they are by no means rigidly separated.

The aerial surfaces of the hydrosphere and of the biogeosphere give off water vapour so actively into the ambient atmosphere that there is in the latter a calculated 3,100 cubic miles or 13,000 cubic kilometres of water more or less all the time (Nace, 1964, 1967). However, the water present in the atmosphere corresponds to a thickness of only about 2.5 cm over the entire 510.23 million sq km of the surface of the globe, or 0.001 per cent of the world's total water of which 97.3 per cent is in the oceans and salt seas, and most of the remainder is frozen in ice-caps and glaciers (*ibid.*); so the cycling must be very active, as is indeed evidenced by the violence of many rain-storms. There is also seepage from the biogeosphere into inner layers of the geosphere where life is normally absent, and corresponding cycling through ground-water movements and springs, etc. The biogeosphere moreover adds materials (including nutrient salts) to the hydrosphere and atmosphere, both of which yield sediments that, in the case of loess, can become deposits many decametres thick. Often of great extent and thickness also are the deposits of particulate matter from the hydrosphere, on ocean or lake floors, of what thus becomes part of the biogeosphere and ultimately, below, of the geosphere in the wider sense. In addition to all this there is, more or less throughout the biosphere, the phenomenon of life in its manifold forms and with its specificity of adaptation and widely unique characteristics. Commonly it needs oxygen, which is plentiful not only throughout the free atmosphere but also in the soil 'atmosphere' and in solution in most parts of the hydrosphere whether marine or freshwater—thus affording further evidence of the continuous flux of materials and energy between the main components of the biosphere.

This degree of 'fluidity' of components of the biosphere seems the less surprising when we consider its origin and development as a single unit. To the extent that what we now think of as life apparently originated on the earth's surface about 2½ thousand million years ago, perhaps half-way back in the temporal span of our planet's existence (Oparin, 1957, 1970), or at most about 3,000 million years ago (Oparin, *in litt.*), the biosphere will have started with it—presumably at some particular geographical point or points, whence it extended gradually with living organisms to envelop in time the entire globe as it does today. But this conquering of the world's surface—particularly of 'dry' land by green plants—to give us the biosphere of recent times, appears from the fossil record to have taken place largely in the last 500 million years. Thus the story of the evolution of the biosphere is surely to a large extent the story of the evolution and extension of life itself on earth, and even as life is eternally changing, so is the biosphere—not merely within its component parts so far as they are separable, but to a considerable extent also between them. In this continual change, the living and inanimate components of the biosphere are both involved, being widely intermingled and often inter-dependent.

AN ECOLOGIST'S VIEWPOINT

Whereas the above categorization of the main components of the biosphere was roughly horizontal, the modern ecologist is apt to think in terms of very different kinds of units which tend to be separated and subdivided vertically. These are the ecosystems—each comprising a broadly characteristic biotic community and its inanimate matrix—and their component biotopes characterized by much more nearly uniform conditions and inhabiting biota. The biotopes are normally made up of phytotopes and zootopes characterizing particular 'ecological niches' and together comprising recognizable biomes. Such units collectively make up the biosphere, which is characterized almost everywhere by free oxygen that is for the most part biogenically produced and envelops the globe as the second most abundant component of the atmosphere. That this global atmospheric envelopment is apt to be complete even as regards relatively minor and casual components became clear to me many years ago when I found spores in the atmosphere over the North Pole (Polunin, 1951: Polunin & Kelly, 1952) and a friend informed me of his discovery of viable Bacteria in antarctic snow and ice, whither they had evidently been carried by air currents (Darling & Siple, 1941). Since then one has tended to think of many things globally rather than regionally!

A wide range of the main ecosystems and component biotopes—of which similar ones comprise a biochore—are so familiar to all of us that I need not dwell on them. It ought to be admitted, however, that judgments concerning them are apt to be subjective, as much depends on one's ecological upbringing and the scale on which one operates; also, that ecologists are apt to vary considerably in their terminology and even basic categorization. Yet to all, surely, the primary ecosystems (or biogeocoenoses) are plant-engendered 'formations' such as forest, grassland, and (relative) desert on land, and planktonic or benthic or other ones in both fresh and salt waters. Within them it seems best to recognize narrower ecosystems—such as different types of forest or grassland—and within these in turn the component biochores down to and including the narrowest of ecological niches with their attendant biota. All these together with the supernascent free atmosphere make up the biosphere, which is thus an enormously complex aggregation of often ill-defined entities.

These ecological or ambient entities making up the biosphere, having as their common attribute some form or forms of life, are moreover in a constant state of change—both internally (autogenically) and externally in their (allogenic) effects on others. Thus we have not merely birth, life, death, and decomposition, together with other autogenic changes leading to changes in particular directions (succession and regression), but also allogenic effects on other communities resulting from dispersal and leading interminably to new patterns of distribution. Beyond all this we have the constant 'struggle for existence' on both the individual and taxonomic scales, and not only with the physical conditions of the habitat but also, usually, among different organisms which compete for the same limited resources—be it of space, light, food, or whatever. Small wonder, then, that the biosphere is endlessly complex and ever-changing—with more than enough for us all, and many in addition, to study and attempt to elucidate. Furthermore, there are changes wrought by evolution and others superimposed by man, of which latter a charming but pungent account has recently been given by Fraser Darling (1971).

In spite of all this complexity and endless change, there are in the biosphere many general tendencies that can be categorized and laws that can be formulated, for it tends to function in a precise and often rigid manner. Thus apart from the intervention of man and drastic natural phenomena, there are various climatic and other cycles—such as those of erosion and deposition —which lead to or permit situations of relative stability or dynamic equilibrium, and it is these which we should watch and study to determine, in the words of my old teacher Sir Arthur Tansley, 'what nature does when left to herself'. Yet this becomes increasingly difficult and problematical as less and less of the biosphere is left without drastic disturbance by—or as an indirect result of the activities of—the world's overwhelming superdominant, man, and clearly we have to recognize that already there is relatively little left on earth that does not show his stamp. This we must surely accept: it is no use trying to be 'purist' conservationists any more!

THE PRESENT TURMOIL

The preceding paper having given us a masterly 'reflective view of the background' of what has happened and is continuing to happen in and to the biosphere as a result of man's all-too-massive intervention, it is not for me to attempt to emulate my distinguished predecessor. Nor is it for me to venture seriously into the fields of specialist speakers to come—the more so as I can assure you that almost every one was, for his particular theme, the first choice in the whole world of the conference's International Steering Committee over which I had the honour to preside. I do, however, feel that I should dwell awhile on the highly alarming situation in which we find ourselves at this stage of the world's unfolding history, only hoping that I can do this without in any way queering the pitch for my very eminent successor on this spot.

There can scarcely be any further doubt that the inexorable build-up of human population pressure, with its concomitants of devastating pollution, degradation of ecosystems, and loss of desirable habitats, constitutes for mankind and nature the very gravest of threats. Meanwhile, human life itself is apt to be widely degraded by over-population and crowding (S. Johnson, 1970). With the expected doubling by soon after the end of this century of the late-1970 figure of slightly over 3.6 thousand millions, and a further doubling about 35 years thereafter (Ehrlich & Ehrlich, 1970; United Nations, 1970, 1971), of the world's most numerous and dominating large species, *Homo sapiens*, more and more of the ecological equilibria that have become established through previous ages will inevitably be drastically disturbed or even destroyed. Already the environments of man and nature are widely quite grossly degraded, and the life to which we are accustomed is changing so extensively and even drastically that the problem may soon become one of sheer survival (Commoner, 1966; S. Johnson, 1970). To many of us it has long been clear that the very biosphere is becoming seriously threatened—that all manner of devastating attacks are converging on the balanced natural system and extremely complex fabric which sustains life on earth, and that the central problem of modern man is this mounting 'environmental crisis' (Helfrich, 1970) or 'environmental revolution' (Nicholson, 1970; Detwyler, 1971).

For by and large there is a widening gap between the number of human mouths to feed and man's capabilities of satisfying them and, quite apart from basic food, of catering for the ever-increasing demands on the world's limited resources of raw materials and even of space. Moreover, in spite of the desperate need to maintain biological productivity as the main basis of life, and to increase production of human foods at least to keep pace with his own numbers, man is adding a fresh complex of depressive catastrophes to the time-honoured ones of drastic climatic or seismic or other 'natural' change—while risking to add more even in these last three categories. Much even of the so-called 'green revolution' of recent years has only been effected through flogging the soil and turning fresh waters and ultimately seas into virtual sewers.

We shall be hearing far more about these problems as this Conference proceeds, and from eminent specialists who will surely inculcate in us the conviction that it is to the impact of many of man's doings and the countering of their ill-effects that the world should now address itself with all possible speed and vigour. Many of these ill-effects are completely avoidable and many others can be reduced to quite minor significance, being due to mere ignorance, uneducated apathy, or sheer greed; yet some, at least, if not effectively countered, may lead to appalling ecodisasters. Of these there are so many and various possibilities that one's inclination is merely to wait and see what blow will fall when and where! The latest really hair-raising one is that of the huge supersonic transport airplanes (SSTs) and also military ones that some nations are now putting or planning to put into the stratosphere, where, according to Professor George C. Pimentel (*in litt.*), 'There is a very dangerous likelihood that [they] will threaten continued existence of life on this planet, plant and animal, by seriously depleting the ozone layer' which filters off the lethal ultra-violet radiation from the sun.

Many of the gravest threats that are having to be faced increasingly by man and nature are global ones, that will need to be tackled at least internationally through the establishment and enforcement of suitable laws and conventions. At present, man is changing important features of the biosphere and destroying the habitats of many plants and animals while widely altering his own (Huxley, 1969; Dorst, 1970). It may not seem to matter so much to him for the time being, as he is extraordinarily inventive and consequently resilient, and meanwhile every now and then some local catastrophe awakens us and makes us feel better when its effects have passed; but still the insidious and sometimes global changes continue. And many of them continue to build up, stealthily, to what could become dangerous proportions. Thus to have grave doubts about our world's future one need only contemplate the widespread destruction of vegetation and concomitant extension of deserts and wastelands, the appalling pollution of the oceans and seas (Heyerdahl, 1971; Cousteau, 1971), the manifold effects of atmospheric pollution both gaseous and particulate (MIT, 1970), the accelerating disappearance of rare species and unique genetic material, the changing of nature's habitats into areas of building, concrete, or monoculture, and the often drastic disturbance of freshwater as well as marine ecosystems by sewage and detergents, insecticides, herbicides, chemical fertilizers, organic mercury compounds, etc.—*ad nauseam* and almost *ad infinitum* (Mellanby, 1967, 1971; Taylor, 1970). These often insidious evils go on together and continue, so that their overall effects have to be considered collectively even if they can only be tackled individually.

One cannot see much hope in the long run unless vegetation, whether natural or of man-controlled crops, etc., continues to fashion most animals' habitats, produce plentiful food, and universally return oxgyen to the atmosphere—particularly through the functioning of marine phytoplankton, which is reputedly responsible for some three-quarters of the free oxygen in the world's air. Yet man's activities are now widely contrary to these three vital needs, besides changing nature in other ways. Nor are matters getting better but generally worse, so that in time there will obviously have to be limitation of human population increases which otherwise seem set to change the biosphere so drastically that life as we know it may become widely impossible. Let us hope that this limitation can be through political enlightenment and medical intervention rather than by the traditional ways of strife, pestilence, and above all famine.

As emphasized very recently by our Conference Scientific Patron Sir Julian Huxley (*in litt. binis*), the effects of deforestation can be quite disastrous, and are proving so all too widely, the underlying soils becoming leached and badly eroded, or rapidly exhausted by cultivation. He also stresses 'the dangers of introducing alien species to a balanced and isolated (e.g. insular) ecosystem . . . Mongooses in the West Indies and Fiji, Mink in Iceland, etc. This results in ground-nesting birds being largely wiped out—in Iceland with grave commercial loss in eiderdown!' Not only are we running short of food but also of water, while the dangers of extracting water from the upper reaches or terminal basin of a river (as opposed to its mouth) are only now becoming at all widely recognized. Sir Julian also stresses 'the need to keep all the world's national and local nature parks and nature reserves intact, and if possible to add to their number', with suitable education on the importance of conservation the key to this and much else besides, and widespread birth-control an especially urgent need. Otherwise at best the areas of open country and natural beauty will become more and more limited and rare, and 'wilderness and in time wildness will vanish from the world'.

It has been suggested by some that relief might come from other planets; but actually, in view of the virtual impossibility at present of maintaining effective quarantine (Alexander, 1970), it should be a matter of relief that it now seems unlikely that any form of life exists in the solar system outside the world's biosphere—apart, of course, from individuals sent by man from earth and maintained only artificially and temporarily. Such widespread use of any other planet or planets in our universe now seems virtually out of the question. Nor is the much-vaunted 'green revolution' likely to help us lastingly; rather, as indicated above, aspects of it may in fact increase our ultimate troubles, although relieving some situations temporarily.

Loss of Diversity

We have already observed that few areas of the world are fully 'natural' any more, undisturbed by the activities of man. At least this is true on land, where even remote arctic regions that seemed (and sometimes were) untouched by man when I worked in them in my youth are now becoming polluted and widely disturbed, as are the limited ice-free tracts of Antarctica (Rudolph, 1970). Various aspects of man-engendered pollution will be dealt with expertly by our colleagues; I suppose this scourge has been existent in some form and degree since Adam first relieved himself (though of course judicious manuring is good), and even before that there were doubtless natural oil-leaks (Allen *et al.*, 1972), obnoxious accumulations of rotting vegetation and/or animals' bodies, and all manner of allied ecological disturbances. Thus pollution is not new so much as increasing quite shockingly in its multiplicity of forms, complexity, and overall effects. Nor, for these and other reasons, is the biosphere at all what it used to be in actuality or, particularly, potentiality.

One of the gravest threats to life on earth as we know it is the ever-increasing loss of diversity—of habitats, vegetation, and biota. An eloquent plea for the support of such diversity has been published by one of our colleagues (Dasmann, 1968*a*), and indeed modern conservation is very largely concerned with its maintenance (Black, 1968; Dasmann, 1968*b*). More and more widely, meanwhile, various landforms get levelled to cultivable plains, 'marginal' lands get torn up and soon eroded, ever-increasing areas get covered with concrete or asphalt, and huge expanses are flooded for water-storage and other purposes. Forests are killed by defoliants or cleared for selfish gain, and not only do the bases of soil fertility and the habitats of wild plants and animals disappear with them, but the surrounding drainage systems may get 'enriched' and degraded by eutrophication, the nitrate concentrations in stream affluents often exceeding the health levels recommended for drinking water (Likens *et al.*, 1970; NAS, 1970).

Tracts of land get treated with pesticides or special fertilizers which favour a particular type of vegetation or animal community—the treatment commonly having to be repeated periodically to maintain what man desires. The extreme expression of this is the monoculture of most agricultural crops and to a lesser extent forests, in which diversity is at a minimum and soil exploitation is apt to be at or near a maximum—at least in the absence of suitable crop-rotation. Erosional and other impoverishment frequently ensues, with a fall in local productivity. Moreover, with the loss of special habitats, many plant and animal species become restricted in their range or even extinct, with concomitant loss of unique germ-plasm (Dorst, 1970; Frankel, 1970; Frankel & Bennett, 1970). Such undesirable phenomena all too commonly advance on an unsuspecting world practically unnoticed—the more easily when they are hidden under seemingly desirable activities such as clearing of scrub or drainage of wetlands. Yet they should be watched and controlled for the wider and longer-term good, as all together they are assuming very serious proportions and having quite alarming effects (UNESCO, 1970; Detwyler, 1971).

In general these changes are being wrought most actively in the industrialized countries, which already use quite disproportionate amounts of the world's renewable and other resources: following technological 'advance' often comes extreme pollution, which in turn leads to loss of diversity. This is commonly expressed in the overwhelming preponderance of particular plant and/or animal species which are alone favoured by the conditions and often also by the unilateral suppression of their normal competitors and predators; the result is too often an extreme simplification of the community and sometimes even a monoculture following the breakdown of the usual intimate association of animals with plants (Pickavance, 1971; Polunin, 1971).

Introductions of exotics are also apt to lead to loss of diversity in some cases, or to be a nuisance in other ways, and should accordingly be controlled and, when made, closely watched for the general good. Examples include the rabbits and cacti which were such a plague in Australia until, most fortunately, they were substantially controlled by biological means without adding long-lasting poisons to the local ecosystems. Living as I do almost in a major airport, with large aircraft bringing people and goods from many parts of the world almost all the time, I often wonder that there are not far more effective introductions of exotic plants and animals: the answer probably is that, even when climatic and other conditions are favourable, 'open' habitats have to be found for successful establishment, though when this takes place we must indeed look out for the local denizens and their maintenance of diversity. Already the floras of some island groups are largely alien, and there are considerable areas, for example in Hawaii, Ceylon, and New Zealand, where the native plants have been largely ousted by alien ones after man has disturbed the local vegetation (Polunin, 1967).

BEAUTY AND THE BIOSPHERE

The first man who landed on the moon was struck by earth's beauty when viewed from afar. Indeed the natural world as a whole is supremely beautiful—meaning the visible part of the biosphere, for we cannot see below it. In contrast, many of man's products and doings are far from beautiful, and whenever he manages to produce a special work of art or utility he is apt to place a great price upon it. When will he learn so to price natural phenomena —other than certain minerals—that he will take proper pride in their existence and care for their conservation? All one can say, in sub-desperation, is 'the sooner the better'! Yet many of the offerings of nature are, surely, far more beautiful than any work of man, and many are apt to disappear because we do not look after them and are apt to take them for granted until it is too late. Beauty being 'in the eye of the beholder', we must teach our children to appreciate it to the full in nature, all insisting together on its preservation for future generations to enjoy.

Not being a poet, I will not attempt to extol the beauties of the biosphere which here in this fairyland of lakes and forests we are all fortunate enough to see and be able to appreciate in fine measure. Yet to an extraordinary degree man's activities destroy this beauty or at least run counter to its full maintenance. As life on earth goes on and human population pressures build up, there is an increasing conflict between the preservationists and the developers. There seems to be a tacit assumption that the interests of the two run counter to each other, whereas really they should go together. That they can do so is evidenced by the simple economy and very beauty of some modern buildings, such as many here in Finland and the Nestlé headquarters on Lake Geneva. Wise recycling can take us much farther, and for such economic activity we commonly have ample knowledge already.

It is said that a happy marriage cannot long exist on love alone, and certainly mankind cannot long exist on beauty alone; but it does help, and much as we may recognize the merits of simplicity, we are bound to admit that the beauty of the world is largely bound up with its extraordinary diversity and striking combinations. Thus we have in the biosphere some three millions of species of living plants, animals, and microorganisms, and probably several times that complement of lower taxa; others are being evolved all the time, while many others have already become extinct. Much the same applies to ecological entities, which I like to call eca. The diversity is enormous—of function as well as form—and we are also blessed with a superb array of different landscapes and seascapes as well as, in most areas, changeable seasons. We can even afford some of the 'new and hurtsome architectures' deplored by the eminent author of the preceding paper, provided they are kept together and so far as possible out of sight. In other words, development can go on but it must be so far as possible hand-in-hand with nature; the biosphere cannot afford and anyway will not long support unbridled human development alone. Nor should we attempt to tamper with its 'absolute asymmetry' (UNESCO, 1970), as this seems to be part and parcel of the situation of relative stability to which it has come naturally through long eons of change.

Sometimes, as a citizen of this harsh but beautiful world, I wish I had a real writer's sensitivity to describe what as a biologist I feel about its unique wonders. Brought up in an artistic home and accustomed to all manner of sights and forms, I can sense them but that is all. Yet surely there is nothing in man's doings as sublime as a spider's gossamer web with dew on it in the early morning, as a view across an Alpine valley with snow-capped mountains towering behind, as a North American maple forest when the leaves turn to brilliant colours in the fall, as an arctic glacier calving into a sunlit sea of dancing waves, or as a field of ripening oats in the sun—unless it be another with raindrops shining on the spikelets! Such and thousands more are the joysome architectures of nature in contrast to the hurtsome ones of man, but in the last instance they bring us back to the reality that much can be done by combining the forces of nature and those of man. For that field of ripening oats was a man-fostered monoculture, and so perhaps was the maple forest—albeit a more enduring product of man's saner activities. There seems no end to the possibilities of man working *with* nature—including various kinds of symbioses such as man with dog and/or horse—but an inevitable end to the world as we know it if he continues to work so widely against her. The constructive possibilities include creative conservation and the enlightened offering of new habitats of which we shall have more to say before closing.

FUNCTIONING OF THE BIOSPHERE

Although the biosphere is endowed with considerable plasticity in its resistance to many agents of potential change, this seems to be in large degree because it has evolved through long ages of what practically amounts to 'trial and error' that does not, however, fit it to resist unaccustomed pressures. Such pressures are now being exerted with increasing force and diversity by man, and often with grave results as we have already seen. Probably the most dangerous of these results, for man's and nature's future, are those which are irreversible, breaking into systems and relationships that in extreme cases have become established only through long geological ages. To appreciate this and have some inkling of what we should do or try to avoid, let us consider in outline a few of the main items in that indescribably complex plethora, the functioning of the biosphere. Two headings will suffice.

Energy Relations and Photosynthesis

As every biologist knows, the surface of the planet earth is bathed by day in solar energy which is fixed and utilized by green plants. Through their possession of chlorophyll, green plants have the particular and all-important ability of synthesizing complex organic substances from carbon dioxide and water with the aid of radiant energy from the sun, which energy is then stored in these organic substances and made available as the basis of the vital activity of practically all forms of life. Thus the biosphere as a whole stores and utilizes vast quantities of energy which reaches it from space and is the basis of its vital activity and very functioning. But tamper with any of the prerequisites—the supply of solar energy, the concentration of carbon dioxide, the availability of water, the functioning of chlorophyll, the ray-filtering activity of the stratosphere, or the breakdown of organic substances needed to give energy for life and growth—and there could be trouble so grave that it might, conceivably, bring life to a standstill or absolute end. Yet such tampering, insidiously and of course unintentionally, is currently going on—though at present only to a degree that probably does not enormously matter in terms of the biosphere's survival.

As examples we may note that the amount of solar energy reaching the earth's surface is being reduced over considerable areas by particulate pollution in the atmosphere (Wendland & Bryson, 1970), though fortunately the resultant reduction of temperature at the earth's surface appears at present to compensate for the so-called 'greenhouse effect' of holding in heat by increased amounts of carbon dioxide in the atmosphere—which increases have totalled at least *ca* 6 per cent since around the turn of the present century and have been due principally to the excessive burning of petroleum and other 'fossil fuels' (F. S. Johnson, 1970; Attiwill, 1971). Again, the functioning of chlorophyll or anyway photosynthesis by some marine planktonic Algae is adversely affected by infinitesimally small amounts of certain chlorinated hydrocarbon insecticides and their persistent breakdown products which have now reached all parts of the globe and also affect respiration (Wurster, 1969 and *in litt.*); yet the return of oxygen to the atmosphere is very largely the result of the photosynthetic activity of planktonic Algae. Photosynthesis and respiration are, of course, practically reciprocal in the matter of oxygen production and use, respectively, and, being two of the most fundamental and universally important activities of life and items of functioning of the biosphere, we had better watch out!

The biosphere is *in toto* a thermodynamically open but generally equilibrated system of living and dead matter (in both cases storing energy) set in an inorganic framework of rock, water, and gaseous materials, that accumulates and redistributes immense amounts of energy all the time. The living matter is in organisms, developed in vast numbers of forms through the long period of evolution since the first manifestations of life appeared probably more than two (some say more than three) thousand million years ago. These organisms exhibit, as another of the main features of the biosphere and items of its functioning, incessant metabolic and motional interactions with their immediate environment (including one another). Indeed they may be visualized as exhibiting activity at three 'levels': internally in their physiology, peripherally in their autecology, and externally in their synecology or relationship to the biome or living component of the biotope and ecosystem to which they belong. As we have already seen, man is apt to change these relationships all too often and, in the case of some important habitats and therefore inhabiting species, drastically. Yet the need for reasonably equable energy-flow is paramount (Odum, 1971), and this normally presupposes the maintenance of existing biotopes.

Growth and Cycling

Another main item of biosphere functioning is the characteristic cycling which takes place so actively that most atoms of carbon existing in living plants must have been back and forth into the atmosphere (which consists as to only about 0.032 per cent of carbon dioxide at any one time) on innumerable occasions. The same may well be true to a lesser extent of oxygen and to a still lesser extent of nitrogen. The total biomass of living organisms *on land* is calculated as being between 3×10^{12} and 10^{13} (3–10,000,000,000,000) metric tons, of which the animal part (zoobiomass) is usually less than 1 per cent, the remainder being the phytobiomass of plants which form up to about 55×10^9 tons of organic matter per year (UNESCO, 1970). Of the animal component from 95 to 99.5 per cent, according particularly to the habitat, is contributed by invertebrates (*ibid.*), of which most live for only a short time. The flow of matter and energy from plants to herbivores depends largely on the number and biomass of the latter, whereas the change of living to dead organic matter is not much influenced by the amount of dead matter present; this last disappears largely through various oxidative processes aided by microorganisms which abound almost everywhere.

On land, vegetation is computed to fix annually the equivalent of some 21.3×10^{16} calories, while 'about the same quantity of energy is fixed by oceanic vegetation' (UNESCO, 1970). Other cycles involve nitrogen, phosphorus, and various other elements (Scientific American, 1970) which are essential components of all or some living organisms, and water which has that significance universally and also cycles in vast quantities all the time through evaporation into the atmosphere and precipitation from it as we have already seen. Details, of course, vary in climatically different areas of the globe, and with the distribution of land and water (which covers about 70 per cent of the earth's surface). There is also cycling to some extent of sedimentary materials, including living organisms and their dead bodies, in the atmosphere and hydrosphere, and of water and mineral salts in the geosphere.

Although crystals can 'grow' in the right medium, the possession of protoplasm, growth in stature based on it, and continuing reproduction of taxa, are characteristics solely of living organisms on which again the functioning of the biosphere depends—as it does in a sense also on evolution, which in some degree seems to go on all the time wherever there is life. Even where new forms are not separable morphologically, they may exhibit differences in their biochemical make-up or physiological activity, or in their ecological impress that is important in the particular 'niche' which they occupy. Such circumstances as unnatural increase in radiation above the amounts which organisms are accustomed to receiving normally from the earth and from space, may increase mutation and lead to monstrosities, etc., as well as to less striking new forms. To a lesser degree, other types of disturbance by man, such as mere clearing of vegetation and offering of new habitats, seems to have a similar effect, while the possibilities of hybridization and gene-flow are increased by invasion of exotics, etc. Thus arise continually new forms and even species that must have their effect on the biosphere, be it usually in only infinitesimally small degree. In the face of all this it should be possible to afford some continued losses through extinction!

Living organisms play an important role in the biosphere also in many and various processes of weathering, soil formation, sedimentation, concentration of calcium and iron compounds, and gaseous exchanges even beyond those already considered, many Bacteria, etc., existing by reducing functions in anaerobic media. These activities have evidently increased in the past as the number and diversity of organisms with different biogeochemical attributes have increased. It would be good to visualize such increases as continuing in future, with life as a whole becoming more complex as more and more ecological niches are filled that have been created by man's *wise* intervention leading to healthy retention of desirable elements in biological cycles! In any case the significance of plants, *inter alia* in concentrating minerals in their tissues and transferring them to the upper layers of the soil on death or making them available to animals which eat the plants, must not be overlooked or too widely interfered with.

Paramount among activities in and of the biosphere is the continuous production of living matter and its accumulation of energy, although in this only a small proportion, commonly less than 1 per cent, of the incoming solar energy is used. Nevertheless something approaching one hundred thousand million tons of organic material are photosynethesized annually on the planet —rather more than half of it on land, and rather more than half of this in forests. Meadows and other grasslands and shallow waters fix an average 0.5–3 grams of carbon per square metre per day, prairies and temperate forests and cultivated fields fix about 3–10 grams of carbon per square metre per day, and tropical forests and intensively cultivated fields and areas of floodplains and estuaries fix 10–20 grams of carbon per square metre per day (Duvigneaud, 1967). The standing crops of phytobiomass varies enormously—from less than 2.5 metric tons per hectare in deserts to up to 1,700 tons per hectare in some tropical forests. Intermediate amounts are up to 25 tons per hectare in tundra, up to 400 tons per hectare in coniferous forests, and 400–500 tons per hectare in broad-leafed forests (UNESCO, 1970). However, these figures may bear little relation to annual production, in which grasslands and savannas may rank high; also, the chemical composition of the organic matter in different ecosystems may vary greatly, with the ash content highest in halophytes (where it may approach 50 per cent of dry-weight) and lowest in tundras and temperate forests (where it commonly ranges from 1.5 to 2.5 per cent) (*cf*. Kovda & Yakushevskaya, 1967).

Biological cycling within ecosystems and biotopes is almost universal. In the oceans and lakes the plankton 'rain' of dead bodies helps to support all manner of deep-water communities, including many in the aphotic abyssal, while on land there is litter which tends to accumulate on the forest floor or other ground. The ratio between litter mass and annual fall gives some indication of the rate of decomposition of the litter and concomitant release of the less-leached chemical elements: the higher it is, the lower will be the intensity of biological circulation in a given ecosystem or biotope (Bazilevich & Rodin, 1967). This index is highest in swamp forests (more than 50) and dwarf-shrub tundra (20–50), which may be considered almost stagnant in this respect. It is considerably lower (10–17) in coniferous forests and still lower (3–4) in broad-leafed forests. In steppes, the decomposition of litter is apt to be very rapid, biological circulation being active, with the index down to 1–1.5. In subtropical forests the index is even lower, being about 0·7, while in savannas it is lower still, being not more than 0.2. In humid tropical forests, owing to the intensive activity of organisms causing its rapid decay and breakdown, almost no litter accumulates and the index is no higher than 0.1.

The transition from one trophic level to another in natural ecosystems commonly involves a loss of biomass of the order of 100 to 1,000, the ratio between the phytobiomass and the total biomass of herbivorous animals present being often of the order of 100 to 10,000 or even 100,000 (UNESCO, 1970). At the best this is far lower than the annual fodder consumption and indicates that the plant resources are only partially used by wild herbivores—suggesting considerable potentialities for changes of ratio from which man might benefit without undue disruption of nature. This could have useful possibilities towards the already desired more-than-doubling of the 20 million tons of protein currently available annually for human food, which would be needed if the present human population of the world were to be adequately nourished. For the future it could have far greater potentialities towards satisfying foreseeable increased needs.

MAN AND HIS BIOSPHERE

Yes, we must face it whether we like the prospect or not, the biosphere is practically man's to do what he chooses with—which, as we have already implied, could be anywhere from utter destruction to the creation of something quite good from his own standpoint and even to some extent from that of nature. For to return momentarily to the extremes which we visualized early in this paper, to continue as latterly would mean in time almost inevitably the destruction of life on earth as we know it, whereas wise use of man's knowledge and unique capabilities, together with the basic necessity of controlling his own future population, should yield for man an attractive and lastingly viable biosphere, albeit a widely unnatural one. But as an early measure to allow such an obvious desideratum, the tendency of humans—having conquered most aspects of their environment apart from the supply of the wherewithal to enable them to go on multiplying indefinitely—to breed uninhibitedly, will have to be curbed, particularly in the industrially less-developed parts of the world (Ehrlich & Ehrlich, 1970; S. Johnson, 1970). For it should not be forgotten that human population growth, like that of most other consumers, is ultimately dependent on increases in available food, even though it is scarcely the *result* of such increases, as has been contended, for example, in the Scientific American (1970).

Need to Limit Human Population

A few years ago I found myself the chairman of a lively symposium on 'Conservation and Environment Concerns' at the Eleventh International Botanical Congress at Seattle, Washington, where a group of students were collecting what in a few days totalled nearly 1,200 signatures of delegates from all over the world to a draft resolution pointing out the dangers to the biosphere of uncontrolled human population increases. Going a little further, I put it to the audience of several hundreds at the symposium that the burgeoning human population would in time confront man and nature with the greatest threats which they had ever faced: there was not so much as a 'peep' of dissension. Yet others elsewhere have dissented, and even continue to dissent, so increasing the dangers from uncontrolled self-interest (or so it seems). Referring to the 3.5 thousand millions in the world at the time of their writing, the Ehrlichs, in their book just cited, wrote, 'Armed with weapons as diverse as thermonuclear bombs and DDT, this mass of humanity now threatens to destroy most of the life on the planet. Mankind itself may stand on the brink of extinction; in its death throes it could take with it most of the other passengers of spaceship earth.' While somewhat dramatic, this is a perfectly real possibility that has been adumbrated by even cautious neo-Malthusian authors; for simple calculations indicate that if human population went on increasing at its present rate for another 600 years, there would be one square metre of land per person, while if it continued for 3,000 years, the total human biomass would approximate the mass of the physical globe! Realization of the 'impossibility' of this kind of situation has led to the rapid expansion of the Zero Population Growth (ZPG) movement in North America (Radl, 1970), whose basic tenet is that two children per family is the desirable norm. If only this movement could effectively take in the rest of the world, our hopes for the future would soar!

Hitherto throughout recorded history man has proved increasingly adept at controlling almost everything but himself: surely his unique intelligence (wishfully indicated in the specific epithet *sapiens*) and extraordinary capability in so many directions will in time enable him to do this, too. That his physical and mental plasticity and resilience are great need scarcely be repeated—except to give us hope in the face of the plethora of pessimistic prognostications that nowadays cloud our horizon. Yet they are in the right direction in making the world and even its governments wake up to a realization at long last of what is happening—insidiously and relentlessly but still far too actively. Education is a great hope—especially of and through the very young, whose world it will be in the future—and ecological and sociological research is another. Hope also lies in the effective intervention of trade unions when it is wisely directed—as, for example, recently with their decision to 'black' all commercial activities which could endanger the Great Barrier Reef of Australia (Connell, 1970, 1971). Great possibilities also lie in wise and efficient recycling—of wastes, water, and many other resources, especially when non-renewable. Meanwhile it need scarcely be reiterated that there is a tremendous amount and variety of cleaning up to do wherever man lives in any great numbers and density—and often even where he does not. To a large extent it can perfectly well be done: witness the return of sunlight to London and of fishes to its River Thames (Wheeler, 1969). Apart from widespread apathy and ignorance, the difficulties are apt to be financial, for the cost of maintaining a clean and viable environment tends to be great; yet more and more industrial concerns are nowadays including the costs of anti-pollution measures in their budgets—usually to conform to local laws, but sometimes seeing beyond them.

Whether the biosphere has yet reached its optimum human population is apt to be hotly debated; probably it has not, apart from the desirability of maintaining existing ecosystems and biotopes, which are already often suffering excruciatingly from man's impress. On the other hand, some countries have already surpassed their desirable complement and have become dependent on others for the satisfaction of human needs. Yet if one thinks of such items as the conceivability of raising the efficiency of photosynthesis by cultivated plants from its present very low level of only 0.2 to 1 per cent up to 5 or even 10 per cent (UNESCO, 1970), of the possibility of increasing markedly the present mere 2–3 per cent of the phytobiomass on land that is utilized by man, of the proven capabilities of geneticists and plant breeders to produce more and more productive strains of plants, of the potentialities for poultry- and fish-farming and even more intensive microbiological synthesis of high-protein foods, and of desalination of water and the vast areas, for example of the Sahara, which could be brought back into production through man's ingenuity, one feels that there should still be food and room in the world for *some* more people to enjoy a reasonable life without despoiling the environment unduly. Thus if human population pressures and ultimately numbers are somehow limited in time, we should be able to look forward to continuing with a reasonably livable world—even though it will inevitably be changed in many ways from what it used to be—in which man and nature will have often changed habits and habitats, and to some extent conceivably altered forms, from their accustomed ones. For this, man will have to change himself again to support nature, even as nature must go through changes to accommodate man; they must learn to live together once more.

Nature Retreating but Still Resilient

Mankind used to fear nature—wild animals, wild places, and the unknown—but latterly he brought nature to bay, and now wild nature is retreating all too rapidly on an increasing range of fronts, so that wildernesses of any kind are difficult to find. Some of these facets are irreversible, having upset complex and delicate situations that took long ages to establish but have now passed the point of no return, while others are fast approaching that point. Yet there are hopes as we have seen, and others of a practical nature that we should mention in concluding. Towards widespread action in the right direction we now have the international Man and the Biosphere project getting under way (Batisse, 1971), various global monitoring and surveying activities such as those of the World Meteorological Organization (Anon., 1970) and the World Health Organization (Anon., 1971) to tell us what is happening, and active preparations for the great United Nations Conference on the Human Environment to which we ourselves are geared and in which we have high hopes as a means of 'getting at' the governments of the world and persuading them to do what is needed and often they alone could accomplish. There are also ideas for a global environmental monitoring and surveying system that would include detailed biological monitoring, though of suitable bases for this too little is known to formulate definite plans as yet (Lundholm & Svensson, 1970). And after all, monitoring and surveying are only the precursors and often prerequisites of real action, which is what man's biosphere needs. Towards such action we shall surely have various proposals from this Conference, and I hope strong and effective recommendations for the outside world. Among organizations which seem clearly needed is an advisory World Council on Environmental Future, which must be entirely free and independent of all governmental and sectional allegiance and, who knows, might grow out of our present Conference.

Fortunately it is not only man that is resilient and 'plastic' but also many wild and domesticated creatures, both animal and plant. Even around the entirely 'new and hurtsome architectures' among which I live, the 'dawn chorus' of birds is great in its variety and considerable in its volume; and one expects it to increase in both these attributes as the planted trees and shrubs grow and the balcony gardens blossom and buzz with bees. Even the most glaring dumps and earthworks are apt to become clothed with vegetation, to the benefit of butterflies and the joy of children who delight to play on them. Great especially are the possibilities of 'creative conservation', the subject of the first 'short communication' ever to be published in my own journal, *Biological Conservation* (Benthem, 1968), and those of multi-purpose 'land consolidation' towards a planned development of landscapes for other purposes besides agriculture and forestry (Benthem, 1969). In these activities, after due study of all foreseeable aspects of the situation and then careful planning and execution, new habitats are offered for invading biota and new biotopes thereby developed. Admittedly they are to a considerable extent man-engendered—but so are an increasing proportion of the landscapes of the world. This we have already emphasized and, one hopes, agreed to accept; for we can never turn back the clock and revert fully to what used to be. Nor was it all unquestionably so good! Clearly we have a grave responsibility, to our descendants and to nature, to make the future world a fit place to live and work and relax in—which means living in unison with nature—and not the ugly hotch-potch of toil and strife which, even at the best, it is likely to become with increasing degradation of the environment if stern action is not taken. It is also clear—indeed axiomatic—that time is not on our side.

Such hopes are not so much utopian as necessary of realization. Towards this we should educate our young and adjure them to watch out—to monitor and survey changes in the biosphere far more actively and thoroughly than as yet we do ourselves, and to act with dispatch whenever the need arises. Often such action will have to be international, and sometimes doubtless global. But here I risk trespassing on the ground of my last-of-all successor on this spot, who has I know been cogitating for some time on these aspects of the biosphere to come.

<h2 style="text-align:center">REFERENCES</h2>

ALEXANDER, Martin (1970). Lunar and Martian quarantine. *Biological Conservation*, **2**(3), pp. 169–70.

ALLEN, Alan A., SCHLUETER, Roger S. & MIKOLAJ, Paul G. (1972). Natural oil seepage at Coal Oil Point, Santa Barbara, California. *Biological Conservation*, **4**(2), pp. 106–7, illustr.

ANON. (1970). *A Brief Survey of the Activities of the World Meteorological Organization Relating to Human Environment*. Secretariat of the World Meteorological Organization, Geneva, Switzerland: iii + 22 pp., illustr.

ANON. (1971). International study of air quality criteria. *Biological Conservation*, **3**(3), p. 207.

ATTIWILL, Peter M. (1971). Atmospheric carbon dioxide and the biosphere. *Environmental Pollution*, **1**(4), pp. 249–61, 1 fig.

BATISSE, Michel (1971). Man and the Biosphere: an international research programme. *Biological Conservation*, **4**(1), pp. 1–6.

BAZILEVICH, N. L. & RODIN, L. E. (1967). Map-schemes of productivity and of biological cycling of the main types of vegetation on dry land of earth. *Izvestiya Vsesoyuznogo Geograficheskogo Obchestva*, **99**(3), pp. 190–4, 2 maps.

BENTHEM, Roelof J. (1968). Creative conservation. *Biological Conservation*, **1**(1), pp. 11–12.

BENTHEM, Roelof J. (1969). Changing the countryside by land consolidation. *Biological Conservation*, **1**(3), pp. 209–12, illustr.

BLACK, John D. (1968). *The Management and Conservation of Biological Resources*. F. A. Davis, Philadelphia: xi + 339 pp., illustr.

COMMONER, Barry (1966). *Science and Survival*. Victor Gollancz, London: 128 pp.

CONNELL, D. W. (1970). Inquiry into advisability of oil-drilling in the Great Barrier Reef of Australia. *Biological Conservation*, **3**(1), pp. 60–1.

CONNELL, D. W. (1971). The Great Barrier Reef conservation issue—a case history. *Biological Conservation*, **3**(4), pp. 249–54, illustr.

COUSTEAU, Jacques-Yves (1971). Statement on global marine degradation. *Biological Conservation*, **4**(1), pp. 61–5.

DARLING, Chester A. & SIPLE, Paul A. (1941). Bacteria of Antarctica. *Journal of Bacteriology*, **42**, pp. 83–98.

DARLING, Sir Frank Fraser. *See* FRASER DARLING, Sir Frank

DASMANN, Raymond F. (1968a). *A Different Kind of Country*. Macmillan, New York, and Collier-Macmillan, London: viii + 276 pp., illustr.

DASMANN, Raymond F. (1968b). *Environmental Conservation* (2nd edn). John Wiley, New York, etc.: xiii + 375 pp., illustr. (3rd edn in press).

DETWYLER, Thomas R. (1971). *Man's Impact on Environment*. McGraw-Hill, New York, etc.: xiv + 731 pp., illustr.

DORST, Jean (1970). *Avant que Nature meure: Pour un écologie politique* (Troisième édition revue et augmentée). Delachaux et Niestlé, Neuchâtel, Suisse, 540 pp., illustr.

DUVIGNEAUD, Paul (Ed,) (1967). *L'écologie: Science Moderne de Synthèse*, Volume 2. *Ecosystémes et Biosphére* (2me edn). Ministère de l'Education Nationale et de la Culture, Direction Générale de l'Organisation des Etudes, Bruxelles: [vi +] 137 pp., illustr.

EHRLICH, Paul R. & EHRLICH, Anne H. (1970). *Population, Resources, Environment: Issues in Human Ecology*. W. H. Freeman, San Francisco: [x] + 383 pp., illustr.

FRANKEL, Sir Otto H. (1970). Genetic conservation of plants useful to man. *Biological Conservation*, 2(3), pp. 162–9.

FRANKEL, Sir Otto H. & BENNETT, E. (Eds) (1970). *Genetic Resources in Plants—Their Exploration and Conservation*. IBP Handbook No. 11, Blackwell Scientific Publications, Oxford & Edinburgh: xxi + 554 pp., illustr.

FRASER DARLING, Sir Frank (1971). *Wilderness and Plenty*. Friends of the Earth, Ballantyne, New York: xi + 112 pp. (Based on the author's Reith Lectures, 1969, Published by the British Broadcasting Corporation, 1970).

GOLDBERG, Edward D. (1970). The chemical invasion of ocean by man. Pp. 63–73 in *McGraw-Hill Yearbook of Science and Technology*, McGraw-Hill, New York: [x] + 477 pp., illustr.

HARRISS, Robert C. (1971). Ecological implications of mercury pollution in aquatic systems. *Biological Conservation*, 3(4), pp. 279–83.

HELFRICH, Harold W., Jr (Ed.) (1970). *The Environmental Crisis: Man's Struggle to Live with Himself*. Yale University Press, New Haven & London: x + 187 pp.

HEYERDAHL, Thor (1971). Atlantic ocean pollution observed by the 'Ra' expeditions. *Biological Conservation*, 3(3), pp. 164–7, illustr.

HUXLEY, Sir Julian (1969). Wildlife in danger. *Biological Conservation*, 1(4), pp. 276–8.

JOHNSON, Francis S. (1970). The balance of atmospheric oxygen and carbon dioxide. *Biological Conservation*, 2(2), pp. 83–9.

JOHNSON, Stanley (1970). *Life Without Birth: A Journey Through the Third World in Search of the Population Explosion*. Heinemann, London: xiii + 364 pp., illustr.

KOVDA, V. A. & YAKUSHEVSKAYA, I. V. (1967). [Evaluation of the terrestrial biomass.—in Russian, with English title and brief abstract.] *Izvestiya Akademii Nauk SSSR (Seriya biologicheskaya)*, No. 3, pp. 331–8.

LIKENS, Gene F., BORMANN, F. Herbert, JOHNSON, Noye M., FISHER, D. W. & PIERCE, Robert S. (1970). Effects of forest cutting and herbicide treatment on nutrient budgets in the Hubbard Brook Watershed-ecosystem. *Ecological Monographs*, 40(1), pp. 23–47, illustr.

LUNDHOLM, B. & SVENSSON, S. (1970). Global Environmental Monitoring System: technical report from Sweden to the IBP-Committee on Global Monitoring. *Ecological Research Committee Bulletin* No. 10, Swedish Natural Science Research Council, Stockholm: [ii] + 64 pp.

MASSACHUSETTS INSTITUTE OF TECHNOLOGY (as MIT) (1970). *Man's Impact on the Global Environment: Report of the Study of Critical Environmental Problems*. MIT Press, Cambridge, Mass., and London, England: xxii + 319 pp., illustr.

MELLANBY, Kenneth (1967), *Pesticides and Pollution*. Collins (The New Naturalist), London: 221 pp., illustr.

MELLANBY, Kenneth (1971). *The Threat of World Pollution*. Lindsay Press, London: 16 pp.

NACE, Raymond L. (1964). Water of the world. *Natural History*, **73** (1), pp. 10–19, illustr.

NACE, Raymond L. (1967). Water resources: a global problem with local roots. *Environmental Science and Technology*, **1**(7), pp. 550–60, illustr.

NATIONAL ACADEMY OF SCIENCES (as NAS) (1970). *Eutrophication: Causes, Consequences, Corrections. Proceedings of a Symposium*. National Academy of Sciences, Washington, DC: vii + 661 pp., illustr.

NICHOLSON, Max (1970). *The Environmental Revolution*. Hodder & Stoughton, London: xii + 366 pp., illustr.

ODUM, Howard T. (1971). *Environment, Power, and Society*. Wiley-Interscience, New York, etc.: ix + 331 pp., illustr.

OPARIN, Aleksandr I. (1957). *The Origin of Life on the Earth* (3rd edn). Academic Press, New York: 495 pp. illustr. (New Edition in preparation.)

OPARIN, Aleksandr I. (1970). Origin of life. Pp. 497–500 in *The Encyclopedia of the Biological Sciences* (2nd edn), Ed. Peter Gray. Van Nostrand Reinhold, New York, etc.: xxv + 1027 pp.

PICKAVANCE, J. R. (1971). Pollution of a stream in Newfoundland: effects on invertebrate fauna. *Biological Conservation*, **3**(4), pp. 264–8, illustr.

POLUNIN, Nicholas (1951). Seeking airborne botanical particles about the North Poles. *Svensk Botanisk Tidskrift*, **45**(2), pp. 320–54, illustr.

POLUNIN, Nicholas (1967). *Eléments de Géographie botanique*. Gauthier-Villars, Paris: xxiii + 552 pp., illustr. (Adaptation of the author's *Introduction to Plant Geography and Some Related Sciences*, Longman, London, and McGraw-Hill, New York, 1960.)

POLUNIN, Nicholas (1971). Vegetation and the animal habitat. *Le Naturaliste Canadien* (Travaux dédiés à la mémoire du Professeur Jacques Rousseau, 1905–1970), **98**(3), pp. 515–28.

POLUNIN, Nicholas & KELLY, C. D. (1952). Arctic aerobiology. Fungi and Bacteria, etc., caught in the air during flights over the geographical North Pole. *Nature* (London), **170**, pp. 314–16.

RADL, Shirley L. (1970). Zero Population Growth, Inc.: past, present, and future. *Biological Conservation*, **3**(1), pp. 71–2.

RUDOLPH, Emanuel D. (1970). Conserving the antarctic terrestrial ecosystem. *Biological Conservation*, **3**(1), pp. 52–4, illustr.

RUSSELL, R. Scott (1969). Contamination of the biosphere with radioactivity. *Biological Conservation*, **2**(1), pp. 2–9.

SCIENTIFIC AMERICAN (1970). The biosphere (and allied articles, by various authors). *Scientific American*, **223**(3), pp. 45–208 illustr. (Subsequently reprinted in book form.)

TAYLOR, Gordon Rattray (1970). *The Doomsday Book*. Thames & Hudson, London: 335 pp.

UNESCO (1970). *Use and Conservation of the Biosphere*. United Nations Educational, Scientific and Cultural Organization, Paris (Natural Resources Research X): 272 pp.

UNITED NATIONS (1970). United Nations Population Division Working Paper No. 37, October 1970.

UNITED NATIONS (1971). *Demographic Yearbook 1970*. United Nations, New York: ix + 830 pp.

WENDLAND, Wayne M. & BRYSON, Reid A. (1970). Atmospheric dustiness, man, and climatic change. *Biological Conservation*, **2**(2), pp. 125–8, illustr.

WHEELER, Alwyne (1969). Fish life and pollution in the Lower Thames: a review and preliminary report. *Biological Conservation*, **2**(1), pp. 25–30, map.

WURSTER, Charles F., Jr (1969). Chlorinated hydrocarbons and the world ecosystem. *Biological Conservation*, **1**(2), pp. 123–9.

DISCUSSION

Dasmann (Chairman)

It seems to me that one of our biggest problems is to know what is going on in the biosphere today, and here I'm reminded of an experience which I had a few years ago on the Channel Islands of California. I was impressed by how remote and undisturbed they were, seemingly untouched by the activities on the mainland. I particularly noticed the Brown Pelicans soaring over the waves or roosting in great numbers on the rocks, and I thought that they were much as they had been in the past. The very next year, however, the discovery was made that the Brown Pelicans had failed to produce any young, and since then the species has been on its way to extinction in California. Even though the adults still survive, they are, because of the effects of DDT, unable to produce hatchable eggs. This is just one illustration of the fact that there are countless things going on around us that we haven't yet detected, but that we may detect in the near or remoter future.

The news which we get is seldom good news, and we rarely find that things are better than we had expected; indeed, we usually find that they are worse. We've been concerned in the International Union for Conservation of Nature and Natural Resources with keeping records of rare and endangered species, and of depleted species, of wildlife. Often we know only how things were five years ago, or in some instances two years ago or last year: we don't know how they are today. To take one example, the Kouprey once survived in Cambodia. Does it still exist? We have no way of knowing. There is great need for a much more elaborate network of information and communication about what really does exist in the biosphere today. Dr Davies, who will speak to you a little later, is in the fortunate position of being one of the few people who is relatively well informed about what is happening to just one thing: world weather. Yet, I am quite sure that he is dissatisfied with his information on the general state of the atmosphere. He does not know what is going on in respect to many of the components of it—which practically means that nobody else does. When it gets to anything as complicated as the actual state of the world's forests, the world's deserts, or the world's grasslands, we simply don't know: we don't have a sufficient network of information and communication, but only odd records from here and there. We must do better than this in future if we are to have a sound basis for action.

Manshard

I am currently in charge of the Department of Environmental Sciences and Natural Resources Research of UNESCO, which works on natural resources, hydrology, and oceanography. One of our main activities is the preparation of the intergovernmental programme on 'Man and the Biosphere' (MAB). I would like to add a few details about this programme, which in the course of the last ten or fifteen years has developed out of our arid zone and humid tropics programmes, the International Biological Programme, and the Biosphere Conference which was held in Paris in 1968.

To simplify, it can be said that MAB has two main axes, one of which is following the main natural ecosystems ranging from the tropical rain forests, savannas, and arid and temperate lands right to the Arctic zone. The other axis covers the 'stretch' from the natural environments which are very little disturbed by man, to the rural environments and then to the other extreme of highly urbanized environments in which we get all the well-known difficulties of pollution.

During the last two years we have selected thirty-one research themes. Within this framework, in November of this year, a Coordinating Council of the 'Man and the Biosphere Programme' will meet and determine the priorities. Perhaps I can give you two pointers: very important will be education in ecology and concerning the environment. We hope also to establish 'Biome Centres', for instance, in tropical rain forests or in savannas, which could be attached to universities or independent organizations in which research as well as environmental education could be undertaken.

In connection with the problems of developing countries that were touched upon earlier this morning, one other aspect seems important—as can be seen by anyone flying across the less desertic tropical latitudes. On one hand we observe marked changes in land-use in these tropical lands with the cutting, burning, or bulldozing, of the forests—changes ranging from 'shifting cultivation' to more sedentary forms. On the other hand we see, even in these countries, the greatly increasing amount of urbanization— for example in Latin America or in south-east Asia. The impact of these two trends on the natural resources of the biosphere is one of the important problems we are confronted with. The MAB programme has been set up as a UNESCO project in cooperation with other United Nations agencies and scientific bodies. It will be organized with the assistance of national MAB committees in member states. We shall be pleased to supply further details from UNESCO headquarters in Paris to anyone who is suitably interested.

Fosberg

I have two things to mention here. One is what I am afraid will be a futile protest against the current general use of the word 'biosphere' in a sense that is very different from its original meaning, which was the actual living component of the earth. I realize that this misuse was perpetuated and popularized by UNESCO and many others, and that it is probably hopeless to try to correct it, but I feel I should point out that the term 'ecosphere' is available for the concept that we are talking about as biosphere.

The other thing I want to say is that a few years ago I was at a conference —and a number of people in this assembly were also there—at Airlie House, Warrenton, Virginia, on 'Future Environments in North America'. This is brought to mind by Professor Polunin's emphasis on the preservation of the beauty of our environment. An economist, of all people, gave the biologists a well-deserved scolding because they didn't have the guts to stand up and say that the preservation of the beauty of North America was one of the primary things that should have been emphasized. In this Conference that we are participating in now, I hope we shall not leave ourselves so open to such criticism from the economists or anyone else. I hope that beauty will be regarded as one of the basic necessities for human happiness and a main component of the quality of life.

Dasmann

Dr Fosberg and I have been arguing for five years about the meaning of the world 'biosphere'. I admit that his definition is strictly correct, but Lamarck, its originator, was also mistaken in some of his concepts about species, and our ideas concerning them have certainly evolved since his time. I think that the term biosphere has also developed from Lamarck's original meaning to that now approved by UNESCO and so many others.

Benthem

In the latter part of Professor Polunin's paper he referred again to the great possibilities of creative conservation and land consolidation, and I think these subjects are important enough to warrant some further details. Changes in the use of land commonly indicate the social and technical developments that are taking place in the densely populated countries, for example, of west and central Europe. Parallel to the replanning of many of the urban districts, there is a growing need to adapt the rural land to the changed conditions of life in today's world. It is obvious that this process will influence, possibly as much as anything, the environmental future which is our discussion subject this week.

Many of the changes in man's rural environment take place in an uncontrolled and haphazard manner, often leading to a decline in amenity or in historic or scientific values. When, however, the changing of the countryside is subjected to a careful, comprehensive country-planning procedure which aims at a multipurpose land-use, it will often be more a challenge than a risk.

Thinking of rural land and landscape, we must bear in mind that in many situations the land-use pattern and the appearance of the countryside no longer reflect the present-day needs of urbanized people. In too many rural districts there is a lack of diversity and an overemphasis of the food production function of the land. We should not make the mistake of thinking of the countryside only in terms of 'existing beauty which has to be protected'. Great tracts of formerly attractive rural landscape have lost their beauty and special character as a result of a single-purpose approach and an insufficiency of land-use planning.

Since 1954, the Netherlands Government has had at its disposal a useful legislative instrument to promote a planned development of the rural areas by land consolidation schemes. Formerly directed purely to the improvement of farming conditions, this Land Consolidation Act now also opens up possibilities for the improvement or rehabilitation of the countryside by the execution of *landscape plans*. The necessity to preserve or to reconstruct the landscape in the process of land consolidation is made a condition by the paragraphs of this Act.

A considerable amount of money and growing areas of land are yearly made available to create new landscape elements by planting trees and plots of woodland, by improving accessibility with roads and trails, and by the acquisition of land for the protection of nature and for recreation. From single-purpose agricultural projects these land consolidation schemes have developed into ones of multipurpose land reconstruction.

Other examples of landscape planning in my country are the land re-clamation projects in the Zuiderzee and Delta regions where, as a part of the creation of landscape, new biotopes are being established for the en-dangered flora and fauna. A team of specialists: agricultural engineers, landscape architects, foresters, city planners, and civil engineers, are co-operating in this multipurpose land-use planning.

It is my opinion, based on a long period of practical landscape recon-struction, that a carefully planned rearrangement of our physical surround-ings outside the urban zones should be handled as an instrument to tackle the problem of deterioration of the countryside. Planning machinery needs to be established with adequate means to assure a design and a manage-ment of the environment in the rural areas that will be just as detailed as for the urban zones.

Paradise no longer reigns in several parts of western Europe, and I think that the rehabilitation and improvement of landscape should be practised in an increasing way. Professor Polunin rightly advocated creative conservation. It is not enough just to preserve what is beautiful. We have to reconstruct, to rebuild what has been destroyed, and in many places to create a more diversified landscape pattern than existed heretofore or at least than we have at present.

Mahler

I wish to speak from the point of view of the Food and Agriculture Organi-zation of the United Nations, which I represent, and as present Secretary of the FAO Interdepartmental Working Group on Natural Resources and the Human Environment. We have just heard a sad story about the Brown Pelicans and their eggs. We have a saying in France that we do not make omelettes without breaking some eggs. This is not to minimize the problem that Dr Dasmann has mentioned. Actually, FAO has a wildlife management section which is actively engaged in protecting wildlife—especially as a source of food and income in developing countries. I would like to put into its proper perspective Dr Polunin's statement about the green revolution being a cause of deterioration of environment. FAO has prepared an Indicative World Plan for Agricultural Development, which shows that, regarding the developing countries and using 1965 as the base, we have to increase the food production 80 per cent just to meet the population increase by 1985. Moreover, if we take into account the need to improve the present diet, the food production will have to increase by 140 per cent. This places a great responsibility on FAO, and therefore we have tried to promote the use of those inputs that can quickly raise food production.

The so-called 'green revolution' is mostly aiming at introducing and using high-yielding varieties wherever possible, increasing the use of fertilizers, and making more irrigation water available. Actually, the less advanced forms of agriculture in the developing countries have often been detrimental to the environment in the past, and in many cases the improvement of the agricultural coverage of soils by crops has provided better protection of the soil. The use of fertilizers has also often proved to be a means to improve the quality of soil. Moreover, if we want farmers to undertake works of basic land improvement and soil conservation, they should have a sufficient income. It is true that the rate at which those inputs are used often disregards the time required for research experiments and extension work. Still, some countries of Asia have recently become self-sufficient in producing cereals, and this in itself is a major achievement. It will, of course, take a longer time to teach the farmer how to use new technological inputs in such a way that risks of deterioration of the environment will be minimal. However, in the immediate future, there is practically no alternative to the use of these inputs to meet the world food demand.

In the FAO Constitution established twenty-five years ago, it said that agriculture must be improved while at the same time conservation of natural resources must be ensured. Since then, while trying to solve food production problems, FAO has also been deeply involved in the protection of the environment.

ADDENDA

[Having been asked to include a selection of comments from invited 'roving eminents' who had expressed particular regret at being unable to attend the Conference personally, we are publishing the following ten involving all six inhabited continents in their alphabetical sequence. Further such contributions from well-wishing invitees who were unable to participate in person will be found at or near the ends of Sections 3, 5, 8, 14, 16, and 18, to which they seem most properly to belong. Some of these additional items were written before or during the Conference, and suggested topics which their authors hoped we would discuss, whereas others were written afterwards. Some were included in letters whereas others were drafted separately; none was, however, brought up for specific consideration in the discussions, even though some of the points concerned were treated or passages cited. —Ed.]

From Professor H. A. OLUWASANMI,
Vice-Chancellor, University of Ife, Ile-Ife, Nigeria

Just as the current level of environmental degradation in the advanced countries is without doubt a source of alarm, so is the poverty, ignorance, and poor management, in the less developed parts of the world a threat to the welfare of man. These facts are beyond dispute. But what is to be done is unhappily a more difficult question which calls for much greater global efforts in the study of the problems of human ecology.

International discussion such as that covered by your Conference is certainly to be commended and it can only be hoped that, when published, the proceedings of this Conference will provide new and stimulating ideas.

We at Ife are planning to make a modest but deliberate effort in the study of environmental problems. I plan to set up a committee as a task-force to plan and coordinate action on some carefully selected interdisciplinary long-term studies. The aim of these studies will be to provide much data on the relationship between man and his environment. We have also approached UNESCO for assistance in establishing an Institute of Ecology at Ife. The latter, incidentally, is a matter which I expect bodies like the one you propose would take an interest in fostering [besides acting as] an umbrella body that might look after future events.

From Professor JOHN F. V. PHILLIPS,
University of Natal, PO Box 375, Pietermaritzburg, South Africa

DETERIORATION OF ECOSYSTEMS IN AFRICA SOUTH OF THE SAHARA

My study of the conditions and circumstances in Africa south of 15°N latitude during the course of over forty years leads me to the following broad conclusions: man's influence upon the great ecosystems of the desert and sub-desert, of the arid, sub-arid, mild sub-arid, and sub-humid, wooded savanna, of the wooded and other savanna derived from tropical, subtropical, and montane, forests, and of the forests of various fasciations, has wrought much harm. Whilst man has for many centuries been the dominant associate within these great ecosystems—except where the upsurge of population increment has been curtailed or impossible because of the lack of water, the existence of disease both human and animal, and internecine wars—it is relatively recently that he has made his presence blatantly evident over a wide range of habitats.

It would be unscientific to assert that everywhere in trans-Saharan Africa the intensity and dimensions of disturbance of biotic communities and their habitats are challenging, but it is true that examples of serious wastage exist in the stupendous gamut of *bioclimatic* regions ranging from the deserts to the humid forests, and from the high montane massifs to the coastal lowlands, the river systems, and the oceans.

Suffice it to mention that among the prime kinds of change induced by man are: the causing of deterioration encouraging desertification of ecosystems adjacent to the deserts and sub-deserts, and of advancement of the aridification in those ecosystems that are normally set within the sub-arid, mild sub-arid, and sub-humid, bioclimates; the reduction in extent and alteration in the nature and biotic and economic characteristics of the forests; and the deterioration of the flow of rivers and streams in volume, in length of season in the less humid sub-regions and, admittedly locally, in the quality of the water for man, his livestock, and wild animals.

One example of the heart running away with the head is seen if there is inefficient development and siting of water points where this element hitherto has not existed; these result in heavy local pasturing and wasteful intensification of and encroachment by woody elements, spinose and other, upon natural pasturage for livestock and wild animals. Another example is the removal of tsetse-fly (*Glossina* spp.) and the unplanned and uncontrolled opening to cultivation and livestock of the land so freed: feckless misuse of the vegetation, erosion of the soil, and related socio-economic distress, follow. A third example is the irrigation of soil without adequate attention to its physico-chemical characteristics and its satisfactory *drainage*, 'brack' or 'alkali' rendering it unproductive within a relatively short period.

The ecology and management of the incomparable wild animals set in an unrivalled range of vegetation and habitats—constituting a complex variety of ecosystems—have been studied all too late in too many parts of Africa. Priceless scientific information and much potential socio-economic wealth have thus been either lost or greatly reduced.

From Professor MICHAEL EVENARI,
Head, Department of Botany, Hebrew University, Jerusalem, Israel

After seeing the detailed programme I am even more sorry to be unable to attend; it looks as if your Conference will be a most important event and I am confident that it will be most successful. If I had been able to attend I would have stressed the following points which I feel may have some importance.

The scientist, remote from reality, has directly and indirectly a capability which has changed the environment in a terrifying way. If nothing is done, this process will gain more and more speed because today the time-lag between scientific invention and practical application is getting continuously shorter.

If man is unable to adapt himself to the environment which he has largely created, he will disappear as have so many genera and species before our time in the course of evolution. The uniqueness of the human race is the fact that man, through his ability to think and through his intellect, has been able to create the technology which is changing his own environment. But man is unique also in that he can adapt himself to the new environment by the very same means by which he has changed it, though in order to do so he needs not only his intellect but also all his emotional faculties. He must also be ready to sacrifice *consciously* some of the possible advances in technology which represent too great a danger to the human environment and the existence of the human race. In order not to use these progresses in technology, man has to use not only his intellect but much more so his sagacity.

From Professor V. J. CHAPMAN,
University of Auckland, Private Bag, Auckland, New Zealand

I believe the following matters are of great importance so far as the environmental future is concerned:

1. Certainly in New Zealand, and probably elsewhere, there are too many acts or statutes that refer in one way or another to the pollution of the environment. This makes it relatively easy for any legal or statutory body to disclaim responsibility. Every country should examine its legislation in respect of the environment, and consolidate it into a few basic acts—preferably one each for air, soil, and water, pollution.

2. In New Zealand, and again probably elsewhere, there are insufficient trained personnel to police the legislation. Intensive training programmes are required and also the acts must carry adequate penalties for being broken. President Nixon's proposals for the USA environmental control would seem to be of the nature required. Financial provision has also to be made to enable the statutory bodies to fulfil their function.

3. It is increasingly important to establish a balance between land-use and potential pollution. For example, where aerial top-dressing of pastures with fertilizers is the normal practice, steps must be taken to see that there is the minimum of run-off into streams. This could be achieved either by replacing powdered fertilizer by liquid fertilizer that is immediately taken up by the soil, or else by planting a protective belt of trees between the pastures and the nearest watercourse or lake.

4. Before any new development project is undertaken, whether it be urban or a new man-made lake, the widest possible preliminary study should be carried out to determine the likely effects upon the environment. In the case of a new man-made lake this should include studies by engineers, ecologists and other biologists, hydrologists, economists, anthropologists, agriculturists, and foresters, and they should work as a team and not as isolated units.

5. In some cases, especially so far as water is concerned, it may not be the major nutrients that are responsible for pollution and consequent excessive growth of weeds and Algae. There may be a minor nutrient or growth-factor, entering the water, which is responsible. In the case of some aquatic plants, small traces of soluble iron may be more significant than nitrogen, potassium, or phosphorus. Such aspects should be studied and countered.

From Sir OTTO H. FRANKEL,
Division of Plant Industry, CSIRO, PO Box 109,
Canberra City, ACT 2601, Australia

GENETIC CONSERVATION

The need for conserving the genetic diversity of cultivated plants is now widely recognized. Urgent action on an international basis is needed to preserve the invaluable 'genetic treasuries' in rapidly developing areas where the genetically rich, but productively poor, ancient land races are giving way to high-yielding but uniform introductions or selections. A proposed five-year emergency programme of collecting and conservation is to be placed before the UN Conference on the Human Environment in June 1972.

The preservation of wild species with little or no economic connotation can be important towards maintaining genetic diversity; without adaptation to ever-changing environments, life cannot continue, and long-term conservation cannot be effective. Adaptation depends on availability of variation.

Man-made and natural systems are identical in requiring a gene-pool for adaptation; but in domesticates man largely controls variation and selection, whereas in nature there must be ample natural variation for natural selection to act upon. Small isolates of relic species, or specimens in botanical or zoological gardens, are unlikely to survive beyond a limited time. To survive, natural communities must be equipped with an adequate range of variation; in practical terms this means an appropriate *size and diversity of nature reserves.*

There is therefore an urgent need to examine the policies of nature conservation in the light of principles of population genetics and dynamics.

From Professor ROGER REVELLE, *Director, Harvard University Center*
for Population Studies, 9 Bow Street, Cambridge, Massachusetts 02138, USA.

I am very much impressed by the list of outstanding people you have gathered together for your Conference. It should be a very stimulating and challenging affair, and I wish it every success.

I hope you can follow through on your idea that similar conferences should be held at intervals of three or four years in the future, and would be interested in participating in the proposed free and independent body which might act as an umbrella *inter alia* to organize such conferences.

The principal idea that I would like to present to the Conference is that the most important long-range problem facing mankind is to create a steady-state, livable world for a human population of around ten thousand million people in the latter half of the twenty-first century. If birth-rates throughout the world can be lowered to between fifteen and twenty per thousand per year by the end of our century, the earth's human population could level off at such a number. The number may seen frighteningly large, but from the point of view of foreseeable resources of arable land, water, air, minerals, and energy, the life-support capacity of the earth is probably sufficient to allow a moderately high material standard of living for this many people.*

If birth-rates continue as at present for about another century, the earth's human population would rise to a level of around fifty thousand million people, but the levelling process would be a terrible one. It would result from an increase in death-rates to match birth-rates, due primarily to widespread malnutrition, and the chances of any future improvement would be minimal. The ghost of Malthus would join the Pale Horsemen of famine, pestilence, war, and death, in a triumphant ride over the earth.

Assuming that a nuclear holocaust can be avoided, the all-encompassing problems of our times are, first, to arrive at a world in which human beings everywhere control their own fertility, so that population does not rise beyond the point at which resources are adequate for all, and, second, to create the social institutions and the shared human values which will make such a world a tolerable one.

From Dr S. DILLON RIPLEY,
Secretary, Smithsonian Institution, Washington, DC 20560, USA.

Perhaps the most important development for future planning for environmental protection is the international aspect. It is always extremely difficult for countries which are known roughly as 'developing nations' to be convinced that the messages passed on to them from the 'developed nations' are objective. It is easy for the more developed countries in the 'western world' to assume a hortatory pose in regard to environmental problems. The possibility of misinterpretation by less wealthy nations is great. It can always be assumed that concern over the environment is merely a by-product of success, and that when once a particular nation has attained a very high standard of living, it is easy for that nation to turn about and urge others to maintain a poorer standard of living so as to protect the atmosphere, the environment, or some rare animal species or other.

How long it will take for all nations of the world to realize that environmental degradation is happening more rapidly than any of us can foresee, and that it is a truly international concern, is difficult to assess. After World War I the League of Nations was founded to attempt to coalesce world opinion on questions of peace and the moral strategies to be developed in

* This passage having been quoted during the Conference, it is only proper to record that Dr Brower stated his 'violent opposition to this position,' and cited Mr Robert S. McNamara —who had himself expressed his personal regret at being unable to attend what he called an 'attractive prospect'—as having pronounced that there will not be a population of even seven thousand millions by the year 2000, for by that time man will either have learned to control his numbers at near or lower than the present level or nature will have to take over the job for him.—Ed.

international relations. After World War II the United Nations was created to mobilize international concern against supra-destructive weapons of war and to attempt to develop strategies for creating a higher standard of living in the world at large through international advice on agriculture, water, and similarly-shared international problems. These great efforts continue, but national ambitions and nationalistic attitudes also continue to prevail. In this atmosphere, environmental problems seem tenuous and more like moralistic sermons to many of our world's citizens.

The key to rational use of the biosphere involves us all, and only through a constant reiteration of the urgency of these matters will we eventually be able to develop an attitude in which all citizens will take this as a matter of course. Thus it seems of the highest use that such conferences should be held in different areas of the world at fairly frequent intervals to underscore the truly international aspects of the threat to our environmental future.

From S. E. Dom HELDER CAMARA, *Archbishop of Recife and Olinda,*
Avenida Rui Barbosa, Recife, Esto de Pernambuco, Brazil

Man, as a co-Creator, will be able to conduct his environmental future; only, he will need to conduct, before, his own egoism.

From Miss SYLVIA CROWE, CBE, PPILA, *Sylvia Crowe & Associates,*
Landscape Architects, 182 Gloucester Place, London NW1, England

The biggest need is for a powerful, disinterested international body that can tackle the problem of pollution caused by industrial and other developments.

We are all working for conservation within a basically unsound framework which is governed by a short-sighted drive for profit, economic growth, and production (regardless of what is being produced). As long as the power rests with economists, we are fighting a losing battle.

Obvious examples are:

(1) Giant tankers, which are bound occasionally to have mishaps. It may be that we should pay more for our oil, delivered in smaller vessels.
(2) At the same time that Zambia's economy is suffering from a fall in the price of copper, Snowdonia is threatened by prospecting for copper.
(3) Jumbo and supersonic planes are developed, when the real need is for quiet, clean, vertical take-off planes.

And so on. This is a desperately difficult problem, but unless we solve it we are largely wasting our time.

From Dr F. T. WAHLEN, *a. Bundesrat, 31 Humboldtstrasse, 3000 Bern,*
Switzerland, a former President of the Swiss Confederation and sometime
Deputy Director-General of FAO.

In a scientific meeting in Zurich on 25 June, attention was drawn to the fact that the running competition which agriculture is forced to maintain with industry in order to obtain equal productivity from labour poses problems that are surely not given enough consideration nowadays. This competition forces on agriculture an ever-increasing use of fertilizers to satisfy the demands of highly productive strains of crops, while also involving the widespread use of pesticides and herbicides, and, in cattle breeding and production, more and more maintenance and feeding methods that are far from nature— including the use of artificial stimulants and antibiotics. However, there must be some maintenance of a natural soil flora and fauna, protection of water and of general environment, and consideration of the quality of the products and the health of the consumer.

There is a top limit of intensity of production that, in the interests of the maintenance of healthy production parametres in the long run, must not be passed. It is to the settlement of this desirable level for the separate fields of agriculture and animal production that agricultural and related sciences should dedicate themselves. We should remember, too, that what nowadays is regarded as micro-contamination can accumulate in the course of years and centuries to constitute macro-contamination that is difficult to control.

3
WHAT HUMANS ARE DOING

Keynote Paper

What Man is Doing

by

JEAN DORST

President of the Charles Darwin Foundation for the Galápagos Islands;
Vice-President, International Council for Bird Preservation;
Professor of Zoology and Director, Laboratory of Mammals and Birds,
Muséum National d'Histoire Naturelle,
55 rue de Buffon,
75–Paris Vᵉ, France

INTRODUCTION

The mark of man on the surface of the earth is as old as the early beginning of mankind. The history of humanity may be envisaged as a struggle against its environment, involving a progressive liberation from the local, natural conditions and the gradual enslavement of the living world by man's own inventions. Biological motivations explain this tendency. But, as in every human activity, cultural traditions and beliefs encourage us to modify our simple actions and reactions. A philosophical attitude is the primary determining factor of any human attitude. Western philosophies emphasize the supremacy of man over the rest of the world, which only exists to serve him— or so they contend. Since the time of Francis Bacon and Descartes early in the seventeenth century, we have been convinced that we are the masters and possessors of nature. The prodigious progress of the sciences seems to give us the right to do what we want and so to confirm this philosophical attitude. Therefore, it is no wonder that protection of wildlife and sound management of the surface of the earth according to biological laws, did not receive any support from this western philosophy.

As we now know, the biosphere functions in a very exact and exacting way, ruled by laws that are often as precise as those of the physical world. Its innumerable components are distributed in well-defined categories between which there exist all manner of definite links. Producers transform physical energy, coming from the sun in the form of radiation, into chemical energy which is stored in organic matter. Numerous consumers live on the producing plants and also prey upon each other, forming food-chains, or, more precisely, a very elaborate food-web. Other organisms, called decomposers, cause degradation and mineralization of organic matter, and recycle its constituent chemical elements. Life has thus evolved a very elaborate mechanism which assures the circulation of a part of the store of chemical elements of the earth and the fixation of a part of the physical energy of the sun, which is then progressively degraded along food-chains according to the laws of thermodynamics (Scientific American, 1970).

At his earliest stages, man was integrated within this natural system, living on fruits, other parts of plants, and animals, and was completely dependent on his natural environment. But this period was relatively short, and even ancient man exerted a dominant influence on habitats—which influence was often already detrimental to his own interests. The primitive situation changed rapidly when man became more numerous and reached a higher level of technology than hitherto. The old usages could then no longer provide enough resources for man as he became more numerous, sedentary, highly gregarious, and socially well-organized. Wild cropping was then inadequate to supply enough food and other products.

Consequently, man 'domesticated' natural ecosystems, and later created entirely artificial ones—thus increasing markedly the proportion of local productivity that was directly available to him, and making it much easier for him to crop the 'fruits of the earth'. Positive effects resulted, and it is clear that this stage was irrevocably reached long ago in our history. But human influence also had numerous negative effects, particularly when industrialization made living conditions more and more artificial. Indeed some of man's actions are to be considered as serious ecological errors, being in complete disagreement with biological laws. At a very early period, human activities already contained the germs of self-destruction which developed dramatically during subsequent phases of history. The problem has latterly developed on a much larger scale and has reached a dangerous point, changing the world to something essentially different (Thomas, 1956).

It would be tedious to give a detailed statement on the present situation in order to make clear where we now stand and what we are doing to the biosphere, for this has already been done many times recently (e.g. by Commoner, 1966; Arvill, 1967; Bell, 1970; Dorst, 1970; Nicholson, 1970). However, to the extent that such an analysis will give us some clues as to how the situation can be improved, and how to avoid an ecocatastrophe which could be the crises of crises, we will briefly survey some of the aspects of the present situation from the ecologist's point of view.

MAN AGAINST THE BIOSPHERE

Overexploitation of Wild Populations
Overexploitation of wild animal populations is probably the oldest impact that man has had on the balance of nature. In the remote past, man exterminated a fair number of species through over-hunting and destruction of habitats. The rate of this phenomenon has accelerated rapidly in recent times, as is particularly evident in regard to birds and mammals for which we have plenty of historic and scientific documentation—see, for example, the lists of threatened species in the *Red Book* published by the IUCN Survival Service Commission (IUCN, 1966–70). Some of these 'endangered' birds and mammals are to be considered as the fossils of tomorrow, and we have little chance of not adding their names to the long necrology of species already exterminated by man. Many other animals and plants, particularly those of smaller size and more obscure habits and habitats, should be added to the better-known ones. Indeed, wildlife as a whole is decreasing at an alarming rate all over the world and could be doomed in the near future in many areas (e.g. Holdgate & Wace, 1961; Le Cren & Holdgate, 1962).

This tendency is a source of great concern, for many reasons. One of these is that we are spoiling a priceless scientific heritage and are depriving ourselves of numerous species of the highest interest for the future development of science. Every species or lower taxon, even the smallest and rarest, plays a role in the biosphere, being a sort of wheel in the complex mechanism of one or another of the world's ecosystems or narrower biotopes. Its extinction means that something is lost in the biosphere's efficiency and capability to transfer energy and chemical elements. Man also deprives himself of valuable resources, which could still be important to satisfy his food or other needs in the modern world. This is particularly obvious in the case of whales, the story of which is a classical example of devastation consequent on direct human influence (Laws, 1960). For many years the Scientific Committee of the International Whaling Commission warned very seriously the several governments involved, but in vain. The total population of Blue Whales, which was formerly the predominant species in Antarctica, is now well under 1,000—as compared with 100,000 only thirty years ago—and their recovery is problematical to say the least.

Over-fishing is even more widespread and therefore serious. Although it seems unlikely that marine species, for example of fish, could be totally exterminated by human action, there is a grave risk that the profitability of fisheries may be seriously affected when pressures become too great. This has happened already in the cases of several species and several vital areas such as the North Sea and northern Atlantic and Pacific Oceans (Burkenroad, 1948; Croker, 1954). Crustacea, molluscs (Angot, 1959), and sea turtles, also are subject to overexploitation. Depletion of fishing zones has caused 'fishing wars', which can be considered as part of our ecological crisis.

All these sad facts are consequences of mismanagement of wild populations (Gabrielson, 1959; Vibert & Lagler, 1961; Fosberg, 1963). In some cases at least, the situation could be remedied by practices in agreement with the laws of the dynamics of populations, which are now fairly well known. The recovery of the Grey Whale, due to strict protection, is a very encouraging fact; also encouraging are recent increases in the numbers of Sea Otters, of several fur-seals, and of some of the larger terrestrial mammals. This shows what we can do with due care, and what we ought to do far more widely. But we should not postpone any longer this reversal of our attitude with regard to wildlife if we want to save it and exploit it on a sustained-yield basis (Dasmann, 1964).

Destruction of Land

Even more serious is the virtual destruction of the land itself. To establish his cultivations and pastures, man has simplified many habitats and replaced over vast areas the natural multiplicity of forms of plants and animals by a few from which he makes direct profit. In doing this he has channelled productivity in a very narrow way, increasing the *quantity* of products that are directly available; for this is the basic aim of agriculture and of animal husbandry. But oversimplification of the food-chains renders the habitat increasingly sensitive to the factors of erosion, and is detrimental to the stability of the entire habitat and above all of the soil, which is no longer protected by an adequate plant cover (Polunin, 1967).

As long as man transformed stable land that was located in flat alluvial plains or in well-balanced temperate or tropical countries, the result was the creation of profitable man-made habitats. Under suitable conditions, wise agricultural management can result in additional fertility while still assuring stability. Spreading of dung and fertilizers, rotation of crops, mixed agriculture in which grazing has an important role, and the maintenance of a mosaic of different habitats, have permitted man to increase soil fertility very considerably over the centuries—particularly in western and central Europe and in some Asiatic lowlands. Even shifting cultivation permits a satisfactory agricultural exploitation, provided crop rotation is rapid and as long as the human population remains below a certain density (Graham, 1944).

But these wise practices were replaced when a real agricultural revolution took place. Man discovered the wealth of the vast 'new' grasslands at the same time as he developed machinery. Farmers abandoned old conservative methods and used the new machines with which to exploit vast surfaces with reduced labour forces. This led to the ecological monstrosity of monoculture— one of the curses of modern agriculture, both economically and politically. Numerous crops, such as cereals (including maize), leave the soil bare during a considerable part of the year. Even during the period of growth, the single stratum formed by the cultivated plant does not protect the soil efficiently against over-heating and water or wind erosion. The classic example of soil degradation is found in the Great Plains of North America, where the original grassy cover was replaced by fields of cereals that afford much less protection to the soil. There resulted the enormous 'dust bowl', where winds stripped off the soil and carried it away in the most dramatic manner (Sears, 1967).

The situation became widely even worse when man began to cultivate 'marginal' lands, including wetlands, which can be transformed only at the price of considerable investment and to the detriment of the soil's stability. This happened in time practically all over the world when human populations increased and made the pressure on the land heavier and more relentless. Instead of concentrating on lowlands, man began to cultivate slopes, where pedological conditions and the slope itself make the soil much more fragile. Dispersal of hard surface materials and loss of their constituents by erosion—especially by run-off following torrential rains—can ruin in a few months a structure which took centuries or even many millennia to form.

The influence of man was particularly disastrous in the tropics, in areas that had already been ravaged for centuries by brush fires and overgrazing (Harroy, 1944; Haden-Guest et al., 1956; Phillips, 1959; Worthington, 1961; UNESCO, 1963). Modern man committed serious mistakes when he installed a predatory economy, the German *Raubwirtschaft*. Cultivating products for export, he introduced monoculture, which has been responsible for much of the disaster that has befallen Africa and Latin America. In many countries, colonists brutally transformed the original habitats and, without any transition, replaced the complex food-chains with simplified ones. Many introduced plants are responsible for degradation of vast areas, as they exhaust the soil and leave it unprotected. Developing countries are desperately seeking funds, and still often sacrifice their future to the present by using agricultural methods that are detrimental to the fertility of tomorrow.

Agricultural misuse adds its effects to those of deforestation—still the first step in the destruction of most natural habitats—overgrazing, and poorly planned urbanization on good farmland, such as is too often seen in western Europe. Practically throughout the world, farmers are destroying a happy balance between hedge-bordered fields that are (or anyway were) interspersed with groves, woods, and marshes. According to a general assumption that is still widespread, any natural habitat can be transformed into an artificial field—thanks to our mechanical skill!

This situation should be remedied with the shortest possible delay. Only land having a definite agricultural potential should be converted into fields and pasture and kept as such, while marginal areas and soils, unsuitable for cultivation in the long run, should be made to fit into the human economy in other ways—by using their natural resources, but with maintenance of their original balance. Biologists and economists should conjure up new methods of taking a reasonable profit from them in the long run rather than on a short-term basis. A good chance is offered now, as radical changes in agriculture are under way in many countries. Ranch management, sensible use of large terrestrial mammals, hunting, and fishing, are some of the mutiple forms of rational exploitation that can bring in useful dividends without altering the stability of the habitats involved.

Marginal areas are vital for conservation, which paradoxically could be the most rewarding exploitation in the quite near future. For tourism and the use of leisure will become a more and more important part of the activities of those portions of humanity who live in developed countries. Many other countries, especially the East African states, have realized that there is a better profit to be derived from exploiting their natural wealth in such a way—rather than converting their original habitats into fields which become ruined in a short time through accelerated erosion after costly investments.

Pollution by Waste Products

Disposal of wastes is also disastrous to the biosphere, causing various pollutions—one of the most serious problems which we have to face in modern times. This aspect of degradation of our environment is the one which is most easily appreciated by the general public, who would never be aware of the present ecological crisis if pollution did not exist. To be sure, it is by no means new; but its proportions have now a completely different scale from heretofore, and for several rather obvious reasons. Thus, human populations have increased tremendously of late and tend to concentrate in particular areas, while human activities are expanding rapidly and generate an ever-increasing amount and variety of waste products. Finally, industry produces resistant substances of great durability, whereas until recent times waste products were mainly organic and could easily be transformed and broken down by microorganisms. So long as the speed of transformation matched the quantity of waste, there was a kind of balance. Today, however, nature can no longer absorb either qualitatively or quantitatively the enormous mass discarded by man; therefore, wastes are piling up and literally poisoning the earth with their accumulative effects (Ternisien, 1968*a*, 1968*b*; Environmental Quality, 1970; Charlier, 1971).

We shall only briefly mention the disposal of radioactive waste, which is perhaps the worst of all. A great quantity has already been produced, and our productive capacity will increase at a very high rate in the near future. Atomic scientists assure us that all precautions are being taken, but we have little chance to check their statements. Outside serious accidents in any atomic factory, there is a risk from wastes disposed of in various ways—including dumping in ocean troughs. The consequences might bring disaster on a world-wide scale (Russell, 1969; Sankaranarayanan, 1971).

Pollutions greatly affect fresh waters, and many of our rivers are converted into open-air sewers by them (Carbenier, 1969). The primary cause is of course the growth of towns, which discard an enormous volume of partially purified water. Another factor is linked to the expansion of industry, wastes from which are commonly discharged into rivers. These wastes contain a great variety of chemical compounds, including detergents, salts of heavy metals (such as cadmium and mercury, which have been widely dumped in waterways and are a serious hazard to living communities, including those of man), and organic substances. Each day the list of such possibilities becomes a little longer and, as René Dubos said, the worst pollution is that which we have not yet identified. Sprayed insecticides and herbicides should be added to the list of iniquities. Most of these substances either reduce the water's capacity to dissolve oxygen, inhibit Bacteria from attacking organic substances, or are toxic to aquatic plants and animals—including fishes. A lot of evidence shows that many rivers and lakes have been virtually sterilized by compounds of heavy metals, or by wastes from coke plants and gas factories. These substances act in various ways in highly complex natural habitats and are generally additive in their effects. Pollution of fresh water is ultimately detrimental to man, for the treatment of highly polluted water is becoming more and more difficult. Also, some of the substances are directly injurious to public health, examples being compounds of metals and nitrites which have already caused severe casualties among children.

Marine waters also are polluted by waste products discharged by littoral towns and industries, and indeed most of the freshwater pollutants end up in the oceans after being washed down by running waters. Oil products are dumped into the sea in huge quantities—which is all the more serious because most of them are remarkably stable. Tankers still pour out sludge from their tanks after their cargoes have been discharged. A further source of oil pollution comes from off-shore wells, the number of which is increasing rapidly over the world. The most spectacular victims are the sea-birds, which die of 'intoxication' or after their plumage has become soaked with in-eradicable oil products. But other marine animals, including fish, suffer extensively from this form of pollution, and the entire marine ecosystem can be disturbed by it (Olson & Burgess, 1967).

The atmosphere is severely polluted by industries which liberate enormous quantities of gases and solid matter in the form of tiny particles that can remain in suspension in the air and be carried for great distances. Big cities are often covered by a grey pall of dust floating in the air. Among gases, the most serious pollutants are carbon monoxide, sulphur dioxide, a series of derivatives of chlorine, fluorine, and nitrate, and a number of incompletely consumed polycyclic hydrocarbons—including such carcinogenic substances as benzo-pyrene. Car exhaust is one of the major sources of pollution; 1,000 automobiles produce 3.2 metric tons of carbon monoxide in a day (when in continuous use, as some are), up to nearly 400 kg of hydrocarbon fumes, and up to nearly 150 kg of nitrate derivatives. This is particularly serious as the number of cars is constantly increasing all over the world, having grown from 83,140,000 in 1953 to 204,120,000 in 1967. It has been said that, in the USA, automobiles pour daily into the atmosphere a quantity of pollutants which is equal in weight to that of a line of cars stretching bumper-to-bumper from New York to Chicago. Industries and domestic fires can also be disastrous in this respect.

Pollution of the atmosphere is a serious hazard to human health, and its effects can be lethal to people who are prone to respiratory and circulatory diseases. Chronic bronchitis is now 2.5 times as frequent as it was ten years ago in the USA, and cancer may be induced by some pollutants (Harris, 1970). Air pollution is also harmful to vegetation, fluorine and sulphur dioxide producing necrosis of leaves over large parts of their surfaces.

Thus man has seriously polluted his habitat and obviously is the only species which 'fouls its nest' to such an extent. Yet he is himself the first victim, and we can only guess what will be the consequences on future generations. We have to control pollutions immediately all over the world, and particularly in developed countries, so getting at the very root of the problem. Thus in producing wastes and disposing of them in the world's habitats, we create open systems, using only part of the raw materials and discarding the rest. Theoretically, by-products are degraded by natural agents and the resultant elements are afterwards recycled; but nowadays many of man's wastes are degraded so slowly that they accumulate, especially when dumped in enormous quantities. Thus man-made systems differ fundamentally from natural systems, which are all well-balanced cycles within which the elements circulate at a fairly regular speed regardless of where in the cycle they may be. For obvious reasons, we are interested only in the active part of the cycle, from which we take profit; we neglect the other phase, which does not produce anything for us and even requires an input of energy to get rid of. If we compare any industrial production with the functioning of a natural ecosystem, the absurdity or anyway impracticability of our attitude becomes obvious.

This attitude ought to be changed. If we take profit from one of the phases of a cycle, we should pay for the others. Hitherto we lived with the idea of an external economy, but somehow we have to realize that we must start paying for pure water and air and a number of services which until now nature has been supplying free. We should be ready to pay the price of our activities, which is the price of western civilization, particularly in regard to their side-effects. We have the technical possibility of controlling most of the pollutions, or at least of lowering them to a bearable level at which our habitat would be clean again and the biosphere would be free from the poisons that are now paralysing some of its essential mechanisms. The effects of the Clean Air Act in Britain provide a good example of what can be done.

Such measures cost money, and we ought to be able to pay for them. The important question is not so much who will pay, as finally society as a whole will be the payer. But when the price is too high, we shall have to give up a project and renounce production if its side-effects would have been too detrimental to man and his environment. Until now, this has not happened, as we have not cared about a true balance sheet; instead, we neglected the negative side and contemplated only the profit.

Pesticides

In recent years, pesticides have become one of the major threats to the environment, combining their effects with those of wastes—such as oil in the sea and numerous substances in fresh water. Many pesticides are persistent and therefore accumulate in the biosphere, where they now reach alarming levels of concentration or at least of total 'presence'. It has been calculated that one-and-a-half million tons of DDT circulate in the biosphere after being sprayed often vast distances from the places where they now exist. Thus their deleterious side-effects cause disturbances of many kinds, often without being balanced to any serious extent by benefits where they were used.

It would be superfluous to go into details of how man courts and even causes disasters by abusing the use of pesticides, for a whole literature has been devoted to this subject (e.g. Mellanby, 1967; Ternisien, 1968a, 1968b;

Carson, 1962). Although synthetic pesticides have performed some notable services in the fields of medicine and agriculture, their generalized use in increasing quantities has become a menace which is so serious that latterly many governments have prohibited or at least severely restricted their use. The persistent pesticides tend to be the most devastating to the biosphere, and most are toxic to man as well as to other animals. They concentrate along food-chains and have delayed effects on numerous animals which may be killed or sterilized by them. There is a lot of evidence of such effects on aquatic birds and raptors, the rapid decline in numbers of which has been attributed to insecticides. These birds are particularly sensitive to chlorinated hydrocarbon derivatives, being at the tops of food-chains along which the latter concentrate. The same is true of many other animals, in both terrestrial and marine ecosystems.

The widespread use of pesticides affects biological balances, often to the detriment of man. Populations of vegetarian insects occurring on cultivated plants are often accompanied by populations of predators which are killed by pesticides at the same time. When the effects of the spraying wear off, the populations of vegetarian insects have a good chance of reviving before their predators do, the increase being slower for animals of a higher trophic level. A sudden swarming of vegetarian insects has often been recorded after a pesticide treatment in the absence of predators to control them.

We have to reconsider the whole problem of utilization of pesticides with a fresh mind. Their use can certainly not be completely banned. But we must avoid the blunder of poisoning the biosphere with long-lasting insecticides that have been considered as a panacea. Pesticides are only one of the tools to be used in the fight against insects and other plagues. They are only one aid to natural defence, and pest combatment should involve at the same time an integration of natural, cultural, and biological, aspects of control. Agricultural methods that are unfavourable to ravagers ought to be more widely used, and pesticides employed merely as an aid. This particularly applies to insecticides, but also to some extent to herbicides which exert a great influence on plant communities and destroy entire terrestrial and aquatic habitats. We should study new products—ones that would be less dangerous and more specific—and seek new methods of 'warfare', among which biological control seems to offer by far the best hopes.

Ecological studies are badly needed towards finding solutions that take whole habitats into account, and not merely combat a particular pest while neglecting the side-effects which often outbalance the positive impact of these substances.

MAN AND THE SEA

It is not only land which has to be cared for by man. In the near future we shall have to give particular attention to the seas and oceans which will be the great new frontier of the next century. The agricultural revolution and, later, the industrial revolution, provided great benefits to man, but at the same time they produced environmental destruction, and in some respects lowered the carrying capacity of land for future human populations. Nowadays man turns to the sea. Until recently his relationships with the oceans were almost the same as they had been in the Palaeolithic. Although technology is now much improved, and we are capable of cropping much more fish and other sea products than was the case thousands of years or even a century ago, we are still at the gathering stage where the sea is concerned: for here we remain hunters and predators, much as were our ancestors.

Now our technology is sufficiently advanced to open up for us another type of exploitation of marine resources. Recently, man has begun to explore the sea thoroughly, even at great depths. He has discovered numerous mineral resources which can be exploited with his new techniques—particularly oil and gas. In 1965, 16 per cent of the oil produced by countries outside the USSR and eastern Europe already came from off-shore wells. Many thousands of such wells are being drilled all over the world, and production from them is growing very rapidly. The depth at which drilling is now possible is increasing. We already know the massive pollution potential of the oil industry, illustrated by the 'Torrey Canyon' and Santa Barbara and several other disasters. Undersea mineral mining will be possible in the near future, and with it, and altogether, the risk of heavy pollution will surely grow apace.

Exploitation of biological resources is a much older aspect of the relationships of man to sea. Obviously, utilization by man represents only a very small fraction of total marine productivity, for he concentrates on some products and even some few species which are easy to crop and highly appraised. Over-fishing has already been mentioned as an example of mismanagement of a natural resource on a sustained-yield basis. It is still the main problem of fisheries, and will presumably remain so as long as the demand increases and technology gives us a better and better chance to enlarge the crop—even if the fishing efforts have to be greater.

In the future, man will at least try to exploit other resources of the oceans, and already research is being carried out on new species which may be used for human consumption. Until now even among fish species only 6 per cent are ever exploited, and only 2 per cent at all regularly. Moreover, 90 per cent of marine animals are invertebrates that are almost inedible; but they will surely in time be examined from the point of view of possible conversion into human food.

Man will also in time surely come to concentrate on lower trophic levels than at present, and some have long advocated the use of marine plankton, which would eliminate a number of intermediate stages in food-chains and so produce a far higher return. Up to the present, however, numerous difficulties have been involved in collecting these microscopic animals and plants. Even with the solution of these problems, there would still be the task of transforming the plankton into edible products. Thus it will probably be some considerable time before man replaces his use of the larger fishes in the food-chains, although this may well be done ultimately.

Marine aquaculture may be a very important provider in the future and is already a major concern in several countries. It will be carried out largely in coastal waters, which it is therefore very important to keep free from the noxious influences of man's other activities. In such manners will man interfere with growing intensity in marine environments, both by direct exploitation and by manipulation of the ecosystems. This will be the 'Marine Revolution' (Ray, 1970).

However, marine ecosystems are very fragile. They have already been severely damaged by heavy pollution in many areas—even in remote regions. The effects of pesticides and heavy metals have already seriously hurt the upper levels of food-chains, so that predators such as ospreys and pelicans have suffered through their lack of breeding success. Further disturbance of the balance of marine environments throughout the world is likely to occur. Owing to overall pollution, many oceanographers already speak about the 'dying oceans', and confirm that in some districts life has diminished by 40 per cent in the past twenty years (as stated by Cousteau, 1971).

As we know all too well, man's actions on land lead to a simplification of the natural ecosystems, and with such reduction in their heterogeneity and complexity, and indeed as a direct consequence of it, they became unstable. Up to now man has not seriously lowered the complexity of marine eco-systems, though he has reduced the number of high-level predators (even apart from whales and seals, for many are commercial fishes that are already overexploited) (Woodwell & Smith, 1969). But persistent over-fishing would be more and more harmful, particularly if combined with a higher degree of pollution which would affect a number of species that are particularly sensitive to it. If man should begin to manipulate marine ecosystems through farming, he would necessarily favour some selected species; these would be ones that are directly useful to him. Yields of useful fishes and of other marine organisms cannot be increased unless the productivity of the ecosystem is channelled in a very narrow and restricted manner. This would lead to the reduction in numbers, and even to the practical extinction, of a wide range of other species, such as those that are reputedly useless or even 'harmful'— exactly as has happened in terrestrial ecosystems. The overall result would be to simplify the existing system and to reduce the stability of the ocean eco-system involved—particularly if mining and other activities were to add their effects. We can easily predict that, gradually, the same situation would occur as the one we have to face on land. Man would then use pesticides or their equivalents to control marine 'pests', and the dramatic, vicious circle of terrestrial habitats modified by man would be repeated in the oceans. For many reasons it is of the utmost importance to preserve the complexity of marine ecosystems as far as we can, and particularly by avoiding over-fishing and monoculture in the districts where marine farming is undertaken.

If we do not succeed in controlling our marine activities, we can easily imagine how an ecocatastrophe might be initiated. The first consequence would be to jeopardize marine harvests upon which human survival may largely depend in the fairly near future. Moreover, we should bear in mind the primary importance of oceans in the stability of the entire biosphere, and in the balance of the physico-chemical conditions on earth. Marine plants, chiefly planktonic diatoms and other Algae, play an important part in a num- ber of vital cycles, such as those of carbon and oxygen. Some seventy-five per cent of the atmosphere's free oxygen is produced by phytoplanktonic organisms as they fix carbon during photosynthesis. We know that already the increase in concentration of carbon dioxide in the atmosphere has been at least 6 per cent since the beginning of this century, due to the widespread use of fossil combustibles (Johnson, 1970). If, as a result of habitat disturbances, this vital regulation no longer worked, the changes in the atmosphere would exert far-reaching effects on the chemical balance of the globe. Moreover, an acceleration of the warming-up process engendered by increased carbon dioxide in the atmosphere would result in some of the most fundamental effects of man on our planet. This threat is another reason to preserve the stability of the oceans, the last general habitat in the world that remains in a relatively primeval condition. Before doing anything drastic to the oceans, we should make a comprehensive ecological survey of them, and the legal status of the high seas should also be modified. Instead of *res nullius*, a *res communis* regime would be much more suitable to preserve oceans against overexploitation and predatory economy, which is already under way (Gros, 1960).

COASTAL REGIONS

Special consideration should be given to coastal seas and also to the interface between land and sea. For a long time, a very high percentage of men have lived within a short distance of the sea. This strong tendency is evident all over the world, but particularly in Europe and North America, and will result in an even higher percentage than at present becoming concentrated along seashores in the near future. Such a drift of population is motivated by easy maritime trade over long distances and by other industrial and recreational facilities.

Large concentrations of man and heavy industries, however, result in the production of great quantities of waste, and subsequently in pollution, after the natural habitats have been destroyed for the benefit of industrialization, urbanization, or recreation. Dumping of solid and liquid wastes, including sewage disposal, within the shallower coastal seas and intertidal marshes, has already had a great influence. Thus a series of very important ecosystems of high productivity have been destroyed all over the world. As we well know, intertidal habitats are among the most productive of all, owing to the ebb and flow of tidal waters which twice a day bring in minerals and other substances.

Swamps in estuaries produce an average of about 25 metric tons of dry organic matter per hectare per year—a figure which is comparable with that of the most productive cultivated fields in western Europe. Salt marshes and mud-flats have particular economic importance because they are the breeding grounds of various marine fishes, and because they are the wintering resort and also often the breeding grounds of a wide range of migratory wildfowl. They are very important also as coastal marine ecosystems to which large quantities of mineral and organic substances are supplied naturally all the time (but also as it happens for the benefit of fisheries that are of the highest significance to man). Yet instead of preserving the interface between sea and land, man makes every effort to separate water from land, and also to separate salt water from fresh water, breaking precisely those well-adjusted systems upon which their high productivity depends. Shore-lines are among the most threatened habitats in the world, and the results of man's onslaughts on them have been heavy pollution of coastal and inland waters, inhibition of the return of coastal fisheries, and rupture of the balance in some vital ecosystems. Thus intertidal zones should have a markedly high priority in a sound conservation policy.

SOME IDEAS ABOUT WHAT WE OUGHT TO DO

Clearly we have to face a crisis of transformation which shakes our very civilization. We are living in a period of historical transition which is apparent in the relations between us and our environment, and also in every other aspect of our life (Fraser Darling & Milton, 1966).

Our present 'evolution' derives directly from the rapid changes that have occurred during the last century and even during the last few decades. We have increased the personal comfort of everyone, at least in the western world, by a very high factor—particularly in regard to communication, heating, transportation, control of diseases, and thousands of other aspects of technology. All this has been achieved with a vastly accelerated speed of technical evolution and, in some directions, of sociological development. Nevertheless we know that if we want to increase something at a geometric rate the effort to maintain the rate becomes greater and greater, and finally the system collapses or comes to a standstill at a particular level. Beyond a certain point it would take too much effort to continue, for we would need a geometrically increasing quantity of energy and of raw materials which would finally exceed our possibilities and those of the environment to produce.

Curb Advancing Technology

To illustrate this last fact, one of the best examples relates to the speed of transportation. We have increased the speed of commercial aircraft to a very high rate, and now we are able to travel through the world in very satisfactory conditions. But we want to go still faster, and there lies the motivation of supersonic transport, or SST, as it is now widely called. We can evaluate the price of flying at supersonic speed, when we calculate how much we have to invest to build the 'plane, to test prototypes, and then to convert them into aircraft that could be operated on a commercial basis. It is a multi-milliard dollar gamble for a great technical achievement but for little materialistic gain. Would it not benefit society much more to allow a few hours to cross the oceans—especially when we calculate the time which we waste at airports or in traffic jams! Moreover, we now know something of the 'cost' of such aircraft as sources of noise—a matter which was considered so important that the assurance was given that the SST would not fly over some countries, among them the United States, until the sonic boom problem had been solved.* We have only an approximate idea of the nuisance it would cause to the environment—particularly in the upper layers of the atmosphere which are already being modified by countless jet flights.

To both ecologists and economists, such great technical achievements would seem to take too great a toll of the biosphere and of society at the same time. What happened recently in the United States seems very symptomatic.

* See pp. 117 et seq., 154 et seq., and 168 et seq., and also the paper on pp. 175–7 and the addendum on p. 178, for discussions of other problems introduced by these aircraft.—Ed.

Public support for technological progress has long been a tradition in that country, and in many others as well. On this occasion, however, for the first time such a technological victory seemed hollow, or at least its price seemed out of proportion to what it would cost the community and the environment. In deprecating the SST, responsible people felt that other problems outranked it, and in this connection many social and economic evils were listed— including pollution. The decision not to proceed forthwith to build fleets of SSTs has been considered as an American reversal of their tradition of being at the vanguard of technology, and many ecologists have praised it as proof of American wisdom while regretting that other nations were not following suit. Meanwhile this decision in favour of the environment is very sympto- matic of a new selectivity about which kinds of objectives are worth pursuing, and at what price.

The story of the American SST is only a small part of a much more general problem, which is the problem of our modern technology. More and more do we come to realize that we are paying too much in terms of resources and effort for what we consider to be progress. Until recently we believed that the faster and the bigger things were, the better they must be. But now suddenly we are beginning to realize that this is not true, and that every technological advance is not necessarily an item of progress for humanity. Industrial ad- vance is not fundamentally to be identified with real progress towards happiness. In many cases its impact on the biosphere is too great in propor- tion to the actual benefit. Degradation of land and sea, and various forms of pollution, are the direct consequences of technological aggression. Until recently the easy answer to the problem of technology was *more* technology. Yet, like science, technology as a whole is neither good nor bad, but depends upon a number of circumstances and how man uses particular aspects of it. Evolving technology will in time give us a chance to control some of the nuisances of today, such as those produced by car exhaust. But in other cases technology often spells trouble, and it would be very dangerous to think that the difficult problems of today could be settled by the technology of tomor- row. Yet technology and imagination, when used together, can still improve our life in the best sense in instances where we make a wise choice—rather than trusting to blind faith in technology to reverse the trends which are responsible for the present crisis.

Control Industrial Growth

To return to the curve reflecting our productions and activities, man still believes that it will for ever continue to show an upward trend, and this is reflected in the economic plans of every government over the world when it is decided that there shall be an increase in productivity of a given per- centage in a particular year. Yet it is sheer nonsense to believe that an ex- ponential curve can be included within a finite envelope, when our world is obviously finite. The curve is in reality an 'S-curve', and is beginning to level off. Increase, so rapid in the past few decades, will necessarily slow down, and we shall have to find a balance between our legitimate needs and the capability of the environment to satisfy them. Instead of *quantity*, we have to look for *quality*: that would be real progress. Optimal conditions for a sound material and psychological expansion of mankind are to be found in a balance between the resources available in the biosphere, the effort to collect them, the noxious side-effects of our activities, and the legitimate needs of everyone. These have to be proportionate to the other parameters of this kind of equation. Increasing them with no limit is probably the most serious complaint against the society which advocates unlimited consumption.

Much controversy occurs when the most desirable rate of expansion comes under discussion. A zero-growth economy has been advocated by many, and not without reason. However, this is probably not feasible for practical considerations, and there is a danger of over-reaction and over-simplification of a problem which ought to be examined with a calm mind. We have to control very carefully any major industrial growth, and check beforehand its side-effects as far as we can. Evolving technology will probably permit on the average a reasonable degree of economic growth—one that is proportionate to what the biosphere can withstand. To stop growth in every sector of economy would have serious sociological and political consequences. We have to be realistic and only be very strict in controlling any new development which would have a serious adverse impact on the biosphere.

We ought by now to be convinced that the resources of our planet are limited—that we cannot use them beyond a certain point and continuously increase our output as we have done in recent decades. Such a reversal will be accepted only reluctantly by mankind, for we have been living for a long time with unlimited faith in economic growth and this will not be easily forgotten. Of course, this need for limitation applies mainly to developed countries and not in the same way to underdeveloped countries in which improvement can and must still be pursued, though under properly controlled conditions (Ciriacy-Wantrup, 1968; Odum, 1971).

In contrast, should we continue to follow the line which brought us to the present situation, we would have a good chance to face an ecocatastrophe within the next decade or so, and this might be the end of our industrial civilization.

Certainly we cannot willingly abandon this way of life—not only because it has brought us a great number of improvements, but mainly because humanity in its present situation could not survive without technology. But we have to revise our thinking about what kind of technology we need, and turn against invention that is aimed only at increasing production and profits.

The Belgian philosopher Henri van Lier (1952) has said that we stand at the beginning of a *dialectical technology*, consisting of a cooperation between the natural world and our artificially created milieu, which may well take the place of the present dynamic technology that tries to make us the masters of the environment in the most brutal way. This new technology, already proposed some years ago by several writers including Lewis Mumford (*cf.* 1967), would be better adjusted to environmental conditions than is the present one, and would cause less degradation in relation to lowered pressure on the biosphere. But it certainly would be less profitable to man on a short-term basis, for it would restrain him from any action which would be disproportionately harmful to the environment.

This new attitude has little chance of being anything more than a Utopia if it is not strongly backed by ecologists, whose main role will be to persuade mankind of the absolute necessity of such a reversal. Yet it will be against what mankind trusts nowadays, and will have to be independent of political opinion or, anyway, motivation.

Remember the Biosphere

Having full confidence in the tools which had been given to us by physics and chemistry, we built the technosphere and progressively forgot the biosphere. Most of us do not even seem to realize that the latter still exists, except for a little fun during weekends, and maybe only because it is fashionable to own a country house. It has rightly been said that our ability to manipulate the physical world has progressed faster and farther than have the social institutions and protective mechanisms which might act as controls over that ability.

For such reasons, we forgot that virtually every human activity takes place in the biosphere, and that our activities are apt to have side-effects which risk the precipitation of situations that are adverse to our objectives and so sterilize costly investments. Ecological conditions are never adequately surveyed and properly considered by planners, still less by decision-makers. Yet we should never allow ourselves to modify any major part or feature of the surface of our earth without first making a global evaluation of the results, including an appraisal of all foreseeable ecological conditions and disturbances which might follow as direct or even indirect consequences.

Need for Ecological Appraisal

In recent years, a number of wide-scale projects have been established without any proper attention being paid to ecological side-effects. A classical example is the building of the Aswan Dam on the upper Nile. The purposes were sound enough, for it provides at the same time a regular supply of water for irrigation and electrical power to industrialize a country that is still mainly at an agricultural stage. But downstream, the flood regime of the Nile has been modified in such a way that the deposition of alluvium has been greatly disturbed and some irrigated areas have become covered with salt carried up from deeper layers by the flood-waters, thus becoming sterilized instead of being opened up to agriculture. Moreover, changes in the water regime favoured molluscs that served as intermediate hosts to flukes causing schistosomiasis, which have increased both in incidence and virulence in Egypt. At the same time the damming has caused serious disturbances in the marine ecosystems of the eastern Mediterranean, where the rich supply of nutrients that was formerly brought down by the Nile is no longer available. As an example, the yield of fisheries has steadily declined, the catch of sardines dropping from 18,000 tons in 1965 to 500 tons in 1968.

Such situations may occur also in the Indo-Chinese peninsula, where a gigantic project will deeply modify the regime of the Mekong River after a number of dams have become operational. Ecological studies have not been carried on at the same rate as the engineering—even in regard to the Tonle

Sap, Cambodia, the great lake from which a sustained yield of fish is collected year after year. Yet here also there appears to be a considerable series of unsettling biological problems which could have very serious sociological implications.

Construction of the pipeline to carry oil southwards from northern Alaska has a good chance of causing serious ecological disturbances in the local arctic ecosystem, which is particularly fragile owing to its hard physical conditions of existence, lack of diversity, and the low recuperative power of the tundra. This project, which would have positive effects on the human economy, could provoke a rupture of balance in the whole area, and not merely among the populations of animals and plants that are of the highest scientific interest (Reed, 1970). Further major projects are under consideration for other northern areas, particularly in the Soviet Union.

Numerous examples of such major damming, etc., projects could be cited in tropical countries. Though advice has sometimes been sought from ecologists, notably by the International Bank for Reconstruction and Development, rarely have their views been taken seriously into consideration. This particularly applies to new cultivation projects, which have had the object of converting, into fields or pastures, land that was still covered by humid forests. As a result, catastrophic erosion has been initiated, notably in Latin America and in Africa, while poor soil management, exaggerated mechanization, and cultivation of land that is unsuitable for agriculture, are still proceeding with funds that are distributed with no proper care by international or national agencies. Even in developed countries, much money is still spent for land reclamation and drainage of wetlands, with no evident purpose unless it be to give engineers a chance to demonstrate their skill!

Importance of Global Viewpoint

It is this regrettable situation that we have to modify without delay. We have an unprecedented opportunity to change our attitude and our relationship with our environment, now that we are undergoing a great historical transition—as is indeed evident in many aspects of our life. It is an urgent need that we give attention to the problems of today from a global viewpoint, for this approach is essential as a basis for sound economic and social development. Instead of the *laissez-faire* spirit of exploitation, we have to adopt a completely different attitude and, as stated previously, reverse the trends (Wolstenholme, 1963; Dubos, 1968; Cox, 1969; Galbraith, 1969; Platt, 1969; Ehrlich & Ehrlich, 1970).

Ecologists have a special responsibility in what will happen. The great hope of mankind will be in what Nicholson (1970) has called *The Environmental Revolution*, and in a better evaluation of relations between man and his environment. Until now, not much responsibility has been given to ecologists, and they have rarely been listened to by planners or decision-makers. Yet they stand at the confluence of academic and social forces, and should be trained to cope with wide-scale problems at the level of ecosystems or even of the biosphere. They have to fight to ensure that ecology, which has been called the subversive science, will be recognized as capable of giving guidelines for finding remedies to the present situation and for any future development. Management of resources of the world of tomorrow should be in their hands, even if the final decision is not taken by them but by the society on which they have to impose a kind of leadership. We hasten to say that ecology is not merely a biological discipline but also a way of thinking and a spirit which can be shared by men without any particular biological training.

The main tasks of ecologists will be monitoring and evaluating the environmental situation and its trends, and also predicting what will happen—thanks to simulation models and computer methods, which offer great hopes of finding solutions to problems with countless parameters. Ecologists must not retire to their laboratories, but move to action and influence political decisions in the right direction. Certainly the 'new Jeremiahs', as they have been called, should not adopt extreme attitudes which would give rise to an 'anti-ecology' movement. But they have to warn, and to be on the positive side in proposing solutions and in setting priorities that everybody can support.

It is scarcely necessary to add that man cannot be dissociated from his natural environment, including all the factors which are essential parts of it. For this reason we have the solemn duty to preserve the remaining stocks of every living species that we possibly can, and also representative samples of all types of natural habitats (Dasmann, 1965, 1968a, 1968b; UNESCO, 1970). We have not to choose between saving the last Whooping Cranes and fighting pollution in our cities; both are facets of the same problem, which we have to solve by good management of the planet earth.

Ecologists should also be what Robert Jungk (1969) called 'the advocates of the future'. We are only usufructuaries of our world, and we have the duty to transmit it to the generations to come in such a state that they will have a freedom of choice such as we had—or should have had if our predecessors had taken care of our wild heritage.

Pessimists think that only a vast catastrophe can change the present trends. We cannot share this opinion, however desperate the situation may look from some points of view. Man has been able to reform his thoughts and actions each time that his future has been in question. But now is the time, and the fight must be won by the present generation. It is getting very late, though not yet too late, to start a new period of history characterized by man living in harmony with his environment—as other living beings do and have done since evolution began in our world.

References

ANGOT, M. (1959). Evolution de la pêche du Troca (*Trochus niloticus* L.) en Nouvelle-Calédonie. Un exemple d'"overfishing' avec ses causes et les remèdes apportés. *Terre et Vie*, 106e Année, No. 4, pp. 307–14, 1 fig.

ARVILL, R. (1967). *Man and Environment: Crisis and the Strategy of Choice*. Penguin Books, London: 332 pp., illustr.

BELL, G. DE (Ed.) (1970). *The Environmental Handbook*. Ballantyne/Friends of the Earth/Intertext, New York: xv + 367 pp.

BURKENROAD, M. D. (1948). Fluctuation in abundance of Pacific Halibut. *Bull. Bingham Ocean. Coll.*, **11**, pp. 81–129.

CARBENIER, R. (1969). Aperçu sur quelques effets de la pollution des eaux douces de la zone tempérée sur les biocénoses aquatiques. *Min. Educ. Nat. Com. Trav. Hist. Scient. Bull. Sect. Géorg.*, **80** (1967), pp. 45–132.

CARSON, R. (1962). *Silent Spring*. Crest, New York: Houghton Mifflin, Boston: xiii + 368, illustr.

CHARLIER, R. H. (1971). Pollution problems. *Intern. J. Environmental Studies*, **1**, pp 129–39.

CIRIACY-WANTRUP, S. V. (1968). *Resource Conservation: Economics and Policies* (3rd edn). University of California Press, Berkeley: xvi + 395 pp.

COMMONER, B. (1966). *Science and Survival*. Victor Gollancz, London: 128 pp.

COUSTEAU, J.-Y. (1971). Statement on global marine degradation. *Biological Conservation*, **4**(1), pp. 61–5.

COX, G. W. (Ed.) (1969). *Readings in Conservation Ecology*. Appleton-Century-Crofts, New York: xii + 595, illustr.

CROKER, R. S. (1954). The sardine story—a tragedy. *Outdoor Calif.*, 15(1), pp. 6–8.

DARLING, F. FRASER & MILTON, J. P. (Eds) (1966). *Future Environments of North America*. Natural History Press, Garden City, New York: xv + 767 pp., illustr.

DASMANN, R. F. (1964). *African Game Ranching*. Pergamon Press, Oxford: 75 pp., illustr.

DASMANN, R. F. (1965). *The Destruction of California*. Macmillan, New York, and Collier-Macmillan, London: vii + 276 pp., illustr.

DASMANN, R. F. (1968a). *Environmental Conservation* (2nd edn). John Wiley, New York: xiii + 375 pp., illustr.

DASMANN, R. F. (1968b). *A Different Kind of Country*. Macmillan, New York, and Collier-Macmillan, London: viii + 276 pp., illustr.

DE BELL, G. *See* BELL, G. DE

DORST, J. (1970). *Before Nature Dies* (transl. C. D. Sherman). Collins, London: 352 pp., illustr.

DUBOS, R. (1968). *So Human an Animal*. Charles Scribner, New York: xiv + 269 pp.

EHRLICH, R. P. & EHRLICH, A. H. (1970). *Population, Resources, Environment: Issues in Human Ecology*. W. H. Freeman, San Francisco: [x] + 383 pp., illustr.

ENVIRONMENTAL QUALITY (1970). *First Annual Report of the Council on Environmental Quality*. U.S. Govt Printing Office, Washington, D.C.: xxv + 326 pp.

FOSBERG, F. R. (Ed) (1963). *Man's Place in the Island Ecosystem. A Symposium*. Bishop Museum Press, Honolulu: vii + 264 pp., illustr. + additional map.

FRASER DARLING, F. *See* DARLING, F. FRASER

GABRIELSON, I. N. (1959). *Wildlife Conservation* (2nd edn). Macmillan, New York: xii + 244 pp., illustr.

GALBRAITH, J. K. (1969). *The Affluent Society* (2nd edn). Hamish Hamilton, London: xxxiii + 333 pp.

GRAHAM, E. H. (1944). *Natural Principles of Land Use*. Oxford University Press, New York: xiii + 274, illustr.

GROS, A. (1960). La convention sur la pêche et la conservation des ressources biologiques de la haute mer. *Recueil Cours Acad. Droit Int.* (1959), **97**, pp. 1–89.

HADEN-GUEST, S., WRIGHT, J. K. & TECLAFF, E. M. (Eds) (1956). *A World Geography of Forest Resources*. Ronald Press, New York: xviii + 736 pp.

HARRIS, R. J. C. (1970). Cancer and the environment. *Intern. J. Environmental Studies*, **1**, pp. 59–65.

HARROY, J. P. (1944). *Afrique, Terre qui Meurt*. Hayez et Office int. de Librairie, Bruxelles: x + 557 pp.

HOLDGATE, M. W. & WACE, N. M. (1961). The influence of man on the floras and faunas of southern islands. *Polar Record*, **10**, pp. 475–93.

IUCN (1966–70). Survival Service Commission. *Red Data Book*. 1. *Mammalia* (N. Simon), 1966; 2. *Aves* (J. Vincent), 1966; 3. *Pisces* (R. R. Miller), 1968; 4. *Amphibia and Reptilia* (R. E. Honegger), 1968; 5. *Angiospermae* (R. Melville), 1970.

JOHNSON, F. S. (1970). The balance of atmospheric oxygen and carbon dioxide. *Biological Conservation*, **2**(2), pp. 83–9.

JUNGK, R. (1969). Imagination and the future. *Int. Social Sci. Journ.*, Paris: **21**, pp. 557–62.

LAWS, R. M. (1960). Problems of whale conservation. *Trans. 28th North American Wildlife Conf.*, pp. 304–19.

LE CREN, E. D. & HOLDGATE, M. W. (Eds) (1962). *The Exploitation of Natural Animal Populations. A symposium of the British Ecological Society.* Blackwell, Oxford: xiv + 399 pp., illustr.

LIER, H. VAN (1962). *Le nouvel Age.* Casterman, Liège: 232 pp., illustr.

MELLANBY, K. (1967). *Pesticides and Pollution.* Collins, London: 221 pp., illustr.

MUMFORD, L. (1967). *The Myth of the Machine: Technics and Human Development.* Harcourt, Brace & World, New York, Secker & Warburg, London: ix + 342 pp., illustr.

NICHOLSON, M. (1970). *The Environmental Revolution.* Hodder & Stoughton, London: xiii + 366 pp., illustr.

ODUM, H. T. (1971). *Environment, Power, and Society.* Wiley-Interscience, New York: ix + 331 pp., illustr.

OLSON, T. A. & BURGESS, F. J. (Eds) (1967). *Pollution and Marine Ecology.* Wiley-Interscience, New York: xvii + 364 pp., illustr.

PHILLIPS, J. (1959). *Agriculture and Ecology in Africa.* Faber & Faber, London: 422 pp., map.

PLATT, J. (1969). What we must do. *Science,* **106**, pp. 1115–21.

POLUNIN, N. (1967). *Eléments de Géographie botanique.* Gauthier-Villars, Paris: xxiii + 532 pp., illustr.

RAY, C. (1970). Ecology, law, and the 'marine revolution'. *Biological Conservation,* **3**(1), pp. 7–17.

REED, J. C. (1970). Effects of oil development in Arctic America. *Biological Conservation,* **2**(4), pp. 273–7, illustr.

RUSSELL, R. S. (1969). Contamination of the biosphere with radioactivity. *Biological Conservation,* **2**(1), pp. 2–9.

SANKARANARAYANAN, K. (1971). Recent advances in mammalian radiation genetics… *Intern. J. Environmental Studies,* **1**, pp. 187–93.

SCIENTIFIC AMERICAN (1970). The biosphere. *Scientific American,* **223**(3), pp. 45–208, illustr.

SEARS, P. B. (1967). *Deserts on the March* (3rd edn). University of Oklahoma Press, Norman: xiii + 178 pp.

TERNISIEN, J. A. (196a) *Les pollutions et leurs effets.* PUF, Paris: 188 pp.

TERNISIEN, J. A. (1968b). *La lutte contre les pollutions.* PUF, Paris: 183 pp.

THOMAS, W. L., Jr. (Ed.) (1956). *Man's Role in Changing the Face of the Earth.* University of Chicago Press, Chicago: xxxviii + 1193 pp., illustr.

UNESCO (1963). *Enquête sur les Ressources naturelles du Continent africain.* UNESCO, Paris: 448 pp., maps.

UNESCO (1970). *Use and Conservation of the Biosphere.* United Nations Educational, Scientific and Cultural Organization, Paris (Natural Resources Division X): 272 pp.

VAN LIER, H. *See* LIER, H. VAN

VIBERT, R. & LAGLER, K. F. (1961). *Pêches continentales. Biologie et aménagement.* Dunod, Paris: xxiv + 720 pp., illustr.

WOLSTENHOLME, G. (Ed.) (1963). *Man and his Future.* Churchill, London: vi + 410 pp., illustr.

WOODWELL, G. M. & SMITH, H. H. (1969). *Diversity and Stability in Ecological Systems.* Brookhaven Symposia in Biology No. 22. Brookhaven National Laboratories, Upton, New York: [v] + 264 pp., illustr.

WORTHINGTON, E. B. (1961). *The Wild Resources of East and Central Africa.* H.M. Stationery Office, London: 26 pp. (Colonial Office, No. 352).

DISCUSSION

Baer (Chairman)

Before opening the discussion I would like to highlight certain points, one of which I feel should be that if we do not want this Conference to become just another esoteric meeting of the 'converted', we must come up with new ideas, some of which may not be very pleasing at first sight. Professor Dorst rightly drew our attention to the fact that the space wherein we live—in which all living creatures live upon this earth, and upon which they feed and find their food—is limited. It is just simple arithmetic: if human population goes on increasing, obviously free space will be reduced as more and more will be needed for this population and less will remain for other animals and for growing food. Like many other resources, space is limited, and I think this is one of the main things that we should insist upon, whenever we have to talk with people who say that expansion is their aim. Expansion is a great modern word: if a nation doesn't expand by so many per cent a year it's on the way down, if not on the way out! This is the kind of supposition that shows how very wrong, biologically speaking, the whole political situation is. I think we've got to face the fact that we live in a world of economists who have made their own system, and that this system has proved itself to be wrong; you cannot go on increasing production, getting people to buy more, throw away more, waste more, spend more on luxury goods, and at the same time have a world worth living in.

Another point which strikes me forcibly is that most of us belong to a generation which has been through two world wars; we have seen the environment deteriorate, but what about the younger generation that has since been brought into this world? How can they understand what our troubles are? Yet we must bring to their attention the facts that we need more young people who understand our problems, and that we cannot go on living above our means as some of us are doing now. Nor, as Sir Frank Fraser Darling pointed out rather nicely in his paper this morning, would it be advisable or desirable to bring all the developing countries up to what we call our standard of living. This would not necessarily do them a good service and it would certainly not help the world as a whole.

Yet another thing that we should not forget when we talk about environment is that there's also an environment which is extremely important for human beings, namely the cultural environment, and many developing countries have a higher cultural development than many other countries which have either lost it or not yet attained it. I think this should be taken into consideration when assistance is given to those countries to help them to reach what may be considered a decent standard of living. But here again, who is going to judge the standard of living? This is a point that has always worried me. Obviously we in the western world judge our standard of living and compare it with that of other countries, and we consider them poor—desperately poor in certain cases—and yet when you look at those people closely, they seem often perfectly happy. They may not always have enough to eat, but then we have too much to eat. They are healthy, their death rate, of course, is slightly higher than ours, and their birth rate is too; but as infantile mortality is also higher, there is some limitation.

Thus I feel that mistakes have been made in giving delusions to some of these developing countries that their inhabitants can all own motor cars and have a very high standard of living if they accept the money that is offered to them and use it to produce more, so that the overdeveloped countries can have more raw material for processing. I think this is economically and humanely speaking entirely wrong, and is another of the important points that we should bear in mind.

Economists look at this promotion from the economic angle, and presumably it is part of what was discussed this morning as the artificial environment that man through his intelligence has created to his own advantage, or occasionally to the advantage of other organisms. But it's the difference between these two—the natural and man-made—that should be bridged, and I am absolutely certain that a problem such as this one which we have before us cannot be solved by biologists alone; we need to explain it to the economists and discuss it with them. We also need to discuss these problems with sociologists and with all those who today decide what's going to happen tomorrow—but without consulting us. For those are the people who keep the ball rolling—I would say often in the wrong direction to where it's gathering a lot of moss. The trouble is that we are too far apart and I think it is necessary in any future discussion of this sort to bring in people from very different social and economical fields, and even from different political fields, so that they can really be made to understand the problem; meanwhile it is our job to show what biologists have done, and what they can do. This can be boiled down quite easily into a short review to be given to people of these other groups in a form explaining how biologists understand what life is: it is not just a number, or a vote. I think such understanding is indispensable if we are to get any further.

Another point is the politically unpopular price that has to be paid. You may have noted how in certain countries and papers where they are aware of the problem, they don't say what is the price they are going to pay, but who is going to pay. This, I think, is a wrong attitude, because the whole world has got to pay, not merely one country or two countries; some will pay more than others, that is obvious, but if this is a global problem, it is a problem that concerns the whole world population and the future of the world population.

Professor Dorst very rightly pointed out that we've got to make ourselves understood by the younger generation, because they are the people of tomorrow who will certainly be able to help most in this world and the world of tomorrow. We've just seen something of the road; we've been shown our mistakes or many of them, but they were made in good faith. At the same time I really feel that we should be closer to the younger generation than we are now. I am glad to see in this auditorium many young people, and I only hope that they will go away with a feeling that what the older people are talking about is not just pure wishful thinking, but that these are hard facts which, even if many of them have already been heard on other occasions, must nevertheless be stressed again and brought to their attention.

But facts are not enough: we need more, we need answers. This is what we've got to stress most—finding the answers. The answer to the population problem has been found. I'm speaking as a biologist. Biologists have solved the problem. But who is going to apply the measures which exist today? This is most unpopular, politically speaking; and yet, it is the only answer. If certain powers, certain authorities, do not understand the problem, it may be that certain countries will apply the measures without necessity or in different ways, and the result could be extremely dangerous. I feel that this is a problem that should be looked at on a global scale; it is unpopular, politically speaking, for the good reason that most politicians think merely of what's going to happen up to the time of the next election*. Thus there cannot be any long-term thinking by them, which is what we really need. We biologists know that nature does not work from election to election but rather in cycles, taking sometimes many years to show her hand, and never doing so within a short period. At the same time it can be unfortunate that those of us who are biologists are inclined to look at these problems from a purely biological viewpoint, though we should understand that sociologists, economists, and urbanists, are also implicated.

Hela

The International Council of Scientific Unions (ICSU) has authorized me to report on the studies of the environment within ICSU.

The programmes of several of the international scientific unions have been concerned with various environmental factors for the last fifty years, but it was not until the International Biological Programme (IBP) was launched in 1964 that the biological community really became involved in an integrated global study of the environment. This programme is concerned with the productivity of communities on land, in fresh water, and in the oceans, together with human adaptability, and is expected to provide the information that is necessary for rationalizing the management of renewable resources. The information obtained up to the present is being assembled and the principal results will be synthesized in a series of volumes. Certain of the IBP research projects will probably be continued within the framework of the Man and the Biosphere programme.†

Various ICSU bodies have continuing programmes which provide information on the state of the environment, which are concerned with the development of methodology to improve the precision and the intercomparability of the environmental data obtained, and which measure the levels of pollution and the effects of pollutants in the air, on the land, and in the oceans and fresh waters.

Studies of the effects on man and on the environment of developments in rural areas, such as man-made lakes, massive irrigation programmes, and replacement of natural vegetation by agricultural crops or of the natural fauna and flora by introduced species, have begun and will continue so as to indicate how to obtain maximum long-term benefits from such changes, or to diminish any deleterious effects.

In spite of the fact that the physical modifications that man makes in the

* But see the comment of Professor Konrad Lorenz, leading specialist on animal behaviour, at the end of this section, page 100.—Ed.

† Described briefly on pp. 53–4.—Ed.

urban environment frequently lead to a deterioration in its overall quality and in the well-being of the urban population, man, because of his great powers of adaptation, rapidly becomes accustomed to the changes. Studies of human adaptability to modifications in the environment, to changes in nutrition, and to certain stresses and hazards, are being undertaken in an endeavour to discover the extent to which these may be deleterious, and in an endeavour to quantify tolerance-limits.

Within the field of nutrition, for example, studies are continuing into various aspects of toxicology—including the effects on foods of additives, of pesticide and other undesirable residues, and of toxins created naturally during storage.

Studies of aquatic environments, both freshwater and marine, are being undertaken: to determine the effects of build-up of waste products within food-chains; to select indicator organisms; to establish baseline conditions; to monitor changes; to estimate the influence of discharges of energy or substances on (a) water quality, (b) reduction of useful productivity, and (c) decrease of amenities; and to examine the sublethal effects of waste products upon biological processes and upon species diversity. Although it is known that in recent years there has been an increase in the proportion of carbon dioxide in the atmosphere, insufficient information is available to provide answers to questions concerning the effect of the oceans and the role of air/sea interaction on the concentration of carbon dioxide in the atmosphere. Additional data are therefore being collected in an endeavour to understand the total effect on the climate of various factors, such as increases in carbon dioxide, in particulate matter, and in condensation trails, and the roles of cloud-seeding and of the generation of heat at the earth's surface.

The Special Committee for the International Biological Programme (SCIBP)* has recommended that an integrated research programme on the analysis and synthesis of the world's major biomes be continued, with the objective of ensuring partnership rather than conflict between man and nature.

The Special Committee on Problems of the Environment (SCOPE), which was established in 1969 under the Chairmanship of Dr J. Eric Smith, has set up the following groups to investigate a number of problems:

(1) Working Group on the Case Study of the Toxicology of Chlorinated Aromatic Compounds;
(2) Working Group on Materials that significantly alter the Biosphere (within the framework of this group a sub-group has been established to study the possibilities of establishing an International Registry of Chemical Compounds, which would provide certain information on those chemical compounds that are produced in amounts greater than 500 kg per year);
(3) Working Group on Scientific Bases for the Creation and Management of Artificial Ecosystems (a work study is being organized within this group that will result in a concise statement on the major relationships in new man-made or man-modified ecosystems and in an analysis of their implications for policy related to present and proposed man-made lakes); and

* Of which the sessional Chairman, Professor Jean G. Baer, was President until recently.—Ed.

(4) Commission on Monitoring, whose function is to design an appropriate broadly-based monitoring system for air, water, soils, and biota (including man), taking into account existing activities. It is not the intention of this Commission to create a monitoring network.

At its second meeting, held recently, SCOPE also set up an *ad hoc* group to consider the objectives and functions of a possible International Centre for the Environment (ICE) and the steps which would be needed for its establishment. A small group was also set up to consider how to obtain the maximum participation of scientists from developing countries in the planning and achievement of SCOPE programmes.

In addition, there are a number of organizations belonging to ICSU that are currently undertaking environmental studies, including the International Unions of Geodesy and Geophysics, Biological Sciences, Geological Sciences, Pure and Applied Chemistry, Geography, etc. These are not only concerned with renewable biological resources but also with the effects of natural disasters—such as earthquakes, volcanic eruptions, tornadoes, and tsunamis —and with the effects on man of modifications in the environment (urbanization, improved transport, synthetic materials and foods, etc.).

It can be expected that, in the future, ICSU will be more and more concerned with the provision of information about the biosphere and its modification—so as to assist in the all-important process of diminishing the deleterious effects of man upon his environment.

Baroda

Standing in front of you is a living specimen of a dying 'sub-species' of the human race, and this is entirely due to man. The population explosion in my country is well-known, and it is because of this explosion that the 'sub-species' to which I belong, the princes and maharajas of India, are about to disappear for ever; for each year millions and millions of new mouths and new stomachs are to be fed, and this grave problem faces my country. I also represent the World Wildlife Fund, of which I am a trustee, and for the last four years I have been minister in one of our largest states, in charge of family planning. I have brought along with me a paper; it was delayed because of the mid-term elections, when luckily I got elected to parliament. I hope that I shall be given an opportunity to present this paper later, for although it is written from a layman's viewpoint, it deals with certain crucial facts.

Meanwhile I just stood up to make a couple of points very briefly. The impact of this paper on me personally has been to ask myself the question, 'Are we today fit to call ourselves human beings? We are beings, but are we human? Do we behave in a humane way towards our fellow beings?' We consider ourselves civilized; but I think we are the most uncivilized of beings on earth today. One could write books and books, even a layman like me, on what man is doing today and what man may do tomorrow and the day after if he is not checked in time.

The other point I wanted to make here is that while I feel bodies and conferences such as ours are doing excellent work, our public relations are apt to be extremely poor. I have always felt this. For instance, this morning I heard the news on the wireless, luckily in English so I could understand it, and it mentioned our Conference being held here; but I do not know how much this will have meant to the vast majority of people who heard that broadcast. Whatever the experts may talk about here, whatever papers are submitted, and books written as a result, all this must be done in a language which is easily understood by those who we feel should understand what we are talking about. And in this direction too, I have always felt that we must have some sort of programme for the education of those to whom we want the message to get through.

These are the two points I felt I should make at this stage. I do not know how important they really are, but personally I feel they are very important, for in my own field of work, which is politics, I am also chancellor of a university that has 18,000 students. However, I talk to them, whenever I get the opportunity, about this subject of conservation and the environment, or what little I know about it. But it doesn't seem to get through to them even with the language I use, and therefore I feel that if we are to get the message out to the masses a far easier language must be used by us when we speak for popular consumption.

Kassas

Mr Chairman, I'd like to accept the challenge which you posed in your first comment: that this Conference should produce some ideas, though they may not be pleasing at first sight. I feel I should convey to you all some ideas that are far from being pleasant ones. The chairman of the first session this morning, Dr Periäinen, posed to us the question: What will be the future of man as a part of the environment? He said that, in trying to answer this question, one should follow the history of evolution of man from its primitive beginnings to the very advanced state reached by western man, and that we should ask a question: When did man make the wrong decision? I'd like to answer by saying that in my opinion man has not yet made the wrong decision. Many people, including myself, think that the future of man as a biological taxon on this earth—whether he will be able to survive during the next three hundred years or the next three million years—will depend on whatever decisions he will take during the next thirty years. One may change the threes into ones or twos or fours, but no more than fives.

What sort of decisions will be taken? We speak about the population of the world in the future. I would like to think of population not in terms of numbers, but in attributes of people. We heard earlier today of the distinction between people living in the underdeveloped world and people living in the developed world; and of people in the north and people in the south. I would like to put it to this Conference that if we let the present cultural gap develop and extend—it is a relatively recent aspect of human society, having largely appeared in the last fifty or sixty years—with the developing countries becoming overdeveloped and underdeveloped countries becoming further and further underdeveloped, we shall be faced with the situation that the human race, the human species, would be almost split into two subspecies. These would not be of the type which His Highness the Maharaja of Baroda has just mentioned, but biological types, different in their biological set-up and different in their psychological set-up—so different that biologically speaking they would constitute two different taxa. I am saying this because if, for the next thirty years or so, things are left to continue as at present, the people in advanced countries will be feeding on substances different from the foods of people in underdeveloped countries. People in developed countries will be suffering from diseases very different from the diseases that are suffered by people in underdeveloped countries. People and their domestic animals and crops will—and this is also important—be suffering from pests that will be very different from those in underdeveloped countries. People in advanced countries will be suffering from certain psychological disorders that will be different from the psychological unpleasantness and worries that will be prevalent in underdeveloped countries, and so on.

If we should allow this to proceed, we would be left within the next thirty years or so with two alternatives. One would be that the people in developed countries—advanced, very well-fed and well-looked-after people—would by their ill-advised development commit what might well amount to ecological suicide. They would have polluted their environment and exhausted its resources to such an extent that life might fail to continue. Now if this should happen, *Homo sapiens* would still be present either in the north polar regions or far to the south near the Equator, and these people would march again as human beings did earlier, and human history would start again. This would be a very sad thing, and we would like to make sure that it would not happen.

The other alternative, to prevent anything like this from happening, would be for the people of the developed countries to take the right sort of ecological decisions and manage to survive. Yet they might still look upon their fellow human beings in the underdeveloped world as centres of danger, because by ridding themselves and their domestic animals and crops of diseases, they would become extremely vulnerable—extremely susceptible to these and other diseases—while people living in the underdeveloped world would maintain a good deal of resistance to these diseases as also would their domestic animals. These people could then represent a very serious danger to the people in the advanced countries. Now what would be the reaction? People in the advanced countries might decide to use atomic bombs to sterilize the world of these sources of infection, which again would be a very sad thing. This is the kind of reason why I say that the future of the human race will depend on whatever decisions we take within the next thirty years or so: whether we allow the present dichotomy to split us apart, or bridge the gap and retain the unity of the human race.

Laird

'What man is doing' can give the unintentional impression that man always 'does', or at least 'has done' up to now, things in an ecologically uninformed and even mindless way. I mistrust generalizations, and would like to question one made by Professor Dorst. He said that 'Sprayed insecticides and herbicides should be added to the list of iniquities'. Now, Professor Dorst made a very good point when speaking of agricultural pesticides. He said, 'They are only one aid to natural defence, and pest combatment should involve at the same time an integration of natural, cultural, and biological, aspects of control'. I most heartily agree with him. I would go further, and say precisely the same thing of public health pesticides. As an ideal, as a goal to work towards, this is in every way sensible.

However, Professor Dorst did not mention the use of pesticides for health purposes—which is often a very selective use indeed, as in the case of the World Health Organization's malarial eradication methodology. Not based upon larvicidal spraying at all, this demands a cheap, safe, and persistent pesticide (usually DDT) for application to inner walls of houses to kill resting adult *Anopheles* mosquitoes. Obviously, any hazard to the general environment here is minimal indeed. The methodology was conceived fourteen or fifteen years ago, with possible ecological hazards very much in the minds of those concerned. Sometimes, though, ecologically hazardous pesticides are used as larvicides too, for example against West African black-flies (*Simulium* spp.) which transmit onchocerciasis to man (in this disease, caused by a filarial worm, the person infected is, all too often, permanently blinded). Many, many thousands of West Africans risk blindness annually from this currently controllable disease, and many of them suffer total blindness at a distressingly early age. Now to some ecologists in affluent countries, Africans with onchocerciasis, but far away, may seem less important than Brown Pelicans, for example, near at hand. Nevertheless, many others (particularly West African health authorities) demand the control of this disease despite side-effects to the environment that may be posed by the pesticides used to control the larvae of the black-fly vector.

As I said at the outset, I wholeheartedly agree with Professor Dorst that integrated and highly selective control is the ideal. But this is still only the year 1971, and neither in this year nor in the near future do we or will we have one single *non*-chemical control procedure that is able to supplement effectively, let alone replace, chemical measures against *Simulium*. Having spent much of my last twenty-seven years working towards biological control, I say this both with very real regret and yet with reasonable confidence that within fifteen, twenty, or twenty-five years, we shall begin to have reliable microbial control procedures, posing no risk to the health of man or other animals.

This is 1971, though, and the demand for control of onchocerciasis is tragically immediate. To control onchocerciasis we must continue to use chemical pesticides as larvicides—and in so doing to bring about at least *some* unwanted side-effects. Do we, then, knowingly harm ecosystems (to some extent at least) before really selective control methodologies become available, perhaps a quarter of a century from now? Or do we turn our backs on huge numbers of people who are at immediate risk from devastating diseases that *can* be averted by not ideally selective methods already at hand and currently in active use? If the former, perhaps those of us in affluent areas should be less prone to make generalizations (even on the basis of very serious ecological evidence) that may lead to the unnecessary prolongation of disease and misery among less fortunate people elsewhere. I submit that these are the kinds of questions that should be faced as the 'moment of

truth' by conservationists and by all of us to whom present-day environmental problems represent our greatest-ever challenge.

Kaprio
Many of us who have seen the conditions either in the villages or in the
towns of the underdeveloped parts of the world do not feel that the people
are all happy, but learn more and more how unhappy many of them tend
to be. Seizing this opportunity to say so, I do not consider the idea to be
generally valid in this connection. But when we ask ourselves about practical
solutions, how we should go ahead, I think there is much need for enlightened discussion among the older generation themselves—especially
among leading politicians, leading economists, leading biologists, leading
medical men, and so on. I think that youth is often much more aware than
we think of the real problems; at least I know that in my own country,
Finland, there is quite a lot of science about, as you can see from this meeting
here, and in a sense they are wondering what the older generation is doing.
So I think I would recommend as a solution more local meetings to try to
find out what can be done, and in this connection I am very happy to
welcome Professor Dorst's paper.

An idea which I bring you today, and am going to speak about the day
after tomorrow at a meeting of western European parliamentarians, concerns the practical problems in everyday environmental health administration in Europe just now. This is the idea that industry and municipalities,
indeed everyone who is producing pollution in any way as a side-effect,
should be responsible for the local ecosystem. Thus wherever you build a
water-supply system, you must analyse the situation completely and provide
for all foreseeable eventualities. It is an old story, and what sanitary engineers
have long been demanding, but it has not yet been carried through in many
places.

Much the same applies to any system in industry; safeguarding the
environment can be developed, it's very expensive, and so the economists and
industrialists like to get out of it. But if the parliamentarians and legislators
demand it vigorously enough it can be done, and in this respect there are
practical solutions on a day-to-day basis. So I am very thankful for this
opportunity to urge that there should come out of this Conference a strong
plea that artificial industrial ecosystems should be made complete in themselves, and leave, in the manner of natural ecosystems, no waste after them.

Allow me to return to the question of sharing funds between developing
and developed countries. We have all read about the cholera epidemic in
and around Calcutta; we also have political problems and a question of
funds. The World Health Organization was asked about ten years ago to
make a feasibility study of an improved water conduit system for Calcutta.
But there has been no money available to carry out the project, even though
all the plans exist; it's just too expensive, both for the Indian government
and for any sources of money that are available for civilian aid. Yet there is
plenty of money available for military purposes, and that is one aspect
where we should hint to the sources that some better balance could and
should be reached in the world.

Johnson

I think it would be a great pity if the population–environment debate got hung up on whether or not population is the cause of pollution. A lot of clever men in the United States—they are very clever—are wasting a lot of time at the moment on this topic, and indeed there is some danger that this rather academic dispute is going to set back the business of establishing the proper relationships for practical action.

I think Professor Dorst is quite right to point out that it is population growth in its widest sense which is one of the prime incentives for economic growth. Back in 1967, Colin Clark wrote a book in which he points this out, saying that it is population pressure more than anything else which has been responsible for major economic and technological advances. Now of course at the time he wrote that, and Colin Clark being who he is, this was meant to be an argument *in favour* of population growth. But we can now see it as an argument *against* population growth. The whole proposition is, in a sense, a simple arithmetical one: you cannot maintain or increase *per caput* income without increasing overall economic growth in a situation in which population itself is growing.

Having settled this, at least in my own mind, I want to go back to agriculture. We have heard a lot of talk about the 'green revolution'. It was a remarkable achievement, I think, which led over a period of four years to such improvements in India and the Philippines, and to the great spread of new varieties. Surely, one would have to be a man of exceptional ill-will to see this as anything but a positive achievement. In 1965–66 India faced famine; now she has a wheat harvest of 30 million tons. The danger of this is, of course, that we have only been presented with a breathing space, a ten- or fifteen-years breathing space, in which the base, the population base, is going to multiply exceedingly in those parts of the world.

Lastly, I come to the question of what governments are doing about the population situation, and wish to point out that the institutional mechanism for remedy does to some extent now exist. The United Nations in 1966 passed a rather far-reaching resolution, which permitted the UN and its agencies to give assistance in a very broad way to governments which wanted to institute and prosecute population and family planning programmes. We now have the UN Fund for Population Activities, which is acting as a single central focus of these matters for the whole UN system of agencies—especially WHO and UNESCO—and helping them to assist governments. There is the World Bank*, which has taken population to heart and is devoting ever-increasing attention to this problem. There is also an organization centred in London, called the International Planned Parenthood Federation, whose budget is now running at the rate of about 25 million dollars annually, and which is supporting population and family planning projects in over a hundred countries.

Now the question is, in a global long-range sense, can the effort be made to work? Will it work? And here I come back to something I tried to say this morning. I think there are very great political dangers in remarks which, whatever their intention, say we cannot expect the developing countries to

* Officially entitled the International Bank for Reconstruction and Development.—Ed.

have what we have. In the same sense this world-wide population control effort, if it is to be made to work, must first be taken to heart by the developed countries themselves. I have some sympathy with those who say that the birth of an American is fifty times as disastrous ecologically as the birth of an Indian, and I really would not mind if that were said about Englishmen as well.*

Lievens

I would like to make a very few brief remarks in the light of what has been communicated here. First, I am sure that the remark of Professor Polunin, saying that the biosphere is the only such phenomenon in the whole universe, merely expresses his own opinion, as a lot of very prominent scientists are of the contrary conviction, and that's a very good thing for humanity.

My next point is that I welcome with enthusiasm the remarks of Professor Baer to the effect that humanity, young or not young, is ill-served by pessimistic publications that are not fully founded scientifically. A typical example of this is Rachel Carson's *Silent Spring*. It was published about ten years ago and said that by this time or soon hereafter there should be no more bird life in a lot of countries in Europe and other parts of the world. Yet we know that in a lot of countries of Europe and in most advanced agricultural countries elsewhere there are now more birds than there were twenty years ago. Nor do I agree with the implication that the 'green revolution' should be considered a bad thing because of the utilization of pesticides for the protection of plants. In my opinion the green revolution was highly beneficial to humanity.

Hadač

We have been told much about what human beings have done against nature, but there are many instances of what mankind can do when he is working *with* nature. Professor Polunin mentioned some examples this morning, and we have a notable one in southern Bohemia, where there was a landscape full of marshes and with poor land on which practically nobody could live. Man has changed the marshes into fish-ponds and fertilized the soils, so that now thousands of people live in that part of our country. On the other hand, of course, we have landscapes that have been entirely destroyed by man—where man has worked against nature. It has been said, I think very wisely, that it is necessary for biologists to discuss problems with urbanists, economists, etc.; but I would say it is not enough merely to discuss, it is necessary to work together with them on the same problems, in the same landscapes. We are now trying in our Institute of Landscape Ecology of the

* Mr Stanley Johnson is an Englishman who, in the opinion of the Conference's International Steering Committee, really knows what he is talking about—otherwise he would not have been invited as a 'roving eminent', in which category he was probably by far the youngest. Having worked in the so-called World Bank and as a Project Director of the UNA-USA National Policy Panel on World Population under the chairmanship of Governor John D. Rockefeller, he latterly became Liaison Officer to International Organizations of the International Planned Parenthood Federation. In 1970 he published his third and most remarkable book, 'Life Without Birth: A Journey Through the Third World in Search of the Population Explosion' (Heinemann, London, xiii + 364 pp., illustr.)—Ed.

Czechoslovak Academy of Sciences, at Průhonice near Prague, to create such a team of workers—including architects, urbanists, economists, and sociologists, as well as zoologists, botanists, agronomists, foresters, and so on. Well, it is an experiment, and we do not know how it will work—we are just starting—but we hope that we shall be able to throw some fresh light on to our own problems and maybe suggest new aspects for others. Yet this is only a small team; I think it would be good if we could create such a body of scientists of different kinds as an international body—perhaps a pioneering institute—in which leading experts of all the world could work together and find a common language. It is particularly difficult for biologists to discuss such matters with economists and urbanists, etc., because we have quite different languages. Yet we need to understand one another, and so the question is how can we find this common language? The answer would seem to be, simply by working together. So I suggest that in future it might be very reasonable to create such a body in the form of an international institution.

Polunin

First, as regards Director-General Lievens's point about the possibility of life elsewhere in the universe, my actual words were: 'It has been suggested by some that relief might come from other planets; but actually, in view of the virtual impossibility at present of maintaining effective quarantine (I there have a reference from a leader in this field, writing in my own journal), it should be a matter of relief that it now seems unlikely that any form of life exists in the solar system outside the world's biosphere'. This involves matters so far removed from any of my specialist interests that I would not venture to express a serious opinion upon them personally; instead, I consult leading authorities—in this instance Professor George C. Pimentel of the University of California at Berkeley, who is, I understand, closely associated with the American NASA programme, and Academician Aleksandr I. Oparin, Director of the A. N. Bakh Institute of Biochemistry of the Academy of Sciences of the USSR, with both of whom I am in fairly frequent touch by correspondence. The latter was expected here by now and I must not anticipate the paper which he has informed me he has prepared for this Conference; but I believe that he holds this opinion and certainly Professor Pimentel did when he last wrote to me earlier this month. I did not say, or at least did not mean to say, that the 'green revolution' should be considered a bad thing because of the use of pesticides for the protection of plants, but merely that it had led to some degradation of soil and waters, which is surely true.

Mr Chairman, I have received a paper of a few pages, prepared by the Executive Officer of the Commission on Education of IUCN, after detailed consultation with his commission chairman, Professor L. K. Shaposhnikov, very recently in Moscow. It is on the vitally important topic of environmental education, and I suggest we treat it as a submitted paper, for discussion if time allows, as unfortunately we have no session in this field. Normally I would ask your permission to read at least parts of this paper, but perhaps you have a better suggestion?

Baer (Chairman)

We'll have it copied and circulated: excellent, excellent.*

Polunin

In conclusion, I merely want to point out a rather interesting problem that appears to be developing here in this Conference, namely some controversy between those who advocate long-term solutions or long-term considerations and those who are more concerned with short-term ones. It seems to me that this has chronically been one of the troubles that we have in this world, and we are stepping right into this trap here.

* The reworked paper is included in Section 18, pp. 601–7—Ed.

ADDENDUM

Written comment from Professor KONRAD LORENZ,
Director of the Abteiling Lorenz, Max-Planck-Institut für Verhaltensphysiologie,
8131 Seewiesen, West Germany

There is one [piece of] advice, really not more than a hint, which I should like to give to the Conference. I sincerely believe that resolutions, even when they are signed by the most important and generally recognized scientific authorities, make a very small impression indeed on politicians. A politician is by definition a man whose chief concern is to be re-elected. The only way, therefore, to influence politicians, is to broadcast scientific truths—in our case the urgent danger to our environment—in such a manner as to influence the electorate. It is only *via* the voters that we can hope to force politicians to listen to us. Serious scientists are generally not good at broadcasting their results, but in our particular case it is a duty to do so. For this reason I hope that the Conference will be successful not only in producing a solid ground for constructive recommendations but also [by gaining] such an overpowering publicity that politicians are simply forced to listen. Those in power turn a deaf ear to all recommendations and resolutions unless it is their voters who force them to listen. Please don't think that I take a pessimistic view of our ultimate success.

Yours very sincerely,
[Signed]   *Konrad Lorenz*

4
MONITORING THE ATMOSPHERIC ENVIRONMENT

Keynote Paper

Monitoring the Atmospheric Environment

by

DAVID ARTHUR DAVIES

Chairman, Functional Group on Human Environment,
Administrative Committee on Coordination of the United Nations;
Secretary-General, World Meteorological Organization,
41 Avenue Giuseppe Motta, 1211 Geneva, Switzerland

INTRODUCTORY REMARKS

It is a good scientific principle to begin a paper by defining the terms which are being used: in the present case, 'atmosphere', 'monitoring', and 'environment'.

Taking first the 'atmosphere', this may be simply defined as the gaseous envelope which surrounds the planet earth—excluding, for our purposes, the gases contained as such or in solution in soils and waters both fresh and saline. But while our definition of the atmosphere is simple, the atmospheric processes are, on the contrary, extremely complex, as will be shown later.

Turning now to 'monitoring', this word is used extensively in modern literature, especially in relation to the human environment. The standard reference books do not, however, offer any definition which could be regarded as appropriate in this context. Perhaps the best description of the concept of monitoring so far put forward is that contained in the recent publication of the Massachusetts Institute of Technology entitled 'Man's Impact on the Global Environment' (MIT, 1970). It reads as follows:

> Accordingly, we think 'monitoring' is best conceived of as systematic observations of parameters related to a specific problem, designed to provide information on the characteristics of the problem and their changes with time.

There is implied in this description not only the making of observations but also their collection and their processing into a form whereby information relevant to the purposes of the system can be deduced—particularly any changes in time. For the needs of this paper, we shall therefore think of monitoring as the purposeful and systematic procedures of observing, collecting, and processing.

As for the term 'environment', to be strictly consistent with the preceding comments a definition of it would be the next stage in developing the theme of this paper. However, this course is not followed for two reasons, the first being that there seems to be a general reluctance to put forward a definition of this much-used word—a reluctance born, no doubt, of the admitted difficulty in formulating any reasonably concise set of words for this purpose. Secondly, the problem is largely irrelevant to the present discussion, because whatever definition might be accepted, it is axiomatic that the atmosphere is an essential component of the biosphere and in some contexts its primary 'element'.

Having thus established, in a very general sense, what this paper is about, one further introductory comment is necessary. The paper is one contribution to a conference which bears the title 'Environmental Future'. The discussion that follows is therefore developed within the overall context of the environment and future trends, but with attention focused on the physics and chemistry of the atmosphere. This is because the biological and social aspects are fully covered elsewhere within the Conference programme—and covered, moreover, by others who are particularly competent to do so.

RELEVANCE OF THE ATMOSPHERE TO ENVIRONMENTAL QUESTIONS

We have defined monitoring as being a purposeful systematic process. The first step in the consideration of an atmospheric monitoring system is thus to establish what purposes it must serve. This is essential not only for clarity of thought in designing the system but also on practical grounds, for monitoring the atmosphere on any significant scale is a complex and costly operation. We therefore pose the question—why is an atmospheric monitoring system necessary?

There are two basic reasons. First, the atmospheric processes have an all-pervading influence upon human life on this earth. In particular, the atmospheric phenomena which we call weather and climate control man's activities to a very great extent—the clothes he wears, the sort of agricultural crops he can grow, and the animals he can breed for food and clothing. They moreover largely control endemic diseases to which man is susceptible, the arrangements that he has to make for safe and efficient transportation systems by air, sea, and land, and the natural water resources which he has at his disposal for irrigation, for hydroelectric power, for human consumption and sewer systems, and for the maintenance of his industries. Also dependent upon weather and climate are the physical recreations and pastimes which man can enjoy and, in one way or another, very many other things besides.

It is therefore inevitable that man should seek to improve his knowledge of atmospheric processes and to apply this knowledge to assist his aims and purposes. The acquisition of such knowledge requires a monitoring system, and such a system has, in fact, been developed over the last century or so by meteorologists and by those who need meteorological information. This system will be described later.

The second reason why an atmospheric monitoring system is needed is because man, by his own activities, is changing the composition of the atmosphere and interfering with the natural sequence of atmospheric processes— mainly by industrial and urban pollution. Sometimes the changes are beneficial, but more frequently they are harmful and, in some cases, very dangerous. It is, of course, largely because of the recognized dangers of atmospheric pollution that the whole subject of the human environment now occupies a front place on the stage of national and international affairs.

It is not within the scope of this paper to analyse the real measure of the threat to the human race which atmospheric pollution presents. It seems safe to say, however, that the full nature and scope of this threat is not at present known, and will not be known until an adequate atmospheric monitoring system has been installed and is functioning.

Before looking further into the details of the atmospheric monitoring system which is required, it may be useful to stress once again that it will need to serve the two basically different objectives referred to in the preceding paragraphs. The first may be described as the outcome of a positive and long-felt need for man to understand the atmospheric processes and to use this knowledge to assist his purposes; the other is the outcome of a defensive and relatively new attitude which man has had perforce to adopt to protect himself from the results of his own lack of thought and foresight. This is not to say, however, that two separate and independent systems are needed; indeed, as we have already pointed out, monitoring the atmosphere is a complex and costly operation, and so duplication of effort and facilities must clearly be avoided as far as possible.

It is important to note also that an atmospheric monitoring system has a relevance in the context of the environment as a whole, which goes beyond the atmosphere itself. This is because there is a constant interplay between the atmosphere and the earth's surface (whether land, inland waters, or oceans). Such an interplay is of course part of the natural environmental processes and is indeed essential to life on earth. To take a very simple example, it may be recalled that it is the process of evaporation from the water surface of the earth which produces the atmospheric phenomenon of rain, without which terrestrial life on this earth could not long be sustained. Such an interplay is, however, present also in the unnatural order of things; for example, the atmosphere is one means whereby pollutants are transported from their sources to the land and the oceans. Thus, the rain produced by natural processes will wash out many of the atmospheric pollutants as it falls through the air. It thus helps to cleanse the atmosphere but, at the same time, it pollutes the land and the oceans.

There is also the possibility of such pollutants having a direct effect on the atmospheric processes and hence producing changes in weather and climate (MIT, 1970). Some scientists believe that such changes may, in the long run, be of much greater overall significance to the human race than the more direct evils of pollution.

The Observing System

The aim of the atmospheric monitoring system must be to observe, collect, and process, data of appropriate atmospheric parameters—in such a way as to make possible the detection of changes in the composition of the atmosphere and of any changes in atmospheric processes, and so to enable the full measure of any actual or potential danger to be assessed. These changes will need to be studied on different scales—local, regional, and global.

For the general advancement of knowledge of the atmospheric processes, a number of observational networks have been set up. Perhaps the most exhaustive listing of these networks is given in the Directory of National and International Environmental Monitoring Activities, published by the Smithsonian Institution in October 1970 (Smithsonian Institution, 1970). Most of these networks which relate to observations of the atmosphere are for meteorological or closely allied purposes, and by far the most complete networks are those operated by the countries of the world under the aegis of the World Meteorological Organization (WMO). Thus, the Global Observing System of WMO's World Weather Watch (WMO, 1967) involves a network of some 8,500 land stations (many of them indicated in Fig. 1) and about 5,500 merchant ships making surface observations, while about 700 stations take upper air observations by using mainly rawinsonde techniques (i.e. measurements of pressure, temperature, humidity, and winds, at various levels of the atmosphere, by electronic means). All such observations are taken at standard hours each day throughout the world (WMO, 1970a), and in the interest of brevity and to overcome language problems in international exchanges, they are converted into internationally agreed figure codes. Internationally agreed technical regulations are also followed, and WMO guides to methods of observation are used widely in all countries and by merchant ships at sea. Fuller details of these networks, and the observational routines, are given in the continuously revised WMO Publication No. 9.TP.4, Volume A, entitled 'Weather Reporting: Observing Stations' (WMO, 1971a).

This system, as already explained, has been developed for general meteorological purposes over a protracted period which extends back into the past to long before atmospheric pollution became a problem. In so far as observations of atmospheric pollution are concerned, the basic need is to maintain a close and constant watch on all variations in the physical and chemical composition

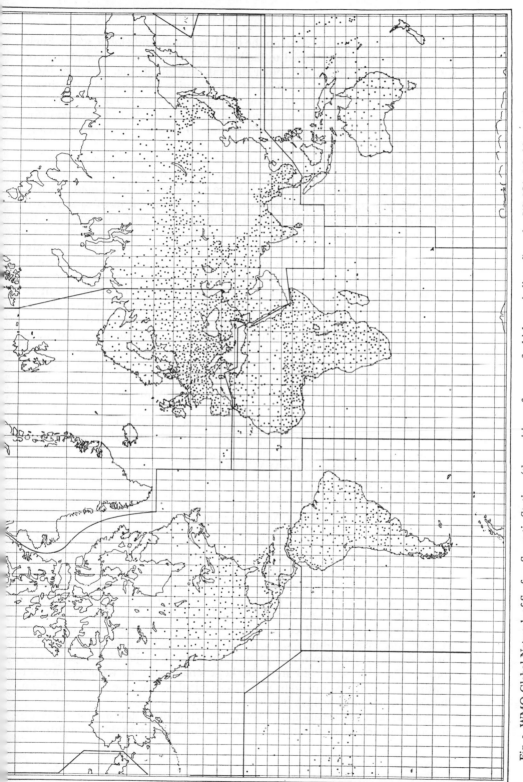

Fig. 1. WMO Global Network of Surface Synoptic Stations (the positions of many of which are indicated) under WMO's World Weather Watch plan.

of the atmosphere, and to do so on the local, regional, and global, scales. Such observations must be designed to facilitate the study of the consequences of such variations upon human, other animal, and plant, life. Many of these consequences will be a direct effect of the pollution (for example, the direct effect of sulphur dioxide in the lower levels of the atmosphere upon human health or crop growth), but some may be an indirect effect of pollution (for example, the possible long-term effects due to changes in climate already mentioned).

The development of an observing system for the purpose of monitoring atmospheric pollution is, of course, far less advanced than that referred to in the preceding paragraphs, although some progress has been made in this direction. Moreover, the purposes which the system will have to serve are multifarious, so that the final analysis of the data will need to be carried out by a range of different specialists. If we recall that the system should have three elements—observing, collecting, and processing—then, clearly, data relating to health questions can only be processed and analysed by medical personnel; similarly, data relating to animals and plants can only be processed by appropriate biological or agricultural experts, etc. The extent to which the observing and collecting systems may be coordinated and combined needs further consideration, but a single basic observing and collecting system seems feasible and is certainly desirable if only for financial and manpower reasons. In any case, as already mentioned, these aspects are beyond the scope of this paper. The monitoring for general meteorological purposes and for the detection of possible changes in climate due to pollution is, however, relevant to this paper—especially the steps that are being taken on the international level.

The plan to be described is that approved by the WMO in 1969 and refined in 1970 and 1971 (WMO, 1970b, 1971b). It aims at establishing a global network of stations to measure background air pollution. Many countries have already responded to the WMO plan and have set up or are setting up the required stations.

BASELINE AIR POLLUTION STATIONS

Two types of stations are included in this network. The first type is known as a 'baseline air pollution' station. The aim of such stations is to document the long-term changes in atmospheric composition that are of particular significance to weather and climate. Very rigid criteria have been set up for these stations, of which only about ten are envisaged throughout the world; already seven stations have been promised. These stations will be located in areas where no significant changes in land-use practices are anticipated for at least fifty years within 100 km in all directions from the stations. They must be located far from major population centres, major highways, and air routes. The observing staff must be kept small, and all requirements for heating, cooking, etc., should be met by electrical power generated away from the site. Many other stringent criteria have to be met.

As regards the observational programme, while these stations may measure any atmospheric constituent, first consideration is given to those constituents that would most affect long-term changes in climate. Two groups of priorities are thus proposed, as follows:

Priority Group I: Carbon dioxide
                   Turbidity (atmospheric particle content)
                   Constituents of precipitation
Priority Group II: Carbon monoxide
                   Sulphur dioxide and hydrogen sulphide
                   Oxides of nitrogen
                   Total ozone
                   Total precipitable water

These priorities are probably not fully acceptable from the point of view of their health aspects—for example, because they do not include the heavy metals—and this is the sort of question which would need to be resolved if the observing part of the monitoring system is to be combined or coordinated. Actually, the atmospheric monitoring of levels of lead, mercury, and cadmium, as part of the observational programme for monitoring air pollution by WMO, is currently under consideration by a special panel of experts. It should meanwhile be noted that the World Health Organization (WHO) has a plan to monitor the lead content of the atmosphere among other pollutants (WMO, 1971*b*).

REGIONAL AIR POLLUTION STATIONS

The other type of station included in the WMO network is the regional air pollution station. The density of such stations is much greater than that of the baseline stations, and each member-country of WMO (and there are at present 135)* is asked to establish one or more such stations, a minimum density of one station per 500,000 km^2 of land being envisaged. However, where a country has several climatic regions, a higher density is considered necessary, and stations should be distributed in such a way that observations become available from each climatic region. Already some twenty-five such stations in twelve countries are operating or are in the process of being installed. The twelve countries so far definitely involved are Austria, Belgium, Federal Republic of Germany, France, India, Ireland, the Netherlands, Norway, Sweden, UK, USA, and Yugoslavia. Canada, Kenya, and Spain, will participate in the future, while stations in Australia have been proposed but are not yet confirmed.

As regards the observational programme, the measurement of turbidity and constituents of precipitation (*see* below) are required, but other measurements, particularly those specified for baseline stations, may be considered. There is thus an element of flexibility in the individual programmes.

For both baseline and regional air pollution stations, the sampling methods, sampling frequency, and analysis procedures, are made according to guidelines determined by WMO and described in the appropriate manual of operations (WMO, 1971*c*). The chemical analysis of precipitation samples includes sodium, potassium, calcium, magnesium, ammonium ion, nitrate

* The membership has since increased to 136.

ion, chloride ion, sulphur, pH (alkalinity or acidity), and electrical conductivity.

In discussing the observational system, attention has been confined to surface stations (whether on land or at sea). The artificial earth satellite is, however, now available as a means of monitoring the atmosphere on a truly global scale and at frequent intervals. Indeed, the advent of the satellite has long been recognized as constituting a turning point in meteorological history, and it is already hard to envisage in the future a satisfactory global weather-observing system without the satellite as one of the main observing platforms.

The role of the satellite as a means of detecting atmospheric pollution is still not clear, but the indications are that here also it will, in due course, be found to constitute an important and, in some ways, a unique means of monitoring on a global scale some aspects of atmospheric pollution. By means of visual and infra-red photographing devices, as well as by the use of infra-red radiometers for measuring vertical temperature profiles, and hopefully the vertical profiles of carbon dioxide and water-vapour content, the satellite will doubtless become an important element in the world pollution monitoring system.

Constant-level balloons and ocean buoys may also become important parts of the global observing system, but the possible role of these as part of the pollution monitoring system is still uncertain.

The Collecting System

We turn now from the first essential element of an atmospheric monitoring system (i.e. observing) to the second (i.e. collecting the data). As before, we shall consider initially the arrangements made for the general advancement of knowledge of the atmosphere and then the arrangements for the pollution aspects.

In the former case, two kinds of collecting systems are needed. The first is for the collection of the data at global and regional centres and their retransmission within a few hours to individual national centres, this process being repeated several times every day. For this purpose, a complex global telecommunication system is essential, and under the World Weather Watch plan of the WMO a greatly improved system is now being developed. This system involves three world centres (Melbourne, Moscow, and Washington) at which all world data are gathered several times each day; it also involves about thirty regional telecommunications centres, as well as a national centre in each country. The main features of this telecommunication system are shown in Fig. 2, which is self-explanatory.

For climatological purposes, however (in contrast to the operational or synoptic purposes already described), exchange of data may take place at a much slower pace and, in general, the data are exchanged by the normal postal services both nationally and internationally. This is the second collecting system, though certain monthly climatological summaries are exchanged on the telecommunications system.

Returning now to the pollution monitoring system already described, the

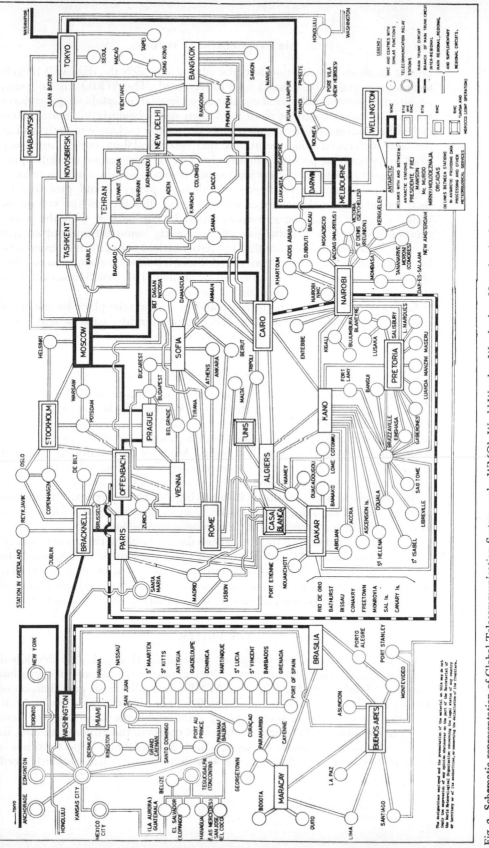

Fig. 2. Schematic representation of Global Telecommunication System under WMO's World Weather Watch plan. Note that in the key in the bottom right-hand corner, WMC = World Meteorological Centre, RTH = Regional Telecommunication Hub, RMC = Regional Meteorological Centre, and NMC = National Meteorological Centre.

precise methods of collection and the places at which the data will be collected have yet to be defined and determined. The WMO air pollution
monitoring system calls on the Secretary-General to establish procedures
whereby member countries shall send their data regularly to central data-
collection centres. At present, no plans exist for the exchange of such data at
the same high speed as for operational meteorological data, nor is it necessary
to do so for studying possible climatic changes. If, however, for specialist purposes (health, agriculture, etc.) high-speed transmission should be necessary,
the existing meteorological telecommunications system could probably be
used for international exchanges without great difficulty, as the volume of
traffic involved would be extremely small in comparison with the many
thousands of groups of data that are constantly being transmitted on this
system. Such use would ensure that the data reached one of the main meteorological centres in the country concerned, though onward transmission to other
specialized centres would of course still be needed. This would, however, be a
national rather than an international problem.

Exchanges of data on pollution could of course take place by means of
normal postal services on a daily, weekly, or monthly, basis provided the
means used would suffice for the purpose involved.

DATA PROCESSING

For general meteorological purposes, a global data-processing system has
been introduced as an essential element of World Weather Watch (WMO,
1967). At the three world centres, powerful high-speed electronic computers
are in constant operation to process the many thousands of groups of weather
data which they receive every few hours. Many of the twenty-one regional
meteorological centres are also computer-equipped. In other cases, the
processing is done by hand. By computer processing, we here mean the use
of numerical analysis techniques in applying the basic physical and mathematical laws of the atmosphere to the mass of observational data received
and the production thereby of the prognostic weather-maps.

In the case of pollution data, the precise data-processing requirements have
yet to be established. Much will depend upon the time-scale applicable to
the warnings and notifications of pollution levels, but it seems unlikely that
such powerful machines will be necessary. The medical, agricultural, and
other specialist experts will, of course, need to advise on this aspect.

THE FUTURE

We have seen from the foregoing paragraphs that a highly-developed
monitoring system for general meteorological purposes is already in operation
under the World Weather Watch of WMO. In addition, as an extension of
World Weather Watch, a global system for measuring the main atmospheric
pollutants is well on the way to being established, the main purpose here
being to detect overall changes in the constituents of the atmosphere and, in
particular, possible climatic changes. This is all useful and important, but is
it enough? Other specialists (e.g. the health authorities) will evidently need

to decide what sort of monitoring system they require—i.e. what pollutants need to be observed, what is the time-scale on which the observational data will need to be collected, to which centres should the data be transmitted, etc.

The sort of question which will then need to be answered is whether a single global observational system for atmospheric pollutants can meet all requirements, or whether the global observing system will in fact need to consist of several separate subsystems. Similarly will arise the question of whether high-speed global telecommunications facilities for air pollution purposes will be necessary and, if so, whether a single system will suffice. The answer in each case is that a single system could probably be devised at least for international purposes. Finally, the question of the national, regional, and global, centres for the processing of the data, will need to be considered. For processing purposes, it seems evident that a single system will not suffice. Data for medical purposes will evidently need to go to medical institutions, and data required for agricultural purposes will need to go to agricultural or biological institutions. The appropriate international organizations are, of course, actively engaged in studying this problem—notably the World Health Organization, the Food and Agriculture Organization, and UNESCO.

It is not possible to predict in detail what the situation will ultimately be, but it seems safe to prophesy that the world's conscience has been so badly shaken by the dangers of atmospheric pollution that within a very few years a system will be evolved which will enable the specialists in different fields to keep watch on the pollution levels and to notify the authorities concerned of any deteriorations or, hopefully, improvements.

It will of course be essential for all activities of this kind to be highly coordinated, and for the procedures to be standardized as far as possible. Steps to this end are already well in hand so far as the agencies mentioned in this paper are concerned; such steps follow well-established coordination procedures. Whether, in spite of this, some new overall international coordinating body will be required will of course also need to be considered. For the atmospheric monitoring alone, this latter course would hardly seem necessary: but the environmental problems as a whole are not only of the atmosphere. This being so, the countries of the world may well find the need for a single central overall coordinating body.

A further point which, although not specifically a monitoring question, is closely allied to it, is that of predicting pollution levels by knowledge of the rates and places of input. There seems little doubt that if standardized data on pollution input as a result of industrial activities could be made available and exchanged, they would constitute a very useful feature of the global pollution monitoring system. Hopefully, these data will aid the development of improved industrial techniques which use available fuels but also result in much lower levels of pollution.

These comments on the future needs and requirements in so far as atmospheric monitoring is concerned, cannot be concluded without a reference to the United Nations Conference on the Human Environment, which is scheduled to be held in Stockholm in 1972. On that occasion, all the problems relating to the environment will be discussed at ministerial level with the object of getting action through the world's governments. As a result, many decisions on future arrangements will doubtless be taken on all aspects of the pollution problem.

CONCLUSIONS

The following conclusions may be drawn from this paper:

(a) The atmosphere is an essential, if not the primary, element of the human environment. In seeking a solution of environmental problems, a knowledge of the composition of the atmosphere and of the atmospheric processes is therefore a *sine qua non*, as is also the establishment of an atmospheric monitoring system which is effective on the local, regional, and global, levels.

(b) A highly developed atmospheric monitoring system has long been in operation for meteorological purposes under the aegis of the World Meteorological Organization, and the same organization has already taken steps to extend this system to include the monitoring of atmospheric pollution. The main aim of this extension is to detect possible changes in climatic conditions.

(c) An atmospheric monitoring system for biological purposes will doubtless be necessary, but these latter are not considered in detail in this paper. The need to coordinate fully any such system with the existing system is, however, stressed.

(d) The concept of atmospheric monitoring is presented as having three main elements:
  (i)   observing the atmosphere;
  (ii) collecting the observed data;
  (iii) processing the data into the most appropriate form having regard to the *raison d'être* of the system.

(e) Study of the atmosphere is also of importance in elucidating environmental questions relating to the land and oceans, in view of the air–land and air–sea interactions. Of particular significance is the transport of pollution, by means of the atmosphere, to the world's lands and oceans.

REFERENCES

MASSACHUSETTS INSTITUTE OF TECHNOLOGY (as MIT) (1970). *Man's Impact on the Global Environment: Report of the Study of Critical Environmental Problems.* MIT Press, Cambridge, Massachusetts: xxii + 319 pp., illustr.

SMITHSONIAN INSTITUTION (1970). *National and International Environmental Monitoring Activities—A Directory.* Smithsonian Center for Short-lived Phenomena, 60 Garden Street, Cambridge, Massachusetts 02138: xvi + 292 pp., illustr.

WORLD METEOROLOGICAL ORGANIZATION (as WMO) (1967). *World Weather Watch: The Plan and Implementation Programme.* Secretariat of the World Meteorological Organization, Geneva, Switzerland: [v] + 56 pp., illustr.

WORLD METEOROLOGICAL ORGANIZATION (as WMO) (1970a). *A Brief Survey of the Activities of the World Meteorological Organization Relating to Human Environment.* Secretariat of the World Meteorological Organization, Geneva, Switzerland: 22 pp., illustr.

WORLD METEOROLOGICAL ORGANIZATION (as WMO) (1970b). *Twenty-second Session of the Executive Committee: Abridged Report with Resolutions.* Publication No. 277.RC.33

(*see* Resolution 12 (EC-XXII) Measurement of Background Air Pollution). Secretariat of the World Meteorological Organization, Geneva, Switzerland: xvi | 253 pp.

WORLD METEOROLOGICAL ORGANIZATION (as WMO) (1971*a*). *Weather Reporting: Observing Stations.* Publication No. 9TP.4, Volume A. Secretariat of the World Meteorological Organization, Geneva, Switzerland. loose-leaf (*ca* 400 pp.), illustr.

WORLD METEOROLOGICAL ORGANIZATION (as WMO) (1971*b*). *Executive Committee Panel on Meteorological Aspects of Air Pollution,* Second Session (Report issued as document for the Executive Committee), pp. 13 + 4 of annexes (Secretariat of the World Meteorological Organization, Geneva, Switzerland).

WORLD METEOROLOGICAL ORGANIZATION (as WMO) (1971*c*). *WMO Operations Manual for Sampling and Analysis Techniques for Chemical Constituents in Air and Precipitation.* Secretariat of the World Meteorological Organization, Geneva, Switzerland; [iii] + [37] pp. variously numbered or unnumbered, illustr.

DISCUSSION

Nyberg (Chairman)

I feel that in this lecture we have been given a lot of facts, and I would like to stress some of them further. Dr Davies mentioned that he felt monitoring is necessary if we are going to understand the questions related to pollution, and he referred to three different parts of the monitoring, namely the observation, the communication, and the processing of the data. He also referred to the World Meteorological Organization (WMO) which for about a hundred years has had experience regarding physical parameters, and their World Weather Watch which is perhaps also known to you. This system is functioning very well, and we have heard about plans for how it will be improved. Also, satellites will be used in this context, and one is already being used. The whole system is very costly, and this is a matter which must be taken into account when new systems are developed. I think that a figure of something like at least a few hundred million dollars a year is used for these observations.

Another fact is that the WMO has established two networks of chemical parameters, and it was also mentioned that observations of other additional parameters, either chemical or biological or physical, may be organized by other agencies but with cooperation offered from the WMO side. Regarding the telecommunication system, it was said that rapid transmission has been developed by WMO; it may, however, not be necessary to use it in connection with air pollution problems, although this is a matter that can be discussed. In some cases warnings may be needed, and rapid transmission of these warnings be necessary, while finally it should be noted that the World Weather Watch has a system of computers, placed in world centres and also in regional centres, that is ready to take on various computational duties.

Whereas you are, of course, free to ask any questions or make any comments that you may desire, I would like to bring before you some questions which I feel come from the lecture we have just heard. One question may be: what are the parameters to be observed in addition to what is now observed—and I already mentioned the necessity of using telecommunication in certain cases? Another question is related to the definition of monitoring. If we consider monitoring as associated with some organized system of observation for a certain time, then it may be too limited. But this is *one* interpretation. In such instances it should be added that special investigations are necessary when you are going into case studies to find a rapid answer to some special question, and I know of such case studies which are being carried on and partly planned to be developed further.

Dr Davies stressed the necessity of coordination between various groups of specialists who are aiming at complete understanding of the processes going on in the atmosphere, and although you have to make a start with meteorologists, these are perhaps not the most important although they are a part of the problem. You have to have the cooperation of doctors, agriculturalists, and biologists working in various sub-fields. We know that there is a UN body of which Dr Davies is Chairman, namely the Functional Group on Human Environment of the Administrative Committee on Coordination of the UN, but other bodies may be established by the United Nations in or after the Stockholm Conference, and I think that comments regarding this might be useful, as well as on the lecture and general topic.

Bryson

I would like to lift one of Dr Nyberg's comments out of context, namely the one in which he implied that meteorologists are a part of the problem. Being a meteorologist, I can say, 'Yes, indeed, meteorologists are a part of the problem'. This leads me into the comment that I wanted to make. The list of pollutants to be monitored, that Dr Davies mentioned, sounds very much like a list put together by a bunch of meteorologists, and I have a suspicion that perhaps it is not a list that represents the proper set of priorities of what ought to be looked at. Meteorologists have a tendency to think in terms of their own equations, their own physical processes, their own needs, their own research interests. I would like very much to know what a group of biologists—thoughtful ones—would have to say about that list of pollutants, and what a group of atmospheric chemists might have to say about it. An example: in the middle of the Priority Group II list is the item 'oxides of nitrogen', while at the top of the Priority Group I list is carbon dioxide. I've a strong feeling that an occasional intensive measurement of the amount of carbon dioxide in the atmosphere, to get some long-term trends, would be perfectly adequate, and this will be done and has been done; but there's no great rush about it. On the other hand, there is some indication that nitrogen oxides, not down here on the ground, but in the stratosphere, might be something for which we should have great concern. There is a recent paper, widely circulated but not yet published, which suggests that the effect of nitrogen oxides in catalysing the conversion of ozone back into oxygen is much more effective than the water vapour effect which has been discussed in the last few years. Professor Harold Johnston, at Berkeley, California, has calculated that a fleet of SSTs, operated in the stratosphere, would release enough nitrogen oxides to effect perhaps a 50 to 90 per cent reduction in ozone. Now there's some serious question about the correctness of Johnston's reaction constants; but the chemists I have talked with recently in the United States National Academy and elsewhere—the atmospheric chemists, who should know about this particular thing—say, 'He just might be right'. Now, if he even *might* be right, then we should be monitoring the ozone and the nitrogen oxides in the stratosphere right now as a very high priority, because there are supersonic aircraft flying at high altitudes *at the present time*—not just the Concorde and the Tupolev, but military aircraft as well. They're flying there *now*.

I'd just like to raise the question as to whether or not others than meteorologists ought to have some input into this matter of priorities for monitoring, and whether there are not some things that we should be monitoring right now—not merely when the World Weather Watch is moving, or some other programme gets going. Perhaps it's even more important than the daily weather information that they are so good at collecting.

Nyberg (Chairman)

Well, perhaps we have some specialist on ozone here. As far as I remember, after having studied ozone, I thought that it was the uppermost part of the ozone layer that was effective, i.e. in the layer of about fifty kilometres, and I don't know whether the airplanes go beyond that level or not. Is there anybody who could speak about this matter, or shall we have to proceed to another question?

Polunin

I know next to nothing of ozone, except its formula and oxidizing instability; but as a biologist I have always understood from my student days that it is the ozone layer in the upper atmosphere that filters off the ultra-violet solar radiation, which forms ozone and which is lethal or at least inimical to life, and that if it weren't for the ozone layer, the ultra-violet radiation would get through and there would quite conceivably be no life on earth.

About this matter of possible danger of SSTs to the ozone layer, I was encouraged—indeed almost adjured—by Professor George C. Pimentel of the University of California at Berkeley to get in touch with his colleague Professor Harold S. Johnston, and I did so with results that belong rather to our next session.

Nyberg (Chairman)

Yes, you are right; but, as I said, it is the top of the ozone layer that is effective, and if this is not destroyed the saving effect will be there. Moreover, we know from observations that the temperatures are much higher above the altitude of fifty kilometres than below that level, showing that the absorption is much stronger there.

Kuenen

Dr Davies told us that there were two problems, one being the interference with atmospheric processes and the other what 'the direct consequence of populations of man' may be, while later on it was indicated that there is collaboration with the World Health Organization. Does that mean that the World Meteorological Organization does not pay attention to plants and animals; have you no relations, for example, with the Food and Agriculture Organization of the United Nations? The second part of my question is the same as has been asked by Professor Bryson: Why in particular are the nitrogen oxides so low on your list of priorities? I suspect that some agriculturalists would be even more upset at your placing of 'total precipitable water' last of all.

Davies

Let me first answer the question about monitoring: this list of priorities was, as I explained, designed by meteorologists, because we felt that our job was to do what was necessary to keep track of possible changes of weather and climate. That is meteorology, and it was on this basis that heating of the lower atmosphere as a result of increases in its content of carbon dioxide, possible cooling through increased turbidity, and things of that kind, came to be watched. This accounts entirely for the priorities we have established, and they are thus established by meteorologists for meteorological purposes. I think I said in my remarks that if the same monitoring system is going to serve other purposes, then it is for the specialists in those fields to make known their requirements and we can perhaps work out a fully coordinated system that meets the needs of everybody without going to the cost—the extraordinary cost, I might say—of duplicating a global monitoring system. I think the answer is as simple as that.

On the question of the ozone effect, of course, what Professor Bryson said is known. This is not a new problem. We studied it several years ago in the context of exhaust, not from supersonic transport aircraft but from very large rockets. I think some rockets which have put outer-space vehicles into orbit release as much as 2,000 tons of exhaust gases, and of course while 2,000 tons is not an awful lot of pollution on the earth's surface, in the extremely rarefied atmosphere at that height, it is a very great quantity. There was some discussion in the scientific literature at that time as to whether these would affect the ozone layer and I think at that time it was felt they would not. The matter has been raised again—and quite rightly so, as Professor Bryson said—in the context of the SSTs, as one of the many problems which this new type of aircraft presents. Although the basic reason for our monitoring priorities is that, as I said clearly, we are meteorologists doing our job of keeping track of weather and climate, I think in the light of comments coming from different specialists that we can and should have another look at these priorities.

Now on the question of whether we like to coordinate our activities with other organizations, I can assure you that these specialized agencies of the United Nations have a very good system of coordinating themselves. The fact that we have been in touch with WHO is mainly, I think, because they themselves have launched quite a substantial programme—quite a different kind of programme from ours—of monitoring the atmosphere. Moreover they are our next-door neighbours, and it's quite natural that we should compare notes—mainly for the purpose of avoiding any duplication, as the nature of the work that WHO is doing in a way overlaps ours. Certainly we are in constant touch with FAO; indeed, this group which the Chairman referred to, of which I am the chairman myself, has the very purpose at the moment of establishing a coordinated statement on the part of all the agencies concerned—and you would be surprised how many of these specialized agencies of the United Nations are directly concerned with this problem. A purpose of this group (the Functional Group on Human Environment of the Administrative Committee on Coordination of the United Nations) is to get these agencies together and to present to the Stockholm Conference next year a coordinated statement of what we in the agencies are doing, what we can do within our existing terms of reference, what our planned programmes will show, and other things of this kind. So there is no question of full coordination between WMO and FAO and WHO and UNESCO, and there are others who are involved, too—including the International Atomic Energy Agency where radioactive pollution aspects are concerned, and so on.

Worthington

It's a pleasure to comment on Dr Davies's illuminating paper, because it isn't so many years ago that he and I were scientific colleagues together in East Africa. Now what worries biologists about atmospheric monitoring is, I think, the difficulty of relating the observable physical and chemical variables (such as we've had explained to us) to biological variables, which should also be monitored but are awfully difficult to select and measure. You mentioned WHO and FAO work in connection with biological variables, but in other branches of ecology, biological monitoring has not made much progress. We have had in the International Biological Programme (IBP) a series of discussions on this extending over two or three years, and still have difficulty in producing even the simplest list of biological variables which can be monitored on a world basis and then related to the chemical and physical variables. Now IBP has handed this problem to the new branch of ICSU, namely the Special Committee on Problems of the Environment (SCOPE), described earlier today by Professor Hela*, which is now getting down to the problem aided by a grant of money from the Ford Foundation.

One example of what may prove useful is the case of birds' eggs and DDT, which has already been mentioned here today and which we shall probably hear more about when the problem of toxic chemicals is discussed tomorrow. Also, there are groups of plants (such as lichens) and of animals (such as many birds) which are particularly susceptible to certain chemical pollutants. It would be splendid if we could get a list of indicator organisms, such as examples from among these groups, and some standard techniques (such as a specific lichen growing on a particular kind of rock) which could be distributed to main monitoring stations and exposed, for example, at different altitudes in the atmosphere. But I do not think there is any chance of this, at least for a long time to come. Rather has the problem to be approached in a more complex and indirect way through population studies—through total ecosystems maybe—and that's what people are working on at the present time.

There is one aspect of our IBP work which is developing just now and looks promising in relation to meteorological monitoring, and that is aerobiology. It's now known that the atmosphere, up to the top of the troposphere, carries a considerable biological load of often living spores, pollen, and some pathogens, which may be distributed around the world in the atmosphere.† Techniques for collecting such items in standard quantitative ways are being developed and I hope will become available soon. This is a case where a direct linkage between atmospheric monitoring and biological monitoring might well be established. Finally, what affects biological situations is not so much the world climate which WMO is primarily concerned with, but the ecoclimates and microclimates around particular associations of plants and animals. This raises intricate problems of its own, in which many other organizations such as FAO and WHO are deeply interested, and which also require close examination from the monitoring standpoint.

* See pp. 89–91.—Ed.

† In the manner of the identifiable dust from the volcanic eruption of Krakatoa.—Ed.

Nyberg (Chairman)

Well, I would like to say there is cooperation between meteorologists and chemists. Also in WMO we have a special working group on pollution in which chemists are contributing in cooperation with meteorologists, and I think it is very essential that we really cooperate, as I said before, over the various borders—both of states and subject-wise—and try to come to satisfactory conclusions. Here I think that Dr Mustelin could tell us something about the project which has been undertaken in Scandinavia and hopefully will extend in western Europe very soon.

Mustelin

I represent Nordforsk, the Scandinavian Council for Applied Research—more specifically the Nordforsk Secretariat of Environmental Sciences, which is located in Helsinki. The Chairman referred to a project we are undertaking that is now in the advanced planning stage. It is a very special atmospheric monitoring project dealing with long-range transport of air pollutants and is to be carried out in cooperation with most of the countries of Western Europe and under the auspices of the Organization for Economic Cooperation and Development (OECD).

The background of this project is the growing concern that has been felt in the Scandinavian countries over the last years about the slowly-increasing acidity of lakes, rivers, soils, and so on—a phenomenon that has already had considerable harmful effects on, for instance, forestry and fishing. The basic mechanism of this acidification is of course well known: the sulphur compounds emitted in the air from oil- and coal-burning plants are transformed in certain ways into sulphuric acid, which then reaches the ground, for instance with the precipitation or through other means. What is not yet clear is how much of this sulphur that is responsible for acidification is due to local sources, and how much is transported to Scandinavian countries from, for example, the heavily industrialized areas of central Europe. Recent evidence, however, seems to indicate that long-range transport on a continental scale plays a considerable role in this context. It was therefore suggested a year or two ago by the Scandinavian delegates to OECD's Air Management Research Group that OECD initiate a cooperative study of long-range transport of air pollutants with particular reference to sulphur compounds, so as to clarify this matter of relative importance of the local and distant sources. A rather detailed plan has now been worked out in close cooperation between OECD and Nordforsk, methods and sampling techniques have been agreed upon in almost all cases, and the project is ready to be launched early in 1972.

I would like to speak briefly about the structure and scope of this project. First, a rather dense network of ground stations covering most of western Europe will be established. Up to a hundred stations have been envisaged, but I think that the actual number will be somewhat smaller than that. At each of these ground stations, all the relevant sulphur compounds will be sampled in gaseous form, on particulate matter, and of course also in rain. They will be continuously sampled and analysed on a twelve-hour or even on a six-hour basis around the clock. At a later stage of this project, probably in

1973, samples will also be taken by aeroplanes up to altitudes of at least 3,000 metres or 10,000 feet. All these measurement data, both from ground stations and from airplanes, together with all available emission statistics and of course meteorological data, will be collected, processed, and evaluated at a central project unit which will be situated in the Norwegian Institute for Air Research outside Oslo.

This project, which as I indicated will probably begin early next year, will presumably go on for a period of three years, and the main emphasis will be laid on particular meteorological episodes when pollutants tend to accumulate in central Europe for some time and then get carried by winds to other parts of the continent. It goes without saying that though this project is of great scientific interest, its main *raison d'être* is situated at a more practical level of environmental protection. What the practical consequences will be if the project clearly proves that transport of air pollutants from country to country has an important effect, is a question which is worth considering quite seriously already now, even if the actions needed will probably be taken only after the proof has been established and is accepted by the countries involved.

Udall

I would like to see this Conference make a very important contribution as a forerunner to the United Nations Conference on the Human Environment to be held in Stockholm slightly less than a year hence. We're getting a bit better acquainted now and we should be ready for a little more give and take, a little more head-to-head conflict. I happen to know, for example, that Dr Wurster has a very serious disagreement with the World Health Organization people who have been telling us that there is no effective substitute for DDT in the human health area. Let's have a blunt discussion of another matter that has already been brought up here. I'm one of those who was in the forefront of the fight against the SSTs in the United States. My concern began over the sonic boom as a new and devastating impact on man's environment. I became interested in the ozone issue only in the final phases of the dispute of last winter. I am a non-scientist. I don't know how serious this issue is, but I am informed by Dr Bryson who is in the middle of it that he believes this issue deserves urgent consideration. So let's have a candid confrontation on this issue.

Where does this issue belong on the list of priorities? From my point of view, if there is one chance in a hundred, one chance in five hundred, that a full fleet of SSTs, operating in the stratosphere, could destroy the ozone shield, this would be a problem of the first magnitude of importance. I was advised by a scientist in Washington who looked at my paper just before I came here: 'Don't emphasize the ozone thing too much.' When I pressed him a little, it turned out that he was merely telling me to be conservative—not to stick my neck out. But when it comes to human life on a vast scale and to the protection of the entire biosphere, to me the conservative outlook—the assumption that what we don't know can't hurt us—is decidedly unwise. Good monitoring is not enough if in fact it is a slow 'death watch' for human life. [Shouts of support from the audience, among which could be heard: 'Surely, if there's a chance in five millions, all such developments should be stopped until the truth is known, and we've been assured it would not take many months to determine.']

Nyberg (Chairman)

We should wait until the paper is published and specialists in the field have given their views.

Kolbig

On behalf of the German Democratic Republic Meteorological Service, I would like to agree with Dr Davies and to add a small example of the usefulness of a network for measuring and monitoring atmospheric pollution nearly continuously over a long period of time. We have in our country a small network of about ten stations for measuring atmospheric dust and SO_2 at all stations, and additionally radioactivity and ozone at some of them. This is the framework for special enterprises which are carried out by our medical service over smaller areas. In this way we are able to generalize and to transfer the results for wider use. I feel that in connection with the global network of Dr Davies, our interpretations become more precise and accurate, furthering the exchange of information and experiences between different countries in general and between neighbours in particular.

Davies

I'm sorry to speak so much but I think as the ozone question has come up I might add a little. This question was studied, as I said, in some detail a few years ago in the context of rockets and SSTs. At one stage it was thought that this could have a very serious effect on the very delicate balance which nature keeps between creation and destruction of ozone, and thereby have the possible effect of letting ultra-violet radiation come through. I think at that time the consensus was that there was really no great danger that rockets would interfere with the natural process, and that even if they did the ultra-violet radiation that would come through would be absorbed by the upper atmosphere anyhow before it reached the ground, although it might constitute a danger possibly to high-flying aircraft, such as SSTs. It's my impression that this was about as far as one could go at that stage.

Nevertheless, it's part of our normal network of observing systems already, and I think something like twenty-five or thirty stations throughout the world have been measuring total ozone for some time. This information has been collected in a systematic way, actually by arrangement with Canada. The Canadian Meteorological Service collects it from all countries by such arrangements as we can make, and publishes it and so makes the information available to everybody. This information is of total ozone determined mainly by using the apparatus of Dr G. M. B. Dobson, which is the most reliable instrument we have for measuring ozone, but other devices are also used, and I wouldn't like you to have the impression that this matter is something we are trying to brush aside. It has been given a good deal of study in the past, but if there are new factors which the SSTs raise, then I can only agree with

E.F.—5*

what the Chairman says: let us face it as a problem, let us study it anew. When we know more about it we shall be able to pronounce.

Hela

I would like to comment on how the problem of air pollution is approached from two different angles. First we have the global meteorological approach, where with great satisfaction we observe that meteorologists are collaborating more and more with the chemists. This seems most important when we think of air chemistry and rain-water chemistry, and I hope it can be expanded to cover the whole globe. Then secondly we have the local approach, and Dr Mustelin has told us about one major case of local approach. We have the factories, we have the big towns and cities, and small towns, and even discotheques and so on, where climate, the local climate, is bad, as everybody knows. This is a local approach which is made by engineers, medical doctors, sociologists even, and here I believe that the meteorologists could be of very great help.

Nyberg

Thank you very much. I can say that we have in my country, and I know there exists in many other countries, good cooperation between meteorologists and engineers and medical doctors, and I think it is necessary to have that cooperation, because the local effects depend very strongly on the local atmospheric conditions.

Goldman

I would like to support what Mr Udall said, and disagree with the Chairman and Dr Davies: I think we can still issue recommendations on behalf of this group. We need not insist on a firm ban against the SSTs, but instead should ask that they be banned until we do know all the consequences of their development and use—that nothing be done until such full knowledge is available. In other words, the burden of proof should be placed on the proponents of the SSTs, not on its opponents. [Again followed by some brief overlapping comments and vocal support from the floor.]

Butler

I am glad Professor Bryson raised the matter he did, because I think he had in mind the same point that I have. I was going to ask what is the real purpose of the WMO–WHO monitoring system, because until you know the purpose you don't know what kind of system to set up. And I would like to tell the Conference about an organization I belong to which has been monitoring the environment of the world for the past sixteen years. It is the United Nations Scientific Committee on the Effects of Atomic Radiation (UNSCEAR), and is the Committee which collects information about levels of radioactive contamination through the world and estimates the risks to human beings of these levels. This Committee publishes reports that are reports to the United Nations General Assembly, and that unfortunately are not very widely read. Yet they are perhaps the most authoritative statements we have so far on levels of world-wide contamination in one particular field. UNSCEAR is provided with information by WHO, WMO, FAO, and IAEA. IAEA does not assess world-wide contamination; they merely assist us in UNSCEAR in doing it.

Nyberg

It seemed to me Dr Davies explained very clearly that the atmospheric monitoring system, which has been set up by WMO, is not primarily for studying the pollution problem but rather for forecasting, surveying the climatology, and so on. In addition to that, a small network has been set up to monitor chemical contaminations in the atmosphere, and I thought everybody would agree to the usefulness of this. On the other hand, Dr Davies stated that further things which anybody wants to know about or to have monitored can be added to the existing system. However, it is not for WMO to present these kinds of observational systems, but rather for other people in other fields to bring them forth.

Miller

Dr Nyberg and Dr Davies have presented us with very interesting things, and I want to respect you both entirely. I am not an ozone specialist, but is that important in the present very grave context? If my dog is run over by an automobile with an internal combustion engine, I do not wish to find an expert on petroleum to satisfy my curiosity or settle my problem: I wish rather to have dogs live. So I would attempt to improve control of traffic or of dogs. In this respect the matter of an ozone specialist is secondary to the immediate problem of what is happening to our life-support system, to what is happening to life.

The Scandinavian project which we have heard is shortly to come into operation seems to have a great value potentially for understanding what is the international drift of pollutants in the air in Europe. Yet this may be less important for international purposes than for individual purposes, as we do want to know what happens to our breathing potential wherever we may be in Europe. What is happening to the recharging of the atmosphere with oxygen from the phytoplankton in the waters of Europe? Maybe the waters of Europe don't recharge the atmosphere any more, and the monitoring should be extended to the oceans to show what the O_2 recharge from oceanic phytoplankton is. I don't think we have any good measurements of what this is per square metre or per cubic metre of the oceans. It certainly links very importantly with that kind of study of atmospheric pollution to know what is the correlation of this atmospheric overlay with the area of oxygen-producing surface lying below. We really need to have some correlation, and consequently in monitoring, as Dr Butler indicated, to have a system designed on what we need to know. And I think this Conference is really intended to find out what we need to know, how to go about getting the information, and how to coordinate it completely towards stemming environmental menaces.

I would like to ask Dr Davies two questions: the first is, how will the parameters be expressed? For instance, I came across the North American continent two days ago, where all of the way there was an overcast. Flying at 30,000 to 33,000 feet, the overcast layer could be seen above us maybe to as high as 50,000 feet. It extended out over the Atlantic Ocean, beyond the Newfoundland coast. Eventually in the middle of the Ocean it was clear, and it was still clear as we approached the continent of Europe. But how do we measure this in terms of sampling: do you have eddies of different kinds of pollutants at these levels, and what is the solar interference relationship to the earth's surface below?

The second question is, what is the WMO specifically asking for at the Stockholm Conference in June 1972? Are you functioning as a branch of the United Nations? I ask this because when we have ventured to pose questions about what's going to come up at Stockholm, we have been told that it is to be a diplomatic session, functioning only with national delegates and their advisers. Delegates will make the decisions, the advisers being there merely to advise them. Will you be there as advisers or are you to be represented by a delegation? As an organ of the United Nations, just what kind of things can you say to them? More specifically, in what terms will your WMO advice have direct relevance to the world life-support system?

Davies

I must be very brief, because my 'plane leaves in thirty-five minutes from the airport here and so if I rush out I hope you'll excuse me. It would take a very long time to answer all the questions of how we are going to observe; we have specialist groups working on this, establishing operational manuals, the first of which will be published very shortly.* These observations are useless unless they are done in a standardized form by agreed international procedures, such as are now being worked out. The remainder will be discussed in Uppsala at another specialist group meeting, mainly of atmospheric chemists—whose side of course has to be very much stressed—in a few weeks' time. Very soon we hope to have a complete operational manual which will tell everybody how to proceed to ensure the complete standardization without which of course the results are not very useful. I think that's about all.

Pavanello

My points can wait until tomorrow morning when we shall have the paper by Professor Bryson who will be speaking further about the effects of pollutants in the atmosphere. I think we should continue tomorrow morning after Dr Bryson's presentation. [Expressions of approval from the floor, whereupon the Chairman terminated the session, thanking 'Dr Davies for his interesting lecture and all the delegates here taking part in the discussion'.]

* *See* the last of the References listed after Dr Davies's own paper, on page 115.—Ed.

ADDENDUM

[In this connection it seems appropriate to quote from a letter dated 22 June 1971 which we received in Finland from the International Organization for Standardization. When first approached verbally about the Conference quite early in 1971, they had indicated that they were not at all ready to participate; but just before the Conference was due to start, they expressed great interest and only regretted not being 'able to nominate effective representation at such short notice . . . this time'.—Ed.]

'The International Organization for Standardization is indeed very much interested in the international standardization aspects of certain important features concerned with environmental pollution, and the ISO has set up . . . specialist Technical Committees which are particularly concerned with these areas. It would therefore have been of considerable interest for the ISO to have taken some part in your forthcoming Conference. Unfortunately, however, there is not enough time now to enable us to arrange for ISO to be represented at the Conference . . . . We would, however, like to communicate to you, for the information of your Conference, the principal activities which engage ISO in regard to environmental pollution. You may like to make use of the following information in any way you think appropriate for the purpose of your Conference:

'The ISO has recently decided to set up two specialist committees to deal with ISO standardization aspects in the field of air and water pollution (purity). These Technical Committees are:

'ISO/TC 146—Air purity. The Secretariat of this Technical Committee is held by the ISO Member Body for Germany (Deutscher Normenausschuss, 4–7 Burggrafenstrasse, 1 Berlin 30).
'ISO/TC 147—Water purity. The Secretariat of this Technical Committee is held by the ISO Member Body for USA (American National Standards Institute, 1430 Broadway, New York, NY 10018).

'The above proposals were approved at the meeting of ISO Planning Committee, held in May 1971, and have now been put up for formal acceptance by the ISO Council. In the meantime, actions to organize the two Technical Committees have been initiated already.
'The proposed scopes and programmes of work of the two Technical Committees are as given in the annex to this letter. It is possible that there might be some minor technical changes to the contents of the proposed scopes and programmes of work, before they are finalized, after the first meetings of the new Technical Committees.
'As you will notice from the statement of the scopes and programmes of work, the committees will be concerned principally with sampling, test methods, classification, and terminology, in their respective fields, but will not deal with standards for the permissible limits for pollution, since the latter would depend very much on the circumstances and would have to be the subject of regulatory decisions of a governmental (or local authority) nature.

'It is expected that the two new Technical Committees will hold their first meeting by the end of 1971.

'In addition to the questions of air and water purity or pollution, for which ISO has decided to set up the two new specialist Technical Committees, mention should also be made of the environmental nuisance due to noise and disturbing acoustic phenomena. In this area, ISO has already a specialist Technical Committee: ISO/TC 43—Acoustics, the Secretariat of which is held by the ISO Member Body for the UK (British Standards Institution, 2 Park Street, London W1A 2BS). The activities of ISO/TC 43 include, for instance, the questions of noise from different sources, its measurement, and effects such as on hearing, conversation, etc.'

Yours sincerely,
[Signed] *Dr N. N. Chopra*
Technical Director, Group 2,
International Organization for Standardization,
1 rue de Varambé,
1211 Genève 20,
Switzerland

ANNEX

ISO/TC 146—Air purity
Scope
Measurement, control, and classification, of air purity and pollution, but excluding limits for pollution.

Programme of work
The following programme of work is proposed:

(a) Sampling, test methods, and methods of analysis, of ambient air, for the determination of its quality and particularly the detection and quantitative determination of pollutants and measurement of pollution of various types.
(b) Test methods and methods of analysis designed for the detection and quantitative assessment of atmospheric pollutants from various products and sources, including industrial nuisances of various types, fuel-burning devices, and effluents from urban pollution sources.
(c) Classification of atmospheric pollutions.
(d) Terminology, including units of measurement and expression of results.

The actual programme of work will be defined at the first meeting of the Technical Committee.

ISO/TC 147—Water purity
Scope
Measurement, control, and classification, of water purity and pollution, but excluding limits for pollution.

Programme of work

The following programme of work is proposed:

(*a*) Sampling, test methods, and methods of analysis, of water, for the determination of its quality and particularly the detection and quantitative determination of pollutants and measurement of pollution of various types.

(*b*) Test methods and methods of analysis designed for the detection and quantitative assessment of water pollutants from various products and sources, including effluents and waste products let out by industries, water transport, and urban pollution sources.

(*c*) Classification of water pollutions and classification of water bodies from the point of view of purity.

(*d*) Terminology, including units of measurement and expression of results.

The actual programme of work will be defined at the first meeting of the Technical Committee.

5
ATMOSPHERIC IMBALANCES AND POLLUTION

Keynote Paper

Climatic Modification by Air Pollution

by

REID A. BRYSON

Professor of Meteorology and Director,
Institute for Environmental Studies,
Meteorology and Space Science Building,
University of Wisconsin, Madison,
Wisconsin 53706, USA.

Introduction

On some 1938 postage stamps of Czechoslovakia are shown the smoking chimneys of factories. These stamps were not issued in support of a campaign against air pollution, but instead were intended to be symbolic of industry and prosperity. To many people of the world this picture still seems true of life, whereas actually, man has so harnessed the energy symbolized by the smoking chimney that the resulting air pollution has become a problem which erodes the prosperity of nations, undermines their health, and even modifies the very physical and biological environments in which we all live.

One of these physical modifications of the environment is the climatic modification associated with air pollution. It is very evident on the scale of a metropolitan region; but if one includes all the sources of air pollution that are directly or indirectly attributable to man's activities, then pollution-generated climatic modification on a larger regional scale, including the global one, can be identified.

The industrial revolution and the harnessing of energy—particularly that contained in fossil fuels—increased the rate at which men could utilize resources and greatly increased the demand for energy that was needed for the use of resources. One can think of industry as powered by 'energy slaves' working for man. These 'energy slaves' not only drive the machines that manufacture goods, but also heat our houses, power our transport systems, plough our fields, print our books, and in many other ways contribute to our welfare. However, these energy-consuming machines 'breathe' and 'excrete', and their 'metabolic' by-products often end up in the air as pollutants.

In addition, just as humans may 'kick up dust' in the course of their activities, so do our machines. Tractors and earth-moving machines, indeed all those things which disturb the land surface and bare the soil, especially in dry areas, increase the wind deflation of soil particles. For the purpose of the discussion in these pages, the materials that are put into the air by man and his machines, and those that enter the air in increased amounts due to a variety of human activities, will be regarded as *atmospheric pollutants*. Increased air pollution can thus result from population increase, mechanization, industrialization, or changed patterns of activity—including those which increase the exposure of dry soils to deflation.

It is not easy to distinguish many of the man-made or man-induced pollutants from those which might 'be there' in the absence of man. Carbon dioxide produced by the burning of fossil fuels is not different from that released from ancient carbonate deposits by natural chemical processes, and, except by isotopic content, is indistinguishable from that produced by oxidation of leaf-litter or soil humus. Dust raised by mechanized farming is not different from that which might have been raised by pre-man dust-storms—unless some distinctive man-made tracer such as DDT has been added. Similar comments might be made about sulphur dioxide, nitrogen oxides, carbon monoxide, and some other compounds which human activities produce.

Nevertheless, careful study and analysis shows that the activities of man may be producing many of these pollutants in quantities that rival nature over large areas, and far exceed nature in local areas. In addition, all over the world, distinctively man-made pollutants may be found—some of which may build up to significant levels unless the use of the atmosphere and hydrosphere as 'sewers' is decreased.

The various major pollutants vary in importance from one environmental realm to another. For example, sulphur dioxide, ozonated hydrocarbons, nitrogen oxides, and carbon monoxide, are important to health, comfort, and biota. Sulphur dioxide is probably the most important among the pollutants causing deterioration of materials, though not in other ways. None of these appears to be particularly important, as yet, in terms of gross climatic effects, unless the reported increased acidity of rain in Scandinavia is regarded as a climatic effect. On the other hand, particulates and carbon dioxide appear to have detectable and physically understandable large-scale climatic effects.

The following pages will explore some aspects of the effects on climate of air pollution, considered on the metropolitan, regional, and global, scales. The emphasis will be on those pollutants which are identifiable as important causal factors, and primarily on the standard climatic parameters. The exclusion of those pollutants which are important to what is generally called 'air quality' is thus due to the focus of this paper rather than to their lack of intrinsic importance to man.

CITY CLIMATE AND POLLUTION

Heat Economy of Large Towns

Large towns and cities* represent significant modifications of the landscape. The modifications consist of many man-made features, most of which contribute to the production of a distinctive city climate: they include tall buildings, paved streets and parking lots, high density of population and of 'energy slaves', minimized open and green space, and maximized storm run-off.

In many respects a city resembles a rough, rocky island in a sea of surrounding countryside and, like an island, tends to develop a 'sea breeze' when the general winds of the surrounding larger areas are light. Two factors are important in the development of the city 'sea breeze'. The first is the heat produced in the city for domestic and industrial purposes, including the metabolic heat-production of the inhabitants (in the terms of our Introduction, all heat produced in a city is metabolic heat of man and his 'energy slaves'). The other factor is the contrast in physical properties between city surfaces and those characteristic of the countryside. These properties favour a heat-balance between sun, atmosphere, and surface, such that the city is warmer than the open countryside—especially at night.

When the sun shines on a city, no matter how wanly through the turbid air, it heats the surface in proportion to how much radiation is reflected and

* The term 'city' is here used in its loose sense of a large and important town, rather than in its strict sense of a town or even a village which has been created a city by special charter and especially when containing a cathedral.—Ed.

how much is absorbed. The fraction that is reflected, the *albedo*, is low in many cities, but not in all. If the surface materials have high specific heats and high thermal conductivities (i.e. high *thermal admittance*), as in the cases of concrete, asphalt, and brick, much heat is effectively stored by conduction from the surface. The loose soil and vegetated layers of the countryside, by contrast, are excellent insulators; in areas covered by them, relatively less heat is stored to be emitted at night.

If this were the only factor involved, the city would be cooler in the day-time than the country, and warmer at night. However, the heat absorbed at the earth's surface is divided into four parts, one of which is that used in subsurface storage. The other three are: first, that dissipated in re-radiation; second, that used in evaporation of water; and lastly, that transferred to the atmosphere which we can actually feel, i.e. as *sensible heat*. As cities are water-proofed over as much as 50 per cent of their area, and also storm-sewered to dispose of precipitation as expeditiously as possible, very little heat is used to evaporate water in the city—in contrast to the country, with its soil moisture and transpiring vegetation. Consequently, more heat is available in cities to heat the air there than in the country, while apparently less heat is re-radiated through the turbid air of the city than through the cleaner air of the country.

At night, the heat that has been stored by day in the town materials is conducted back to the surface to counteract the nocturnal cooling, while in the country the temperatures drop down lower at the top of the insulating blanket of loose soil and vegetation than is the case in the city. On balance, then, the city would be warmer than the countryside even without the considerable artificial heat input due to fuel combustion. It is estimated that, in New York City in midwinter, the combustive heat-production is two-and-one-half times the solar energy input. Generally, the combustive heat-production is less than—but still an appreciable fraction of—the solar energy input even on annual averages. The mean annual temperature excess of the city over the country is often 1–2° C, and in some cases more. The warmer area of the city is called the *heat island*. As it is in significant part the result of addition of waste heat to the atmosphere, it is a climatic indicator of *thermal pollution*.

The Dust Dome and City Ventilation

Because of the 'heat island', the city develops a distinctive air-circulation pattern very much like a sea breeze on an island—except that it does not reverse at night as does the sea breeze. The warm air rises from the city centre, while the cooler suburban air sinks and flows in towards the area thus 'vacated'. As the central air rises, it flows out towards the suburbs and sinks. Particulates such as specks of mineral dust and other particles generated near the surface by traffic, industry, and inefficient domestic heating, are kept in suspension by the turbulence near the rough city surface, and are swept in towards the centre of the city. As the air rises, the turbulence diminishes and a large fraction of the particulates settles back into the in-flowing lower air. As a result, the turbidity of the air tends to be highest in the middle of the 'heat island'. In profile, the particulate-laden air may be seen as a dome-shaped cap of dirty air over the city. This 'dust dome' identifies for the viewer the characteristic course of the heat-pollution-generated city air circulation (Fig. 1).

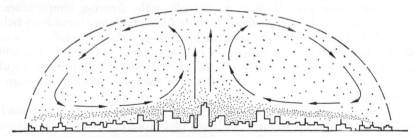

Fig. 1. Schematic air-circulation pattern over a city, produced primarily by thermal pollution. The pattern is much more complex over cities which are coastal, complex in plan, or situated in topographic basins.

The 'dust dome' and city air circulation are well developed only with light winds and a compact city form, and are poorly developed with a less compact city form, broad green belts, lakes, broad rivers, etc. Clearly they can be nearly eliminated with careful planning of green belts, industrial centres, and the like.

With winds stronger than 5–8 metres per second, the 'dust dome' breaks down into a downwind 'plume' that may extend for many miles. The dust plume of New York has been followed to Iceland, and that of Los Angeles to Nebraska, for example. The more pronounced the heat island is, the higher will be the wind-speed at which the dome breaks down into a plume. The most severe air-pollution episodes occur when the dome is restricted in its vertical development by the presence of a low inversion. Even under plume conditions, the vertical structures of the city modify the aerodynamic roughness of the area and, in turn, the rate at which the wind may disperse the pollutants generated in the city.

The aerodynamic roughness is characterized by a roughness length, usually designated z_0. It has been shown by J. E. Kutzbach (in Lettau, 1969, cf. 1970) that the roughness length is proportional to the square of the height (h) and to the width (w) of the buildings, and inversely proportional to the surface area devoted to each building—i.e. to the lot size or square of the average distance from building centre to building centre (D). The factor of proportionality is about 1/2, so that

$$z_0 = 1/2 \frac{h^2 w}{D^2}$$

A characteristic value of z_0 in the open countryside is about 5 cm, while in a metropolitan centre it might be 1,000 cm. With a standard wind-profile, this would reduce the wind at 30 m or so by 80 per cent or more. This reduction of wind-speed increases proportionately the length of time required for the wind to flush the pollutants from the city.

The pollutant concentrations in the city, produced by industrial and domestic sources and by traffic, and exacerbated by the special wind modification by the city, produce other climatic modifications (Peterson, 1969). Of unusual interest are the varieties of particles that are put into city air: some are especially effective as nuclei on which condensation of water may occur, some are effective at controlling the freezing temperature of water droplets, and some promote condensation at relative humidities below saturation. As a result, cities tend to have more rain (especially on week-days!) and much more fog than do country areas (*ibid.*), and apparently they may produce downwind effects which result in rather spectacular changes in the quantity and character of the precipitation (Changnon, 1969).

The particles in the city air also change the radiation regime, reducing sunlight by 15 to 30 per cent and ultra-violet radiation by up to 90 per cent.

In summary, the heat pollution of a city modifies the temperature regime of the city and produces a distinctive wind-circulation pattern which traps particulate and gaseous pollutants. The special vertical structure of the city further modifies the wind-flow. The trapped pollutants in turn modify the fog, cloud, radiation, and precipitation of the city—as well as detract from the quality of life in the city.

It is clear that man and his machines can modify the climate of a metropolitan area through pollution of one sort or another. In the next section an example will be given of how man's activities and pollution can modify regional climate.

Dust, Goats, and Deserts

The Dusty Regions

Polynesian sea-voyagers used to sail towards islands over the horizon by watching for the characteristic features of land-clouds—features that differentiate them from sea-clouds. Similarly, an air pilot may see a distant city indicated by its 'dust dome'—usually brown by day and glowing with the internal city lights at night. But the pilot with an educated eye may see far more than local pollution. He may see city dust-plumes merging into regional palls that extend from hundreds to thousands of kilometres downwind, perhaps rising along a sloping internal atmospheric surface and flattening into a dust layer at a height of 10 km or more—a layer that the ground-bound observer would not see or understand, for dust in the atmosphere is not routinely measured. The pilot knows that the upper surface of the hazy or dusty layer near the ground marks an inversion and smooth flying. He knows that the dusty layers produce a glare of scattered sunlight, and that a dusty region is a bright region.

Travelling about the world, an air pilot will see tremendous variations in the turbidity of the atmosphere, ranging from the crystal clarity of arctic skies with 300 km visibility to the brown air and bronze-blue zenith of West Pakistan and north-west India, where the ground may not be visible at all from a height of only 3 km. He will wonder about the source of the dust and its significance. From the ground he might watch the red twilight glow not on the western horizon, but as a weird orange-red oval some 15° above the black, dust-obscured horizon. If he is also a climatologist, the pilot will ask himself what effect this dense dust might have on the climate.

Without instruments, the attenuation of the sunlight is obvious. Looking at the sun is not painful in these dusty regions, but the glare of scattered sunlight is great. Prolonged exposure of human skin to sun without tanning indicates that the ultra-violet light is attenuated also. The slow evening cooling after the 40°C summer day in the Indian or Rajputana Desert indicates that outward infra-red radiation from the ground is also reduced.

Measured Effects of Dust over India

Instrumental measurements verify the sensory evidence. Of particular importance to the climate of the area is the radiation variation with height, for the vertical divergence of the radiation is a measure of the diabatic or direct radiative cooling of the atmosphere which is necessary to maintain the mean subsident motion that is characteristic of deserts. Over wet northeastern India the mean motion is upwards, but west of New Delhi it is downwards. Downward mean motion implies mean compressional warming of the air and in turn an average *in situ* warming which is greater than that observed.

Das (1962) calculated the sinking motion and its relation to the temperature change, and found that in mid-troposphere, perhaps 5 km above the ground, diabatic cooling of 2.4°C/day was necessary to sustain the subsidence. Calculating the infra-red diabatic cooling that would occur in the air over northwestern India, with the observed temperature and moisture distribution, Das found that he could account for only 1.8°C/day. He had, of course, made the calculation in the standard way, assuming that water vapour, carbon dioxide, and ozone, were the significant radiating gases. Without data on the distribution of particulate matter in suspension, and a much more complicated and less certain calculation, he could not have allowed for the effect of dust.

Shortly after Das's paper was published, a series of balloon-sonde measurements of the infra-red radiation divergence was started on the fringes of the Rajputana Desert, in New Delhi, in Poona, and later in the desert at Jodhpur (Bryson *et al.*, 1964; Mani *et al.*, 1965). These measurements showed that the discrepancy between observed and calculated cooling-rates was very nearly the same as the discrepancy found by Das (1962) between required and calculated cooling-rates—and that the discrepancy depended on the dustiness of the air!

To the uninitiated, the difference between 1.8 and 2.4°C/day may seem small, but it means a difference of 33 per cent in the sinking rate of the desert air—and it is sinking air primarily that causes aridity—leading one inevitably to the conclusion that the dusty desert air makes the area more desertic. Subsidence increases air stability (usually) and decreases relative humidity, thus inhibiting precipitation.

In short, the radiative effect of dust in the air over north-west India and West Pakistan is enormous when compared with the effect of particulates in North America and Europe. But then the amount of dust in the air is enormously greater in the former region, too. In order to put numbers on the sensory evidence of greatly reduced visibility in the Rajputana Desert, a series of research flights were made in 1966 (Peterson & Bryson, 1968).

The effect of dust content of the air on the infra-red radiation divergence, as measured during these flights, is shown in Fig. 2.

The measurements of dust concentration made in the air over north-west India suggest that even on the average, away from the cities, there are 300–800 micrograms of dust per cubic metre in the lowest 5 to 10 kilometres of air. Compare that with 150–200 micrograms per cubic metre in the lowest

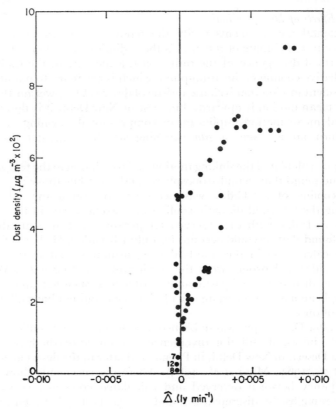

Fig. 2. Infra-red radiation effect of atmospheric dust as measured over north-west India. The ordinate is in hundreds of micrograms per cubic metre. The abscissa indicates the difference between observed and calculated upward radiation flux-gradient, corrected for variation in ambient temperatures and downward fluxes. (After Peterson & Bryson, 1968.) This figure shows that the upward radiation flux decreases less rapidly in dusty air than in clear air.

1 to 2 kilometres over Chicago, and one sees that if Chicago air is turbid, Rajputana Desert air is *very* turbid and covers a much larger area. During pollution episodes, city air is as turbid as the average air over the Rajputana Desert, but to lesser heights.

Instrumental observations are not available to assess the areal extent of this turbid air, but visual observations indicate maximum dust density over the Rajputana Desert area. In all directions from there the dust density diminishes—especially to the east and south—though remnant layers may be traced to Cambodia, northern Malaya, and at least as far south as Madras. To the west, the dust density decreases somewhat along the Mekran Coast and then may increase over Arabia and the Sahara in some seasons. Over the mountains to the north and north-west of the Rajputana Desert, the air appears to be less turbid.

If one uses the homely principle that the smoke is densest near the chimney, then one would conclude that the Rajputana Desert itself was the source of the dust. Indeed, this appears to be the case. Samples of the airborne dust were composed of 36 per cent quartz and 20 to 22 per cent each of carbonate, mica, and either feldspar or clay minerals. Of particular interest in this assemblage is the clay. E. D. Goldberg's studies (personal communication) of wind-borne dust on the ocean floor near India show the major clay to be montmorillonite, which is rather effective as a nucleating agent for cloud-seeding. With their very large characteristic dust-loads, one would suspect that the few clouds would be typically over-seeded, and that the region would be a poor prospect for artificial rain-enhancement.

The thick blanket of turbid air affects the incoming solar radiation as well as the outgoing, absorbing or scattering a considerable portion of the radiation before it reaches the ground. This diminishes the day-time instability that might promote convective showers if moisture were present (incidentally, the air of the Rajputana Desert is surprisingly moist for a desert—there just isn't much rain). At night, the large radiative cooling of the upper part of the dusty blanket and suppressed radiative cooling near the ground increase the instability and keep the ground warmer than it would otherwise be. This reminds the scientific traveller of the night-time difference in near-surface temperatures between the city and the countryside in less desertic, better vegetated, areas. The reason is different, but there *is* a relationship, as will be seen hereafter.

Several comments in the preceding paragraphs may have alerted the reader to some rather special circumstances of the particular desert under discussion. Thus he may have asked himself some questions, such as why this particular desert is so dusty, and why it is a desert if the air is moist.

The Rajputana Desert does have some unusual features:

1. It is probably the dustiest of all deserts.
2. The air over the part of this desert having the least rainfall has a total water-content which is comparable with that of some very rainy tropical forest areas.
3. The dew-point of the air is quite high during the summer, and there are quite a few clouds.
4. It is the most densely-populated desert in the world.
5. Much of the desert area was once occupied by a high culture with an agricultural base—the Indus civilization.
6. The region appears to be more barren than the measured rainfall would lead one to expect.

The remains of the Indus civilization suggest that the region was not always as desertic as it is now, and palaeobotanical studies verify this suggestion. Gurdip Singh (1970), studying the pollen in the bed of Sambhar

Salt Lake near Jaipur, in Rajasthan, found that during the time of the Indus people, the lake held fresh water and the vegetation of the surrounding land was indicative of much moister conditions. Then the lake became salty as the culture disappeared, and about 1000 B.C. the lake dried up entirely. After a long dry interval, scattered settlements reappeared, to be replaced by the extensive Rangmahal culture by the fourth century A.D. Then extensive nomadism developed. Many dust-storms in south-west Rajasthan were reported in the seventh century A.D., and it appears that by A.D. 1000 considerable spread of the desert had occurred, to be accentuated in the recent past.

One acquires, at this point in the investigation, a nagging suspicion that perhaps this region should not be desertic at all, but rather some sort of savanna. This suspicion is compounded by awareness of cities buried under sand-dunes, great castles in areas that are now too poor to have provided the excess capital to have built them, and ancient paintings which depict a lusher, wetter land.

If the Rajputana Desert is really anomalous, how might one change it back to a more productive land? We know that the air over this desert subsides, more than it otherwise would do, because of the high dust-content and its effect on radiative cooling. Without the dust there would be less subsidence—and more frequent showers! If there were more rain there would be more grass, and as the dust is from the surface soil, the grass would reduce the deflation from the surface and result in there being less dust carried into the atmosphere (Bryson & Baerreis, 1967).

Now think of the contrast between the concrete, brick, and asphalt, of the city on one hand, and the grass and loose soil of the countryside on the other. Just as the night-time temperatures fall lower in the country than they do in the city, so lower nocturnal temperatures would prevail over the desert grass than over the compact, bare desert soil—and the night temperatures would be still lower if the dust blanket were not there. With the high dew-point of the Rajputana Desert, heavy dew would form on the grass (and does to some extent in the areas which are grassy, even now).

With dew to help the grass grow and hold down the desert soil, there would be less dust in the air. In turn, there would be less radiative cooling of the top of the dusty layer of air, less subsidence, and more frequent showers to make the grass grow, etc., etc.

Obviously, more grass, if it improved the climate and so made possible the growth of still more grass, would be a good thing for the goatherds of the desert—except that it appears that their herds are the reason why the grass is sparse, the air dusty, and the land unproductive in a semi-desert climate!

The evidence for this influence of goats is to be found in a simple experiment that was performed at the Central Arid Zone Research Institute in Jodhpur. There, a barren plot of land (Fig. 3) was fenced to exclude goats, sheep, and other grazers. Nothing was done inside the fence except to let nature have its way—and in less than two years there was tall, rich native grass except within one goat-neck distance from the fence (Fig. 4).

This gets at the heart of the whole matter, for it indicates that *a significant fraction of the dust over the Rajputana Desert is there because of human activity*. Such

Fig. 3. A grazed area adjoining the Central Arid Zone Research Institute in Jodhpur, India. The surface of the soil is bare of vegetation except for a few highly unpalatable plants that are avoided by the goats. The fine-textured soil is roughened by thousands of hoof-prints, and deflates readily. The scale is indicated by the large vultures perched on the tops of trees in the background. (Photo: Professor Reid A. Bryson.)

Fig. 4. Photo taken inside the area of an enclosure protected from grazing on the grounds of the Central Arid Zone Research Institute in Jodhpur, India. The [...] The grass growth is natural—no seed, water, or fertilizer, having been applied. Control of goats has made the soil less prone

dust falls within the definition of air pollution as used in this paper, and it thus appears that over-use of the land can change regional climates even without the 'blessings' of mechanization and industrialization.

THE HUMAN VOLCANO

In order to understand more fully and in detail the role of human activity in modifying the climate of the Rajputana Desert, it will eventually be necessary to unravel the story of climatic change in India and the world, for until this is done we will not know how much of the history of human occupation of the region was related to natural climatic change, and how much was due to human modification of the local ecosystems by over-use of the land. The same kind of analysis will be necessary if we are to know whether man is modifying the climate of the whole world.

The non-linear, explosive growth of human population on the earth suggests that if air pollution is significant in the modification of world climate, the effect will be most evident in an examination of the latter half of the past hundred years. Towards the end of trying to identify such effects, among others, the following pages will deal with the observed climatic variation of the past century, and with its causes.

While the complete numerical modelling of world climates in detail is not yet within the grasp of atmospheric science, we may gain considerable insight into the problem by using a simple model of the world annual mean temperature (Mitchell, 1961).

The Theory

The earth has a surface temperature that results from near-balance between income of heat from the sun and output of heat radiation from the planet to space. If the income and output were exactly balanced, the temperature of the earth would be constant. If the income and output were not balanced, the temperature would change until the heat omitted from the earth once again balanced the income. The change would not be instantaneous, for the earth has a considerable 'thermal mass' that takes some time to heat and cool—just as a thermometer with a large bulb does not respond instantly to the temperature of the medium in which it is immersed.*

In symbolic form,

$$I - O = m^+ \frac{dT}{dt}$$

where
I = heat income from the sun,
O = heat radiated to space from the earth,
m^+ = effective heat capacity of the earth,
T = mean annual temperature of the earth, and
t = time.

The heat income per unit area at the surface of the earth is equal to the absorbed direct solar radiation with cloudless skies fractionally reduced by the presence of clouds, K_1 (R_{dir}), plus the absorbed diffuse short-wave radiation

* The reader who does not wish to follow the development of this equation may skim through to the next side-heading (on page 145) without great loss.

from the sky, K_2 (R_{diff}), plus the downward long-wave radiation from the atmosphere and clouds (R_{LW}).

The output of heat from the surface of the earth is equal to the infra-red radiation emitted from the earth ($e\sigma T^4$), plus the net flux of heat from the surface by convection and latent heat of evaporation, which we will lump together and symbolize as A. If the income and output do not balance, the mean temperature of the earth will change ($m\,dT/dt$). The approximate equation then becomes

$$K_1(R_{dir}) + K_2(R_{diff}) + (R_{LW}) - (e\sigma T^4) - A = m\frac{dT}{dt}$$

where
$\qquad\qquad e$ = effective emissivity of the earth,
$\qquad\qquad \sigma$ = the Stefan–Boltzmann constant,
$\qquad\qquad T$ = surface temperature of the earth, and
$\qquad\qquad m$ = effective 'thermal mass' or heat capacity of the earth.

Unfortunately, we do not have all the appropriate information to know the values of the variables in this equation, or even the coefficients, for the past century. However, we can make some approximations and use whatever information is available, determining the appropriate coefficients (K_1, K_2, etc.) statistically where previous research has not provided the information, or the needed basic data are not available.

Over the small range of temperature involved, the temperature itself may be substituted for the temperature raised to the fourth power without much loss of accuracy. The various radiation fluxes may be regarded as consisting of constant mean parts plus small variations. The diffuse radiation varies, in part, due to particulates in the air, as does the absorption of solar radiation in the air. The downward long-wave re-radiation of a part of this absorbed heat, and that transferred to the air by condensation and convection, also varies with the particulate matter content of the air. The variation of the carbon dioxide content of the air also affects its infra-red absorption and emission. These complex relationships may be summed up in a few simplifying approximations:

1. The infra-red emission from the earth's surface is approximately pro-portional to the temperature of the surface within the range of tem-peratures considered, i.e.

$$(e\sigma T^4)/m \approx C_1 T.$$

2. The diffuse radiation term and the long-wave radiation term are proportional to some function of the dust content of the atmosphere, plus some function of the carbon dioxide content of the atmosphere, plus some term that combines all other factors not considered here, i.e.

$$[K_2(R_{diff}) + (R_{LW})]/m = C_3(\text{dust}) + C_2(CO_2) + b.$$

3. All the coefficients that modify the direct solar radiation may be com-bined into a single coefficient, i.e.

$$K_1(R_{dir})/m = C_4(R_{dir}).$$

4. The factor, b, above, the flux of energy by convection and as latent heat, and all other factors not considered, may constitute a residual term after we have considered the factors mentioned specifically above, i.e.,

$$(b + A/m) = \text{residual}.$$

In these approximations, $C_3(\text{dust})$ is some exponential function of the particulate content of the atmosphere, and C_1, C_2, C_3, and C_4, are constant coefficients. Several calculations of the value of $C_2(\text{CO}_2)$ are available, such as that of Manabe & Wetherald (1967). The purpose of these approximations is to reduce the complete equation to a form that will enable us to examine the role of possible pollutants such as particulates and carbon dioxide:

$$C_1 T + \frac{\mathrm{d}T}{\mathrm{d}t} - C_2(\text{CO}_2) = C_3(\text{dust}) + C_4(\text{R}_{\text{dir}}) = \text{residual}.$$

Bearing in mind that the direct solar radiation reaching the surface through cloudless skies is also in part a function of the turbidity of the atmosphere, we may now examine the evidence. This we shall do by means of a series of graphs.

Northern Hemisphere Temperature and the 'Greenhouse Effect'
Fig. 5, modified slightly from Mitchell (1970), shows the variation in the mean annual temperature of the northern hemisphere over the past century. The variation of world mean annual temperatures is similar, but there are far

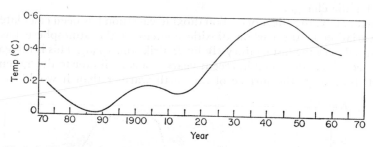

Fig. 5. Variation in the mean annual temperature of the northern hemisphere over the past century, expressed as ten-year overlapping means of the departures from the 1885–90 mean. This figure is an extension and modification of one given by Mitchell (1970).

fewer data for the southern hemisphere. The curve is based upon mean annual values for several hundred stations, weighted for the area represented by each station, and while the data are not ideal, there seems to be nothing better to use. This curve is essentially that of the term $C_1 T$ in our equation.

It is a rather simple matter to add the second term, $\mathrm{d}T/\mathrm{d}t$, to $C_1 T$, using the common technique for correcting the response of a thermometer of large lag-time. This requires knowing the lag of the earth in response to the variables which cause the temperature to change and, in this case, experimentation suggests that a half-response time of ten years is appropriate. The sum of $C_1 T$ and dT/dt is given by the heavy line in Fig. 6.

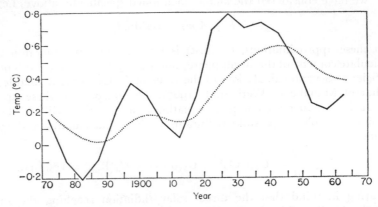

Fig. 6. The observed temperature variation of the northern hemisphere corrected for the lag of the ocean–atmosphere–soil system in responding to variation of the factors which cause the variation of temperature. A half-response time of ten years was used. The stippled line is the temperature curve of Fig. 5 repeated for comparison.

In essence the variation of the mean temperature of the earth is a measure of the integral of the imbalance of heat input and heat loss. To measure the imbalance, therefore, we must calculate the rate of change of the temperature curve. To the best of my knowledge, this has not been done by scholars studying climatic change.

Fortunately, the effect of carbon dioxide variation has been calculated and the variation in the carbon dioxide content of the atmosphere has been measured over the last century (Bolin & Eriksson, 1959). This is the gas that has been widely discussed in recent years as a contributor to the 'greenhouse effect' that keeps the surface of the earth warmer than it would be if the

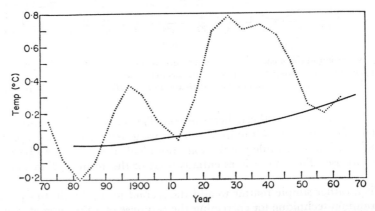

Fig. 7. The calculated temperature effect of the secular increase in atmospheric carbon dioxide (solid line) compared with the variation of northern-hemisphere mean annual temperature adjusted for lag (stippled line).

atmosphere were completely transparent to infra-red radiation (Johnson, 1970). It is generally agreed that more carbon dioxide in the air makes the air less transparent to infra-red radiation, the increased absorption of the radiation increasing the re-radiation of heat from the air to the ground. It is also generally agreed that the increase of carbon dioxide over the last century is the result of burning large amounts of fossil fuels—and is therefore the result of air pollution. One might suspect that increased population and land-use might also have caused part of the increase, by adding the carbon dioxide resulting from oxidation of more and more soil organic matter.

Using the calculations of Manabe & Wetherald (1967), we may draw the curve of temperature effect due to increasing carbon dioxide, $C_2(CO_2)$ (Fig. 7). This may then be subtracted from the sum of $C_1 T$ and dT/dt to give the form of the left-hand side of our equation (Fig. 8).

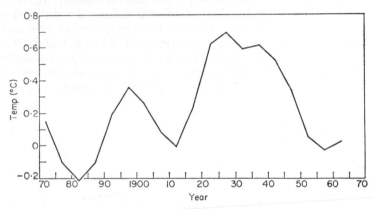

Fig. 8. The northern hemisphere mean annual temperature variation over the last century, adjusted for lag, with the warming effect of the secular increase in carbon dioxide removed.

It is particularly interesting to note that the increase of the 'greenhouse effect' due to carbon dioxide is rather small compared with the variation of the temperature corrected for lag—or, for that matter, compared with the uncorrected temperature variation. About three per cent of the variance of the corrected temperature is explained by variation in the amount of carbon dioxide present.

The Role of Dust

Particulate matter in the atmosphere is observed primarily in either the lowest few kilometres of the atmosphere or in the stratosphere. Stratospheric dust is known to increase following volcanic eruptions, and its scattering effect is demonstrated by the many accounts of brilliant sunsets following volcanic eruptions. The low-level, or tropospheric, dust may be from many sources: it may be the composite particulate plume from thousands of cities; it may be smoke from slash-and-burn agriculture; it may be soil deflated from deserts such as the Rajputana, or stirred up by heavy equipment used in building highways in Italy; it may be from mining activities in Arizona, or from mechanized farming in the Ukraine. It may be 'natural', it may be man-made, or it may be man-augmented.

Whatever the source of the dust or its location, it causes scattering and absorption of radiation. There are almost as many viewpoints on the relative importance of scattering and absorption as there are authors writing on the subject. In part this is because many assumptions about particle-size distribution, refractive index, density, particle shape, distribution with height, etc., are possible, and there are inadequate data to indicate which set of assumptions is most representative. We shall, therefore, for the present purpose, by-pass the theoretical arguments and use an empirical approach. Here the data problems are formidable but perhaps tractable.

There are no measurements of the amount of volcanic dust in the atmosphere which reach back over the past century or even the past month. However, in his characteristically thorough and careful manner, H. H. Lamb (1970) has catalogued historical eruptions and estimated a dust-veil index. We shall assume that his dust-veil index is correct; but, as attenuation of radiation is exponential, we shall use an exponential function of the dust-veil index rather than the linear form (Fig. 9). Lamb would undoubtedly concede that, while the dust-veil index record is carefully constructed, it can only be regarded as an approximation of what actually occurred.

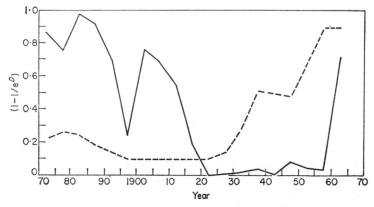

Fig. 9. Exponential plots of the dust-veil index of Lamb (1970), based on volcanic eruptions (solid line), and of the dust-fall on the Caucasus glaciers according to Davitaya (1969) (dashed line). The magnitude indicated by the solid line should be proportional to the effect of stratospheric volcanic dust on radiation, and the magnitudes indicated by the dashed line might crudely parallel the effect of tropospheric dust.

Estimation of the tropospheric dust-load of the atmosphere for the past century is essentially impossible because there are so many potential sources of such dust and so few measurements of it. Even the man-made and man-induced sources can only be estimated roughly. Certainly the assumption that the only sources of particulate pollutants are ash particles ('fly-ash') and soot from chimneys, as was suggested by Mitchell (1970), is totally inadequate in view of such other sources as those mentioned above.

About the only possibility of estimating approximately the tropospheric dust-content variation over the past century is to assume that the amount of dust suspended in the atmosphere was, at least in part, proportional to the amount that settled from the atmosphere, i.e. the dust-fall. Unfortunately, there are very few records of dust-fall, though there are a number of possible places to obtain such information. One of these is in the dust that becomes trapped in snow accumulating on glaciers. If the location is chosen such that there has been no loss of the trapped dust by snow-melt and run-off, then study of the profile of dust content down through the past century's accumulation of snow will provide a measure of local dust-fall.

One such study of the dust-fall, which would include both 'natural' and man-related dust, was made by Davitaya (1969) in the high Caucasus. This is hardly the ideal set of data from which to estimate the world load of suspended particulates in the troposphere. However, if its variation does not parallel any part of the climatic trend that theoretically might be due to tropospheric dust, that failure will appear in our statistical analysis as the non-significance of the explained variance attributable to this variable. Bad as the data are, there does not appear to be a better substitute available. An exponential function of the Caucasus dust-fall data appears in Fig. 9.

It would be scientifically satisfying to compute the temperature effect of the tropospheric and stratospheric dust directly, but the necessary information to parametrize the variables correctly is not available. As a crude substitute, we may regress the dust values shown in Fig. 9 against the temperature adjusted for lag and carbon dioxide effect, and determine the transfer function statis-

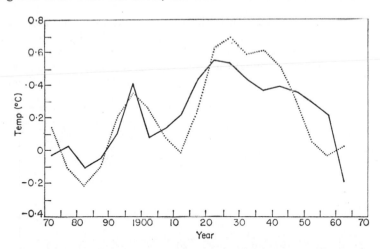

Fig. 10. Predicted form of temperature variation over the past century, due to stratospheric and tropospheric dust (solid line), compared with observed temperature variation adjusted for lag and carbon dioxide increase (stippled line). Comparison with Fig. 9 indicates that the agreement of these two curves would not be very close in the last forty years if the stratospheric (volcanic) dust alone had been considered.

tically. The effect thus estimated is shown as the heavy line in Fig. 10. The dust effect, C_3(dust) in our above equations, clearly explains most of the variance of the adjusted temperature over the last century. 63 per cent of the variance of the adjusted temperature may be assigned to stratospheric dust of volcanic origin, and 17 per cent to tropospheric dust—perhaps more than half due to man.

Direct Radiation and More Dust Effect

The difference between the adjusted mean northern-hemisphere temperature and that predicted from the crude estimates of stratospheric and tropospheric dust is shown in Fig. 11. If our equation is correct, this curve should

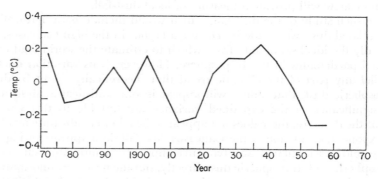

Fig. 11. The difference between the two curves plotted in Fig. 10, i.e. the difference between observed temperature variation (adjusted as described in text) and that predicted from the variation in dust.

look like the observed variation in direct solar radiation with cloudless skies obtained by Budyko (1969). The comparison is made in Fig. 12, and is really quite good considering the crudeness of the data regarding dust.

Thus far we have examined the causes of climatic change in terms of the heat-balance at the surface of the earth. In so doing we took the direct solar

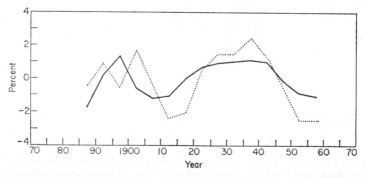

Fig. 12. The difference curve of Fig. 11 (stippled) compared with the variation in direct solar radiation with cloudless skies (cf. Budyko, 1969) (solid line). The unexplained residual difference is surprisingly small in the light of the crude data used.

radiation as an independent variable. We now see that the variation of the direct solar radiation with cloudless skies is important, and we must ask why it varies.

The reason cannot be variation in cloudiness, clearly; but it could be variation in the attenuation of the sunlight by dust, primarily by varying the albedo of the air itself and perhaps by absorption. For Ångstrom (1962) has shown that the albedo is rather sensitively dependent on the turbidity of the air.

Regressing the stratospheric and tropospheric dust against the direct solar radiation, shows that about a third of the variance of the direct radiation may be attributed to volcanic dust and about a quarter to tropospheric dust of diverse origins. The fraction of the temperature variance remaining, eleven per cent, contains various sorts of errors and is the source of the difference of the two curves in Fig. 12.

Despite the accumulation of errors, the residual error remaining after our analysis is quite small, and some useful information may be obtained from it. Specifically, the small size (i.e. 11 per cent) of the residual error demonstrates:

1. That there is no *large* cause of climatic change which has been overlooked, such as sunspots, internal feedback within the earth–atmosphere system, etc.
2. That the transfer of 'sensible' and latent heat through the atmosphere, when averaged over the hemisphere, is not very significant to this problem.

From the preceding analysis, we may additionally conclude:

3. That the dominant cause of climatic change is variation in particulate matter in the atmosphere, at least on the time-scale of a century.
4. That dust in the atmosphere reduces the mean temperature of the northern hemisphere.

How Much of the Change is Due to Man?

The whole range of hemispheric mean annual temperatures in the past century was of the order of 0.6°C, or, adjusted for lag, about 1.0°C, while the whole range due to carbon dioxide increase has been 0.25°C. As the increase of carbon dioxide is generally attributed to the burning of fossil fuels, the change of climate due to carbon dioxide pollution is a significant fraction of the whole change of the past century, and is globally detectable.

Since the recent temperature maximum, about 1945 (Fig. 5*), the adjusted temperature has fallen 0.4°C, instead of rising about 0.1°C as the increase in atmospheric carbon dioxide in recent decades would lead us to expect. We have attributed this 0.5°C difference between expected rise and observed fall to the effect of increasing particulate loading of the atmosphere. In effect, the dust caused more cooling of the earth than the carbon dioxide caused warming (Wendland & Bryson, 1970). Perhaps 70 per cent of the cooling is attributable to volcanic dust mostly in the stratosphere, and 30 per cent to tropospheric dust.

In order to assess the role of particulate air pollution in changing the climate of the earth, it is now necessary to estimate the fraction of the tropo-

* *See* footnote on page 173.—Ed.

spheric dust increase that can be attributed to human activities. Although it is not possible to do this with any degree of confidence based on actual measurements, it is my personal opinion that most of the increase which has taken place since at least the 1930 period is anthropogenous. This opinion is based on many isolated observations, such as personally seeing the dust blowing from disturbed portions of desert surfaces but not from the undisturbed parts, and watching the visibility change drastically in North America according to whether the air trajectory was over virgin lands or over heavily used lands. Perhaps it is a reasonable first approximation to say that the *increase* in tropospheric dust over the last half-century is due to human activities.

THE FUTURE

If the analysis of the preceding pages is correct, then the most important factor in climatic change on the scale of a century is the injection of dust into the atmosphere by volcanoes. However, there is now something new in the world—a human population nearing saturation of the earth's living-space, and rapidly harnessing fossil energy supplies to drive its machines. The 'excreta' of these 'energy slaves' have entered the atmosphere in quantities sufficient to have had an effect on global climate that is significant in comparison with the effect of volcanic dust. Indeed, mankind is in this respect equivalent to a volcano that is showing signs of increased activity. If projections of energy use and population growth are correct, the climatic role of man in the next century could be greater than that of volcanoes in this century!

Lest one be misled by the small value of global cooling which has been observed since 1945, it should be pointed out that local changes may be quite different from the global average. For example, while the direction of change in the mean annual temperature of Iceland has roughly paralleled that of the rest of the northern hemisphere, the magnitude of the change has been about four times as great. In terms of the recent cooling, this has meant a dramatic increase in the drift-ice in Icelandic waters, and a return to the severe conditions that characterized the nineteenth century. It is unfortunate that we must attribute at least a fraction of this change to air pollution by non-Icelanders, though the man-made increase in carbon dioxide has at least mitigated the change through the 'greenhouse effect' described above.

We might summarize and conclude by saying that man, by concentrating in towns, has modified the climate of built-up areas through his proliferating use of energy and materials. Man, in too large numbers and by over-use of the land, appears to have modified the climate also of certain large regions such as north-west India. Indeed, man is so numerous, and so profligate in the use of energy, that he can now change the climate of the world.

Through the use of his intelligence, man may change his effect on climate to his advantage. However, this requires that he have an open mind and alter his habits and the way he has habitually done things. This change will be more difficult than the needed new technology, but without it the technology will be insufficient.

REFERENCES

ÅNGSTROM, A. (1962). Atmospheric turbidity, global illumination and planetary albedo of the earth. *Tellus*, **14**, pp. 435–50, 1 fig.

BOLIN, B. & ERIKSSON, E. (1959). Changes in the carbon dioxide content of the atmosphere and sea due to fossil fuel combustion. Pp. 130–42 in *The Atmosphere and the Sea in Motion, Rossby Memorial Volume* (Ed. B. Bolin). Rockefeller Institute Press, New York: 509 pp., illustr.

BRYSON, R. A. & BAERREIS, D. A. (1967). Possibilities of major climatic modification and their implications: north-west India, a case for study. *Bull. Amer. Meteor. Soc.*, **48**, pp. 136–42, 3 figs.

BRYSON, R. A., WILSON, C. W., III & KUHN, P. M. (1964). Some preliminary results from radiation-sonde ascents over India. Pp. 501–16 in *Symposium on Tropical Meteorology, Rotorua, New Zealand, Nov. 1963*. New Zealand Meteorological Service, Wellington: xiv + 737 pp., illustr.

BUDYKO, M. I. (1969). The effect of solar radiation variation on the climate of the Earth. *Tellus*, **21**, pp. 611–19, 6 figs.

CHANGNON, S. A. (1969). Recent studies of urban effects on precipitation in the United States. *Bull. Amer. Meteor. Soc.*, **50**, pp. 411–21, 2 figs.

DAS, P. K. (1962). Mean vertical motion and non-adiabatic heat sources over India during the monsoon. *Tellus*, **14**, pp. 212–20, 10 figs.

DAVITAYA, F. F. (1969). Atmospheric dust as a factor affecting glaciation and climatic change. *Annals Assoc. Amer. Geogr.*, **59**, pp. 552–60, 5 figs.

JOHNSON, F. S. (1970). The balance of atmospheric oxygen and carbon dioxide. *Biological Conservation*, **2**(2), pp. 83–9.

LAMB, H. H. (1970). Volcanic dust in the atmosphere; with a chronology and assessment of its meteorological significance. *Phil. Trans. Royal Soc. London A*, **266**, pp. 425–533, 28 figs.

LETTAU, H. H. (1969). Note on aerodynamic roughness-parameter estimation on the basis of roughness-element description. *Jour. Appl. Meteor.*, **8**, pp. 828–32.

LETTAU, H. H. (1970). Physical and meteorological basis for mathematical models of urban diffusion processes. Pp. (2) 1–26 in *Proceedings of Symposium on Multiple-Source Urban Diffusion Models* (Ed. A. C. Stern). *Air Pollution Control Office* (U.S.) *Publication* No. AP-86, ix + 421 pp., illustr.

MANABE, S. & WETHERALD, R. T. (1967). Thermal equilibrium of the atmosphere with given distribution of relative humidity. *Jour. Atmos. Sci.*, **24**, pp. 241–59, 31 figs.

MANI, A., SREEDHARAN, C. R. & SRINIVASAN, V. (1965). Measurements of infra-red radiative fluxes over India. *Journ. Geophys. Res.*, **70**, pp. 4529–36, 8 figs.

MITCHELL, J. M., JR (1961). Recent secular changes of global temperature. *Annals New York Acad. Sci.*, **95**(1), pp. 235–50, 6 figs.

MITCHELL, J. M., JR (1970). A preliminary evaluation of atmospheric pollution as a cause of the global temperature fluctuation of the past century. Pp. 137–55 in *Global Effects of Environmental Pollution* (Ed. S. F. Singer). Springer-Verlag, New York: ix + 218 pp., illustr.

PETERSON, J. T. (1969). The climate of cities: a survey of recent literature. *National Air Pollution Control Administration* (U.S.) *Publication* No. AP-59, v + 48 pp., 7 figs.

PETERSON, J. T. & BRYSON, R. A. (1968). Influence of atmospheric particulates on the infra-red radiation balance of north-west India. Pp. 153–62 in *Proc. 1st National Conf. on Weather Modification*, Albany, New York. American Meteorological Society, Boston: xii + 532 pp., illustr.

SINGH, Gurdip (1970). *History of Post-Glacial Vegetation and Climate of the Rajasthan*

Desert. Birbal Sahni Institute of Palaeobotany, Lucknow, unpublished report, 173 pp. (manuscript), 9 figs, 5 plates.

WENDLAND, W. M. & BRYSON, R. A. (1970). Atmospheric dustiness, man, and climatic change. *Biological Conservation*, 2(2), pp. 125–8, 4 figs.

POSTSCRIPT*

If we concentrate on changes in what may be considered the normal constituents of the atmosphere, but which are altered by the presence of pollution, some things are simply not important. For example, over the history of the earth the argon level in the atmosphere has been gradually increasing from the decay of radioactive potassium. It is totally unimportant whether we have 1 per cent of argon in the atmosphere or 2 per cent, so we shall not consider that. We can also think about short-term and long-term imbalances—those things that have an immediate effect and those that might have a long-term effect.

My greatest concern about short-term effects is with regard to the ozone in the atmosphere. I am not an expert on ozone, but I have had the benefit within the last few weeks of going through some rather extensive discussions of the ozone problem as a member of the Environmental Studies Board of the National Academy of Sciences of the United States. We are concerned with the ozone levels in the stratosphere and how they might be affected by man, because there is some new information. We have for some time been discussing the possible effects of large numbers of supersonic transport aircraft operating in the stratosphere, presumably at a height of about 20 kilometres (which is near the level of the maximum *concentration* of ozone, although as Dr Nyberg implied yesterday, the maximum *production* is at about 50 kilometres). It was suggested a year or two ago that water vapour released by high-flying aircraft would not only impede the sun's rays but also modify the amount of ozone somewhat, and calculations—very difficult calculations, to be sure—suggest that this would increase the intensity of ultra-violet light at the surface of the earth. This would have both its good points and its bad points: an increase in ultra-violet rays would increase the natural production of vitamin D, but it is estimated—and I have checked this with cancer experts—that the predicted amount of ozone decrease would result in an ultra-violet increase yielding 10,000 extra cases of skin cancer per year in the United States alone. This is a rather questionable figure—it might be 2,000 or it might be 15,000, it is not very clear—because the reduction in ozone due to water vapour produced by high-flying aircraft would be small. Recently, however, it has been suggested that there are a number of reactions—perhaps fifty different reactions—for the destruction of ozone, which are catalysed by nitrogen oxides which aircraft engines also produce in large quantities.

The first calculation on this, done by Professor Johnston at Berkeley, suggests a 50–90 per cent reduction in ozone and a correspondingly very large increase in the amount of ultra-violet light reaching the surface of the earth.

* As an addendum to the above keynote paper and to complete the background for the continuing discussion, it is considered desirable to publish the following excerpt from the recorded script of Professor Bryson's verbal presentation.—Ed.

It is not at all clear what the appropriate rate coefficients for these reactions are—the experimental work has not been done. Nor do we know the ambient levels of nitrogen oxides at an altitude of 20 kilometres in the atmosphere. This could obviously be resolved very, very rapidly, and it would seem to me that one of the first priorities of atmospheric science should be to establish whether or not Johnston's results are indeed valid, because if a full fleet of supersonic transports can reduce the amount of ozone by 50 per cent, then we must say that we should not operate that type of engine at those altitudes in the atmosphere even for military purposes (and they are flying there now). So I would strongly suggest that one of our recommendations from this Conference should be to resolve, by an immediate crash research programme, whether or not these results are correct. They may not be correct, *but they still might be*, and surely we ought to know!

There is another possibility of a short-term effect on the atmosphere. The natural production of methane on earth is about 10^9 metric tons per year. A few years ago that figure was approximately doubled. It is said that the oil companies in the Near East put out the flames of the gas exhausts from their wells because the people of the area apparently had been saying: 'You are burning our resources and wasting them.' They could see these big flames, so the oil companies simply put them out. Now one can't see that they are wasting the resources, but the amount of methane thus added to the atmosphere is of the same order of magnitude as the total natural production in marshes, etc. There is a very good chance that the increase in the total amount of water vapour as one goes upwards above the tropopause is due to the diffusion of methane through the tropopause, and then its oxidation, in sunlight, to yield water and carbon dioxide. Now doubling the methane might then double the water vapour production, and as the water vapour in the high atmosphere does have an effect upon the production of ozone, this would appear to be another priority item for study and resolution.

There are some longer-term changes, too. I have heard a number of environmentalists express concern about the oxygen supply—if we destroy our plants we will destroy our oxygen supply to the atmosphere. This is, of course, true. It is equally true that you can destroy the nitrogen in the atmosphere, because both molecular oxygen and molecular nitrogen are in the atmosphere as a result of life. The denitrifying Bacteria are very important— that's why we have nitrogen instead of nitrogen oxides in the atmosphere. But this appears to be a non-problem. There seems to be an atmospheric homeostasis—a tendency to balance the oxygen amount because it is so non-linear in its reactions—in which a small increase of oxygen increases greatly the oxidation rate and therefore removes some oxygen, and a small decrease greatly increases the amount of energy required for oxidation and therefore tends to stabilize the oxygen amount. Oxygen supply apparently is a non-problem, because long before the amount of oxygen available became reduced significantly we would have been wiped out by other things. If we reduced the world's plant growth enough to destroy the oxygen supply—as this is a long-term process—we would be in such desperate straits that the oxygen supply would not matter to us.

DISCUSSION

Pavanello (Discussion Leader)

We have always been puzzled by these facts of dust and carbon dioxide, and have been following them in the literature through the many, many articles which have appeared in recent years. We have never before been able to find such a clear and penetrating analysis, though, as you yourself admit, and as a good scientist should indeed admit, you used the best data available, pointing out that they were often the only ones, and that you were not by any means always satisfied with them yourself. Your observations are surely of enormous importance for giving the trend towards more studies along the two main lines you have indicated—that is, on the short-term effects of what you have indicated as priority items, and also, even more important, I think, on the long-term effects of climatic changes.

In view of the time and our likely need for long discussion, I think we should try to be brief but remember Professor Polunin's suggestion of adjourning to the evening if necessary. We should also recall his comments as a biologist on ozone.

In connection with the ozone problem, Professor Bryson indicated an apparent effect through skin cancer as a result of ultra-violet radiation. He also made some remarks about carbon dioxide, putting this aspect into proper perspective, and indicating that this has caused a variation of perhaps not more than 3 per cent in the average temperature of our planet. We had known for some time that even if all the reserves of fossil fuel which are known to exist in this earth were burnt in one year, it would not cause a great disruption in the climate of the earth.

The effects of vapour trails are very interesting, as we started to note yesterday in connection with SSTs. Water vapour, just like carbon dioxide, can absorb the outgoing infra-red radiation. But it can also block the incoming solar radiation, and it has been calculated that a rise in the amount of stratospheric water vapour from 2 to 6 parts per million would increase the earth's average surface temperature by about 0.5°C. I don't know if we should trust this figure but I put it as a question to Professor Bryson and ask if he has any better information. What is important, however, is that, below the stratosphere, water vapour disappears rather quickly whereas above in the stratosphere the average residence time of water vapour has been thought to be about 18 months, because it mixes very very slowly with the lower atmosphere. At the present time the commercial jets fly mostly below the stratosphere but the SSTs are meant to fly much higher, and it has been calculated that if the water vapour stays in the atmosphere for an average of 18 months, and that we have something like 500 supersonic transports operating over the Atlantic and over the Pacific, they could increase the water vapour content of the stratosphere by about 0.2 parts per million.

As regards the 'heat island' effects of a city, as Professor Bryson points out, the mean annual temperature excess of the city over near-by rural areas is often about 1–2°C or sometimes more. This is just through the heat generated in the city. But in addition to the difference in temperature, cities are frequently covered by clouds, and the frequency of fog in winter can be twice that in surrounding rural areas. You might be interested in the following details which give some idea of the sort of climatic changes produced by cities as compared with near-by rural areas. Not only is the annual mean temperature often 1–2°C higher in cities than in surrounding areas, but cloudiness is 5–10 per cent more, the fog in winter in the temperate zone may be 100 per cent more and that in summer 30 per cent more, the precipitation may be 5–10 per cent more, while annual mean wind-speed is 20–30 per cent less. Wind-speed has great importance particularly in dispersion of locally-generated, down-to-earth pollutants, and this reduction starts the reverse cycle: less speed means more accumulation of pollutants, more accumulation of pollutants means more retention of heat, and so on.

Professor Bryson's main concern here has been with world-wide climatic modification, but whereas we in the World Health Organization are, of course, interested in these matters, we are more concerned with what happens much lower—not so much with happenings in the stratosphere at 30,000 metres but for ourselves at 1.50 metres, which is about the height of our noses. We're concerned with the air which people breathe every day in the city, and this I would classify as an immediate or short-term effect. We do know that there is a wide variety of pollutants emitted today in the cities. We have heard much about sulphur dioxide and particulate matters such as soot, though there is still disagreement among scientists as to the real effects on health of low concentrations of each of these types of pollutants. But there is no doubt that any effects on health would be enhanced by the simultaneous presence of sulphur dioxide and particulates in the air. Besides these there are, as you know, many other pollutants—depending on the industrial and transport, etc., activities going on, whether in the town or in surrounding areas. We are much concerned with these problems and the health effects of this form of pollution which we call urban pollution.

Yesterday Dr Davies and some other speakers here mentioned the WHO monitoring programme. We're using the same words, but the monitoring we do is of a different kind: it is global in the sense that we're doing it in many parts of the globe, but nevertheless it is chiefly of local significance. We are not trying to detect global patterns but to see similarities of problems in different urban areas—particularly in large cities, which have more or less the same degree of development or industrialization, but which can hardly afford, especially in the developing countries, to undertake all the very expensive and elaborate research that is needed to ascertain what the effects of these pollutants are on their people. So by using parameters which are simple indicators, such as SO_2 and particulate matter, we try to find out where the problems of urban air pollution lie, and to alert the government where these problems are becoming so serious that something has to be done. We do find that air pollution in cities such as Taipei, for instance, or Bombay, is much worse than in Chicago or in Milan, which are among the most polluted places in North America and Europe, respectively.

There have been health effects detectable from famous episodes of air pollution—for example in London and New York—and we do know that certain effects occur when the concentration of pollutants goes beyond certain limits. So what can we expect, as health effects, in towns in developing countries where human beings are already under stress from many other things—including communicable diseases, malnutrition, and low standards of living? We are certainly not trying to force governments to do anything, but just putting the data in their hands, whereupon it is up to them, of course, to set up priorities towards any action. Certainly if they had to cope with an epidemic of cholera they would not worry about pollution—cholera is far more dangerous, and the same goes for smallpox. But they should know—and this is the important thing—that our monitoring is really directed at detecting these problems where they are and then, of course, at ascertaining the trend, because this is also important. Many of those countries are unable to do anything at all now, and we want to know whether, if nothing is done, the problem remains where it is—whether the concentrations stay or grow worse, or do new pollutants come into the picture and make the situation still more dangerous?

Hdač

I'm no meteorologist but a botanist; however, as a botanist I can corroborate some of these facts. I've seen in Iraq such fenced areas in the so-called desert, and in the time-space of two or three years there developed plenty of grass and plenty of very nice flowers in them. So it seems that originally the area was not at all a desert but maybe a semi-desert or even steppe. It was caused, of course, by overgrazing by sheep and other animals, and when comparing all the data about vegetation in Iraq it is quite interesting to see the correlation between tribal wars and peace in this region. During peace-time, people could go with their sheep to the desert and the vegetation ceased to exist. During the tribal wars the vegetation could, step by step, cover the desert. So there, without any experiment, you can corroborate these results.

A similar situation can be observed in Iceland: when the first settlers came there a thousand years ago it was said that the forests reached from the coast to the mountains. Perhaps this is exaggeration but there was thick vegetation. Now, after a thousand years, much of the ground is covered by stony desert with only islands of higher vegetation. So it is not only in the southern regions but also in the subarctic regions that we have desertic areas which might be caused by overgrazing. Talking about Iceland, I think you could find interesting data about volcanic dust in the atmosphere from the so-called tephra layers in loess deposits that have been studied by S. Thorárinsson and which I believe go back for about a thousand years.

Laird

We've all heard of the ozone depletion dangers that may or may not be associated with supersonic transport fleets. However, for years past certain military aircraft have been operating and indulging in what might be generously thought of as a form of research at great altitudes. Clearly the results of such operations are sometimes placed in the burn-without-reading category. I assume that there is, however, an accumulation of knowledge of various kinds relating to these military activities. Several countries are, of course, involved. Totalling up all their past and present SST operations, and adding to these the massive introductions of contaminants to the upper atmosphere due to rockets (which, of course, have been launched in earnest since late in World War II), one wonders whether we might not perhaps already have experience of something approaching the equivalent of the SST fleets that we read about as being likely in the immediate future.

I would be very interested in learning from Professor Bryson whether in his view the analysis of such already-existing information has perhaps engendered an air of confidence in high places that SSTs on the scale now envisaged are *not* really very likely to trigger major ozone depletion?

Bryson

Being an American, I do not share your view that an air of confidence in high places is very meaningful. In particular, the question that you raised as to whether or not the high-altitude military flights provide us with this information is a question that I have raised also. I have tried for several years to get information from the US Air Force by direct and indirect methods, but have been able to glean so very little by these various methods that one can reach no conclusion from it. However, at the height of the argument over whether there should be an SST built with the subsidy of the United States government (the argument that Mr Udall referred to yesterday), I did speak out to the point where those in support of supersonic transport started calling me—and one of those who called me was the man who presumably knew the most about the high-altitude SST flights of the Air Force—to tell me that their experience indicated there was no problem. I said, 'What data do you have?' 'Well, we have flown there quite a bit', he said. 'What did you write down?' I asked. 'Well, nothing', he said, 'but we didn't seem to have any problems!' 'Where are your data?' I asked. 'Well, we have no data but we have a lot of experience and so we are confident that there will be no effect.'

My confidence in his confidence is nil. If one makes a calculation of the amount of water vapour produced by rockets and by the military aircraft that have been operating in the stratosphere, it is really quite small compared with what would be produced by a fleet of 500 SST's. Let me give you some idea of the fuel consumption. The oil companies have been telling us, through their advertisements which try to convince us, (*a*) that we ought to build a trans-Alaska pipeline, and (*b*) what a wonderful job they're doing environmentally. (Again I have no confidence.)

Oil companies told us recently two 'facts': (1) that there is enough oil on the North Slope of Alaska to last the United States a whole year (!), and (2) that there's enough oil there to last the SST fleet three years. Now does this mean that the SST fleet will use as much in three years as the entire United States uses in one year? For every pound of fuel that SSTs burn you get about 1.3 pounds of water vapour. That is an enormous amount compared with the rather minute amounts (by comparison) that you are producing by the existing flights.

Pavanello (Discussion Leader)

Thank you, Professor Bryson. I can only confirm what you say about the availability of information. I've tried myself desperately in various connections—such as the effects of the supersonic bang—to get some information from the military, from the Oklahoma City Study, and even from the private company flying the Concorde—but with the same experience that you have had.

Goldman

I was very much impressed with Professor Bryson's really exciting paper, but would like to remark on a few things as an economist. First of all, I think it is important, especially after yesterday's discussion, to recognize that it's not just industrialized societies which are capable of affecting our environment, though we often tend to miss this point. As our colleague from Czechoslovakia pointed out, there were civilizations in the Near East which at one time flourished but brought upon themselves a considerable amount of self-destruction without the advent of the industrial revolution. I think the fact that the dust over Chicago is about one-fourth of that over the Indian desert again is significant. Thus the dust over this wider region may be more harmful than the dust over the smaller area of a city, and presumably the total effect of many small farmers, each acting in his own small but destructive way, will cause more devastation than that which can come from an industrialized society.

An important thing, I think, is not to blame everything on the over-developed economies that we sometimes talk about. Certainly they bear a very great share—perhaps the greater share—but they are not solely to blame. Similarly, yesterday, some of the biologists tended to blame everything on the economists. Well, as an economist I'm prepared to shoulder more than my share. But don't forget that it was the biologists and other scientists, not the economists, who developed and used DDT; it was the physicists, not the economists, who developed the atomic bomb; and it was the chemists, not the economists, who developed so many chemical components which we now have. So one of the things I think it is important to recognize in discussions of this kind is that we're all in this together, and it really does nobody any good to say, for instance, that 'The economist comes along to underdeveloped countries and foists economic development on to them.' I don't think it is done that way, and in any case it certainly is not the fault only of the economists. The biologists and other scientists also have a share in what has been going wrong.

As for the paper itself, I was very excited by it and by Professor Bryson's presentation. But there is a problem concerning it where I think he is right, though perhaps for the wrong reason, and this has to do with the dust over the Caucasus. Maybe the Russians who are here will say something about it themselves. The dust figures which Professor Bryson has in his chart indicate that the amount began to increase greatly in 1929. The 1929 period is the beginning of the first Five Year Plan—the big push of industrialization in the Soviet Union. It also happens that in 1929 or 1930 the level of the Caspian Sea began to fall—again, this is associated with the rapid development of economic resources in the Soviet Union. Now, the dust-fall and the fall of the Caspian Sea may well indicate industrialization in the Soviet Union itself, and therefore prove what Professor Bryson is trying to demonstrate for that immediate area. But considering the world as a whole, I'm a little concerned that this may not be the best indicator, though he acknowledges this in referring only to small dust-falls as opposed to larger ones. Finally, if you look at the figures for 1939–45, which was the period of World War II, you will see that the dust-fall declines, or in other words there was apparently less dust in the atmosphere. The same thing happened with the Caspian Sea—it stopped falling in this period or soon after its beginning, so that the particular region with which we are concerned reflects what was going on in the Ukraine and in the Caucasus. In World War II the Germans in effect stopped industrial activity in this portion of the world. Your indicators reflect that local effect and not, it seems to me, the industrialization which was going on at a great pace in the world as a whole during World War II.

Bryson

I excluded from the slides which I showed you before, plottings of the capital input to the Russian economy and the dust-fall of large particles in the Caucasus (and, therefore, local dust). The two are quite parallel. What Professor Goldman says is absolutely true and corroborated by the data. However, the pattern is different if one only looks at the very small particles that are carried long distances and do not settle out rapidly. This fraction does not show an increase in 1929, but gives a more global view—and I get better results with my own analysis.

Baroda

I have some very brief questions. We have talked since yesterday about air pollution through SSTs and dust. But this most illuminating paper, which I have gone through carefully, does not, I see, make any mention of possible air pollution due to nuclear tests, and we've heard much of this radioactive fallout. Is it because it falls down and doesn't remain in the air? However, some time ago and even nowadays occasionally, we read in the newspapers that if we shoot duck we shouldn't eat them—we should be careful because they might be radioactive, and so on. I wonder if Professor Bryson could educate me, particularly on whether this is a threat. We've also heard about nuclear tests having an effect on weather, and I would like to ask whether there are any data now available indicating that weather has been affected as a result of nuclear tests?

My remaining question concerns the dust in India. I have suffered from it as a photographer and as a naturalist, and what Professor Bryson said has shaken me considerably. Now this is all true—we can see it there, we can feel it, and in fact occasionally I almost have to use a knife to walk through the streets—but what is the solution? As an Indian interested in my country and the world generally, I would like to know if there is a solution.

Bryson

Atomic bombs? We like to think of man as being a powerful creature, but compared with an ordinary thunderstorm an atomic bomb is rather weak, while the kind of rain that is occurring over Scandinavia today is the equivalent of perhaps 200 atomic bombs an hour. So power-wise, atomic bombs just aren't very important. They don't put that much energy into the atmosphere. They are also scarce enough, fortunately, to make the amount of dust which they put into the atmosphere quite minute when compared with the quantities we're talking about. From the standpoint of radioactivity, the results of atomic bombs are known to be dangerous—all of us know that. But I would like to point out one thing here with regard to radioactive material in the atmosphere which is related to the question of atomic energy, and it is that a coal-fired electric generating plant releases radio-activity into the environment, much as does a well-built nuclear-powered plant. The ash from a coal-fired plant is 'hot' radioactively.

As for doing something about the dust situation in India, I would like to talk with the Maharaja about this because I have been trying to get Indian government officials interested but without apparent success.

Pavanello (Discussion Leader)

Let me disagree a moment with Professor Bryson. I'm fully aware of the radioactivity which is emitted by fossil fuels, but we shouldn't forget about the liquid wastes. You are presumably speaking here merely of what comes out of the stack.

Bryson

Yes, the environment of the factory.

Polunin

Mr Chairman, as our time is now up if we are to have our coffee break and start the next session promptly as is so desirable, yet there are several other participants wishing to speak, I would like to suggest adjournment of this session to 1900 hours. [This was carried *nemine contradicente*.]

RESUMED DISCUSSION

[in a smaller hall making direct dialogue possible]

Bryson

Again I would like to add some comments about man-made modifications of the climate which I didn't consider this morning—to get the discussion going. Somebody mentioned condensation trails and the difficulty of finding some data indicating how much cloud is actually made by jet aircraft. For, in reality, such condensation is a cloud, and at times you can see the condensation trails of aircraft spreading—practically covering the entire sky and making it overcast by clouds. The figures are very difficult to get; however, there is one place where we do have some hard data on the amount of cloud produced by jet aircraft, and it happens to be Iowa City, Iowa. A young astronomer there was trying to make observations on the solar spectrum and was always running into trouble with these jet trails, so he started to record the losses of solar radiation due to jet aircraft which were actually observed there and measured. In Iowa City the condensation trails are the equivalent of twenty overcast days per year. This is significant when you consider that the total number of overcast days per year in the vicinity is only 120 or something like that—to which should now be added another 20 due to condensation trails.

Having got this information, here is something that I came across inadvertently. A marine biologist in Scotland wrote to me saying that he had observed a later-than-normal 'blooming' of the diatoms and reduced numbers of zoophytes in certain parts of the North Atlantic, and did I have any information on changes in ocean currents.

Well, I didn't; but just for exploration I wrote back and asked whether it was possible that where he found this delayed spring bloom of diatoms lay under the trans-Atlantic jet route and not in other places, which would be suggestive that the additional shadows cast by the jet trails was the explanation. Those of you who cross the North Atlantic may know that you can usually look out and see one aircraft every six minutes, and consequently it seems possible that their condensation trails may so reduce the intensity of sunlight, and therefore the penetration of light sufficient for photosynthesis, that we have this effect of reducing planktonic life and perhaps a slowing of the warming of the North Atlantic. And the answer came back, 'Yes, that is possible.'

By the meteorological officers at Bracknell, in England, I have been told that they frequently notice times when they get cirrus clouds drifting over England that are quite obviously derived from jet trails, and this, of course, can only have been for the last 20 or so years—during the jet era. So this is something to think about and consider when we are talking about environmental matters: here are the data, here is the prediction, but what are the facts?

Butler

I would like to ask you a question about your paper this morning; you hinted, I think, that a greater source of dust in Asia was from mainland China rather than from India. Is this actually the case?

Bryson

It doesn't seem to cross the Himalayas very much.

Butler

But you indicated that there was a great deal of dust.

Bryson

There is a great deal of dust. There has been for quite 3 to 4 million years. Thus the Pleistocene sediments in the North Pacific are clearly formed from Chinese dust in large part; indeed, the silica in Hawaiian soils has been identified as airborne silica from Asia, rather than of local Hawaiian origin. So there is a lot of dust transported. The important thing is the suggestion— there are not enough real observations—from Hong Kong that the dust coming over China is increasing, which is hardly surprising!

Butler

It's pretty hard to get aerial observations on that, isn't it?

Bryson

Yes, as a matter of fact, within two minutes after I took that picture I showed you there was a MIG 17 coming up.

Seidenfaden

Our political need is to get the underdeveloped countries interested in pollution problems in general, and here is one question that is typically a question related to the less developed countries: therefore, I would like to see such people as you speakers consider the matter of how we can formulate a resolution in this field? Indeed I think we might be able, on the basis of this discussion, to think of two resolutions: one about the SSTs and the ozone problem, the other about the dust in the atmosphere. I would like you to consider what form and content we could employ to give force to our input to the Stockholm Conference in this field.

One thing more I would like to say is about dust. Professor Bryson has his experience of the Indian dust and the goats. But in my opinion it is geographically a much wider problem, as he has indeed already indicated. I have, as a sideline, worked for the last ten years on the frontier between Burma and Thailand, and I have gone by helicopter over those mountain areas. The frightful problem in these countries is the deforestation that has taken place, and it is even more dangerous than that in India where it might be possible to find a solution for the dust problem. Our Indian friends may tell us that there are difficulties in getting remedies started, but after all there is top-soil still there—some of it has gone up as dust but most of it is still there. But with deforestation, in the mountainous monsoon areas, the top-soil is washed away when the forest is burnt, and this creates a permanent desert in the mountains, so therefore the problem is much larger, and if we try to formulate resolutions my private idea is that we should not only speak about your Indian problem but speak of deforestation generally as a problem with very serious consequences for the less developed countries.

Bryson

I couldn't agree more. It is in the underdeveloped countries, I think, that the problem exists most forcibly, because they are so vulnerable in the matter of food supply, and I am concerned with the stability of climates because we can do without one more variable; if things could be just a little more stable, the outlook would be less unpromising.

If we examine the number of people in the whole scientific community who are working on such questions as 'What is the amount of dust suspended in the air?', 'What is its source?', and 'What are its characteristics?', we could probably name them all on fewer than ten fingers. They are so very few that I feel there is a question of reordering our priorities here, which is the point I have been trying to make with Dr Davies—that when we look at the list of things to be monitored and hope that some day they can all be studied, this just offends my sense of priority, because I think there are some pieces of research that should be tackled immediately by far larger numbers than have yet been employed on them. For example, considering the Indian desert question which I told you about this morning: how many people are working on this—perhaps two or three? But it's too important to be left to two or three people; and there ought to be some really brilliant meteorologists, instrumentationists, and so on, working on the wider problems of world-wide climates. Yet I can name the very few persons who are concerned with this particular question of atmospheric dusts: Davitaya in Russia, Mitchell and myself in the United States, and Lamb in England. Surely it is too important to be left just to us, and there is a real question of priorities here—of what to observe and what to monitor for future study.

Should we monitor the things that feed the big computers? I have a sneaking suspicion that it is mostly for the care and feeding of big computers that what goes on now is designed. Or should we monitor the things that have a direct impact upon the welfare of man? Surely it's the latter we should be doing, rather than more of the same of what we have been doing for the last twenty years. Now this is heresy among meteorologists, but I think we should really look at our priorities very carefully.

Nyberg

Yes, but if you will allow me, I think that the monitoring system which we now have has been established wholly for the purposes which have already been explained. But if you come up with a new purpose, well, things might be added to the problems that we already have, while there is no reason to stop the observations which we make for very good reasons. I could give you examples of the value of the activities of the meteorological service.

Bryson

I can undoubtedly add to your list.

Nyberg

I agree they are very important, and that is why I am opposed to your formulation of this; it is not a mistake, it is not a question of priorities, it is something which is now coming in because it has not been observed before as a problem.

Personally, I would like to be quite clear as to the effect of the dust. If you told me that, at these latitudes here, dust in the air will lead to a cooling of the atmosphere, I would agree with you; but there may be a different effect of dust in air over the latitudes of India. Are you sure about the effect; will it be a cooling or will it be a heating of the upper atmosphere? I think this is a question which is not yet settled, and I should like to say also that we have some activities going on to simulate what is happening in the atmosphere. It is very difficult to come to a clear picture; if it were not, we would certainly have done it some time ago. In the case of the dust over India and some other regions, I think this may be more complicated than it at first appears, and I would be grateful for your very open reply.

Bryson

I agree with you that this matter is too important to leave to just a couple of people working on it. It is too important to leave to my one paper to examine, but should be looked at carefully by someone else. And I agree with you one hundred per cent that it is a very complicated thing. But am I right or am I wrong? If there is any chance that I am right, then we ought to know; but it's too important just to take my word as I presented it to you, and, of course, that was not the complete picture either.

Panikkar

I would like to comment on the subject of the dust in Rajasthan, and seek guidance here on how we may handle it from the point of view of climate. We have work going on in the desert from various angles, one of which, as you may know, is the problem of forestation in the Rajasthan area to prevent the marching of the desert all the way to Delhi. Another problem is the effect of dust on the climate of the desert; we say that the Delhi climate is determined by the amount of dust in Rajasthan and the amount of snow in Kashmir.

Seidenfaden

Speaking again as a practical man, I understand that you would first of all have to have some more monitoring time—you will need to know more about these matters.

Butler

The committee that is preparing the monitoring aspects for the UN Conference will be meeting in Geneva this coming August 16 to 20 and I know that in the monitoring group in Canada they are preparing a position paper and studying the problem before going to Geneva. On our list of reasons for doing monitoring we have the study of climatic trends, and this dust study is a good example of what that topic meant in our priority list. Now that I have a good example, this subject will be included in the discussion of the working group on monitoring.

Wurster

Perhaps as a partial answer to the problem of this morning and where to begin, the data would suggest that at least a beginning might be made by eating some of the goats!

Goldman

I would like to follow that up: it may not be just simply eating the goats, but I would approach it in the same way as an economist should approach the question of industrial pollution in a developed society. I would begin to diminish the goat population just as I would begin to diminish the production of paper pulp by the sulphite method, by imposing a tax on the goats and trying to switch the dominant form of livestock to some other form of milk supply. But I think the important thing is to start switching the production means, and one of the ways of doing this would be gradually to impose a tax on goats or on livestock more generally.

Bryson

If I may differ from you, you are talking about something that doesn't work in underdeveloped countries—imposing a tax on people who are already hungry and poor is not the way to do it. I think there are ways to do it, but they would require a change in land-tenure patterns—a change in the mode of handling the areas. It may not be that there are too many goats; it may be that they are handled wrongly. For example, in Wisconsin the farmers have started, even though they have plenty of grass, to pen-feed their cattle because they find that they get more grass, more milk, and more meat, by putting the cattle in pens, cutting the hay, and taking it to them. It may very well be that all they need to do in India is to pen-feed the goats and not reduce the goat population at all—in which case they might well get more grass, more milk, and more meat too. I think it is more complicated than just saying, 'Let's put a tax on them'—scarcely an economic approach with people who can't pay taxes. Nor can they do without their animals without starving. Yet it has got to be a simple and cheap solution, and I would like to see working on this problem some experts on range management, and others on the social structure and on land tenure. I think what we need at the international level is true interdisciplinary work, rather than to leave the science to the scientists and the social stuff to the social people: put them together and find a solution. Perhaps what we really need to do is to restructure some of our UN units so that people of diverse backgrounds can apply their expertise to common problems that require an interdisciplinary and practical solution.

Holopainen

In order to deal properly with possibilities of global atmospheric pollution and their climatic effects, we obviously have to know and understand the behaviour of the atmosphere fairly well. The question is, do we at present understand the atmosphere well enough for this purpose? One measure of our knowledge concerning the behaviour of a physical system is our ability to formulate a model which successfully simulates the system. This is something everybody would agree to. With regard to the atmosphere, we have at present numerical models which simulate fairly well the behaviour of the atmosphere in the time-range of from one to three days, though there is room for improvement as we know from the frequent failure of forecasts. Yet I think we are on a very good road in this respect, as we carry on the modelling of the atmosphere.

The climatological events in the atmosphere enveloping the earth are, as you know, so complex, and involve so many feedback mechanisms, that they cannot be easily studied by any simple means. The very same computers which have provided tools for solving physically realistic models for short-range forecasting appear also to be indispensable here. Previously, questions such as the effect on the air circulation and the world climate of melting arctic ice or the irrigation of vast desert areas, could only be speculated upon;

also, the question of the effects of the man-made increase in carbon dioxide has so far been tentatively studied only by assuming that all other factors which are important for the earth's temperature remain constant. A rational basis for attempts to answer these questions in their very complexity is, or will be, provided by numerical simulation experiments on large computers based on the relevant physical laws—not merely on one of them. The experiments so far performed on the simulation of the present climate have been very encouraging, and the results really give us some confidence that the meteorological problems of climatic change which we are confronted with can be solved.

Development of numerical general circulation models which successfully simulate the present climate and the behaviour of the atmosphere in long time-scales is a natural first step in attempts to predict what happens to the atmosphere as a result of man's activities. Development of these models is the ultimate goal of the Global Atmospheric Research Programme, which is a joint research effort of ICSU and WMO. I think the fundamental importance of developing these numerical models should also be recognized and stressed here. It was one of the most strongly emphasized matters in the MIT meeting last year.

Concerning Professor Bryson's presentations, I would like to say that of course there is, apart from these large-scale complicated numerical simulation models, a need also for simplified models, such as the one he offered. But I would agree with Dr Nyberg's comments that these simplified models imply many assumptions and hypotheses, and the results depend on how good these are. I would like to make two specific points: Professor Bryson's first conclusion was that there is no large cause of climatic change which has been overlooked, such as internal feedback within the earth's atmospheric system, etc. But does not his model implicitly involve the feedback mechanism between the atmosphere and the ocean, as he speaks about a 'thermal mass of the atmosphere' and takes a response-time of ten years? So I wonder where he got that? And if you take a number from his Figure 6 for the air temperature at the earth's surface. and then you consider the thermal mass temperature there, the difference is quite large, and implies that heat is somehow put into the ocean.

Polunin

There was talk yesterday and this morning about the SST ozone matter which, as a biologist, I would like to hear continued by the meteorologists and others who should really know about these things. But only after, if you will permit me, reading from a letter I have just received this afternoon from Professor Harold S. Johnston, who has been referred to as perhaps *the*, or certainly *a*, leading specialist in this field.

Here I should hark back to my mention yesterday of hearing recently from Professor George C. Pimentel, an old correspondent and former contributor to my journal, *Biological Conservation*, that we really ought to invite Professor Johnston, 'to talk about the probable effect of commercial supersonic transport planes (SSTs) on the ozone layer. There is a very dangerous likelihood that these planes will threaten continued existence of life on this planet, plant and animal, by seriously depleting the ozone layer. Needless to say, this should be aired at an international forum, since it affects all of us and there are four major countries who must be dissuaded from using these planes.' Both Professor Pimentel and Professor Johnston are scientists of high repute, being *inter alia* members of the US National Academy of Sciences which is perhaps the most select body of its kind in the world, and immediately I heard from the former I wrote to the latter—I ought to have telephoned, and did so later—who replied with the long letter which I have just received and from which I would like to quote the following passages:

'I have written three reports on this subject: (1) a fairly lengthy, qualitative, preliminary paper was written primarily for US governmental scientists and agencies concerned with the SST; (2) simultaneously I was working on a brief technical article for *Science*; and (3) a long technical report, including the quantitative aspects of (1) and supplementary details in support of (2). The first report was 'leaked' to the press by some person unknown to me. I regret this premature publicity, because the case should be presented first to the scientific community for evaluation, modification, and correction. The second report has been accepted for publication by *Science*, and it will be published within a very few weeks.* The third report (over 100 pages in length)* is being issued by the Lawrence Radiation Laboratory, University of California at Berkeley, for release at the same time as publication of the *Science* article. Copies of the third report are available to interested parties upon request.

'Since the newspapers discovered the first report, I have noticed two extremes of response. Some people feel that the report is irresponsible and without scientific basis and that it is ridiculous to imagine that the SST could have any effect on the environment of the earth. Other people feel that I have proven that the SST would destroy most plants and animals of the earth. In view of the manner in which my arguments have appeared, I cannot blame anyone who embraces either of these extreme views. However, I do not want to make any announcements, defenses, or other response, until the two scientific articles are published. I can tell you that the scientific articles do not fall into either extreme indicated above. On the basis of detailed considerations, I point out that the oxides of nitrogen are a very important variable in this problem, and that they have been either overlooked or incorrectly discounted by SST planners. Ozone is very strongly reduced by NO and NO_2; but there are many technical questions, as, for example, how fast are NO and NO_2 converted to nitric acid in the stratosphere?

'As you are a biologist, I want to propose a question and perhaps a line of research. I think it is clear that if stratospheric ozone were reduced almost to zero (a most unlikely prospect), then the radiation between 240 and 300 nm would destroy most living things on the surface of the earth. However, what would be the biological effects of reducing the world-average ozone from 100 per cent to 98 per cent, to 95 per cent, to 90 per cent, to 75 per cent, to 50 per cent, to 33 per cent? The absorption spectrum of ozone is such that these reductions of ozone would greatly increase the radiation between 280 and 300 nm at the earth's surface. However, we need quantitative statements from biologists to establish the relation between the amount of ozone in the stratosphere and the biological effects to be expected.

'The timing is such that my articles will appear in a few weeks, and the articles are sure to receive a strong rebuttal during the next year. There is not time to get

* *See* the end of this section (pp. 176 and 177) for full citations of both these papers—Ed.

this subject on the agenda of your meeting. If you think it desirable to do so at your meeting, you could mention to those who are interested that there will be new material and perhaps a vigorous debate concerning NOx and the SSTs during the coming year. Those who are interested in this subject may want to watch for the article in *Science*.'

Before hearing from Professor Johnston I had telephoned him in California and heard some further details and formulae which he undertook to put in another paper and send to me for our (extended) proceedings. [This paper is published at the end of the present section, on pp. 175–7.] So I will not detain you now with the details which he gave me. But if you will allow me I would like, before giving over to those of you who know far more about these things, to spend about two minutes explaining why, as a mere biologist, I feel so strongly on this matter. The scientific reason is that it has long been my full understanding—I was for years almost the closest neighbour of Dr G. M. B. Dobson on Shotover Hill near Oxford—that it is the ozone layer which makes life on earth possible, so that anything which could conceivably weaken that all-important shield against lethal solar radiation is surely to be countered at all costs.

A seemingly supernatural reason is an extraordinarily vivid dream which I had only some weeks ago but *before hearing* of this possible threat to the ozone layer. I dreamt that I was standing alone on the dome of a hill and saw a dark blotch perhaps fifteen degrees above the horizon—seemingly at a great distance but still far above the horizon—which gradually but visibly extended as I watched. It was not really black but a horrible murky tinge that extended more and more widely—especially to the sides—while getting darker in the centre. It seemed far enough away to have been stratospheric, but anyway was horrible, murky, and ever-spreading, with the centre now getting quite black. I looked behind me and saw to my further amazement that the entire sky was criss-crossed by an unprecedented number of maybe hundreds of condensation trails of large jet aircraft. This was not so remarkable for me as I live near an international airport and have counted up to twelve contrails at a time in a few observations made over our countryside outside Geneva. But these ones were extraordinarily numerous and blackish, fluffy, and petering or sizzling out at the narrow ends where in several cases the aircraft could be seen falling from the sky. The dream ended and I awoke, but unable to forget it. My chemistry being limited and largely forgotten, all I could think of was that nitrogen dioxide was brown and that there might have developed a sudden catalysis of atmospheric nitrogen and oxygen to form it, with a concomitant chain-reaction leading to rapid use-up of all the free oxygen. I told only my wife and a very few friends about this dream, knowing how matters can get exaggerated; and then I heard about the possible threats posed by the SSTs. But as there have been examples in my family of unexplained predictions coming true and of things being 'felt' over vast distances, I think you will understand why I feel so strongly with Stewart Udall and some others that, even if there is only an infinitesimally small possibility of Professor Johnston's suggestions proving to have serious foundation, all SST aircraft should be grounded until the full truth is known about their various possible effects, which Professor Bryson assures us should not take many months to determine in the case of what now seems most worrying.†

Bryson

In the careful look which we had in the National Academy of Sciences a few weeks back at Johnston's paper, outside factors were considered as he had performed the great service of pointing out that there are other possible reactions with regard to ozone—other, that is, than the catalysis by water vapour as had been suggested earlier. The MIT summer study people said that nitrogen oxides produced by SSTs were not a problem. Johnston's real contribution up to this point was to prove that you cannot say it's not a problem. He had identified several reactions that are catalysed by nitrogen oxides and had calculated some of the rates at which his catalytic destruction can occur. This paper has now been discussed and studied for about two months by top-class atmospheric chemists and they have identified something like forty-eight other reactions that can involve ozone and nitrogen oxides. There are many ways in which nitrogen oxides catalyse the destruction of ozone. Now, the result of this discussion was to say there is an urgent need for us to know more about the reaction rates and coefficients of these various catalytic reactions, because they are not well known and many of them are not known at all.

It is also important for us to know whether there are large quantities of nitrogen oxides in the stratosphere at the ozone levels now, because if there are large quantities of nitrogen oxides at the ozone levels now, and there is still ozone, it would be fairly clear that the mere presence of nitrogen oxides is not enough to destroy the ozone. This is the kind of question we could answer within a couple of months by simply going there and seeing if there are nitrogen oxides in any quantity. We have the instrumentation, capability, and aircraft, and it can be done; so I think the recommendation should be to do it post-haste.

As regard the ozone, we need much more sophisticated calculations than have yet been made of the rates of movement and general dynamics of the ozone system in the stratosphere. But as in the opinion of experts who have examined this matter and I have talked with, there is a chance that Johnston could be absolutely right, then there must be no delay in finding out whether or not these reactions are significant. And I think we should also say that as there is apparently a chance that this analysis is correct, we should be very reluctant to do any flying in the ozone layers with engines that produce nitrogen oxides until we find out what the values are; nor need it take too long.

Vallentyne

I think it would be intolerable if at the United Nations sessions on environmental questions they came up with such unsettled problems, perhaps even without any possibility of getting an informed opinion. The general impression I get, at least from the things I hear in Canada and the United States, is that there is a scientific input into the UN planning now but that it is

† *See* footnote on page 173.—Ed.

likely to get so reduced that by the time of the actual sessions it may have become rather negligible. I think it would be a very serious situation if the political components found themselves there without a scientific body whom they could go to and get answers to such questions from. They must, I think, have such a body and be prepared to accept what that body says, and I'm just wondering whether this sort of thing has been identified in the planning —it would be very embarrassing if it hadn't.

Pavenello (Discussion Leader)

I think we have been aware of the problem all the time but haven't got anywhere in answering your question.

Seidenfaden

No, but I think we should discuss it more, because this is what we all have to think of: what is the practical significance of this gathering—not only that we have a nice chat together and express ideas, which can be important, but I also see this Conference as some sort of an input to something we are trying to do in the United Nations. For this we are having our third preparatory conference this autumn, and I would like to go with as much material as possible—to which end I would like to see something formulated that we should discuss among ourselves during the coming days.

Kangas

Returning to that dust problem, I understood it is possible afterwards to calculate the past quantity of dust in the atmosphere.

Pavanello (Discussion Leader)

It is possible but it has only been done in two places by one man, from studies of dust in glaciers.

Kangas

A practical step would be to recommend in our resolutions that such investigations be done immediately in very many places, so that results from them could be compared, and then afterwards to have an international monitoring system to include this matter.

Seidenfaden

I wouldn't even go that far: I think what we can do today is simply to ask the Monitoring Committee to take this monitoring of the dust into their system in order to see, for example, whether Professor Bryson is right or wrong. We have to have that material first, and then if we feel there might be something in it we can go further and, as Professor Goldman suggested, get at the Indian Government to do something about the goats. But we cannot be in a position to do that without some more monitoring—that's my own practical solution of where we have to start, and fortunately we are having a Monitoring Committee meeting next month.

Panikkar

May I just add one word about this dust? If we do have such a monitoring system it should extend, as far as India is concerned, to the Arabian Sea. Oceanographers come across enormous quantities of dust practically throughout the northern Arabian Sea area during most months of the year.

* [Footnote to page 151: Although his Fig. 5 suggests 1943 rather than 1945 as the year of temperature maximum, Professor Bryson writes (*in litt.* 4 October 1971) that he is 'unalterably opposed to substituting 1943 for 1945 ... No one can state with certainty that the date was 1943! That implies identification of the highest point of a bompy curve that simply is impossible'.—Ed.]

† [Footnote to page 171: Cf. the Addendum on page 174 contributed by Dr Francis S. Johnson, who had been unable to attend our Conference owing to the concurrent meeting of the United States Committee on Space Research while also Acting President of his University. His survey paper on 'Ozone and SSTs' is in press for *Biological Conservation.*—Ed.]

ADDENDUM

From Dr FRANCIS SEVERIN JOHNSON,
Director, Center for Advanced Studies, University of Texas at Dallas,
Box 30365, Dallas, Texas 75230, USA.

The possibility that exhaust products from a large fleet of supersonic transports (SSTs) may seriously perturb the earth's ozone layer needs intensive examination, because the consequences of a substantial reduction in the layer could be disastrous to life on earth. The important exhaust constituents are water vapour and nitrogen oxides, both of which act to reduce ozone concentrations; nitrogen oxides are especially important as they act as a catalyst for ozone decomposition and hence are not used up in the process. However, much additional information is needed before accurate predictions can be made—especially data on the ambient concentrations of water vapour and nitrogen oxides in the stratosphere, on atmospheric transport processes in the stratosphere, on reaction rates for all the relevant reactions, and on nitrogen oxide concentrations in jet exhausts.

Because of the many uncertainties, predictions of reductions in atmospheric ozone that would be caused by a fleet of SSTs range from a few per cent to a factor of two or even more. The sensitivity of life to ultra-violet radiation that is kept from the earth's surface by ozone is so great that even a few per cent reduction in the ozone must be considered serious. The few measurements that are available do not confirm the predicted effect, as stratospheric water vapour and total ozone have apparently both increased over the past decade, but natural variability may have masked the real effect. Consequently, further study is of crucial importance and urgency.

Catalytic Reduction of Stratospheric Ozone

by

HAROLD SLEDGE JOHNSTON

Professor of Chemistry, University of California,
Berkeley, California 94720, USA.

The photochemistry of ozone in the presence of water vapour and the oxides of nitrogen represents a complicated situation involving scores of elementary chemical reactions. Many of these reactions act to interchange related 'species'* with each other: O and O_3, NO and NO_2, HO and HOO, etc. A relatively small number act to increase or decrease 'odd oxygen'— that is, the interconvertible pair, O and O_3. Under stratospheric conditions of temperature, pressure, and solar irradiation, some of these reactions are much more important than others. In terms of formation and destruction of 'odd oxygen', the dominant reactions are:

A. Creation of 'odd oxygen'
- (1) $O_2 + h\nu$ (below 240 nm) $\rightarrow$ O + O
- (2) $NO_2 + h\nu$ (below 400 nm) $\rightarrow$ NO + O

B. Interconversion of related 'species' of 'odd oxygen'
- (3) $O + O_2 + M \rightarrow O_3 + M$
- (4) $O_3 + h\nu$ (190–350, 450–650 nm) $\rightarrow O_2$ + O

C. Destruction of 'odd oxygen'
- (I) (5) $O + O_3 \rightarrow O_2 + O_2$
- (II) (6) $NO + O_3 \rightarrow NO_2 + O_2$ } catalytic cycle
-       (7) $NO_2 + O \rightarrow NO + O_2$

      net: $O + O_3 \rightarrow O_2 + O_2$

- (III) (8) $HO + O_3 \rightarrow HOO + O_2$ } catalytic cycle
-        (9) $HOO + O \rightarrow HO + O_2$

      net: $O + O_3 \rightarrow O_2 + O_2$

* I.e., similar molecules.—Ed.

The oxides of nitrogen (NO, NO_2) act as a catalytic couple for the destruction of ozone, and the free radicals based on water (HO, HOO) also act as a catalytic couple with the same net chemical reaction. The catalysts are not consumed in this process, and one molecule of NO_x in time can destroy a large number of ozone molecules. The steady-state assumption is quite good for NO_2 and for HOO:

$$d[NO_2]/dt \approx 0, \; d[HOO]/dt \approx 0;$$

and the differential equation for 'odd oxygen' including these steady-state assumptions is:

$$\frac{d([O_3] + [O])}{dt}$$
$$= 2j_1[O_2] - 2k_5[O] [O_3] - 2k_7[O] [NO_2] - 2k_9[O] [HOO]$$

As a first approximation, the rate of formation of ozone and atomic oxygen, $2j_1[O_2]$, is the same, with and without the catalysts NO_2 and HOO. The destruction of 'odd oxygen' (essentially ozone) is $2k_5[O_3] [O]$ in pure dry oxygen, but the destruction rate is increased by the additional amount $2k_9[O] [HOO]$ in the moist stratosphere, and it is further increased by $k_7[O] [NO_2]$ by oxides of nitrogen. The rate constant k_7 is of about the same order of magnitude as k_9; but, according to my estimates, the concentration of NO_2 in the natural stratosphere so greatly exceeds the concentration of HOO that the rate of the catalytic cycle III is negligible compared with the catalytic cycle II. At 220° K, a normal temperature in the lower stratosphere, the rate constant k_7 exceeds the rate constant k_5 by the factor 4,600. Thus if NO_2 is one-tenth of one per cent of ozone, the rate of ozone destruction by NO_2 catalysis is 4.6 times faster than the rate of ozone destruction in the natural oxygen system, and the steady-state concentration of ozone would be reduced by the square root of one plus 4.6, $\sqrt{5.6} = 2.3$. With an increase or decrease of NO_2 about this reference point (0.1 per cent of O_3), the reduction of ozone varies relatively slowly, very nearly as the square root of NO_2 concentration.

For the projected fleets of supersonic transport 'planes, a large portion of the lower stratosphere would be loaded with NO_x(NO and NO_2) in amounts as great as 0.1 per cent of the present ozone concentration. Large reductions of ozone are indicated. The problem is too complicated to be stated simply in terms of fractional reduction of the ozone shield.

The total problem involves many technical considerations: the rate of radiation absorption through the stratosphere and how it is changed by a reduction in ozone, the present distribution of NO_x in the stratosphere, the rate of conversion of NO_x to HNO_3, and the role of turbulent diffusion and large-scale air transport. These problems are considered in the forthcoming report in *Science** and in the supporting document which is being issued from

* Now published as 'Reduction of Stratospheric Ozone by Nitrogen Oxide Catalysts from Supersonic Transport Exhaust'. Harold Johnston in *Science*, **173**, pp. 517–22, 6 August 1971. —Ed.

Berkeley at the same time*. The simple argument is that the catalytic cycle II is very much faster than the natural process I, which it imitates, and the amount of NO_x to be added by full-scale SST operation is sufficient to have a strong effect on the ozone layer.

* H. Johnston (1971). *Catalytic Reduction of Stratospheric Ozone by Nitrogen Oxides.* Lawrence Radiation Laboratory, University of California, Berkeley: vi + 114 columns on half as many pages (UCRL–20568. UC-4 Chemistry. TID-4500 (57th edn.), June 1971).—Ed.

6

FRESHWATER SUPPLIES AND POLLUTION

Keynote Paper

Freshwater Supplies and Pollution: Effects of the Demophoric Explosion on Water and Man*†

by

JOHN R. VALLENTYNE

Fisheries Research Board of Canada,
Freshwater Institute, 501 University Crescent,
Winnipeg 19, Manitoba, Canada;
Environmental Protection Service of the
Canada Department of the Environment

* *See* page 185 for a definition of demophoric.
† The author has requested this footnote indication that the preamble to his paper which he considered essential has been deleted editorially, though an attempt has been made to preserve its spirit in the introductory paragraphs.

INTRODUCTION

I had seriously thought of beginning this global account of freshwater supplies and pollution with a porcine analogue to the human population explosion. Projection of the latest fifteen-year period for which figures are available, indicating a pig population doubling-time of about twenty years up to 1967–68, suggests that the global balance in numbers between pigs and men will shift in favour of pigs by the year 2060 (*cf.* United Nations, 1970). Each pig being more or less equivalent to two humans in terms of food consumption and physiological waste production, a still more meaningful shift in these terms will take place approximately one pig doubling-time earlier, namely about the year 2040. These facts prepare the ground for a question posed at the end of this paper—namely, are we really solving our problems today? They also help to establish a proposition pertaining to human populations that, for some reason or other, seems acceptable only when applied to some animal other than man, namely: that the world population explosion of pigs will persist on its seemingly inevitable course only as long as humans want to have more and more pigs around them. In a like manner, the world population explosion of humans will persist on its seemingly inevitable course only as long as humans want to have more and more humans around.

Should it ever occur to humans that there are too many pigs around to suit humans, or too many humans around to suit humans, then ways will be found to reduce the numbers to more desirable levels. These ways—almost regardless of what they may be—will readily be accepted in the knowledge that a better life will be available to all thereby. We will accept them because they will be behavioural adaptations towards our survival—adaptations on the part of the individual and of society. Some of us may hesitate to think of this as true; yet we all know deep within ourselves that it is. Our rationality as humans is such that we would consider it immoral not to adopt these ways. If one accepts this—and it is really impossible to avoid such a conclusion— then it follows that there is no basis for assuming without question that the population explosions of pigs or humans will continue indefinitely, or even into the immediate future.

Why, then, is it that world-renowned specialists on water-supply problems typically begin their learned discourses with a statement that such-and-such a quantity of water must be supplied by the year so-and-so in order to meet the rapidly rising demands of some exploding, hyper-consumptive population? We are all too familiar with this sort of thing. Here is an example taken from an article by Kalinin & Bykov (1967): 'In the next thirty years or so, it will be necessary to meet not only the multiplied demands for water of a doubled world population, but to employ water as a global coolant to prevent over-heating of the planet.'

Statements such as this are, of course, nonsense. The authors might more appropriately have said that *if* the human population of the world actually does double during the next thirty years, and *if* a concomitant decline in the mean global style of living is to be avoided, then at least twice as many of the 'multiplied demands' of humans will have to be met by the year 2000 as would have been the case in the absence of population growth. In this form the statement fittingly poses more questions about the future than it answers. It also phrases the problem in terms of total demands rather than the demand for a single item such as water—which, though vitally important for many different aspects of our existence, still does not provide all the necessary conditions for human survival or well-being.

Following such an introductory statement, the authors could pose a number of questions, most of which are hidden and unwarranted assumptions in the statement of Kalinin & Bykov (1969):

(1) Can the 'multiplied demands' of the *present* world population be met by the year 2000?
(2) If met, can these demands be fulfilled perpetually in the years following 2000?
(3) If (1) and (2) are answered in the affirmative, can the same answers be given for a doubled world population?
(4) Are there unforeseen consequences in the fulfilment of any of these demands that might indirectly result in markedly diminished overall returns, thereby reducing the chances of their fulfilment?
(5) What grounds are there for believing that the predicted population growth will, in fact, take place?

Having raised these and other questions, the authors could finally state that their prime function is to assess the significance of water supplies in relation to a number of conceivable situations, thereby offering their customers a *menu* from which to choose. Under such conditions they would be, as they should be, not irresponsible peddlers of technological intoxicants for the human population, but interpreters of human behaviour relative to the distribution and use of water in the biosphere. That is the point of view taken in this paper.

Consumption Rises to Meet Supply

In an abstract sense, an imbalance in the relationship between supply and demand can equally well be interpreted as a deficiency of supply, an excess of demand, or some combination of both. Being human, however, we tend to view such imbalances solely in terms of a deficiency of supply. On the basis of past experience, this has not been unreasonable, for it has been possible to increase the supply of most of the needs and comforts of life—not infrequently with the development of improved substitutes. We have grown accustomed to thinking that supply is not restrictive—that there is no problem which modern technology cannot solve. With the increased magnitude of demand from a large and rapidly-growing human population on a finite earth, however, something must eventually become limiting in supply. What most people do not realize is the rapidity with which resources become exhausted during the terminal growth-stages of an exponentially growing population (Ehrlich & Holdren, 1971).

Supply and demand, as every economist knows, are terms that like to chase each other around—one now serving as the cause and the other as the effect, and then, an instant later, doing the reverse. The supply part of this relationship requires the production of some marketable commodity for its expression in response to an increased demand. Demand, on the other hand, is a purely psycho-behavioural phenomenon. As is well known to those in the advertising business, the mere suggestion of the possible existence of some item can be sufficient to create a demand that supply will later rise to meet. To this one need only add that, in an expanding economy, supply and demand chase each other up a circular staircase rather than in a closed circle.

As people, we often use these relationships of supply and demand to our momentary advantage. The managers of organizations involved in supplying water and energy for various domestic and industrial uses, for example, like to point out that their past predictions of future demand have almost invariably turned out to be correct. These future predictions, in fact, serve as the cause that induces them as willing (perhaps over-willing) servants of the public to increase the supply. They argue with a certain amount of reality in dealing with us, the whimsical public, that their proposals for expansion have an urgency that cannot be ignored.

As many have noted, however, the argument is not compelling, as the very act of providing the supply is the *sine qua non* that makes possible the fulfilment of the demand. The case only illustrates a general resource utilization law—one that will be intuitively obvious in terms of individual behaviour, particularly to the parents of small children—namely, that *consumption rises to meet supply*. In the evolution of human societies, two fundamentally different mechanisms come into play to bring about this end result. One is by increased *per caput* consumption, which is most prominent in relation to the comforts of life; the other is by adding heads to the population, through immigration or birth.

There is an important corollary to this law which, likewise because it is so obvious, seems to have eluded us in the collective management of our affairs— a principle well known to the hosts of cocktail parties and to managers of taverns near the closing hour—namely, that *consumption is controlled by supply*. Rational arguments may induce rational individuals in a population to exercise control over their consumption; but such mechanisms are ineffective for the total population because of the well-known rule that what one man does not consume, another man will.

Those who are familiar with the writings of C. Northcote Parkinson will recognize the similarity between the above resource utilization law (*consumption rises to meet supply*) and Parkinson's Second Law (*expenditure rises to meet income*). If my interpretation is correct, Parkinson's Second Law is really only a special case, pertaining to matters of finance, of the more general law enunciated here.

It is one of the most curious and interesting aspects of human behaviour that, when we are presented with behavioural laws such as those so successfully formulated by Parkinson and others, we laugh, nod our heads, and, after a moment's reflection, return to what we were doing before. In spite of this—or, *more accurately, because of this*—it is my firm and scientifically well-founded opinion that until the managers of the human race recognize the significance of this resource utilization law, there will be no hope of protecting the biosphere or, for that matter, mankind, *from man*. The greatest need today is for the development of national and global strategies that will permit governments to find familiar and legitimate bases for the creation of conditions which will cause people to control themselves collectively.

The Impending Crisis from the Demophoric Explosion

The problem at this point in the world's history is that an uncomfortably large number of people seem to be living under the general impression that supply can always rise to meet demand. To anyone familiar with the growth of populations, such a proposition is ridiculous. It is so ridiculous that, should it ever be suspected that a significant fraction of the managers of the human race believed it, the potential danger would be immense.

Prior to the onset of the agricultural revolution some 11,000 years ago, the total population of the human race was probably less than ten millions. According to Clark (1967) it was about 250 millions in Caesar's day, 500 millions when Shakespeare lived, 800 millions at the onset of the industrial revolution, and should be 3,700 millions in 1971. The most recent estimates of the United Nations suggest a median predicted population of 7,000 million humans in the year 2000. The high momentum of population growth at the present time can be appreciated from the fact that the global increase in population from 1960 to 1970 was equivalent to the entire population of the earth that existed in Shakespeare's time. The predicted population increase in the next twenty-nine years (1971 to 2000) equals the total build-up in population of the last 400 years.

The impending crisis is not only the result of population growth; it is also a result of technological growth—both in the sense of increased *per caput* production and consumption, and indirectly in that technology has permitted the growth of population and urbanization to take place. To appreciate the current momentum of the man–machine system, we need a concept that encompasses both the combined effects of population in a biological sense and production–consumption in a technological sense.

As we have no words for such a concept, I feel it appropriate to invent one: *demophora* (as a noun) and *demophoric* (as an adjective).* They take their origin from the Greek words *demos*, meaning population, and *phora*, meaning production. They are intended to encompass all aspects of the biology of human populations and technological production–consumption. The joint notion of production–consumption is used rather than consumption alone, in order to encompass the common situation in which biospheric degradation occurs through both production and use (e.g., resource utilization and pollution from steel production and car manufacture; then further resource utilization and pollution through the use of the car).

The concept of demophoric growth, focusing attention jointly on the internal and external (technological) metabolism of man, gives rise to a far better understanding of recent changes in the relationship between man and the rest of the biosphere than is implied in the term 'population growth'. Our current situation is much more of a demophoric explosion than it is a population ex-

---

* The suggested pronunciation is demóphora and demophóric. I am indebted to H. L. Tracy for suggesting these words to fit the concept.

plosion. In addition, the notion of demophora may be useful in creating an atmosphere within which people in developing and developed countries may jointly find some common expression of unity and purpose. The concept of global demophoric stabilization might be appealing to all.

THE CURRENT SITUATION WITH REGARD TO FRESHWATER SUPPLIES AND POLLUTION

Water in Relation to Man

To any casual visitor from outer space, the most impressive feature of the earth would surely be the abundance of water at its surface. This immense quantity of water, covering 71 per cent of the earth's surface to a mean depth of 3.8 km, has been derived over geologic history from the water present in magmatic rocks that accreted to form the earth some 5,000 million years ago. As a result of heating and degassing processes deep within the earth's crust, water and a number of elements that exist in volatile forms (carbon, nitrogen, sulphur, chlorine, and others) came to the earth's surface in steam vents, fumaroles, geysers, and volcanoes. Interacting with surface rocks and soils, the gases mostly condensed to form the hydrosphere (Rubey, 1951). Some components (N_2 and a small fraction of the CO_2) remained in the atmosphere. Molecular oxygen (O_2), vital for the respiration of all aerobic organisms, accumulated in the atmosphere as a result of the activity of photosynthetic plants—due to the burial, without oxidation, of some photosynthetically produced organic matter.

Table I shows an inventory of the quantities of water in various forms in the biosphere. The water-renewal times listed in the right-hand column provide

TABLE I

Inventory of Water in the Biosphere. Modified from Kalinin & Bykov (1969)

Inventory item	Volume (thousands of km³)	Per cent of total	Renewal time
Oceans	1,370,000	97.61	37,000 years†
Polar ice, glaciers	29,000	2.08	16,000 years
Ground-water (actively exchanged)*	4,000	0.29	300 years
Freshwater lakes	125	0.009	1–100 years‡
Saline lakes	104	0.008	10–1,000 years‡
Soil and subsoil moisture	67	0.005	280 days
Rivers	1.2	0.00009	12–20 days§
Atmospheric water vapour	14	0.0009	9 days

* Kalinin & Bykov (1969) estimated that the total ground-water to a depth of 5 km in the crust amounts to 60 million cubic kilometres. This is much higher than the U.S. Geological Survey estimate of 8.3 million cubic kilometres to a depth of 4 km. Only the volume of the upper, actively exchanged ground-water is included here.

† Based on net evaporation from the oceans.

‡ Renewal times for lakes vary directly with volume and mean depth, and inversely with rate of discharge. The absolute range is from days to thousands of years for some saline lakes.

§ Twelve days for rivers with relatively small catchment areas of less than 100,000 km²; twenty days for major rivers that drain directly to the sea.

rough estimates of the time required under natural conditions to replace the volumes shown in the left-hand column. Note the relatively small amounts of water that occur in the form of freshwater lakes and rivers, and the short water-renewal times for the atmosphere and rivers as compared with lakes and ground-water. Other things being equal, the extent of pollution problems in freshwater systems tends to be inversely related to the volume of the receiving body of water and directly related to water-renewal time. For pollutants that are primarily removed by sedimentation, the depth of a water body can be of major significance—the deeper the water, the more likely is it that the pollutant will be permanently removed from the active zone of the biosphere by burial.

Although the standing stock of water in the biosphere is of interest in relation to the earth's history and to some human uses of water such as recreation and transportation, the rate of supply is generally more important—particularly for fresh water. The ultimate source of this freshwater supply is the precipitation which falls on the land surface of the earth, and which amounts to about 105,000 km³/year. If it were evenly distributed over the land surface, it would correspond to a precipitation of 72 cm per annum. The problem, of course, is that this precipitation is not evenly distributed; nor is it all available to man.

A better indication of the potential supply to man of fresh water on a sustained-use basis is provided by the volume of fresh water annually delivered to the oceans as river-flow. This totals about 37,500 km³ per annum—roughly one-third of the total precipitation that falls on land. The remaining two-thirds is returned to the atmosphere by evaporation from exposed water surfaces and as a result of plant transpiration. The importance of the latter can be appreciated from the fact that forest transpiration generally approximates the evaporation from an open water surface under the same climatic conditions.

A rough idea of what this river-flow amounts to *per caput* of human population can be obtained by dividing the potential supply of 37,500 km³ by the 3,700 million humans now present on earth. The result is 10,000 m³/*caput*/year, or 27,000 litres/*caput*/day for 1971—or about half these values for the year 2000, if current population predictions turn out to be correct.

In relation to the human physiological requirement for water, about 2 litres/*caput*/day, these values seem immense. This is also the case relative to a number of other uses of water—domestic consumption which averages 40 to 250 litres/*caput*/day, depending on ease of access and affluence of the user population; average industrial consumption up to 1,500 litres/*caput*/day in technologically developed nations; and agricultural uses up to several thousand litres/*caput*/day in countries with hot, dry climates. Why then is it that many countries, even including Canada with her 9 per cent of the world's river-flow and only 0.7 per cent of the population, have water-supply problems? The answers are several:

(1) People have not distributed themselves over the earth's surface in proportion to rainfall or river-flow.
(2) Supply problems typically develop during periods of low flow in hot, dry weather.

E.F.—7*

(3) *Per caput* demands have increased with increased availability and economic well-being. Total consumption has increased with demophoric growth.

(4) The use of water for certain purposes is consumptive—e.g., water lost from the system by evapotranspiration.

(5) Pollution lowers the quality of water, thereby reducing the supply for certain purposes.

Most man-made problems of water-supply have originated from demophoric growth, urbanization, and the direct discharge of inadequately treated wastes into water. Additional serious effects have come about through destructive land-use practices such as deforestation, overgrazing, improper cultivation practices that lead to soil erosion, and over-irrigation of flat, downstream areas of semi-arid lands (leading to the salinization of soils and the creation of desert conditions).

Four general classes of water pollutants are commonly distinguished by agencies involved in waste treatment and water-supply:

(1) pathogens (Bacteria, viruses, protozoans, worms), potentially the most dangerous because of their virulence and powers of multiplication;

(2) biodegradable organic pollutants that consume oxygen in water and give rise to smells and fish-kills;

(3) persistent (non-biodegradable) pollutants such as many salts, ions, and organic compounds that degrade slowly or not at all; and

(4) toxins, separated off as a class because of the danger attached to their use.

In terms of pollution from animal sources we often forget the obvious—that the waste output from a non-growing adult equals the food intake. An average human, 70 kg in weight, annually eliminates about 100 kg of carbon in the form of CO_2, about 28 kg of BOD_5 (organic substances that create a *biochemical oxygen demand*, measured over 5 days), 3.4 kg of nitrogen, and 0.45 kg of phosphorus—all as physiological waste. The ratio of physiological waste produced by livestock and poultry in most countries to that produced by the human population is about 10:1 for BOD_5, 8:1 for nitrogen, and 11:1 for phosphorus. In heavily industrialized nations, the waste associated with the external 'technological metabolism' typically exceeds that of the internal biological metabolism by a factor of up to 3 or more in terms of BOD_5 prior to treatment.

It cannot be overstressed that all air pollutants are potentially pollutants of land and fresh water, and that the ultimate fate of all non-biodegradable pollutants in fresh water is either transport to the sea or sedimentation. These elementary and obvious facts are often forgotten in the naïve belief that pollutants will somehow or other magically disappear when added to certain environments (e.g., high smoke-stack emissions to air).

The two sections that follow pertain to existing situations in developing and developed countries. Only the most generalized statements can be made. The plain fact of the matter is that there is at present no systematized body of information that would permit a comprehensive and reliable assessment of water pollution on a global scale. The situation in regard to water-supply is more amenable to measurement, particularly in urban areas; but, even in those cases, the existing data are only of the crudest sort. Finally, in all settled areas of the world it is now virtually impossible to determine with any accuracy the nature of pre-settlement conditions.

Developing Countries

The most comprehensive review of urban water-supply conditions is that of Dieterich & Hendrickson (1963) which was based on a survey of 75 developing countries in Africa, southern Asia, and Latin America. Of the total urban population in these countries in 1962 (319 millions), the authors found that 107 million people (33 per cent) had piped water on their premises, 83 million (26 per cent) had access only to public outlets, and 129 million (41 per cent) had no access to piped water at all (Table II). The areas in most

TABLE II

Urban Population and Water-supply in 75 Developing Countries.
From Dieterich & Hendrickson (1963).

Area	Number of countries	Total urban population, 1962	Urban population without piped water in home, 1962	Anticipated urban population increase, 1962–77
Africa	31	39,000,000	26,000,000	24,000,000
Latin America	20	102,000,000	41,000,000	77,000,000
Asia	24	178,000,000	146,000,000	105,000,000
Totals	75	319,000,000	213,000,000	206,000,000

critical need of improved water-supply conditions were south-central Asia, south-east Asia, and Africa south of the Sahara. All governments seemed to consider their urban water-supply conditions as unsatisfactory, but few had taken the direct initiative of establishing national water policies, plans, legislation, or funds. Without such action, governmental policy statements have no meaning.

A World Health Organization report (WHO, 1969b), completed six years after the publication of the study by Dieterich & Hendrickson (1963), stated: 'From available evidence it would appear that in many developing countries the present rate of increase in urban community supplies [of water] is not even sufficient to make up for past neglect, let alone to keep pace with population growth.' This can be sensed from data presented in Table II. If one had to cite one area where the problems of high population density, high population growth-rate, and a backlog of constructional needs, were all compounded to the greatest extent, it would be in southern Asia.

Most developing countries are located in tropical or semi-tropical areas where climatic and geographic factors can be particularly destructive to soils under conditions of land misuse. The Food and Agriculture Organization report entitled 'The Influence of Man on the Hydrologic Cycle' (FAO, 1969) cites a number of common instances of land misuse, pointing out that most problems stem from a lack of knowledge and experience of sound soil conservation practices. Dangers from overgrazing and the misuse of arable cropland by the expansion of subsistence agricultural populations are cited with particular concern. Salinization problems due to over-irrigation are especially common in the lower flat areas of river systems in countries with hot, dry climates. If drainage is not sufficient to remove surplus water, the result is a rising saline water-table which, when it comes into contact with plant roots, causes wilting. The farmer assumes that the wilting indicates a need for more water. When he adds it, the salt-laden water rises still farther, the plants are killed, and the area is abandoned as a biological desert.

In the absence of standardized surveys, little can be said of pollution in developing countries. A World Health Organization report (WHO, 1969a) provides one of the better summaries available in terms of geographic coverage. It cites the general lack of sewerage systems even in towns and cities that are provided with piped water. The description of 'sewage usually being disposed of in pit latrines and septic tanks or by dumping of night soil into a river or sea' is reminiscent of nineteenth-century conditions in Europe.

Perhaps the best indication of present conditions of water-supply and pollution in developing countries is provided by mortality data for water-borne diseases using *Homo sapiens* as an indicator species. The statistics show that infant mortality rates from enteric diseases in developing countries are many times greater than in technologically developed countries. India and Pakistan remain focal centres for cholera and a number of other water-borne diseases. Pollution from human pathogens ranks without question as the most serious of all pollution problems in developing countries, with high economic costs on top of the heavy penalties to individuals.

Developed Countries

Most urban areas in technologically developed countries are provided with adequate supplies of fresh water that is piped into the home, and they also have facilities for the collection (though sometimes not treatment) of sewage. Dramatic reductions in the incidence of water-borne diseases such as typhoid fever, cholera, dysentery, and the like, have come about during the twentieth century, paralleling the installation of water-transport and systems of waste disposal. The situation is now such that most citizens of developed countries do not normally think of pollution as having a pathogenic component. On the other hand, the number of beach areas that are closed to swimming for reasons of health does not seem to be on the decrease.

Most water-supply and pollution problems in technologically advanced countries occur in the vicinity of urban centres where high demophoric growth-rates create a heavy upstream demand for pure water and a low downstream quality. The consequences are that more and more distant sources of supply are utilized, and greater attention is given to the multiple use and recycling of water. For drinking, bottled water tends to be used rather than the municipal supply. Los Angeles and the Ruhr Valley provide two of the more extreme cases of man's behaviour in relation to water in technologically developed parts of the world. In the former case the sources of supply extend into other states, with water even from Canada considered as a future possibility; in the latter case multiple use and recycling are used to the fullest extent, the entire volume of water received being subjected to waste treatment.

Table III shows water-use values for the United States in 1965, with projected values for the year 2000. Note that somewhat more than 25 per cent of all the water used in the United States in 1965 was used consumptively. Table IV shows industrial process and waste-water usage in the United States in conjunction with data on BOD_5 and suspended solids in the waste-water before treatment. In neither of these tables is any allowance made for water as a medium for waste dilution, which is perhaps the major use of water in the United States.

TABLE III

Water-use in the United States in 1965, and Projected for the Year 2000.
From U.S. Water Resources Council, 1968 Water Assessment.
(Per caput *Values for 2000 Estimated on the Basis of a Population of 320 millions.*)

	Total population use (thousand millions of litres/day)		Per caput use (litres/day)	
Water-use	*1965*	*2000*	*1965*	*2000*
Rural, domestic	9	11	45	40
Municipal* (public-supplied)	90	192	460	600
Industrial (self-supplied)	175	480	900	1,520
Steam-electric power	320	1,780	1,640	5,600
Agriculture	420	580	2,200	1,820
Total use (rounded)	1,000	3,000	5,200	9,600
Consumptive use (rounded)	300	500	1,500	1,600
Non-consumptive use (rounded)	700	2,500	3,700	8,000

* Domestic and some industrial.

There has been a pronounced deterioration in the quality of water in technologically advanced countries during the past two hundred years. Although detailed statistics are not available for time-comparisons, it is probable that the overloading of rivers with organic matter in the United Kingdom and Europe reached maxima in the middle of the nineteenth century and during the first third of the twentieth century. The overall situation in regard to water pollution in the New World has probably been a steady deterioration—one that is still taking place.

There has been a dramatic increase in the incidence of cultural eutrophication problems in developed countries during the present century, in large part due to urbanization and the development of sewerage systems. As a result of the by-passage of the soil, phosphorus and nitrogen compounds delivered directly to the receiving water stimulate the growth of Algae and rooted plants. This results in increased turbidity, gives rise to plant accumulations on beaches, causes undesired changes in fish populations, results in taste and odour problems in drinking water, and so on. Problems have been accentuated in recent years from the use of phosphates in detergents, drainage of untreated wastes from feed-lot areas, and increasing fertilizer use (Vollenweider, 1968). As a control measure, a number of municipalities in

TABLE IV

Estimated Quantities of Industrial Wastes Before Treatment, USA 1964.
Data from T. J. Powers, cited in Council on Environmental Quality (1970).

Industry	Process water intake in 10^9 gallons*	Waste water volume in 10^9 gallons*	BOD_5 in 10^6 pounds*	Suspended solids in 10^6 pounds*
Food and kindred products	260	690	4,300	6,600
Textile mill products	110	140	890	NE†
Paper and allied products	1,300	1,900	5,900	3,000
Chemical and allied products	560	3,700	9,700	1,900
Petroleum and coal	88	1,300	500	460
Rubber and plastics	19	160	40	50
Primary metals				
blast furnaces and steel mills	870	3,600	160	4,300
all others	130	740	320	430
Machinery	23	150	60	50
Electrical machinery	28	91	70	20
Transportation equipment	58	240	120	NE
All other manufacturing	190	450	390	930
All manufacturing	3,700	13,110	22,000	18,000
For comparison: sewered population of U.S.A.	—	5,300	7,300	8,800

* 1 gallon = 4.546 Litres; 1 pound (lb) = 0.454 kg.
† NE = not estimated.

Europe (especially in Sweden and Switzerland) are now treating sewage to remove phosphate.

Commoner *et al.* (1971) have drawn attention to the role of new technologies relative to a number of pollution problems that have been accentuated in the United States since World War II. On the basis of such data as are shown in Table V, Commoner *et al.* concluded that increases in population

TABLE V

Percentage Changes in per caput *Production or Consumption of Some Natural and Synthetic Products in the United States. (From Commoner et al., 1971.)*
Data Corrected for Population Growth.

Item	Period	Percentage increase per caput *of total country*
Non-returnable beer bottles	1946–69	3,778
Mercury for chlorine and sodium hydroxide products	1946–68	2,150
Plastics	1946–68	1,024
Nitrogen fertilizer	1946–68	534
Synthetic organic chemicals	1946–68	495
Detergents	1952–68	300
Pesticides	1950–68	217
Wood pulp	1946–68	152
Motor fuel (consumption)	1946–68	100
Meat (consumption)	1946–68	19
Calories (consumption)	1946–68	−4
Lumber	1946–68	−23
Work by animal horsepower	1950–68	−84

(43 per cent) and affluence (59 per cent, as measured by the increase in Gross National Product) were inadequate to account for changes in pollution that ranged from 200 to 1000 per cent. In attributing a major role to changing technology, however, these authors neglected to stress that the increased population accounted for about half of everything produced or consumed. They also neglected to contrast the effects of new and old technologies based on the same extent of usage. If, for example, we covered the same distance today by horse-drawn vehicles as we do by car, our roads would literally be paved with horse dung.

Brief reference to the situation in the St Lawrence–Great Lakes region will illustrate some of the problems that arise in developed countries. It is important to note that none of these waters is truly international, although the boundary line bisects four of the five major lakes. As is shown in Table VI, the Great Lakes Drainage Basin covers an area of 764,500 km^2 (land plus water) and contains 1 per cent of the world's human population. One out of every seven citizens of the United States, and one out of every five citizens of Canada, lives in the Basin.

TABLE VI

Some Characteristics of Lakes in the St Lawrence Drainage Basin, from Beeton & Chandler (1963). Population Data from T. R. Lee (personal communication).

Lake	1970 Population (thousands)	Surface area (km^2)			Mean depth (m)	Volume (km^3)	Discharge (m^3/sec)
		Water	Land	Basin			
Superior	700	82,400	124,600	207,000	148.5	12,240	2,080
Michigan	13,400	58,000	118,000	176,000	84.2	4,880	1,560
Huron	2,100	59,600	128,400	188,000	59.5	3,550	5,040
St Clair	} 12,900	1,300	17,900	19,200	3.0	4	5,040
Erie		25,700	58,500	84,200	17.7	455	5,520
Ontario	6,100	19,500	70,600	90,000	86.3	1,680	6,630
Total	35,200	246,500	518,800	764,500	—	22,800	—

The total human population in the Great Lakes Basin in 1810 was only 290,000. By 1910 it had risen to 13,800,000, and it is about 36,000,000 now in 1971. The predicted population for the year 2000 is 57,000,000. As the centre of the steel industry, the Great Lakes Basin is sometimes referred to as the industrial heartland of North America.

A recent report to the International (Canada/United States) Joint Commission (Anon., 1969) on pollution in Lakes Erie and Ontario cites the following changes:

(1) An increase in total dissolved solids in the water from 145 mg/litre in 1910 to 200 mg/litre in 1967;
(2) An increase in the polluted area in the western end of Lake Erie from 263 km^2 in 1930 to 1,020 km^2 in 1960;
(3) Vast changes in the composition of fish populations;
(4) Increased incidence of algal blooms and of *Cladophora,* a nuisance Alga that lives on rocky substrates; and

(5) Immense quantities of greases, oils, BOD sources, nutrients, and other wastes, delivered to waters in the drainage basin from various centres of population and industry.

One cannot help but be impressed with the vast changes that have taken place in the Great Lakes Basin since William Francis Butler (1872) wrote: 'But this glorious river system, through its many lakes and various names, is ever the same crystal current, flowing pure from the fountainhead of Lake Superior. Great cities stud its shore, but they are powerless to dim the transparency of its waters. Steamships cover the broad bosom of its lakes and estuaries; but they change not the beauty of the water, no more than the fleets of the world mark the waves of the oceans.'

THE FORESEEABLE FUTURE

General

The only certain prediction that can be made about the future is that it will be increasingly unpredictable. There are several reasons for this: (1) the high momentum of the man-machine system, (2) the susceptibility of monocultures (e.g., human) to violent perturbations, (3) the difference in rate constants and time-lags between technological growth and population growth, (4) unexpectedly erratic changes in population behaviour for bizarre reasons, and (5) the frustrating and inadequate response-times of organizations when one organizational crisis is compounded upon another.

The most critical single factor that will act to determine the course of future events between man and environment, using the term environment in the broadest of all possible senses, is human population. This is because of the influence of such population on all matters of life—individual and social behaviour, resource utilization and depletion, incidence and transmission of diseases, effects on economic and political stability, and so on. I anticipate that most of the global increase in population currently projected to the year 2000 will take place, but that markedly decreased birth-rates over those currently projected will be observed in developing countries prior to 1980, and in developing countries prior to 1990.

I do not believe that the human species is in danger of extinction, even from the full-scale consequences of nuclear war and all the probable after-effects. The species is simply too cunning to exterminate itself, even by accident. The more probable danger, which I think will also be avoided in the long run, though not in the short run, is adaptation to a continuously declining quality of life while the human races affectionately cling to meaningless symbols of physical prowess. On the other hand, continued demophoric growth will increase the probability of major global catastrophes—the most probable of which are pestilence, war, and famine, as has been the case for millennia.

The Developing Countries

The disparity in affluence between developed and developing countries will continue to widen for a number of reasons: (1) the heavy investment of many developing countries in population growth to the detriment of technologically-based economic expansion, (2) the heavy health-drain in many developing countries because of inadequate facilities for medical treatment and environmental measures to limit the spread of diseases, and (3) the decreasing dependency of developed countries on the importation of natural products from developing countries. The crux of the situation is the unlikelihood of achieving birth control among the poorly educated segment of the population. In such circumstances, any attempt to improve health will lead to higher population and less investment in technological expansion. The natural consequence of this with respect to water supplies and pollution is that conditions in regard to both will probably progressively deteriorate. The situation will be worst on the fringes of urban areas with high population densities, high population growth-rates, and a large backlog of constructional needs.

As a result of power struggles during rapidly changing times, one can expect increasingly serious economic breakdowns in countries with a relatively rapid technological build-up. There will be ever-present dangers of land misuse that could be catastrophic during times that are calling for increased production of food. Famine, however, is more likely to result from disruption of transportation systems induced by economic and political instability, than from a shortage of food supply *per se*.

It is probable that at least one major global outbreak of disease will occur before the year 2000. The consequences are difficult to predict; however, the focus of origin will almost certainly be somewhere in Asia, probably in south-central Asia. Non-viral infections can probably be contained or largely limited to the continent of origin. Viral infections, on the other hand, can spread with disastrous consequences around the world. The reasons for this are the comparative lack of knowledge of viral diseases and control, and the comparative ease with which viruses can be distributed in water-supply and sewage systems.

Conditions of water-supply and pollution in urban areas will continue to deteriorate relative to the population present; however, in no sense could any improvement of these conditions alone be expected to lead to an amelioration of total environmental situations. The overall long-term effect would probably be just the opposite, due to excessive growth of population and population density. If this analysis is correct, it would in large part explain the reluctance of local authorities to press actively for improved systems of water-supply and waste disposal. Their innate intelligence may be a good deal higher than public-health engineers appreciate!

The Developed Countries

Water-supply problems in developed countries will continue to be solved by increasingly larger systems of diversion and storage, and in industry by multiple use and recycling of water. Desalination of sea water, coupled with the development of nuclear power-plants, will become economically viable ventures in areas of rapid demophoric growth located in arid and semi-arid regions. It is unlikely that any global engineering scheme to modify the circulation of water on the planet will be put into effect in the next thirty years, for the possible consequences to the expanded population will not be foreseeable to the necessary extent. On the other hand, it is possible that some stages of an overall plan may be initiated on a try-as-you-go basis.

Continued demophoric growth can be expected to occur in technologically developed countries, though at a slower average rate than latterly. For this expected slowing there are a number of reasons, including: (1) the increasingly rapid exhaustion of rich deposits of non-renewable resources, (2) the probability of acceptance of measures for population stabilization within the next generation, and (3) the increased cost of measures for pollution abatement and biospheric protection.

Assuming economic stability, a continuous decrease in the inputs of environmental pollutants can be expected for the next few years, probably extending over the next thirty years. The improvements in this regard will be most accentuated in the well-to-do countries, less so in countries that are striving for rapid economic improvement. On the other hand, it is probable that *environmental problems*, using that phrase in the broadest of senses, will increase generally—particularly in and around urban centres. One of the most interesting situations to follow will be the development of nuclear reactor facilities for atomic power production. Although it has been predicted that 50 per cent of all power in the United States will be nuclear by the year 2000, no analysis has been made of the detailed consequences in terms of a reasonable spectrum of possible situations.

The rate of substitution of new synthetic chemicals for old functions will probably slow down as the need for environmental testing and governmental restriction increases. Many of the products with noxious side-effects from current and past technologies will, however, probably continue to be used in developing and moderately developed countries because of the more favourable benefit/cost ratios in terms of increased food production and protection from disease.

WHAT CAN AND SHOULD BE DONE

(1) Although it is generally recognized that the most urgently-needed solutions to environmental problems are of a political nature, because of my own inexperience I have no suggestions to make along these lines. Rather, it is my purpose to identify certain areas in which our concepts and assumptions are in need of re-examination and re-formulation. If we cannot think clearly, stating in succinct terms the nature and origin of our problems, we cannot be expected to solve them.

(2) There should be a general recognition that we are now in the middle-to-terminal stages of a *demophoric* explosion; that if mechanisms are not discovered and put into practice to control this explosion before the year 1980, then harsher controls will be imposed by adverse economics operating in conjunction with the idiosyncrasies of human behaviour and the cold reality of nature. The recognition of a need for a global control of demophora will not come about through any positive thought-pattern, but rather through a recognition of the adverse consequences of operating without control. Income taxation schemes are essentially demophoric in content, though with a greater control exerted over production-consumption power than over population

increase. (The latter is in fact widely uncontrolled—which is in large part why population growth is so serious in its implications today.) We all hate income tax; yet we all recognize its necessity, in principle if not in detail. The same will pertain to demophoric control.

(3) One of the major aims of governments individually and collectively through the United Nations should be to obtain a general recognition prior to the end of the twentieth century that *man is an animal*. Secondly, man must be recognized as a product of the biosphere and therefore as a part of the biosphere. Without political recognition of these two fundamental and scientifically well-documented propositions, there can be little hope for the future of man and/or his environment.

(4) The most prominent of the myths that we live by is that we can maintain a collective control over death (through improvement of health and survival) and yet not over birth. The current *laissez-faire* attitude in respect to human population is the basic cause of environmental problems. Any conference on environmental matters that fails to face this issue squarely is doomed to failure from the start.

(5) There is a need for the formulation of new words and concepts pertaining to the 'environment' of man. 'Environment' currently means so many different things to different people that its use in general discussion is apt to be confusing and misleading. Just as the Eskimo has many words for ice in his language, so must modern man have many words for environment. The Stockholm Conference on Environment in 1972 could provide an avenue for the development of such concepts.

(6) There is a general belief among citizens, industrialists, and politicians today, that most or all of our environmental problems will disappear following the application of measures for pollution abatement. In actual fact, however, only those problems that are caused by pollutants will be solved. Other environmental problems will remain—resource depletion, 'living space', overpredation and species extinction, spread of pathogens and pest species, land misuse, and a variety of politico-socio-economic ills that hinge upon uncontrolled demophoric growth. As a word encompassing these concepts, including pollution, I propose *biotribe* to mean the devastation to the biosphere brought about by man. The origin is Greek, from *bios* (a word with the connotation of our biosphere) and *tribë* (waste—in the sense of laying waste or devastation). *Brotobiotribe*, though lengthier, may be useful in accenting the causal role of man (*brotos* = human race—a somewhat poetic Greek word with a slight suggestion that humans are a sorry lot). These words are intended for use in a local as well as biospheric sense—in the former case representing localized examples of widespread processes.

(7) Global statistics should be gathered on water pollution in terms of rating waters on a scale of 1 to 5, from pre-settlement conditions to grossly polluted conditions—measured in terms of length of river system or lakeshore.

(8) There is a need for rigorously controlled experimental manipulation of entire ecosystems to obtain an improved understanding of the laws governing their behaviour, the mechanisms by which they can be controlled, and the effects and persistence of introduced chemicals in these systems. Canada

has made a major commitment in this regard in setting aside a Canadian *Experimental Lakes Area* in which forty-six small lakes and their land-drainage basins are available for ecosystem manipulation. A description of the rationale and initial phases of development has been published (Freshwater Institute, 1971). This concept should be extended to other geographic regimes.

A Closing Question

Is it possible that we may be living in some kind of a Faustian world, in which we do not solve our problems, but merely replace them with other problems? The primary reason why I began this account of freshwater supplies and pollution with a comment on swine and man was not so much to ask this question, as to ask a deeper, more probing, and perhaps inwardly disturbing, question. *Is it conceivable that we may have been living in such a world for over a century without having known it?*

I ask this question in the sense that many of our problems of today were created by a solution that we employed to solve another problem in the middle of the nineteenth century. The problem at that time was the high death-rate in urban areas—approximately twice that in adjacent rural regions—from enteric, water-borne diseases. The problem was solved by the introduction of the water transport system of waste disposal. As a result of that change, and of subsequent improvements in the technology of medical practice, we have inherited all of the problems that stem from urbanization and un-restricted population growth. The process has been continuing in the twentieth century with the extension of environmental health measures to the control of insect-borne diseases.

All of these changes have been good changes in the short run, leading to improved health and happiness of those who have been fortunate enough to receive the benefits. What has been apparent for some time, however, is that we have instituted only a half-technology—one that will return to plague us because of our failure to parallel population measures for the control of death with those for the control of birth.

The time is late. The brakes have long been removed from a train that is now rapidly gaining momentum on its way down the bumpy road of life. Have we, like Dr Faustus, made a blood pact with the Devil—one that we are required to keep?

Conclusion

Problems of water-supply and pollution are of our own making. It will be futile to attempt to solve them on a global scale by increasing the supply of pure water and decreasing the extent of pollution in the absence of measures for demophoric control. We will collectively accept measures for global demophoric control, perhaps through some universal taxation scheme, not because of their positive virtues, but through fear of the consequences of a lack of demophoric control.

References

ANON. (1969). *Report to the International Joint Commission on Pollution in Lake Erie, Lake Ontario, and the International Section of the St Lawrence River.* International Joint Commission, Washington, D.C., and Ottawa, Canada: Vol. I, xiv + 151 pp., illustr.; Vol. II, viii + 316 pp., illustr.; Vol. III, viii + 329 pp., illustr.

BEETON, A. M. & CHANDLER, D. C. (1963). The St. Lawrence Great Lakes. Pp. 535–58 in *Limnology in North America* (Ed. D. G. Frey). University of Wisconsin Press, Madison, Wisconsin: viii + 734 pp., illustr.

BUTLER, W. F. (1872). *The Great Lone Land.* [First Hurtig edition of M. G. Hurtig, Edmonton: xvi + 388 pp., illustr., 1968.]

CLARK, C. (1967). *Population Growth and Land Use.* Macmillan, London: [ix] + 406 pp., illustr.

COMMONER, B., CORR, M. & STAMLER, P. J. (1971). The causes of pollution. *Environment,* **13**(3), pp. 2–19.

COUNCIL ON ENVIRONMENTAL QUALITY (1970). *The First Annual Report of the Council on Environmental Quality.* U.S. Government Printing Office, Washington, D.C.: 421 pp.

DIETERICH, B. H. & HENDRICKSON, J. H. (1963). Urban water-supply conditions in seventy-five developing countries, *World Health Organization, Public Health Papers,* **23**, pp. 1–92.

EHRLICH, P. R. & HOLDREN, J. P. (1971). Impact of population growth. *Science,* **171**, pp. 1212–17.

FOOD AND AGRICULTURAL ORGANIZATION (as FAO) (1969). *The Influence of Man on the Hydrologic Cycle.* FAO SC/HYMIDEC/20, Rome: 55 pp.

FRESHWATER INSTITUTE (1971). Experimental lakes area. *J. Fisheries Research Board Canada,* **28**(2), pp. 121–301, illustr.

KALININ, G. P. & BYKOV, V. D. (1969). The world's water resources, present and future. *Impact of Science on Technology,* **19**(2), pp. 135–50.

RUBEY, W. W. (1951). The geologic history of sea water. *Bull. Geol. Soc. Amer.,* **62**, pp. 1111–47.

UNITED NATIONS (1970). *Statistical Yearbook 1969* (21st issue). Statistical Office of the United Nations, Department of Economic and Social Affairs, New York: 821 pp.

VOLLENWEIDER, R. A. (1968). Scientific fundamentals of the eutrophication of lakes and flowing waters, with particular reference to nitrogen and phosphorus as factors in eutrophication. *Organization for Economic Cooperation and Development,* Paris DAS/CSI/68. 27, pp. 1–159.

WORLD HEALTH ORGANIZATION (as WHO) (1969a) Water pollution in developing countries. Report of a WHO expert committee. *WHO Technical Report Series* No. 404, pp. 1–38.

WORLD HEALTH ORGANIZATION (as WHO) (1969b). Community water supply. *WHO Technical Report Series* No. 420, pp. 1–21.

DISCUSSION

Skulberg (Chairman)

Dr Vallentyne is an expert of international repute on biological problems of inland waters and water pollution who has performed a formidable amount of research on primary production, algal vegetation, and freshwater ecology. As Scientific Leader of the Eutrophication Section, Fisheries Research Board of Canada, he is surrounded in the Freshwater Institute in Winnipeg by colleagues whose specialist fields combine to cover those of research on inland waters and pollution. Yet it is important in our discussion that we keep in mind the overall purposes of our Conference. We have now heard the account of the global situation on freshwater supplies and pollution, and look forward to hearing your views on what is most likely to happen in these respects in the foreseeable future, and what can and should be done to avoid further contamination and degradation.

Personally, I feel a great sense of urgency about our task. There is a real question as to whether the world can afford to wait for more study and more knowledge before acting to restrict water resources degradation. It is necessary to apply, all over the world, scientifically sound and effective projects of water management. But this is a gigantic task, and failure is far-reaching. Wise political action must be based on a greatly strengthened science of environment. A massive effort by the rich nations, now, while they are still rich, is needed to understand and teach the broadest aspects of the problem. Only by sustained attack can the world provide the foundations for an enduring solution. Action of this magnitude requires convincing knowledge of the consequences of failure, and a clear basis for engagement. Environmental control should be locked into our future by legislation, expanded budgets, and governmental programmes.

With the increasing international emphasis on inland water pollution abatement, a full knowledge of a variety of control measures is needed for a proper solution of the problems related to water quality management. There is no general remedy for the prevention of pollution. At present very little is known about many aspects of the several factors that act together in various environments and cause undesirable effects. Dr Vallentyne's paper is of general interest and will stimulate diverse thinking on possible approaches to solutions and methods of combating pollution of freshwater supplies.

I am going to make one principal suggestion, namely that we emphasize the role of biology in the struggle to avoid concomitant catastrophes to man and nature. Dr R. O. Brinkhurst, now of the University of Toronto, has formulated it in this way (*Water and Sewage Works*, **117**, p. 6, June 1970):

> Pollution and eutrophication are words which describe largely undesirable changes in the ecology of man. The problems are biological, in that we are dealing with processes which determine the lives of living things and which are themselves subject to the action of living things. Strange, then, that we turn to chemistry and engineering to solve the difficult problems with which we are confronted.

Our group is intentionally diverse and interdisciplinary, and surely capable of very interesting discussions. Let the Conference be an exercise in cross-disciplinary communication. We must look beyond the confines of any single branch of science for a multidisciplinary approach.

Professor Jean G. Baer yesterday raised the question of communication, as did Dr Vallentyne in his lecture. The scientific community is aware of the fact that present methods of communication fail to keep pace with the growing mass of data that is flooding the scientific literature. It is sometimes forgotten, however, that communication is effective only when information is conveyed to and understood by another human mind. Unless this basic goal of understanding is achieved, we will fail in the primary purpose. In the situation of today, with its increasing problems of environmental degradation, the need for real communication, for instance between biologists and engineers, is strongly felt. It is to my mind only through intimate cooperation between the various fields of science which are involved in the study of the biosphere, that control of environmental degradation may be possible.

[At this point the discussion was adjourned, pending the finding of an interpreter for a representative of an international organization situated in an Eastern European country. Subsequently, an interpreter was found but the representative declined to address the reduced audience in a more intimate atmosphere making direct dialogue possible. The continuing discussion was led by Dr Vallentyne at the request of the Chairman.]

Vallentyne

In resuming, I want to draw your attention to some of the concepts that I introduced in my talk, as owing to my late completion of the basic paper you did not have the usual opportunity of reading the full text in advance. Particularly do I wish to throw those words 'demophoric' and 'biotribe' back at you. They represent concepts which I have been struggling with for about eight or ten months, and I am convinced that they will be useful. To stress this I would remind you that when Lavoisier undertook to change the whole concept of chemistry in the latter part of the eighteenth century, working with a number of colleagues in France and elsewhere, the one thing which he reserved for himself to do, and which he would not let anyone else touch, was the definition of the terms, because of their importance in the formulation and expression of concepts. We have now entered into the beginning of a revolutionary change in our approach to the biosphere, and need new words for our new conceptions. I would like you to try the ones I have given you. If they are useless, throw them away; but if they happen to be useful, use them. And if the concept is good but the word is not, put a better one in.

Butler

There are two comments that I want to make about this paper—especially about those parts of it which deal with the population problem. I think it would be useful for some suitable group of people, such as this, to emphasize that there is not only a human population problem in the world but also a problem of the population of certain other animals. You can see this in India where the animals wandering around are almost as numerous as the people, and not by any means all of them serve any useful function. You can see it in large cities in North America and Europe, where there are tremendous numbers of dogs and cats fouling up the sidewalks and roads, and this, I think, is a problem in pollution which must be faced too.

Another thing: I took a statement from what Dr Vallentyne called his preliminary notes, as that was the only pertinent document that was available to me before today, and on the last page he says: 'Most prominent among the myths that we live by is the notion that we can maintain a collective control over death (laws and social customs pertaining to health and survival) and yet not over birth (which is what we can and must control). The current *laissez-faire* attitude to human population is the basic cause of environmental problems. If the UN Conference on the Human Environment, to be held in Stockholm in 1972, faces this issue squarely, there will be hope for the future. If it does not, then those individuals, agencies, and governments, that feel strongly on the matter, should become obnoxious in bringing the issue into uninhibited discussion.'

I share Dr Vallentyne's view about the necessity of having an objective discussion of this problem, but it is not practicable to do it at the United Nations Conference in Stockholm, and I'll tell you why: I'll tell you my experience during the first meeting of the Preparatory Committee for the Stockholm Conference which was in New York in March, 1970. I was chairman of the working group which was deciding on what the subject matter of the Conference should be, and I was so starry-eyed about this population problem, the way Dr Vallentyne is, and thinking if I did one useful thing I would get it on to the agenda for the Stockholm Conference—even against the advice of all my experienced friends in the UN who said you just can't debate the population problem in the UN. The reason why you can't debate it there is that there are some developing and developed countries which have as one of the elements in their national policy—a very strong element—that they will not admit that they have a population problem; they want more population, not less. As soon as you raise this matter in any committee there will be so much argument that you will never get any document accepted or any business done. And this is precisely what happened: after a lot of advice against it, we got in two sentences in our report to the effect that we thought the fundamental problem was the population one. But as soon as we presented the report for acceptance by the committee at the end of the meeting, the representatives of the rather few countries that are opposed to this policy began to debate, and the two sentences had to come out and be dropped immediately—just like that! You will never get a direct discussion of this problem in the Stockholm Conference, and consequently I think one of the most useful things this present Conference can do is to bring it right into the open. We are scientists, we don't have political problems here, and we can discuss the matter freely and objectively and perhaps be able to make some statement on the subject.

Caldwell

I fully agree with this and also observe that the Economic and Social Council has called for another conference on population, in 1974. The attempt to get resolutions through the United Nations on an International Declaration of Human Rights has been a long and slow one, but some progress has been made: fewer and fewer countries are now adamant about this matter of population. The agenda for Stockholm is already largely established, so it seems to me that it would be spinning out wheels to try to do much about that occasion; but it does seem that we could do something here, though whatever is done, I am convinced, needs to be done in a constructive and realistic way.

When we talk about population—and I thoroughly agree with the need here for elaboration of our vocabulary—what we really get is a problem of population policy coupled with the whole question of the quality of life and the standard of living. It is very difficult to talk about optimum population unless you have some yardstick for optimality; practically no one uses mere survival as the yardstick, although to hear some people talk you would suspect that they are thinking of this, because they never really introduce the question of what kind of lives people are going to have. And if you go into this question of population, you run into the point Dr Butler has just made: you get into a confrontation with countries—with representatives from countries—that see this whole thing as somehow derogatory, as contrary to their ambitions for economic development and growth. The President of Mexico said not long ago that they need more people to develop their resources: well, I think he couldn't have been more wrong, but that is the way he put it, the way he was thinking about it.

I don't want to divert our attention from the population issue but I do want to add just another dimension to it, which is that, until we get a more sophisticated way of talking about what we mean by 'standard of living', I think we are going to find this debate about population levels a rather futile one, with mismatched argument and semantic confusion. Now I don't know what kind of vocabulary we need, but we certainly need some concepts that would be more meaningful—that could be more readily translated into action or the conditions of life of people—than the term 'standard of living' or, for that matter, 'economic growth'. Supposing one took the example of the conditions of life in non-industrial societies—for instance, in a Cambodian village—one could make for many such villages a list of human resources and amenities that the inhabitants enjoy, having, by a good many elements on such a check-list itemizing the quality of life, a fairly decent kind of existence. Now this list doesn't apply to such people as were referred to by the World Health Organization as being exposed to conditions that exist in heavily populated areas, or in villages near national capitals, and so on, where you have conditions that are different from those found in a traditional society. On the other hand, you have the kind of standards found in industrial states. In the United States (and I still argue with European friends that their public standard of living is probably higher than ours in most places, at least as regards civic amenities) we have a great deal of redundancy built into our standard of living. Thus one might ask: is your standard of living at a particular level if you have one television set, and higher if you have three—simply duplicating one another? Is living standard only a matter of 'more'; may it not also be qualitative?

I would argue that to do anything very constructive about the question of population policy we must relate it to this problem of the quality of life.

You may deal with population policy in economic terms if you want to, though it's more than that. The economic limits of human numbers have been extended by technology, but the basic issues are ecological. We need not seek to discover just how many people the earth can hold, because that really isn't the question. Rather does it seem to me that the question even in the less developed countries is, how many people ought there to be in relation to the hopes that we have (and the life-support capabilities can allow us to have) for economic and social welfare?

Johnson

If I might give a very brief résumé of the background, the United Nations were unable to take a hand in matters of population until 1966, when their General Assembly passed an enabling resolution permitting organs of the United Nations to give advice on population problems when so requested. In due course the agencies concerned—especially UNESCO and WHO—evolved their own parallel mandates to reflect the overall mandate of the UN General Assembly. In 1967 the Secretary-General established a Trust Fund for Population, but because of the usual internecine warfare in the United Nations system they had trouble in deciding where to locate the Trust Fund—whether in the UN Development Programme or in the UN headquarters itself. So contributions to the fund remained at a very low level—roughly 1.25 million dollars—until the summer of 1969, when the fund was firmly and decisively placed in the UN Development Programme and renamed the United Nations Fund for Population Activities. Governments, especially of advanced industrial countries, rallied around and contributed ever-growing amounts of money to the fund, with the result that it hopes to receive commitments of 25 million dollars next year and expects to have 100 million dollars to spend annually by, roughly, 1975. Here you have a situation where a small number of countries acted really under the UN mask to get something going.

I entirely agree with Dr Butler as to the extent of the opposition, but I would go much farther than he would in defining the opposition to population control and family planning action. It includes the governments of Latin America—who either suspect the hand of Yankee imperialism in UN efforts or want to fill up their own countries—and it also includes Catholic governments elsewhere. Particularly involved are the old Catholic countries of Europe: France, Belgium, Italy, Ireland. The opposition also includes African countries that have similar suspicions of the motives of the Fund and of family planning programmes in general. And it includes all the nationalist regimes or other regimes that have ethnic problems themselves—minority problems which make them internally suspicious and distrustful of having population programmes.

All this being certainly true, the question really is: whether it is so true and so important that the 1972 Stockholm Conference and the Secretariat which presumably should take instructions from governments is still to be allowed to get away with not having it on the agenda at all. As for entering by the back door of certain items on the Stockholm agenda—namely, the section on human settlements—I think we have learnt enough from our own discussions here so far to realize that you cannot have any paper on agriculture which doesn't make some pretty remarkable reference to the effect of population growth, and to the environmental and ecological effects of population growth on the countryside. But these are rather incidental allusions to the subject, and now our question is, are we or are we not going to get anywhere: can this unique group of leading scientists and others say anything which the UN Secretariat will be able to act upon or at least take effective notice of?

I think there is a way out of the political dilemma—a way which Dr Vallentyne's clever coining of words suggests, indeed helps to make clear—and it is this: if you put forward the population problem and emphasize that it is in fact a *demophoric* problem, a combination in different measures of peoples and wealth, then point the finger at the industrial societies because of their impact, you should have a chance of persuading even the Brazilians!

The developing countries are immensely worried about this whole environment exercise which they fear is a way of stopping what they consider their legitimate aspirations for development. I think Mr Maurice Strong, the Secretary-General of the UN Conference on the Human Environment, would himself be quite amenable to recommendations which tended to point out the population problem in a politically acceptable light by saying, 'OK, it's a universal problem that should be discussed at Stockholm, though, of course, not just concerning developing countries.' There is to be a UN World Population Conference in 1974 and I think this would be a second possibility for our present Conference to consider making recommendations to. The UN 1974 World Population Conference is part of the activities of World Population Year 1974, and in spite of all opposition one of the major subject-areas on the provisional agenda of that Conference will be the demographic future—particularly population and environment—and I think that such things as we have been saying here will strengthen the hand of those who are on the preparatory committee for that Conference and Year and wish to keep the environment on the agenda. So far there have been two meetings of the preparatory committee and environmental matters remain firmly on the agenda; but the agenda list has to go before the Population Commission and then before ECOSOC, and if we are to follow the current form there will be a lot of pressure to take this kind of thing off it. So I think anything we can say here in support of the need for far more consideration of population and environmental problems would be helpful.

Polunin

[*It has been gratifying indeed to my organizer's ear to hear these frank and pungent comments from people who are really qualified to make them. Mr Stanley Johnson's latest book, *Life Without Birth: A Journey Through the Third World in Search of the Population Explosion*, should surely be read by all who are interested in this vital subject; to my mind it gives an objective and courageous appraisal of an appalling situation and prospect. Now his revelation that there have already been two meetings of the preparatory committee of a United Nations conference which is to be held as far away as 1974, seems typical of how long it takes to 'get anything going' in those august

[* Square brackets are used to indicate that not by any means all of the details given were spoken out on this particular occasion.—Ed.]

circles. It reminds me that an acquaintance of mine, who recently retired from the post of head of the office taking care of conferences in one of the largest UN Agencies, told me that whereas it used to take fully two years to 'get anything going' in the United Nations, it now takes considerably longer. Yet how in these circumstances and given an increasingly beleaguered world, can they possibly be 'on the dot'—when I am not sure that we of this relatively modest Conference can claim to be, who have settled our agenda, prepared our papers, and convened ourselves all in the last very few months.

Mr Johnson mentioned Mr Maurice Strong's openness of mind on this matter of population *versus* environment to which I, too, can testify. Indeed he expressed keenness to me that we should debate it and some other matters quite frankly and let his people have the results of our deliberations in good time for the drafting of the papers for Stockholm. And being unable to come here himself because of prior engagements in Africa, Mr Strong has sent the UN Conference's newly-appointed Scientific Adviser to our conference as his first assignment, and also their Senior Programme Director (who will be with us tomorrow). So you see our hopes of contributing indirectly but usefully to the Stockholm Conference ought to materialize, especially as several of us here are acting as consultants to it—all of which throws on us a burden of the highest responsibility.

As for the Brazilians, we invited as 'roving eminents' one of their leading ecclesiastics, with a wide reputation for fearless outspokenness, Archbishop Helder Camara, and also one of their leading conservationists, Dr José Candido de Melo Carvalho, who is a Consulting Editor on my own Journal. To his expressed regret, Dom Camara could not come owing to a prior engagement in Rome, 'to participate [in] a big program, through Italian television, around "Populorum Progressio", the Encyclical of Paul VI, about the development'.* Dr Carvalho accepted our invitation to participate but in the end could not find his fare which, owing to his not being on our main programme and in view of the shortness of time and funds, we were unable to contribute. But the long cable which he sent me may be indicative of his country's viewpoint, as it starts: 'At this moment of history when man has acquired ascendency over the biosphere so much so that now for the first time in history he is even able to pose a technological threat to demographic growth by vastly destructive war and by imperilling the existence of his own habitat...'

Somewhat similar things happened with the East, West, and South, Africans, and I fear our hopes are dwindling of seeing here Professor David Wasawo, of Kenya, whose wife cabled me recently that he was 'still hospitalized after operation . . . article ready soon' and 'doctor agreeable attending . . . conference'; thereupon we asked two outstanding West Africans to redouble their efforts to participate if possible. We also invited South Africa's most eminent ecologist and he accepted; but there were problems about his coming and in the end he didn't. So you can see that although we did our best to muster fully representative invitees in the short time available to organize this Conference after the (delayed) passage of the Finnish National Budget, circumstances were often against us. Thus as regards representatives from the two Germanies, the Eastern one died after acceptance and the expected West-

* He did, however, send us a pungent message, which is published on page 63.—Ed.

ern one broke her leg. The Academia Sinica (the Academy of Sciences of Mainland China) cabled me that they could not send anybody at the last moment 'since our work schedule has been arranged'.* But still in the end I hope you would agree with me that we have not managed too badly in the matter of wide representation by invited participants, having somehow exceeded our optimum number!

To return finally to the United Nations Organization: there seems no question that it does much good work through some of its diversified family of agencies which are reasonably effective, so that as a whole it represents the hope of the world. But I would like to place on record my thoughts on why many of its activities seem to be sadly ineffective nowadays. I live in the midst of what must be by far the greatest agglomeration of United Nations specialized and other agencies, in Geneva, and it seems to some of us more ardent well-wishers that they need urgently to remedy certain aspects of their form and functioning. Of these aspects which we feel require constructive reconsideration I'll now give you a 'round dozen', as follows:

1. The present method of recruitment of staff which is very largely according to geographical distribution rather than qualifications, professional competence, or even general suitability, so that real leadership is lacking and efficiency suffers.
2. The frequent lack of a sense of urgency, of real work-rigour, and of any feeling of global mission, in marked contrast to their early stages which I well remember at Church House, Westminster, around the end of World War II, were so full of hope and enthusiasm.
3. The 'empire-building' tendencies of individual heads or would-be heads and concomitant internecine warfare exhibited so widely in their midst.
4. The extreme bureaucratic ponderousness of their mechanisms which makes swift and effective action virtually impossible.
5. The often arrogant attitude adopted by many officials and, particularly, agencies, that they were set up to look after such and such a matter, and that, therefore, the matter is being looked after throughout the world.
6. Concomitant with the last item, the insistence (and, often, active attempts to ensure) that no other agencies should exist or, particularly, be newly organized in, the field or fields concerned.
7. The frequent lack of decision on the part of perfectly competent individuals who find themselves stymied by the all-too-established system.
8. The almost unbelievable amount of duplication of effort and personnel, e.g. in environmental matters, in different agencies it seems often without proper liaison and certainly without coordination even in the interests of reasonable economy.
9. The frustration felt by many would-be-active officers to the extent that it is said 'a good man cannot last'.
10. The chronic production of far too much printed or cyclostyled paper, whose very volume renders it impossible to digest and which is consequently largely overlooked and therefore wasted.
11. The widespread administrative incompetence such as would preclude

* *See* footnote on page 211.—Ed.

viability in commercial or even academic circles, and which often seems
to be due to the employment of *far too many* people.
12. The continuing shortage of funds for really worthy projects at least of
an urgent nature.

I could go on with other items and document them all—adding, for
example, the nonsense which gives the same voting weight to the smallest
nation as to the largest, and the intense nationalism that commonly precludes global consideration—but the details would so often be tedious or
actually painful that I presume you would rather take my word for it: that I
have checked each and every one 'back and forth'.]

Vallentyne
Just as a point of verification, my reference to the United Nations in the
preliminary notes which I sent you some months ago is not in the final paper.
I was informed in Canada that the Brazilians flatly refuse to discuss population, and that it could not be brought up at Stockholm in 1972. So I took it
out.

Polunin
You should jolly well put it back.

Vallentyne
Put it back in?

Polunin
Yes, please.

Vallentyne
I'll be glad to do so if it will not inhibit the development of global discussion.

Polunin
I remember those remarks very well and I thought, well, here is another
who really understands the true situation and has the courage to speak out
about it.

Kangas
Mathematically speaking, if you have a suitable formulation and then a
high level of production (or, better speaking, consumption), it is roughly the
same as the use of national resources. Then the bigger the population is, the
bigger will be the production or consumption, and the greater the use of
national resources. This means that if you have a small population but large
production, you have a big use of national resources.

Skulberg
I would like to have your views on the fact that in the developed countries
we have increasing pollution of the fresh waters.

Vallentyne
I think we can look forward to a decreasing degree of pollution in what
some have called the overdeveloped countries. The way I put it in the paper

was, a 'continuous decrease in the inputs of environmental pollutants can be expected for the next few years, probably extending over the next thirty years'. There has just been a fantastic change in awareness, and in the pressure of the public, in this respect. We have seen it on the North American continent—in the United States and Canada—and I think it is a great deal more universal than that.

The politicians today are receiving quite a different kind of pressure on pollution from what they received ten years ago, and this change has had a very profound effect. As a result, a number of things have come about—new laws, new regulations, the creation of new environmental departments— whereas before there was a scattering of interests concerned with land, air, or water. Now it's all under one roof—which compresses and, I think, eases, the control. I don't believe that those pressures are going to disappear. Although public awareness and reaction are on their way downhill at the moment— and I think they're probably going to sail down farther still—it seems merely that the peak which they hit a year or two ago in North America could not be sustained indefinitely. It was an almost purely emotional reaction, and I believe its effect will be to make the issue a permanent one at a lower, more rational, sustainable level. For in my opinion virtually all pollution problems are remediable, and there is nothing, even in an economic sense, that we do not have in the way of remedies at this moment, and that could not be applied. The city of Montreal pours what is essentially raw sewage into the St Lawrence river, as is still the case with many communities all over the world. We have had the knowledge of what to do in the way of secondary treatment of sewage for a hundred years, yet it hasn't been applied in these places.

The knowledge of how to treat another problem in technologically developed countries, the eutrophication problem, has been in existence for twenty years, and there is no reason why it could not be applied. The impetus that is required is the impetus from the public, who at the moment are very prone to point the finger at the industrial polluter. What they are going to find is that, having forced politicians to control industrial polluters, politicians will make laws that also force communities to do their job with sewage treatment plants. This is certainly happening, yet I don't think the public is really saying, 'Well, I'm a polluter and I must stop immediately.' But the effect of getting the politician to go after the industrial polluter is going to have repercussions on the attitude of the public and ultimately of municipalities.

The 1971 report of the Royal Commission on Pollution in England was referred to earlier in connection with air pollution. Also cited were some figures for water pollution that are semi-comparable. One thing I didn't mention in my paper is that our statistics on pollution are non-existent. What we need is a UN Statistical Yearbook on pollution. At present, no one would know what to put in—but it could be done very easily if we had, as they did in the English system, Grades 1–5 or Grades 1–4. Grade 1 might be unpolluted, and Grade 5 excessively polluted. Something of this sort needs to be done. In England things look rather promising, in spite of their far-too-large population. They can say that the fish are moving back towards and even through London in the Thames now, and I think this will continue.

They can also point to the sunlight increasing by 70 per cent over the central part of London.

Skulberg

It seems to me that in some countries where there are very rapid developments in industry and new settlements, more and more of the area will come under the influence of civilization and more and more polluted waters will occur. But I would like to hear comments on the situation, e.g. in Canada. Is it thought necessary to secure catchment areas for freshwater supply in the future?

Butler

We do so in certain areas, though the big dam in Saskatchewan isn't a catchment one in the sense usually employed for the term—it isn't for catching rainfall—it's for storing river-flow, as Saskatchewan is an area that is very much subject to drought and there is an enormous project there to build this big lake which is, in a sense, a catchment area. Yes, we do store water in certain places in Canada and they have an enormous project at Winnipeg to control flooding of the Red River and also to effect storage.

Vallentyne

Actually, there is no storage in the Winnipeg flood-control diversion channel—it is just an alternative route for water around the city. But I think the situation that you refer to is widely mixed in Canada. We suffer no lack of water, having, as mentioned in my paper, about 9 per cent of the world's river-flow and only about 0·7 per cent of the world's population. There are many river basin projects under study or development now to aid in water regulation and use.

As for increasing freshwater pollution with modern development, my feeling is quite the opposite. Situations with new and rapidly developing communities and industry are the ones that are going to get good waste treatment. The ones that we are beset with in Canada are ancient structures that are just on the verge of being economic. The pulp and paper industry is probably the worst offender, the problem being that if you ask outdated plants to upstage their treatment facilities they will say, 'Well, I'm sorry we just can't do it—we'll go broke', and so it generally degenerates into a non-solution. But to new industry governments can say, 'No, I'm sorry, no building permit until you do'.

Butler

It's in old cities and old industries that the greatest trouble lies. The city of Montreal has a rather interesting attitude economically: I am told that they have looked at this problem objectively and have calculated that it costs much less to treat drinking water than it does to treat sewage. So they put raw sewage in the river because everybody else along the Ottawa/St Lawrence River does, and subsequently they treat the drinking water. This is their way of thinking and acting.

Vallentyne

In the mid-nineteenth century we put human waste on the soil. It then passed to plants and sooner or later to food, the water and much else being brought into the recycling system. Then we broke the cycle with the institution of the water-transport system of sewage disposal by which man's waste goes directly into the rivers—skipping the soil and wending its way to the sea, though actually not all of it gets there because some is taken up by plants. Soon it became necessary to put into the soil fertilizers containing nitrogen, phosphorus, and potassium, which were being robbed from the soil. These are now going one way through the system and so are detergents containing phosphorus, though there is no need for them to create all the problems that they currently do. At present we are pitching away a raw but material resource of human waste that, if we shoved it back into the soil, would give us fine plant growth again, and there are many places where, of course, this is done. The systems that are operated, for example, in Tel Aviv, Mexico City, and Singapore, could well repay study towards possible emulation elsewhere.

[* Footnote to p. 207: The cable from the Academia Sinica, also thanking us for our 'kind invitation', was in response to my letter to their president written only a matter of days before our Conference started and following a decision in Finland that no governmental approach could be made in spite of the 'ping-pong episode' which spurred me to suggest it. Usually for similar reasons of lateness we were repeatedly out of luck in the matter of leading industrialists whom we had hoped to entertain in Jyväskylä, and I shudder to think of my telephone bills over those last few weeks of organization.—Ed.]

7
MAJOR WATER ETC. DEVELOPMENT PROJECTS

Keynote Paper

Ecological Consequences of Water Development Projects

by

M. KASSAS

Professor of Applied Botany,
Faculty of Science, University of Cairo, Giza, Egypt

INTRODUCTION

Each of the main land-masses of the world is largely divided piecemeal into catchment areas of drainage systems supplying major rivers, the example of Africa being illustrated in Fig. 1. A river may be defined as a mixture of water, rock detritus, and other materials, flowing in a channel having pro-

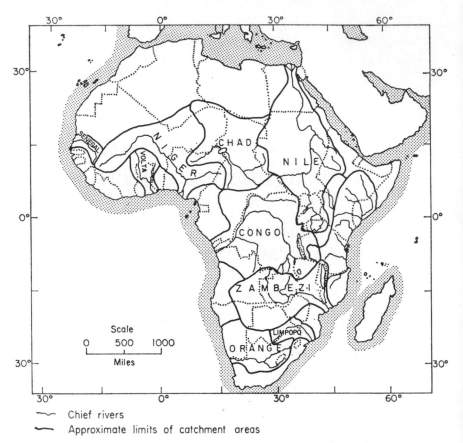

Fig. 1. Map of the main catchment areas in Africa. 1 mile = 1·609 km.

gressively lower levels. Strahler (1951) quotes from John Playfair's Law (published in 1802): 'Every river appears to consist of a main trunk, fed from a variety of branches, each running in a valley proportioned to its size, and all of them together forming a system of valleys connecting with one another, and having such a nice adjustment of their declivities that none of them joins the principal valley either on too high or too low a level; a circumstance which would be infinitely improbable if each of these valleys were not the work of the stream which flows in it.' This statement comprises three main points: (1) valleys are proportioned in size to streams flowing in them, (2) stream junctions are accordant in level, and (3) therefore, valleys are carved by streams flowing in them.

Whereas this may be true for simple rivers comprising a single drainage system, complex rivers do not always conform to the postulates of Playfair's Law. Thus, the River Nile is an example of a complex system composed of a number of drainage systems that joined later in their history. This union was not due to intrinsic development of the pre-Nile rivers, but was due mostly to climatic changes, tectonic events, and geomorphic development (Butzer & Hansen, 1968). The present hydrologic regime of the River Nile is apparently no older than 20–30 thousand years (Fairbridge, 1963; Wendorf & Said, 1967; Wendorf et al., 1970).

For riparian communities a river is a flow of water, and water is a most important natural resource. But rivers are apt to be very inconsistent: sometimes in devastating flood, and sometimes too low to provide for even the local needs. A natural river seems wasteful and awesome; its challenge has throughout history urged in man the will to control.

We may cite the discharge regime of the River Nile at the turn of this century as follows (Willcocks, 1904): of the mean discharge of 3,400 cubic metres per second which passed Aswan, 400 cubic metres per second were utilized in the irrigation of 2,320,000 acres (ca 928,000 ha) in Upper Egypt, while 540 cubic metres per second were utilized in the irrigation of 3,430,000 acres (ca 1,372,000 ha) in Lower Egypt, the remaining 2,100 cubic metres per second being discharged into the Mediterranean. Barning & Banson (1969) stated that the average discharge of the Volta River to the sea off West Africa was 40,000 cubic feet (ca 1,100 m^3) per second. These are examples of wastefulness from the viewpoint of utilization by man (Rodier, 1963).

To illustrate the danger of flooding by the Nile we may quote Willcocks (1904): '. . . in 1887 I witnessed a scene which must have once been more common than it is today. The news that the bank had breached spread fast through the village. The villagers rushed out on to the banks with their children, their cattle, and everything they possessed. The confusion was indescribable: a narrow bank covered with buffaloes, children, poultry, and household furniture. The women assembled around the local saint's tomb, beating their breasts, kissing the tomb, and uttering loud cries, and every five minutes a gang of men ran into the crowd and carried off the first thing they could lay hands on wherewith to close the breach. The fellaheen meanwhile, in a steady, business-like manner, plunged into the breach, stood shoulder to shoulder across the escaping water, and with the aid of torn-off doors and windows and corn stalks, closed the breach.' Similar stories may be quoted for other rivers; in 1887 the Hwang Ho in China inundated 50,000 square miles (129,500 km^2) and killed a million people.

Comparable threats are related to changes in position of river channels. Fig. 2 (simplified from Strahler, 1951) shows a series of surveys of the Mississippi River carried out within the period 1820–1932, and illustrates notable shifts in the river's course. Each shift would mean destruction of farms, villages, etc.

Annual variation in river flow is universal. As an example we may quote the flow of the River Zambezi in southern Africa. The mean flow for March is 110,000 cubic feet (ca 3,000 m^3) per second (average of 1925–54); in March 1949 the flow was only 30,000 cubic feet (ca 840 m^3) per second; in March 1952 it was 190,000 cubic feet (ca 5,300 m^3) per second. Man's legitimate concern is to make these annual variations more even.

Armed with modern technology and the powers which it provides, man ceased to worship the river gods and began his world-wide venture of river-control schemes. By 1966 there had been created 8,613 dams (above 15 metres

in height) in all continents (2,810 in the USA alone), and, as Obeng (1969*a*)
stated, '. . . it is much easier to list the *without-dams* countries rather than the
with-dams countries.' A dam is often built as a multipurpose construction: to
transform a water supply that is seasonally and annually variable to a man-
controlled supply, to conserve a considerable volume of water that would
otherwise be discharged into seas and utilize it in expanding agricultural

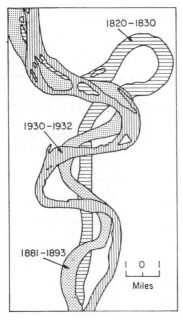

Fig. 2. Map of results of surveys of part of
Mississippi River, USA, indicating some notable
shifts in its course within the period 1820–1932.
Simplified from Strahler (1951). 1 mile = 1·609
km.

potential, to harness river energy for providing cheap power, and to curb
destructive floods. But river control means that a natural system is substantially modified, and that its physical and biotic attributes are transformed. These are seeds of ecological problems. Dams form man-made lakes,
and these are fertile beds for those seeds.

MAN-MADE LAKES

Conservation of Water (quantity)

Evaporation is an inevitable process; dam-planners will have to consider
it as one of their calculation parameters. How big is the loss? Hurst *et al.*
(1966) estimate the average annual evaporation from Lake Nasser (above
the High Dam of Aswan, Egypt) to be 2.7 metres* depth of water. Hammouda
& Elnesr (1964) give a very similar estimate of 2,658 mm. The estimated area
of the lake at survey datum 182 m will be 5,736 square kilometres and the
total annual loss of water will be about 15.5 thousand million cubic metres.
Amissah (1969) estimates the average depth of water lost by evaporation at
the Volta Dam in Ghana as 65 inches (1.62 m) per year, and the total annual
loss of water from this lake to be about 12.6 thousand million cubic metres. To

---

* According to Professor Reid A. Bryson (*in litt.* 24 Sept. 1971) this is 'a low estimate, as
events have demonstrated'.—Ed.

appreciate these volumes, we may mention that 8 thousand million cubic metres will irrigate one million acres (400,500 ha) in Egypt for a year.

The evaporation from reservoir lakes poses two questions. Can this loss be reduced or, alternatively, will it be increased? The possibility of reducing evaporation from open bodies of water by the application of monomolecular films has been the subject of world-wide investigations which were initiated in Australia in 1952—*see* the comprehensive review by Frenkiel (1965). On an experimental basis, such action seems feasible, but for large bodies of water various practical difficulties and cost are limiting factors.

The likelihood of increasing evaporation from man-made lakes by invading water-plants is a serious menace—*see*, for instance, Little (1966). The 'explosive spread' of water-weeds has numerous examples to be quoted—*see*, for instance, Chapman (1970). Stories of the 'most beautiful menace', *Eichhornia crassipes* (Water-hyacinth), have been related in popular weeklies. Several investigations dealing with the effect of water-plants through increasing rates of water-loss (e.g. Migahid, 1948*a*, 1948*b*, 1952; Hammouda, 1968) show that water-plants may increase evaporation losses up to three times; or even, according to Penfound & Earle (1948), up to six times. Thus any increase in water-loss by evapotranspiration may upset the calculations of reservoir planners.

Conservation of Water (quality)

The quality of water in man-made lakes is related to its physical and chemical attributes, and these are mainly influenced by: features of water collecting from the often vast catchment area upstream of the dam, features of the terrain that the lake covers and adjoins, the length of time during which water will remain in the lake before flowing farther downstream, and the types of human industries skirting the lake.

The physical features of water as it reaches a reservoir-lake are related to its load of rock detritus—a load that varies in texture and will eventually settle and cause the problem of silting. But this load may include such fine colloidal components as were recorded in the water of the River Niger and described by White (1969*a*) as '. . . . not removed by filtration through glass-fibre filters'. The alluvial load is influenced by the geomorphological characters of the whole drainage system—for details, *see* Leopold *et al.* (1964). That the chemical features are also related to the country which a river drains may be shown by reference to the River Ob (USSR), that drains extensive areas of the Siberian marshes which enrich its water with organic matter that causes a chain of chemical reactions including deoxygenation (*cf.* Hynes, 1969).

Available data seem to indicate (e.g. Harding, 1966; White, 1969*a*, 1969*b*) that on the closure of dams, the concentration of chemicals in the water at first rises but then falls gradually until a stable situation is reached. The rises are apparently due to leaching from the inundated soils. The sudden rise in fish production in Lake Kariba from 1960 to 1963 (Harding, 1966), and its drop in later years, are indications of the early phase of fluctuation in the physical, chemical, and biological, qualities of stored water.

The quality of water has two aspects: its *in situ* impact (e.g. on the hydrobiology of the reservoir) and its downstream impact. The silt-free water running downstream below a dam is an active agent of erosion. Leopold *et al.* (1964) give measurements of degradation below several dams in the United States (partly reproduced in our Table I), adding that ' . . . sixteen years after closure of the Denison Dam approximately 35,000 acre-feet of sediment have been removed from the Red River channel over a reach extending 100 miles downstream from the dam. This removal represents both a lowering of the bed and erosion of the banks of the channel.' The problems of the silt-free water of the Nile downstream from Aswan, Egypt, are thoroughly discussed by Ahmed (1960, 1961). The so-called Nile-cascade scheme of building a series of barrages between Aswan and Cairo, aims at protecting the downstream channel against the erosive action of the silt-free water.

TABLE I

Degradation below Selected Dams in USA (after Leopold *et al.*, 1964).

River—Dam—Location	Period	A*	B+
Missouri, Fort Peck, Montana	1936–50	1.01	0.067
Missouri, Garrison, N. Dakota	1949–57	0.65	0.093
Arkansas, John Martin, Colorado	1943–51	0.33	0.041
North Platte, Guarnsey, Wyoming	1927–57	2.00	0.066
Red, Denison, Oklahoma–Texas	1942–48	1.63	0.102
North Canadian, Canton, Oklahoma	1947–59	1.82	0.150
South Canadian, Conchas, New Mexico	1935–42	2.65	0.378
Salt Fork, Arkansas, Great Salt Plains, Oklahoma	1936–45	1.00	0.125
Smoky Hill, Kanopdis, Kansas	1946–61	0.76	0.051

$A*$ = average lowering of bed at all sections (ft).
$B+$ = average degradation per year of record (ft/year).
1 ft = 30.48 cm.

Long-term storage in a reservoir means that some of the waters will be stored for several years. During this time their biota will develop successively and their chemical attributes will become changed as a consequence of re-action of the biota on the aquatic habitat (*cf.* Houghton, 1966). Even minor changes in certain chemical attributes of water, e.g. pH value, may have far-reaching influences on the fertility of land and on the efficiency of fertilizers applied to it.

Invasion by Water-weeds

The initial phase, namely of filling a reservoir—it will take about ten years to fill the High Dam Reservoir of Egypt—and the episode of dramatic fluc-tuations, will eventually come to an end, and a man-made lake will result and provide habitat features that are not in general different from those of a natural lake. Invasion by water-weeds will follow sooner or later, subject only to their migration efficiency and local conditions of water depth, etc. The development of mats of *Salvinia auriculata* on Lake Kariba (River Zambezi) followed the establishment of the dam almost immediately (Hattingh, 1961; Boughey, 1963). According to Little (1966), the invasion reached its peak of 400 square miles (1,036 km²) in 1962 but declined to 200 square miles in

1966. The Jebel Auliya Dam on the White Nile (Sudan) was completed and filled to a level of 375.8 m in 1937 and to a level of 377.2 m in 1942 (Hurst *et al.*, 1946); yet, as an example of 'later' invasion, it was not until 1957 that *Eichhornia crassipes* appeared in its lake (Gay, 1958; Gay & Berry, 1959). The *Eichhornia* has now become a serious menace, and it is costing about £50,000 per annum and a manpower of about 200 men to combat this weed in the White Nile. Further examples of weed invasion are cited by Little (1966), Lawson *et al.* (1969), Mahal (1969), Chapman (1970), Lawson (1970), and others.

Little (1969) enumerates the following troubles that may be caused by weed invasion of reservoir-lakes:

1. By making movement of boats difficult.
2. By forming large mats which may drift and block hydroelectric installations and harbours.
3. By choking feeder streams and irrigation outlets.
4. By forming dense cover that may make fishing difficult, or even induce deoxygenation and hence mass fish mortality.
5. By reducing the effective capacity of the reservoir.
6. By the weeds' transpiration, water-loss may be greatly increased.
7. By reducing or eliminating recreational utility of the lakes.
8. By providing excellent breeding-grounds for many disease-transmitting insects, snails, etc.*

The floating water-weeds—such as *Eichhornia crassipes, Pistia stratiotes, Salvinia auriculata*, etc.—represent one order of menace that is not deterred by depth of water. Reed-swamp growth is a menace of a different and more serious order. Deep water may prevent the initial establishment of reeds, but when once established on the shallower peripheries of a water body, they may form floating swamp vegetation that may expand over deep water. Reference may be made to the floating swamps of the Danube Delta (Pallis, 1939) and to the Sudd Region in the Sudan. Invasion of man-made lakes by reed-swamp vegetation is recorded from the Dnieper Reservoirs (USSR) and elsewhere, as was discussed in several papers at the IBP-UNESCO symposium on 'Production, Ecology, and Hydrological Implications, of Aquatic Macrophytes' held in Romania during 1–10 September 1970.

Extensive literature has accumulated during the last decade on the control of water-weeds. Use of numerous herbicides for this purpose, although with variable success, has been reported on by Ivens (1967), Mahal (1969), Medani (1970), and others. Experiments on methods of biological control include studies on snails (Seaman & Porterfield, 1964), manatee (Allsopp, 1969), etc. A number of papers in the IBP-UNESCO symposium (*see* preceding paragraph) reported on biological control studies using geese (e.g. *Anser anser*) and Muskrat (*Ondatra zibethica*) in Czechoslovakia, Grass Carp (*Ctenopharyngodon idellus*) in New Zealand, and various insects (e.g. *Lipara lucens*) in the Netherlands.

* We might venture to add the possible loss of photosynthetic activity of phytoplankton and benthic Algae at lower levels due to reduction of light at the surface, with concomitant loss of biological productivity in the body of water.—Ed.

The Silt Problem

Reference has been made to the problem of erosion by clear water flowing below dams in place of the more usual sediment-laden flow. Deposition of sediments in reservoir lakes is a common problem. Thus Barning & Banson (1969) quote examples of 'dams which have been rendered dry and ineffective or even useless by the rapid filling with fragmented sediments. New Lake Austin on the Colorado River in Texas lost 95.6% of its capacity in 13 years, the Grand Reservoir on Toulumene River in California lost 83% in 36 years, and the Habra Reservoir on the Habra River in Algeria lost 58% in 22 years.'

Allen (1971) describes problems of the Anchicaya Hydro Project in Colombia, where the dam was closed in April 1955. These include sedimentation so that, 'by the end of 1955, which was a year of heavy flow, it was clearly evident that the reservoir was filling rapidly.' The first survey of the sediments was made in December 1956, 21 months after closure of the dam. 'Calculations revealed that the total sedimentation in this period was 1,188,000 cubic meters, or 23.4% of the reservoir volume.' In the second survey, made in October 1957, the new deposit amounted to 167,000 cubic metres.

With large reservoir-lakes, room may be available for accumulation of sediments. According to Hurst *et al.* (1966), the capacity of the High Aswan Dam Lake in Egypt, at its maximum level of 182 m, is 157.4 thousand million cubic metres. This is made up of 30 thousand million cubic metres (up to a level of 146 m) as silt trap (dead storage), 90 thousand millions (up to a level of 175 m) for over-year storage, and 37.4 thousand millions (up to a level of 182 m) for flood protection. The silt trap is estimated to fill up in 500 years.

Duchoň (1967) discusses the two aspects of the silt problem, namely fluvial erosion of the catchment area, and loss of valuable soil materials (silt + organic compounds) either by their being deposited in reservoir-lakes or by their being washed out to sea. He suggests that silt-retention basins be built upstream of dams, and that the silt be collected from these basins and applied to fields; alternatively, technological means and machinery should be developed for quarrying silt from reservoir beds. Duchoň estimates that rivers in Czechoslovakia carry away every year 28 million tons of soil material.

Climatic Changes

Man-made lakes may be considered as bodies of water giving off into the atmosphere considerable amounts of water vapour and changing the local heat-energy balance as land surface is replaced by water surface. Climatic changes in the form of increased rainfall, reduced temperatures, and increased humidity, in the country adjoining the lake, may be speculated upon.

Microclimatic modifications of limited extent in space and in value may be expected (e.g. Goswami, 1958), but large-scale climatic modifications are not likely. Amissah (1969), dealing with the Volta Lake (Ghana) which, when fully formed, will have an area of about 3,000 square miles (7,770 km^2), concluded that there was no evidence of climatic change.

A plant ecological survey of the Red Sea coastal chain of hills and mountains between Suez (lat. 30° N) and Jebel Elba (lat. 22° N) on the Sudano-Egyptian border (Kassas & Zahran, in press), shows that a body of water of the size of the Gulf of Suez (*ca* 10,000 sq km) is not sufficient to provide for perceptible orographic rainfall; only the full stretch of the Red Sea may provide for the formation of orographic-rain-fed mountain oases of the Erkwit type described by Kassas (1956).

Social Problems (displacement)

Creation of man-made lakes entails relocation of people. In Africa alone have been moved: 100,000 people from Nubia (Egypt and Sudan) in connection with the Aswan High Dam; 75,000 (1 per cent of the population of Ghana) in connection with the Volta Dam at Akosombo; 50,000 in connection with the Kariba Dam (Zambezi River); 50,000 in connection with the Kaingi Dam (Nigeria); etc. The problems arising depend on a complex of physical, biological, ecological, cultural, and economic, factors that relate to (a) the attitude of the relocated people, and (b) the approach of the relocating authority. The problems are different in different parts of the world. Thus the problems associated with population displacements 'in order to facilitate construction of reservoirs and flood storage basins' in the United States, as enumerated by Humphrys (1958), sound like pleasant fairy-tales as contrasted with the distressing problems of population displacement consequent on the creation of man-made lakes in Africa as described by Scudder (1966, 1971) and others. Humphrys (1958) remarks: 'the most significant conclusion is that the problems associated with moving people cannot all be solved with money. There are endless, intangible values associated with social, religious, recreational, legal and amenity factors.' Scudder (1966) quotes a paper entitled 'The Lusito Tragedy' which describes the sudden onset of high and rapid mortality in about eight relocation villages, one of which lost 10 per cent of its population within a few months of their resettlement.

Timing and carefully-planned programmes of action may avoid a good deal of the human suffering that is commonly associated with uprooting people. As Scudder (1966) points out, the time between initiation and completion of dam construction is too short to implement research programmes that are needed for effective rehabilitation. Resettlement accordingly becomes a 'crash programme'. At Kariba (Zambezi River) the water level rose approximately 50 feet (15.24 m) during the first week, and to 88 feet (26.82 m) within a month from sealing off. After the Volta River (Ghana) was sealed on 19 May 1964, water was up by 20 feet (6.1 m) on the first of June, to 70 feet (21.3 m) two months later, and exceeded 150 feet (45.7 m) by the end of the year. This means that moving people should follow a carefully planned schedule.

Crises arise during or immediately after resettlement, when people go through a period of mental fluidity or 'culture shock'. Such crises may be partly alleviated by effective programmes aiming at helping people to reorientate themselves to their new environment and, probably, new way of life: fishermen become cultivators, shift-cultivators become permanent cultivators, dispersed populations in numerous hamlets become congregated into larger villages, etc.

Social Problems (health hazards)

Health hazards of man and beast associated with man-made lakes are particularly obvious in the tropics—*see*, for example, Waddy (1966) and Hughes & Hunter (1971). Notable sources of hazard are: schistosome-(bilharzia-) transmitting snails (Obeng, 1969*b*; Paperna, 1969; Shiff, 1971; etc.), malaria-transmitting mosquitoes, and filaria-transmitting flies (*Simulium*). All are associated with aquatic environments.

Running waters of rivers are often free from bilharzia-transmitting snails, whereas man-made lakes provide habitats that are suitable for these snails which are especially favoured by the presence of water-weeds (Paperna, 1969). Large-scale application of molluscicides may sound feasible, but Shiff & Clarke (1967), Shiff *et al.* (1967), and Shiff (1971), all report adverse effects of these chemicals on fish, microflora, and microfauna, of water, with secondary effects on water quality.

Malaria, through its local vector *Anopheles quadrimaculus*, was successfully controlled in the Tennessee Valley development project (USA) by raising and lowering the levels of lakes by about one foot (30.48 cm) every 7–10 days throughout the summer. However, when the same solution was proposed in connection with the Volta Lake (Ghana), tests indicated that the local vector (*Anopheles gambiae*) would be greatly encouraged by this measure (*cf.* Waddy, 1966)!

To save the labour force building the Owen Dam in Uganda from the threat of swarms of *Simulium damnosum*, 'it was necessary to eliminate the fly by dosing the White Nile with DDT. . . . Provision for repeating the treatment, if it becomes necessary, is actually built into the dam structure' (Waddy, 1966). The measure was successful (A. W. A. Brown, 1962). For the Volta Lake, the river was dosed with DDT periodically during the construction period. DDT was also used in the Kaingi Lake, on the River Niger, to protect the workers from the bites of *Simulium* (Kershaw, 1966). This was all very well, but we now know that DDT poses very serious problems on its own (e.g. Wurster, 1969).

Social Problems (archaeological salvage)

On 8 March 1960, the Director-General of UNESCO inaugurated the 'International Campaign to save the Monuments of Nubia' by saying: 'Work has begun on the great Aswan Dam. Within five years, the Middle Valley of the Nile will be turned into a vast lake. Wondrous structures, ranking among the most magnificent on earth, are in danger of disappearing beneath the waters . . . It is, therefore, with every confidence that I invite governments, institutions, public or private foundations, and men of good-will everywhere, to contribute to the success of a task without parallel in history. . . .' André Malraux, then French Minister of State for cultural affairs, responded: '. . . Your appeal is historic, not because it proposes to save the temples of Nubia, but because through it, for the first time, world civilization publicly proclaims the world's art as its indivisible heritage.'

The Nubia campaign did not only result in the salvation of numerous monuments including the Abu Simbel temples, but also attracted archaeological expeditions from thirty countries to work in Nubia (Egypt and Sudan). Greener (1962), Keating (1962), and others, narrate some of the exciting stories of this truly international endeavour.

Other man-made lakes in Africa were less fortunate in this respect. Thus Davies (1966) states: 'At Lake Kariba little attempt was made by the government ... to carry out archaeological salvage .... Dr Bond and Dr Clark undertook an extended survey of the Zambezi terraces and their archaeological content as part of the regular museum field-work.' He adds, 'The building of the dam at Akosombo and the imminent creation of Volta Lake led to considerable effort to record and salve what was possible .... There was little chance of obtaining international help ....' River valleys were probably the cradles of human infancy, so the archaeological sites that are likely to be associated with their terraces should not be allowed to drown without record. The examples quoted by Davies (*ibid.*), and there are surely others in all continents, may stimulate us to consider the establishment of an international fund for archaeological surveys in river valleys that are threatened with permanent inundation.

Social Problems (recreational possibilities)

L. H. Brown (1966) and Stroud (1966) refer to extensive studies carried out in the United States on 'the recreational use of water works reservoirs'. Recreational activities associated with man-made lakes are varied, and L. H. Brown (1966) enumerates fourteen activities—including sailing, fishing, swimming, water skiing, etc. Jackson (1966) mentions that the Tennessee Valley Authority reservoirs yield 36 lb (16.3 kg) of fish per acre per annum, of which 27 lb go to anglers and 9 lb to commercial fishermen. Opperman (1965) estimates that 3 million pounds are spent annually by anglers alone in the Transvaal Province of South Africa.

The need for this aspect of utility of man-made lakes is likely to expand. The Rockefeller Committee (1962) predicts that the amount of recreational fishing in the year 2000 will be three times what it was in 1960. This aspect of human pressure on man-made lakes will require the introduction of management measures that will maintain the productivity of waters to satisfy fishing requirements and also water quality. Water-use conflicts will arise. The Rockefeller Committee (*ibid.*) states: 'Public action is needed to resolve conflicts between recreation and other uses of water as well as among recreation activities themselves.' This aspect of the problem is thoroughly discussed by Biswas (1969), who firmly believes that 'all these problems can be overcome by proper planning' and extra cost. He emphasizes that recreational use of man-made lakes necessitates careful control of water quality: 'Polluted water just will not do.'

THE JONGLEI CANAL PROJECT

We shall here discuss briefly one example of a water development project that will illustrate the complexity of ecological processes and the diversity of interests involved.

The Sudd Region

Two river systems drain the Nile catchment of the Equatorial Plateau of Africa. One comprises Lakes Albert, Edward, and George, while the other comprises Lakes Victoria and Kioga. The two rivers meet, pass over the Murchison Falls (Lat. 2° N), and form the Bahr-el-Jebel that enters the Sudan over the Fola Rapids at Nimule. The River eventually reaches the extensive swamp known as the Sudd Region (Fig. 3). This is described by Willcocks

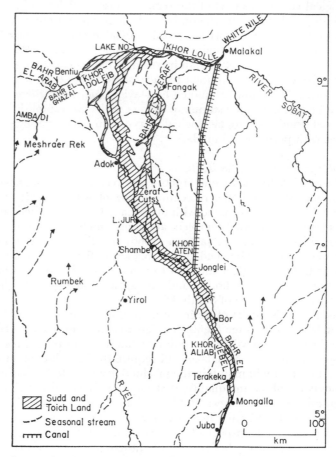

Fig. 3. Sketch-map showing location of the projected Jonglei Canal and area of the Sudd Region of Sudan. 1 km = 0·622 mile.

(1904) as 'the delta of the river in a very embryonic stage . . . an old lake which has silted up and become full of peat and sand deposits. At one time the lake must have had an extreme length of 400 kilometres and width of 400 kilometres . . . . The Sobat River flowed into it . . . dense masses of papyrus and water grasses shut out the horizon in every direction . . . .' The area of the swamp, estimated on the basis of air survey maps of 1930–31, totals 8,000 square kilometres (Hurst & Phillips, 1938).

Plant life in the Sudd Region is described by Migahid (1948a, 1948b, 1952), Drar (1951), the Jonglei Investigation Team (1954), and others. Reed-swamp (*Cyperus papyrus, Typha australis,* and *Phragmites communis*) and floating reed-swamp (*Vossia cuspidata, Echinochloa pyramidalis,* and *E. stagnina*) vegetation types characterize the permanent swamp. Freshwater mangrove is represented by *Aeschynomene elaphroxylon.* Floating plants are numerous; *Eichhornia crassipes* appeared after 1957. Higher grounds (islands, banks, floodplains that are mostly above inundation, etc.) have a variety of plant cover ranging from grasslands of the *Hyparrhenia rufa* and *Setaria incrassata* types to savanna forest types; there are also palm forests (*Hyphaene thebaica, Borassus aethiopium*) and mixed *Acacia* forests (*Acacia seyal, Balanites aegyptiaca*).

Three principal soil types were recognized by the Jonglei Investigation Team (1954):

1. Sudd soil, of the ectomorphic complex, with the surface organic horizon varying in thickness from one inch (2.54 cm) to four feet (122 cm).
2. *Toich* soils, of the hydromorphic group, occupying ground that lies between the permanently water-saturated sudd soil and the periodically water-saturated soils of 'intermediate' land. Seasonal anaerobic conditions prevent total decomposition of organic matter in such soils, which comprise a predominantly clay *toich* soil and a predominantly sandy *toich* soil.
3. Cracking clay soils, of heavy alluvial clay of montmorillonitic type which shrinks considerably on drying, occupy periodically-flooded ground.

Of the swamp animals we should mention particularly crocodiles and Hippopotamus. The latter is an ecological agent of special importance, its tracks through the reed-swamp often initiating new channels in the river system; it would thus risk destroying the muddy embankments that have been envisaged in the so-called Embankment of the Bahr-el-Jebel Scheme. Other animals that are commonly found in the region include African Elephant, White Rhinoceros (now rare in Africa), Black Rhinoceros, Wild Buffalo, Giraffe, Zebra, antelopes (several kinds), Lion, Leopard, Hyaena, etc.

Aspects of Human Ecology

Prevalent ecological conditions (seasonality of climate and hydrological regime of river and swamps, soil types, vegetation, etc.) have produced a way of life that comprises cattle-rearing, agriculture, and fishing, and includes a cycle of seasonal movement of man and cattle. Several ecological systems may be recognized (Barbour, 1961):

(a) The Nile and other permanent bodies of water (e.g. lakes).
(b) Permanent swamps of papyrus and other reed-like vegetation.
(c) Floodplain (*toich*) inundated for 4–6 months every year.
(d) 'Intermediate' land, not flooded from the river but flooded because of impeded drainage of rain-water, and crossed by numerous water-courses.
(e) High areas that are not flooded from the river, and have soils which are sufficiently permeable to drain quickly after rain.

Permanent villages in this region are built on high ground. They are surrounded by land that is cultivated during the rainy season, and are occupied
from May to October. Grazing resources are limited. As floods recede and
underfoot conditions become bearable, cattle are moved to 'intermediate'
land. As water supplies dry, cattle are further moved to cattle camps on the
floodplains (*toich*). Here grass and water are in ample supply and fishing is
bountiful during early January to late April. By May the rainy season is on,
cattle are moved towards the permanent villages on high land, and the
seasonal cultivation is resumed. A variety of crops are grown, but mainly
sorghums and millets.

This pattern of life is closely associated with the present hydrologic regime
in the Sudd Region and its floodplains, with water flooding the *toich* and
'intermediate' land during summer (with maximum flow in Bahr-el-Jebel)
and receding during winter (of minimum flow). This pattern involves a
human population estimated to be 666,939, with 829,900 cattle and 686,800
sheep and goats.

Hydrology of the Sudd Region

Table II shows the discharges, in thousands of millions of cubic metres per
annum, at the head of the Sudd Region (Mongalla) and at the tail of the
Region (below Lake No—*see* Fig. 3). Two points are obvious: (1) a considerable volume of the river water, amounting normally to 12.7 thousand
million cubic metres per year, is lost during passage through the Sudd, and

TABLE II

*Discharge in Thousands of Millions of Cubic Metres per
Year, at Mongalla (Head of Sudd Region) and at Tail of
the Sudd.* From: Jonglei Investigation Team, *Vol. I, p. 67* (1954).

Years	Mongalla	Tail of Sudd
Average: 1912–42	27.0	14.3
1915	27.9	14.0
1916	37.9	15.5
1917	55.8	18.0
1918	47.1	21.3
1919	31.2	17.8
1920	25.8	13.9
1921	16.6	12.8
1922	15.3	11.0
1923	19.3	11.4
1924	20.4	11.4
1925	18.9	12.5

(2) the greater the volume of water entering the Region at Mongalla (e.g.
55.8 thousand million cubic metres in 1917), the greater will be the volume of
water lost (37.8 thousand million cubic metres in 1917, as compared with 4.3
thousand millions in 1922). The first point suggests that something should be
done to reduce this loss, as was early discussed by Garstin (1904). The second
point indicates that the increase of equatorial supplies of Nile water by dam
reservoirs on Lake Victoria, Lake Albert, etc., will have little effect on the

volume of water flowing northwards from the Sudd Region if the capacity of its channels remains as it is. It is obvious that the present channel of Bahr-el-Jebel and its adjoining streams cannot carry all the water flowing past Mongalla, as it spills over the banks and forms the swamp system of the Sudd Region. Evapotranspiration and other agencies of water loss consume an annual average of 12.7 thousand million cubic metres of the river water, plus rainfall water amounting to 7.5 thousand million cubic metres (the average rainfall in the Sudd Region being 900 mm per annum).

Three projects have been proposed for the purpose of reducing 'water-loss' in the Sudd Region and to increase the capacity of the water channels:

(a) Embankment of Bahr-el-Jebel.
(b) Cutting a new channel to carry the whole normal supply, leaving Bahr-el-Jebel as a flood escape.
(c) Leaving Bahr-el-Jebel to carry as much as it can without undue loss, and cutting a new channel to carry the remainder (Jonglei Canal Diversion Scheme).

The third is accepted as a part of a complex project comprising the equatorial sources of the Nile.

Bahr-el-Jebel attains its maximum flow in August–September; this is the so-called 'untimely season', because it is the season when the Ethiopian sources (Blue Nile and River Atbara) provide more water than can be used for irrigation in Egypt and Sudan. Minimum flow is attained in January–February; this is the 'timely season', when water is needed.

The objectives of the water conservation projects in this part of the Nile system are: the equatorial sources of the Nile should be made to provide more water, to provide this water during the 'timely season', and saving the water that is currently lost in the Sudd. To fulfil these purposes:

(a) Lake Victoria will be used as a reservoir for 'over-year' storage. Regulators at the exit from Lake Kioga and below Lake Albert will control the quantity of water entering the Sudan.
(b) Between Mongalla and Jonglei the capacity of the existing river channel will be increased by dredging.
(c) A regulator at Jonglei will determine the distribution of water between Bahr-el-Jebel and the Jonglei Canal. In the 'untimely season' (August–September), Bahr-el-Jebel will be made to carry the minimum water required for navigation. In the 'timely season' (winter), the flow in Bahr-el-Jebel will be increased to a maximum that will usually not spill over the floodplains (Fig. 3).

This proposed regime will reverse the present seasonality of maximum and minimum flow. It will also eliminate the overflow of water on to the *toich* and network of lagoons and streams occurring across the floodplain. But how would this changed ecological set-up influence the life of people and their cattle? The Sudan Government appointed a team of experts to examine this question. After several years of work, the team published a report of four volumes (Jonglei Investigation Team, 1954). The following 'ecological consequences' comprise the essence of the results from this truly monumental work.

Ecological Consequences

As we have seen, the life pattern and economy of the Nilotic tribes living in the Sudd Region and its surrounding country is closely related to the existing regime of Bahr-el-Jebel and its associated rivers and water bodies. The essence of the Jonglei Canal proposal is to eliminate flooding and consequent loss of Nile water. It will also reverse the present seasonality of the hydrological regime of the whole system. These changes will have considerable effects on pasture and animal husbandry, and on the availability of water (and fish) to man and beast within the vast stretch of country lying farther from the river channel.

The drainage of the swamps of the Sudd Region seems likely to provide considerable areas of cultivable land, and experiments with rice, sugar-cane, tobacco, etc., are showing encouraging promise. But the various types of soil that are at present kept moist will behave differently when drained. The peaty soil will probably subside as it dries and becomes subjected to oxidation; the clay soil will shrink (60 per cent shrinkage has been indicated by Migahid, 1948b, and Jonglei Investigation Team, 1954) and hence subside, forming depressions; the sandy soils will not shrink and so will remain high. The variable topographic patterns will present land reclamation projects with further extensive problems that may prove expensive to remedy.

The change in the present way of life of the inhabitants to become sedentary cultivators will need a good deal of applied sociology to effect, and will surely entail hardship to many of them.

FUTURE PROSPECTS

It is no exaggeration to say that within the not very distant future practically all rivers will be brought under technological control. Some rivers will even be sealed off by estuary barrages (e.g. barrages across Morecambe Bay and Solway Firth in the United Kingdom, cf. Gilson, 1966). Yet rivers represent an important agency in the hydrologic cycle, collecting surface drainage and discharging it into the oceans and seas. Young (1969) estimates the total run-off of water from land to sea (mostly by rivers) in the world as 24,000 $\times$ 10^9 gallons (103×10^9 m^3) per day. This is equivalent to about 7 per cent of the total evaporation from land and sea.

Rivers normally bring to coasts an abundance of sediments that contribute to the building of deltas and to beach accretion. Elimination of such alluvial deposits might cause coastal erosion with serious repercussions that could amount to man-made marine transgression (e.g. the case of the Nile Delta, cf. Kassas, 1971). Fresh water and its load of alluvium influence the biological processes within the coastal water; a river flow brings to the coast an annual load of valuable fertilizers for fish life. Reduction of this river flow will entail reduction in fish production (e.g. the case of the eastern Mediterranean described by George, 1971).

Roden (1967) estimates that rivers discharge into the northeastern Pacific

Ocean between California and the Aleutian Islands approximately 21,000 cubic metres of water per second, and that freshwater discharges into the Bering Sea by Alaskan and Siberian rivers average 10,000 cubic metres per second. The Columbia River discharges about 3,200 cubic metres per second, its influence on the surface water of the ocean being perceptible several hundred kilometres out to sea (Duxburg *et al.*, 1966). Under the influence of the northward movement of water masses emerging from Bering Straits to the Chukchi Sea (McManus & Creager, 1963), fresh waters and sediments are carried northwards, together with warmth. What would be the effects of sealing off these river and other discharges, as has been proposed?

The effects of disrupting the hydrological cycle are, of course, more obvious on inland seas than on oceans. Goldman (1970) refers to the gradual lowering of levels of the Aral and Caspian Seas. Consequent on river control and irrigation schemes, less water is discharged into these seas than formerly. From 1961 to 1969 the surface of the Aral Sea dropped 1.3 metres, and during the last twenty years the level of the Caspian Sea has fallen $2\frac{1}{2}$ metres. This has drastically affected fish population. Various projects to remedy or at least relieve the situation are proposed, including the diversion of some north-flowing rivers in the Soviet Union to flow southwards. This, however, would involve large-scale changes of natural systems, with ecological consequences that would need to be carefully considered before any such major diversion was effected.

Large-scale regional and inter-regional water transfer projects are envisaged by certain United States authorities. These include the transfer of waters from Alaska and Canada to Arizona or even to Mexico, as proposed by the North American Water and Power Alliance (NAWPA). McGauhey (1969) comments, 'In exploring the physical implications of truly large-scale water transfers it might be revealing to consider the physical effects of not making such transfers.' He refers to thirst.

The ecological effects of water impoundment and diversion are discussed by Thomas & Box (1969), who emphasize that 'There *is* evidence of significant change in certain ecosystems as water projects are developed. There *is* evidence of loss of habitat for certain biota. There *is* evidence of changes in local environment which call for new approaches to wildlife or plant management.' One cannot but agree vehemently with their concluding comments: 'We do not argue against such large-scale water transport *per se*. Rather, we present an urgent plea for a better understanding of the ecological implications of these schemes. We urge that sound ecological studies be incorporated in the initial planning for large-scale water movement.'

Let us heed this wise counsel in considering also the even wider range of major projects on which man seems to be bent, guided by his urge to exploit the resources of the salt seas and oceans as well as the land.

REFERENCES

AHMED, A. (1960). Recent developments in Nile control. *Proc. Instn Civ. Engrs.*, **17**, pp. 137–200, 13 figs.
AHMED, A. (1961). Discussion on papers Nos. 6102 and 6370. *Proc. Instn Civ. Engrs*, **19**, pp. 337–415, 9 figs.

ALLEN, R. N. [1971]. The Anchicaya hydro project in Colombia. In *The Careless Technology*, Proc. Conf. Ecol. Aspects International Development, Warrenton, Virginia, 1968. Published early 1972 by Doubleday, Garden City, N.Y. 11530: pp. 318–42, illustr.

ALLSOPP, W. H. L. (1969). Aquatic weed control by manatees—its prospects and problems. Pp. 344–51 in *Man-Made Lakes*. Proc. Accra Symposium, 1966; Ghana Acad. Sc. and Ghana University Press, Accra: 398 pp., illustr.

AMISSAH, A. N. De Heer (1969). Some possible climatic changes that may be caused by the Volta Lake. Pp. 73–82 in *Man-Made Lakes*. Proc. Accra Symposium, 1966; Ghana Acad. Sc. and Ghana Universities Press, Accra: 398 pp., illustr.

BARBOUR, K. M. (1961). *The Republic of The Sudan*. University of London Press, London: 292 pp., illustr.

BARNING, K. & BANSON, J. K. A. (1969). Possible sedimentation and seismic effects on the Volta Lake. Pp. 83–90 in *Man-Made Lakes*. Proc. Accra Symposium, 1966; Ghana Acad. Sc. and Ghana Universities Press, Accra: 398 pp., illustr.

BISWAS, Asit K. (1969). Planning and evaluation of recreation on man-made lakes. Pp. 373–86, 2 figs, in *Man-Made Lakes*. Proc. Accra Symposium, 1966; Ghana Acad. Sc. and Ghana Universities Press, Accra: 398 pp., illustr.

BOUGHEY, A. S. (1963). The explosive development of a floating weed vegetation on Lake Kariba. *Adansonia*, **3**, pp. 49–61.

BROWN, A. W. A. (1962). A survey of *Simulium* control in Africa. *Bull. Wld Hlth Org.*, **27**, pp. 511–27.

BROWN, L. H. (1966). The multi-purpose use of reservoirs. Pp. 183–7 in *Man-Made Lakes*. Proc. Symposium Roy. Geogr. Soc., London, 1965; Institute of Biology and Academic Press, London: xiii + 218 pp., illustr.

BUTZER, K. W. & HANSEN, C. L. (1968). *Desert and River in Nubia*. University of Wisconsin Press, Madison: 562 pp., illustr.

CHAPMAN, V. J. (1970). A history of the lake-weed infestation of the Rotorua Lakes and the lakes of the Waikato hydro-electric system. *New Zealand Department of Scientific and Industrial Research, Information Series*, No. 78, pp. 1–52, 12 figs.

DAVIES, O. (1966). Archaeological salvage in man-made lakes (Lake Volta, Ghana). Pp. 109–11 in *Man-Made Lakes*. Proc. Symposium Royal Geogr. Soc., London, 1965; Institute of Biology and Academic Press, London: xiii + 218 pp., illustr.

DRAR, M. (1951). The problem of the Sudd in relation to stabilizing and smothering plants. *Botaniska Notiser*, Hafte II, pp. 32–46, 8 figs.

DUCHOŇ, F. (1967). Údolní přehardy a ochrana půdního fondo. [River dams and soil protection, (in Czechoslovak)]. *Vesmir*, **48**, pp. 306–7, 2 figs.

DUXBURG, A. C., MORSE, B. A. & McGARY, N. (1966). The Columbia River effluent and its distribution at sea. *Univ. Wash., Dept/Oceanog. Tech. Report,* No. 156, 105 pp.

FAIRBRIDGE, R. W. (1963). Nile sediments above Wadi Halfa during the last 20,000 years. *Kush*, **11**, pp. 96–107, 2 figs.

FRENKIEL, J. (1965). Evaporation reduction. *UNESCO Arid Zone Research*, **27**, pp. 1–79, 12 figs.

GARSTIN, W. E. (1904). *Report upon the Basin of the Upper Nile*. National Printing Department, Cairo: vi + 196 pp., illustr.

GAY, P. A. (1958). *Eichhornia crassipes* in the Nile of the Sudan. *Nature* (London), **182**, pp. 538–9.

GAY, P. A. & BERRY, L. (1959). The Water-hyacinth: a new problem on the Nile. *Geog. Jour.*, **75**, pp. 89–91.

GEORGE, C. J. [1971]. The role of the Sadd-el-Aali in the fisheries of the southeastern Mediterranean. In *The Careless Technology*, Proc. Conf. Ecol. Aspects International Development, Warrenton, Virginia, 1968. Publ. early 1972 by Doubleday: pp. 159–78, illustr.

GILSON, H. C. (1966). The biological implications of the proposed barrages across Morecambe Bay and Solway Firth. Pp. 129–37, 2 figs, in *Man-Made Lakes*. Proc. Symposium Roy. Geogr. Soc., London, 1965; Institute of Biology and Academic Press, London: xiii + 218 pp., illustr.

GOLDMAN, M. I. (1970). The convergence of environmental disruption. *Science*, **170**, pp. 37–42.

GOSWAMI, P. C. (1958). Reservoir submergence and ecological studies in the Damodar valley. *I.U.C.N. 7th Technical Meeting*, Athens, Greece, paper 51, 6 pp.

GREENER, L. (1962). *High Dam Over Nubia*. Cassell, London: xi + 198 pp., illustr.

HAMMOUDA, M. A. (1968). The water outlay by *Eichhornia crassipes* and observations on plant chemical control. *Phyton*, **13**, pp. 97–106, 5 figs.

HAMMOUDA, M. A. & ELNESR, M. K. (1964). On the estimation of evaporation from Lake Nasser. *Univ. Coll. Girls Ann. Rev.*, Cairo, No. 4, pp. 3–10.

HARDING, D. (1966). Lake Kariba: the hydrology and development of fisheries. Pp. 7–20 in *Man-Made Lakes*. Proc. Symposium Royal Geogr. Soc., London, 1965; Institute of Biology and Academic Press, London: xiii + 218 pp., illustr.

HATTINGH, E. R. (1961). The problem of *Salvinia auriculata* Aubl. and associated aquatic weeds on Kariba Lake. *Weed Res.*, **1**, pp. 303–6.

HOUGHTON, G. U. (1966). Maintaining safety and quality of water supply. Pp. 173–82 in *Man-Made Lakes*. Proc. Symposium Royal Geogr. Soc., London, 1965; Institute of Biology and Academic Press, London: xiii + 218 pp., illustr.

HUGHES, C. C. & HUNTER, J. M. [1971]. The role of technological development in promoting disease in Africa. In *The Careless Technology*, Proc. Conf. Ecol. Aspects International Development, Warrenton, Virginia, 1968. Publ. early 1972: pp. 69–101.

HUMPHRYS, C. R. (1958). Social problems resulting from the displacement of people by water management projects. *I.U.C.N. 7th Technical Meeting*, Athens, Greece, paper 54, 7 pp.

HURST, H. E. & PHILLIPS, P. (1938). *The Nile Basin*. Schindler's Press, Cairo: Vol. V, x + 251 pp., illustr.

HURST, H. E., BLACK, R. P. & SIMALKA, Y. M. (1946). *The Nile Basin*. S.O.P. Press, Cairo: Vol. VII, 178 pp., illustr.

HURST, H. E., BLACK, R. P. & SIMALKA, Y. M. (1966). *The Nile Basin*. Government Printing Offices, Cairo: Vol. X, 253 pp., illustr.

HYNES, H. B. N. (1969). Life in freshwater communities. Pp. 25–31 in *Man-Made Lakes*. Proc. Accra Symposium, 1966; Ghana Acad. Sc. and Ghana Universities Press, Accra: 398 pp., illustr.

IVENS, G. W. (1967). *East African Weeds and their Control*: Oxford University Press, Nairobi: 244 pp., illustr.

JACKSON, P. B. N. (1966). The establishment of fisheries in man-made lakes in the tropics. Pp. 53–73 in *Man-Made Lakes*. Proc. Symposium Royal Geogr. Soc., London, 1965; Institute of Biology and Academic Press, London: xiii + 218 pp., illustr.

JONGLEI INVESTIGATION TEAM (1954). *The Equatorial Nile Project: Report of the Jonglei Investigation Team*. Sudan Government, Khartoum: Introduction and Summary lxix pages; Vol. I, A Survey of the Area Affected, pp. 1–397, illustr.; Vol. II, The Equatorial Nile Project: Its Effects and the Remedies, pp. 399–816; Vol. III, Special Investigations and Experimental Data, pp. 819–1077, illustr.; Vol. IV, Maps and Diagrams, 8 maps + 241 figures.

KASSAS, M. [1956]. The mist oasis of Erkwit, Sudan. *Jour. Ecol.*, **44**, pp. 180–94, 1 fig.

KASSAS, M. [1971]. Impact of river control schemes on the shoreline of the Nile Delta. In *The Careless Technology*, Proc. Conf. Ecol. Aspects International Development,

Warrenton, Virginia, 1968. Publ. early 1972 by Doubleday, Garden City, N.Y. 11530: pp. 179–88, illustr.

KASSAS, M. & ZAHRAN, M. A. (*in press*). Plant life on the coastal mountains of the Red Sea, Egypt. *Jour. Ind. Bot. Soc.,* Jubilee volume.

KEATING, R. (1962). *Nubian Twilight.* Hart-Davis, London: 112 pp., illustr.

KERSHAW, W. C. (1966). The *Simulium* problem and fishery development in the proposed Niger lake. Pp. 95–7 in *Man-Made Lakes.* Proc. Symposium Royal Geogr. Soc., London, 1965; Institute of Biology and Academic Press, London: xiii + 218 pp., illustr.

LAWSON, G. W. (1970). Lessons of the Volta—a new man-made lake in tropical Africa. *Biological Conservation,* **2**(2), pp. 90–6, illustr.

LAWSON, G. W., HALL, J. B., LAING, E. & HOSSAIN, M. (1969). Observations on aquatic weeds in the Volta Basin. Pp. 331–6 in *Man-Made Lakes,* Proc. Accra Symposium, 1966; Ghana Acad. Sc. and Ghana Universities Press, Accra: 398 pp., illustr.

LEOPOLD, L. B., WOLMAN, M. G. & MILLER, J. P. (1964). *Fluvial Processes in Geomorphology.* Freeman, San Francisco & London: xiii + 522 pp., illustr.

LITTLE, E. C. S. (1966). The invasion of man-made lakes by plants. Pp. 75–86 in *Man-Made Lakes.* Proc. Symposium Royal Geogr. Soc., London, 1965; Institute of Biology and Academic Press, London: xiii + 218 pp., illustr.

LITTLE, E. C. S. (1969). Weeds and man-made lakes. Pp. 284–91 in *Man-Made Lakes.* Proc. Accra Symposium, 1966; Ghana Acad. Sc. and Ghana Universities Press, Accra: 398 pp., illustr.

McGAUHEY, P. H. (1969). Physical implications of large-scale water transfers. Pp. 358–63 in *Arid Lands in Perspective.* A.A.A.S. and University of Arizona Press, Tucson, Arizona: viii + 421 pp., illustr.

McMANUS, D. & CREAGER, J. S. (1963). Physical and sedimentary environments on a large spit-like shoal. *Jour. Geol.,* **71**, pp. 498–512, 7 figs.

MAHAL, M. S. (1969). Aquatic weeds and their control. Pp. 337–43 in *Man-Made Lakes.* Proc. Accra Symposium, 1966; Ghana Acad. Sc. and Ghana Universities Press, Accra: 398 pp., illustr.

MEDANI, M. A. (1970). [*Water Weeds: Methods of Control.*—in Arabic.] Government Printing Office, Cairo: 232 pp., illustr.

MIGAHID, A. M. (1948a). *Report on a Botanical Excursion to the Sudd Region.* Cairo University Press, Cairo: 159 pp., illustr.

MIGAHID, A. M. (1948b). An ecological study of the Sudd swamps of the Upper Nile. *Proc. Egypt. Acad. Sc.,* **3**, pp. 57–86, 8 figs.

MIGAHID, A. M. (1952). Further observations on the flow and loss of water in the Sudd swamps of the Upper Nile. *Bull. Fac. Sc., Cairo University,* 16 pp.

OBENG, L. E. (1969a). Man-made lakes—some perspectives. Pp. 19–24 in *Man-Made Lakes.* Proc. Accra Symposium, 1966; Ghana Acad. Sci. and Ghana Universities Press, Accra: 398 pp., illustr.

OBENG, L. E. (1969b). The invertebrate fauna of aquatic plants of the Volta Lake in relation to the spread of helminth parasites. Pp. 320–5 in *Man-Made Lakes.* Proc. Accra Symposium, 1966; Ghana Acad. Sc. and Ghana Universities Press, Accra: 398 pp., illustr.

OPPERMAN, R. W. J. (1965). The recreational potential of the Orange River Project. *South Afr. Jour. Sc.,* **61**, pp. 147–50.

PALLIS, M. (1939). *The General Aspects of the Vegetation of Europe.* Taylor & Francis, London: 66 pp.

PAPERNA, I. (1969). Snail vector of human schistosomiasis in the newly-formed Volta Lake. Pp. 326–30 in *Man-Made Lakes.* Proc. Accra Symposium, 1966; Ghana Acad. Sc. and Ghana Universities Press, Accra: 398 pp., illustr.

PENFOUND, W. T. & EARLE, T. T. (1948). The biology of Water-hyacinth. *Ecol. Monogr.*, **18**, pp. 447–72.

ROCKEFELLER COMMITTEE (1962). *Outdoor Recreation for America.* Outdoor Recreation Resources Review Commission Report, Government Printing Office, Washington, D.C.: 245 pp.

RODEN, G. I. (1967). On river discharge into the northeastern Pacific Ocean and the Bering Sea. *Jour. Geophysical Res.*, **72**, pp. 5613–29, 7 figs.

RODIER, J. (1963). Hydrology in Africa. *A Review of the Natural Resources of the African Continent.* UNESCO Natural Resources Research, Vol. 1, pp. 181–220, 2 figs.

SCUDDER, T. (1966). Man-made lakes and population resettlement in Africa. Pp. 99–108 in *Man-Made Lakes.* Proc. Symposium Royal Geogr. Soc., London, 1965; Institute of Biology and Academic Press, London: xiii + 218 pp., illustr.

SCUDDER, T. [1971]. Ecology and development: the Kariba Lake basin. In *The Careless Technology.* Proc. Conf. Ecol. Aspects International Development, Warrenton, Virginia, 1968. Publ. early 1972 by Doubleday, Garden City, N.Y. 11530: pp. 206–42, illustr.

SEAMAN, D. E. & PORTERFIELD, W. A. (1964). Control of aquatic weeds by the snail *Marisa cornuarietis. Weeds*, **12**, pp. 87–92.

SHIFF, C. J. [1971]. The impact of agricultural development in aquatic systems and its effect on the epidemiology of schistosomes in Rhodesia. In *The Careless Technology*, Proc. Conf. Ecol. Aspects International Development, Warrenton, Virginia, 1968. Publ. early 1972 by Doubleday, Garden City, N.Y. 11530, pp. 102–15, illustr.

SHIFF, C. J. & CLARKE, V. DE V. (1967). The effect of snail surveillance in natural waterways on the transmission of *Schistosoma haematobium* in Rhodesia. *Central Afr. Med. Jour.*, **13**, pp. 133–7.

SHIFF, C. J. CROSSLAND, N. O. & MILLAR, D. R. (1967). The susceptibilities of various species of fish to molluscicide N-tritylmopholine. *Bull. Wld Hlth Org.*, **36**, pp. 500–7.

STRAHLER, A. N. (1951). *Physical Geography.* John Wiley, New York: vii + 442 pp., illustr.

STROUD, R. H. (1966). American experience in recreational use of artificial waters. Pp. 189–200 in *Man-Made Lakes.* Proc. Symposium Royal Geogr. Soc., London, 1965; Institute of Biology and Academic Press, London: xiii + 218 pp., illustr.

THOMAS, G. W. & BOX, J. W. (1969). Social and ecological implications of water importation into arid lands. Pp. 363–74, 7 figs, in *Arid Lands in Perspective.* A.A.A.S. and University of Arizona Press, Tucson Arizona: viii + 421 pp., illustr.

WADDY, B. B. (1966). Medical problems arising from the making of lakes in the tropics. Pp. 87–94 in *Man-Made Lakes.* Proc. Symposium Royal Geogr. Soc., London, 1965; Institute of Biology and Academic Press, London: xiii + 218 pp., illustr.

WENDORF, F. & SAID, R. (1967). Palaeolithic remains in Upper Egypt. *Nature* (London), **215**, pp. 244–7.

WENDORF, F., SAID, R. & SCHILD, R. (1970). Egyptian prehistory: some new concepts. *Science*, **169**, pp. 1161–71, 9 figs.

WHITE, E. (1969a). The place of biological research in development of the resources of man-made lakes. Pp. 37–49 in *Man-Made Lakes.* Proc. Accra Symposium, 1966; Ghana Acad. Sc. and Ghana Universities Press, Accra: 398 pp., illustr.

WHITE, E. (1969b). Man-made lakes in tropical Africa and their biological potentialities. *Biological Conservation*, **1**(3), pp. 219–24.

WILLCOCKS, W. (1904). *The Nile in 1904.* National Printing Dept Egypt, Cairo: 225 pp., illustr.

WURSTER, C. F., JR. (1969). Chlorinated hydrocarbon insecticides and the world ecosystem. *Biological Conservation*, **1**(2), pp. 123–9.

YOUNG, G. (1969). Import alternatives. Pp. 382–97, 14 figs, in *Arid Lands in Perspective.* A.A.A.S. and University of Arizona Press, Tucson, Arizona: viii + 421 pp., illustr.

DISCUSSION

Kunin (Chairman)

Professor Kassas has devoted his paper to an extremely important and highly complex variety of problems, such as the analysis of the diverse influences of management and conservation of stream-flow and of large reservoirs on the different aspects of nature and the biosphere. I think the experiences of my country in these respects are of great interest—especially our extremely large projects on the management and conservation of the stream-flow running into closed or semi-closed basins. Elsewhere in the world, only Lake Chad and perhaps Lop Nor offers such conditions on a comparable scale.

It might seem that in such conditions it would be relatively easy to forecast the changes which should take place after the completion of the projects. For we really are diminishing the input of water into a basin of known volume, which should lead to such and such a degree of lowering of the water level. On this one might expect to be able to construct a chain of logical considerations which might seem to be more or less indisputable. Our experience has shown, however, that in reality matters are much more complicated.

A number of people think that the level of the Caspian Sea has become lower owing to the conservation of the Volga river-flow by the chain of great reservoirs. A number of people are also of the opinion that the construction of the large reservoirs has led to increased loss of water due to evaporation. But both these contentions are, in general, incorrect. During the period of the filling up of some of the greatest reservoirs of the Volga River, the level of the Caspian Sea did not become lower but even became slightly higher. Hence it seems that the volume of water in, and the area occupied by, the Caspian Sea are so large that long-term variations of the natural conditions, which are barely known to us, are more powerful than man's influence, at least so far in this instance.

As for the loss of water due to evaporation from the surface of reservoirs, we have found that if the water has flooded an area covered by vegetation under temperate or humid climatic conditions, we can be sure that the evaporation from the water surface will be of the same order as that from the same area before filling of the reservoir. The total balance would be approximately the same.

An exactly opposite picture is represented by the Aral Sea. Its volume and size are relatively small, and for this reason man's influence appears to be more powerful than the influence of nature. But during the first year of our project, the behaviour of the Aral Sea was not entirely clear: we had doubled the area of irrigation around the Sea, but this measure did not affect its level. It was discovered later, however, that the aquatic vegetation which existed within the deltas of the Syr-Darya and Amu-Darya Rivers consumed and transpired about the same amount of water as was taken for irrigation. The disappearance of this vegetation, due to the lack of water in the rivers' deltas, gave additional input of water into the Aral Sea. Now that the big project on the Syr-Darya River is near its completion, and some others are under way on the Amu-Darya River, the level of the Aral Sea is going down.

The importance of the Caspian Sea is clear to all Soviet scientists—this unique phenomenon must be protected. For this we have to work out its optimum level for the future. As for the Aral Sea, there are different opinions and we have great discussions about the matter; but personally I believe there is no adequate reason for keeping this so-called sea at all. But perhaps we can discuss these matters later, after some of our earlier would-be speakers have had a chance?

Holthoer

In my capacity of Lecturer in charge of Egyptology at the University of Helsinki, I would like to point to some matters in Professor Kassas's paper: Nothing would be better than to create an international committee, for example under the supervision of UNESCO, in order to save the archaeological monuments threatened by dam-building plans in different parts of the world. However, it has proved in the past to be far easier to collect a team of archaeological experts to explore and to dig for something 'new' than to preserve already known monuments just in case some problems emerge later, e.g. after their removal and relocation. The problems are of the character classified by Professor Kassas as social problems. Thus when we are concerned with archaeological monuments, it is not always enough merely to explore and save those which are situated in the area to be occupied by the artificial lakes. The social problems in connection with the archaeological salvage works, include also further preservation of the relocated monuments.

In connection with the construction of Lake Nasser, two archaeological problems have occurred in Egypt and Sudan. The first one concerns the monuments saved from the Sudanese Nubia, such as the temples of Buhen, Semneh, and Kummeh, which have already been transferred to Khartoum and put on display in the garden of the local museum. Here they are exposed to the weather, including rains which did not occur on their original sites in Nubia. A fall of rain which occurred in 1965 in Khartoum partially destroyed some of the paintings on the blocks from the temple of Buhen, when they were temporarily stored in crates in the open air. Unless precautions are taken to prevent such damage caused by an unsuitable climate, monuments will rapidly deteriorate. The second problem concerns the temples that were rescued from the flooding and rebuilt at a high level but close to their original site. It always has to be remembered that the monuments which have come down to us constitute only a fraction of those originally built. They have been preserved owing to the suitable and positive conditions of their environment. The others, not having these protective conditions, have long since decayed. When these protective conditions are changed by man, as for example by exposing them to the winds, this exposure will soon cause severe damage, as happened to the temples of Abu Simbel during a sandstorm in April 1969, a few months after their rebuilding.

There is an additional problem connected with the influence of artificial lakes upon the antiquities, the effects of which do not show up in the neighbourhood of the lakes themselves but on sites situated far away from them. It is the archaeological monuments of Egypt that suffer from these effects, and when I was last in that country two months ago and discussed this subject with the Antiquities' Service authorities there, they told me that, owing to the raising of the level of the subsoil ground-waters combined with the capillarity of the rock (mainly sandstone), the temples of Middle Egypt and some temples of Upper Egypt show a tendency to fall into decay. The constant, non-fluctuating flow of the River Nile also provides a constant amount of water which reaches a certain level of the tomb's or the temple's wall, where the water evaporates, leaving an accumulation of potassium carbonate and sulphate. The accumulation of these and other undesirable and destructive salts has been noted for the first time at the site of el Kab, some hundred kilometres to the north of the High Dam. Even farther north, at Luxor, the frescoes of several tombs are reported to have suffered damages for the same reason. Thus the salvage of the archaeological monuments is a social problem which did not cease to exist in 1964, when the water of Lake Nasser started to rise, but will remain for quite some years to come.

Turning to the social problems involved in the relocation of people and to concomitant health hazards, as a member of several archaeological expeditions to Sudan I have received some personal information given on the spot about these subjects, but concerning Sudan only. Concentrating on the health hazards, it must be remembered that 100,000 Nubians were transferred to different places—the Egyptian Nubians to Kom Ombo, where, I think, the climate is not different from that of their original habitat, and the Sudanese Nubians to Khashm el Girba, near the Ethiopian mountains. Here the climatic circumstances are completely different, according to Hassan Dafallah, former Commissioner of the Northern Province and Chairman of the Wadi Halfa Resettlement Committee. This resulted in a great increase in the incidence of tuberculosis among the population, owing to the fact that the Nubians are not accustomed to rainy periods, and other strong climatic changes. This epidemic of tuberculosis does not only concern the Nubians themselves but has been brought in this manner also to the Shilluk tribes who are the original inhabitants of the area in which the Nubians were resettled after the construction of the High Dam. Thus the health hazards occur some 700 to 800 kilometres south-east of the Sudano-Egyptian border, which is quite far away.

Finally I will comment on some other social problems connected with the construction of the High Dam. Owing to the specific character of the ecosystem of the Nile Valley, construction of an artificial lake on the River has been fatal to most of the land animals which are dependent upon the so-called 'green strip'—the fertile strip, on both sides of the River, that is very sharply distinguished ecologically from the neighbouring desert lying to the East and to the West. The disappearance of the land animals that had lived close to the river resulted in the disappearance of the carnivorous fauna of the near-by desert. However, 'new' species may become established and when the resettlement of the population was effected many domesticated animals such as dogs were left behind. They became wild and have since been threatening the inhabitants of the only unresettled town of the Lake Nasser district, namely Wadi Halfa. In 1971, despite the increased hunting, they still threaten the local people *inter alia* with rabies. This communication serves to show that social problems in connection with an artificial lake are not restricted to the neighbourhood of the lake only, but also have widespread and far-reaching consequences in districts that may be situated far away from the artificial lake itself.

Kuenen

Professor Kassas twice mentioned loss of water, which I interpret to mean waste of water. One case concerned 2,100 cubic metres per second flowing into the Mediterranean, the other being the water that is lost in the Sudd area. Now I don't believe that the botanist Kassas can mean quite that, because water is obviously needed both in the Mediterranean and in Egypt. In particular, as you may know, invasion of the Red Sea fauna into the Mediterranean is speeded up not only by the de-silting of the Bitter Lakes but also as a result of the reduction of outflow of Nile water. Loss of water is not the right term in this case, and the same applies to the region in the south. Just imagine, if that were drained, what would happen to the wild flora and fauna! The idea of Professor Kassas that what man can control he should legitimately be allowed to control—and he specifically mentioned all rivers—implies the fast destruction of much wildlife. Whether we object to this for practical reasons, or just to preserve the beauty of natural life on earth, we all agree, I think, that it cannot be allowed.

Worthington

I would like to pick up three points from these interesting discourses, the first two from Professor Kassas on a specialized subject, and the other from the Chairman on a generalized subject. The specialized subject relates to aquatic vegetation, and is a matter of importance in all man-made lakes. Early in his paper Professor Kassas refers to floating vegetation as being responsible for a lot of water-loss—as much as three times the water-loss from a free water surface. But there is a serious anomaly here between the biological results and the physical theory. H. L. Penman and other eminent hydrological physicists claim that theoretically it is impossible for water-loss from vegetation to be more than 1.3 times that from free water surfaces. Now here is a big anomaly: the observed results show something quite different from the theoretical possibility, and this is important in relation to the construction and management of man-make lakes.

A second point about vegetation relates to water quality. If you refer to Professor Kassas's second table you will see that the quantity of water flowing out of the Sudd area of the Nile is about half as much as that flowing into it. Now if one studies the quality of the water one finds that the water flowing into the Sudd area carries a heavy load of calcium carbonates whereas in that flowing out there is substantially less of this and other salts. The effect on the water going through the Sudd area is to purify it of the kind of salts which are very dangerous when it comes to using that water for irrigation down below. The effect of cutting the Jonglei Canal would be to increase significantly the salt content carried by the White Nile to Egypt. I think this is a point which is not fully taken into account in some of the long-term plans for the Upper Nile project.

My general point is that the whole subject of man-made lakes is one of great significance for this Conference, as they afford perhaps the best-documented major effects of man altering large areas of his environment. There have already been three international symposia on man-made lakes, their physical effects and geophysics, their meteorology, and their biological, physiological, sociological, archaeological, and other influences. The first was in London in 1965, the second was in Accra in 1966, and the third was held a few weeks ago in Tennessee. Each of these resulted in much discussion and accumulation of data. An important point came out in the recent Tennessee symposium, that a very large number of the biggest man-made lakes are in the USSR.

Your country, Mr Chairman, is a long way ahead of the rest of the world in this particular form of human alteration of the environment. Some of the African man-made lakes have been subjected in advance to intensive study of social influences, physical influences, biological influences, and so on. Others have been very poorly studied. One of the sad things about the world's knowledge of these man-made lakes is that when it comes to describing them, journalists are tempted to concentrate on the ancillary effects and forget the primary purpose. Thus recently there has been a lot of publicity about Lake Nasser, where, as a point of fact, the ancillary effects had been rather thoroughly studied and predicted in advance, four or five years of research having been taken into account. But now, as a result af bad newspaper reporting, a great many people think that Lake Nasser is a disaster for Egypt and the Mediterranean. It is by no means so. The primary purposes were to improve Egyptian irrigation and to make hydroelectricity, and they have been achieved. The undesirable ancillary effects are, in the opinion of Egyptians, relatively incidental.

Goldman

I would like to discuss some of the developments in river transformation in the Soviet Union. Though I could be talking about the United States and the North American water alliance, where the effects, when carried out, will presumably be very much the same, it happens that I have been working on the Soviet Union. Ironically, perhaps the best place to begin is to go back to Friedrich Engels. I'm not a Marxist, but Engels, I think, has to be given credit for recognizing some of the problems that I believe are just coming into their own—that we are just beginning to realize now. One of the things that Engels said was that we can often anticipate the primary effects of what we do, but that it is very difficult for us to anticipate the secondary and tertiary effects when we change nature and such things as agricultural patterns and water-flows. When we begin these changes it seems that sometimes we do not anticipate all the effects—especially tertiary effects—as they begin to work out, and I think it's likely that, as our technology grows in the future, the effects that do take place will become harder and harder to predict. Thus as we develop, say, atomic power for peaceful purposes of blasting river channels, the temptation may be to take on more and more of the earth—to change more and more of the environment just to show that we can do it.

If I might return to the Chairman's comments, I find myself agreeing very closely with Professor Kassas on practically all he had to say. But I would like to supplement the discussion with some details of what seems to be taking place in the Soviet Union by discussing what's happening to the Volga, the

Amu-Darya, and the Syr-Darya, that Professor Kunin mentioned. Meanwhile with regard to what Professor Kunin said about what is happening to the Caspian Sea, all I can do is to refer to other Russian scientists who find that the water level of the Caspian Sea is falling. What Professor Kunin disputed was whether it fell or not during the final build-up of the reservoirs that were completed in the 1930s. Now according to the information which I have, the Caspian Sea did fall sharply, so that from 1929 to 1970 the level fell by 2.6 metres. There were, however, some variations; thus at one time the level rose for more than two years during World War II, when industry and agriculture were interrupted and dust accumulation decreased slightly.

The surface of the Aral Sea fell 1.7* metres from 1960 to 1967, and I refer to Professor Kunin's statement about his willingness to let the Aral Sea dry up. He is not alone in this: there are many in the Soviet Union who feel this way—especially those who want more irrigation. But those who live in the vicinity of the Aral Sea are not so keen that it should disappear, so economic calculations are being made to determine whether or not the Sea should be allowed to go. The calculations indicate that there would be about 40 million roubles' worth of fish lost annually, and also transport losses, if the Sea should disappear. As in the case of the Caspian Sea, the ports are now situated inland and what were once fishing villages are now farming villages. But there may be milliards of roubles' worth of grain in the agricultural land; yet as an economist I am sad that these cost benefits are being utilized in this manner—there should also be inclusion of social costs, for example, of the disappearance of the Sea.

What is the water being used for? The Volga is being used as a sewer, as it flows down the centre of the country; but it is also being used for irrigation, for the generation of electric power, for industry, for households, and for transportation. Part of the Volga water is being drawn along the Volga-Don Canal. The same kind of thing can be said of the Amu-Darya and Syr-Darya. But use of the water thus has given rise to secondary effects that were not anticipated. The Aral Sea and the Caspian Sea are shrinking. If nothing is done to correct for these effects, they in turn are likely to set off other effects.

Because of what has happened, some think that the thing to do for those who want to preserve the Caspian and Aral Seas would be to re-route several of Russia's major rivers. There are two chief programmes that have been offered: one is to re-route the rivers in western Siberia, the Yenisei and the Ob, and move them south over the continental divide, for the longest rivers in the Soviet Union, with the exception of the Volga, flow north. Instead, the rivers would be re-routed to flow south, which would mean that they would have to cross over the mountains and come down ultimately in the Aral Sea and so in the western part of the Soviet Union. The other plan is to re-route the Pechora and Vychegda Rivers so that they would run into the Volga *via* the Kama River, similarly being brought south.

Now what kind of problems have Russian scientists anticipated from this kind of thing? They would presumably encounter all the items that Professor Kassas talked about. In addition, some argue that the building up of reservoirs has in fact already caused as much land to be flooded as would pre-

* *See* footnote on page 246.—Ed.

sumably be gained through the use of irrigation in the future. There would also be salination of the soil; in western Siberia there are already many marshes, and the building of reservoirs could conceivably lead to an increase in the marshes. There are also those who fear that windstorms should be anticipated, especially in western Siberia. The winds can be very strong, and flooding of land and the disappearance of trees could create a smooth flooded basin which in fact would make it possible for windstorms to develop much greater velocity. This is similar to the 'build another highway' syndrome that we are so familiar with the United States, where, as we build more highways, we have all the more need for more and more highways. The same is true of dams and more water. Why? Because we make water available for agricultural industries at a cheap price when very often it is being subsidized as it is also used to generate electricity. Then what happens is that more farming comes in, more industry comes in, and they need more dams—just as we need more highways, and so do they. Indeed, we never build enough highways. We discovered that long ago; nor will you ever build enough dams. In fact, you'll have to seek even farther out for water, and then it becomes even more expensive. Fears of what may happen also include one that underground water-flows will be cut off by dams.

As for the question of what effect all this would have on the Arctic, some say that the reversal of the rivers to flow south would remove the fresh water and that therefore there would be less fresh water in the Arctic. The warm water would move south, so that ice-caps would spread. In contrast, there are those who say the removal of fresh water would instead make the Arctic more saline, and that the ice-caps would melt. You can choose whichever dire result you want, but in any case something would happen if these things were done, and some changes will doubtless take place as a result of what has already been done. There will also be effects on other countries: what happens to the Caspian Sea will also affect Iran, and so on. There is even the question of a possible effect on the rotation of the earth. If a baseball pitcher ruffles the seams of the ball, it starts wobbling in flight. The same could happen to the axis of the earth if some of its major rivers were ruffled or displaced. It seems conceivable that this could spark a global catastrophe, a new kind of general ecodisaster.†

Matthews

My country has a dismal record of dam-building, I'm ashamed to say. Would it be possible for you to consider some of the advantages which might have accrued from your *not* having built the Aswan Dam? It seems to have been responsible for quite a lot of problems—e.g. decline in the sardine and shrimp fisheries, increasing dependence on fertilizers, spread of some terrible diseases, and rising salinity of the eastern Mediterranean Sea. Also, any other such problems which you could point out would be of interest.

Mahler

Some general data about the efficiency of water use for agriculture: it is estimated that at least 70 per cent of the water consumed is used for agri-

† *See* footnote on page 246.—Ed.

culture—mostly for irrigation. The efficiency of the use of water for irrigation is of the order of 30 to 40 per cent. This means that from 30 to 40 per cent of the water available to them is actually used by the crops in the farmers' fields. In the best conditions an efficiency of up to 70 per cent can be reached. Any wastage may cause environmental problems in an irrigation project by salinization of the soil, and also waterlogging by raising the water-table. However, these problems should not prevent us from developing water resources as one of the best means of increasing agricultural production quickly. The main problem which we face is that, whereas it is relatively easy to get the funds to build a dam, it is difficult to obtain the means also to implement the improvement of water management in the network of irrigation. The improvement of water management practices by the farmer is a prerequisite to our deriving full benefits from irrigation projects.

There is another environmental problem that is sometimes related to the building of dams and canals: earth movements. However, environmental problems related to the development of water resources can in general be more easily solved than those related to the management of the resources, as these latter involve a much greater number of people and much larger areas. It is therefore in this direction of management improvement that efforts should be made.

Laird

I found Professor Kassas's contribution a most interesting and valuable one. My only comment is that while it covered hot-climate man-made lakes very well, it did not discuss man-made lakes in cold climates. To turn an Orwellian phrase, some countries are more equal than others: and some parts of individual countries (even of countries that are usually thought of as 'developed') are less well-developed than neighbouring regions. Some such cold-climate areas, including the western part of Canada's Province of Newfoundland and Labrador, also have ambitious projects for man-made lakes. Thus the impoundment behind Churchill Falls, at the edge of the Labrador plateau, will have a final area of 6,900 square kilometres (one-quarter the size of Belgium). This lake is in an area that only a handful of Europeans had visited until quite recently, and it is going to pose various ecological questions. One currently under investigation concerns the blood parasites of wildfowl which breed in or migrate through this area. It has been suggested that the filling of the impoundment may affect the relative incidence of local biting insects which transmit birds' blood parasites. There could, for example, be a decline in the populations of bird-biting black-flies and hence of harmful avian blood parasites (e.g. leucocytozoonosis) transmitted by these insects; this could be linked with a rise in mosquito populations and a parallel rise in the incidence of bird malaria. Related mortalities could lead to fluctuations in wildfowl populations, which would be a matter of concern both to conservationists and to those who are primarily interested in water-birds from the recreational standpoint.

This particular problem is already under investigation, and long-term monitoring of the avian blood-parasite situation at the Churchill Falls impoundment is planned. An African equivalent could be a transition from tsetse-borne sleeping sickness to mosquito-borne malaria through fundamental alterations made to the vector habitats. Perhaps some general guidelines might be established for the monitoring of changing vector-borne disease situations involving other animals, as well as man himself, in cold-climate as well as tropical developing areas? Needless to say, such monitoring should be securely founded upon baseline data of the pre-existing situation prior to filling of major impoundments—a matter which calls for the closest possible collaboration among biologists and other scientists and engineers, etc., from the earliest planning stage onwards.

Udall

I want to make three or four observations about the larger, planetary aspects of the problem of dam-building. Having been for eight years the head of the United States Department of the Interior which supervised the Bureau of Reclamation—the agency which pioneered large dam-building in the world—I have to confess that my own views with regard to the building of dams changed about 180 degrees in the eight years that I was in office between 1961 and 1969. In this I was helped by Dr Brower, who is here, and by others who opposed the building of dams in the Grand Canyon, one of our great national parks. Now there is growing scepticism in the USA as regards further building of large dams—particularly on those rivers that are already controlled. There is even a growing feeling that we should not look at rivers in terms of their potential for dams for flood control or irrigation, but also at the value of leaving large stretches of rivers in their natural condition for their value to man as undeveloped resources.

Personally I am sceptical of the people in my country today who favour water projects, moving water from region to region, or who propose that huge engineering contraptions be built to bring water from Alaska or Canada to the southwestern United States. I hope that Canadians are sceptical themselves about this project, and I've been telling people in my part of the country (the Pacific South-west) that from now on we must play the hand that nature dealt us—we must learn to use wisely the water we have, and not think that we can go to some other country or some other region and bring in new supplies when we already waste enormous amounts of water.

Another point which I wanted to make is that I think it is clear from experiences with the Aswan Dam and others in Africa, that there are ecological problems associated with large dams of large rivers in semi-equatorial climates that are not present in temperate zones. The United States a few years ago proposed a series of big dams for the Mekong River in southeastern Asia. I have mentioned this project in my paper and I'm very sceptical about it. Last year some of the scientists in the USA who had studied it came back with a report which raised many environmental impact issues. Irrespective of the benefits of dams that have been built up to this point of time, I think we are now in a new era when all benefits and detriments of dams must be analysed. It is interesting that we have very different attitudes today towards dam-building from what we had only five or ten years ago. This should lead to far different assessments of proposed large dams in the future, with particular emphasis on long-term ecological impacts and on costs.

Kassas

Initially I would like to make a comment on the Chairman's point that evaporation from natural vegetation is approximately equal to evaporation from a similar area of reservoir. This water transpired by plants represents part of a process which is building new raw material. But water evaporating from a dam is not doing anything of this kind—it is not recycled in the physiological process. This is the difference.

My comment on Professor Kunin's observation is that living in a country like Egypt, or anywhere in a desert area, one feels the great value of water. Earlier I mentioned verbally that we are living on barely 0.5 per cent of the water in the world. The oceans and seas contain over 95 per cent of the water resources of the world, but this is not available to us. Perhaps if more of the world's scientific potential could be directed towards doing something about these resources of water, then we should be able to save the beauty of rivers and maintain their natural streams!

As for the problem of decline of fisheries in the eastern Mediterranean, from the Egyptian point of view there has been such a decline, but at the same time an equally great increase in fisheries in the Aswan reservoir. Concerning the problem of utilizing more fertilizers, I would only say that Nile silt is not present everywhere in the world; there is agriculture all over the world depending on fertilizers, and the problems so introduced are ones that can be solved. As for more bilharzia in the delta of the Nile, there could hardly be more!

Miller

I'm from Nevada in the USA where the first irrigation project of the United States Department of the Interior created lands by taking water from the river feeding Pyramid Lake. My students are there now, studying the Lake. The Indians who live there and have an economy from that lake are now suing the United States Government to restore water to the Lake which for the past fifty years has been declining and has still not reached its stable level. In lectures in California in the 1950s, we were given predictions that in eighteen years the water behind the Aswan High Dam would be established and crops watered, but that during these eighteen years the population would reach such a point that it would have consumed all of the increase in agricultural products. Now what will be the situation in Egypt?

Kassas

The population in Egypt is increasing, this is true. If the increased population would erode the benefits of the high dam, should we then not build the high dam? I don't see the relationship. In Egypt by 1950 there was only one-third of an acre of agricultural land per head, when the minimum that would satisfy a reasonable standard of life would be two acres per head. By 1980, after the building of the high dam, after utilization of all underground water in the desert oases, and after the reclamation of certain semi-arid areas on the northern coast of Egypt, with the projected increase in population the one-third would drop to one-quarter per head. This is why we say that agriculture would not be the answer to the increase in population; expanding industry and population control will be the answer. Meanwhile, people are increasing the population and the government is doing its best; but population control cannot happen at once—it takes time to change people's habits in such matters as family control.

Kunin (Chairman)

As to the question of Dr Goldman concerning the change of the regime of the Arctic Ocean in connection with the measures we have taken in respect of the Siberian rivers, I can state the following: as far as the total flow of these rivers for hydroelectric purposes is concerned, there will be no change at all. There will be only a certain change in the annual distribution of the run-off: hydroelectric installations use water, but do not consume it.

As for the switching of part of the stream-flow of one or two of the Siberian rivers into the southern parts of the USSR, the situation is as follows: the total annual stream-flow of the most important Siberian rivers—the Ob with the Irtysh, the Yenisei, the Lena and some other rivers—exceeds 2,000 cubic kilometres. But we envisage switching only 20–30 cubic kilometres out of this total. It will be clear to everybody that this cannot provoke any noticeable changes in the regime of the Arctic Ocean. However, this whole problem is a very serious one which requires detailed and comprehensive study.

[* Footnote to page 241: Asked to verify this figure in view of the 1961–69 one of 1.3 m given by Professor Kassas in his formal paper (p. 231), Professor Goldman replied (*in litt.*) that 1.76 m is given in *Soviet Geography in Review and Translation*, No. 3, 1969, p. 46.—Ed.]

[† Footnote to page 242: Thus claims in the Soviet press have, for example, indicated that the Kama River will alone carry 40 cubic kilometres of water south annually, that 20 per cent of the water of the Ob and Yenisei will ultimately be diverted south, and that the Siberian river diversion (exclusive of the northwestern project) may be designed to move from 45 to 70 cubic kilometres of water a year southwards.]

8
MARINE PRODUCTIVITY AND POLLUTION

Keynote Paper

Marine Productivity and Pollution

by

ILMO HELA

Chairman, Finnish National Commission for UNESCO;
Professor and Director, Institute of Marine Research,
Tähtitorninkatu 2, Helsinki 14, Finland

Introduction

When we consider the theme of 'Marine Productivity and Pollution' within the framework of an International Conference on Environmental Future, we find it necessary to deal in some detail with the topic of how pollution is affecting marine productivity at the present time, before attempting any prediction for the future. In such a prognostication of what in our opinion is most likely to happen in this highly important matter, a clear distinction must be made between the ultimate results that are to be expected from the present trends and the effects of man's decisions to apply remedial measures—or, practically, between scientific predictions and political decisions. Without legislative and other counter-measures, the present trend would be amenable to prediction with some accuracy (and despondency). However, man's counter-measures may well result in greatly reduced trends or even in reduction of the eventual pollution. One worthy instance of this nature is the present downward trend of smoke and sulphur dioxide pollution of the air above the United Kingdom (Royal Commission on Environmental Pollution, 1971).

If predictions are to be more than mere suppositions or emotional lamentations, simply extrapolated from some of the present, often frightening, trends, they must be based upon veritable understanding of the present situation, upon true knowledge of current trends, upon suggestions for remedial measures and due consideration of their applicability, and upon estimates of integrated effects of these remedial measures if and when they are applied. Obviously, this is more difficult and also more profitable than alarming predictions derived from the present situation and estimated simple trends.

Much of the 'news' that is given out on our topic nowadays is unduly sensationalistic or actually wrong, as in the case of the statement that the primary production of the oceans has been reduced by 40 per cent as a result of the world-wide use of DDT. I shall not speak any more of such misleadingly sensational or otherwise untrue items but of the actually possible effects, as they are known and understood at present, of pollution and other man-made depressants on marine productivity. Man is menacing also, through over-fishing, the most valuable biological resources of the salt seas and oceans, and is thus affecting the balance of marine ecosystems; however, this serious threat does not fall within the framework of this article, though it is to be hoped that it and other aspects of marine productivity *per se* will be dealt with in the discussion.

One has to admit that we do not know and understand by any means all of the facts, yet have to make every possible effort to stick to them! The field of items that could, hypothetically, lead to various forms of marine pollution or other degradation contains a vast range of difficult, often unsolved, scientific problems and unknown facts. Therefore it would be a mistake to take a definite personal stand on every problem, being safer to refer to other authors whenever appropriate. However, even the scientific literature on the problems of pollution, including the marine ones, tends to be biased: every pessimist, regardless of the reliability of his scientific results, is anxious to publish his warnings, while every optimist, even following a serious scientific study of the situation, is rather reluctant to present his less sensational findings to the public at large.

The task of writing this article has been made the more interesting and in some ways easier by the wealth of information available in many recent reports, books, and scientific papers. Only a few of them have been actually cited, though many more have affected my thinking. On the other hand, my task was made difficult by the limits of length in spite of the wealth of available information, the selection of items dealt with being governed more by the immediate theme than by the general character of the Conference.

ACTIVE USES OF THE SEAS

In earlier times the salt seas and oceans were considered to be limitless and invulnerable. Everyone was entitled to use them for his own purposes— that is, for navigation, for fisheries, and for the discharge and dumping of wastes. Today the seas are used actively and increasingly for the following additional peaceful purposes: aquaculture, mining, acquisition of water, and many and various types of recreation. To these must be added, unfortunately, naval and military uses—and not only during wars!

The present uses of the seas are not independent of one another. Our subject of today covers marine productivity (or, indirectly, fisheries and aquaculture) and pollution (or mainly the discharge and dumping of wastes into the seas). These topics are closely interrelated, and with the increasingly active uses of the seas for various other purposes, they, too, have tended to become interdependent. The days are gone when man could use the seas for one purpose without paying due attention to others. Today the seas must be considered *res communis* of the whole of mankind and not any longer *res nullius* (*cf.* Ray, 1970). This is the starting point of our discussion: how can we make use of the seas for certain purposes without endangering the other uses? Or, to be more specific, how can we save marine productivity from the dangers created by an ever-increasing range and volume of polluting activities?

GENERAL BIOLOGICAL PRODUCTIVITY

For our further discussion we have to know the basic features of the biological primary production of the salt seas and oceans. Of solar energy some 5×10^{20} kcal is absorbed every year by the biosphere, which, however, uses for biological production less than 10^{18} kcal per year, or only some 0.2 per cent of the incident amount. Nevertheless at least 6×10^{10} metric tons of organic material (dry-weight) is produced per year. Of this huge amount, it has been estimated (Duvigneaud, 1967) that 36 per cent is produced in the seas and the remaining 64 per cent on land (*cf.* also UNESCO, 1970). As some 72 per cent of the incoming solar radiation hits the sea while only the remaining percentage hits the land, it is easy to observe that, according to this calculation, per unit area, the lands on an average are 4.6 times as productive as the seas. Nevertheless, the annual primary production of the seas is some 3×10^{10} or 30,000 million tons of organic material

E.F.—9*

(dry-weight), which is equivalent to some 8,000 kilograms per head of the world population. At the same time some 14,000 kilograms per head is produced on the land areas.

Thus by the land areas of the world every one of us human beings is provided—daily—with some 38 kilograms (dry-weight) of vegetation and, at sea, with some 22 kilograms (dry-weight) of phytoplanktonic or other Algae. However, most of us wish to eat, in addition to 'grass', also meat or fish. Studies of the trophic levels have revealed that each step involves a *ca* 90 per cent or often greater loss of energy. Thus 38 kilograms of dry grass could make available some 4 kilograms of (dried) meat per day. Even here the seas, in spite of their tremendous area and volume, are less successful than the land because of the complexity of their trophic levels: the phytoplankton is followed as a secondary level mainly by zooplankton (so far not much consumed by human beings) and benthic animals, while the 'primary' carnivores, such as herring or cod, appear only as a tertiary level. As all the above figures refer to the dry-weights, one may multiply them by the round figure of 10 to get wet-weights. Thus, schematically, 200 kg of wet phytoplankton per day would be enough for the production of 20 kg of zooplankton per day and of 2 kg of fish per day for every person of mankind.

It has been estimated that the annual world catch of marine fisheries is, in these years, approximately 60×10^6 tons, or some 15 kg per person per year or 35 grammes per person per day. Thus, theoretically, the world fisheries catch currently only about 2 per cent of the annual production of fish of all the seas and oceans, or some 0.02 per cent of the marine primary production.

Obviously, in all such estimates a great number of uncertain factors are involved, making the resulting figures almost inevitably inexact. Moreover, for practical reasons anything approaching 100 per cent of the fish of the seas and oceans will never be caught. But even 5 per cent would be enough to cover the protein needs of everyone currently on earth, including all the poor and suffering nations. Towards helping them, marine productivity could be of the greatest significance, and such considerations have led many to propose its exploitation at lower trophic levels. It is against this background that we have to study the problem created by the present trends of marine pollution and other degrading influences, though to understand their ill-effects upon marine productivity we have to be familiar with the basic features of the latter.

The 'other degrading influences' include drastic disturbance of habitats, of which we shall give instances hereafter, and over-fishing, which is getting more and more serious. Thus to keep up the needed catch, new methods have to be used and fresh areas exploited—to which, unfortunately, there are all manner of limits!

MARINE PRODUCTIVITY

On land there are rather many factors affecting the photosynthesis and growth of plants, the dominant ones being illumination, temperature of the surrounding air, nutrients and water available in the ground, the type of substratum, and the humidity of the atmosphere. But whereas many of these factors still play an important role in the growth of estuarine and intertidal plants, in the open sea it is primarily the amount of light and availability of nutrients that have to be taken into account.

The amount of light in the seas is locally affected by suspended solids and consequent turbidity. Nevertheless, the availability of nutrients alone is in most areas the decisive factor in the primary production of the surface layers of the open sea, assuming that light is plentiful. Ordinarily, the nutrients available in the homogeneous, mixed surface layer are rapidly exhausted: they are used up by the growing and reproducing phytoplankton and, finally, they are removed from the mixed surface layer by the death and sinking of the organisms. The local run-off from rivers is a significant fertilizing factor only in estuarine and coastal waters. In the open ocean, the large-scale renewal of the nutrients of the surface layer is possible only within the framework of vertical mixing, winter turnover, and upwelling from deeper layers which brings decomposed organic material and nutrient salts back to the euphotic zone where photosynthesis can proceed.

When considering nutrients one should remember that some 'trace' metals—such as iron, manganese, copper, zinc, cobalt, and molybdenum—are also important for the growth processes of marine organisms. In other words, nutrients should not be considered in isolation, as other limiting factors—for example, bioactive trace-metals, organic growth-limiting and growth-promoting substances, and the penetration of solar radiation—are also important in controlling plant growth. Moreover, as pointed out recently by Allen (1970): 'A huge harvest of fish from aquatic systems fertilized with animal wastes, including those of man, takes place in the world. This fact is rarely mentioned in the scientific literature of western industrialized societies. Nutrients in sewage wastes can be used to grow harvestable aquatic products in sanitary, managed systems.' Significant economic and social benefits can result from acting on Athelstan Spilhaus's thesis that 'Waste is simply some useful substance which we do not yet have the wit to use.' Thus we should remember that domestic raw sewage and agricultural run-off are, up to a certain level, highly desirable additions to the marine environment.

Moreover, as pointed out by Lundholm & Svensson (1970), the oceans have always been the ultimate 'sink' for many contaminants. 'Pure' water never existed: it was always 'polluted' by a number of dissolved compounds, organic substances, and particles emanating from erosion. Of primary interest, therefore, are the rate of increase of these substances in marine waters and, increasingly nowadays, the introduction of completely new substances through human activity *via* agricultural and industrial complexes.

FORMS OF MARINE POLLUTION

An overoptimistic layman might think of the oceans as being so wide that man-made pollution would affect only a narrow strip of their coastal waters. Unfortunately, this is by no means the case. Yet about 50 per cent of the world's total fish supply is derived from coastal regions of upwelling waters comprising about 0.01 per cent of the ocean's surface (Halstead, 1970).

The remaining half is produced in other coastal waters and in a few regions that are more remote from land but nevertheless of comparatively high fertility. Thus the most productive portions of the world's oceans are concentrated in the neritic rather than in the oceanic (pelagic) realm. Most of the fishing operations are performed in coastal zones, and, surely, aquaculture will always be practised only along or near coasts. Yet these same neritic regions, being the ones of greatest human activity, are also those most susceptible to the destructive forces of man-made pollutants.

Estuaries constitute a rather poorly-defined category of waters in which there are many interactions between coastal and oceanic waters on one hand and land-borne ones on the other. The biological productivity of estuaries is naturally very high, but among man's aquatic resources they are probably the most susceptible to damage from pollution by various waste materials. This fact becomes the more serious when we realize that, of the fish species which are harvested, for example, in the United States (Rice *et al.*, 1970), more than 70 per cent spend part of their life-cycles in estuarine waters.

In more general terms one may state that the coastal waters, defined by the continental shelves, play the major role in determining harvestable marine productivity. These shelf areas are equal to some 20 per cent of the total land area on earth. In man's design to provide for an expanding population, the coastal regions are important—economically, aesthetically, and as sources of food (Blumer, 1970). One-half of the total world fish production, and nearly all of the shellfish production, comes from the coastal regions; but oil pollution threatens the coastal environment, and adds to the growing stresses from sewage, pesticides, chemicals, over-fishing, hot-water discharge, and the destruction of natural environment through construction works.

Thus the coastal waters and, in particular, the estuarine areas, are of the greatest importance for the production of living marine resources, but it is these very areas that are most gravely threatened by marine pollution and other devastation.

In the following sub-sections, the various forms of marine pollution (in the widest sense) will be described after outlining in each case the main troubles that may be caused by it. Some of these forms of pollution are known to have effects which may become at least locally dangerous—say, to the ecosystems and to the fish—whereas others may have only very limited harmful effects. Such a comprehensive list of actual or potential pollutants or, rather, contaminants, should serve a useful purpose in defining the full set of dangers and effects that may, sooner or later, possibly affect the health of the seas and oceans—including their living resources. At the present stage of pollution research we do not know for sure which forms of pollution will finally become the most detrimental and which, for instance as a result of the adaptability of nature, will be of academic interest only.

Petroleum (Crude Oil) and its Distillates
The main dangers and/or harmful effects of these pollutants are: squalor, toxicity causing risks to the health of fish, and effects on the quality and marketability of fish.

In discussing the various groups of pollutants or contaminants entering the sea, our sequence does not necessarily follow any known or predictable degree of fatal character or importance of the different groups. We start the discussion with petroleum (crude oil) and its distillates simply because the general public is more aware of some petroleum catastrophes than of any other kinds of marine pollution

To quote from the final report of the *Seminar on Methods of Detection, Measurement and Monitoring of Pollutants in the Marine Environment* (FAO, 1970), 'Oil pollution* is the almost inevitable consequence of the dependence of a growing population on an increasingly oil-based technology. The widespread production and transportation of oil and its use as fuel, lubricant and chemical raw product leads to losses which are wide, but not evenly spread. Production estimates for 1970 and 1980 are 2,200 and 4,000 millions of tons. Estimates for the amount of oil spilled, introduced deliberately or accidently into the ocean, vary widely between 1 and 10 million tons per year.' At any one time, about 30 million tons of oil are at sea in tankers (Ray, 1970). At present (in 1971) some 20 per cent of the oil produced by that part of the world which discloses its production figures is produced off-shore, while the figure predicted for 1980 is 32 per cent. Moreover, oil transport is not evenly distributed over the ocean surface but tends to be concentrated along the continental shelves in coastal areas and regions of upwelling water which are also areas of intensive production and utilization of living marine resources.

Petroleum pollutants in the ocean may occur at any concentration ranging from bulk oil to oil at a very low level of concentration (FAO, 1970). They may occur as floating material, as an emulsion dispersed in sea water, in solution in water, or absorbed on sediments; they may also be taken up by marine organisms at several trophic levels.

Serious efforts are being made to reduce to a minimum the oil that is spilled from intentional rinsing of oil tanks, from the discharge of used, dirty lubricants, and from accidental leaks and the shipwrecks of oil tankers. Although these efforts are proving successful to a considerable extent (*cf.* Boyle, 1969), they will never succeed fully. The probability of oil pollution, say, per oil ton, is certainly becoming smaller, but it is inconceivable that any measures could be devised to make oil pollution of the seas and oceans non-existent.

Unfortunately, the varying degrees of danger posed by different incidents of oil pollution are not properly understood, as can be seen from the controversial results and/or opinions expressed in the scientific and less scientific literature. Nevertheless, everyone has to admit the reality of two harmful effects. The first of these is the fouling of the intertidal zone of coastlines—in particular of bathing beaches—by crude oil, which constitutes an effect that is not only unaesthetic but can be really harmful.

The second harmful effect is on sea-birds, which may suffer from the oil squalor most grievously. Fouled birds are usually condemned to death (Bourne, 1970), and hundreds of thousands of them are killed annually by

* 'Oil pollution' here refers to the forms of pollution that are brought about by heavy crude oil and its various fractions.

oil pollution in the English Channel and North Sea alone. I myself photographed moribund oil-covered sea-birds in the North Sea already in 1947. Moreover, birds with oil-coated feathers may transfer oil to their eggs during breeding, whereupon the eggs often fail to hatch (Davis, 1970).

Petroleum pollution effects have been studied following spillage disasters. Fuel products appear to be more damaging to biota—especially to macrobenthic populations—than does crude oil (*cf.* Cowell & Baker, 1969). The most immediately toxic, low-boiling fractions of oil (Blumer, 1970) are somewhat more readily water-soluble than the others. Therefore, recovery of oil-slicks is often futile, except for the aesthetic improvement and the chance of saving sea-birds. Treatment with emulsifiers, even the 'non-toxic' ones, is 'dangerous' because it disperses oil into droplets that are ingested and retained by many organisms. On the other hand, more optimistic views have been presented even on the use of emulsifiers, as in the statement that 'Emulsifiers of the type commonly used in oil pollution emergencies, although more toxic than fresh crude oils, do not cause large mortalities of littoral organisms unless used heavily' (Cowell *et al.*, 1970).

A full range of statements of varying degrees of reliability has been given recently concerning the actual effects of oil contamination; from these we will quote a few examples.

Halstead (1970) states: 'Crude oil (petroleum) and refined oils are toxic for all marine organisms and for man. Poisoning may be immediate or slow and long-lasting. Oil may be taken up in the tissues of shellfish and make them unfit for the market. Toxic hydrocarbons produce anaesthesia, narcosis, cell-damage, and death, in a variety of lower animals. Crude oil contains hydrocarbons which are carcinogenic. To what extent these toxic hydrocarbons become protein-bound and carry over in the food of man is not known.'

Blumer (1970) writes: 'All crude oils are poisons for all marine organisms. Many crude-oil distillates are more severely poisonous because they contain higher proportions of the immediately toxic compounds. Long-term toxicity may harm marine life.'

On the other hand, Cowell *et al.* (1970) observe: 'Studies of accidental pollutions and experimental plots have verified that oil, except in large quantities, has little effect on the intertidal fauna and flora' (*see also* Cowell & Baker, 1969).

One must assume that the following general statement (FAO, 1970) comes closest to the actual truth: 'Different oils and oil products vary in their toxicity and in the mode by which they interfere with marine life-processes. Generally, distillates are more severely toxic on a short time-scale than the higher-boiling fractions.'

The immediate dangers of marine pollution by oil, as opposed to some other pollutants, seem to be relatively limited. Nevertheless, because of the huge, ever-increasing amount of oil transport, the hypothetical dangers of oil pollution cannot be underestimated, and all feasible measures must be applied to reduce their possible effects. Particularly alarming is the surface pollution by floating lumps of asphalt-like material often accompanied by dead invertebrates observed by Heyerdahl (1971) over the central part of the Atlantic Ocean during his papyrus-raft crossings in 1969 and 1970.

At the same time, the actual effects of oil pollution must be studied further in spite of the difficulties of the problems involved. As indicated in the recent seminar (FAO, 1970), 'In general, the background organic level of the sea is sufficiently large to mask detection of many of the introduced pollutants. It has been estimated that 4.5×10^6 tons of petroleum products will be added to the world ocean per year by 1980. Such pollution will be detectable as an increase in hydrocarbon level as its concentration in localized regions will exceed that of the naturally occurring organic sea-water components.' Moreover, 'monitoring of oil should aim not only at the detection of spills but also at ascertaining long-term changes in marine systems and in the degree of pollution of the ocean. Because insufficient knowledge exists on the long-term effects of pollution, monitoring of oil in water, organisms, and sediments, is urgently required.'

Petroleum-derived, Halogenated Hydrocarbons (including Pesticides)
The main dangers and/or harmful effects of these pollutants are: toxicity, risk to health of fish, and risk to public health; they also depress the photosynthetic rate of some Algae.

Halogenated hydrocarbons constitute a group of synthetic chemicals that have latterly come into widespread use in both industry and agriculture. Global production figures for the chlorinated hydrocarbon insecticides alone are currently of the order of 200,000 metric tons per year, while production of industrial halogenated hydrocarbons has expanded with the development of a global technology, so that the current production figures exceed those of the allied insecticides. The relative chemical stability of many of these compounds, and their mobility, have resulted in the transfer of a significant fraction of the total production to the marine environment. Large amounts are also transferred to the sea in sewage outfalls and by dumping.

The halogenated hydrocarbons are of concern to us mainly because of their eventual toxicity, which may create a risk to the health of marine life—including fish—and thus, at least theoretically, to fish-consuming animals, including man. Infinitesimally small amounts of some of them can depress the photosynthetic rate of marine plankton (Menzel *et al.*, 1970), which could have far-reaching effects and profound implications (Wurster, 1969).

In reality, a great part of the marine pollution problem is toxicological and concerns the eventual toxic effects of chemical substances on the cellular systems of marine organisms. Laymen sometimes ask why the degree of toxicity is not clearly defined and stated, in order to make the limits of permissible discharges known to everyone. Unfortunately the answer is that we do not know enough about this subject. Even more serious is the fact that we shall never know enough to understand all such limits, because of the evasive character of the concept of toxicity in the marine environment. Thus a particular substance is not equally toxic to every form of marine life. Moreover, the degree of toxicity—even to the same animal or plant—depends also upon other environmental factors, and upon its age, etc. A growing amount of evidence also indicates (Halstead, 1970) that pollutants may trigger 'natural-occurring' marine biotoxicity cycles, at least in tropical insular regions. When the proper mix of chemical constituents is present in the environment of certain types of marine organisms, biotoxins are produced.

Aubert *et al.* (1970) have studied chemically-polluted wastes along the coasts of France. They examined the effects of such wastes on a marine biological chain (phytoplankton, zooplankton, fish, and the higher mammals), and in this way determined the toxicity thresholds (lethal doses) of each type of polluted water on the constituents of the chain. Furthermore, by following the successive stages of passage at various levels of this biological chain, they were able to determine the transmitted or induced toxicity due to factors of nutrient (and hence pollutant) concentration. By this method it was possible to identify more readily the influence of such pollution on the elements of the marine environment, and to determine the toxic effects which the pollutant might have on the final consumer in the trophodynamic chain. The studies covered over a hundred types of industrial wastes, and included testing effluents from petrochemical, wood chemistry, metallurgical, plastics, and ceramics, industries, as well as from cement works, canneries, etc.

Such results, based upon a great amount of labour, offer a realistic approach to the dangers to the marine environment and its nutritional utilization that may result from pollution by chemically-contaminated water. But such studies have been performed only in rather rare instances, Moreover, as pointed out by Mitrović (1970), some of the criteria on permissible levels of toxic substances in water will have to be changed, as they have been derived from the results of short-term bioassays, in which mortality of fish was taken as the measure of toxicity. For results of long-term bioassays and some field observations indicate that quantities much lower than the lethal ones could either cause functional and morphological disturbances in fish or change environmental conditions in the aquatic ecosystem to such an extent that the existence of natural populations would be endangered.

Concerning the toxic effects of pollutants on marine organisms, Halstead (1970) writes: 'Thousands of halibut, croaker, sea-bass, sole, sand-dabs, and other shore fishes, in the vicinity of sewage outfalls, have had an alarmingly high incidence of cancerous growths, skin ulcers, malformations, emaciation, and genetic changes. These pathological disturbances are believed to be due to the toxic effects of pollutants. The precise causative agents are unknown. The possible public health implications to man are of growing concern.' It is thus evident that fundamental biological, chemical, and pharmaco-toxicological, data are urgently needed to clarify the situation.

Of the halogenated hydrocarbons—some of them ill-famed for their known toxicity—that are being produced today, the following have so far been detected (FAO, 1970) in the marine environment:

Aliphatic by-products of vinyl chloride production (AHCS)
DDT compounds and breakdown products
Polychlorinated biphenyls (PCBS)
Dieldrin
Endrin
Benzene hexachloride (BHC).

However, many halogenated hydrocarbons have not yet been looked for in the sea.

Very few analyses for organochlorine (chlorinated hydrocarbon) pesticides appear to have been carried out on sea water (FAO, 1970). Actually, the present methodology is not always capable of detecting the levels of these compounds that are present in open-sea waters. Whereas the adsorption characteristics of these pesticides on particulate matter are not understood, it is known that surface slicks of crude oil are apt to contain concentrations of them which are considerably higher than those found in sea water. Meanwhile, deposition in sediments is assumed to be a major pathway whereby those pesticides or their breakdown products leave marine ecosystems (*ibid.*).

Butler *et al.* (1970) have presented data to support the hypothesis that estuarine areas and river deltas are probably major depositories for the persistent pesticide chemicals which have been applied world-wide in the past twenty-five years. Yet according to Dybern (1970*a*), 'a serious feature of the Baltic Sea pollution is the high content of DDT and PCB compounds in fish and other organisms in the open sea. The concentrations clearly exceed those from the North Sea animals.' Meanwhile Holden (1970) remarks: 'The analyses of seal blubber have demonstrated that, by comparison with the Arctic, Antarctic, and Pacific Oceans, the levels in the contamination in the Baltic, North Sea, and Irish Sea (west of Great Britain), are very much higher, as judged by the presence of both pesticides and PCB residues. Dieldrin and PCB levels are highest around Great Britain and DDT levels highest in the Baltic and Gulf of St Lawrence. There is no evidence that seals in good condition are affected by these residues, but when fat is mobilized the higher residue concentrations which are produced in the remaining lipids could have a detrimental physiological effect.'

Pesticide residues of the chlorinated hydrocarbon type have been shown to follow a pattern of increasing concentration with trophic level in many aquatic systems (Kneip *et al.*, 1970). At this stage we know that already in some limited areas of sea the DDT and PCB residues have reached a concentration which is potentially dangerous to fish. Moreover, we know the approximate sizes of the industries involved and the amounts of their wastes. For instance, Jensen *et al.* (1970) state: 'The unwanted by-products formed when chlorinating aliphatic hydrocarbons amount to at least 75,000 tons per year in northern Europe alone.'

In order to save marine life from the eventual dangers of the toxicity of the petroleum-derived, halogenated hydrocarbons, including the pesticides, we need:

(*a*) Precise and wide scientific knowledge of the toxic effects of the hydrocarbons under consideration.

(*b*) International chemical inventories of the waste discharges and dumpings that are currently going on or in preparation.

(*c*) Reduction of such actions.

(*d*) Both national and international monitoring systems.

Other Organic Compounds (including Detergents)

The main dangers and/or harmful effects of these pollutants are: toxicity (of the non-biodegradable compounds) with risk to health of fish, oxygen demand (of other compounds), and the consequent effects on eco-systems.

No doubt the field of these 'other organic compounds' is broad and important; however, it has so far been investigated only superficially. The organic compounds in question may be divided into two groups, namely those which are classified as hypothetical pollutants because they are non-biodegradable and thus possibly toxic, and those which are considered to be 'pollutants' because they are biodegradable and consume the dissolved oxygen of the water, having a high 'biological oxygen demand'.

Which organic compounds must be considered pollutants and under what circumstances? This seemingly simple question covers in reality an endless succession of sub-questions, most of which cannot yet be answered. For in too many cases the organic pollutants cannot be distinguished from naturally occurring organic compounds. Moreover, the behaviour of an organic compound in the marine environment depends upon all manner of other factors. Furthermore, the number of organic compounds, existing at present or to be synthesized in the future, is virtually inexhaustible, and any of them might be classified as potential pollutants. At the present time only a few have been demonstrated to be harmful. The task remains to test the toxicity of these additives and to develop suitable analytical methods for their isolation, determination, and identification, in sea water.

The detergents form an important group of organic chemicals. According to FAO (1970), the detergents are either (*a*) of the 'hard' type, being not readily biodegradable and having the toxicity to living organisms increasing with the increasing complexity of their molecules, or (*b*) of the 'soft' type, which are less toxic to marine organisms than the former group, and more rapidly degraded by living organisms.

Nutrient Chemicals (including Domestic Raw Sewage and Agricultural Run-off)

The main dangers and/or harmful effects of these are that they cause over-fertilization (possibly leading to depletion of oxygen) and adversely affect ecosystems.

The nutrients are those compounds of nitrogen, phosphorus, and silicon (FAO, 1970), that are necessary for the growth of marine plants in general and of marine phytoplankton in particular. These are nitrate, nitrite, ammonia, orthophosphate, and orthosilicate, compounds, together with biologically derived organic nitrogen and phosphorus compounds which can be used after microbiological breakdown. Other forms of phosphorus and nitrogen, such as the polyphosphates and nitrilo-triacetic acid occurring in detergents (*see* above), must also be considered here. All these substances are of importance because of their role in promoting eutrophication, which produces far-reaching effects in the biogeochemical cycle.

As a young student I was told that the low productivity of the Baltic Sea, and especially of the Gulf of Bothnia, was caused by the lack of nutrient chemicals, and even now one should remember that nutrient chemicals are, up to a certain limit, most welcome for the primary and higher productivity of a sea area.

Over-fertilization and consequent eutrophication of the seas will probably always be limited to estuaries, fjords, some coastal zones, archipelagos, and parts of the semi-closed inland seas. Here in Finland we speak a lot of this kind of nutrient pollution. The sources of nutrient chemicals and potential nutrients that are likely to cause eutrophication are domestic sewage (including the 'soft' detergents), certain industrial wastes, and agricultural run-off.

Especially in connection with the monitoring of the nutrient chemicals, limnologists and marine scientists should work together. (Finland is one of the relatively few countries where this collaboration has been established.) In addition to the study and monitoring of the rivers and points of direct discharge, the estuaries and other receiving areas must also be studied and surveyed regularly. The aim should be to arrive at more reliable knowledge of the fate of chemical nutrients in the sea, and also of sediments which may play an important part in the balance, since they act in eutrophic waters as reservoirs from which nutrients may be regenerated under suitable conditions.

In some sea areas, eutrophication as such could be a welcome process. However, because of its secondary effects (FAO, 1970), it may be extremely harmful: in it, oxygen is initially over-produced by photosynthesizing Algae, but when these die, oxygen is rapidly removed from the water, leading in extreme cases to its total depletion which may be followed by the formation of hydrogen sulphide. This is what was observed in the deepest basins of the Baltic Sea in the 1960s. We who live around this inland sea are convinced that the situation is basically caused by the natural, periodically occurring stagnation of the deep waters. We also agree that both the biological oxygen demand (originated by biodegradable organic wastes from industry) and the recently excessive input of nutrient chemicals leading to eutrophication, have acted as additional factors to the same end. However, we have not been able to agree fully upon the respective significance of the said two additional factors, even though the application of remedial measures will depend to a large extent upon such agreement.

Inorganic Chemicals, including Metals (e.g. Mercury, Lead, Copper)

The main dangers and/or harmful effects of these result from their toxicity (with risk to the health of fish), from their ill-effects on the quality and marketability of fish, and from the risks which they pose to public health.

In some cases (e.g. cyanogen and compounds of copper, phosphorus, and arsenic), serious dumpings have occurred with harmful effects (FAO, 1970) on marine life (such as fish-kills, 'green' oysters, 'red' herrings, etc.). In other cases the dumpings have given rise to finely-divided solid materials (such as iron and aluminium oxides) which have caused harmful slime excretion in shellfish.

There are also other highly-toxic elements that are currently being produced in large quantities; their possible entry into the marine environment should be considered and the concentration levels in the sea measured. For instance, cadmium is used in some quantity by plastic industries; sooner or later the products become waste. Vanadium is present in fossil fuels and can thus be introduced into the marine environment through the atmosphere.

Some of the heavy metals are particularly toxic. Thus mercury and lead are considered to be among the most threatening of all marine pollutants, and will be discussed below together with airborne chemicals in general.

Lead is a 'trace element', an enzyme inhibitor, and also impairs cell metabolism in the human body. In prehistoric times, an estimated 1,300 tons of dissolved lead were chemically precipitated annually in pelagic sediments together with 500 tons of lead in settled silicate particles. Today, 20,000 tons of dissolved lead enter the oceans annually from rivers, and a similar amount is introduced from the atmosphere by wash-out of aerosols originating from leaded automobile fuels (FAO, 1970). Man has thus contaminated the mixed, upper layer of the oceans of the northern hemisphere with industrial lead to such an extent that average concentrations have been elevated by a factor of about five. However, the (presumably adverse) effects on marine life of this increase of lead are not yet known.

A similar increase in the concentration of mercury in sea water has not yet been shown, although some effects of it on coastal marine life are known. Actually, the mercury concentration (Kečkeś & Miettinen, 1970) in sea water is low, but due to mercury's high chemical reactivity and biological toxicity its increase has a strongly deleterious effect on living organisms. At present the world production of mercury is about 9,000 tons per year, and it is estimated that about 5,000 tons of this is released into the sea from the industrial and agricultural use of mercury compounds. Thus mercury pollution has become an urgent problem not only to the fisheries of the world but also in marine ecosystems.

The biological transformation of relatively less toxic forms of mercury into those with high toxicity, and its bioaccumulation directly from sea water or through the food-chains, returns the mercury to man in a concentrated form, which apart from direct toxic effects can also have a genetic effect. In Japan, several persons are reported to have died as a result of eating mercury-contaminated fish, and elsewhere considerable consignments of fish have been condemned as unfit for human consumption because of an unduly high content of mercury.

The biosphere being one continuous envelope, in the monitoring of global atmospheric pollution particular attention should be paid to items which are suspected of influencing climate to a high degree—for example, carbon dioxide and turbidity of the atmosphere. Indeed, carbon dioxide supplies the classic example (Eriksson, 1970), whose concentration in the atmosphere is to a considerable extent dependent on the physical and chemical state of the oceans. At present it seems likely that at least one-third of the 'fossil' carbon dioxide released by man's activity enters the oceans through their surfaces.

The most important sulphur compound (Lundholm & Svensson, 1970) in the air is sulphur dioxide, which is also probably the most important atmospheric pollutant. It is, however, estimated that roughly 80 per cent of the sulphur in the atmosphere has been emitted as hydrogen sulphide, and roughly 20 per cent as sulphur dioxide.

Both sulphuric acid and sulphates exist as aerosols and will disappear from air either through gravitational or precipitational fallout to different 'sinks' (soil, lakes, oceans). Sulphur dioxide has harmful effects on the health of man and other animals, and causes injuries also to plant tissues. A serious decrease in the pH of precipitation, and a concomitant decrease in the pH of lakes and rivers with a low buffering capacity, has been noted in the last decade. This decline may affect aquatic life, as most forms cannot exist at a pH of below four. Fortunately, the pH of the sea will not change to a measurable extent for this reason, because of the high buffering capacity of sea water.

The rapid global spread for example of DDT and lead, clearly indicates also the significance of the atmospheric transport of marine pollutants, and thus the need for close coordination of oceanic and atmospheric monitoring systems.

Enteric Bacteria and Viruses (from Domestic Sewage)

The main dangers and/or harmful effects of these are their risk to public health and the effects which they may have on the quality and marketability of fish.

In estuarine areas, lagoons, and archipelagos, a great number of bathing beaches have latterly been closed in many countries because of the enteric Bacteria and viruses that have got into the local sea water. Moreover in eastern Canada, sewage pollution has resulted in the closure of more than 50 per cent of the former molluscan shellfish-growing areas (Blackwood, 1970). Thus the disposal by municipalities of raw sewage into the marine environment without consideration of the multiple-use concept for coastal waters has been a major oversight.

Because of the 'self-cleaning' power of sea water (simply resulting from the death of the said microorganisms), the risk to public health and to marine biota created by the discharge of wastes containing enteric Bacteria and viruses, should always remain relatively local. However, with the ever-increasing human population of the world, the number of such local, small contaminated areas is increasing rapidly, and they are tending to 'join up' in the manner of (and with) towns. Particular care should be exercised practically throughout the world to avoid the contamination of bathing beaches and fishing grounds by raw domestic sewage.

Suspended Solids and Turbidity

The main dangers and/or harmful effects of these are through their interference with the functioning of ecosystems.

The seas have always been characterized by their natural suspended matter: inorganic materials (sand, clays, and minerals), living material (phytoplankton, zooplankton, Bacteria, yeasts and other Fungi), and dead organic material (detritus). In the open sea the concentration of suspended matter is much less than in coastal waters or in estuaries. Approximately, the total amount of suspended solids is inversely related to the transparency of the water and directly related to the so-called turbidity, which is normally expressed in terms of light attenuation coefficient.

The artificially-added load of suspended solids consists of domestic sewage, waste products from industry, and material stirred up by coastal constructions, etc. The additional organic material, as always, may lead to increased productivity, to over-fertilization and/or high oxygen consumption, and to changes in the ecosystems. The solid inorganic pollutants may at least locally hamper also light penetration into the sea and thus reduce the primary production. Moreover, the inorganic waste deposits may modify the composition and very structure of the sea-bottom. The additional suspension may also affect the well-being of biota even directly.

Man is in some cases reducing the amount of suspended solids in sea water as a result of diminishing the sediment load of water that is discharged from rivers. The effect of the Aswan Dam upon sea water of the easternmost part of the Mediterranean Sea is one of the well-known examples: according to Ellsaesser (1971), the building of the dam has already been blamed also for reducing the sardine catch in the eastern Mediterranean by 97 per cent. How much man-made changes will affect marine productivity in the long run remains to be seen, as the factors and their effects may be complex and manifold.

On the other hand, even without an increase of the actual load, the turbidity may be changed locally: the effect of effluent pipelines discharging into the sea differs from that of rivers in that the residence time of materials in the pipes is shorter, so that practically no decomposition takes place before the materials reach the sea. This is an additional reason why the pipelines must be connected with purification plants.

Dumped Containers

The main dangers and/or harmful effects of these are that they affect fishing operations; they are also often aesthetically obnoxious.

An ever-increasing amount and variety of solid and liquid waste products are being dumped into the open sea. The possible effects of such actual pollutants, for instance leaking from corroded containers, have been covered in the preceding subsections. Here it remains only to observe that the dumped containers on the bottom can affect fishing operations directly in the shallow-sea areas, while the mind of decent man revolts at the thought of the ever-increasing flotsam of plastic containers, etc.

Coastal Construction and Exploitation of the Sea-bottom

The main dangers and/or harmful effects of these are through affecting the local ecosystems.

In many parts of the globe, man is changing the 'morphology' and ecology of the coastal waters through new constructions and new kinds of exploitation of coastal resources, as the following examples will indicate.

Serious ecological problems arise from the tapping, for agricultural or other purposes, of rivers which flow into lagoons and coastal estuaries (Lemus *et al.*, 1970).

Perhaps even more serious than over-fishing is the inshore habitat destruction (Ray, 1970). The most effective way to extirpate a species is by environmental disruption, and this is being done inshore at a rapid pace.

Waste discharges do great harm, but even more damaging are apt to be the permanent environmental changes that are being caused by widespread dredging and filling in of coastal areas (Wastler & Guerrero, 1970). The changes have often resulted in the destruction of estuarine nursery areas of shrimps and other important commercial biota, and in the alteration of water movement patterns which may affect entire estuarine systems. Actually, numerous lagoons, natural harbours, estuaries, and mangrove swamps, are now being threatened in many parts of the world by the development of new resorts, communities, and heavy industries.

Finally, the underwater exploitation of off-shore and other resources is apt to affect the biota through added turbidity, changing of the morphology of the sea-bottom, and destruction of natural habitats and ecosystems.

Especially in connection with this subsection, which deals with the effects of some man-made and other changes in the natural habitats of the biota, can one observe that nature is able to adapt herself to the changing conditions, at least in some cases, in a favourable way (seen from the point of view of man). Thus here around the Baltic Sea we are happy to observe that our most expensive delicacy, the salmon, when its traditional spawning grounds in the inland rivers were cut off from the sea by hydroelectric power stations, apparently learned to spawn in some coastal zones.

Radioactive Wastes

The main danger and/or harmful effects of these is as a source of radio-activity and consequent risk to biota and public health.

In the future, assuming that nuclear explosions continue at their present low rate, the major concern with artificial radionuclides in the marine environment will be from the expansion of nuclear power programmes, and the resulting local contamination which should be limited (Russell, 1969). Environmental monitoring requirements for waste-disposal operations will be mainly national in character, and the present and foreseeable need for global monitoring can be controlled through the inventory of rates of introduction (FAO, 1970).

Condenser Waters

The main danger and/or harmful effects of these are through increased water temperatures affecting ecosystems.

The condenser waters, in particular from the nuclear power-plants, may alter, in limited areas, the breeding seasons of some biota and allow warm-water species to breed in areas that would otherwise be too cool for them. Correspondingly, the cool-water species may avoid the areas with increased water temperatures. It is expected, however, that such changes will not prove significantly harmful. Only in the tropics may the additional heat cause critical local problems, as here some organisms live close to the upper limit of their temperature tolerance.

It should not be overlooked that condenser waters may affect local micro-climate in an undesirable manner.

THE PRESENT SITUATION

Although the probability of large-scale contamination of the marine environment from planned and unplanned waste-disposal is slowly becoming greater, it is encouraging to observe man's increasing awareness of the threat which certain pollutants pose upon the marine environment. Public attention has centred on the more dramatic incidents involving major oil-spills and uncontrolled off-shore oil and gas wells, but the insidious attrition of the productive capacity of near-shore and estuarine environments is probably of greater concern on a world-wide basis. As was pointed out by the FAO Technical Conference (1970), the increases in uncontrolled industrialization and in other waste-producing activities constitute, in the absence of new and increased remedial measures and preventive action, the major threat to the success of any measures for alleviating marine pollution, and this threat is aggravated by the increasing world population. It is also becoming clear that marine pollution must be considered as a part of the overall problem of the pollution of the human environment.

Even the sanitary engineers and industrialists who have been using the seas for the solution of some of their waste-disposal problems are starting to realize the fact that the seas have become *res communis*—the property of all of us, which can be used for various purposes only within the framework of all-embracing programmes. Since the publication of the Report of the ICES Working Group on Pollution of the North Sea (Cole, 1969; *cf.* also Cole, 1970), there has been a considerable development of research in several countries bordering the North Sea, and this has led to sharpened appreciation of the need to limit the discharges of toxic and persistent wastes such as organochlorine pesticides, polychlorinated biphenyls, and heavy metals such as mercury, lead, and copper. The importance of international cooperation in developing standards and effective controls of pollution discharges into the seas has latterly become quite strikingly evident.

Marine pollution has confronted marine scientists and engineers with an urgent and demanding challenge. The decision-makers of the world are badly in need of reliable and critical scientific and technical advice concerning the problems of marine pollution and the practicability and efficiency of various remedial measures that may eventually have to be applied. This advice can be obtained only from the appropriate scientists and qualified technologists.

Are the scientists really ready to cope with the problems of marine pollution? Edward D. Goldberg (FAO, 1970) has answered this most serious enquiry with the contention that 'The world's scientists are now ready to measure the health of the oceans.' This straightforward reply does not, however, mean that the scientists already know the answers to all the problems, many of which are still irrational even to them. Ray (1970) has observed: 'Many maintain that we do not yet know enough about the sea, nor do we have sufficient experience with it, to change our *modus operandi*.' Nevertheless, as pointed out by Lopuski (1970), a general scientific motivation is now needed for introducing legislative measures. Even at the risk of committing errors, marine pollution should cease to be considered an 'unknown', while limits of 'permissible pollution' must be scientifically defined, and proper controls enforced, well before those limits are reached. Scientific advice is needed to establish legally recognized methods of measuring the concentration of pollutants, and the advice of scientists is needed on the legislative measures necessary for implementing research and monitoring programmes.

As one of the first practical steps to this end, the recent FAO Seminar (FAO, 1970) delineated as an urgent requirement the gathering of data on the world production of both organic and inorganic chemicals as a guide towards evaluating their potential dangers to the environment. In addition, knowledge of their paths of consumption and disposition would help to make feasible the formulation of survey programmes towards defining their oceanic dispositions.

In more general terms, marine scientists should either know or find out the modes of entry, pathways, and fates, of pollutants in the seas. The possible modes of entry or sources of pollutants include: discharge (by rivers, pipelines, etc.) whether domestic, industrial, or agricultural; coastal dredging, etc.; intentional dumping; in the case of petroleum, intentional rinsing, waste oil, accidental leaks, and shipwrecks; rain-water and atmospheric dust; and re-entry from sediments.

Other problems of pathways and fates to be dealt with are: dispersion and distribution of pollutants in the sea; absorption and adsorption of pollutants by sediments in suspension; biological accumulation and transport (whether by direct intake or by transfer of pollutants from one trophic level to another); and degradation of various harmful substances into harmless ones in the natural environment (including the role of marine Bacteria).

When it comes to the actual pollutants, an immediate increase in research activity is needed to examine more closely the scientific problems associated with oil pollution effects on the marine environment and its living organisms, so that action can be taken to avoid dangers that could arise.

Detailed investigations are needed, among other things, into the distribution of chlorinated hydrocarbons in the components of marine ecosystems—including the water, particulate material, plankton, dominant animals and plants of the biomass, and sediments and surface films.

In designing a global network of baseline and impact stations, considerable difficulty arises on account of our ignorance of the present state of the oceans and their natural variability. Permanent changes and variability induced by pollution must be detected and measured against the spectrum of natural variation. This means also that it is necessary to have long-term data on several significant factors. For instance, experimental work (Glover *et al.*, 1970) has shown that pesticide residues may depress the rate of photosynthesis, but there are no long-term data concerning pesticides in the open ocean. Moreover, we do not know whether there have been natural changes in the vertical distribution of plankton or in the rates of production and turnover.

There is also a critical need for increased biological information on lifehistories of the units of fauna and flora that appear to be most suitable for monitoring purposes or to have the greatest ecological importance. Moreover, the spectrum of organisms that can be used as indicators, particularly as greater areas of the world come under surveillance, should be broadened.

Finally, it goes almost without saying that much more scientific work is needed to develop criteria for intercalibration of methods of chemical analysis of all significant pollutants, to develop water quality criteria to be used as a guide for controlling the discharge of effluents into coastal waters, and to evolve methods of sewage and industrial waste treatment with a view to minimizing pollution from these sources.

LEGISLATIVE AND ADMINISTRATIVE MEASURES

Political decisions leading to various legislative and administrative measures for effectively combating marine pollution are not feasible without thorough scientific knowledge of the problems that have been briefly indicated above. On the other hand, without the necessary legislative and administrative measures, all the scientific knowledge in the world would not solve the acute problems of marine pollution. One might list the forms of such measures schematically as follows:

(National) monitoring of territorial waters
National legislation
Regional cooperation
Open-sea monitoring
International monitoring arrangements
Collaboration with monitors of inland waters, atmosphere, and land
International conventions
An international 'agency' for concerted action.

It may well take an international 'agency' to gather data on the world production of both organic and inorganic chemicals as a guide to evaluate their potential dangers to the environment. In the past it has been difficult to acquire such data, because producers and users have not been required to furnish them to the world public. Yet it should be recognized by everyone that when pollution extends to a world-wide scale, such organizations *must be obliged* to furnish production and dissemination data to international bodies. The obvious success of the International Atomic Energy Agency in the field of global control of radioactive material is a proof that such a scheme can be feasible.

As was pointed out by the FAO Technical Conference (1970), the member nations should, among others, be requested to increase research on ecologically less harmful substitutes for the control of pests; also, better control of losses into the environment of polychlorinated biphenyls and other potentially hazardous chemicals should be instituted immediately. Governments should require advanced techniques to be adopted for mercury recovery in all factories producing mercurial products or using mercury or its compounds for any purpose. Moreover, mercurial compounds should be replaced by other, non-mercurial substitutes whenever possible.

The deliberate dumping of toxic and solid wastes on recognized and potential fishing grounds and other shallow-water areas should be prohibited. Further studies of the conditions in the deep sea should be performed before dumping is allowed.

The FAO Seminar (FAO, 1970) considered the key word—monitoring—to be the systematic observation of properties related to specific problems concerned with the marine environment, the observations being carried out in such a way as to show how these properties vary with time at a number of fixed locations or geographical areas. In designing a world-wide ocean monitoring system, it will* be essential to consider this in relation to similar systems for monitoring the atmosphere and terrestrial environments.

Such a programme of monitoring is needed to provide information on long-term trends in certain basic characteristics of the marine environment. From the basis of such a continuous programme, warnings can be issued when certain pollutants exceed their maximum permissible concentrations in the water or in marine biota. Moreover, the monitoring programme will give information on the changes in the areal distribution of polluting substances in the seas and oceans.

The monitorings of the coastal waters and of the open seas will be basically somewhat different from one another. Thus the aims of the coastal monitoring must include maintenance of health of fish and shellfish stocks, prevention of risk to public health, and preservation and balance of the ecosystems. Correspondingly, the pollutants to be monitored in coastal waters must include at least the following ones: DDT, polychlorinated biphenyls, mercury, pathogenic microbes, toxic marine organisms, detergents, and agricultural run-off.

The open-sea monitoring must cover, though often in a less detailed manner, at least lead, mercury, radioisotopes, persistent hydrocarbons and petroleum products, sulphur dioxide, sulphuric acid, carbon dioxide, and DDT and its toxic breakdown products.

The present plans for marine monitoring call for approaches through local (national) monitoring systems, regional networks, and global systems—the last comprising a network of baseline stations, a network of impact stations, remote-sensing systems (using satellites and airplanes), and special systems for specific items.

The baseline stations will follow large-scale changes, particularly of those pollutants that are transported over great distances in the atmosphere or in the sea, while the impact stations will measure the most marked changes and be sited in areas where such changes are likely to be harmful to the marine ecosystem, to food resources, and eventually perhaps even to man. A global marine monitoring system must measure also the amount of pollutants in rain-water and atmospheric dust entering the sea.

Finally, the selection of suitable organisms, by means of which the changing degree of pollution could be monitored, offers interesting possibilities, particularly in coastal waters. The selected organisms or communities of organisms to be used for monitoring should reflect not only the presence or absence of pollutants but also relative pollution levels and periodic fluctuations of polluting chemicals in a circumscribed geographic area (FAO, 1970). Their usefulness will usually be directly related to their ability to concentrate pollutants either from the physical environment or from lower trophic levels. Also, changes in population density and species diversity in some ecological niches may serve as guides to pollution from a variety of known materials or even to

* It may be noted that the conditional is no longer used in referring to such systems as they are considered inevitable.—Ed.

unidentified toxic conditions. The composition of the below-tide benthic communities seems most promising as an object to be monitored.

In reality, the global oceanic monitoring system must evolve from a set of regional networks which themselves will surely grow out of national systems. The North Sea and the Baltic Sea offer good examples of how such regional systems have been developed—in these cases by the International Council for the Exploration of the Sea (cf. Cole, 1969; Dybern, 1970b).

A general appraisal of existing legislation on marine pollution (Lopuski, 1970) indicates the need for a programme both for international legislation and for fostering national legislation. The creation of monitoring networks, and the introduction of international legislation, are possible only at the highest intergovernmental level. This will be one of the great problems to be tackled by the United Nations Conference on the Human Environment, to be held in Stockholm in 1972.

THE FUTURE

In order to prosper as the most advanced animal species on earth, or perhaps even to survive as a species at all (Lundholm & Svensson, 1970), man has to enter the field of environmental management to preserve, control, and improve, his natural resources, and to do so with all his available power. He has to meet the challenge of the side-effects emanating from his own destructive activities, and to do this in an integrated effort at all levels of his society—political, administrative, public, and scientific. The seas and oceans are one of man's most important natural resources.

A pessimist, tired and exasperated, would base his predictions upon the assumption that nothing will be done to combat marine pollution or to protect the biosphere against the dangers of more and more pollution. According to him, we continue with accelerating speed on the road to extinction of the human race. On the other hand, a nonchalant optimist shows little concern for environmental alterations and insists that the powers of technology can overcome any inconveniences resulting from the dispersion of man's wastes.

The position of every scientist who is interested in the problems of the human environment should surely be the following: We observe around us and also in the marine environment some alarming signs. We know for sure that we do not yet realize all the other, possibly harmful or even dangerous developments in the same environment. With the introduction of effective scientific programmes and of legislative and administrative measures, both nationally and internationally, we must be able to rescue not only the human race from threatened extinction but also the marine environment from drastic deterioration of its food resources and other important attributes.

The salt seas and oceans could never become perfectly 'pure'. They never were 'pure', and fortunately this is not even desirable. The world needs from the scientists the development of ecosystem-based conservation practices. The world needs from the governments and intergovernmental agencies, assisted by scientific expertise, the development of international legislation with enforcement for coordinated, balanced, active uses of the seas—one of them being their use as discharge areas. Both these goals, of scientific direction and governmental application, can be achieved if we so wish and if we are prepared to pay the expenses involved. All this is feasible.

References

ALLEN, G. H. (1970). The constructive use of sewage with particular reference to fish culture. *FAO (1970) Seminar* . . . 26 pp., illustr.

AUBERT, M., AUBERT, J., DONNIER, B. & BARELLI, M. (1970). Utilization of the trophodynamic chain in the study of the toxicity of chemically-polluted waste water. *FAO (1970) Seminar* . . . 8 pp.

BLACKWOOD, C. M. (1970). Canadian experience on sewage pollution of coastal waters: effect on fish-plant water supplies. *FAO (1970) Seminar* . . . 14 pp., illustr.

BLUMER, M. (1970). Oil contamination and the living resources of the sea. *FAO (1970) Seminar* . . . 11 pp.

BOURNE, W. R. P. (1970). Oil pollution and bird conservation. *Biological Conservation,* **2**(4), pp. 300–2.

BOYLE, C. L. (1969). Oil pollution of the sea: is the end in sight? *Biological Conservation,* **1**(4), pp. 319–27, illustr.

BUTLER, P. A., CHILDRESS, R. & WILSON, A. J., Jr (1970). The association of DDT residues with losses in marine productivity. *FAO (1970) Seminar* . . . 13 pp., illustr.

CIFUENTES LEMUS, J. L. *See* LEMUS, J. L. CIFUENTES

COLE, H. A. (1969). Report of the ICES Working Group on Pollution of the North Sea. *Cooperative Research Project, A* (13), International Council for the Exploration of the Sea, Charlottenlund: 61 pp., illustr.

COLE, H. A. (1970). North Sea pollution. *FAO (1970) Seminar* . . . 12 pp.

COWELL, E. B. & BAKER, J. M. (1969). Recovery of a salt marsh in Pembrokeshire, South-West Wales, from pollution by crude oil. With an appendix by D. H. Dalby. *Biological Conservation,* **1**(4), pp. 291–6, illustr.

COWELL, E. B., BAKER, J. M. & CRAPP, G. B. (1970). The biological effects of oil pollution and oil-cleaning materials on littoral communities, including salt marshes. *FAO (1970) Seminar* . . . 11 pp., illustr.

DAVIS, C. C. (1970). The effects of pollutants on the reproduction of marine organisms. *FAO (1970) Seminar* . . . 13 pp., 2 figs.

DUVIGNEAUD, P. (Ed.) (1967). *L'écologie, Science Moderne de Synthèse,* Volume 2. *Ecosystèmes et Biosphère* (2me edn). Ministère de l'Education Nationale et de la Culture, Direction Générale de l'Organisation des Etudes, Bruxelles: vi + 137 pp.

DYBERN, B. I. (1970a). Pollution in the Baltic. *FAO (1970) Seminar* . . . 17 pp., illustr.

DYBERN, B. I. (1970b). Report from the ICES Working Group on Pollution of the Baltic Sea. *Cooperative Research Project, A* (15), International Council for the Exploration of the Sea, Charlottenlund: 86 pp., illustr.

ELLSAESSER, Hugh W. (1971). Air pollution: our ecological alarm and blessing in disguise. *Eos,* **52**(3), pp. 92–100.

ERIKSSON, E. (1970). Global monitoring of atmospheric pollution; its possible relation to a global marine monitoring scheme. *FAO (1970) Seminar* . . . 3 pp.

FAO (1970). Seminar on Methods of Detection, Measurement and Monitoring of Pollutants in the Marine Environment. FAO, Rome, 4–10 December 1970; final report, 94 pp.

FAO TECHNICAL CONFERENCE (1970). *Technical Conference on Marine Pollution and its Effects on Living Resources and Fishing.* Abstracts of the Papers Presented. FAO, Rome, 9–18 December 1970, iii + 35 + 44 pp.

GLOVER, R. S., ROBINSON, G. A. & COLEBROOK, J. M. (1970). Plankton in the North

Atlantic: an example of the problems of analysing variability in the environment. *FAO (1970) Seminar* . . . 14 pp., illustr.

HALSTEAD, B. W. (1970). Toxicity of marine organisms caused by pollutants. *FAO (1970) Seminar* . . . 21 pp.

HEYERDAHL, Thor (1971). Atlantic Ocean pollution and biota observed by the 'Ra' expeditions. *Biological Conservation*, **3**(3), pp. 164–7, map.

HOLDEN, A. V. (1970). Monitoring organochlorine contamination of the marine environment by the analysis of residues in seals. *FAO (1970) Seminar* . . . 14 pp.

JENSEN, S., JERNELOV, A., LANGE, R. & PALMORK, K. H. (1970). Chlorinated by-products from vinyl chloride production: a new source of marine pollution. *FAO (1970) Seminar* . . . 8 pp., illustr.

KEČKEŚ, S. & MIETTINEN, J. K. (1970). Mercury as a marine pollutant. *FAO (1970) Seminar* . . . 34 pp., illustr.

KNEIP, T. J., HOWELLS, G. P. & WRENN, M. E. (1970). Trace elements, radionuclides and pesticide residues in the Hudson River. *FAO (1970) Seminar* . . . 11 pp., illustr.

LEMUS, J. L. CIFUENTES, KESTEVEN, G. L., ZARUR, A. & MEDINA, A. (1970). Aspects of contamination of sea water in the Gulf of Mexico. *FAO (1970) Seminar* . . . (summary only).

LOPUSKI, J. (1970). Present needs for scientific advice in the process of legislation on pollution. *FAO (1970) Seminar* . . . 6 pp.

LUNDHOLM, B. & SVENSSON, S. (1970). Global Environmental Monitoring System: technical report from Sweden to the IBP-Committee on Global Monitoring. Swedish Natural Science Research Council, Stockholm, *Ecological Research Committee Bulletin* No. 10, [ii] + 64 pp.

MENZEL, David W., ANDERSON, Judith & RANDTKE, Ann (1970). Marine phytoplankton vary in their response to chlorinated hydrocarbons. *Science*, **167**, pp. 1724–6, illustr.

MITROVIĆ, V. V. (1970). Sublethal effects of pollutants on fish. *FAO (1970) Seminar* . . . 10 pp.

RAY, Carleton (1970). Ecology, law, and the 'marine revolution'. *Biological Conservation*, **3**(1), pp. 7–17.

RICE, T. R., BAPTIST, J. P., CROSS, F. A. & DUKE, T. W. (1970). Potential hazards from radioactive pollution of the estuary. *FAO (1970) Seminar* . . . 9 pp., illustr.

ROYAL COMMISSION ON ENVIRONMENTAL POLLUTION (1971). *First Report*. Her Majesty's Stationery Office, London: 52 pp.

RUSSELL, R. Scott (1969). Contamination of the biosphere with radioactivity. *Biological Conservation*, **2**(1), pp. 2–9.

UNESCO (1970). Contemporary scientific concepts relating to the biosphere. (Based on a draft submitted by V. A. Kovda and collaborators.) Pp. 13–29 in *Use and Conservation of the Biosphere*, Natural Resources Research, X, UNESCO, Paris: 272 pp.

WASTLER, T. A. & GUERRERO, L. C. de (1970). Estuarine and coastal pollution in the United States. *FAO (1970) Seminar* . . . 42 pp., illustr.

WURSTER, Charles F., Jr (1969). Chlorinated hydrocarbon insecticides and the world ecosystem. *Biological Conservation*, **1**(2), pp. 123–9.

DISCUSSION

Panikkar (Chairman)

Professor Hela has given us a critical survey of our knowledge of pollution of the marine environment and its effects on productivity. Beginning with a brief appraisal of the living resources of the sea— both the current harvest and the probable yield in future—the account which we have heard covered the grounds of principles of production of living matter in the sea and the likely manner in which it may be influenced by different forms of pollution.

Among the various categories of pollution, the dangers of that from crude oil and its distillates were dealt with first. It is uncertain whether this is really the most dangerous type of pollution in the long run, but there is no doubt that oil-spills in the sea, whether from ships or escapes from the sea-bed, are spectacular and often receive wide publicity. While the hypothetical dangers of large-scale oil pollution cannot be minimized, the opinion seems to be hardening that the dangers of marine pollution by oil are limited and not as catastrophic as was once believed. The problem, however, is complex and requires the most careful study, as some of the early methods of dealing with oil-spills are by themselves harmful, because oil in emulsified form is likely to be more dangerous than oil in film or other states.

The second category of pollution dealt with by Professor Hela is that caused by the petroleum-derived halogenated hydrocarbons, including pesticides, and it is here that we diagnose the greatest possible danger. Cumulatively, too, this poses serious world-wide problems; for these compounds are toxic, affect fisheries, are hazards to public health, and intervene in fundamental biological processes such as photosynthesis. Because of their widespread employment in industry and agriculture, the chlorinated hydrocarbons are currently manufactured in amounts of something like 200,000 metric tons per annum, and their production and use are still increasing. The greatest drawback here is that, among the large number of chlorinated hydrocarbons utilized, the high toxicity-rates of certain compounds are well known, but the relative toxicities of the different types of these compounds under different conditions and on different organisms have not been adequately studied. The fact that they are extremely stable and not liable to biological degradation enhances their danger as enemies to mankind.

The increasing interest in the toxicity of this group of compounds has led to a considerable number of studies and is summarized in the recent report of the British Royal Commission on Environmental Pollution. A point to be emphasized is that not enough research has yet been done to prove conclusively that the less toxic of these compounds are the ones which are least likely to have cumulative effects. What the world would like to see is the changeover from the well-known and effective pesticides such as DDT to less stable, harmless ones that do not leave residual effects after their use. In this direction, both research for the development of new pesticides and their production in economically large quantities at low cost to replace those currently employed, are urgent necessities.

In the category of other organic compounds including detergents, the dangers are diagnosed as much less; but relatively little is known about them. The rise in the use of detergents during the past twenty years points to the need for a closer assessment of the dangers of their use—from the long-term aspects of their interference with the environment, and particularly from their effects on ecosystems.

The next category of pollutants discussed by Professor Hela was that of nutrient chemicals, including those in domestic and agricultural wastes. Here dangers are through excesses of nutrients rather than through their use in optimal quantities. They are essential for life; but in excess they can lead to explosive increases in the populations of particular and often undesirable organisms. Such phenomena are not uncommon even in the normal course of events in the sea, and are exemplified by 'red tide' and other phenomena that are apt to be followed by mass mortalities of other marine organisms.

The last category of chemical pollutants dealt with are the inorganic chemicals of direct toxicity, such as compounds of mercury, lead, and copper. Some of them cause considerable damage even as trace elements. The attention of the world has recently been drawn to the occurrence, well above the normal thresholds that are considered safe for humans, of mercury in canned tuna fish and of cadmium in edible molluscs.

The review was concluded by a summary of the present thinking on pollution through domestic sewage, suspended solids, turbidity, coastal construction, exploitation of the sea-bottom, radioactive wastes, and thermal pollution. From the discussion point of view I should like to emphasize a few aspects.

As regards sectors of the marine environment where the effects of pollution are likely to be manifest in an alarming measure, it has already been indicated that estuaries, backwaters, fjords, coastal lakes, and finally the inshore environments, have to be specially singled out as being vulnerable areas—as opposed to the open ocean where the dangers are less. Organic and inorganic pollutants from industrial and domestic sources can obviously attain high concentrations in such environments. The Baltic Sea is a good illustration. It is a matter of regret that adequate studies on the differential effects of polluting substances have not been carried out in many parts of the world. The inshore and estuarine environments have great significance from the point of view of living resources of the oceans, and Professor Hela has already indicated how more than half of the total catch of the world's fisheries comes from coastal regions. The tropical regions where the estuarine fauna and flora are particularly developed have a special significance, because many major commercial species of the tropics use the inshore and estuarine environments either for breeding or as nursery grounds during their life-cycle. These involve the very same biotopes as can be used for aquaculture. It is obvious, therefore, how important it is to protect the coastal ecosystems from the influences of pollution.

May I draw the attention of this Conference to an important aspect that is based on our own experience in India. From time immemorial the large rivers of India have been the recipients of raw domestic sewage from the cities which have developed on the banks of rivers along their courses. With recent industrialization, factories have sprung up within the cities and the industrial effluents are discharged into the rivers in increasing measure. We have not reached the stage where the effects of pollution are apparent; but pollution there is, and we should not wait until the effects become obvious through destruction of the natural fauna and flora. The pollutants flow down to the estuaries, where they tend to accumulate because of the tidal influences of the coast that extend many miles into the interior. A feature that is peculiar to large river systems is the increasing salination of estuarine waters of the lower reaches of the river systems with the increased use of the river waters for irrigation and power-generation.

The importance of monitoring the marine environments on a continuing basis has been emphasized by Professor Hela. The initial handicap here is the absence of figures of natural variability of the environment. But there is no room for complacency; indeed, studies in different parts of the world must be initiated immediately. It would be an extremely sad day for the world if the harmful effects of pollution were diagnosed only after environmental calamities had taken place. The scientific techniques and information already gathered should be put to good use in the establishment of world-wide monitoring systems. It is also evident that there is much need for standardization of methods and reporting employed for this purpose, so that the results can be readily compared.*

Very interesting possibilities of utilizing biological indicators of pollution, and their quantitative measurement, open up a promising new approach in this connection. The use of certain widely-distributed benthic and neritic species on a quantitative basis, to assess the intensity of pollution, offer promising fields for research and application on pollution survey.

Experimental studies of pollution have been lagging far behind. A clear lead is needed in this direction, as has also been emphasized at the FAO Seminar on Pollution which is so widely cited by Professor Hela in his formal paper.

In conclusion I should say that it is a common but melancholy experience in the world today that, in many fields, the application of knowledge already available to us is not put to good and effective use. I am constrained to emphasize this with reference to many developing countries, where with some foresight and circumspection the dangers inherent in pollution could be avoided. The all-too-familiar tale is that many countries continually wait for the same cycle of harmful effects and possible correction to be re-enacted in their own environment. Conferences of this type provide us with the opportunity to create world opinion to encourage the taking of timely action on a global scale.

Miller

In discussing the productivity of the oceans as harvested by man, we should be greatly concerned to see that some effective moratorium is imposed on the destruction of whales. I wish to introduce this by saying that in the Antarctic the whale fleets are still active in harvesting whales although some of the species involved are supposed to be protected. A year ago a group of concerned whale people in the United States, and officials of our government going to the Tokyo Conference—a consultative Conference on the Antarctic Treaty which takes place every two years and involves the twelve or so

---

* *See* the material from the International Organization for Standardization published on pp. 127-9.—Ed.

countries who are the signatories of that treaty—requested consideration of a programme for total protection of whales over a certain period of time. This, however, was apparently not propitious, and we didn't get any consideration or even discussion. Yet the Antarctic is one of the main breeding and productive areas of whales, and supports many species. Apparently the excuse among those harvesting whales is that they can handle this matter by some kind of action of their own, and that there is another forum, a London meeting on sealing, at which there could be discussions. Moreover, there has just been a meeting of the International Whaling Commission—a commercially-oriented organization without any real commitments to the world public.

Some people have felt that this is a matter for the United Nations, and indeed it will probably take that course eventually. Meanwhile I'm pleased to say that the United States Government has taken action, and that there is a bill before Congress now to bolster previous action by imposing a moratorium on any importation of whale products. Dr Brower's organization, the Friends of the Earth, has an active programme towards making the public aware of the problem, and I hope that this Conference will see fit to initiate some kind of resolution on the subject.

Hashimoto

As Japan has experienced, twice in the past ten years, miserable and bitter incidents of methyl-mercury poisoning, I think we should be responsible for reporting on the scientific problems involved in those incidents, to avoid their being repeated in the world again. It is to be noted that the concentration of methyl-mercury in the ambient water was below the sensitivity of the chemical analysis methods used, and that this is a pitfall of water-quality science. Many fishes that are contaminated with methyl-mercury are alive and look like normal fishes. The problem of biological concentration of mercury in fish in ambient water having low concentrations of it is of particular importance, as they may concentrate the mercury as much as several thousand times and still remain alive and seem normal. The food habits of fishermen should also be noted. They are heavy fish-eaters, often eating fish up to three times a day continuously over long periods of time. The amounts of fish eaten by affected persons have been estimated as at least 300 grams per day continually for more than a few months. Some of them eat 1,500 grams per day.

A nationwide survey has been conducted for the past six years, from which it emerged that the range of mercury content of fish is usually from 0.03 ppm to 0.3 ppm, though it is not uncommon to find fish with 0.5 ppm of total mercury. In areas with a high geochemical content of mercury, the average concentration of total mercury in fishes is around 1·5 ppm. There are no extremely high-concentration fishes nor low-concentration fishes locally, the content of mercury being related rather to size and ecological behaviour. Large fishes and those living near the bottom of watersheds seem to be relatively high in their content of mercury. Usually the content of methyl-mercury ranged from *ca* 30 per cent to 80 per cent of the total mercury. In the areas of incidents of mercury poisoning, we always found fishes with concentrations of several ppm or even of the order of 10 ppm; so as a provisional measure we use the pollution level of the fish population. If 20 per cent or more of fish samples exceed 1 ppm of total mercury, it is necessary to make more detailed investigations. If we find several ppm in fish samples, especially if the content exceeds 10 ppm, it is necessary to sound the alert. If we find a person with a mercury concentration in the hair exceeding 50 ppm, we ban all fishing and fish-eating. The usual figure of mercury content in the hair of the population is more or less 5 ppm, and from 30 to 50 per cent of this is methyl-mercury.

The effectiveness of control of trade effluent containing mercury can be observed within a few years in the case of fish. However, matters are different in shellfish, owing to the precipitation of mercury in bottom sediments. The route of intake of mercury by fish is considered to be through the food-chains, though gill respiration cannot be excluded in cases of high man-made pollution. We studied the mercury content in various kinds of foods and in water and air. At present, our estimate of mercury intake by the Japanese population is an average of about 30–40 millionths of a gram per person per day of total mercury. In areas of geochemically high concentration it is about double, or 60 μg per day. Concerning toxicology, we have estimated the daily intake of total mercury in cases of methyl-mercury poisoning incidents, and it was found that 1 to 1·5 milligrams per day was minimal. In cases of Minamata disease, it was estimated that 3 to 5 milligrams intake per day continuously for more than two or three months is necessary for incidence. The usual intake of fish by the average Japanese is 80 grams per day, based on an annual nutrition survey.

In the case of tuna fish, we have recognized that they have rather a high content of mercury—about 1 ppm of total mercury, though the percentage of methyl-mercury is low, being around 30 per cent of the total mercury. The tunas were caught in the open ocean and we do not know how they came to have such a content of mercury. But based on our investigation results on daily intake in two incidence cases, and also on the national daily intake of fish, we do not consider these tuna fish to be harmful to human health. This is the consensus of opinion of all our experts who have been engaged in research on mercury poisoning to date.

Man-made mercury pollution has to be controlled on the strictest possible basis. With the one exception of seed dressing with phenyl-mercury pesticides, the use of organic mercury pesticides is prohibited in Japan. Trade effluent is controlled very strictly, and the pulp and paper industry abolished the use of organic mercury for slime control purposes already several years ago. Water pollution control laws provide effluent standards for mercury at less than 0.01 ppm of total mercury, and also demand that it be not detected by either of the two analytical methods of gas chromatography and thin-layer chromatography with sensitivity of the order of parts per thousand million (ppb). It is our principle that man-made mercury pollution must be controlled very strictly, and our belief that it is possible to combat mercury poisoning at present and for the future.

Panikkar (Chairman)

Concerning the point raised by Dr Hashimoto, there is a feeling in many circles, and particularly among Japanese fishery scientists, that the standards imposed by the FDA in the United States regarding mercury are quite unrealistic—that the permissible limit for the amount of mercury in tuna could be far above what they now prescribe. Meanwhile there is insufficient information available concerning naturally occurring mercury in particular species of fish; yet the feeling of alarm persists that tunas are dangerous because they accumulate mercury.

Brower

Looking at this map of the world, with all the blue representing the oceans, I'm reminded of the perspective that Jacques-Yves Cousteau, the great undersea explorer, employed to explain things to architects. He said that if the earth were reduced to the size of a hen's egg, all the water in all the oceans would be represented by only one drop of water on that egg's shell. The drop of water would be less than five millimetres across. It looks as if there is a great deal more than that, as the oceans and seas occupy more than 70 per cent of the earth's surface. But they are on average only about two miles deep, whereas the Earth is four thousand miles deep, and that gives us the perspective of the drop of water representing the oceans. The atmosphere, if you put it on the same scale and reduce it to the density of water, would be only about ten metres deep. I think that if we were living on a lake which was only ten metres deep, we would hesitate to throw as much garbage into it as we are now throwing into the air. Or if we realized how small the ocean really is on this scale, we would hesitate to put into it what we are now putting in. Especially do I think we should be mindful of René Dubos's contention that the worst pollution is that which we have not yet identified.

Most of the people in the audiences that I appear before in America are quite young, but this is scarcely the case here, and I think that if there were more young people in this audience they would be beginning to feel impatient about the things that are not being discussed: their future, I think, has not been discussed with enough concern. I know from those with whom I have talked of the great apprehension they feel about the forthcoming Stockholm Conference—that it should have been held five or six years ago instead of next year. I'm hopeful, and I think they are, that the things we are discussing here will be considered at the Stockholm Conference, and make the following year start, and subsequent years start, with the concern we need to have. I think the young people have the feeling that my generation, and those of you who are younger than I am, are not beginning to do nearly enough. There has been talk about everything being almost under control; but the Baltic Sea is dying, Lake Erie is dying, and Cousteau can say that the oceans, in twenty years, have lost 40 per cent of their living productivity. But somehow I don't really feel the sense of emergency that I should like to feel.

Surely some of the most drastic pollutants going into the oceans are the chemicals that we now contrive to make, and that nature does not know how to handle. I define pollution in terms of the time-lag between when man invents or anyway makes something and throws it into the environment, and when the environment figures out what to do about it. We are putting pollutants into the environment now that it never had to cope with before. We have invented some very beautiful new ones. I think perhaps the worst of all that was not discussed at great length but perhaps we will consider later is radioactive pollution, which we have not yet found a solution for.*

One of the things which worries me most is that we somehow imagine we can go right to the very brink, until we reach the absolute limits of the earth, and then we will stop and think hard about what we shall do next—instead of about what we have been doing. I would urge that this Conference, in its discussions and in its resolutions, adjure man to apply the brakes and stop before we overrun the last unspoiled places on this planet. He should go back over where he has been and do much better. Those wild places, those international ecological monuments containing information that comes from the beginning of life on earth, are far more important than we seem to recognize. They hold answers to questions that man has not yet learned how to ask. Yet we seek to pave them and pollute them, to destroy the incredible bank of information that has been passed on to us. I think we somehow assume that we are the last generation, though I trust we will not so assume at all in any of our discussions here. There should be thousands of years of mankind to come, but I think that mankind must realize that he will not stay on this planet unless he shares it with other living beings and gives them all the consideration he possibly can.

Vallentyne

I want to accent briefly Dr Miller's comment on whales, the population of which is going down dangerously—particularly in the matter of Blue and Humpback Whales. We should all feel concerned and join in the *biodrive* to save them.

With regard to the rather common contention that much higher biological production may be looked forward to from the sea, I would like to draw this Conference's attention to an assessment of the potential of marine fisheries that was made a few years ago by W. E. Ricker, who concluded essentially that production might go up to double the present level but that would be the limit.

Finally, I would like to comment on the frequent contention that Lake Erie is dead. To be sure, there is apt to be so much oil on the inflowing rivers that their surface may catch fire, as has happened also in the Soviet Union. Indeed, lots of things are funnelled into Lake Erie, including mercury. But there is one thing that Erie is not, and that is, dead! The problem with Lake Erie is that there is too much life of some kinds in it, resulting from the nutrients that have been put in there—which nutrients are stimulating the growth of plants and causing innumerable changes, including oxygen deficiencies which largely eradicate insects and greatly affect the fish population. But if you look at the total plant life and the total animal life in the lake over the past half-century, you will find that it has not changed much; if anything it has increased, and this is true of the fish production. So I would like to modify the statement that Lake Erie is dying or dead, as the problem is rather that it's too much alive with the sort of things that people don't like.

* *See*, however, the International Atomic Energy Agency observer's 'Statement on Nuclear Energy' published on pp. 354–5.—Ed.

Panikkar (Chairman)

With regard to the world production of fish, I think the assessment of a possible two-fold increase to which Dr Vallentyne referred is reasonable. With the present total tonnage around 60 millions,* it should be possible to raise it to, say, 120 or even 150 millions—something like that. But the point I'd like to emphasize is that whereas the increase which is possible in certain areas of the world is very limited, in certain other areas it is really great. Thus, whereas the Indian Ocean at present produces 2.5 million tons of fish per annum, a very conservative estimate of its possible yield is something like 15 to 20 million tons; on the other hand, a proportionate rise in production in the North Sea could scarcely be conceivable. The order of possible increase in the Indian Ocean at present being from 6 to 8 or even 10 times, such countries as India and Australia could expand their fishing efforts very substantially.

As for our approach to the pollution problem, if for example there is a ban on the use of certain types of insecticides on the theoretical possibility that they will be washed down into the Indian Ocean or certain regions, shall we be justified in introducing such a ban until a certain danger has been realized, the present ill-effects being so small? It is this kind of thinking which makes many people hesitate about accepting point-blank a ban on certain insecticides, as exemplified by the problem of DDT with reference to the Indian Ocean.

Nuorteva

Professor Hela pointed out that marine fishing is mainly restricted to coastal waters. However, the polluting effect of man is concentrated on the coastal waters, too. In this world of exponentially increasing technological activity, one bit after another of the coastal waters is taken over and polluted. As a consequence, our possibilities to obtain fish for the exponentially increasing human population is steadily decreasing. So I think as a matter of urgency it is necessary to calculate how much fish the exponentially increasing human population needs. After this calculation has been made, we should reserve for the world's fisheries as much coastal area as is necessary, requiring that industry restrict its activities to the remaining areas.

Concerning the methyl-mercury problem, Mr Chairman has pointed out the need to know the amounts of natural mercury in tuna and other fishes. I think, however, that natural mercury is as dangerous for man as is the mercury of industrial origin.

Matthews

I wonder whether we are being too optimistic. In this connection I would like to refer you to Professor Hela's paper in which you will note an example:

[* The latest figures obtained from FAO (*in litt.* 17 August 1971) indicate a total world fisheries catch, in millions of metric tons, of 64.3 in 1968, 63.1 in 1969, and 67.0 (estimated) in 1970. Of these the marine components were 57.1, 55.7, and 59.5, respectively. These figures include 'Fish, Crustaceans, Molluscs, etc.' but 'not Whales and Seals'. The Chief, Fishery Statistics and Economic Data Branch, Fishery Economics and Institutions Division, FAO, Rome, commented (*ibid.*) 'The important feature of the last three years is not so much the actual drop in 1969, but a slowing down in the consistent increases that had occurred in the 20 years up to 1968.'—Ed.]

'Serious efforts are being made to reduce to a minimum the oil that is spilled from intentional rinsing of oil tanks, from discharge of used, dirty lubricants, and from accidental leaks and the shipwrecks of oil tankers. Although these efforts are proving successful to a considerable extent . . ., they will never succeed fully', though there is a probability of oil pollution per ton transported becoming smaller. I have four questions for Professor Hela:

1. What serious efforts exist to combat oil pollution at sea, and what evidence does he have that they have been effective?

2. What is the minimum intentional rinsing that should be permitted?

3. What are the bases for his conclusion that the probability of oil pollution per ton transported is decreasing?

4. In view of the rapidly increasing world consumption of oil, including increasingly vulnerable means of transporting and storing oil, what is the basis for continuing optimism?

Hela

I was being somewhat absent-minded but think I can answer the questions, at least to some extent. First as to oil accidents, they are surely bound to decrease proportionately. We may compare the situation with automobile accidents on the world's roads: when the roads are getting better, the automobiles are getting better, and power brakes are introduced, etc., the probability of accidents per kilometre travelled is reduced, but at the same time the numbers of people who die from them are increasing, as the total numbers of people and of cars are increasing enormously. I think it's much the same with oil accidents. I'd say that everyone who has been studying the problems of oil pollutions is of the opinion that their number is decreasing per oil ton transported, but at the same time the probability of accidents is increasing because of the increasing amount of oil transported.

Concerning the intentional rinsing of oil tanks, it is my personal view that this should be completely forbidden, and I believe it could be done. There are ways of remedying matters, but in our country we have the big problem that the coastal waters are very shallow, and the people who are transporting oil into our ports are trying to make the waterways safer, trying to have better-educated pilots to guide the ships in, and so forth. Consequently on the average the likelihood of accidents should become smaller. However, this is not the case in every country, and we know, for example, that in the English Channel there are certain countries which drive their tankers through with very little care, so that the possibilities of accidents are still rather high. But I believe the international agencies are becoming so interested in these situations that something will be done fairly soon on an international scale.

Fosberg

I have gained the impression that several speakers seem to think that because there is a certain amount of natural mercury in water, this in some way mitigates the seriousness of the industrial and other pollutional mercury. Surely if you die from mercury poisoning you are just as dead if it's natural mercury or industrial mercury that has caused your demise, so the existence of natural mercury is no justification at all for pollution. We had exactly the same difficulty some years ago with the United States Atomic Energy Commission, who justified or anyway excused the current amounts of radioactive contamination of the atmosphere by saying, 'Well, but this is really no more than you get naturally if you go up to a high altitude in the Rocky Mountains, so why worry?' I don't think that the fact that something is natural reduces its seriousness or the seriousness of adding to it.

Butler

Although I would agree with the last speaker that the fact that mercury occurs naturally doesn't excuse chemical companies' dumping it in the effluents from their plants, it does have a bearing on what is the maximum permissible level of mercury in fish and other foods. For the argument goes that if fish have such-and-such a natural level and people have been eating these fish for many years without showing any ill-effects, then this is one level that can be considered as tolerable. This is the point really at issue, and the same thing applies to the level of natural radiation; it's difficult to say what is a tolerable level of radiation and what is not. But one that could be expected to be tolerated by the human race is one that they've had ever since the human race began.

Fosberg

I would merely like to say that if the natural mercury level in these fish brings them practically to the maximum level of human tolerance, then this is all the more reason why we should be careful rather than complacent.

Panikkar (Chairman)

I come from a place that is near to coastal sands with natural radiation at a very high level, and people have been living in that area for thousands of years with apparently no ill-effect—yet when scientific investigations are made, they all raise their eyebrows and think they are living at a very dangerous level. But there it is, things have not changed much so far as we know.

Pavanello

I would like to give this Conference some additional information apart from that recorded by Professor Hela. One point of interest is that seven of the international agencies of the United Nations family, namely IMCO, FAO, UNESCO, WMO, WHO, IAEA, and the UN itself, formed about three years ago a group which is called the Joint Group of Experts on the Scientific Aspects of Marine Pollution. This group has already met three times, and it is advising the heads of the respective organizations on the scientific aspects. I have in my hand the report of the last session which was held very recently and which reviews several of the topics that have been discussed here. The report has just come off the press and I would be happy to send a copy to anyone interested.

A second piece of information that is even more recent is connected with the United Nations Conference on the Human Environment to be held in Stockholm next June. As you know, certain intergovernmental groups are being formed to prepare proposals for action to be submitted to that Conference. One of these groups, the first one to be convened, met just ten days ago in London, and had very long and heated discussions. But I would like to reassure Professor Hela regarding international conventions that, on the proposal of the United States delegation, a draft convention has been submitted against dumping at sea. Admittedly this is a relatively minor matter where the pollution of the oceans is concerned, but I think it was a useful start in so far as something specific was submitted and is going forward.

Söyrinki

I would like to add only a little to the discussion of marine oil-pollution. There has really been success up to a point, particularly here in the north, where we have a Nordic committee against oil-pollution. This committee has been actively fighting against the pollution at sea here in the north, and I think we have somehow succeeded in protecting our waters. Now it's a question of the waste oil on the seas of the world, for not all states have yet ratified the pact against polluting the seas with waste oil. This has delayed very much the solution of this important question, and I think here the best remedy would be to create small regional committees to work actively like this Nordic one against oil-pollution. Such committees are needed in all states, on all coasts, and if there is one man who is active enough, such a committee can do much more locally than a big conference where people give out much knowledge and where the specialists come together from all over the world and then go back home—so that nothing will be done until the following conference comes along and the same wise men come together again and speak a lot and make a big book, etc., etc. One must work actively, one must *force* the governments, everyone in his own country. That's the way!

Ojala

I would like to make a comment concerning the fishery industries of the world and the aquatic faunal resources available. It is an overoptimistic conception that the oceans should yield enough animal protein for the ever-growing population of the world. But an important problem today in this field is that a considerable part of aquatic animal protein is used for secondary purposes, particularly as food for domestic and even pet animals in northern America and western Europe. Stopping the flow of animal protein to highly industrialized countries with a relatively high average living standard would be one of the most important tasks for global environmental planning. Unfortunately, this seems to be impossible in the political situation of today, as are most of the things that are needed for real improvements in the environment of the world.

E.F.—10*

Udall

I hate to be so ubiquitous, but I had the unusual experience ten years ago of beginning the task under two presidents of heading up the natural resources department of the United States. That ten years' span keeps fascinating me because I look back with amazement at the assumptions my colleagues and I operated on then. My experts were optimistic about the potential of science and technology, and they gave off the impression that most of our problems were manageable—that if we just monitored them we would understand which ones needed priority attention!

In fact, if we had the kind of international scientific analysis which we ought to have today, we would have a map here before us that would show the estuaries and the coastline areas of the world which in the last decade have been closed to fishing because of pollution. And despite all of the forecasts that were given me ten years ago about the increased potential world catch of fish, the FAO report for 1969 revealed that the total catch decreased in that year.* Swordfish, because of the mercury problem, has been taken off the list of edible fish in the United States, and in many other ways the damaging effects of man's errors are now being felt.

I'm disappointed that we've had so little mention today of the serious plight of the Mediterranean, the Baltic, and the Great Lakes. Everything that I have read about the status of the Mediterranean, for example, leads me to believe that the situation there is very serious indeed. I don't pretend to know much about the Baltic, but I know enough about the Great Lakes to indict the failure of the United States and Canada over the last twenty years to curb pollution by effective action. Meanwhile they have done a good job of monitoring worsening conditions; but the best monitoring is not good enough—that's what I'm trying to say. All the time we appear to be scaling up for disasters—we know not of what kinds and where. In this connection another thing that disturbs me is that if this Conference had been held two years earlier there would have been no discussion of mercury poisoning of fish-life and people. We didn't know that industrial polluters we causing a hazard to human health. We know it now, and my guess is that there are going to be more mercury and other surprises. There may be no shellfish on our menus if we do not act soon to curb the fingers of poison that are creeping outward on the coastlines of the world. That, at least, is my fear.

Polunin (Jr)

Professor Hela emphasized that public interest has been drawn particularly by spectacular events such as big oil-spills, but it is sad to have to say that most of this concern was simply that of local people for their income from tourism. Perhaps this is why detergents were accepted so readily for purposes of dispersion. Well, some concern is better than very little, which might have been the case if private interests had not been involved, but I think that these motives reflect a sad state of affairs. It would be gratifying to feel that people were really attempting to save the marine environment rather than their own ice-cream stalls. I would like to ask a question, too.

* *See* footnote on p. 280.—Ed.

Do you think that the addition of fertilizers to shallow marine enclosures, such as lagoons, to enhance fish production, is a truly feasible project?

Panikkar (Chairman)

I shall answer the question right now. There are many lagoons in the warm parts of the globe where this is done successfully, though, of course, one has to be extremely careful not to over-fertilize those areas.

Polunin (Jr)

I might mention something else: the case of a species of starfish, the Crown-of-thorns Starfish (*Acanthaster planci*), that feeds on living corals. This underwent a population explosion in about 1962 in the western Pacific, and people immediately thought that it was probably heading towards devastation of all the world's, or at least the Indo-Pacific's, coral reefs and, ultimately, coral islands. A year or so ago a British zoologist, P. J. Vine, published a paper on the subject, following widespread studies in the areas involved—in some of which I myself have been privileged to work—and one of his views, perhaps a rather extreme one, is that this population explosion is conceivably just a cyclical, natural event. If this is indeed the case, then we have an interesting situation: for if the damage intensifies, we may have to make the choice of whether this really is a man-produced event and therefore to effect some kind of control if this is possible, or whether one should leave the starfish to carry out what may be a natural ecological function. So here is another instance of where our horizon and possible course of action are restricted by lack of scientific knowledge.

ADDENDUM

From Dr THOR HEYERDAHL, *Colla Micheri, Laigueglia, Italy,*
and Kon-Tiki Museum, Oslo, Norway

Man had to reach America before Columbus could come back and testify that the earth was round. Man had to reach the moon before the astronauts could come back and tell us that the earth was not only round, but it was small as well—very, very small. And if we destroy it, we have nowhere else to go.

If it does nothing more, this should serve to teach us that we had better take good care of this little ball which is our parent and supporter. Do we? Not yet! Indeed, while our planet soars through the universe, we struggle to invent, hoard, and release, all the explosives and all the poisons that the human brain can possibly contrive to eradicate life, both human and other. We construct steamships and jet planes to cross at leisure all natural obstacles, and we divide our little planet instead by artificial frontiers, on each side of which we stack enough high explosives to eliminate all inhabitants on the opposite side of the line. Our ancestors' worries about wild animals' teeth, horns, and claws, were child's play compared with our own justified worries about man-contrived rockets, laser-rays, and nuclear explosions.

Yet, the main troubles for us and our descendants may never become the horrors that we and our foes have in store for one another. Today we barely begin to realize that, more treacherous than the missiles which openly face our front door, are the modern venoms we carelessly throw away around our own feet: non-human traitors which already accumulate and sneak silently up on all of us from behind, where we have prepared for no defence. We have suddenly an enemy in common, we and our fellow creatures on the other side of any political borderline. The winds and the ocean currents, which no man can stop, take care in distributing this ever-growing menace of pollution evenly among us. Air and sea form a common mobile human heritage which no politician can delineate and no military barrage can halt. With its irresistible global rotation, the east and west, the north and south, the rich and poor, receive an equal dose of harmful refuse that none of us wants— residues we believe we can get rid of by merely spewing them into the air and the sea.

Neither Columbus nor the astronauts have been able to convince us that no chimney is tall enough to pierce our own atmosphere and no sewer long enough to project beyond the edge of the world. Anything we want to get rid of remains within the thin peel of air, soil, and water, which covers our hot little ball of fire in proportion to the skin of a tomato. Thanks to gravity, nothing falls off the edge into space. Sulphur, lead, mercury, or DDT— anything we dump, spray, send up in smoke or down into the sea, remains forever with us. This has always been so; but formerly everything man ate, burnt, or threw on his refuse heap, was part of nature's own perpetual cycle. It was altered by Bacteria and Fungi or through chemical transformation, and served directly to support new life.

This was the situation before, but is no longer so. Man has now discovered the existence of molecules and atoms. He has started to split them and to alter their composition, concocting new elements. To our immediate delight we have brought into existence materials either not needed or not desired by Mother Nature—indestructible substances which fall outside the functional life-cycle of evolution and maintenance in the biological world. Although a blessing to man in their primary use, some of these modern synthetics, such as plastics and DDT and other chlorinated hydrocarbons, are eternally dead and non-transferable—like extra bolts and nuts falling inside a ready-made and perfectly functioning machine. Nature never asked for these dead-end synthetics which were created by man while God held his Sabbath. Nor does nature know how to handle them, how to incorporate them, or how to transform or dispose of them. They simply accumulate perpetually out of context within nature's smoothly rotating mechanism. As they build up, they begin to become visible among the cog-wheels. We ourselves threw them in, but we don't know how to get them out. In the meantime we have given this man-made surplus a name which is suddenly on everybody's lips: pollution.

'Pollution is rich man's problem', says hungry man in undeveloped and developing countries. 'Give us industry, give us oil, give us progress and we shall be happy to take pollution with it. Let the tourists worry about plastic containers and oil that replace seaweed and shells on the beaches; let the movie stars lose sight of the Hollywood sun behind the smog. We want development: to Hell with aesthetics!'

Indeed an empty stomach is worse than plastic bottles on the beach. Discarded containers and oil-clots are ugly, but hardly harmful to man. Seen as a symptom they tell us of welfare. In fact, we should perhaps even bless their presence, for they give us a most timely warning of what we might otherwise have overlooked: they ought to ring a bell, wake us up, poor and rich alike, to start pondering. For each unsightly tube, each rusting can, each solid oil-clot that we see washed ashore or floating about, gives us reason to think of the invisible pollutants dissolved in the water between this flotsam—liquids or particles which cannot be distinguished by the naked eye and yet must be there. Man does not dispose of empty containers only. It is the lost contents, not the empty cartridge, that ought to scare us. Where is the spray, the paste, the powder, the liquid that is no longer inside the empty packing? If washing-powder, it was carried by the sewer into the ocean, if insecticide, it was carried by the rain, the drain, the brook, and the river, into the ocean. All sewers and drains from all cities and fields in the whole world end somehow in the ocean. All the polluted rivers and all the polluted lakes in the world empty into the ocean.

I can testify to the claim of the astronauts that the ocean is not endless. With my friends I have stepped on board a raft of logs in the Pacific, as well as on to some bundles of reeds in the Atlantic, and travelled across what we like to think of as an endless abyss. The ocean is not endless. Put seven Lake Eries end to end and they span the whole Atlantic. Lake Erie is already polluted and largely destroyed. Half-a-dozen fair-sized cities and a few ships send their refuse into Lake Erie. All the cities in the world, all the industry, and all the world's shipping, join together in using our common oceans as our common sewer. About one per cent of the thousands of millions of tons of crude oil transported yearly by tankers is intentionally pumped overboard as sludge, and other vessels loaded with nuclear refuse and industrial poisons too dangerous to dispose of ashore are heading into deep water where no laws exist, to dump their deadly cargo among fish and plankton, out of human sight. This is how we treat our most important body of water, the earth's only indispensable purification system, the home of living plankton which has the double function of producing oxygen and providing nourishment for fish and other sea-foods that form a staple for the family of man. A dead ocean means empty stomachs and empty lungs for rich and poor alike.

There is plenty of time to ponder about these problems when you sit on a raft for weeks and months, at the level of the ocean's surface, observing plastic containers, nylon, empty cans and bottles, drifting slowly by. In 1947, when we crossed 4,300 nautical miles (7,998 km) of the Pacific in 101 days with the balsa raft *Kon-Tiki*, no trace of man was seen until we spotted an old wreck up on the reef where we were to land. In 1969 it was therefore a blow to me to observe from the bundles of the reed-boat *Ra* that entire stretches of the Atlantic Ocean surface were densely packed with oil-clots—first off the African coast, next in mid-ocean, and finally in front of the Carribean Islands. Repeating the same general itinerary with *Ra II* in 1970, we carried out a day-by-day survey and found sporadic oil-clots floating by, within the reach of our small dip-net, during 43 out of the 57 days that it took us to cover the 3,270 miles (6,100 km) from Safi in Morocco to Barbados in the West Indies. With our sail we moved faster than the pelagic pollution, and since the Equatorial Current runs westwards with a speed of half-a-knot, the pollution we saw *en route* from Africa to America in 1969 was, during our next crossing a year later, washed ashore in tropical America—or else was on its way back to Europe with its direct extension, the North Atlantic Gulf Stream.

This means that visible pollution is already bridging a major world ocean. We know from tests on whales and polar bears in the Arctic and on penguins in the Antarctic that DDT is carried by the rotating ocean even to the most remote parts where no insects have ever been sprayed. A laboratory analysis of the crude oil-clots which we collected shows a variety of nickel and vanadium contents and thus discloses that the oil does not originate from a leakage in any single area, but must represent discharge from different sources—probably from tankers preparing for fresh loads.

In the long run—and it may not be very long either—we shall learn that the producer, the transporter, and the consumer, are all 'in the same boat'. We shall float or sink together. The problem is complex and can hardly be solved by producer and transporter alone, for the consumer demands his oil, and he wants it at its present price. The price we shall all have to pay in the end may be an extremely high one. While we delay action, each year more than a hundred thousand tons of crude oil are dumped, intentionally, by tankers into the closed Mediterranean alone. This is more than the accidental spill from the *Torrey Canyon* which caused a world sensation when it ran onto a reef in the English Channel a few years ago.

We do not know the durability and effect of this pelagic oil, but we can see that it does accumulate. The lumps we saw were often densely covered with barnacles, crustaceans, and other marine hitch-hikers, and thus are a tempting prey for fish. Whether swallowed or stuck in the delicate sieving mechanism of filter-feeding fish and whales, these constantly increasing quantities of oil-clots can hardly avoid affecting marine life.

Back from the open Atlantic ocean, I have personally made random visits to islands and continental shores all around the land-locked Mediterranean Sea. The oil-clots washed up on the beaches are now familiar to most tourists and carpet cleaners, but only the poor fisherman has apparently begun to notice that a greyish to black band a few feet wide begins to darken the yellow coastline of the cliffs and boulders just above the waterline. It looks as if a devilish painter has impregnated with a thick brush the most important habitat of shell and seaweed—the birth-place and irreplaceable nest of so very many marine species at some stage in their life-cycle. The darker the oil paint is, the poorer becomes the growth of living creatures: and where the coat is thick enough to be black, the waterline is sterile, dead as coke, devoid of any kind of life. Is it the oil itself that acts as impregnation against biological birth? Or is it because, as we know, the invisible insecticides, the chlorinated hydrocarbons, are increasingly present in the sea and, as we also know, are absorbed wherever in contact with oil? The waves serve as the painter's brush; the oil containing DDT and other man-made poisons, intended for killing, will then do the job of impregnating against the life we want and need, rather than against the bugs and beetles of the field. For the man-made nuts and bolts rattling about in nature's fine machinery do not know where they belong and where they are expected to strike.

It is not the oil-clots, not the toilet flush or the empty containers which the rich man can see, that ought to occupy all our attention, but the invisible and indestructible pollutants that move about as ghosts, unseen.

9
EFFECTS OF PESTICIDES

Keynote Paper

Effects of Insecticides

by

CHARLES F. WURSTER

Chairman, Scientists Advisory Committee,
Environmental Defense Fund;
Associate Professor of Environmental Sciences,
Marine Sciences Research Center,
State University of New York,
Stony Brook, New York 11790, USA.

INTRODUCTION

World opinion has been awakening to a variety of man-made environmental problems during the past few years, and few of these have received more public debate than 'the pesticide problem'. Strong emotions are evoked in people when they get the idea that they or other animals are being poisoned, regardless of whether the threat is real or imagined. 'The pesticide problem' is by no means a single problem, but instead consists of a host of individual and highly diverse problems depending on the pesticide and circumstances involved. In considering the effects of pesticides on non-target organisms, I propose to organize my remarks into several categories, touching only on those aspects of pesticides that seem more important, and omitting much that in my view appears less critical.

The word 'pesticide' is generally applied to any chemical that is used to kill pests, but I shall restrict myself to insecticides. The various herbicides, fungicides, rodenticides, and nematocides, certainly introduce problems of their own, but it is my impression that they are generally less serious and widespread than are the insecticide problems. In any event, I cannot discuss these other pesticides with any real competence, and will therefore leave their consideration to others (e.g. Moore, 1967).

NON-PERSISTENT INSECTICIDES

The insecticides can be divided roughly into two large groups—those that are stable (persistent) and those that are not. The non-persistent insecticides currently in use are mainly organophosphates and carbamates (O'Brien, 1967). Being chemically unstable, they do not retain their original identity and associated biological activity sufficiently long to permit them to be transported to distant regions. Most of them break down rapidly into non-toxic products. The effects of these non-persistent insecticides are therefore primarily restricted to the treated areas, and their residues do not accumulate extensively in the biosphere.

This is not to suggest that organophosphates and carbamates do not pose problems, however. Some of the organophosphates, such as Parathion, Systox, and TEPP, are extremely toxic, making them potentially hazardous to farm personnel and other non-target organisms that may be present in the vicinity of the application (US Department of Health, Education & Welfare, 1969). Other organophosphates, including Malathion, Chlorthion, Dibrom, Ronnel, and Dipterex, have lower acute toxicities to vertebrates than has DDT, and DDT is not an especially toxic material when compared with most pesticides.

Another major problem with some non-persistent insecticides, in common with many other insecticides, is their tendency to be disruptive within insect communities, often aggravating, rather than alleviating, insect control problems (Bosch, 1970; Huffaker, 1971). By destroying beneficial insects that are natural enemies of the pests, and by eliminating the susceptible individuals, use of insecticides may generate outbreaks of insecticide-resistant, injurious insects that are far worse than those which existed prior to the treatment. The solution to most of the problems with non-persistent insecticides involves careful regulation and wise usage, rather than a complete prohibition of their use.

However severe the effects of non-persistent insecticides may be, they are principally restricted to the vicinity and time of application. Non-persistent pesticides cannot become a world problem by contaminating or affecting non-target organisms in areas that are remote in distance or in time from the treated areas. In this regard they contrast dramatically with the persistent insecticides, and I will therefore accord primary attention to the latter in this paper.

PERSISTENT CHLORINATED HYDROCARBON INSECTICIDES

Stability or persistence confers an entirely new dimension on an insecticide because its unintended effects can, and sometimes do, extend thousands of miles and many years beyond the area and time of application, thereby involving a wide variety of non-target organisms. The persistent chlorinated hydrocarbon ('CH') or organochlorine insecticides have thus become one of the world's most serious pollution problems, involving many non-agricultural interests and values. This family of insecticides includes DDT, Aldrin, Dieldrin, Isodrin, Endrin, Chlordane, Telodrin, Heptachlor, Strobane, Toxaphene, Mirex, and a few others.

Of this group, DDT has long been, and still is, by far the most widely manufactured and applied; nearly 3 thousand million (10^9) pounds (1.36×10^9 kg) of DDT have been produced in the United States alone since 1944 (Fig. 1; US Department of Agriculture, 1970). Production was 123 million

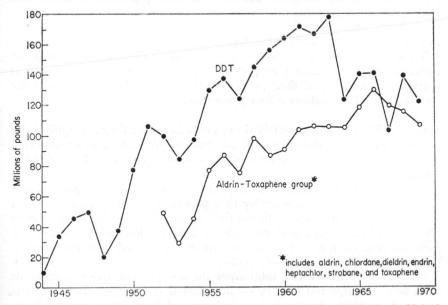

Fig. 1. Production of DDT and of the Aldrin–Toxaphene group of insecticides in the United States (US Department of Agriculture, 1970). 1 pound = 0.454 kg.

pounds (55.8×10^6 kg) in 1969 (the latest year for which data are available), which is just under the average rate of 145 million pounds (65.8×10^6 kg) produced annually during the 1960s. The world's largest DDT manufacturing plant, and now the only one in the United States, is that of the Montrose Chemical Corporation in Los Angeles. The data in Fig. 1 further show that, except in one year (1967), more DDT has been, and continues to be, produced annually in the United States than the total for Aldrin, Chlordane, Dieldrin, Endrin, Heptachlor, Strobane, and Toxaphene, combined. Although we read that DDT is being 'restricted' and 'phased out' in many countries, it continues to be used in greater quantities than any other insecticide.

As we continue to add to the nearly 3 thousand million pounds (more than 10^9 kg) of DDT already released into the environment, and with some unknown fraction of it still circulating in the biosphere, it should hardly be surprising that DDT poses by far the most serious of our persistent pesticide problems. I believe that DDT has had a greater impact on non-target organisms and ecosystems than has any other pesticide, and possibly a greater one than all other pesticides combined. For these reasons, and to bring the issue up to date and correct misinformation, I shall discuss the CH insecticide problem in some detail, with primary emphasis on DDT (C. F. Wurster, 1969a). The polychlorinated biphenyls (PCBs), a mixture of CH compounds of industrial origin (used as plasticizers, flame retardants, insulating fluids, adhesives, etc.) that are now widespread in nature and exhibit environmental behaviour which is similar to that of the persistent insecticides, may also represent a serious environmental hazard (Peakall & Lincer, 1970). The PCBs are another example of the large-scale release of a material into the environment before adequate research on their potential environmental impact had been performed.*

Properties of the Chlorinated Hydrocarbons

To appreciate the environmental behaviour of the CHs, along with the associated hazards which they pose to various non-target organisms, it is necessary to understand their properties. Their behaviour results from the combination of the following four properties:

1. *Mobility*. CHs unfortunately do not remain where they are applied. By various mechanisms they enter the air and surface waters, to be dispersed often over great distances within world circulation patterns (C. F. Wurster, 1969a).

Although these materials have very low vapour pressures, volatilization is an important mechanism whereby they pass into the air (Edwards, 1966). Co-distillation with water facilitates their passage into air from wet surfaces (Bowman *et al.*, 1964), and CHs adsorbed to particulates, especially soil particles, and existing as suspensions, are also dispersed to remote regions by the winds (Risebrough *et al.*, 1968).

Exceptionally low water solubilities do not prevent these compounds from being transported in very dilute solution by flowing water, but the transport capacity of water is greatly increased by the tendency of CHs to

* *See also* the next section, particularly pp. 337–8.—Ed.

form suspensions in water and to adsorb to particulates, all of which pass downstream within watersheds (Bowman *et al.*, 1964; Edwards, 1966).

These dispersal mechanisms transport CHS to most parts of the world after they have been released into the environment, thus explaining their presence in remote, untreated regions such as Antarctica (Peterle, 1969; C. F. Wurster, 1969*a*).

2. *Persistence.* The persistence of the CHS varies with the compound and the conditions. DDT is slowly converted to DDD, then to other metabolites, and eventually to the non-toxic DDA, by various conditions and organisms (O'Brien, 1967). DDT is also converted to DDE, which is very stable though not very toxic, but which shows a variety of environmentally important enzyme effects. DDE is the most widespread of all CHS in the environment. DDT, DDD, and DDE, are commonly called 'DDT residues', and these biologically active materials remain in the biosphere for many years and probably decades after their use (Edwards, 1966; Nash & Woolson, 1967).

In the environment, Aldrin and Isodrin are gradually converted into Dieldrin and Endrin, respectively, both of which are very persistent (Nash & Woolson, 1967). Mirex appears to be unusually stable (Valin *et al.*, 1968).

3. *Solubility Characteristics.* Being typical non-polar organic compounds, CHS have extremely low solubilities in water, but high solubilities in lipids or fatty tissues. Water is saturated with DDT at only 1.2 parts per thousand million (10^9) (ppb, i.e. parts per milliard or American billion), and Mirex is evidently still less soluble; Aldrin and Dieldrin have somewhat higher (but still very low) solubilities of 27 and 186 ppb, respectively (Park & Bruce, 1968; C. F. Wurster, 1969*a*). As all living organisms contain lipids, CHS are much more soluble in living tissues than in water, and the partition coefficient strongly favours accumulation and retention of CHS by the tissues of living organisms.

The solubility properties explain why CHS are not 'lost' by dilution in the inorganic components of the environment—the water, air, and soil. Instead, CH residues, especially DDT, have become nearly universal in animal tissues in most regions of the world. Birds, fish, and mammals, including man, are almost invariably contaminated.

4. *Broad Biological Activity.* The toxicity and biological activity of the CHS are by no means limited to the target species of insect, but instead can affect a great variety of animals, including all classes of vertebrates; furthermore, they can operate by several different mechanisms. They are nerve poisons— an effect that can be lethal (O'Brien, 1967). In addition, most are inducers of hepatic enzyme systems and inhibitors of certain other enzymes (Conney, 1967; Kupfer, 1967; Peakall, 1970*b*). DDT and Aldrin have oestrogenic activity (Welch *et al.*, 1969), and several CHS inhibit photosynthesis, possibly by inhibiting electron transport (C. F. Wurster, 1968; Menzel *et al.*, 1970; Bowes & Gee, 1971). DDT, Aldrin, Dieldrin, Heptachlor, Strobane, and Mirex, are carcinogenic in rodents (US Department of Health, Education & Welfare, 1969), and DDT has shown mutagenic activity as well (M. S. Legator, in

preparation). Although effects are by no means predictable, contamination of non-target organisms with compounds that have such a broad spectrum of biological activity clearly carries the potential for affecting those organisms. The realization of that potential is the major topic of this paper.

Biological Concentration

When CHs are absorbed into food-chains, they tend to remain in them because of their solubility characteristics. Each organism feeds on many organisms from the next-lower trophic level; food organisms are metabolized and excreted, but the CHs are retained, thus leading to a higher concentration of CHs in the predator organism than was present in the food organism. Concentrations of CHs thereby increase with each step in the food-chains. This biological or trophic concentration causes CHs to reach levels that are many thousands or even millions of times higher in organisms than are found in the surrounding inorganic environment (Woodwell et al., 1967; Korschgen, 1970). Analyses of soil, water, or air, showing only minute quantities of CHs to be present, can therefore be misleading indicators of environmental quality because they ignore the importance of these highly efficient biological concentrating mechanisms. Analyses of predatory organisms that are high in the food-chain are a more relevant measure of environmental contamination with CHs.

Significance of these Properties

In summary, the CHs can travel great distances from application sites, are sufficiently stable to retain their identity for years, are accumulated by non-target organisms because of their solubility characteristics, reach the highest levels of contamination in carnivores, and are hazardous to these organisms because they have a broad spectrum of biological activity. CHs are therefore inherently uncontrollable materials after they have been released into the environment. Few major, widespread environmental pollutants combine these properties.

Effects on Birds

It has long been known that CHs can cause extensive mortality among birds. Bird mortality following attempts to control Dutch elm disease with DDT has been documented on numerous occasions (D. H. Wurster et al., 1965), and other CHs, especially Dieldrin, have frequently killed birds following their use (Rudd, 1964; Stickel et al., 1969). Rather than being restricted only to treated areas, mortality of certain raptors has sometimes resulted from general environmental contamination with CHs. Deaths of Bald Eagles (*Haliaeetus leucocephalus*) from Dieldrin poisoning in the United States is an example (Mulhern et al., 1970). It is hard to know just how extensive direct mortality among carnivorous birds from general environmental contamination might be; it may be far more important than is immediately obvious. The available evidence suggests, however, that the sublethal effects of CHs on avian reproduction have a greater overall impact on birds populations than does acutely lethal direct mortality, even though a bird-kill may seem more spectacular.

The effects of DDT residues on avian reproduction have only recently become well understood, and the many years of research that developed this knowledge make a fascinating and alarming 'science detective story' (C. F. Wurster, 1969b; Peakall, 1970a). By 1967 it had become clear that extensive and widespread declines in populations of many species of carnivorous birds and DDT contamination of these birds were correlated, but only in the past four years have cause–effect relationships been confirmed and mechanisms of action partially clarified.

DDT contamination inhibits avian reproduction by causing the birds to lay abnormally thin-shelled eggs, which break prematurely in the nest and therefore do not produce chicks (Peakall, 1970a). Additional symptoms include late ovulation and nesting, abnormal behaviour, hatching failure, and failure to lay eggs. The thinning of the eggshells may be caused by inhibition of carbonic anhydrase, an enzyme that is essential to the formation of calcium carbonate eggshells in the shell-gland of the oviduct (Peakall, 1970b). DDE, the most widespread CH pollutant that was considered to be innocuous for many years, is an inhibitor of this enzyme. This explanation has recently been challenged, however (Dvorchik et al., 1971). Jefferies & French (1971) recently suggested that the thin eggshells result from a hypo-thyroidal condition caused in the birds by DDT.

DDT residues, as well as most other CHs, are inducers of hepatic hydroxy-lating enzymes that metabolize steroids, including sex hormones (Conney, 1967; Kupfer, 1967; Peakall, 1970b). Enzyme induction by DDT thus reduces the level of circulating endogenous estradiol, which is partially responsible for various secondary sex characteristics and breeding behaviour in female birds (Peakall, 1970a, 1970b); this apparently explains the additional symptoms mentioned above. Evidently by simultaneously affecting different organs in different ways, contamination with DDT residues can reduce the reproductive success in wild bird populations to only a small fraction of what is normal.

Abnormally thin-shelled eggs have become commonplace among populations of many species of carnivorous birds in recent years (Blus, 1970; Ratcliffe, 1970; Cade et al., 1971). Controlled experiments have shown that the levels of contamination with DDT residues regularly found in wild populations cause the thin-shelled eggs and other symptoms of reproductive failure that have now become typical of those populations (Wiemeyer & Porter, 1970). As a consequence of these phenomena, DDT has suppressed or even extirpated some populations of many species of birds of prey and sea-birds in the United States—including the Bald Eagle, Peregrine Falcon, Prairie Falcon, Sharp-shinned Hawk, Cooper's Hawk, Marsh Hawk, Black-crowned Night Heron, Double-crested Cormorant, Osprey, Common Murre, Brown Pelican, Ashy Petrel, and Common Egret.

The role of CHs other than DDT in avian reproduction is less clear, partly because they are much less widespread in the environment and partly because they have been studied less. Various evidence does not indicate that complacency about them is justified, however. Dieldrin also causes birds to lay thin-shelled eggs (Lehner & Egbert, 1969); it inhibits carbonic anhy-drase (Verrett & Desmond, 1959), is a powerful hepatic enzyme inducer

(Peakall, 1970b), and was evidently the major factor in the low reproductive success of the Golden Eagle in Scotland (Ratcliffe, 1970). As Dieldrin is very widespread in nature, it is presumably a contributor to the above problems.

Effects on Fish

CHS have long been known to be highly toxic to fish. Widespread mortality of Atlantic Salmon (*Salmo salar*) resulted from spraying of the coniferous forests of New Brunswick with DDT in the 1950s (C. F. Wurster, 1969a), and large, spectacular fish-kills resulted from the application of Dieldrin to a Florida salt-marsh and the discharge of Endrin into the Mississippi River (Harrington & Bidlingmayer, 1958). As with birds, however, it is probable that acutely lethal effects of CHS on fish are less important to fish populations than are the less obvious sublethal effects.

CHS can inhibit reproduction in fish, but the mechanism is quite different from that which inhibits avian reproduction. Macek (1968a) showed, by controlled experiments, that concentrations of DDT in the diet which are sublethal to adult fish may be lethal to fry after they hatch from contaminated eggs. The DDT is passed into the egg-yolk; the embryo develops and hatches and, after hatching, at the stage of final yolk-sac absorption, the fry will die if the concentration of DDT in the yolk is sufficiently high. This form of reproductive failure has occurred several times in nature, has sometimes been severe, and is probably more widespread than published accounts indicate. Reproduction of Lake Trout (*Salvelinus namaycush*) in Lake George and other New York lakes has failed completely for the past dozen years, with 100 per cent mortality of the fry occurring annually (Burdick *et al.*, 1964). Similar, though less severe, fry mortality has involved the Coho Salmon (*Oneorhynchus kisutch*) in Lake Michigan (Johnson & Pecor, 1969), trout (several salmonids) in Alberta and New Zealand, and Spotted Sea-trout (*Cynoscion nebulosus*) in the Gulf of Mexico (Butler *et al.*, 1970). As the concentrations of DDT at which fry mortality has been shown to occur under both controlled and field conditions are now being approached or equalled in some freshwater and marine fisheries, it is hard to escape the conclusion that these fisheries are threatened by contamination with DDT (Risebrough, 1969). Unfortunately, few data are available on the possible effects of CHS on the reproduction of marine fish, so it is hard to know what might be happening to marine fishery resources.

CHS have other sublethal effects on fish. A few ppb of DDT in the water upset the temperature-regulating mechanism of young Salmon (Anderson & Peterson, 1969), and controlled experiments by Macek (1968b) showed that the stresses of falling temperature and starvation killed most Brook Trout (*Salvelinus fontinalis*) that were subjected to sublethal amounts of DDT, whereas very few of the control fish died. DDT-induced susceptibility to stress presumably explains the delayed salmon mortality in New Brunswick that coincided with colder weather several months after the DDT application and initial fish-kill (C. F. Wurster, 1969a). Sublethal exposure to Toxaphene and DDT also affects the behaviour of fish (Anderson & Peterson, 1969).

Chlorinated Hydrocarbons and Photosynthesis

Recent studies have shown that a few ppb of DDT, Dieldrin, Endrin, or PCBS, in the water, decrease photosynthesis, as measured by ^{14}C uptake, in certain species of marine phytoplankton—an effect that could result from inhibition of electron transport by these substances (C. F. Wurster, 1968; Menzel *et al.*, 1970; Bowes & Gee, 1971). I do not, however, subscribe to the theory frequently advanced in the public media that these findings indicate that DDT will ultimately eliminate oxygen production in the oceans, thereby greatly diminishing the oxygen supply in the atmosphere.

The effect of CHS on Algae appears to be highly selective, affecting certain susceptible species and not others. Selective poisoning of some algal species in areas near sites of CH application could lead to an undesirable imbalance within the flora, and a bloom of the resistant species might then occur. An alteration in species composition of phytoplankton communities could have profound ecological consequences, but too little research has yet been done on these phenomena to allow the drawing of any conclusions.

Effects on Ecosystems

Many of the activities of man tend to simplify ecosystems by reducing species-diversity. An agricultural ecosystem generally contains fewer species of organisms than the ecosystem it replaced, and the same is usually true of cities, towns, and the human environment generally. Fire, ionizing radiation, a variety of pollutants including pesticides, and other forms of human disturbance, all tend to degrade and simplify the structure of ecosystems in a somewhat similar manner. They tend to favour small, rapidly reproducing organisms that are low in the food-chain—at the expense of larger but more slowly reproducing carnivores that are higher in the food pyramid. These processes have been articulated with unusual clarity by Woodwell (1970).

The effects of persistent CHS on ecosystems are better understood than are those of most other pollutants. For a variety of reasons, their maximum impact tends to involve organisms that are high in the food-chain (Moore, 1967; Harrison *et al.*, 1970). Biological concentration subjects predators to the greatest dosages of CHS, and by virtue of their fewer numbers and slow rates of reproduction the predators are less capable of sustaining increased mortality than are the smaller, more rapidly reproducing organisms farther down the food pyramid. The latter can quickly develop populations that are resistant to CHS, whereas the predators cannot afford the mortality that is always the price of resistance.

The effects of CHS on predators is apparent in a number of instances (Moore, 1967). The large predatory fish are diminished by decreases in reproductive success, and declines in populations of carnivorous birds for the same reason are even more obvious. Perturbations among other components of the ecosystem inevitably follow decreases of predators.

Losses of predators and parasites following the use of insecticides is especially marked among insect communities—a phenomenon that has been well documented (Ripper, 1956). Phytophagous (plant-eating) insects are well equipped for chemical warfare, but entomophagous (insect-eating) insects are not so endowed (Krieger *et al.*, 1971). Losses of predatory and parasitic insects frequently cause enormous outbreaks of phytophagous insects—an effect that may be highly detrimental to agriculture (Huffaker, 1971). The strategy of attempting to control insects by inflicting mortality with broad-spectrum, persistent poisons would appear to be counter-productive over the long term because it is ultimately beneficial to populations of phytophagous insects and other herbivores, and deleterious to many higher, non-target organisms—thus degrading the structure, diversity, and stability, of ecosystems.

Human Health Implications of Chlorinated Hydrocarbon Insecticides

Apparently all human beings carry residues of DDT in their tissues, and most of them contain Dieldrin and other CH residues as well (US Department of Health, Education & Welfare, 1969). What is the significance of these residues to human health? After several decades of using these materials, there is still no adequate answer to this question.

Humans are very poor experimental animals. They tend not to volunteer for experiments that terminate with their sacrifice and dissection; yet such experiments may have to be done to evaluate the biological effects of a chemical or drug. Laboratory animals therefore 'volunteer' their services in these experiments, and most of our knowledge of these subjects depends on their dedication and self-sacrifice. Mice and rats are not men, but their similarities to man are greater than their dissimilarities. In actual practice the correlation between findings in laboratory animals and those in man is quite high. Results in animals therefore indicate the *probability* that man would react similarly. Often we have no choice but to accept results on experimental animals, and prudence dictates that we base our actions on these experiments where experimentation with human subjects is inadequate or lacking. Studies on laboratory animals suggest at least four areas in which human populations may be affected by current levels of exposure to CHs, especially to DDT residues.

Behavioural Effects

CHs are nerve toxins (O'Brien, 1967). At concentrations well below those producing obvious toxic symptoms, a variety of behavioural changes are known to occur in experimental animals (Desi *et al.*, 1966; Anderson & Peterson, 1969; C. F. Wurster, 1969*a*). At the concentrations of CHs which are present in the tissues of the general human population, such effects would be extremely difficult to detect—especially in the absence of controls, in the presence of a host of other variables, and with inadequate testing procedures. We do not know whether or not a threshold exists—a concentration of CH above which effects occur but below which they do not. Nevertheless, until better evidence is available, we should assume that behavioural changes in laboratory animals are indicative of comparable effects within the human population. Such effects could be of great importance to human society, but they have not been studied. The absence of knowledge, however, is not evidence of safety.

Hepatic Enzyme Induction

Most CHS are enzyme inducers, i.e. they induce a substantial increase in the synthesis of relatively non-specific hepatic enzymes that hydroxylate steroid hormones and various other substrates (Conney, 1967; Kupfer, 1967; US Department of Health, Education & Welfare, 1969; Peakall, 1970b). The effect has been noted in experimental animals at dietary levels of a few parts per million—concentrations that are legally permissible in some human foods in the United States. Enzymes induced by DDT have reduced the concentration of endogenous oestrogen in the blood of birds—an effect that causes a variety of behavioural and reproductive changes (Peakall, 1970a, 1970b). Induction of these enzymes has been shown to occur in men who had been occupationally exposed to DDT and Endrin (Jager, 1970; Poland et al., 1970). In man it is possible that these enzymes can reduce the level of circulating steroid hormones sufficiently to affect behaviour and other parameters that are influenced by these steroids, and to affect various drug interactions— including the function of oral contraceptives containing steroids—and other biochemical processes. Furthermore, it is not known whether there is a threshold concentration for CHS below which these effects would not occur. But, once again, the absence of knowledge is no indication of safety, and animal experimentation suggests that hepatic enzyme induction by CHS, especially by DDT residues, may be a human health hazard.

Cancer

The evaluation of chemicals, drugs, and pesticides, for carcinogenic activity in humans, presents numerous inherent difficulties. These include (1) the inability to use human subjects, necessitating the employment of laboratory animals as substitutes; (2) the presence of cancer from numerous other, usually unidentified, causes within the human population; and (3) the difficulty of testing at environmental exposure-levels and attaining statistical significance when those levels might produce only a single tumour in thousands of individuals. Detection of carcinogenesis at environmental concentrations would require enormous and unmanageable numbers of animals to demonstrate a statistically significant increase in the frequency of tumour induction (Epstein, 1970). Nevertheless, indication of cancer in the general population at a rate of 1 in 10,000 individuals would involve about 20,000 persons in the United States alone—a number that would clearly be of serious public-health significance.

Some technique must be employed to increase the sensitivity of the testing procedure so that smaller, more practical numbers of test animals can be used. One way of doing so is to increase dosage levels, thereby also increasing the incidence or frequency of tumour formation. There is no evidence that an increase in dosage converts non-carcinogenic materials into carcinogens. Carcinogenesis is a specific, relatively rare biological event, and the ability to induce it is possessed by few chemicals. The standard procedure for evaluating carcinogenesis involves high dosage-levels with both positive and negative

controls in laboratory animals, usually rodents (Epstein, 1970). This procedure shows 'a remarkable degree of concurrence . . . between chemical carcinogenesis in animals and that in man where it has been studied closely' (US
Department of Health, Education & Welfare, 1969). In the absence of better
techniques, prudent public policy should be based on results obtained in this way.

Four different laboratory experiments on mice, rats, and trout, have shown
an elevated rate of carcinogenesis by DDT, while Aldrin, Dieldrin, Mirex,
Strobane, and Heptachlor, proved carcinogenic to mice (US Department of
Health, Education & Welfare, 1969). Carcinogenicity thus appears to be
rather common among CH insecticides. Cancer induction in these animals
indicated a high probability, but not a certainty, that these chemicals are also
carcinogenic to humans. Evidence is lacking that there is a threshold or safe
tolerance-level for carcinogens, above which they cause cancer and below
which they do not. The frequency or incidence of cancer induction by such
chemicals may fall to zero only at a zero concentration of the chemical concerned. In the United States the Food, Drug, and Cosmetic Act prohibits the
presence of carcinogenic additives in human foods, but the federal government has not enforced this law adequately.

A further suggestion that DDT and Dieldrin are human carcinogens is
found in two studies showing that victims of terminal cancer contain substantially elevated concentrations of DDT and Dieldrin residues in their adipose tissues, as compared with the general population (Casarett et al., 1968;
Radomski et al., 1968). These elevated CH levels did not correlate with, and
are therefore not explainable by, the loss of weight in these people prior to
death. The presence of these elevated CH residues does not prove that they
caused the cancers, but the findings are certainly consistent with the hypothesis that they did, and also with the results obtained with test animals.

One must conclude, based on the standard procedures for evaluating
carcinogenesis, that these CHS represent a significant cancer hazard in the
human environment.

Mutagenesis

Genetic toxicity of a chemical can manifest itself as carcinogenesis, mutagenesis, or teratogenesis, depending on the location and maturity of the
damaged cell, and often two or three of these phenomena may be caused by
the same chemical (Legator, 1970). In addition to being a carcinogen, DDT
has been shown to be a mutagen, as is indicated by recent studies by the US
Food and Drug Administration using the dominant lethal test in rats (M. S.
Legator, in preparation). The argument regarding mutagenesis is similar to that
for carcinogenesis: mutagenesis in rats indicates a high probability, though
not a certainty, that DDT is a human mutagen. The present level of contamination of human tissues with DDT could mean that future generations of
human beings will be burdened by an increased incidence of genetic defects.

The ubiquity of CH residues in the human environment, together with the
above-cited evidence of genetic toxicity, at least of the most prevalent of these
chemicals, rather strongly suggests that man has, during the past quarter-
century, increased the burden of genetically toxic agents throughout the
entire human population of the earth. But although thousands or millions of

people may be affected, a cause–effect relationship may remain unproven for many years, if, in fact, it can ever be proven. The logistic difficulties of such experimentation with humans may be insurmountable.

Several studies of the physiological effects of DDT, Aldrin, Dieldrin, and Endrin, have involved human subjects (Jager, 1970; Hayes *et al.*, 1971). These studies were deficient in experimental design, failed to consider the most relevant parameters, and were more concerned with levels of CH storage than with physiological or biochemical effects. They establish only that under current environmental conditions, excluding accidents and suicides, members of the general population are not dying of acute CH insecticide poisoning, nor are they suffering overt, toxic symptoms. Long-term, chronic effects were inadequately studied.

To be more specific, the investigations by Hayes *et al.* (1971) and those conducted in the Shell laboratories (Jager, 1970) had only men in their samples; women, children, infants, and foetuses, were not studied. The small numbers of men involved were completely inadequate to evaluate biological events (such as carcinogenesis or mutagenesis) that may occur once in many thousands of individuals. Periods of exposure were too short to detect biological effects involving induction periods that may be many years or decades. Emphasis was given to reviewing the men's attendance records at work, and many of the other simple blood and other routine tests performed were largely irrelevant. When two of twenty-two men who were being fed high dosages of DDT became severely ill after months on this diet, they were dropped from the experiment and excluded from the data with the conclusion that 'at no time was there any objective finding to indicate a relationship between illness and DDT storage' (Hayes *et al.*, 1971).

It is unlikely that these tests on men could have detected behavioural changes, hepatic enzyme induction, carcinogenesis, mutagenesis, or other effects that might be anticipated in man because they occurred in experiments with laboratory animals. The authors concluded, nevertheless, that exposure to these CH insecticides involved no ill-effects on human health—a conclusion that has been widely quoted by the pesticide industry. It seems remarkable that, although hundreds of millions of people have been exposed to these substances for more than two decades, their effects have been so inadequately tested by such primitive studies on such a small number of men!

INSECT CONTROL WITH CHLORINATED HYDROCARBONS

The introduction of the CH insecticides during and shortly after World War II was accompanied by the optimistic belief by some people that these 'miracle' substances would eliminate our insect pest problems. These dreams proved naïve. Although the control of insect populations is a fundamentally ecological problem, these materials were developed and introduced by chemists and medical authorities with almost no ecological sophistication (Smith & Bosch, 1967). The CH insecticides are ecologically crude, powerful, and highly disruptive poisons within insect communities, so it is hardly surprising that problems soon appeared among populations of such rapidly reproducing and adaptive organisms.

The following are among the more serious problems that have occurred following the use of these materials in an attempt to control insect populations:

(1) *Resistance*. When a high rate of mortality is inflicted by a poison on an insect population, a few insects survive because they have certain traits (detoxifying enzymes, behavioural mechanisms, less permeable cuticles than the others, etc.) that protect them from the poison (Brown, 1961). These survivors repopulate the region, and so the protective traits become more prevalent. Repeated insecticide applications further the process, resulting in heavy selection for those traits with survival value. The population soon consists of insects that can no longer be killed by the original insecticide at the original dosage. Insect resistance to CHS is now widespread, rendering these insecticides far less effective than they once were.

(2) *Pest Resurgence*. Even in the 'monocultures' of modern agriculture, insects live in complex communities containing hundreds of different species (Smith & Bosch, 1967). Most of these species are maintained under biological control, so that only a very few achieve pest status, do economic damage, and require human intervention. The potential pest species are phytophagous (plant-eating) ones, and primary among their control agents are the entomophagous insects—the insect parasites and predators of other insects.

Most CH insecticides destroy phytophagous and entomophagous insects alike because they are broad-spectrum, highly toxic poisons to all arthropods (Ripper, 1956). The entomophagous insects cannot recover, for lack of food or hosts, until after recovery of the phytophagous insects, which may vigorously rebound with an ample food-supply (the crop), less interspecific competition, and the absence of biotic pressure from their natural enemies. The pest insects may thus resurge to much greater proportions and numbers than were present before the insecticide was applied, thereby making the pest problem worse and creating the apparent need for more insecticide (Ripper, 1956; Smith & Bosch, 1967; Huffaker, 1971).

(3) *Creation of New Pests*. A phytophagous insect species that was not previously present at pest densities may be 'elevated' to pest status by the resurgence in numbers that follows destruction of its natural enemies by broad-spectrum toxins such as the CH insecticides (Smith & Bosch, 1967).

In many instances, then, the use of certain insecticides aggravates the insect pest problems that they are intended to solve, or creates new ones. Without realizing what has happened to him, the farmer may find himself with nightmarish insect problems such as he has never known before. Farmers sometimes get 'addicted' to this insecticide treadmill, just as a person becomes addicted to drugs. The farmer, the consumer, and the environment, all suffer while the insecticide manufacturer benefits. As insect control is an ecological problem, it requires the employment of ecological principles and techniques to achieve a long-range, satisfactory solution for the agricultural community and the environment.

The Alternative: Modern Integrated Control

In contrast with the purely chemical approach to insect pest problems, modern integrated control employs an ecological approach to pest management by combining and integrating biological, chemical, and other effective measures into a single, unified pest-management system. Insecticides are used only when and where necessary, and in a manner that is least disruptive to beneficial regulating agents in the environment (Smith & Bosch, 1967). Crop yields and farmers' profits are thereby generally increased, and environmental damage is minimized or eliminated. Integrated control is not a dream for the distant future, but is already available in many instances and can readily be developed in most other cases (Bosch, 1970; Huffaker, 1971). Most CH insecticides are incompatible with integrated control and, in fact, they destroy its operation.

Modern agriculture must adopt effective, economical, and ecologically sound, integrated insect-pest management systems to avoid the numerous shortcomings, hazards, and high costs, of complete reliance on insecticides. An increasingly hungry and polluted world can ill afford to continue on its present course; for if it does, the adaptable insects will be the ultimate winners.

Choices for the Future

The current excessive dependence on insecticides, especially persistent CHS, seems to be filled with troubles for man. CH residues, particularly those of DDT, are diminishing the richness and diversity of the human environment by causing widespread declines in populations of many species of carnivorous birds—in some cases to very low levels or even to extinction. These residues threaten freshwater and marine fisheries by inhibiting the reproductive success of the larger predatory fish, thereby threatening an important source of proteins. They exhibit genetic toxicity to experimental animals, and are therefore probably adding to the existing burden of cancer and mutations within human populations. And finally, these materials are frequently counter-productive in achieving their intended objective of controlling insect populations.

Man can choose to continue these trends by maintaining current pesticide practices, with further deterioration indicated. Or he can choose to reverse them by adopting ecologically sound insect-pest management using modern integrated control systems. These choices may seem simple, but they are less simple than they appear. It will not be easy to reverse the momentum of current policies, to adopt existing knowledge, to seek new knowledge *via* imaginative and unbiased research, and to re-educate a whole generation of people who believe that insecticides represent the only approach to insect control. The adoption of new approaches will be resisted by many, and will be actively opposed by powerful economic interests; the faint-hearted will not prevail over these forces. Ecological pest-control without environmentally dangerous materials is essential, however, if we are to preserve the integrity of the biosphere as we know it.

REFERENCES*

ANDERSON, J. & PETERSON, M. (1969). DDT: sublethal effects on Brook Trout nervous system. *Science*, **164**, pp. 440–1.

BLUS, L. J. (1970). Measurements of Brown Pelican eggshells from Florida and South Carolina. *BioScience*, **20**, pp. 867–9.

BOSCH, R. Van Den (1970). Pesticides: prescribing for the ecosystem. *Environment*, **12**(3), pp. 20–5.

BOWES, G. W. & GEE, R. W. (1971). Inhibition of photosynthetic electron transport by DDT and DDE. *Bioenergetics*, **2**, pp. 47–60.

BOWMAN, M. E., ACREE, F., LOFGREN, C. S. & BEROZA, M. (1964). Chlorinated insecticides: fate in aqueous suspensions containing mosquito larvae. *Science*, **146**, pp. 1480–1.

BROWN, A. W. A. (1961). The challenge of insecticide resistance. *Bull. Entomol. Soc. Am.*, **7**, pp. 6–19.

BURDICK, G. E., HARRIS, E. J., DEAN, H. J., WALKER, T. M., SKEA, J. & COLBY, D. (1964). The accumulation of DDT in Lake Trout and the effect on reproduction. *Trans. Amer. Fish. Soc.*, **93**, pp. 127–36.

BUTLER, P. A., CHILDRESS, R. & WILSON, A. J. (1970). The association of DDT residues with losses in marine productivity. *Food and Agriculture Organization (UN) Technical Conference on Marine Pollution and its Effects on Living Resources and Fishing*, 9–18 December 1970, Rome, Italy. FIR: MP/70/E-76, 11 Nov. 1970, 13 pp.

CADE, T. J., LINCER, J. L., WHITE, C. M., ROSENEAU, D. G. & SWARTZ, L. G. (1971). DDE residues and eggshell changes in Alaskan falcons and hawks. *Science*, **172**, pp. 955–7.

CASARETT, L. J., FRYER, G. C., YAUGER, W. L. & KLEMMER, H. W. (1968). Organochlorine pesticide residues in human tissue—Hawaii. *Arch. Environ. Health*, **17**, pp. 306–11.

CONNEY, A. H. (1967). Pharmacological implications of microsomal enzyme induction. *Pharmacol. Rev.*, **19**, pp. 317–66.

DESI, I. FARKAS, I. & KEMENY, T. (1966). Changes of central nervous function in response to DDT administration. *Acta Physiol. Acad. Scient. Hungaricae*, **30**, pp. 275–82.

DVORCHIK, B. H., ISTIN, M. & MAREN, T. H. (1971). Does DDT inhibit carbonic anhydrase? *Science*, **172**, pp. 728–9.

EDWARDS, C. A. (1966). Insecticide residues in soils. *Residue Rev.*, **13**, pp. 83–132.

EPSTEIN, S. S. (1970). Control of chemical pollutants. *Nature* (London), **228**. pp. 816–9.

HARRINGTON, R. W. & BIDLINGMAYER, W. L. (1958). Effects of dieldrin on fishes and invertebrates of a salt marsh. *J. Wildl. Mgmt*, **22**, pp. 76–82.

HARRISON, H. L., LOUCKS, O. L., MITCHELL, J. W., PARKHURST, D. E., TRACY, C. R., WATTS, D. G. & YANNACONE, V. J. (1970). Systems studies of DDT transport. *Science*, **170**, pp. 503–8.

HAYES, W. J., DALE, W. E. & PIRKLE, C. I. (1971). Evidence of safety of long-term, high, oral doses of DDT for man. *Arch. Environ. Health*, **22**, pp. 119–35.

HUFFAKER, C. B. (Ed.) (1971). *Biological Control*. Plenum Press, New York: 468 pp.

JAGER, K. W. (1970). *Aldrin, Dieldrin, Endrin and Telodrin: an Epidemiological and Toxicological Study of Long-term Occupational Exposure*. Elsevier, Amsterdam: 234 pp.

JEFFERIES, D. J. & FRENCH, M. C. (1971). Hyper- and hypothyroidism in pigeons fed DDT: an explanation for the 'thin eggshell phenomenon'. *Environ. Pollut.*, **1**, pp. 235–42.

* Documentation is not exhaustive, but is intended to guide the reader to important papers, reviews, or recent sources, in which additional references will be found.

JOHNSON, H. E. & PECOR, C. (1969). Coho Salmon mortality and DDT in Lake Michigan. *Trans. 34th North Amer. Wildl. Nat. Res. Conf.*, 3–5 March, Washington, DC, pp. 159–66.

KORSCHGEN, L. J. (1970). Soil-food-chain-pesticide wildlife relationships in Aldrin-treated fields. *J. Wildl. Mgmt*, **34**, pp. 186–99.

KRIEGER, R. I., FEENY, P. P. & WILKINSON, C. F. (1971). Detoxication enzymes in the guts of caterpillars: an evolutionary answer to plant defenses? *Science*, **172**, pp. 579–81.

KUPFER, D. (1967). Effects of some pesticides and related compounds on steroid function and metabolism. *Residue Rev.*, **19**, pp. 11–30.

LEGATOR, M. S. (1970). Mutagenic effects of environmental intrusions. *Assoc. Food & Drug Offic. US*, **34**, pp. 3–5.

LEHNER, P. N. & EGBERT, A. (1969). Dieldrin and eggshell thickness in ducks. *Nature* (London), **224**, pp. 1211–19.

MACEK, K. J. (1968a). Reproduction in Brook Trout (*Salvelinus fontinalis*) fed sublethal concentrations of DDT. *J. Fisheries Research Bd Canada*, **25**, pp. 1787–96.

MACEK, K. J. (1968b). Growth and resistance to stress in Brook Trout fed sublethal levels of DDT. *J. Fisheries Research Bd Canada*, **25**, pp. 2443–51.

MENZEL, D. W., ANDERSON, J. & RANDTKE, A. (1970). Marine phytoplankton vary in their response to chlorinated hydrocarbons. *Science*, **167**, pp. 1724–6.

MOORE, N. W. (1967). A synopsis of the pesticide problem. *Adv. Ecol. Res.*, **4**, pp. 75–129.

MULHERN, B. M., REICHEL, W. L., LOCKE, L. N., LAMONT, T. G., BELISLE, A., CROMARTIE, E., BAGLEY, G. E. & PROUTY, R. M. (1970). Organochlorine residues and autopsy data from Bald Eagles, 1966–68. *Pesticides Monitoring J.*, **4**, pp. 141–4.

NASH, R. G. & WOOLSON, E. A. (1967). Persistence of chlorinated hydrocarbon insecticides in soils. *Science*, **157**, pp. 924–7.

O'BRIEN, R. D. (1967). *Insecticides, Action and Metabolism.* Academic Press, New York: 332 pp.

PARK, K. S. & BRUCE, W. N. (1968). The determination of the water solubility of Aldrin, Dieldrin, Heptachlor, and Heptachlor epoxide. *J. Econ. Entomol.*, **61**, pp. 770–4.

PEAKALL, D. B. (1970a). Pesticides and the reproduction of birds. *Scientific Amer.*, **222** (4), pp. 72–8.

PEAKALL, D. B. (1970b). p,p'-DDT: effect on calcium metabolism and concentration of estradiol in the blood. *Science*, **168**, pp. 592–4.

PEAKALL, D. B. & LINCER, J. L. (1970). Polychlorinated biphenyls: another long-life widespread chemical in the environment. *BioScience*, **20**, pp. 958–64.

PETERLE, T. J. (1969). DDT in antarctic snow. *Nature* (London), **224**, p. 620.

POLAND, A., SMITH, D., KUNTZMAN, R., JACOBSON, M. & CONNEY, A. H. (1970). Effect of intensive occupational exposure to DDT on phenylbutazone and cortisol metabolism in human subjects. *Clin. Pharmacol. Therap.*, **11**, pp. 724–32.

RADOMSKI, J. L., DEICHMANN, W. B. & CLIZER, E. E. (1968). Pesticide concentrations in the liver, brain and adipose tissue of terminal hospital patients. *Fd. Cosmet. Toxicol.*, **6**, pp. 209–20.

RATCLIFFE, D. A. (1970). Changes attributable to pesticides in egg breakage frequency and eggshell thickness in some British birds. *J. Appl. Ecol.*, **7**, pp. 67–115.

RIPPER, W. E. (1956). Effect of pesticides on balance of arthropod populations. *Ann. Rev. Entomol.*, **1**, pp. 403–38.

RISEBROUGH, R. W. (1969). Chlorinated hydrocarbons in marine ecosystems. Pp. 5–23 in *Chemical Fallout: Current Research on Persistent Pesticides* (Ed. M. W. Miller & G. G. Berg). C. C Thomas, Springfield, Ill.: 531 pp.

RISEBROUGH, R. W., HUGGETT, R. J., GRIFFIN, J. J. & GOLDBERG, E. D. (1968). Pesticides: Transatlantic movements in the north-east trades. *Science,* **159**, pp. 1233-6.

RUDD, R. L. (1964). *Pesticides and the Living Landscape.* University of Wisconsin Press, Madison: 320 pp.

SMITH, R. F. & BOSCH, R. Van Den (1967). Integrated control. Pp. 295-340 in *Pest Control: Biological, Physical and Selected Chemical Methods* (Ed. W. W. Kilgore & R. L. Doutt). Academic Press, New York: 477 pp.

STICKEL, W. H., STICKEL, L. F., & SPANN, J. W. (1969). Tissue residues of Dieldrin in relation to mortality in birds and mammals. Pp. 174-204 in *Chemical Fallout: Current Research on Persistent Pesticides* (Ed. M. W. Miller & G. G. Berg). C. C Thomas, Springfield, Ill.: 531 pp.

US DEPARTMENT OF AGRICULTURE (1970). *The Pesticide Review 1970.* Agric. Stabiliz. Conserv. Serv., Washington, DC: 46 pp.

US DEPARTMENT OF HEALTH, EDUCATION & WELFARE (1969). *Report of the Secretary's Commission on Pesticides and Their Relationship to Environmental Health.* E. M. Mrak, Chairman, Parts I and II, Washington, DC: 677 pp.

VALIN, C. C. Van, ANDREWS, A. K. & ELLER, L. L. (1968). Some effects of Mirex on two warm-water fishes. *Trans. Amer. Fish. Soc.,* **97**, pp. 185-96.

Van Den BOSCH, R. *See* BOSCH, R. Van Den

VERRETT, J. J. & DESMOND, A. H. (1959). Inhibition of carbonic anhydrase by chlorinated hydrocarbons. *Pharmacologist,* **1**, p. 72.

WELCH, R. M., LEVIN, W. & CONNEY, A. H. (1969). Estrogenic action of DDT and its analogs. *Toxicol. Appl. Pharmacol.,* **14**, pp. 358-67.

WIEMEYER, S. N. & PORTER, R. D. (1970). DDE thins eggshells of captive American kestrels. *Nature* (London), **227**, pp. 737-8.

WOODWELL, G. M. (1970). Effects of pollution on the structure and physiology of ecosystems. *Science,* **168**, pp. 429-33.

WOODWELL, G. M., WURSTER, C. F. & ISAACSON, P. A. (1967). DDT residues in an East Coast estuary: a case of biological concentration of a persistent insecticide. *Science,* **156**, pp. 821-4.

WURSTER, C. F. (1968). DDT reduces photosynthesis by marine phytoplankton. *Science,* **159**, pp. 1474-5.

WURSTER, C. F. (1969a). Chlorinated hydrocarbon insecticides and the world ecosystem. *Biological Conservation,* **1**(2), pp. 123-9.

WURSTER, C. F. (1969b). Chlorinated hydrocarbon insecticides and avian reproduction: how are they related? Pp. 368-89 in *Chemical Fallout: Current Research on Persistent Pesticides* (Ed. M. W. Miller & G. G. Berg). C. C Thomas, Springfield, Ill.: 531 pp.

WURSTER, D. H., WURSTER, C. F. & STRICKLAND, W. N. (1965). Bird mortality following DDT spray for Dutch elm disease. *Ecology,* **46**, pp. 488-99.

DISCUSSION

Moore (Chairman)

Dr Wurster has restricted his excellent review to the organochlorine insecticides which, as he said, provide the main pesticide hazard owing to their persistence, fat-solubility, and extensive use. But we must remember that most pesticides are not very persistent; DDT, thank goodness, is not a typical pesticide. As Dr Wurster indicated in his paper, we need better forms of crop protection which integrate the use of less persistent and more specific chemicals with appropriate biological methods. But how are we to get the research done and applied? This is one thing I hope we can discuss.

Despite the great importance of environmental contamination by the organochlorine insecticides—and I think this *is* a very important problem— we must remember that many industrial pollutants also exist, and their effects have been very much less studied; they may be much more serious than is often considered likely. I think we must get things in proportion: pesticides, bad as some of them are, provide only a part of the total pollution problem.

The ecological effects of pesticides are extremely complicated; it takes a very long time to study the effect of *one* chemical on *one* species of organism, as extensive work on the effects of DDT on the Peregrine Falcon has shown. This means that those responsible for the control of pesticides often have to act on insufficient knowledge if disaster is to be avoided in time; and this, of course, puts the advisory biologist in a very difficult position. In general, environmental biologists have the very difficult duty of explaining the environmental crisis to administrators and politicians whose training and preoccupations make it particularly difficult for them to apprehend it.

How in practice should we go about this task? We must appreciate the strength of those vested interests which prevent, either consciously or unconsciously, a more responsible and scientific use of pesticides. On the other hand, I personally regret the polarization of people into pro- and anti-pesticide groups, because by allowing that, conservationists lose the help of enlightened industrialists and enlightened agriculturalists, and these are the people who can help us most. I dare make the claim that in Britain we have succeeded, to some extent, in avoiding this polarization and thus have achieved some success. For example, the numbers of several species of British birds of prey had declined, and their breeding capacity had been reduced as the result of the use of Aldrin, Dieldrin, and other organochlorine insecticides. But subsequent restrictions on the use of these chemicals, which had been suggested by British conservation biologists and were agreed to by industry, have caused recoveries both in breeding success and numbers of all the threatened species.

If we scientists in the environmental field are to be *effective*, we have got to retain both the fire in our belly *and* our scientific integrity and accuracy. All of us here, including Dr Wurster and myself, know how extraordinarily difficult this is to do. The issues at stake are so important that scientists must ensure that the people with political power apply the results of our research. But how are we to achieve this in practice?

Mahler

Without wishing to dispute the facts and interpretations that Dr Wurster has presented in his well-prepared paper, I do feel that this picture is far from complete, and that, as such, it scarcely provided a suitable basis for this group to make resolutions and recommendations to politicians and to decision-makers. I would therefore like to broaden slightly the scope of the discussion and not to place emphasis on negative side-effects only, but also on some positive and direct effects of pesticides. In this I will leave aside the aspects of health and concentrate on the use of pesticides for agriculture.

The increased use of pesticides over the years does not show that they are ineffective, but rather that the farmers who pay for their cost have found that significant benefits can be derived from their use; and I think the farmers are very good at knowing where they can find some benefit from using one chemical or another. Actually, considerable quantities of food are apt to be involved. In 1967, 100 million tons of rice and 200 million tons of sugar-cane were lost because of insect damage, and this was mostly because of insufficient pest control in developing countries. One can easily imagine what could be the result of reducing or banning the use of some of the pesticides in developing countries. I agree with the speaker that well-integrated pest control techniques can prove much more efficient than the sole use of pesticides; however, they should not merely use biological control but start at the land-use planning stage, choosing the right cropping pattern on the right land, and going on with sound management practice.

FAO has been actively engaged for many years in promoting these techniques through expert committees, seminars, training courses, research projects and demonstrations, and assistance in developing legislation for the registration and use of pesticides. But one should stress that this integrated pest control still relies substantially on pesticides. Biological control is still in its infancy, and it also may prove to involve dangerous manipulation of the environment. (FAO is actually engaged, with the International Atomic Energy Agency, in the study and promotion of biological control.) One can therefore, I think, say that for the time being we have mainly to rely on pesticides for pest control. A considerable amount of research is being done towards the employment of more selective and less persistent pesticides, but these are usually two or three times more costly than the broad-spectrum, persistent pesticides, and without considerable financial assistance, the farmers of developing countries cannot afford their use—at least for the time being.

Wurster

The last speaker appears to be assuming that the use of pesticides is equivalent to pest control, which I do not consider valid. That assumption has been made repeatedly in this Conference—that the more pesticides we use, the more and better pest control we'll get, and the better human health will be. That assumption is open to very serious question, because it has failed completely in numerous countries. I certainly agree that we need more and better pest control, but I do not agree that the use of more insecticides is going to give it to us.

I should also like to point out that biological control is not nearly as much in its infancy as one might imagine. There are something in excess of a million species of insects in this world. At least half of them eat plant material, and yet only a few thousands of these are pests. All the rest are under biological control, which consequently should not be considered in its infancy at all. What we really need to do is to preserve the biological control which is given to us automatically—which we get for nothing—and that's really what integrated control is all about. Further, integrated control is not in its infancy either; integrated control is already far advanced in some directions, and most integrated control programmes have come out of disasters caused by pesticides. It seems that it takes an agricultural disaster, where the farmer is getting hopelessly squeezed between pesticide bills and insects, before an integrated control programme is developed. It apparently takes disasters to develop integrated control. Many of our environmental problems seem to have that characteristic.

Laird

I suppose that I can be considered as among the apostles of integrated control in medical entomology and, as such, on the side of the angels in environmental issues. When in the mid-1950s mine was the voice in the wilderness advocating (within WHO's Expert Committee on Insecticides) the earliest possible development and exploitation of biological and other non-chemical controls, I never thought I'd live to see the day when, without the slightest change in my basic views on the subject, I would be putting in a good word for chemical insecticides.

Dr Wurster's paper is entitled 'Effects of Insecticides'. It reviews selections of the literature of some aspects of this topic, but it leads up to statements of apparent fact that have yet to be proved or disproved. It deals with ill-effects and, as its author has admitted, it ignores disease-vector control. Dr Wurster has mentioned adverse effects that have been associated with the use of insecticides, but not one word about the good things that have been associated with these same uses.

In 1955 the World Health Assembly voted to undertake the Global Malaria Eradication Programme. In 1969, about 1,778 million people were living in the areas that had been malarious in 1955. Malaria eradication, thanks to the highly selective use of DDT as a spray on the *inner walls* of houses, had progressed to the point where 1,402 millions of these people—79 per cent of them—were now living in areas from which in fourteen years malaria had been eradicated, or in which eradication was under way. This is truly no small achievement against a disease that was formerly called the greatest single killer of mankind.

Let us look at some relevant facts and figures. At the height of WHO's malaria eradication operations, up to 63,000 tons of technical DDT—one-fifth of the world output—were being applied annually to the inner walls of houses, most of it in developing areas. Great care was taken to avoid any insecticidal contamination of either householders or the personnel involved, and, of course, the general environment was not at risk in anything like the same measure as it is when the same pesticides are misused by aerial spraying against certain agricultural crops in some more fortunate areas. There is no record that exposure to pesticide during the peak year of that malaria eradication campaign had adverse effects on any of the 130,000 spraymen, or on any of the 535 million people occupying treated houses.

Wurster

First, I would not disagree with a more limited title for my paper if desired. I do not oppose the use of DDT for malaria control in those countries that cannot afford the alternatives, but I think they should switch as quickly as possible to such materials as Methoxychlor, which are effective but more expensive.

Fosberg

I am going to take what will probably be a fairly unpopular position on some of these matters. I am particularly going to refer to remarks that Professor Laird made on this subject a day or two ago, which were more or less in the same vein as what he has just said, namely, that you cannot refuse to extend to a great many people relief from malaria or other diseases in order to keep from polluting the general environment with pesticides. I think this is a philosophical position which needs discussion, and that there are certainly two sides to it. And this does not only apply to this matter of DDT, but I would say to any treatment, any activity that tends to contaminate the environment—especially the world environment, the environment of others than the ones who are supposed to be the beneficiaries of the operation. I think it also applies to the activities of those who risk the release in the environment of radioactive materials, regardless of their motives. I think that the other people in the world, of whom there are a considerable number, if we are to accept the idea that all people have DDT now in their bodies, have a legitimate basis for objecting to being subjected to this kind of physiological abuse. I suggest that the benefit of, shall we say, a relative few, even though they may turn out to be millions, is not sufficient reason to contaminate the world environment and to subject the other thousands of millions of people to a risk of cancer, or of any number of other, as yet unknown, physiological difficulties and disadvantages.

I think that the burden of proof is on the agency that plans to apply these things, even though we freely admit that they may be beneficial to the people at whom they are aimed. I think that the rest of us have a legitimate reason to demand that we be not subjected to such risks for the benefit of other people. I would not demand that someone else be subjected to such a risk for my benefit, and I think this should work both ways.

Gootjes

Being the economist of the National Institute of Public Health in the Netherlands, where in recent years we have been doing a lot of research on the hazards of pesticides to human health, the excellent paper of Dr Wurster gave me a lot of data, but also some familiar facts. One of the facts is that, even after a long period of research, we are not sure of the dangers. Dr Wurster spoke several times about a lack of evidence, and also of how difficult it is to sell the results of research to policy-makers. This is notably the case in the country with the highest income in the world per square kilometre, because of the consequences for agriculture, industry, and national income; but this is a part of my duty.

I think it is easy to say, as we have already heard it said, that it does not matter who pays when in fact we all have to pay. But this seems to me unrealistic in a world with far more needs and priorities than income can pay for. Even when our research concerns the residues of pesticides and other hazards, we try to get benefits for our research costs, while important limits are set by the technical possibilities and practical handiness. Thus analyses for materials in concentrations lower than 0.01 ppb can only be realized in extreme cases; for many materials, concentrations of 0.1 to 1 ppb are necessary for a significant quantitative and qualitative analysis. For the River Rhine this, my colleagues tell me, corresponds to daily amounts of the order of 20 to 200 kilos. This means that in the first place we have to look at the bulk products and not at highly specialized research products.

We have found that the persistence of pesticides in general in surface waters is higher than on plants, and that resistance is fairly difficult to forget in changing environments. Many pesticides contaminate fairly fast with sludge. Such observations make it possible to give tolerable norms, and I think that in the USA and the USSR there have been some failures because of insufficient calculation of indirect hazards—even when chain-reactions and inter-reactions have been demonstrated in the environment.

I think Dr Fosberg was right when he said that he didn't want to risk his body for the benefit of others. But the first thing of all is to prove: does he risk his body at all, for if he does not, you can't withhold those benefits from the others.

Baroda

Though a layman in these matters, it is my understanding that, in the part of the world whence I come, we have had no evidence of any harmful effects either to plant or human life. In this we have the advantage of being a developing or an underdeveloped country as opposed to a developed or over-developed one, inasmuch as both the chemical fertilizers and such things as DDT are only distributed through government agencies. No one can walk into a shop and buy a can of DDT in India, nor can a farmer walk into a shop and buy a bag of fertilizer. Therefore the problem, if it has to be tackled at all in my country and others like it, is not going to be an easy one, for it is quite impossible at this stage to convince the vast majority of our people—I think almost all, from the Prime Minister downwards—that the use of chemical fertilizers and DDT in a country like India is harmful, and will have harmful effects in the future; because I feel, as has been said already, we have seen the benefits of both chemical fertilizers and DDT.

Professor Laird mentioned malaria. I myself have experienced malaria. As a child I used to get malaria at least two or three times a year. Now I haven't had malaria for I don't know how long. This is a common experience in India where we know that malaria has been practically eradicated through the use of DDT. Indeed, we thought it was completely eradicated until a couple of years ago when, thanks to our complacency, it reared its ugly head again. Now we are back on the attack and I am sure that with DDT we are again going to eradicate malaria. I know there are alternatives to DDT, but I don't think we can afford them. Presumably most of what we have been hearing about is the result of over-use of both the fertilizers and DDT and allied products. The remedy for us would seem to lie, if all these dangers exist for the future, in educating our government and people. So as far as I am concerned, and for the people of countries like mine, the solution or the control should not be too difficult.

Wurster

I would suggest that if there seem to be no ill-effects in India, perhaps no one has looked for them. Unfortunately the effects of DDT and Dieldrin often emerge only many years after, and very far removed from the sites of, their application. People do not drop dead from DDT and they don't get sick from DDT; but when a person dies thirty or forty years later of cancer, nobody knows what caused it. We are talking about short-term palliatives *versus* long-term effects, which are always very difficult to prove.

Another speaker mentioned that nobody was hurt or harmed of the 400 millions or so who have been intimately in contact with DDT. Unfortunately, nobody has studied those people in a systematic way, and nobody has really looked at the question. When we do look carefully, through experimental animals, we find a very different story. We can only accept those findings until something better comes along.

Laird

Remembering Mr Udall's plea on our opening day that we bring our disagreements right out into the open, I would like to substantiate my earlier remarks and spread my criticisms well beyond this one paper.

Now to start off, I am going to disagree with Dr Wurster, who stated that 'In addition to being a carcinogen, DDT has been shown to be a mutagen . . . .' This is simply not true. DDT has been *alleged* to be these things. On present evidence, it is *not* a carcinogen. Again, DDT has not been as universally demonstrated in the environment as has been asserted this morning—and the same analytical technique that 'detected' it in antarctic penguins and arctic polar bears has recently 'shown' chlorinated hydrocarbons to be present in soil samples that had been sealed up since 1909–11—as long before the first environmental introduction of DDT as this year is after that event!

I belong to a generation that, like many another before it, inherited an imperfect world—or at all events, a changing world—and I would venture to suggest that generations yet to come will, as they succeed one another, be just as rebellious about some things as earlier generations were. Yet as one who has tried very hard to advance biological control in public health entomology (having, like many others, been well aware for over a quarter of a century of the environmental threat posed by unselectively used pesticides), I was deeply disturbed by the overall vein of Dr Wurster's contribution and, I might add, by much of what I have heard and *not* heard in the past two days.

The recent rediscovery of 'The Environment' in some quarters, notably journalistic ones, was a blinding revelation of the obvious, if ever there was one. It has promoted the growth—the very rapid growth—of instant 'expertise' in environmental fields. Thankfully, some of us have been spared the tag of 'expert' in this Conference; but, of course, our classification as 'roving eminents' strongly suggests that we do not belong to that fulminating body of which Dr Brower spoke so eloquently yesterday. Aided and abetted by the mass media, youth today is admittedly more heard (and better supplied with research opportunities) than it was in earlier generations. But all of us were formerly young, and the current crop of youth will assuredly age—hopefully acquiring wide practical as well as laboratory experience and gaining wisdom in doing so. Dr Brower, I noticed, said nothing about wisdom, founded upon long practical experience of complex environmental problems.

Of course, this sort of approach goes down well with those committed to 'ecotactics', the methodology of 'ecopolitics'. Saying that Lake Erie is 'dying' falls into the same category and certainly catches headlines. Horrendous news still sells more newspapers than dull objectivity. Now I shall summarize, factually, what Dr Wurster could have said, but didn't:

> In some areas, certain pesticides have been irresponsibly used. This irresponsible use (and, sadly, some responsible use, too) poses ecological threats and perhaps even long-term hazards to man—about which there is much speculation but distressingly little factual information. In those same areas that have been most notable for past misuse of pesticides, consequences of this misuse are being extrapolated to less fortunate parts of the world where the same chemicals have been, and are being, used selectively and otherwise intelligently with great saving of human life through disease control (I shall not speak of the food production these chemicals have made possible, without which many would be facing famine; Mr Mahler of FAO has touched upon this).
>
> For the present, there are no available alternatives to the continuing intelligent use of chemical pesticides in vector control for disease eradication. Among these pesticides DDT (a chemical which has been alleged—not demonstrated—to be carcinogenic and mutagenic) is (because of its persistence, wide effectiveness, and relative cheapness and safety) of particular importance. Thus, if mankind is to be spared unbelievable suffering, we must resist the temptation to *ban* this or that chemical (DDT included). Instead, we must move as fast as possible towards the development of alternative and supplementary procedures not yet in existence, to make integrated control a reality—not just a dream—in public health entomology as well as economic entomology (in which latter field, effective integrated methodologies are much easier of achievement and have already become available for some purposes).
>
> In the meantime, even at the cost of some unfortunate effects on non-target organisms, we must continue to rely largely on chemical pesticides, used as selectively as possible, where human life and human well-being are at stake—unless, of course, we want to play God, and in doing so turn our backs on hundreds of millions of people already in existence and, whether we like it or not, our responsibility.

I would like to end with a plea that this Conference put forth a resolution calling on Member States of the UN and its specialized agencies to consider, as a priority issue, the vigorous promotion and support of research in their territories towards effective and selective integrated control methodologies in public health as well as agricultural entomology. It is further advocated that every effort be made by all concerned (1) to promote necessary governmental/industrial/university collaboration in such research, and (2) to share its results with the world at large, all of us being deeply involved in this issue. [Adjournment to evening.]

RESUMED DISCUSSION

[in a smaller hall making direct dialogue possible]

Hashimoto
Speaking from the standpoint of OECD, I wish to explain that Dr Roderick submitted his request to make a comment in this discussion, but unfortunately time did not allow it this morning and now he has had to leave to honour a prior commitment in Paris. However, I am of the same opinions and therefore trust I can be accepted to speak at this point.

First, I would like to describe the activities of OECD concerning environmental problems in relation to pesticides. OECD has been conducting cooperative studies on the unintended occurrence of pesticides since 1966, while a group for the study of bioactive chemicals was established early in 1971 on the basis of a decision of the Environment Committee. The cooperative research programme is proceeding and the fifteen member laboratories send fish samples periodically to the central laboratory in the United Kingdom where analyses are made for DDT, etc. Not only organochlorine pesticides but also polychlorinated biphenyls and mercury are considered important.

Concerning the role of international organizations in tackling this problem of organochlorine pesticides, as a Japanese I feel that at first each individual government should do what it can itself, before coming to the appropriate international organization. This is a very important point: that we should not expect the international organization necessarily to remedy matters and meanwhile use the organization as a camouflage for doing nothing ourselves. If a government thinks that nothing need be done it should say so, but if it thinks that there is something to be done it should say so and do all it possibly can. For pesticides, WHO and FAO set the tolerance-limits in the *Codex Alimentarius*, but what we often find now exceeds them by several times— sometimes by ten times—and people get quite worried about this. Each individual government must face the situation, explain the risks, and act. Concerning the reports about carcinogenicity and mutagenicity, these are undeniable though not yet conclusively proved for humans. This is a very difficult and delicate problem not only scientifically but also administratively and politically, but we cannot avoid it as a really serious challenge to environmental health.

With regard to industry in Japan, its attitude has long been that, if it is to be blamed for pollution, it expects to be shown the results of scientific investigations indicating that it is guilty. But now matters are changing and the public are saying they must have complete proof of safety; in other words, the burden of proof of harmlessness is shifting to industry.

Moore (Chairman)

I would like to endorse what Dr Hashimoto says about OECD, for it is very much to their credit that they have got onto doing something really useful by checking that different laboratories come to the same results when they look at samples of the same material, and consequently that you can make meaningful comparisons of the data from the laboratories concerned. I think also that this work indicated a lot of the problems of setting up a monitoring system. And I hope very much that when this is done by the United Nations they will take full account of the OECD experience which is now quite considerable—as I know personally because of being involved with the British contingent.

Coming to the main points—and I think they're the ones a lot of us want to talk or hear about—these whole questions remain as to how relevant is information about carcinogenicity, to what extent could you withdraw DDT in the tropics, and so on? All of us here who are biologists are interested in Peregrine Falcons—not so much because they are fast-flying birds that are widely used in falconry as because of the indications they give of much wider problems. I feel we really must try and make some sort of judgment about the immediate problems, such as people dying of malaria if we don't use pesticides. All of us would surely agree that we have got to use pesticides; but are there any practical alternatives to DDT at this moment, or will there be within the next few years? And what shall we do about substituting them? Here, Dr Wurster made the very positive suggestion that in some cases we could use Methoxychlor. If this is the case, and I believe it is in some circumstances, ought we not to press for the use of Methoxychlor?

Wurster

Many different points have been raised, but I will take first the one concerning the order of priorities in dealing with these environmental problems. I think the order is determined by how much we have already dumped out there; we have unloaded in excess of 3,000 million pounds of DDT, and so it is almost automatically the greatest problem although, pound for pound, it is probably not the worst. Had we unloaded that same quantity of Dieldrin, I think the problem would be yet worse. But because there is so much DDT, and because it's such a subtle compound in that its effects are often very remote from the site of application, in both time and distance, I think we are in a very serious difficulty with DDT, and that this problem is very far out in front. I think that Dieldrin is in second place, and when you say Dieldrin you have to include Aldrin because Aldrin is converted into Dieldrin in the environment, and so these two are really a pair constituting one problem. Probably in third place and needful of urgent tackling have to come the PCBS—again because there is so much of them 'out there', though unfortunately we know a great deal less about their biological effects. Beyond these three groups are others, and though I don't know how they should be ordered, I would probably as a guess put Heptachlor a close fourth.

Among the other matters that have been raised was that of tolerances, and it was suggested that there are safe tolerances—that to exceed these tolerances is not safe, but as long as we are below them it is safe. Actually, there is no scientific basis for establishing these tolerances, which with us in America are a hocus-pocus by our Food and Drug Administration. They merely take a level at which they notice effects on test animals, such as rats, and then they move the decimal point over two places and that becomes the 'tolerance'. But this just isn't the way things work, not being based on any scientific criterion at all. Further, there is no proper basis for the assumption that any tolerance at any level of carcinogenic material is safe; for though it is conceivable that there is some level of a carcinogen that is safe, we have no evidence to support such a statement.

As for steps that should be taken by governments, it seems that so far the main steps taken by the United States Government have been to generate propaganda. Thus the US Department of Agriculture has the habit of cancelling certain uses or registrations of various pesticides. They usually cancel those that are no longer used, which makes good publicity and doesn't change usage patterns at all. They have hundreds and hundreds of such registrations and, when enough public pressure builds up, they cancel fifty or a hundred and then the newspaper headlines say, 'Department of Agriculture bans 47 uses of 32 different vegetables', which sounds great. But it doesn't do anything, it's a completely useless step. The intricacies of Federal Law are such that the effect of cancellation in any event is to do essentially nothing, because all it does is initiate an administrative procedure that goes on virtually for ever without any conclusion. There has never been a cancellation proceeding that has gone to termination, except where the manufacturer agreed to it. In other words, there have been many so-called steps taken by the US Government to restrict the use of DDT; but as of this moment there is no restriction whatsoever in the United States at the Federal level on the use of DDT. There are some state restrictions, particularly in Wisconsin, to a lesser extent in New York, in Arizona, in Illinois, and a few other states; but at the Federal level it's been all talk and no action.

One more point that has been raised is, I think, a very good one, to which I'd like to give further consideration. It was about the burden of proof and the necessity of governments or industry proving safety. I think this is a crucial point because industry, in the United States, has on a number of occasions taken the great democratic position that chemicals are innocent unless proven guilty. But chemicals don't have human rights—they are guilty until proven innocent! Otherwise, if they are innocent until proven guilty, then human beings are being deprived of their rights to good health. In other words, we must assume that any chemical which is being released into the environment is a dangerous material until we know it's not a dangerous material. Meanwhile, of course, materials of this nature are being released constantly, every day, without any such indications of safety.

Moore (Chairman)

I would like to pose this question of controversial chemicals in its most acute form. Supposing we agree that DDT is a carcinogen at very low concentrations, should we decide to use it, even so, in order to save a lot of lives at the moment in developing countries? This decision is really the problem we face in a great deal of the world, and though I'm all for getting rid of DDT eventually, it seems to me that we must get to grips with this most critical decision. This is the kind of dilemma mankind is faced with chronically nowadays.

Butler

Before we go any further in this discussion, I feel I should say that I don't at all like some of the language in which it is being conducted. Nothing is safe—let's admit that; and you don't talk about a thing being safe or not safe, you talk about whether the risk is acceptable or not. We have been all through this in the radiation game, and we're quite familiar with this philosophy. We conduct a debate on that basis, not on a basis of being safe or not safe. Nor is it fair to say the burden of proof is on the taxpayer or on the manufacturer. The burden of proof is with science, which has to develop knowledge to tell us about the toxicity of these things. You can't say the burden of proof is on the manufacturer to prove something safe when you can't prove anything is safe; and you can't say the burden of proof is on the taxpayer to prove it dangerous. The burden of proof is not on anybody except on science to do the necessary research.

Wurster

The burden of proof is legally on the manufacturer before any pesticide can be registered in the United States—it's stated in Federal Law where the burden of proof is.

Butler

I'm not talking about law. If you want to talk about law you will only be talking about American law, whereas I can tell you that Canadian law does quite a lot about DDT.

Mellanby

We have got to be extremely careful about these issues. Obviously a thing must be proved safe or reasonably safe, but one of the great difficulties is that any screwball can make any statement and then somebody will say: 'So and so has said something does so and so, and now the industry must prove this isn't the case.' This I think is one of the worrying things. Another is the lack of proportion and even of self-discipline: we still have people getting up in a meeting and saying 'we mustn't have this terrible carcinogen' with a cigarette hanging out of the corner of their mouth.

Polunin (Jr)

Yes, but there's a radical difference: at least the cigarette was there by their own choice whereas DDT is thrust on us, and that's what much of this discussion is about.

Laird

There is not one single biological control technique that is ready for use at this moment against any vector of a human disease: I say this with full authority and confidence because this is the field in which I have worked for the greater part of my life. There are three leading candidate organisms for mosquito control, but all seem rather remote possibilities in the present state of our knowledge and experience. Yet some such alternative methods must ultimately be found in the direction of integrated control, and for this we need to keep DDT and Dieldrin in our armoury.

Moore (Chairman)

This leaves us with the need to get industry and government to look for these desired alternatives. Thus if we allow the present compounds to go on being used, which I agree with you we ought to do in such countries as India, we must still find some ways of getting the research done on practical alternatives.

Mellanby

The way to accomplish this is for some chaps to get into a lab and do some work. The idea that a government committee or an international organization is going to start this or ever invent anything is simply not reasonable, though that is where we need to exert more pressure. Perhaps we ought to have a few less international conferences and people attending them, but instead working in their labs.

Wurster

Whereas one must concede the use of DDT for malaria control in those countries that cannot afford the alternatives, perfectly good alternatives do exist. One of these is Methoxychlor, which can also be sprayed on the inside of houses and huts, and this will work. It tends to be less stable than DDT, and so it doesn't last so long but has to be used somewhat more often and costs more in the first place—about twice as much. But the cost of the programme is not the cost per pound of chemical; it's the cost of shipping it, applying it, etc., etc. In other words, doubling the cost of the chemical does not double the cost of the programme. Thus Methoxychlor is an acceptable alternative, and so is DDBP. Dichlorvose is another effective alternative, impregnating those Shell strips we have in every gas station in the United States. For malaria control I think the benefits would vastly exceed the risks in those areas where we have widespread resistance to DDT, and, in fact, it's more widespread in Africa for malaria control than is DDT, because DDT doesn't work any more. Indeed, as part of my argument, DDT isn't all that good!

It has also been claimed that for control of onchocerciasis there is no effective alternative to the use of DDT. Onchocerciasis is a disease that is transmitted by a black-fly which breeds in rapids. It has been found and already published in a World Health Organization bulletin that Methoxychlor is an excellent alternative—in fact, it's better than DDT—to do the job of controlling onchocerciasis. So there *is* an alternative!

Even if we agree that until there's a definitely better way to do it, malaria control by DDT may continue in certain countries, I will certainly not concede the use of 10 to 20 million pounds annually in the United States on cotton—a crop of which we have a surplus, and which the taxpayer subsidizes the raising of more of. Yet we're subsidizing the use of this costly and exceedingly destructive chemical for the growing of cotton that we don't need—at the expense of our own environment. Furthermore, you can grow cotton much better without DDT in spite of the fact that the cotton farmers keep screaming that they have to have it for cotton.

Finally, Professor Laird indicated that we must keep such materials as DDT and Dieldrin in our armoury for effective integrated control, but the integrated control people say that DDT and Dieldrin are so destructive of entomophagous insects that they can play no role whatsoever in an integrated control programme. Paul DeBach, who is certainly one of the world's leading authorities on biological and integrated control, says that DDT is the most destructive, disruptive material one can throw into an agricultural ecosystem. It is so disruptive that it completely fouls up integrated control, so that you can't *manage* anything any more until you get rid of the DDT.

Laird

But the sad fact of the matter is that there are no entomophaga which attack mosquitoes and black-flies. You see, in agricultural entomology there is a whole range of parasites which do not occur in mosquitoes or in black-flies. In mosquitoes and black-flies the only chance we've got of developing meaningful biological control is (primarily) by microbial pathogens—instead of endoparasitic insects—and (secondarily) by various predators. Genetic control is usually considered separately from biological control nowadays, so I won't refer to it here.

Wurster

Professor Laird has shifted from an agricultural ecosystem that I was talking about to disease-vector control. I am not talking of biological control of malaria—it's not going to happen, at least it's very hard to picture how it could happen. I'm talking about agriculture, I'm talking about that darned cotton in the United States that we keep pouring all these awful things onto.

Laird

This is fine so long as we don't generalize from agricultural experience and give the impression that this covers the whole subject—there is no argument there. But I think that what this Conference must do is to make it quite clear that there are two very distinct components: one is agricultural and economic, and the other is concerned with public health. If we can get people to see that we recognize this distinction, I think we won't get our wires crossed so frequently, because extrapolation from one to the other is very dangerous and can lead to a lot of errors.

Wurster

I didn't intend to make an extrapolation, and I don't think I did. The problem as I see it has to be tackled step by step, and the first thing to do is to stop the use of DDT in the United States and in Europe. They don't need it and in fact can't afford the destruction that it causes. So I'm not arguing really with you at all on the disease-vector situation, except in the case of onchocerciasis.

Ojala

Although I think we have talked too much already about the DDT problem, I would nevertheless like to add a few words. I feel that enough evidence has been collected to demand that the use of DDT and most other organochlorine pesticides and related compounds should be prohibited in the whole world; but there is one thing outstanding, and that is malaria. I have many times searched in WHO publications for indications of efforts to find other methods of malaria control; maybe there have been such efforts, but at any rate every time WHO experts talk about this problem they try to deny any evidence of the harm caused especially by DDT. I think it would be better for them to make efforts to find other methods, for they are surely needed; then these environmentally undesirable compounds could be prohibited even in tropical areas.

I would like to add some compounds to those that have so far been discussed. In Finland a special Council for Poisons was established last year, and we have tried to list what we call the environmental poisons, finding out some things that have not yet been spoken of here. For example, besides the heavy metals we must not forget the metalloid elements such as selenium which are harmful; so can other groups be, as, for example, wood preservatives, among which the most important, at least in Finland, is pentachlorphenol. Then there are the anti-slime chemicals used in the wood-pulp industry. The whole mercury problem in this country resulted from the use of phenylmercury acetate, but now the pulp industry has begun to use organobromine compounds. Yet enough evidence has not been gained to indicate their 'guiltlessness', and they are still used without knowledge of possible harmful effects. Another group, taken very seriously in the Soviet Union, are organo-tin compounds, which are used as some kind of plastic additives. Other chemicals used in Finland, including a source of nitrous acid and formaldehyde, may even come out in the environment.

Over-fertilization with nitrates and nitrate poisoning is a 'disease' that is usually restricted to industrialized countries, which use some 90 per cent of all the fertilizers that are applied in the world—especially the nitrate fertilizers. We should also mention the military use of herbicides. In Vietnam, already 50,000 tons of 2,4-D and 2,4,5-T have been applied, and also cacodylic acid which is still more toxic and probably has mutagenic effects. Other chemicals have been used experimentally, so that we really have those human experiments that were mentioned earlier.

Polunin

As Editor of *Biological Conservation* I had some correspondence about two years ago with Dr M. G. Candau, the Director-General of WHO, concerning their continued use and advocacy of DDT for malarial control, and he wrote me then that they had for several years had an extensive research programme on alternative possibilities and were continuing to search for something else effective. With his permission I published a footnote about this in my journal, and I have since been given the impression, living as I now do within easy walking distance of the WHO headquarters, that they have hopes of finding and applying effective other methods; certainly they do not accept the use of DDT as the last possible thing.

Now I come to what I wanted to say this morning but time did not allow. I have listened 'back and forth' to arguments on this and other occasions— often very vital and at times brilliant arguments such as I feel we have been having in good measure here. Yet they are rarely unbiased to the extent of being strictly truthful in all respects—even within the limits of available knowledge. I am a scientist by basic training as well as lifelong practice and devotion; not perhaps a particularly outstanding scientist, and certainly not a great one, though I have had my 'eureka' occasions. But this I stress as a background for the unhappy contention which I feel it my solemn duty to advance, namely, that our scientific leadership to industry, to Uncle Tom Cobley and all—but particularly to industry—often leaves much to be desired. Indeed in some connections it is apt to be downright lousy!

We have the case of the chemists developing the chlorinated hydrocarbons, of industry pushing them—probably at first in good faith—and now of the biologists showing them up. We have the case of what to avoid putting into detergents to reduce their tendency to cause eutrophication, of which my son spoke this morning*: I suspect that industry's switch from phosphates was a very costly one, and now we have been expertly informed that there is no clear answer anyway. But I feel sure you can think of further instances and believe you must agree that this kind of thing often involves poor leadership from those who ought to know better—or at least to determine their proper bases before pronouncing. Yet we should strive to give firm guidance where it is needed, as it is so widely and often desperately today.

Speaking of industry, one sometimes wonders whether they are really interested—that is, beyond the immediate confines of profits, amenities, and actual laws. Thus it is said—I hope only jocularly—that the big oil companies spend far more on advertising what they do for conservation than they actually spend on it. To be sure, we cannot reasonably expect one firm to undertake costly improvements on behalf of the environment, thereby adding to the price of its products, if its competitors do not do likewise; but we can expect them all to show some concern for the welfare of the world, and I would have thought we could reasonably expect them to have some interest in such an occasion as this Conference—when the future of their environment and everyone else's is being discussed. Of several outstanding foreign industrialists and financiers who claim or are widely reputed to have environmental interests, and whom we invited, though admittedly rather late, two undertook to come but only one has turned up (unless Mr Augustine Marusi, Chairman and President of Borden, Inc., has now arrived—he promised to be here today†). But the International Chamber of Commerce and some other international bodies undertook to send representatives—and yet we do not hear a single word from any of them‡.

One would expect them to be aroused by some of the remarks that have been passed, but so far we have not had so much as a peep from any captain or even corporal of industry, though we have a brigadier with us all the time; are they afraid, or are they just not interested? In any case, the lack of a voice from industry is to be deplored, I feel, when we made considerable efforts to get it here. For we would surely like to hear what they have to say, to consider their viewpoint, and to see fair play. I say this not merely in my present

* *See below*, page 349, the present discussion being a continuation of an earlier one.—Ed.
† *See*, however, his comments received later and published on pp. 511–12.—Ed.
‡ But *see* their later intervention, published on pages 498–501.—Ed.

capacity here but also as a long-time micro-investor and, I hope, general *amicus curiae*. We would indeed have welcomed the 'Club of Rome'.

Moore (Chairman)

I think we all regret the lack of the voice of industry here. One of the things we are rather proud of in Britain is that we do have a dialogue with industry—I won't say they're all angels—but they do at least come and talk, and they frequently come to me before they release a new chemical, tell me about it, and say 'We're a little bit worried about it in water: what tests should be done?', and so on. Thus we have a good practical relationship which has worked reasonably well, and I suspect that one of the reasons why this happens in Britain is a rather odd one—that we don't control pesticides by law but have a voluntary scheme, as Dr Mellanby mentioned this morning*. This, though it may appear paradoxical, does have a very good effect, because it means that industry can't look for holes in the law if the law doesn't exist; it's up to them to see that their own members in the British Agrochemicals Association carry out the wishes of the interdepartmental committee which controls pesticide use in Britain.

This system seems to work pretty well, and I suspect that one of the troubles in the United States is the polarization there into two camps which, when once you've got it, makes constructive dialogue very difficult, though you can always have a slanging match. Thus if a conservationist suggests that DDT has some value, he is thought a traitor; and if an industrialist says that we must be more careful of this or that use of a pesticide, he is considered 'soft' by his colleagues. So you get an unscientific situation of opposing forces —of armed camps—and once you've got that, and often actual legal strife, there's very little you can do about amicable settlement.

I have great sympathy with Dr Wurster who is involved in this legal strife, but I think if you can avoid it and get hold of the many people in industry and the agricultural departments who really are as keen on preserving the environment as a lot of conservationists, you can really get something done. I don't know how exportable our system is, but it's surely worth considering and, as I say, the practical results are very clear: our Dieldrin levels are going down in food and they're going down in wildlife, our birds of prey are increasing, and we have not let through any new chemicals that have really done harm in the last ten years. I am not saying we won't make any mistakes; as with drugs, etc., we are bound to make mistakes sometimes. But we seem to manage well enough by any objective assessment, and I would very much like to see other people—particularly those involved in the control of pesticides—similarly pooling their experience, because this is the type of thing which can give really practical results.

Wurster

I can't speak about industry in general but I can say a few things about the pesticide industry in the United States. As the Chairman indicated, I've been involved in a variety of legal activities concerning the use of DDT, Dieldrin, and Aldrin, in the United States. I've gone to lots of conferences

* *See below*, page 343.—Ed.

and been in quite a few legal forums. A few years ago the industry tended to appear on these occasions but fared extremely badly. Now they don't appear any more but are remarkable by their absence. This has become a general pattern; you can't get them to appear, in fact it's reached a point where we can't even subpoena them because they're out of the range of a Federal subpoena.

In Madison, Wisconsin, where we had extended hearings on the use of DDT, our Environmental Defense Fund side of the issue had so many witnesses that we could scarcely begin to put them on; we could have had a hundred scientists up there. The industry was able to put up a handful of people who fared very badly, and then their representative, the 'great ecologist' representing the National Agricultural Chemicals Association, who were the defendants in the case, disappeared when it became time for them to put on their case. He had been sitting in the room, but he disappeared because we would have subpoenaed him to get him up there. So then he was gone—he's been gone ever since. Whenever there are scientists around he disappears; meanwhile he gives lectures all over the United States to horticulturalists, to agriculturalists, to various people who will not ask difficult questions. But when the chips are down he's not around, he vanishes, and he's become typical of a number of people who are spokesmen for the pesticide industry. They are remarkable by their scarcity in real scientific circles.

Heinø

I have got to speak when asked in this way. I'm not a specialist on the subject, which is why I haven't spoken up before. But I do happen to know the detergent field, and, as you all realize, this is very much in the headlines in many parts of the world nowadays. So I came here hoping to learn something, and looked forward to the leadership that Professor Polunin has spoken about—the scientific leadership—though I must say with some disappointment that I haven't yet seen all that much of it.

Why doesn't an industry man speak up? Well, in a group where one has to listen to accusations of almost the whole of United States industry and agriculture in one sentence, how can a single man say something without having to defend a lot of things he has no influence over or working understanding of! I think it is very difficult for any industry man to talk without immediately being put on the defensive. He is expected to justify all the past actions, some of which may have proven to be wrong, and to be content with only a defensive point of view in the light of current knowledge. He has been learning in the past few years, just as science has, that he still carries with him all of the negatives and the problems that have arisen. Though I speak with certainty only for myself, I think in industry we're all in some such position. Personally I believe that such discussion is useful when it is frank and open and as long as one doesn't start out with having to justify one's own existence.

Hashimoto

The assessment of industrial or other risks is a very difficult matter, and I am of the opinion that we badly need to develop a *relative risk spectrum* based on available scientific data and experiences in various fields. In medical treatment, the extent of risk in many cases of surgical operations and drug administration is known. In public health, immunization programmes also involve a certain risk of side-effects. So one would think it ought to be possible to develop an ecological risk spectrum indicating the consequences of various intensities of human activity in an environmental setting. Economics is often involved in problems of probable risk, and various kinds of insurance are based on the principle of pooling risks. But atomic science is too remote and independent; it should be more mixed with other sciences and systems. Meanwhile the world is changing: scientific knowledge is no longer the monopoly of scientific groups, and mass-communication interests are becoming more and more involved in controversial issues particularly in relation to environment.

Kassas

We have been talking about chemicals and biological control and so perhaps, to make the picture complete, somebody would tell us about the prospects of chemosterilents and the use of sterile males, for we would like to learn the lessons of DDT from the point of view of their possible application to birth-control pills, etc. There are lots of chemicals that are being produced all the time, and that go into our medical, agricultural, or physiological, systems. What we would like is to see a certain code of ethics to be practised on how to use and release these chemicals, to hear what precautionary measures should be taken by industry, and to know what specifications should be set before these chemicals are released. We are not proposing that they be banned but just want to make as sure as possible that they are safe. We don't want in ten years' time to meet at a conference like this and, instead of talking about DDT, find ourselves discussing some substance that we are using today as human beings and yet within the next ten years we find has accumulated in the bodies of ourselves and of wildlife sufficiently to do the kind of harm that DDT—which for years was considered harmless—is now doing all too obviously.

Laird

You have asked, Mr Chairman, how we may develop ecologically less hazardous alternatives to DDT and other pesticides, and Dr Ojala indicated that perhaps WHO might have been remiss in not actively searching for such alternatives, whereupon this point about chemosterilents led right into what I had proposed to say. So to enlarge on Professor Polunin's point about the World Health Organization, I think it should be very clearly understood that, since 1958 when its expanded medical research programme started, WHO has had an extremely active programme directed towards the discovery of alternative and supplementary means of vector control. I personally was a member of the Expert Committee on Insecticides which in 1957 decided that insecticide resistance was developing faster than our capacity to deal with it. And it was at that meeting that a lot of things began, including a move towards the biological control research programme.

Since then a very effective chemical screening scheme has been developed, which I think it would be only fair to bring to the notice of this Conference;

it would also be only fair to industry to do so, because there are men of good will in industry as well as everywhere else. Thus industry has contributed most handsomely to the insccticide testing scheme of WHO's. Briefly, chemicals that have been developed for pest control have, in the past, been almost entirely developed on a rather *ad hoc* basis, with agricultural use in mind. They have only come to be used in vector control through the back door, as it were.

Over a period of twelve or more years an increasing number of chemical companies in many countries have supplied to WHO samples of their new products—to such an extent that each year a total of approximately 300 new compounds arrive, having been screened out from the 2,000 to 3,000 new compounds which have been developed during that year by industry. Those 300, approximately, substances have been, over this period of years, farmed out among collaborating laboratories, for WHO has no laboratories of its own; its total budget for its entire global operation comes to about one-half the budget of the National Research Council of Canada. By effective use of existing laboratories in various parts of the world, WHO gets dispassionate assessment of these new chemicals, and each year something of the order of two compounds are 'put into mothballs' for future use when resistance problems become so complex that our present means of controlling certain vectors fail. Thus important developments that have come out of this chemical screening programme to date have included new means of controlling body-lice and hence typhus, so that even if the currently-used pesticides end up with a total resistance situation, there will be 'mothballed' chemicals to fall back on.

Another pertinent aspect of WHO activities is a very effective biological control research programme that has been developed so that it now involves collaboration from scientists in, I think, 119 of the member states of WHO. Individual scientists are supplied with a pocket-sized collecting kit that has been developed to enable any conceivable pathogen, or parasite of any conceivable vector, to be preserved in both fixed and viable states for inten- sive laboratory investigation. These kits are sent out from WHO head- quarters at Geneva, and, after use, are dispatched directly to the address on the pack. This is WHO's International Reference Centre for Diagnosis of Diseases of Vectors, which is at Ohio State University, USA, where the incoming kits are screened. The material having been analysed, reports are sent to the collectors in the field, and also to experts on the taxon concerned —together with material for further study in cases that might have some interest from a biological control standpoint.

Such work has grown to such a point, and so rapidly, that the world output of literature on biological control as related to medical entomology has leapt forward enormously since 1964. In 1964 a literature survey going back to the year dot—which was in the middle of last century in this case—indicated that something like 4,000 papers had so far been published on the subject of biological control and pathology as it related to disease vectors. In the period since 1964, approximately 1,000 further such papers have appeared, and there has been a much higher incidence of papers with a direct relevance to biological control rather than just reporting yet another parasite in yet another area or insect host.

It should thus be realized that WHO is actively working, in a very constructive way, towards alternative methods, one of which is genetic control. A considerable group of people and a number of study centres are critically evaluating genetic control procedures for use against mosquitoes, for use against tsetse flies, and for use against muscoid flies. There are varying opinions on how effective these procedures are likely to be, and we know it is going to be a long time before they're really ready for use to give reproducible results, but at least we know a great deal more about the topic than we did a very few years ago. Yet we need to know far more still—hence my appeal this morning for a resolution designed to bolster research on integrated control. This might help a lot of people, including WHO, to increase their efforts in what is still a woefully under-supported field of endeavour. It might even stimulate industry to dip deeper into its pocket at a time when it is suffering from sales losses from the impact of the issue of deleterious environmental consequences of chemical pesticide misuse.

Apollonov

With each technology speaking for itself, I would like to say something about the benefits from the use of nuclear energy in this field, which was scarcely touched on in my statement circulated today.* I just wanted to say that nuclear energy is used fairly extensively to further some of the items we have been discussing. Thus radioactive isotopes are used to check the path of pesticides, and in some circumstances they can be a substitute for the use of pesticides—I mean pesticides generally, not DDT. The International Atomic Energy Agency conducted a project in South America to combat fruit-flies by using the method of sterilization of the males, employing a certain dose of radiation for their sterilization and then placing them in the population. The conclusion was that this population will not continue.

Polunin

[† Returning momentarily as I hope to conclude this already too-long session, I would like to outline some further thoughts on the matter of quality of scientific leadership and advice which I raised earlier. It seems that those of us who have been brought up on ecology and really trained in environmental studies are largely to blame—for not, on one hand, 'sticking our necks out' and pronouncing firmly when we really have reached a conclusion and have something to say and, on the other, for not getting together and insisting on set standards. The difficulties are, of course, that we are actually very few and commonly voiceless—a true scientist rarely makes pronouncements without double-checking his facts, which is particularly tricky to do in ecology with its extreme complexity and the ever-changing facets of life—and that it is difficult to decide on standards in a relatively young and ill-defined composite science. An unfortunate result is that all manner of ill-qualified or even totally unqualified people hop on the environmental bandwagon, pronounce themselves loudly in often ill-founded ways, and give us all a bad name. My own experience is that, although I am still, I think, the only one ever to offer ecology as a 'special

* *See* pp. 354–5.—Ed.   † *See* footnote on page 205.—Ed.

subject' in the Final Honour School of Natural Science at Oxford, subsequently continued studying it at both Yale and Harvard, and have researched in and written on the subject widely since, I used not to call myself an ecologist because of the need to explain *ad nauseam* what it meant, and I now do not normally do so because it has become something of a loose term or even 'dirty word'—smacking of rabid bandwagoners and bogus 'experts'.

If we take the case of the medical profession throughout the world, they have long organized themselves into a strong professional union *inter alia* insisting on set standards of training and practice, and this has been demanded by human beings with whose individuals they have largely to contend. Their training to deal with these highly complex organisms is long and multifarious; but I put it to you that the ecosystems making up the biosphere which ecologists have to deal with are even far more complex, the training which they need—in botany, zoology, geology, pedology, physics, chemistry, meteorology, oceanography, limnology, etc., etc.—is at least as exacting as that required for medical practice, and it often takes (and surely should take) as long or longer. Nor are the problems with which ecologists have to deal any less vital but commonly far more important than the lives of individual human beings in a locally already often overcrowded world. Yet because sometimes of their lack of authority—especially where the bandwagoners are concerned—the real ecologists are rarely listened to and, as consultants, command only a small fraction of the fees which are, it seems, automatically paid out to medical, legal, and some other organized practitioners.

The remedy all around would seem to me to lie in a proper international organization which would insist on adequate minimal standards of qualifications based on both training and experience. Only those so accepted at least by their national chapter of the wider, controlling international body should be allowed to call themselves and seek employment and make pronouncements as real ecologists. For there ought to be a considerable diffusion of *suitably qualified* ecologists in the higher echelons of industry and government, if we are to get the kind of environmental future we are dreaming about, and this is a vital matter which I would adjure some of you to get together and do something about before the situation gets quite hopelessly out of hand. At present the people who are listened to tend often to be the wrong ones, lacking adequate bases for their pronouncements, and this can do great harm to our cause—the future of man and his entire environment.]

10

UNWISE USE OF CHEMICALS
OTHER THAN PESTICIDES

Keynote Paper

Unwise Use of Chemicals other than Pesticides

by

KENNETH MELLANBY

Editor of Environmental Pollution;
Director, Monks Wood Experimental Station,
The Nature Conservancy,
Abbots Ripton, Huntingdon, England

INTRODUCTION

Pesticides are toxic substances that are deliberately released into our environment to kill organisms which, from the point of view of man, are undesirable. The perfect pesticide would eliminate the target organism and be otherwise harmless. Unfortunately, as Dr Wurster and others have shown, some pesticides become environmental contaminants and have harmful effects that are often distant in time and space from the place where they were applied. These are calculated risks which have to be taken when the pesticide is used; the user believes that the advantages of application outweigh the disadvantages when, or perhaps more particularly if, he himself will not suffer from the side-effects of his actions. My present purpose is to deal with some of the other chemicals which man may introduce into his environment—usually accidentally, but sometimes deliberately, as in the cases of wastes discharged into the air or the sea as a method of disposal—which can also be the cause of environmental degradation.

This is an immense subject, for almost every substance in sufficient concentration in the wrong place can be a 'pollutant'. Poisons such as cyanide or mercury are obviously potential dangers, but so also are other substances that are not generally so recognized. Thus nitrates are essential for the growth of green plants, and on them the whole economy of life on this planet depends. A suitable concentration of nitrates in the soil is needed for the optimum growth of a crop; but a higher concentration may upset the system, or even prove to be highly phytotoxic. Sulphur deposited from the air onto many areas of grassland can rectify a soil deficiency and stimulate growth, but at a slightly higher level of sulphur concentration the grass may be poisoned and killed. So when we consider the unwise use of a chemical, we need to be concerned not only with processes which liberate poisonous substances at effective levels, but also with almost every activity of man that changes the world in which he lives.

Clearly, I cannot hope to tackle all aspects of this subject. Therefore, I shall not deal in any detail with the many cases where chemical pollution is produced, either deliberately or carelessly, when the possibilities of local damage are fully realized. This happened frequently in Britain in the early days of the industrial revolution, and we have, in areas of the resultant dereliction, many continuing monuments to this process. Unfortunately, some developing countries seem to be repeating our mistakes. These latter might perhaps be avoided if, when aid is given by the developed countries, clauses were included in all agreements to safeguard against environmental or other damage. My main concern in this paper is with cases where chemicals have been used with apparent care, taking what appear to be reasonable precautions, and yet their use has given rise, generally unexpectedly and often quite insidiously, to damage to the environment.

I have not mentioned several topics which further experience may show to be important. Thus silver salts are increasingly used for 'seeding' clouds in attempts to cause rain to fall in drought areas. This could cause local pollution with silver—a very toxic element. More seriously, it could upset at least the local weather pattern with unexpected results. Atomic wastes also present an increasing problem, notwithstanding the responsible attitude of most authorities.*

There are two very different types of problems caused by harmful chemicals. Most such substances do not have long-term effects. They may cause serious damage to the environment and acute poisoning to some at least of its inhabitants when they are present at sufficient concentrations, but if they are diluted down to a level where they are harmless, the problem is solved, for they then decompose or are absorbed or recombined into harmless compounds. The long-term dangers come from substances which, like the organochlorine pesticides described in this Conference by Dr Wurster, are not easily decomposed and which, after having been diluted to harmless levels, may be reconcentrated by living organisms up to a level where they once again have damaging effects. It is clear that we must

* *See*, particularly, the *Addendum* at the end of this section, pp. 354-5.—Ed.

be very cautious in introducing into general use any chemicals having these properties.

POLYCHLORINATED BIPHENYLS

This principle of concentration and the need for caution have both been demonstrated recently by the polychlorinated biphenyls ('PCBs'). These are substances which are synthesized for industrial purposes but have become world-wide contaminants, and which may have harmful effects on wildlife. Although they are not sold commercially as insecticides, they have considerable insecticidal properties, and are toxic to many other organisms. The reason for their importance as contaminants, however, is that they are persistent, very sparingly soluble in water, but readily soluble in lipids. These properties account for the fact that they may be concentrated in the fatty tissues of animals when they occur at low levels in the environment. Although much of the information about the PCBs is well known to many scientists, I make no apology for any repetition, for the experience we have obtained with these chemicals may be taken as a warning of the possible dangers of their industrial development, and perhaps of how these dangers may be avoided.

Polychlorinated biphenyls have been known to chemists for about a hundred years, and have been used in industry for half that time (Penning, 1930). They are manufactured in large amounts in the United States, in several European countries, and in Japan. They have a wide variety of uses as plasticizers in cosmetics, paints, sealers, and protective coatings. They are incorporated in electrical apparatus, and in liquid forms they are used as hydraulic fluids and in cooling systems employing transformers. It has been suggested that they could be used to extend even further the active life of persistent organochlorine insecticides! There was concern that workers exposed to them might be at risk, and safety precautions in factories have been enforced, but until 1966 no one suspected that widespread environmental contamination was resulting from their use.

In 1966, Jensen showed that previously unidentified peaks on chromatograms produced in the determination of insecticide residues in wildlife were caused by PCBs. Then he and his colleagues (Jensen *et al.*, 1969) found PCBs as well as known pesticides in a wide range of marine organisms from the Baltic, with particularly high levels (approaching 20,000 parts per million in fat) in White-tailed Eagles. There have been many other such reports from various parts of the world: for instance, by Holmes *et al.* (1967) and Prestt *et al.* (1970) from Britain; by Koeman *et al.* (1969) from the Netherlands; and by Peakall & Lincer (1970) from the United States. Other occurrences, including those in Finland (Helminen, 1970), were reported at the special PCB conference held in Stockholm in September 1970 (PCB Conference, 1970). Levels have varied widely, but have been roughly parallel with those of DDT and its metabolites, i.e. they have been highest in predators and particularly in predators of fish, such as herons. In the autumn of 1969 a serious sea-bird wreck* occurred in the Irish Sea, and in

* 'Wreck' is used here in the sense adopted by meteorologists to signify an incident where many birds died.

many of the dead sea-birds high levels of PCBs were found (Holdgate, 1971). These reached nearly 1,000 ppm in guillemots—many hundred times the 'normal background' level which we have now come to expect.

We are still not clear as to how the PCBs have entered our environment. Holden (1970) has shown that substantial amounts of them may be found in sewage sludge, and that it is probable that marine contamination arises from sewage and similar disposals and from accidental spillage from factories (*cf.* Nimmo *et al.*, 1971). It is suggested that industrial smoke and engine exhausts contribute to the levels of PCBs found in the air, as temperatures over 800°C are required for their molecular destruction. Some PCBs have been deliberately dumped at sea or into sewers, though such procedures are widely condemned by industry. But the high levels that have sometimes been found are still difficult to explain.

Although there is no doubt that PCBs are widely dispersed, and that quite high levels are found in many organisms, the actual significance of this contamination is less easy to assess. There are conflicting reports on their toxicity; this is probably in part because different workers have used different chemicals from among a large group of substances that have been lumped together as 'polychlor biphenyls'. However, it would seem that the chemicals of this group that are found in the environment are only about a tenth, or less than a tenth, as poisonous to birds as is DDT, and that Dieldrin may be as much as a hundred times as lethal as they are. Thus, though high, the levels of PCBs so far investigated would seldom seem to be high enough to be directly lethal as acute poisons.

The question of chronic toxicity is less easy to determine. Laboratory experiments have shown that PCBs at quite low levels may have sublethal effects on some animals, as do the organochlorine insecticides, and that they may affect fertility and breeding success, while effects on behaviour are also reported. The higher levels, such as those found in White-tailed Eagles and herons, are certainly of an order which could have harmful effects.

Both ecologists and industrialists have been worried by the appearance of these substances, and it may be that action is being taken *before* serious ecological damage has occurred. The Monsanto Chemical Company, the main producers, have announced their willingness to withdraw those chemicals whose use is most likely to cause pollution if other firms will do likewise.

DETERGENTS

Personal hygiene is one of the less undesirable qualities of civilized man. For generations he has used soaps, made by the reaction of alkalis with animal fat (producing, for instance, sodium stearate), to clean his skin and his garments. Most soaps, even when sophisticated and adulterated with ingredients purporting to give them additional appeal to their users, did little damage to the environment except in the highest concentrations, and soaps passing into sewage treatment-plants were normally decomposed to harmless products. Unfortunately, ordinary soaps were inefficient in 'hard' waters, and in the last fifty years have been largely replaced, at least for laundry purposes, by synthetic detergents. These, and their additives, have had marked effects on the environment.

The most spectacular effect of detergents was the production of masses of foam ('detergent swans') in turbulent rivers to which the otherwise-purified effluents of sewage works had been added (Mellanby, 1967). This was because the so-called hard detergents (e.g. sodium tetrapropylene benzene sulphonate or 'TBS') were not broken down in the manner of soaps. In recent years these hard detergents have been largely replaced by 'soft' detergents, such as sodium alkane sulphonate, which do break down; thus the foam problem is much alleviated, though some industries still prefer the hard compounds and, in parts of Yorkshire in England, certain notorious rivers do not share in the general improvement. The detergent foam was unaesthetic, but had remarkably little effect on most aquatic life, so that some rivers polluted with it were still good centres for 'coarse' fishing. In most cases, these detergents did not appear to have any long-term ecological effects.

One interesting case which, though in itself of advantage to man, shows the risks which detergents may produce, has been studied in the Netherlands (Seventer, 1970). Substantial levels of Teepol CH53 are found in the polder ditches. This is largely derived from domestic sources, with the result that the level is highest immediately after 'washing day'. Although amounts in excess of 1 ppm are found, no foam 'swans' appear in the still ditches of this flat country. The detergent is sufficiently concentrated to kill the larvae of *Anopheles* mosquitoes; in the dry July in 1969, levels rose sufficiently, because of the reduction in the dilution of the effluents, to reduce the mosquitoes almost to extinction. This appears to have contributed to the disappearance of malarial transmission from the Netherlands. So far, no harmful effects on other organisms have been detected, but it is unlikely that only mosquitoes have been damaged, and it is to be expected that other incidents of this kind will be reported or, in other circumstances, will occur without detection.

Many detergents contain optical brighteners which, in advertising parlance, make clothing treated with them 'whiter than white'. One widely-used brightener is DBT (2,5-di-[benzoxazole-2-yl] triophene). This appears not to be broken down in sewage treatment, and it is accumulated and concentrated in the fat of fish (Jensen & Pettersson, 1971). It is possible that it is a more serious environmental contaminant than has been generally realized, as it is not detected (as were the PCBS) by gas liquid chromatography.

Recently, detergents have been incriminated as contributing to the eutrophication of inland waters. A very substantial proportion of the phosphate in such waters comes from the breakdown of detergents (Owens & Wood, 1968). This has caused serious damage to many lakes and reservoirs, and the results may in some cases be irreversible. So far, replacements by new detergents low in phosphate have not been entirely successful, as some of the chemicals proposed have themselves been much more toxic than those which they were intended to replace.

It thus appears that the substitution of synthetic detergents for soap has had considerable environmental effects of kinds which were not foreseen when this apparent improvement to the armament of the housewife was made. The substances themselves have been more toxic to some organisms (so far only mosquitoes) than was foreseen. The non-biodegradable detergents produced troublesome foam on many rivers. The optical brighteners are possible long-term pollutants which may be accumulated by aquatic animals and concentrated in food-chains. Finally, the eutrophication of inland waters may be greatly accelerated by the phosphates released by detergents.

Recently, Webb & Earle (1972) have reported that detergents, particularly sodium alkylbenzene sulphonate, affect drainage of beaches—possibly by causing polymerization of the water. If indeed detergents can thus cause the production of 'anomalous water', then their possible effects on the environment are even greater than has been previously suggested.

HEAVY METALS

Environmental pollution by heavy metals is an increasingly serious problem. However, it must be realized that toxic levels of metals may often occur naturally, without any human intervention. Thus in some parts of Britain, lead occurs in the soil at such concentrations that many crops are unable to grow, and at slightly lower levels vegetable crops may take up the metal to such an extent that their consumption has to be forbidden. Lead may also contaminate water dangerously. Copper, zinc, mercury, and arsenic, are also widely dispersed naturally—not infrequently at toxic levels.

Such natural contamination may make it difficult to distinguish some cases of man-made metal pollution. Thus mercury is becoming a world-wide pollutant, though in some cases, as in fish from the open ocean, the levels found are due at least mainly to the metal occurring naturally. Nevertheless, the fact that such natural contamination does occur should not be allowed to divert attention from the possible effects of heavy-metal pollution arising from man's activities.

Man introduces mercury into his environment in many ways. Until recently, 'calomel' (Hg_2Cl_2) was used widely as a purgative, and its prescription is still sanctioned by most pharmacopoeias. Hg_2Cl_2 is, clearly, comparatively non-toxic, but danger could arise from its wide use and subsequent turning, by bacterial action in sewage sludge, into very poisonous methyl-mercury compounds. Fortunately, mercury in any form is now little used in human medicine, so that this form of pollution is likely to decrease.

Organomercury compounds have been used widely as fungicides, particularly as seed dressings. This is a case of their use as pesticides, which is not my subject. It is sufficient, therefore, to say that in Sweden there is good evidence that methyl-mercury seed dressings have poisoned seed-eating birds and have seriously affected their predators (Borg et al., 1969), though in Britain there is little evidence of damage from organomercury seed dressings—perhaps because less-toxic phenyl-mercury compounds have generally been used there (Mellanby, 1967).

Serious pollution has occurred from the presence of mercury in industrial effluents, particularly from the wood-pulp industry (e.g. in Canada, see Fimreite, 1970). Such mercury can be concentrated by freshwater and estuarine fish and molluscs, and fatal cases of poisoning of man after eating these animals have been reported. The ability of natural systems to transform comparatively non-toxic inorganic salts into such extremely poisonous and persistent substances as methyl-mercury compounds makes the control of mercury levels in all effluents something that deserves the highest priority.

Lead poisoning of man and of domestic animals is serious and widespread (Anon., 1969; Chisholm, 1971). The commonest cases in humans are among children in slum areas, and the source has been from old and flaking paint-work. Recently, much concern has been expressed about lead from motor-car exhausts, derived from tetraethyl lead used as a petrol additive (US Public Health Service, 1965; Air Pollution and Health, 1970). There is no doubt that the soil near highways can become contaminated, and quite high levels of lead (e.g. 500 ppm of dry-weight) are found in the vegetation of roadside verges. Such materials could be harmful if consumed. Crops grown for human consumption adjacent to roads might be seriously contaminated, but in practice the levels in lettuce (which is particularly efficient at taking up lead) have not been found to reach an obviously dangerous level. Most observations on men exposed to high intensities of car-exhaust gases suggest that they are not harmfully affected by lead, though not all authorities agree, and the effects on children are being subjected to further intensive investigation.

Many would agree that lead poisoning is such a serious possibility that greater efforts should be made to eliminate all possible sources, including that from petrol additives. Others consider that the improvement in automobile performance from these additives outweighs the disadvantage of possible, but generally unproven, dangers. I would wish to dissociate myself from this latter viewpoint.

EUTROPHICATION CAUSED BY FERTILIZERS

World-wide agricultural productivity has increased with the greater use of chemical fertilizers—particularly of nitrogenous compounds. This widespread and often excessive application of fertilizers has given rise to environmental damage by its acceleration of the eutrophication of many inland lakes and rivers—particularly from the use of nitrates which, instead of being taken up by the plants, are leached out of, or washed off, the surface of the soil.

Commoner (1970) has reviewed the situation in the United States of America. He has shown that in many areas rises in nitrate levels in inland waters can be directly related to increases in fertilizer application in the surrounding arable land. This has been demonstrated for the Missouri river, enriched by the farmlands of Nebraska, and for rivers in Illinois. Commoner discusses the importance of sewage and fertilizers in this connection, and shows that the latter make by far the greatest contribution.

Though Commoner's (1970) data indicate a close correlation between fertilizer application and nitrate levels in ground-water and rivers, others have suggested that the relation is much more complicated. Thus Tomlinson (1968) has studied fertilizer application in the catchment areas of seventeen British catchment areas and river systems. Though there were rises in nitrate levels in many rivers in the period 1955 to 1968, these rises seemed, in many cases, to bear no direct relation to fertilizer use. Owens & Wood (1968) indicate that the rise in river nitrogen comes mainly from arable land, though the intensity of cultivation, rather than the actual local use of nitrogenous fertilizer, seems to have the greatest effect on the constitution of the run-off water. As, however, there is almost invariably an increase in fertilizer use when more arable crops are grown, and as less than 50 per cent of the nitrogen applied is recovered in the crops, the long-term increase in nitrate levels in inland waters almost certainly arises mainly from the wasteful use of these chemicals.

Eutrophication, the process in which the levels of nutrient salts in water are increased, is not always harmful. It occurs naturally as a river, derived from relatively 'pure' rain-water, with a paucity of salts in solution, runs down from the hills and picks up salts that have been leached from the land through which it flows. The levels of salts in the water largely control the typical vegetation found in natural waters. Man-made eutrophication may be more rapid and may promote undesirable algal blooms which may harm the whole system, though when properly controlled, as in a fish-pond, eutrophication can lead to increased food production. Under some circumstances, algal blooms seem to be triggered off by increased concentrations of phosphates, arising from the residues of detergents in sewage (see pp. 339–40). At other times, nitrates derived from fertilizers cause the trouble. A balanced nutrient medium is obviously required, and it is impossible to generalize as to which substance causes most damage. If the water is naturally well-supplied with phosphate, additional nitrates may produce dramatic effects. If nitrates are present in adequate amounts, additional phosphate will trigger off the algal development. Often we find nutrients at levels where damage might be expected, but where it does not occur. This happens in lakes where there is a balanced system, and when grazing animals (e.g. crustaceans such as *Daphnia*) keep the Algae in check. In such cases the accidental contamination of the lake by persistent pesticides may kill off the Crustacea and allow a severe and harmful algal bloom to take place (Bays, 1971).

When we know that the cause of damage is some particular chemical, we know how to control the damage. Unfortunately in the case of fertilizers, world-wide changes in agricultural practice are all contributing to an increase in conditions which are likely to make the situation worse. Therefore there are those who consider that this may be the most serious case of the unwise use of chemicals, and certainly greater efforts should be made to ensure the more efficient use of such agricultural chemicals—in the interests of economy as well as to try to obviate a particularly dangerous form of pollution which is ruining, for mankind and nature, so many of the world's finest inland waters as well as countless others.

CONCLUSIONS

In conclusion, I would like to try to consider this whole question of the use of chemicals, and their possible harmful effects, in proper perspective. We see once again that we have to consider the whole world as a unit; abuses in one area may have their effects in distant parts of the globe. We see also that it is by ecological studies of whole systems, as well as of particular animals or plants, that we can sometimes discover that chemicals are having an effect on the environment. We obviously wish always to act before serious damage has occurred, and so we must try to anticipate such damage.

The idea that a chemical is 'safe' until it has been proved dangerous must be avoided; no new chemical, particularly a persistent chemical, should be allowed to be used at all widely until it has been shown to be safe. We know that we must exercise particular care with any substance which is toxic, persistent, and more readily soluble in fat than in water. We therefore need some system which will prevent such a chemical, if it is used for example in a novel industrial process, from being produced in large quantities if it is toxic and likely to become a dangerous environmental pollutant. I have described how a possible global danger from the polychlorinated biphenyls can be avoided by cooperation between ecologists and industry.

For the future, we need some organization which can ensure even closer liaison to prevent, if possible, such contamination from occurring at all. Something that works, on a global scale, in a manner similar to the British Pesticides Safety Precautions Scheme, but which copes with *all* industrial processes, is envisaged. The Pesticides Safety Precautions Scheme considers confidentially the data provided by industry about any new pesticide chemical, and its independent scientists, who include ecologists, have to be satisfied as to the safety of the product before a particular use is approved. This scheme has been a remarkable success, for so far as we know it is only in Britain that the populations of predatory birds, which had become so seriously diminished as a result of the unwise use of organochlorine insecticides (particularly Dieldrin seed-dressing) have made a significant recovery. I consider that it could serve as a model for an international 'watchdog' to control possible pollution from all industrial sources.

Poisonous chemicals occur naturally throughout the world. Some of these are at dangerous levels; more often they are too dilute to do any damage. In the same ways the products of industry are not necessarily damaging the environment when our skilful chemists can detect their presence in minute amounts. Often such analyses, which may be quoted as evidence of danger, are in fact evidence that dangerous levels have not been so much as approached.

Some ecologists harm their cause by overstating their case, and by condemning any industrial development—even if they do not hesitate to make use of the products of that industry! We need to recognize real risks, and to concentrate on eliminating them, while at the same time using our technology properly for the benefit of mankind.

REFERENCES

AIR POLLUTION AND HEALTH (1970). *Report by the Committee of the Royal College of Physicians of London.* Pitman, London: 80 pp.

ANON. (1969). Lead astray? *Fd Cosmet. Toxicol.,* **7**, pp. 255–60.

BAYS, L. R. (1971). Pesticide pollution and the effects on the biota of Chew Valley Lake. *Environmental Pollution,* **1**(3), pp. 205–34.

BORG, K., WANNTORP, H., ERNE, K. & HANKO, E. (1969). Alkyl mercury poisoning in terrestrial Swedish wildlife. *Viltrevy,* **6**(4), pp. 301–79.

CHISHOLM, J. J. (1971). Lead poisoning. *Scient. Amer.,* **224**(2), pp. 15–23.

COMMONER, B. (1970). Threats to the integrity of the nitrogen cycle: nitrogen compounds in soil, water, atmosphere and precipitation. Pp. 70–95 in *Global Effects of Environmental Pollution* (Ed. S. Fred Singer). D. Reidel, Dordrecht: 218 pp.

FIMREITE, N. (1970). Mercury uses in Canada and their possible hazards as sources of mercury contamination. *Environmental Pollution*, **1**(2), pp. 119–31.

HELMINEN, M. (1970). PCB-experiences in Finland. Pp. 26–8 in PCB CONFERENCE, National Swedish Environment Protection Board, Stockholm, 100 pp. (mimeographed).

HOLDEN, A. V. (1970). Source of polychlorinated biphenyl contamination in the marine environment. *Nature* (London), **228**, pp. 1220–1.

HOLDGATE, M. W. (Ed.) (1971). The sea-bird wreck of 1969 in the Irish Sea. Supplement: analytical and other data. *Natural Environment Research Council Publications*, Series C, No. 4, Suppl. pp. 1–18.

HOLMES, D. C., SIMMONS, J. H. & TATTON, J. O. G. (1967). Chlorinated hydrocarbons in British wildlife. *Nature* (London), **216**, pp. 227–9.

JENSEN, S. (1966). Report of a new chemical hazard. *New Scient.*, **32**, p. 612.

JENSEN, S., JOHNELS, A. G., OLSSON, M. & OTTELIN, G. (1969). DDT and PCB in marine animals from Swedish waters. *Nature* (London), **224**, pp. 247–50.

JENSEN, S. & PETTERSSON, O. (1971). 2,5-di-(benzoxazole-2-yl) thiophene, an optical brightener contaminating sludge and fish. *Environmental Pollution*, **2**(2), pp. 145–55.

KOEMAN, J. H., BRAUW, M. C. ten Noever de & VOX, R. H. DE (1969). Chlorinated biphenyls in fish, mussels and birds from the River Rhine and the Netherlands coastal area. *Nature* (London), **221**, pp. 1126–8.

MELLANBY, K. (1967). *Pesticides and Pollution*. Collins (The New Naturalist), London: 221 pp., illustr.

NIMMO, D. R., WILSON, P. D., BLACKMAN, R. R. & WILSON, A. J. (1971). Polychlorinated biphenyl absorbed from sediments by fiddler crabs and pink shrimp. *Nature* (London), **231**, pp. 50–2.

OWENS, M. & WOOD, G. (1968). Some aspects of the eutrophication of water. *Water Res.*, **2**, 151–9.

PCB CONFERENCE (1970). National Swedish Environment Protection Board, Stockholm,; 100 pp. (mimeographed).

PEAKALL, D. B. & LINCER, J. L. (1970). Polychlorinated biphenyls. Another long-life widespread chemical in the environment. *BioScience* (Washington, DC), **20**(17), pp. 958–64.

PENNING, C. H. (1930). Physical characteristics and commercial possibilities of chlorinated diphenyl. *Ind. Eng. Chem.*, **22**, pp. 1180–2.

PRESTT, I., JEFFERIES, D. J. & MOORE, N. W. (1970). Polychlorinated biphenyls in wild birds in Britain and their avian toxicity. *Environmental Pollution*, **1**(1), pp. 3–26.

SEVENTER, H. A. VAN (1970). Anionic detergent and chlorine concentrations in polder ditches in a former malarious area. *Environmental Pollution*, **1**(2), pp. 105–17.

TOMLINSON, T. E. (1968). *Nitrate contents of English Rivers*. ICI Agricultural Division, Research and Development Department, Bracknell, Berks: 14 pp. (mimeographed).

US PUBLIC HEALTH SERVICE (1965). *Survey of Lead in the Atmosphere of Three Urban Communities*. US Government Printing Office, Washington, DC: 99 pp.

van SEVENTER, H. A. *See* SEVENTER, H. A. van

WEBB, J. E. & EARLE, C. M. (1972). Possible polymerization of water by sodium alkylbenzene sulphonate. *Environmental Pollution*, **3**(2) (*in press*).

DISCUSSION

Mikola (Chairman)

I would like to compliment Dr Mellanby for the elegant way in which he gave his very interesting paper and, before leaving the discussion free, to make some opening remarks. As Dr Mellanby mentioned, the problem of unwise use of chemicals is so wide that it may be impossible to give a complete review of the whole subject, and therefore in his paper he concentrated on some illustrative examples, namely polychlorinated biphenyls, heavy metals, detergents, and fertilizers.

One fact which I particularly noticed was how rapidly problems can arise, but also how rapidly we can act when necessary. Polychlorinated biphenyls had been known and used for several decades, but it was only about five years ago that their harmful side-effects as environmental pollutants were first detected. Today these side-effects are under intensive research all over the world and, as an outcome, numerous scientific papers have already been published on them in these last years. Remedial measures are also under way and can be expected in the near future. As Dr Mellanby mentioned, the main producer of these substances is willing to stop their production if only other producers will do the same, so that in this case effective action will very probably be taken before any serious ecological damage has occurred.

These examples also show that one necessary prerequisite for effective monitoring and control of environmental pollutants is available, namely analytical methods. Thanks to recent developments in analytical chemistry, today extremely minute concentrations of almost all kinds of substances can be determined, which was not possible even a few years ago. Thus, the skill of modern chemists gives us some hope that the occurrence of potential pollutants in our environment can be continuously observed, and that appropriate counter-measures can be taken before concentrations reach dangerous levels.

Another aspect which I would like to point out in Dr Mellanby's paper is that he spoke on *wise* and *unwise* use of chemicals. Any chemical can be used wisely and unwisely, or in other words, as we used to say in Finland, even oatmeal is poisonous if you eat too much of it. The difficulty is to know which use is wise and which is unwise, or to find out where is the boundary between wise and unwise use. I think that if this question could always be answered, many of our environmental problems would be solved rather easily. Let us take fertilizers as an example. The day before yesterday several speakers mentioned the 'green revolution', which involves liberal application of fertilizers, and questioned whether it is good or bad. We must admit that the 'green revolution' has saved millions of people from starvation or near-starvation and, accordingly, chemical fertilizers have to that extent been beneficial. But, as we have heard, fertilizers may have harmful side-effects, such as eutrophication of lakes, rivers, and even seas. In regard to such harmful side-effects, there is not only a question of the amount of fertilizers which are used, but as much or even more of the kinds of fertilizers and the techniques of using them. We cannot very well reduce the application of fertilizers in the world at the present time, but we must try to develop new kinds of them and improve the techniques of application in order to maximize the benefit of using fertilizers and to minimize their undesirable side-effects.

Now the subject is open for disccussion, and I'd like first to call Mr Mahler, the representative of FAO, which is the United Nations agency most concerned with these matters.

Mahler

Thank you, Mr Chairman, I think you have stressed most of the points I wanted to make. However, I feel that fertilizers are a minor contribution to eutrophication of lakes*. We have actually still very few data in this respect, but we are undertaking studies on the problem in FAO. However, from the information we have so far, it seems that the nitrates which participate in the eutrophication of lakes mostly come from sewage and from cattle feed-lots, and that nitrogen from fertilizers is only a small fraction of the nitrogen causing the eutrophication. Moreover, when nitrates cause eutrophication it can be from run-off, so that the problem is not with the fertilizer but with the control of soil erosion. With regard to phosphates, well, we know that almost all the phosphate in the soil is insoluble, and again, if phosphates reach the lakes it is because of erosion; so once more the need is for a measure of soil conservation, but certainly not any restriction in the use of fertilizers. Finally, most of the phosphates causing eutrophication of a lake come from detergents, so altogether I am somewhat reluctant to see fertilizers put in the list of pollutants together with polychlorinated biphenyls and heavy metals. Rightly the speaker has placed them at the very end; but I still wonder whether they should be even there.

Goldman

I thought I had said enough yesterday, and therefore resolved to be quiet today! But I've become fearful, particularly after the last speaker, and to some extent from last night and earlier this morning. Nobody seems to be responsible for anything when it comes to these tricky questions of environment: it's always the other guy! And somehow the fear I have is that this attitude will be carried over to next year in Stockholm. Nobody, it seems to me, will ever acknowledge that his activities or his department or the people he is associated with ever contribute in any way to pollution or, if they do contribute, that it is more than a very small portion of the problem. Somehow the problem always comes from some larger interest outside one's own. If we're ever going to do anything effective about the environment or environmental pollution or destruction, I think we have to acknowledge that we are all involved. It's important, of course, to assess proper responsibility; but I fear we shall get nowhere if we keep saying, 'Well, you are looking in the wrong direction if you look at me'. In some cases, of course, there have been mistakes and there's good room for argument; but if we consistently say that we

* The figures given by FAO show a remarkable rise in recent decades in the application of fertilizers as plant foods. Thus in the world (apart from mainland China, North Korea, and North Vietnam) there were applied in 1930–31 some 1,499,000 tons of nitrogen, 2,986,000 tons of P_2O_5, and 1,959,000 tons of K_2O—a total of 6,444,000 tons. In 1969–70 the corresponding figures were 25,620,000 tons of N, 17,820,000 tons of P_2O_5, and 15,520,000 tons of K_2O—a total of 58,960,000 tons in all. These figures were sent to us by the Director-General of F.A.O., Dr A. H. Boerma (*in litt.* 30 November 1971), and are all in metric tons (tonnes); we might comment that even the human population had not increased at anything like such a rate!—Ed.

must have all kinds of artificial fertilizers, we must have all kinds of pesticides, we must have all kinds of population, then nobody is responsible, nobody is going to take the first step towards remedy, and I'm sure we're not going to get very far. Therefore, I have fears for the results of next year, and some doubts even about the outcome of our deliberations this year.

Mellanby

Quite frankly, I don't understand what Dr Goldman is talking about. Obviously we are all of us to blame, and we've been trying to say what we want to do by introducing some kind of a system. Every time we visit the lavatory we contribute to pollution, of course we do, but we don't all want to be permanently constipated. So I don't see really how every country can take the blame for what everybody is doing, when we are all of us to blame, though I'm not quite sure what it is we are supposed to do about this situation.

Goldman

Perhaps I didn't make myself as clear as I should have done. Really, I wasn't referring directly to Dr Mellanby, though maybe he should be involved as much as I should be. But in these matters of personal reactions it's interesting to see what is going on in the United States today. There may be a certain tendency to change one's mind after one loses power, but we've noticed that, especially in military questions having to do with Vietnam, the moment one is out of office one naturally changes one's attitude. And Mr Udall mentioned the other day that some of his positions have changed 180° from what they were before. Well, one of the things I think it's important for us to do is to be self-critical, to analyse our own situation. And if our governments, if our organizations, if our countries, are doing things that deserve to be criticized, or if there are questions about what they are doing, I think it's important to bring this out into the open—to recognize this situation ourselves, and to acknowledge it.

One of the most interesting things about the United States today is the degree of self-criticism. This may be an unfair sample of mostly outstanding Americans that you have in the group here, but almost all of them are critical of what is being done in their country—by themselves, by the government, by industry, by agriculture. And I think one of the most remarkable developments which we have not properly acknowledged is that as a result of this criticism the government is beginning in a sense to respond—not as much as it should, not as much as we'd like, but it is responding. An important instance to recognize is what has happened with our SSTs. This is a remarkable phenomenon, but if you had asked me two months ago, last year, or five or more years ago, whether the Congress of the United States, under pressure from some of the people in this hall, would have said, 'We will not produce the SST, we are going to cut back on the millions of dollars that have already been spent, and just let them go to waste', I would have bet that this would never happen. And I doubt if anybody here, even the strongest defenders of the environment, would have dared to bet otherwise. The point that I'm trying to make is that we all have vested interests, but that it's important to recognize them, because the environment is bigger than our particular vested interest, and surely bigger than all of our interests put together.

E.F.—12*

So I wish and I would hope that all peoples, not just those in the United States, not just those in England or France or the Soviet Union or wherever the problem may be, but all peoples everywhere, would have the integrity and the love of self to stand up when necessary and ask the simple question: Am I doing the wrong thing? This is what I am referring to. As you sit in the audience through all of these talks, and through wider relays elsewhere, I would like you to know that I hate to pick on the FAO, when in some directions they've done a very good job; but every time something is wrong their representative stands up and he says, well, it's not the FAO, we've got to have this, and there are these problems. And earlier the same defence came repeatedly from the World Meteorological Organization, and I could name some others. It's just that, having gone through three days of hearing such things, I'm reacting this way and I apologize for becoming emotional about it. But, you know, nobody is responsible, and yet we are all responsible—we have to face up to it. I'm sorry, but there it is. Yet the sooner the United Nations outfits come down to earth and start looking at themselves critically in the light of the latest scientific and other information, abandoning the attitude that they are the sole doers and arbiters and nobody else must be allowed in, the better it will be for the rest of us and, I would like to think, for themselves in the long run. In this I concur wholly with Professor Polunin.

Greve

In the Netherlands National Institute of Public Health we have been working for some time on surface waters and have found that the pollution especially of pesticides in them is not attributable in the first place to agriculture but rather to industry. So if we are going to do something about it, we feel that we must invest not only money but also in manpower and the use of knowledge. To get rid of these pesticides we have to act not so much where they are applied as where they are synthesized and formulated. The main pollutants in our part of the River Rhine are not at all as in America, namely DDT and derivatives, but α- and γ-benzenehexachlorides and hexachlorobenzene, so we feel that our problem is mainly an industrial one. This is the case also in some other western European countries.

I would also like to add that among the so-called non-persistent pesticides, the phosphorous derivatives are much more persistent in surface waters than in plants or animals. They are actually found in significant amounts in the Rhine and its tributaries. Also, regarding carcinogenesis of members of the DDT family, experiments done in the Netherlands indicate that in fact o.p'-DDD is an anti-tumour agent.

Mellanby

One point about industrial pollution in Britain is exemplified by a particular factory I know of on a river which was notorious for the amount of pollution it received from insecticides coming from this factory. A new manager was appointed who is chairman of the local Salmon and Trout Fishing Society and is himself a keen fisherman. Since then there has never been another pollution incident: therefore, give the manager of every chemical factory that makes pesticides a fishing rod and you'll have no more trouble!

Butler

Dr Mellanby's formula for the correction of erring commercial enterprises brings to mind two cases in which its application could have been most useful and interesting. You may have heard that in Canada we have a mercury pollution problem, and in one river this was caused by chlor-alkali plants which used mercury as one of the electrodes in an electrolytic process. When the situation was investigated it was found that there was somebody in this plant who knew from its inventory that it was losing ten kilograms of mercury a day, which amounts to a great deal of mercury in two hundred operating days in each year. Yet nobody thought of telling anybody in authority.

Another case is now documented: it's apparently the first recorded one of poisoning of humans by polychlorinated biphenyls. In Japan there is a plant that makes rice-oil by pressing rice in a hydraulic press, and in this case the hydraulic liquid is a polychlorinated biphenyl. When the press developed a leak, the hydraulic liquid found its way into the rice-oil, causing an epidemic of poisoning by polychlorinated biphenyls. Some men in that plant must have known from the inventory that they were losing polychlorinated biphenyl at a certain rate every day, but nobody said anything. This is something for Dr Goldman to think about: there was at least one man in that plant who knew precisely what was going on: but his job was to run the plant, and not to cause any trouble. Yet this kind of thing is probably the basis of a lot of environmental trouble.

Polunin (Jr)

We should not forget that science also can withhold known facts or otherwise mislead the ways of industry. Thus it appears that whereas it used to be said that nitrates are the leading cause of the effect of over-fertilization which is now generally referred to as eutrophication, more recently it became the stated (or anyway quoted) view of research workers that phosphorus compounds could be more important in this, and so industrial concerns were persuaded to produce detergents with no or little phosphorus. Now we are being told that in marine environments, particularly, it is after all nitrogen which is the more limiting, and that this can also be the case in some fresh waters. So what are the industrialists to believe, who are often striving to do the best they can for the public and the environment? Please don't think I claim to have any specialist knowledge in these matters: I merely dug this one out of the *Scientific American*, and would hope we can hear from those who really know*. But there are doubtless other such instances of scientific vacillation misleading industry and the general public, albeit unintentionally.

Mellanby

This is just a short comment: another problem which has occurred in some cases is that, in the attempt to produce a phosphorus-low detergent, we have been faced with substances that have at times been marketed but are in fact

* *See* the explanations given next by Dr Mellanby and subsequently by Professor Vallentyne (p. 352), and also the portion headed 'Eutrophication caused by Fertilizers' (pp. 341–2) of Dr Mellanby's final paper which he kindly expanded in this respect at our request.—Ed.

more acutely toxic than the original substances. In this kind of thing one has to be extremely careful. The question of what is causing eutrophication—whether phosphate or nitrate is the more important—is, I think, one that is practically unanswerable because under certain circumstances there is no doubt that one causes it when there is a shortage of one element, whereas in other cases there is a shortage of the other, so that one can never say dogmatically that one is the baddie, and the other is the goodie. They are both baddies under some circumstances, they are both goodies under other circumstances, and it's a terribly complicated question. But unless you have both present at a certain level you'll not get any trouble. This is the one obvious truth.

Wurster

With regard to the comments from the Netherlands, I should mention that there are materials which tend to induce tumours but inhibit the development of those same tumours—in other words, carcinogens are often tumour-allaying. DDD was mentioned as an anti-tumour agent, and DDT can be the same, but that doesn't make them anti-canceral materials; they merely inhibit the development of a tumour after inducing it.

As for the effluents from chlorinated hydrocarbon plants causing problems in the Netherlands, apparently such plants are characterized by bad effluents, and we have the same problems in the United States. The prime one has been caused by the Montrose Chemical Corporation in Los Angeles, which is the world's largest plant manufacturing DDT. For many years they have had the habit of discharging between 500 and 1000 pounds of DDT daily. into the Los Angeles sewer system, which then flows to the sewage treatment plant and into the Pacific Ocean. This has been going on for many years, and is responsible among other things for the story that you've heard about the pelicans of the California coast laying omelettes instead of eggs. Last year the Environmental Defense Fund, with which I am associated, brought suit in the Federal Court against Montrose, and this convinced them that the thing to do was to clean up; now they have stopped this effluent and the case has been dismissed from the Court.

As for Professor Laird's earlier strictures, unfortunately there is not time to deal with them all now but I should say that, far from neglecting literature, I had great difficulty in boiling down my original reference material to something that would be both manageable and within the limits I was set. What remains is chiefly that published in recognized journals by recognized scientists all over the world, and is surely deep. I could have used an entirely different set of references to support practically all the statements in my paper. What I would now like is the references in support of some of Professor Laird's statements, such as the one that the tests show DDT to have been present in soils collected in 1910*. When people come along and say there is DDT in those soils, they are merely demonstrating that they don't know how to run the analysis. There was no DDT present in the world environment prior to the 1940s.

Now concerning the carcinogenesis of DDT, this substance has not been demonstrated to be a human carcinogen although there are findings which

* *See* page 316.—Ed.

show that some people who died of cancer had from two to three times as much DDT in their adipose tissues as had those who died from other causes. But, while suggestive, this still does not prove a cause-and-effect relationship. Yet although we have not proven such a relationship, repeatedly, in different laboratories in different parts of the world, DDT has caused cancer in experimental animals. The burden of proving that DDT is not a carcinogen accordingly lies with Professor Laird, not with me. The *prima facie* case has been made that DDT is a carcinogen, and so we should regard it until it's proven to be otherwise.

Miller

It's been eighteen months since the IUCN at their Tenth General Assembly in New Delhi passed a resolution urging an immediate ban on the use of DDT, with the implication that this should be extended to some related poisons. But this was only after a countryman of mine, representing the Government of the United States, had interceded to make sure that a clause was included to the effect that this ban should be operative 'except for emergency human health purposes'. We fight this battle over and over again in different forms, and I think that one of the opportunities of a forum such as this is to advocate possible means of action based on the better data from which we have to operate. We are all arguing here for the sake of environment, of which public health is a segment, and agreeing, I hope, that the environment of the planet and of all the organisms on it is the main concern of the future.

Some of the proponents of DDT seem actually to be advocating that we consider public health as the primary concern; it has been a good tool for their mission, whether of FAO or WHO, in India or in Holland, and these are very valid things to fight for. But I would like to suggest that, because we all have the larger view as well, we leave some of that battle for those who are being paid to wage it. I doubt whether anybody speaking here is being paid to advocate that industry continue to produce a poison which shows up in so many places in the world as anti-life. I feel that what we must think about is the striking fact that, as Professor Polunin indicated, all manner of people were invited and encouraged here to represent the producers of various environmental poisons, but they didn't come. The last one I saw was at the New Delhi meeting—the representative of the Shell Corporation, a worldwide producer of various kinds of chemicals. These people have no entity; when they come to us it is merely as public relations people, so perhaps it's just as well that they didn't come here. It's as though their mouths say, 'Oh, everything is fine, I feel fine today'; but inside the stomach or some other place they are saying, 'I'm sick, sick, sick . . . ,' because one part is going on saying something and the other part is actually producing something else. What I feel is that even if we had representatives of industries here to speak it would be in their 'public relations' capacities. This is a part of the credibility or incredibility that we have to face in modern corporations, and though I used to think it was the American corporations that were this way, I now believe the disease is world-wide.

Yet I think we must realize that we are all culpable to some degree. For as has been brought out by previous speakers, whether we want to look at it philosophically or practically, we are all part of the same general problem, and part of the solution is to change our ways after some internal viewing and appropriate soul-searching. As Dr Goldman said, it's love of self that ought to be considered here: if we love ourselves we are not going to be the servants of somebody else, we are not going to be slaves. At least we should see that money does not go to corporations that have no proper concern, and meanwhile we should speak about these matters uninhibitedly in such a free atmosphere as this. And even if our recommendations are not based on exhaustive fact, but on many truths and a widespread conviction, they will speak on behalf of humanity. As a counter-measure, we shall be causing industry to pay people to come to our meetings, and pay them doubtless extremely well—they'll pay for advertising, they'll pay for representation and much costly travel—which will have the one advantage for us of raising the cost of their products. Hopefully, they'll raise the cost of DDT to the point where the manufacturers will gladly produce an alternative, which is certainly within their power. Then we'll have accomplished our purpose. Indeed if we look at the whole structure of industry and commerce, we see that it is easy to produce something as long as there is a ready and submissive market for it, but that matters change when the market becomes difficult for any reason—wherein I think could lie the solution to many of our environmental problems.

Mellanby

Could I just have one word? I don't think we want industry merely giving industry's views—we've come here to speak the truth. I hope everyone is speaking the truth; for not all people who call themselves conservationists and environmentalists speak the truth. It's unfortunate, but it's the case.

Vallentyne

I just wanted to make a comment on the point that Nicholas Polunin, Jr, contributed concerning the relative importance of nitrogen and phosphorus in causing eutrophication. In most instances in fresh water, phosphorus is a little more limiting, sometimes quite a bit more, than nitrogen. In the sea it's the other way around: but in both environments, if you want to cause eutrophication, you have to have both these elements, as Dr Mellanby indicated. The question concerning phosphorus and eutrophication is one of control. We have a technology that's available for phosphorus removal, and most people think it is sufficient to reduce the phosphorus levels to control plant growth—that even if phosphorus is not a limiting element in an aquatic environment it can be made so, whereas nitrogen cannot. So if you really want to cause eutrophication, you need both phosphorus and nitrogen, and if you want to control it, the only technology available is through phosphorus.

Regarding the substitute for phosphorus that is under discussion, NTA, I think it's a compound which has been very extensively tested by industry and by governments, and about which there is a good deal of information to go on at the present time. So I think that, in relation to this particular compound, the environmental testing that has been done shows science in a very promising light for the future.

Mikola (Chairman)

I have just received a message from Professor Polunin to the effect that news has been received that the three Russian astronauts have died after twenty-five days in space. May I ask you to carry out the suggestion that the entire Conference express our deep sorrow for this tragic accident by observing a three minutes' silence and then sending an appropriate cable to the Soviet Government.

[After observance of the silence, the Chairman closed the session with an expression of thanks to Dr Mellanby for his 'valuable introduction and comments, and to all who contributed to the discussion on this very important subject'. He also suggested that, as there were a number of people who evidently desired to continue the discussion further, this might be done at or after the resumed session on pesticides on the same night—the two topics being in any case scarcely separable.]

ADDENDUM

Statement on Nuclear Energy

Circulated to the Conference by G. I. APOLLONOV,
International Atomic Energy Agency Observer

Environmental problems are of growing concern to the whole of mankind. The impact of modern society's activities on the environment is well and fully demonstrated by the deliberations of this Conference.

Among them we must not neglect nuclear energy, which is part of our life today. It has ceased to be the realm of scientists and has become an important contribution to development and progress towards a better life for the whole population of the earth.

Development and environment are linked in one chain, and the fact that the development of peaceful uses of nuclear energy went alongside the development of measures for protection of the environment, sets a good example for other technologies. To judge the impact of nuclear energy on the environment in its true perspective, one must have in mind the following considerations:

1. It is true that nuclear energy is one of the man-made sources of radiation. No less true, however, is the fact that the radiation to which man is exposed by using nuclear energy for peaceful purposes is only a very small fraction of the radiation he receives from the natural background.

2. Radiation caused by the peaceful applications of nuclear energy presents a minor environmental problem in comparison with the effects of other technologies and industries—for instance, the chemical industry, insecticides, combustion products of cars, etc.

3. Nuclear energy presents a practical way out of the gloomy perspective facing the world with regard to the lack of energy sources and the rapidly growing need for energy.

In the IAEA booklet distributed here at the Conference—'Nuclear Energy and the Environment'—it is pointed out that, by the year 2000, energy consumption will probably have increased to four times, and electricity production to eight times, the amounts used in 1970.

By providing an alternative to fossil fuels, nuclear energy will diminish pollution and contribute to a cleaner environment. The Symposium on Environmental Aspects of Nuclear Power Stations, held in August 1970, concluded that nuclear power stations contribute far less to environmental degradation than do other forms of power production. However, this does not mean that nuclear energy is not facing certain problems. One of them is the management and safe disposal of radioactive wastes. The IAEA is devoting its efforts towards the solution of this problem, and we are sure that consolidated work towards this end at the national and international levels will be fruitful.

As I mentioned before, the development of the nuclear industry went alongside the development of measures for the protection and preservation of the environment. A few examples of this will follow.

Since 1958, the IAEA has issued thirty-six guidebooks giving standards designed to ensure safety, from the environmental point of view, for every kind of activity where nuclear energy is used for peaceful purposes. This work was carried out in collaboration with the World Health Organization, and the standards and guides, based on the most authoritative advice, were compiled jointly by IAEA and WHO, and addressed to member states under the joint sponsorship of these two organizations.

A number of these standards have also been sponsored by other specialized agencies, such as the International Labour Organization and the Inter-Governmental Maritime Consultative Organization. All questions relating to the impact of radiation on man's food resources are dealt with internationally by the Joint FAO/IAEA Division of Atomic Energy in Food and Agriculture. The 1970 decision of the United Nations Scientific Committee on the Effects of Atomic Radiation—UNSCEAR—to devote more attention in future to the peaceful uses of atomic energy, is leading to a further strengthening of the excellent working-level cooperation that has already existed for more than a decade between IAEA and UNSCEAR. The Agency is preparing for active participation in the Conference on the Human Environment, to be held in Stockholm in 1972. A number of our contributions to the conference papers have already been prepared and sent to the secretariat.

We have also been actively promoting research through coordinated programmes of contracts and through the Monaco Laboratory on Marine Radioactivity since 1961. UNESCO and FAO are now also participating in the work of that Laboratory. We have promoted the exchange of information in the course of twenty-three symposia and about four times that number of smaller meetings on radiation and environmental questions during the last ten years. Together with WMO, we have set up a world-wide sampling network to measure radioactivity in rain, snow, and other forms of precipitation, and together with UNESCO we have done the same thing with regard to the world's major rivers. We have arranged safety reviews for a dozen nuclear reactors and helped member states to select locations for about the same number of nuclear plants. A substantial part of IAEA's technical assistance programme is designed to help developing countries to introduce nuclear energy safely and with the minimum of environmental impact. Altogether, the Agency's environmental and related activities represent an expenditure each year of more than one million dollars, or about 7 per cent of our current budget. To this total must be added the complementary activities of WHO, ILO, etc.

Nuclear techniques are being increasingly used as a means of combating the environmental impact of *other* technologies and industries. They are used, for instance, to measure pollution of the atmosphere, to follow the movement of sewage in rivers and in the sea, and to follow the path and test the effects of food additives and chemical pesticides. In certain cases, they are providing an alternative means of insect control.

11

SOIL PRESERVATION

Keynote Paper

The World's Soils and
Human Activity

by

V. A. KOVDA*

President, International Society of Soil Science;
Director, Institute of Agrochemistry and Soil Science, and
Corresponding Member, Academy of Sciences of the USSR;
Professor, Subfaculty of Pedology,
Moscow State University, Moscow V–234, USSR.

* Presented by Professor Vladimir Nikolaivich Kunin, Corresponding Member of the Academy of Sciences of the USSR and Vice-Chairman of their Scientific Council on Environment, as well as Scientific Adviser to the United Nations Conference on the Human Environment, who explained the absence of his friend, Professor Kovda, on an urgent mission in Rome: 'He cannot be in three places'.

Soils as a Component of the Biosphere

The soils of the world's land areas, together with the bottoms of the seas and lakes of planet earth, form a specific biogeochemical sphere. As a product of the continuous interactions of living matter and the earth's crust, the soils and their counterparts in the hydrosphere represent a zone of concentration: of different living organisms, of the products of their metabolism, and of their remains. The living organisms (plants, animals, microbiota) and other components of soils constitute integral parts of the complicated ecological systems (ecosystems or biogeocoenoses) that both change and in turn depend on the history and peculiarities of their particular environments, which vary according to their geographical positions and circumstances. The most striking differences in the mosaic of these systems can be observed in progressing from the equator of the earth towards the poles, and from the high mountain areas towards the lowlands and seas.

The ecosystems (of organisms and their physical habitats) in the biosphere are the centres of the most important functions permitting the existence and continuation of life. These functions are: (a) permanent photosynthesis and accumulation of energy originating from the sun, together with transformation and redistribution of this energy, and (b) maintenance of regular cycling of such chemical elements as oxygen, hydrogen, carbon, nitrogen, phosphorus, sulphur, calcium, magnesium, potassium, copper, zinc, cobalt, iodine, etc. These leading functions of soil/organism systems are performed through the regular formation, by plants, of organic matter which is consumed by herbivorous organisms. The zoobiomass of the animals is in turn broken down by a long chain of parasitic and predatory organisms, and by saprophagous soil invertebrates and microbiota.

Importance of Humus and Underground Parts

Soil humus is the most important product of the soil-forming process and also the last link in the trophic chain of decomposition of organic matter ending in 'mineralization' to water and carbon dioxide, ammonia, oxides of nitrogen, hydrogen sulphide, methane, oxides of iron, aluminium, and silicon, and carbonates, sulphates, phosphates, and nitrites. The influence of living organisms on the formation of the hydrosphere, of the atmosphere, and of sedimentary rocks of the earth's crust, has been increasing during the past two thousand million years which constitute the actively biogenic part of the history of the earth. But the influence of life became important for our planet particularly after plants and animals invaded the land comprising the surface of continents. This was around the beginning of the Devonian period nearly 400 million years ago. The weight of living matter on land is now estimated as being of the order of 10^{12-13} metric tons (Table I). The biomass of the forests is the dominating part of this, amounting to 10^{11-12} tons, while the zoobiomass is equivalent to only 0.5–1.3 per cent of the phytobiomass, being usually less than 1 per cent locally (Kovda, 1970).

Little is known about the total biomass of the microorganisms inhabiting the world's soils, etc., though it may be tentatively suggested as being of the order of 10^{8-9} tons.

TABLE I

Weight of Living Matter of the Planet Earth

Biomass	Tons
On the whole planet	10^{13}–10^{14}
On the land	10^{12}–10^{13}
Forests	10^{11}–10^{12}
Grasslands	10^{10}–10^{11}
Animals	10^9
Microorganisms	10^{8-9}

It is necessary to bear in mind that 30 to 90 per cent of the phytobiomass is represented by roots and is consequently concentrated inside the soil, where the soil animals and microorganisms mostly live. The plant litter, other remnants of dead plants and animals, and the products of metabolism, are mostly accumulated and remain on the soil surface or just beneath it, only a small part of the litter and organic remnants being normally washed away by surface or other waters.

The particular importance of soils as a basic site for living matter (roots, insects and other invertebrates, etc.) is well illustrated in the extremely difficult and unfavourable conditions of deserts, polar territories, high plateaux, etc. In such conditions the roots comprise from 95 to 97 per cent of the total phytobiomass of the ecosystem. The phenomenon of the concentration of phytobiomass in a wide range of soils is well illustrated by the data given in Table II.

TABLE II

Ratio of Overground Phytobiomass to Mass of Roots Alone

Tundra	1:6, 1:8
Fir taiga	4:1
Aspen woods on solod of wooded steppe	3:1
Grassland of typical chernozem	1:9
Grassland associations of chernozemic meadow soils	1:6
Grassland associations of solonetz	1:20

The rather general predomination of roots in relation to overground parts of vegetation is evident. Only in the case of trees does the above-ground biomass clearly predominate over the roots. But if one takes into account the content of humus in the soils, the total amount of organic matter in them

TABLE III

Distribution of Organic Matter in Ecosystems (tons per hectare)

Type of vegetation	Overground phytobiomass	Litter and roots, etc.	Humus
Lichens and mosses, etc.	10–20	100	128
Tundra	3–10	270–380	320
Fir taiga	278	189	97
Grasslands, steppes, and meadowlands	6–16	360	335

when compared with the overground parts of the plants in many forest ecosystems appears to be about equal. Yet in the majority of other ecosystems, and particularly in grasslands, the totals of organic matter in the soil, including humus, considerably exceed those in the aerial parts of the plants (Table III).

If we calculate the potential energy involved (Table IV), it becomes evident that the order of magnitude of the total energy resources that are bound

TABLE IV

Energy in Aerial Phytobiomass and in Soils

In phytobiomass above ground on land	10^{19-20} kcal
Annually fixed by photosynthesis	10^{17-18} kcal
In soil humus normally	10^{19-20} kcal
Maximum possible in soil humus	10^{22} kcal

up in the humus of all the soils of the world will be about equal to or even exceed (10^{19-22} kcal) the total energy accumulated in the overground parts of the vegetation (10^{19-20} kcal).

If the energy that is stored in the roots is added to the energy in the soil humus, the total energy resources of soils become strongly dominant over those of aerial vegetation; in other words, one can conclude that the main part of the energy accumulated in living and dead matter on land is located in the soils of the continents. The top-soil, and particularly the humic horizons comprising the humosphere of the land and the beds of shallow waters, are sites of active accumulation and redistribution of the energy obtained through photosynthesis; they also form a kind of universal screen that keeps in the biogeosphere the most important biophilic elements (such as nitrogen, phosphorus, and potassium), preventing them from being leached out and transferred into the geochemical stream and ultimately into the world's oceans.

Functioning of Terrestrial Ecosystems

Under natural conditions, each mature ecosystem (biogeocoenosis) is a self-regulating mechanism resulting from many thousands or even millions of years of history and evolution. Such an individual ecosystem on land represents an advanced and definite level of organization that has been reached by living and mineral matter interacting together. The members or components of the ecosystem—such as plants, herbivorous animals, predators, microorganisms of various trophic categories, soils with their contained soil atmosphere, and subsoil waters—are all more or less closely interrelated and interconnected throughout any homogeneous territory. Thus there is a common source of energy, exchange and cycling of biophilic chemical elements, synchronization of seasonal physical and biochemical dynamics, and conformity of trophic relationships engendered by the mutual adaptabilities of numerous populations inhabiting the same territorial unit. The biomass formed inside an ecosystem, and the energy combined within this biomass, will be consumed, redistributed, and dispersed inside the same ecosystem. As a product of biogeocoenosis, the soil is at the same time a kind of mirror reflecting the history and properties of the biogeocoenosis, and recording its peculiarities (Kovda, 1944, 1956, 1966, 1969, 1970, 1971).

As a result of the above-described processes, the soils accumulate humus and other organic materials and simpler compounds, biogenic minerals, and many biophilic chemical elements such as phosphorus, nitrogen, sulphur, calcium, potassium, magnesium, sulphur, cobalt, zinc, iodine, and others. Thus the soils, and particularly their humic horizons, are enriched by highly-dispersed secondary minerals and by important organic compounds—to uphold the level of natural productivity (or soil fertility).

The stores of energy, of biophilic chemical elements, and of biogenic compounds, that have been accumulated after many thousands of years of soil formation, explain the extreme importance of humus to the fertility of soils. The humus is the basis of the soils' internal biology, of their absorption capacity, and of their biological activity and productivity. The loss of humus through exhaustion of soils, or through erosion and deflation, is equally disastrous to the agriculture of the tropics and of steppes and prairies of cool regions of the earth.

Even worse, major losses of humus from the upper horizons of the soil will be fatal to many aspects of the normal dynamics of the biosphere (Kovda, 1971). For the regular synthesis, transformation, cyclic destruction, and final mineralization, of organic matter, the accumulation of energy and its redistribution through trophic chains of organisms, the selective absorption of chemical elements and ions and their concentration through trophic chains in the humic horizons of soils and in pure natural waters, all together represent the most important global functions that are being performed by the systems of organisms and soils in the biosphere.

THE INFLUENCE OF MAN ON SOILS AND ECOSYSTEMS

Human Activities

From the beginning of his appearance on earth, man entered the biogeocoenological mechanism of the biosphere—as a herbivorous animal and also as a predator, consuming increasing amounts of the biomass of both vegetable and animal origin. This relationship of man to the biosphere has, in essence, remained to this day. Nevertheless, there have been considerable changes under the influence of the activities of man and with the changing nature of human society.

During what might be termed the zoological period of his history, the influence of man on ecosystems and on their soil components was probably no more important than was the influence of other animals. However, since the Palaeolithic and particularly since the Neolithic, the influence of man on the top-soil has been increasing progressively. Although man and his society have long existed under social, economic, and political, rules, this existence has been—and must surely remain—closely connected with the biosphere and with its main components, namely the ecosystems and their soils. The soils are the basic physical conditioners of the existence of man, being the main object of his labour activities and usually determining the places of his settlements.

The various types of biological production, formed through the systems of soils and living organisms, are the main (and in many aspects the only) sources of food, various raw materials, and fuel, which are absolutely necessary for man. Systems of soils and living organisms are the bases of agricultural husbandry and forestry, the objects of amelioration, and the sources of many branches of industry and manufacturing. The availability of biologically pure water and of air and suitable foods, and the conditions of normal work and of resting, are properties of changing environments in relation to which man has developed and become adapted through many thousands of years of evolution. They are necessary to his very existence; but the stability of these environments surrounding man is provided and supported through permanent cyclic activities of the systems of soils and organisms (Kovda, 1971).

It need scarcely be stressed further that man and his biology and labour activities are closely connected with environments which he has increasingly altered and moulded to his needs—often so drastically that these needs are no longer served satisfactorily. His hunting, discovery and use of fire, deforestation of land, ploughing of the soil, grazing, artificial irrigation, draining of swamps, protection against floods, terracing of slopes, fertilization of soils—all these activities have considerably influenced and changed natural ecosystems and soils. So, too, have accumulations of litter and refuse around villages and cities, and wastes from industry and mining in the forms of dust, smoke, fog, ash, and gases.

The natural ecosystems and their soils have been widely disturbed through building activities (including roads and airports, etc.), bombing and other military devastations, and applications of poisonous materials—to mention only a few of the worst sources of desecration of vegetation, particularly. All these destructive actions of contemporary man as an elemental calamity emerged spontaneously, and simultaneously with the development of 'modern' civilization, as an influence disturbing the normal biological cycling of the chemical compounds in soils, ecosystems, and the biosphere in general.

As a result of these processes, there arose all manner of secondary biogeocoenoses—artificial, cultural, and post-cultural, ecosystems created by man or resulting from his labours. Notable in this connection are agroecosystems, grassy pasturing ecosystems, and ecosystems of managed forests. In such cultural biogeocoenosis, man has tried to influence the process of biomass synthesis, desiring to obtain particular biological products and the productivity required for his existence and rising standards of living. But in the majority of cases this pragmatic activity of man was without deep knowledge and consciousness, and without proper understanding of the possible consequences of his practical activity. Only recently have we come to realize in general terms that environments, organisms, and soils, form about the closest interrelating systems imaginable. This modern knowledge stems from widespread researches, of which those of V. V. Dokuchaev, V. I. Vernadsky, and V. N. Sukachev, are among the most notable—cf. Vernadsky (1926, 1934), Sukachev (1948), and Sukachev & Dylis (1968).

Only after coming to realize the closeness of this interrelationship has man started deliberately to apply the complex of measures and actions on different elements of ecosystems which are aimed at obtaining from them the maximum of useful biological production. Up to the end of the nineteenth century and even in the first decades of the twentieth century, there was no proper under-standing and enlightened discussion of the relationship and unity of environ-ments and organisms. The practical activities of man were aimed at the pro-duction and utilization of biological materials for fuel, building, food, raw material for industry, and other purposes, being as a rule anarchical and very often directed at obtaining a high and easily acquired profit. As a result there appeared more and more secondary and artificial ecosystems created by man and having very many features that were quite different from those of the natural, primary ecosystems. For man tries to provide, in the field, for the domination of the populations of those types of plants and animals in whose production he is most interested for the furtherance of his own needs. This leads of necessity to man's protection and support especially of those kinds of organisms that help to supply his needs, and this he does through a system of agrotechnical measures, amelioration of environments, and appropriate zootechnical methods.

Disruption of Ecosystems and its Remedy

Of the biomass that is created in man-made agroecosystems, up to 40–80 per cent will commonly be removed by man as the product which he requires. Under this influence of human activities, the stream of energy and normal cycling of biophilic chemical elements in the system of soils and organisms that existed earlier will be disturbed and even broken. The reserves of energy, both biological and chemical, that had earlier been accumulated in virgin soils as a component of the biosphere, will become exhausted—especially with a marked decrease in the content of humus and at the same time of nitrogen, phosphorus, potassium, and important trace-elements. As a result of the lasting domination of man-made artificial ecosystems of one sort of population and especially of monocultures, and following the concomitant shortening of trophic food-chains, the soils of given ecosystems can be adversely affected by accumulations of toxins, and by pathogenic microorganisms provoking so-called soil fatigue. This leads to the necessity of application of fertilizers to compensate for the elements that have been removed and to expand their biological cycle.

As a result of all this, man has become obliged to leave cultivated fields for long periods of fallow, or to introduce rational rotation of leading economic plants with, particularly, grasses together with clover or alfalfa. He may also have to practise inoculation with mycorrhizas or specific microorganisms for the reinforcement of nitrogen fixation, or to undertake periodical deep-plough-ing of soils to bring up rich lower horizons into the agricultural stratum. All these and other measures are being applied in order to minimize the con-sequences of man-provoked disturbance in the functioning of the soil/organ-ism system. Consequently in man-made ecosystems, and particularly in agroecosystems, much labour of man, and capital investment for such pur-poses as liming, draining, irrigation, chemical and physical amelioration, and mineral and manure fertilizers, must be regularly applied in order to stabilize artificial agroecosystems and so support their functioning and productivity. Otherwise the artificial ecosystem will be destroyed and productive life will perish.

Increasing World Bioproductivity

In spite of all this, in the course of history the productivity of the world's land as a whole has increased considerably at the hand of man. In many cases, unproductive natural landscapes of desert and semi-desert, areas of saline and alkaline soils, and swampy territories, have been improved by man through irrigation, drainage, or leaching, and so transformed into usefully productive ecosystems. For instance, highly productive lands of Denmark, the Netherlands, and Belgium, are located in what were formerly swamps but have been effectively drained. The productive soils of drained areas of the swampy delta of the River Rion in Georgia, USSR, and the cotton plantations of Uzbekistan, which are situated in a desert of Asia, are further examples, as are extremely productive palm and citrus plantations in irrigated areas of Egypt, Algeria, Morocco, etc. Such works as those of Black (1968) and Dasmann (1968) indicate the situation in the United States as well.

In such artificial man-made cultural ecosystems, not only was a new type of soil created and the most favourable regime of moisture and nourishment of plants introduced, but a very reasonable type of grading or levelling of the territory was applied. Moreover, in some cases new varieties of plants of extremely high value and productivity have been introduced. For striking examples of highly productive artificial ecosystems we may cite the terraced fields of irrigated rice situated on the hills of southeastern Asia or in valleys and on deltas of such rivers as the Amu-Darya and the Syr-Darya, the Indus, the Ganges, the Nile and, more recently, the Kuban and Rhône.

As a result of the efforts of man, the general level of the fertility of soils and of productivity of agricultural husbandry was markedly and widely increased. This can be illustrated by referring to the yield of cereal grain: from the fifteenth to the eighteenth centuries the yield of grain in Europe was 6–7 quintals* per hectare*, whereas in the nineteenth century in most advanced countries of Europe the average yield was about 15–16 quintals per hectare. In the middle of the twentieth century the average yield of grain reached the level of 30–40 quintals per hectare in industrially advanced countries, while towards the end of the twentieth century yields of the order of 60 to 70 quintals per hectare, or even higher, can be reached in the most advanced countries. Such an intensive rate of increase in the average yield of grain can be explained by the extremely rapid development of science, of industry, and of the technological means of influence of man on nature and particularly on soils and living organisms.

In the countries that now have the highest yields of grain, there has been accomplished a great degree of amelioration of the land. This has often involved repeated liming, introduction of irrigation, and the use of the most advanced types of rotation of plants and, what is most important, of the optimum rate of application of chemical fertilizers and chemical means of protection of plants by herbicides, insecticides, and so on.

However, modern industrial development, with its characteristic concentration of humans in big cities, has provoked vast changes in agriculture and forest husbandry, and these have had simultaneous consequences on both the general biosphere and the more limited biogeocoenological sphere. In com-

* 1 quintal (q) = 100 kg = 220.5 lb; 1 hectare (ha) = 2.471 acres.—Ed.

parison with prehistoric times, the cover of forest has been reduced to only about 60–65 per cent of its former area, while the grasslands have expanded greatly in many areas that were previously under forest. According to the data of FAO (1967), the total surface of arable land is nowadays some 10–11 per cent of the area of the continents, while meadows and other grazing lands occupy about 16 per cent (Table V).

TABLE V

The Surface of Agricultural Land of the Earth

Total surface of land	14.8×10^9 ha
Arable	1.5×10^9 ha
Meadows and other grazing lands	2.6×10^9 ha
Forests	4.06×10^9 ha
Total of arable, grazing, and forest lands	8.16×10^9 ha

Thus the total agricultural (in the wide sense) utilization of the world's land area is now nearly 28 per cent, while if forests are included it approaches 60 per cent.

Consequences of Deforestation

Deforestation of such vast territories of the continents has probably provoked important changes in the biosphere and particularly in its soils. Carbon which was formerly combined in the biomass of the forests, has been transferred to the atmosphere in the form of carbon dioxide. Replacement of forest by grassland has resulted in a general acceleration of biological cycling of such biophilic elements as carbon, nitrogen, phosphorus, and many others. This acceleration has reached the level of 10–100 times because of the longevity of trees, which is measured in centuries and even millennia, whereas the lifetime of grasses is measured in months or, at the maximum, a few years.

Decomposition and disappearance of forest litter, and burning of 'fossil' fuels which in prehistoric times kept in storage colossal amounts of organic and mineral matters together with potential energy, have greatly augmented the rate of return of carbon dioxide to the atmosphere and reinforced some of the other tendencies and changes that take place in the biosphere after deforestation (Johnson, 1970; Wendland & Bryson, 1970).

The water regime of the soils, and the general hydrology of the continents, must have changed considerably after their deforestation. Water comprises about 50–60 per cent of the raw biomass of forests, and this water became liberated and added to the global cycling which reached some trillions of cubic metres. Deforestation reinforced by 2–3 times the surface run-off of water on the resultant bare land, such run-off being due to an approximately equivalent reduction in the infiltration of water into the soil and subsoil (Fig. 1).

As a result of deforestation and the concomitant reinforcement of surface run-off of water, the development of erosion became a most menacing factor in the destruction of soils. Particularly destructive was, and still and perhaps

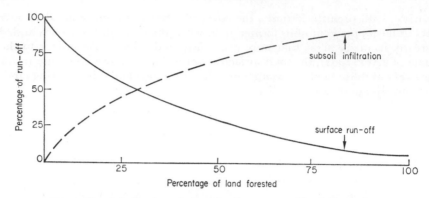

Fig. 1. Graph indicating relationship of water run-off to deforestation.

increasingly is, the erosion of soils on deforestated slopes and on mountains, while tillage of steppes, prairies, and savannas, and their mechanical treatment and ploughing, provoked considerable changes in their soil cover as well. In such landscapes the water erosion became accompanied by wind deflation, dust-storms, and a general destructurization of the soils which in many cases was accompanied by salinization. Periodical burning of grasses and bushes in savannas and steppes—for agricultural purposes or hunting, or merely by mistake—provoked additional factors of loss of humus reserves, impoverishment of soil fauna, and destruction of useful microorganisms. All these items additionally weakened, and continue to weaken, the capabilities of soils to withstand water and wind erosion and salinization.

Such a general increase in the surface run-off of water, combined with reduced infiltration into the subsoil, is followed by general xerophytization of landscapes and lowering of the level of ground-water. Construction of wells, pumping of subsoil water into towns and villages, and its use for irrigational, industrial, and transportation purposes, in turn considerably reinforced the general tendency to desiccation of the land and xerophytization of its vegetation. This in turn resulted in more frequent appearance of drought combined with a decreasing rate of yield of grain, with decreasing fertility of the soils, and with general aridization of the territories. Such phenomena can be observed on the Great Plains of North America, and widely in Europe, Asia, and Africa, being reflected in the appearance of the soils and in their chemical, physical, and biological properties.

As a general consequence of increased water erosion and wind deflation, there has been very considerably accelerated mechanical run-off and loss of solid particles and dissolved chemicals from the land into rivers and lakes. This has resulted in widespread pollution of water, in increasing the concentration of soluble residual salts in the water, and in the process of silting of water basins, irrigated meadows, and tributaries, as well as of the mouths of rivers, deltas, and estuaries. Without a rational plant of plant rotation, and without application of mineral and organic fertilizers, the long-tilled soils of steppes and prairies are getting much too poor in their content of humus. The content of humus after fifty to seventy years of utilization can be reduced substantially, while the depth of the humic horizon can be depressed by 5–15 cm or sometimes even by 30–50 cm. Subsoil-infertile, stony or salty horizons, would then be much shallower, coming nearer to the surface, while the resources of nitrogen, phosphorus, potassium, and micronutrients, in the tillage horizon, will be considerably reduced.

The application of mineral fertilizers is insufficient to combat the general process of degradation of soils following erosion, deflation, xerophytization, and salinization. Instead are required some at least of a whole complex of preventive measures such as contour cultivation, creation of a network of protection belts of forests or lines of trees, regular introduction of grasses into the rotation, construction of local basins in ravines, stabilization and terracing of steep slopes, or even total prohibition of tillage of land that is at all subject to erosion. All these preventive measures, coupled with high doses of mineral and organic fertilizers—including proper utilization of organic remnants and wastes of villages and cities—could preserve the soils and will increase the reserve of humus, nitrogen, and biophilic elements. The most important need, however, is for the measures adopted to reinforce the biological potential and activity of the soils.

In the USSR, there have been successful trials of restoring and increasing the fertility of meadow chernozem soils in trans-Uralian areas through the application of high doses of mineral and organic fertilizers coupled with a grass type of rotation and introduction of anti-erosion forestation. After 5–6 years the content of humus became even higher than it had been before the tillage had been started, while the average yield of grain increased by up to 0.5 to 1 ton per hectare.

Effects of Overgrazing

Not less serious are the consequences of overgrazing of many types of land. In the course of millennia, the waste territories of steppes, prairies, and meadows, served as a basis for nomadic cattle-breeding. In many of these areas nomadic cattle-breeders existed even earlier than did people practising field cultivation. After hunting, the use of fire and some degree of deforestation, the domestication of certain mammals and birds, and the establishment and development of nomadic cattle-breeding, were probably among the most important events in the history of the struggle of man with the forces of nature, and particularly in that of his struggle with hunger. But nomadic cattle-breeding was followed by a long chain of seemingly endless consequences and changes in the environment of man and in local habitat conditions (Brown, 1971; Kovda, 1971). Organic matters of animal origin (meat, fat, skins, wool, milk products, etc.) are already materials of the secondary biological productivity of ecosystems. The level of secondary biological productivity, quite apart from other factors, depends on the level of the primary productivity of the phytobiomass, and depends on it through the vegetation that in its turn depends very largely on the properties of the soils (UNESCO, 1970).

In natural ecosystems the primary and secondary productivity are interrelated and equilibrated. Over-charging of grassland and landscapes by numerous grazing animals, involving overgrazing, coupled with extremely high and irreversible alienation of the animals' bioproduction, results in very strong degradation of the vegetation through destruction of the sward and devastation of the soils. Trying to graze the maximum number of cattle with the aim of obtaining the maximum possible productivity, the nomadic cattle-breeders in the past and even now were and still are the strongest destroyers of the ecosystems and soils of steppes, woodland, prairies, meadows, and savannas (Brown, 1971).

The vegetation and the sod of the soils of arid areas of the Mediterranean, of the Near and Middle East, and of Central Asia, were literally eaten by vast numbers of sheep, goats, horses, donkeys, camels, and other livestock, quantities of which have been growing there permanently from prehistoric time, so that the productivity of these areas has tended to get less and less. Searching for fuel, the nomadic cattle-breeders cut and burned all the bushes and other plants that were not eaten by domestic or wild animals, and go on doing so to this day. In these areas traditionally the dung of animals is utilized for making briquettes of fuel or bricks for building. As a result of all these activities of destruction, the normal exchange and cycling of components of ecosystems could not occur, vegetation became physically degraded, and the unprotected soil was eroded, deflated, blown-out, salinized, and finally deserted.

Particularly suffering were the Quaternary and Tertiary sand-deposits of deserts after their shrubby vegetation had gone. When the psammophytic vegetation had been destroyed, previously-fixed sandy soils became mobile and subject to strong deflation. Mobile shifting sands formed dunes which occupied wells and fields, villages and roads, irrigation canals and watercourses. Even in the temperate climate of Europe, deforesting the sandy soils, tilling them, and overdraining them by means of deep canals, contrived to transform previously useful 'fixed' lands into shifting dunes. If shifting sands are protected and forested, with the numbers of grazing animals and rotation of grazing properly controlled and planned, their areas can be transformed into useful lands, as has been done, for example, in parts of southern France, in the Buchara area in central Asia, and in some tracts on the Baltic Sea coast. But in many parts of central Asia and northern Africa, this problem is not yet resolved or even understood.

After the termination of the glacial and pluvial periods, there appeared on earth some semi-arid and arid areas. But the soils of these territories had been formed in part in conditions of much higher moisture and under much more developed and often flourishing vegetation. That is why, even in areas of currently arid conditions, these soils are characterized by a high level of potential fertility inherited from their past history. Anarchical utilization of these grasslands for grazing by numerous nomadic herdsmen in the course of the last two millennia has very strongly reinforced the natural process of desiccation of the lands and has added to this process anthropogenically in many semi-arid and sub-arid regions where irreversible and often catastrophic desertification of the land has been accompanied by degradation and destruction of the soils.

Unwise Use of Chemicals and Disposal of Wastes

The vitally important subject of the preservation of the fertility of soils now includes the problem of their protection from alien chemical compounds. Even a wrongly-selected spectrum of mineral fertilizers can provoke acidification or alkalinization of soils, accompanied by decreasing fertility. For instance, for soils of arid regions that are inclined to alkalinization, preference must be given to mineral fertilizers, such as ammonium sulphate or superphosphate, that combat this tendency of the soil solution. For soils of acid reaction, on the other hand, preference must be given to mineral fertilizers that are capable of neutralizing or slightly alkalinizing the soil, examples being sodium and calcium nitrate. It should, however, be remembered that too-high doses of soluble fertilizers such as nitrates or potassium chloride can provoke additional problems and even cause the death of young and tender plants.

Very disastrous can be the influence of excessive applications of different biocides such as insecticides, herbicides, defoliants, and so on (Mellanby, 1967). It is established that highly stable, long-living pesticides, in spite of their positive role in the protection of the yields of plants, and in the protection of animals against parasites and diseases, nevertheless can provoke the strongest oppressive effects on soil fauna, microorganisms, and ultimate fertility. The residual pesticides or products of their transformation and metabolism enter the soil and subsoil water and can contaminate human food and poison men and particularly children. They can also have disastrous effects on animal populations even far from their point of application (Wurster, 1969).

If pesticides are applied repeatedly to the same fields, one can observe cases of considerable decrease in the germination of seeds, weakness of plants, withering of vegetation, and perishing of animals. The worst offenders in such respects are the persistent pesticides which can remain in soils for 2–3 years or more without losing their toxicity. There are known cases of extensive sickness of people in areas where the soils have been polluted by excesses of DDT or by the disposal of compounds of mercury, cadmium, or zinc, which accumulate in soils and water in the areas of mining or industrial use of these elements. Time will show what further effects they may have.

Modern industry, means of rapid and easy transportation, mining enterprises, and cities, are very important sources of many other polluting compounds, which poison soils and decrease their fertility: the gases of metallurgical plants and oil refineries, the emissions of cars and locomotives, and the dust and acid compounds emanating from mining and cement enterprises, are particularly bad sources of contamination. Others include salt water pumped into petroleum fields and huge mountains of mineral material excavated from mines, etc. (MIT, 1970). We must have, and rigorously enforce, laws that forbid all such desecration and poisoning of the world's soils. The technologies of industrial processes must be modified in such a way as to preclude the very existence of poisoning by waste products and the disposal of toxic substances which enter the soils and waters of the biosphere (Helfrich, 1970).

There are known and often quite different cases of destruction of soils, including instances of poisoning of vast territories through fallout of radio-active nucleids. Remember the case of the Government of the United States having to export many tons of soil that had become polluted by radioactive productsfollowing their careless use by military personnel in foreign countries! Nobody has forgotten that all living beings, including those in soils, were killed and devastated by the war-time explosion of atomic bombs in Japan. Even so-called 'conventional war' is accompanied by numerous losses of fertile soil through the construction of trenches and anti-tank defences, through explosions, and through the application of poisoning gases, solutions, or other preparations. War as a means of attempted solution of economic and political conflicts should never again exist in the life of man.

IMPROVING THE PRODUCTIVITY OF SOILS

The relentless increase in human populations and their ever-growing demands for improved standards of living provide the most powerful stimulus towards attaining more and more highly intensified agriculture and animal husbandry. Improved quality and increasing rates of application of fertilizers, many-sided mechanization of labour, newly-created and highly productive varieties of plants, and the use of pesticides and of correctly-designed crop rotations, have all played extremely effective roles in the whole process of increasing agricultural productivity.

Importance of Soil Amelioration

The fundamental advances by man in attaining the highly productive agriculture of today have been achieved only through the amelioration of soils in order to eliminate unfavourable features of the land. Very often this important role of amelioration, as executed in the past, has been forgotten; yet the different types of amelioration, from the earliest beginnings of civilization, aimed at elimination of negative properties of the general environment, of soils, and of organisms.

In countries of high yield, the liming of acid soils has been practised and repeated for more than a century, so that soils which were previously acidic are now fully neutralized. Swampy and waterlogged areas of western Europe and North America have been drained. Heavy, unproductive soils have been improved through super-deep tillage and application of high rates of manure and sand. In arid and semi-arid areas, irrigation has been introduced, so that the people can harvest crops twice or thrice or even more times in each year. In areas of semi-arid climate, protective forest belts have been created. In many parts of Europe, Latin America, and particularly south-east Asia, anti-erosional terraces have been constructed for the effective control of erosion. One can observe the extension nowadays of irrigation into more and more humid areas having a temperate climate.

Newly created, highly productive varieties of cotton, wheat, rice, maize, sunflower, and sugar-cane, are particularly sensitive to their environments, and require for the most part optimization of the biological, water, air, and nourishment, regimes of arable soils. This is why one can confidently predict that the general requirements of different kinds of improvements of natural environments and low-productive soils, will grow considerably in the forth-coming 30–50 years. First of all irrigation, and then more general amelior-ation, will be called upon to create the most widespread and favourable environments possible—for effective operation and in order to obtain stabi-lized high biological production in the fields, grasslands, forests, and other sources of our biologically-based economy.

The amelioration of soils and improvement of geographical environments can thus to some extent liberate agricultural and forest economy from their traditional dependence on natural features. Apart from this, amelioration of soils must prevent such negative phenomena as erosion, drought, dust-storms, shifting sands, salinization and alkalinization of fields and meadows, and desiccation of rivers, lakes, and subsoil waters. Amelioration of environments must also assist in the creation of more beautiful and healthy conditions for man, his work, and his rest (Kovda, 1937, 1944, 1946, 1954; Graham, 1944).

Irrigation the Common Key

Universally known is the role of artificial irrigation of soils in the history of civilization, and in providing for the growing human populations of the world with their ever-increasing needs of food and raw materials. Irrigation of land is the most ancient form of amelioration of an environment, long practised to create artificial, highly productive ecosystems in order to im-prove the life and lot of man in arid and desert regions. It was not accident-ally that the most ancient civilizations occurred and successfully developed simultaneously with the establishment and expansion of ancient irrigation systems in the valleys and deltas of such rivers as the Murgab, Amu-Darya, Syr-Darya, Hwango-Ho, Yangtze, Nile, Ganges, Indus, Mekong, Tigris, Euphrates, Tiber, and others.

The process of establishment of irrigation systems represents one of the most complex actions and many-sided influences of man, on different com-ponents of the landscape, which have as their aim the creation of highly-pro-ductive artificial agroecosystems. For purposes of irrigation it is necessary to construct high dams, irrigation and drainage canals, and basins of different sizes and types; it is also necessary to grade and level the surface of the fields, to apply a high rate of fertilizers, and to introduce specific plants and pro-tective forest belts. Now the world's total area of irrigated land is of the order of 230 to 240 million hectares.

The soils of ancient irrigation systems have quite specific and peculiar characteristics. After several thousands of years of irrigation there have been created, for example in the deltas of the Nile, Murgab, and Indus, 3–7 metres-deep, artificially deposited soils with very favourable physical and biological properties, including valuable reserves of humus, nitrogen, phos-phorus, and micronutrients. By applying irrigation correctly, man can obtain from two to four harvests per year (in the delta of the Chu-dzjan River near Canton in China, up to six or eight harvests per year).

Thus by means of irrigation, man creates artificial agroecosystems with extremely high bioproductivity such as never appeared in the past under natural conditions. In our time, artificial irrigation penetrates more and more into areas with a moderate, sub-arid climate—for example in the steppes of the USSR. Realization of a huge programme of irrigation of land in the semi-arid steppic regions of the USSR, started in 1966, has been followed by excellent results and increasing production of agricultural material. Fully fertilized and correctly irrigated arid soils of the USSR are now producing yearly over large areas 50 quintals per hectare of grain, 60–65 q/ha of rice, and 40–45 q/ha of raw cotton. Similar results have been achieved in areas of the northwestern part of the USSR, where recently drained, limed, and fertilized, soils that were previously swampy are now producing yields of grain of the order of 30 to 40 and even 50 to 60 q/ha.

Dangers and Remedies of Unwise Irrigation

Nevertheless, in contradistinction to brilliant achievements in the agricultural economy of mankind that have been attained through the application of various means of amelioration, undesirable consequences are not rare, and unexpected negative results may lead to decreasing fertility of some ameliorated soils. Several forms of negative consequences of misguided 'ameliorations' of soils are known, including secondary salinization and secondary waterlogging of irrigated soils and adjacent territories—also cases of over-draining of swampy areas in lowlands and river valleys followed by decreasing productivity of the over-drained lands. The main remedies against such secondary salinization and waterlogging of the soils are, respectively, deep drainage of irrigated land in order to promote the washing out of excesses of toxic soluble salts from the soils and saline ground-water, and lining of irrigation canals in order to prevent infiltration and seepage of water into the subsoil strata.

Unfortunately in our time the majority of both ancient and newly-constructed irrigation systems lack any means of deep horizontal or vertical drainage and also lining of the irrigation canals for the prevention of salinity and waterlogging, respectively. Because of these technical mistakes, only 20–40 per cent of irrigated lands are producing good harvests; the remaining 60–80 per cent are getting gradually more and more saline and infertile. One has to recognize that the construction of irrigation systems without drainage of ground-water and lining of the canals is hazardous in provoking both salinization and waterlogging of the soils. Depending on the chemical content of the irrigation water and the salinity of the soil, subsoil, and ground-water, the long-term consequences of wrongly constructed irrigation systems can be very various. The first-developed and most widely existing form of degradation of irrigated soils is their cementation and destructurization. Very often this is accompanied by a high degree of alkalinity, with a pH of up to 9–11, and by a strong accumulation of soluble salts in the upper part of the soil, where their concentration can be as high as 2 to 3 per cent.

The causes of destructurization, alkalinization, and salinization, of irrigated soils have been and still are the subject of many studies in different countries. An important role belongs to the quality of the irrigation water: the presence of colloidal compound of silica, of sodium and magnesium carbonates and bicarbonates, and of toxic soluble salts such as chlorides and sulphates, can be deleterious. No less important are chemical compounds in the ground-waters. If the depth of ground-water in the absence of artificial drainage exceeds 1.5–2.0 metres, its evaporation and transpiration will be followed by surface accumulation of soluble salts and colloidal components that are present in it.

In various arid and sub-arid regions, some tens of millions of hectares of previously productive soils are more or less affected by alkalinization and salinization, while many millions of hectares of previously irrigated soils have been transformed into unproductive saline soils or even into the so-called 'saline deserts'. The most representative examples of such territories are to be observed in some valleys and deltas of rivers in Iran, India, Pakistan, Mesopotamia, Egypt, and so on. There are also examples of newly-constructed irrigation systems which were not provided with adequate artificial drainage, with consequent strong salinization of the irrigated land. Examples can be observed in the countries of North Africa, central Asia, North and South America, and southern Europe. In such cases, again, salinization has been provoked by the evaporation of saline subsoil ground-waters after their level had been raised.

The main reasons for the degradation of lands after irrigation are: (*a*) underestimation of the importance of specific soil conditions and of the low quality of the irrigation water used; (*b*) the inclination of designers and constructors of new irrigation systems not to build drainage mechanisms (horizontal deep drains or vertical deep wells) in attempting to keep down capital investment; and (*c*) excessive application and losses of water in the field, through seepage from irrigation canals which are usually not lined and consequently provoke inevitable rising of the level of the ground-water. One can estimate that, in different countries of the world, there are not less than 20–25 million hectares of saline, infertile soils that have deteriorated after the introduction of incorrect irrigation.

The losses of irrigated lands in different countries are still continuing, and can probably be estimated as high as from 200 to 300 thousands of hectares annually. So the damages of secondary salinization and secondary over-watering and swamping of irrigated land are among the most destructive of all for countries having an irrigation economy. This can, however, be prevented; for in accordance with experience in the USSR, the United States, and some areas of the United Arab Republic, the introduction of deep horizontal (2.5 to 3 m) or vertical drainage (pumping tube-wells) and effective lining of irrigation canals can fully prevent the process of salinization provoked by high levels of ground-water. Moreover, by applying drainage and special types of leaching and washing-out of soluble salts, one can effectively desalinize the saline soils and restore their fertility. There are many examples of this in trans-Caucasian and central Asian parts of the USSR and in western parts of the USA.

Swamp Draining and Its Problems

Another type of amelioration of soils is the draining of swampy lands, which considerably changes the soil-forming processes and productivity of these soils. Thus toxic compounds accumulated in swampy soils before they are drained will be oxidized after the draining. The potential productivity of drained swampy soils can be very high, while their subsoil water is very useful for so-called sub-irrigation—the subsoil moistening of soil and root systems of plants through water raised by capillarity. This is the reason for the high productivity of drained but previously swampy tracts of prairies in the United States, and of lowlands in England, the Netherlands, Belgium, Denmark, West and East Germany, Sweden, and Canada.

However, if the rate of draining of swampy soils is excessive, and after the draining the subsoil water is located deeper than 1–1.5 metres, the productivity of the drained soils will be low. For the humus and peat will be oxidized very soon in a kind of 'burning' of the organic matter, while the deeply installed network of draining canals will evacuate much of the store of important nutrient compounds. Sub-moistening in such cases will be very limited. Indeed, if such mistakes are made, not only will the productivity of the drained area be low, but also the productivity of neighbouring territories and forestated lands will be reduced owing to over-draining.

Because of this, when designing a projected draining of swampy lands, it is most important to consider not so much the question of simple draining and transportation of excess water, as that of undertaking a much more complicated set of tasks: how to utilize the hydrotechnical installations to manage the water budget of the territory, and how to create optimum moisture, temperature, and nutrient, regimes in the soils. These adjustments together should aim at obtaining the maximum biological production possible, and on a sustained-yield basis.

In some sea-shore lowlands in deltaic and estuarine regions of humid temperate and tropical climates, one can sometimes observe a specific form of degradation of drained soils through the formation of free sulphuric acid. Examples are to be seen in drained littoral swampy areas in Scandinavia and elsewhere in northwestern Europe, in Florida and Texas in the United States, in Senegal, Guinea, and Ivory Coast in West Africa, in the Central African Republic, and in Burma and Thailand. After the draining and aeration of these soils, there is oxidation of iron sulphides into sesquioxide and free sulphuric acid, causing extreme acidity with a pH as low as 2–4. In the same soils may be formed sulphates of iron and aluminium, which are again acidic and toxic, so that such soils finally lose their fertility.

For amelioration of such extremely acidic soils, the strongest liming and periodical artificial over-wetting are required in order to lower the redox potential and increase the average pH to a level of 5.5 to 6.5. Nevertheless there remain cases showing that the restoration of fertility and productivity of such 'sulphuric acid soils' is almost impossible.

Effects of Damming

Many forms of losses and deteriorations of highly productive soils are known following swamping, flooding, and construction of high-level dams and basins in the valleys of rivers. After dam construction, the productive soils of the lower terraces in valleys downstream get an under-flow of basin water, while the higher terraces can be virtually submerged by an infiltration of water from the newly-created basins. Within a period of 10–20 years these effects can extend for tens or even hundreds of kilometres as a result of a regularly-formed subsoil infiltration-water stream.

If the newly created and raised subsoil ground-waters are fresh (sweet), and if they are stabilized at a level of the order of 1.5 to 2 metres, the productivity of such semi-submerged territories can be even higher than it was earlier. But if the ground-water is stabilized at a higher level than this so-called critical level, and if it is salty and so transports soluble salts which reach the surface of the soil, there will follow processes of destructurization of the tillable horizons of the soil by cementation or even by alkalinization and salinization.

It has been observed that newly-created man-made lakes can provoke the strongest phenomena of erosion, abrasion, and landsliding, of the shores and high banks, followed by loss of valuable agricultural lands, villages, and even towns. All such possibilities must be foreseen at the time of designing of future constructions of dams, basins, and canals; their economic consequences must be evaluated and measures must be taken for their prevention where necessary.

Other Results of Human Activities and Their Remedy

Mistakes in man's activities have been followed by other forms of degradation of soils. For example, the phenomenon of so-called 'petrification' of productive soils can be followed by their full loss of fertility. In the soils of the humid tropics, after draining and deforestation, this 'petrification' may occur through dehydration and crystallization of the soil colloids, and particularly of hydroxides of iron and aluminium. This is accompanied by the formation of a strongly cemented lateritic stratum (quirasse) of hard-pan. Cementation and petrification of irrigated soils can be provoked by accumulation of silica or calcium sulphate or carbonate following evaporation of shallow subsoil ground-water. This has been experienced in many regions of northern Africa, South America, and central Asia. Petrification of soil considerably decreases its productivity, though there are measures of prevention—such as introduction of alfalfa or of woody plants, application of pan-breakers, and loosening of the 'petrified' horizons by means of special explosions.

In savannas, steppes, and meadows, one can often observe the phenomena of destructurization, peptization, and 'slitization' of soils (formation of vertisoils), which occur mostly where there is circulation in the soil and subsoil of water of alkaline reaction with slightly concentrated solutions of colloidal and molecular silica. Inadequate draining or serious overgrazing of meadow areas can provoke and reinforce the phenomenon of formation of cemented structureless vertisoils. After ten or twenty years of wrong utilization of such soils, they become very heavy, and sticky and viscous when moist. Such soils are cemented, impermeable to water and air, and crack after drying. The real reasons and causes of the phenomenon of vertisoil formation are not fully known, but it is indisputable that complications and negative consequences are often the results of inadequate knowledge or poor scientific justification of the measures selected for attempted amelioration and development.

Many mistakes are made in establishing irrigation, drainage, and other soil reclamation systems. Sometimes the real reason is inadequate under-

standing of the basic principles and required tasks; for the amelioration of
the soils of a territory is obliged to involve a very complicated programme of
actions in which the construction of dams, basins, or canals, represents only
the beginning. The most important requirement consists in transformation
of infertile and low-productive lands into highly productive ones, and these
tasks involve requirements in additional labour and capital investment in
chemical, physical, and biological, methods of soil amelioration—including
often the necessity of execution of long and difficult programmes of de-
salinization, etc. There may also be the need to execute complicated cultural–technical programmes of levelling, grading, enrichment with organic
matter, and rational reorganization of the whole territory—including the
location and distribution of buildings, of roads, of means of mass communication and information, and even of schools and apartments for the
population.

The final efficacy of all types of land amelioration work must be measured
in terms of the levels of productivity reached and the total cost of the additional production obtained. Here must be taken into account all the expenses
required for prevention of negative effects and for liquidation of all complications provoked by unforeseen consequences of amelioration. The most
important thing to bear in mind is that profound scientific research is
required before amelioration is introduced through irrigation or drainage.
The elaborated design must be studied and critically discussed, and special
prognoses must be produced in order to forecast the entire spectrum of
possible consequences in the near and remote future.

Conclusions for the Future

Soil degradation is a subject engendering the highest anxiety among
scientists, agriculturists, administrators, and governments. The soils of our
planet have been formed during millennia, and in conditions which have
now widely disappeared. But their destruction has occurred through the
mistakes of men in the course of often only a few years. Usually this degradation and destruction of soils is either irreparable or can be remedied and
the soils restored with much effort and loss of time. That is why, in many
parts of the world, national and regional research institutions and laboratories have been established for the study of the origin, evolution, and
properties, of soils, the object being to elaborate scientifically sound measures
of prevention of degradation and methods of restoration of fertility. The
International Society of Soil Science, FAO, and UNESCO, particularly,
are promoting the broadest possible international cooperation of scientists
and of governments in this vital field.

The soils of our planet, as a source of fertility and as a component of the
biosphere, must be guarded from degradation and preserved for future
generations of people. Their importance in the biosphere is not limited to
the 'service' which they render to plants in promoting photosynthesis, for,
particularly in their humosphere, they are also the feeding substrata of much
of the zoobiomass. Indeed, as a vital component of the biosphere, the soils
represent a kind of universal global accumulator and very economical distri-

butor of the energy that is contained in humus. The soils regulate the normal exchange and cycling of chemical elements and compounds in nature. Consequently the biological productivity of the planet earth is based on a normal, harmonized functioning of both soils and organisms in the biosphere.

Until man interfered with the biosphere, it functioned as a self-regulating system, producing biomass and regulating the qualities and properties of soils, of water, and of air. But then came the interference of man in the biosphere through agriculture, forest and water economy, and exploitation and exportation of the bioproducts. This was followed by man's scientifically sounder operational management of the biosphere and its components— with soils, living organisms, water regime, and ecosystems, functioning as units. The higher the production obtained by man is, the more exact must be our understanding and the more thorough must be our methods and technology of management of the ecosystems.

Mistakes in such measures and in management can have the most disastrous consequences, and could become more and more widely serious as the scale of operations becomes larger with the need to satisfy growing and increasingly voracious populations. Ameliorated and developed territories with highly fertile soils, high productivity of plants and animals, and extensive modern technology, represent now the highest level of operational management of a man-made ecosystem. Isolated and closed, artificially existing ecosystems (for instance, greenhouses and hydroponic operations) are an industrial imitation of natural ecosystems.

The principle of unity of nature and interdependence of organisms, including the universality of interrelations of different phenomena, is very helpful to scientists in their attempts to establish the places of soils and of organisms in the biosphere. Having accepted this principle, it is impossible to think that increasing the productivity of soils and of ecosystems could be achieved by any one single method; rather will it need a many-sided complex of different methods and measures based on scientific knowledge and understanding of consequences in both the biosphere and its component ecosystems.

According to our contemporary level of scientific knowledge and technology, the soils among the components of the biosphere are the most manageable of all—through tillage, application of fertilizers, protection, and various forms of amelioration. Water is much less manageable, although still in many respects remaining in the hands of man to manipulate in irrigation, drainage, etc.—but again through soils. Living organisms are manageable only to a small extent—through genetics, selection, and protection. The atmosphere and climates are not yet at all extensively manageable; nor do they seem likely to be in the foreseeable future.

To supply the needs of his ever-increasing numbers, mankind is now forced, with the help of science and its application in technology—through fertilizers and amelioration, through the application of desalted water, through condensation of moisture, through reduction of evaporation, and through various other means—to raise the productivity of the earth by concentration of his efforts first and foremost on the protection, improvement, and utilization, of soils (Table VI).

E.F.—13*

TABLE VI

The Biosphere and Its Components

Components of the biosphere	Degree of manageability	
	Now	In the future
Light, thermal climate	—	Artificial light?
Atmosphere	—	Increasing of concentration of CO_2?
Water	+	+++
Organisms	+	++
Soils	+++	++++

The problems of biological productivity, preservation, and management, of ecosystems and of the biosphere, with the active participation of Soviet biologists, soil scientists, and geographers, have become the subject of very widespread international research and cooperation. UNESCO and other United Nations organizations have now initiated a major long-term programme entitled 'Man and the Biosphere', which will coordinate and concentrate the efforts of the scientists of different countries on the elaboration of measures to increase the productivity of the biosphere (Batisse, 1971). For the biosphere and its component ecosystems, organisms, and soils, must be secured and protected against anarchical utilization by contemporary human society. Particularly must the world's soils be protected against destruction through erosion, salinization, and pollution by industrial effluents and radiation of various kinds, as well as by the waste accumulations of cities and villages. Consequently for the future of man and nature there should be every possible support for the branches of science and technology that deal with these vital problems of the world's soils.

REFERENCES

BATISSE, M. (in press). Man and the Biosphere: an international research programme. *Biological Conservation*, 4(1), pp. 1–6.

BLACK, J. D. (1968). *The Management and Conservation of Biological Resources*. F. A. Davis, Philadelphia: xi + 339 pp., illustr.

BROWN, L. H. (1971). The biology of pastoral man as a factor in conservation. *Biological Conservation*, 3(2), pp. 93–100.

DASMANN, R. F. (1968). *Environmental Conservation* (2nd edn). John Wiley, New York, etc.: xiii + 375 pp., illustr.

FAO (1967). *The State of Food and Agriculture 1967*. Food and Agriculture Organization of the United Nations, Rome: vii + 202, illustr.

GRAHAM, E. H. (1944). *Natural Principles of Land Use*. Oxford University Press, London, etc.: xiii + 274 pp., illustr.

HELFRICH, H. M. Jr (Ed.) (1970). *The Environmental Crisis: Man's Struggle to Live with Himself*. Yale University Press, New Haven & London: x + 187 pp.

JOHNSON, F. S. (1970). The balance of atmospheric oxygen and carbon dioxide. *Biological Conservation*, 2(2), pp. 83–9.

KOVDA, V. A. (1937). [*Solontchaks and Solonetz.*—in Russian.] Academy of Sciences of the USSR, Moscow: 245 pp.

KOVDA, V. A. (1944). Biological cycles of movement and accumulation of salts. *Pochvovedenie*, Nos. 4–5, pp. 144–57.

KOVDA, V. A. (1946–47). [*Origin and Regime of Saline Soils.*—in Russian.] Academy of Sciences of the USSR, Moscow: Vol. I, 568 pp.; Vol. II, 336 pp.

KOVDA, V. A. (1954). [*Geochemistry of the Deserts of the USSR.*—in Russian and French.] Academy of Sciences of the USSR, Moscow: 152 pp.

KOVDA, V. A. (1956). Mineral composition of vegetation and soil-forming. *Pochvovedenie*, No. 1, pp. 6–37.

KOVDA, V. A (1966). The problem of biological and economic productivity of the dry land. *Selskokhozyaistvennoya Biologiya*, **1**(2), pp. 163–77.

KOVDA, V. A. (1969). [Contemporary studies on the biosphere.—in Russian.] *Journal of General Biology*, Academy of Sciences of the USSR, **33**(1), pp. 3–17.

KOVDA, V. A. 'and collaborators' (1970). Contemporary scientific concepts relating to the biosphere. Pp. 13–29 in *Use and Conservation of the Biosphere*. United Nations Educational, Scientific and Cultural Organization, Paris (UNESCO Natural Resources Research X): 272 pp.

KOVDA, V. A. (1971). [*Soil Cover and Influence of Man on it.*—in Russian.] Institute of Agrochemistry and Soil Science of the Academy of Sciences of the USSR, Pushino, Moscow: preprint of 37 pp.

MASSACHUSETTS INSTITUTE OF TECHNOLOGY [as MIT] (1970). *Man's Impact on the Global Environment: Report of the Study of Critical Environmental Problems*. MIT Press, Cambridge, Mass., and London, England: xxii + 319 pp., illustr.

MELLANBY, K. (1967). *Pesticides and Pollution*. Collins (The New Naturalist), London: 221 pp., illustr.

SUKACHEV, V. N. (1948). *Phytocoenology, Biogeocoeology, and Geography*. Trudy & Vsesuyoznogo Geograficheskogo Sozda, Vyp. 1, Geografgiz, Moscow: pp. 186–201.

SUKACHEV, V. N. & DYLIS, N. V. [1968]. *Fundamentals of Forest Biogeocoenology*. Oliver & Boyd, Edinburgh & London: viii + 672 pp., illustr.

UNESCO (1970). *Use and Conservation of the Biosphere*. United Nations Educational, Scientific and Cultural Organization, Paris (Natural Resources Research X): 272 pp.

VERNADSKY, V. I. (1926). [*The Biosphere.*—in Russian.] Nauchnoe Khimiko-Tekhricheskoe Izdatelstvo, Leningrad & Moscow: 147 pp.

VERNADSKY, V. I. (1934). [*Problems of Biogeochemistry. Part I: Significance of Biogeochemistry foe Studying the Biosphere.*—in Russian.] Izdatelstvo Akademii Nauk SSSR, Leningrad: 47 pp.

WENDLAND, W. M. & BRYSON, R. A. (1970). Atmospheric dustiness, man, and climatic change. *Biological Conservation*, **2**(2), pp. 125–8, illustr.

WURSTER, C. F., Jr (1969). Chlorinated hydrocarbons and the world ecosystem. *Biological Conservation*, **1**(2), pp. 123–9.

DISCUSSION

Køie (Chairman)

There are many important points in Professor Kovda's paper but I would like to single out for discussion his statement that if the energy that is stored in the underground parts of plants, particularly roots, is added to the energy in the soil humus, the total energy stored in soils becomes strongly dominant over that in the aerial parts of plants. In other words, one can conclude that the main part of the energy in living and dead matter on land is located in the soils of the continents. The soils also form a kind of universal shield that keeps in the biosphere important biophilic elements even though some tend to get leached out and transferred into the geochemical stream and ultimately into the world's oceans. Under natural conditions each major ecosystem is a self-regulating mechanism resulting from many thousands or even millions of years of history and evolution. Such an individual ecosystem on land represents an advanced and definite level of organization that has been reached by living and non-living materials reacting together.

The living components of the ecosystem—the plants, animals, and micro-biota—and the non-living components such as soils with their contained soil atmosphere and water, are all more or less closely interrelated and interconnected throughout any homogeneous area. Thus there is a common source of energy, an exchange and cycling of biophilic chemical elements, a synchronization of seasonal, physical, and biochemical dynamics, and general conformity of relationships, attained by the numerous populations inhabiting the same territorial units. The biomass formed inside the system, and the energy combined within this biomass, will be dispersed and consumed mainly inside the same ecosystem. As the product of biogenesis, the soil is at the same time a kind of mirror reflecting the ecosystem's history and recording its peculiarities.

As the result of these processes, the soils accumulate humus and biogenic mineral elements such as phosphorus, nitrogen, sulphur, calcium, potassium, magnesium, copper, zinc, and various others. Thus the soils, particularly in humid regions, are enriched by highly-dispersed metallic and other mineral ions and in important organic compounds giving them an often high level of natural fertility. These stores of energy and important chemical elements in biochemical compounds that have been accumulated after many thousands of years of soil formation, explain the extreme importance of humus to the fertility of soils. Humus is the basis of the soil's internal absorption capacity and hence of its biological activity and productivity.

I would like just to draw your attention to another aspect of the soil mentioned in Professor Kovda's paper and instancing the close connection with plant physiology. It is a well-known fact that plants should obtain somewhere between twelve and fifteen different elements from the soil, but we scarcely know at present which these elements fit in particular cases—merely that application of very small and economically niggardly amounts of trace-elements (such as copper, boron, and molybdenum) will often save a harvest or make an otherwise poor soil fertile. Yet if we knew more precisely what the requirements of particular crops are, maybe in many cases land could be saved and successfully used. So it seems strange that more force has not been put into these investigations of circumstances which actually form the basis of our existence.

Mäde

The discussions of the last few days have dealt with world-wide problems. But there are also heavy problems of a more regional character which are worthy of consideration.

Professor Kovda mentions in his paper the activities of mining enterprises. In the GDR, one effect of these activities is through the need of farmland for outcrops of lignite: quite frequently such an open-cast lignite working requires 90 to 100 hectares of farmland or woodland a year for mining purposes. The great expansion of these areas brings a notable loss of farmland and total transformation of the landscape relief, of the geological structure, of the soil, of the flora and fauna, and of the economic function of the entire region. Considering the fact that in our country one hectare of farmland has to nourish approximately three persons, there is an urgent need to regain all disused mining areas.

The area in question totals about 3,000 hectares or 30 km² a year, which means for my country a loss of 1 per cent of its whole territory within three years. This shows you the importance of recultivating the waste areas in a relatively small country. Until now, 48 per cent of all the land that has been devastated by lignite mining since the beginning of such activity has already been regained by agriculture or forestry. In addition to this, extensive remnant 'craters' are today used for purposes of water-supply and recreation. But in view of the need to recuperate the losses of the past, the percentage of the area recovered has constantly to be increased, and today we have a relationship between devastation and recovery of approximately 1:1. This has proved possible on the basis of systematic scientific investigations that have been pursued since 1952.

The next aim of the research work will be to elaborate a complex basic plan as the starting point for models of recultivation and amelioration with multipurpose utilization of the territory according to the task which has been given to us by the Environment Preservation Law from the year 1970. It may be of interest to you to know that one of these multipurposes is the retention and increase of the recreational value of the reclaimed areas.

Budowski

It is undoubtedly a fact that, because of the increased population which we shall acquire in the next years, we are already witnessing a tremendous increase in the invasion of what will clearly be marginal areas throughout the world and particularly in tropical countries and on tropical soils, and I wanted to bring one point out in this connection. There are, of course, many types of marginal areas, such as steep slopes or very dry areas, some of which can be remedied as Professor Kovda has indicated by suitably adapted earthworks or irrigation systems. But the greatest danger which I have witnessed in the last ten years in Latin America, whence I come, is the invasion of marginal areas of high rainfall. This is a point which has not been illustrated in Professor Kovda's excellent paper but should, I feel, be emphasized.

[At least two-thirds of tropical Latin America is comprised of these areas which are marginal for agriculture and grazing, and so far most of them have remained more or less untouched. They are the large forests of the unpopulated parts of, particularly, Brazil, Bolivia, Peru, Ecuador, Colombia, and Venezuela; but because of the recent facilities in communication and of the ill-conceived 'development' plans, there has been, in the last few years, a tremendous invasion of these areas. This constitutes a threat, in a sense to the whole biosphere, because of the elimination of an extremely useful type of vegetation cover and its replacement by often terribly degraded lands. There is a further pitfall in all this: most of our agriculture has hitherto been in areas of alternating dry and wet seasons; however, where there is no such alternation but continuously high rainfall, and when the type of agriculture of drier areas is carried over, deforestation leads to very quick degradation of the soil, with devastating erosion on slopes.

Areas totalling possibly hundreds of millions of hectares are involved in this invasion of marginal lands, and certainly it will result in the deforestation of vast tracts of tropical rain-forest. These are, I repeat, areas of poor soils and very high rainfall. What could be a solution is extremely difficult to say, as long as population continues to increase at the alarming rate that is all too familiar in many tropical countries. But I would suggest one ecological guideline, namely that experience so far has shown that it pays much more, and brings ultimately much better results, to concentrate production on the best soils in areas already settled and which can be adapted to intensive types of techniques, rather than to move on to some of the marginal soils of the wet hinterlands.

My main point was to bring this matter to the attention of this Conference and the world because it involves tremendous areas of what may be considered an indispensable green belt in some of the tropical countries in which vast forest tracts are being destroyed, as well as the soils underlying them, because of poor planning and increased demographic pressure.]

Gootjes

In my view Professor Kovda is right in stressing the need to look at the entire biosphere—to integrate specialized studies of air, water, and soil. Sound policies cannot be constructed separately, as we have attempted to do in recent years without consideration of wider aspects than those with which at first sight they may appear to be exclusively concerned. Thus certain measures to reduce air pollution have led to industries switching to techniques causing water pollution. When this is forbidden too, the last way out is the soil. But what will be the result if the soil is in the neighbourhood of a drinking-water basin or is on land where the cows walk around and graze?

Clearly, what we need for the future is an integrated environmental policy with a multidisciplinarian basis and outcome. It is no longer sufficient for policy-making in such matters to be left to specialists in air pollution, to chemical engineers, to mathematicians, or even to biologists or others. Such people, however expert they may be, are at once isolated by partial policies—regional, national, or international—that do not take into account the consequences for the other components of the total environment, especially on the borders of other countries. So I think far more international cooperation is needed, and maybe the economists can help us in this through use of their classical knowledge of price theories and economic order for the attainment of new objectives. Surely we should take action in an integrated way, considering the biosphere as a whole, and stressing this overall aspect in our discussions.

Mellanby

I was very interested in Professor Mäde's contribution about the recovery of land which has been destroyed by open-cast mining. In Britain in the nineteenth century, as in many other countries, we destroyed enormous areas of our countryside by open-cast mining and by removal of iron ore. But today we have a law that requires people who destroy such areas to rehabilitate them afterwards, and there is a very complicated system by which the land is recovered and paid for in various ways. It has been very interesting to see how successful this has been in many cases. There are areas where coal mining was rife but now good agricultural crops are being produced within five years of all the coal having been dug out, and on the iron ore areas such rehabilitation has been sometimes even quicker. A good deal of scientific work has been done on the soil cover and how to replace the organic matter and so forth. In most cases the top-soil is stored separately from the subsoil and is carefully put on top, though it is doubtful whether this is always necessary.

I was interested last year to see a case in Durham, in the north of England, where they had been very careful over one area to put back the top-soil properly and on top. In another case they had taken no trouble—they had simply been in a hurry and the weather had been getting bad, so that over a huge area they had put the subsoil on top. Yet after two years there was absolutely no discernible difference. I think that sometimes we are being too careful here—not in all parts of the world, with all climates and with different types of rainfall, but at least in many temperate areas. I think that we may be not rehabilitating many areas because we think it is too difficult, whereas if we did not take quite so much trouble, and were more careful with fertilization and so on, we might be able to recover the fertility of what is a very unpromising subsoil much more quickly than many of our soil scientists would have us expect.

Johnson

The question of the rain forest of the Amazon region is most interesting. A couple of years ago Sir Frank Fraser Darling made a very powerful statement in which he said in effect that the forests of the Amazon were being burned and bulldozed at a fearful rate to provide indifferent grazing for cattle of inferior quality. I can even go along with his phrasing. For not very long ago I had occasion to fly, from the Brazilian-Colombian border, all the way down the Amazon via Manaus to Belém, and I also went up into the frontier state of Maranhão. From this experience I would like to support the suggestion that there is in the making here an ecological disaster of some magnitude. There is no doubt, if you fly over this State, that you are a witness of a random process of despoliation and destruction. The forest is being burned at an immense rate. Nobody knows for sure precisely the rate at which it has been burnt, but it certainly far exceeds the rate of natural regeneration.

The reason is not far to seek: the Brazilian government has made one of its principal plans and facets of economic strategy the extension of the trans-Amazonic highway into the interior, with the result that you have the constant leap-frogging of small settlers along the road as the highway pushes on into the interior. Well of course in a couple of years they exhaust the fertility of the soil, up sticks, and move on again. Behind the people come the cattle, eating down the secondary growth, and behind the cattle comes the desert, though admittedly this is taking a somewhat dramatic view of the situation.

Two questions are involved: first, what is the international significance of destroying this great green area? I think frankly this is something we probably don't know enough about, though there have been suggestions that the Amazon forest is responsible for quite a lot of the free oxygen in the world. Yet as we have already been informed more than once in this Conference, most of the free oxygen in the atmosphere is produced by the seas, and so perhaps after all the Amazon forest is not so very important. But all this wanton vegetational desecration would seem to be economically ill-founded and an aesthetic tragedy, if not anything else. So the other question is: what are the alternatives?

The Brazilians over the last twenty years have had an immense problem of migration from their north-east zone into the south-central area. One of the alternatives to this, and to the consequent urbanization and slum problems in São Paulo and Rio, is to try and develop other parts of the country. When I had occasion to go up to an area in Maranhão, I found there a British team from Hunting Technical Services trying to devise a pattern of settlement—a pattern of exploiting the rain forest which would at the same time provide a livelihood for the settlers. Without destroying the forest, the basic thing that was being done was to give a 50-hectares plot to each settler—rather a large plot, of which 20 hectares were to remain under forest and were to be exploited as timber but along properly-designed commercial lines. Within the remaining 30 hectares—recognizing the social limitations on agriculture and the sort of agriculture that for generations had been practised there—they tried to evolve a system of shifting cultivation, designed carefully to permit the natural fertility of the soil to be maintained in the long run.

Well, I did not come out in any clear way on either side, but feel this case in Brazil is a terribly important one. You talk to Brazilians but simply cannot get them to see why they should not push ahead with the road through the Amazon. And I have some sympathy with them when they reject suggestions from outsiders who are trying to stop such development. It does mean, however, that very great importance must be placed on the possibility of devising systems for exploiting the forest which are not ecologically harmful.

Kuenen

Professor Kovda in his important paper reintroduces the concept of general conservation from which in particular yesterday we were drifting away. He also introduces the prospect that we might go so far as to decide where we should do what, at least in the matter of soil use and conservation. Carrying this further, we might even decide that certain areas of the world should be set aside as world parks and not just as national parks which is the highest level most of us strive for at present. This might also imply that we believe, for mankind as a whole, that we might take the responsibility for saying where people can live and where not—where it is reasonable to have a settlement, and so on. Indeed, if you start from the point of view of the soil, this seems reasonable enough. But now I suggest that we might also look at it from the point of view of human health, as for the last twenty to thirty years we have always assumed that if somebody wants to live somewhere it is therefore the duty of the medical officer to make the environment such that he can live there healthily. Never has the medical officer asked the question of whether it is sensible for people to live there!

So I would like to suggest that in looking at the problems of the use of insecticides to make certain parts of the world habitable for man, the same reasoning might be applied in the matter of human health as in the case of soil. Then in certain cases it could be said: this area is not habitable from the point of view of medical care, because of the consequences of using insecticides. Though it is evident from the discussions yesterday that for medical reasons insecticides must continue to be used, it is also quite obvious that certain ones are poisoning the biosphere. Man wants health and he wants food; but man also requires ethical and aesthetic satisfaction. It is these last two which are endangered by the present exploitation of the earth. We should be very careful not to destroy one aspect of man's requirements because of the idea that just plain health and enough food are all we need.

Fosberg

The last two contributions have called to mind something which I think is quite worth bringing to your attention, namely an interesting little book which is being published about now. It is called *Amazonia*, and is by one of American's more thoughtful and competent anthropologists, Dr Betty Meggers. The subtitle is 'Man and Culture in a Counterfeit Paradise', which tells you a great deal, for the book brings out and documents extremely well the fact that the glowing pictures we have been given of the fertility of the Amazon basin and the prospects of this being a future solution of the world's food problem are an absolute delusion. She does this with what is perhaps one of the best available brief presentations of the nature of an ecosystem, and particularly of the rain-forest ecosystem. This is astonishing, coming from an anthropologist, as most of them are quite ill-informed in such fields. But I would like to recommend this book with the suggestion that you read it with Professor Kuenen's remarks in mind.

I believe that the attempts in the past to relieve the population pressure in other parts of tropical countries by inducing people to emigrate to the rain

forest have largely been failures, and I think they have often been quite
unfair to the people who have been resettled in these areas. I saw this in
Colombia, where people were persuaded because of poverty in the uplands
to migrate down into the lowland areas; yet inevitably within a year or two
they were crying for help, and, in one way or another, went back home up
to the places where they had been poor but at least not quite starving. They
did get a good crop of maize and bananas the first year in the lowlands, and
they got half of this crop the next year; but after that they got virtually
nothing. And they were too far away to get any relief, to get any help from
anyone else. They were down in the abandoned part of Colombia, and I
have seen the same sort of thing in other parts of the world; but it was most
obvious there.

I think it is a pretty poor policy to promise people something and get them
out into a situation where they really cannot help themselves. It may be a
temporary relief from their impoverished condition, but their disillusionment
is perhaps far worse than the poor conditions under which they are living
at the present time, and I think, as Professor Kuenen suggests, that there are
other far better land-uses for at least some of these tropical forests than chop-
ping them down and converting them into submarginal agricultural land.
Tropical rain-forest is one of the most magnificent biological phenomena
the world has produced, and I would recommend saving a substantial part
of it until we have advanced in our civilization and culture to a point where
we can appreciate it.

Mahler

I would like to give you some information about the meeting on soil
conservation which has just been taking place in Rome. It was called for by
the UN Secretariat in connection with the Stockholm Conference, and was
hosted by FAO who provided the technical help. We had about thirty-five
governments represented, involving an approximately equal proportion of
developed and developing countries. After reviewing general problems, the
group set up guidelines for action, including an outline plan, and I would
like briefly to mention the main points which have emerged from this
meeting.

There was first a recognition of the need for better delimitation and
assessment of soil resources. As is probably known to most of the participants
here, there has already for many years been a project shared between FAO,
UNESCO, and the International Society of Soil Science, for a Soils Map of
the world, and several sheets have now been prepared for Europe and Latin
America. It was felt, however, that it was not sufficient to indicate the
boundaries of this resource without identification of soil conservation
problem areas, and actually we have come to the same approach about the
water resources. Thus we are in favour of defining soil problem areas, on
which basis some action can be instituted. It was also felt that, so far, in many
cases soil scientists have failed to convey their message to the users and
especially to the planners, because they employ a rather special scientific
terminology and very often their maps are not easy to understand—especially
by the planners who are commonly engineers or economists. So one of the

proposals was: place more emphasis on land classification and soil-maps' interpretation.

We have now started in FAO what we call a 'soil data bank', to provide information to those governments which require it on the land capabilities in different areas. This is based upon existing knowledge, and should enable us to transfer experience gained in one area to all other similar areas, so helping people to avoid some of the mistakes that have been made. Emphasis is also placed on soil survey interpretation because we feel that a major part of the soil degradation problem has to be tackled at the stage of land-use planning—at the stage where it is decided to use a particular piece of land for a given purpose—and very often when a mistake is made at this stage it will be very difficult to solve any degradation problem afterwards. For such interpretation we feel that the planners and the soil scientists have to come to a better understanding, with a language which comes closer to each other's, and we have at present a project on the way to develop norms for an international system of land classification.

As for the need for multipurpose interpretation for multidisciplinary approaches in land-use planning, we talked very much in our meeting about systems of management for soil conservation, and particular emphasis was placed on legislation and on the licensing of the use of land. It has transpired that very often land uses are decided by different ministries in a country, each ministry giving out licences for the use of land—for example, for roads, for buildings, for airports, for development of irrigation projects, etc.—and some coordination of this licensing is necessary to avoid conflicts in land-use.

It was also felt that there is already existing legislation in some countries for soil conservation, and that we have already a system of information on this legislation in FAO which could help the governments of developing countries to establish their own legislation in this respect.

Kassas

Concerning the very important issue of whether we should intensify land-use in our limited fertile areas or encroach and expand our land-use into the so-called marginal areas, the problem in many parts of the world, including much of the continent of Africa, is not so much that we are encroaching on marginal areas as actually the other way round—marginal ecosystems are encroaching on land use areas. Many people, including myself, have studied the problem of desert encroachment in Africa. It is estimated that in one country, Sudan, the desert has encroached within the last 15–20 years over land-used areas to occupy a belt no less than 150 kilometres in width. This is happening very widely in the Sahelian belt of Africa—from the Sudan to Niger, where the great Sahara is extending at a very alarming rate—and all land reclamation work in the whole continent of Africa is gaining for man much less land than man is losing by the desert encroachment. Now this desert extension is mostly due to man trying to intensify land-use, particularly by too-heavy grazing, and people should be extremely careful about this, especially in these marginal areas.

My other point concerns the importance of interdisciplinary and integrated studies, which I feel should not only bring soil scientists and hydrologists and climatologists together but also—and this is very important —sociologists and anthropologists. In this connection I would like to quote an example of work done with all good intention by FAO in Egypt. It started in 1964 and involved the expenditure of millions of dollars on a project having the intention of releasing land from overgrazing pressure by bringing into the area a good deal of animal feed (dried cake) and also food for people. But after five years of this excess feeding the herds had increased in number so that they did more overgrazing, and when once the project and its flow of feed stopped these animals had insufficient to eat. This is the sort of thing we need to consider in properly integrated studies, including sociological and anthropological studies to enable us to predict how people will react and behave, and biological studies to help us towards doing the same for animals.

Cain

I want to make one point which I don't believe has come before us yet: in almost any place in the world, whatever the sophistication of soil science or lack of it, there remains a very human problem—the hard-headedness of the bankers' approach to development which tends to make them ignore the environment. Let me illustrate how this possibly may be overcome. Nearly all developments need credit. There has been some scattered experience in the United States of private banks extending credit to a farmer only if he has a soil-and-water conservation plan, and this credit would be discontinued if he does not follow the plan. This puts the emphasis on any soil management in a very practical position. I think, then, that we need to note the typical bankers' approach and try ultimately to educate them.

Now I will turn to a different situation. The biggest bank that I know of is the International Bank for Reconstruction and Development, commonly referred to as the World Bank, with its great funds to spend internationally. After more than two decades of history, with little thought given for the ecological sciences which integrate information about the environment, the International Bank had no one to look at the environmental impact of development plans. When Mr Robert McNamara, who is used to looking at whole systems, became President of the Bank, he got on his staff a competent ecologist to review the development of a new iron mine and harbour in Brazil. A control over money is often a control over soil as well as other natural resources. It took the World Bank a long time to become alert to the environment. And when in the United States, with over 2,000 counties, we have only a few county banks that require good soil management plans before they will make a loan on farm equipment, there must be some kind of imbalance in the human ecosystem that goes far beyond the realm of soil science.

I wish to make one more point. I know of a case in which a mine was to be developed and the developers had become alerted to the public requirements for the handling of spoil from mining. In planning this mine it was computed that about $1\frac{1}{2}$ per cent of the capital investment would be required to restore the land after mining was complete and meanwhile to avoid serious disturbances of the physical environment during mining. The point is that when an investment is being planned, the amount of capital which it takes to protect the environment, whether it be from air pollution, from water pollution, or from soil disturbance, seems relatively small. It may be in some cases less than 1 per cent, it may be 3 or 4 per cent; but when once the operations are established, or when once the plant is older, it is nearly impossible to get any money out of a private or even a public enterprise to repair the damage that has already been done. My point accordingly is: let's talk to bankers, let's talk to people who handle investments, and see if we can convince them that they had better hold on tight to their money until they have got some agreement, some contract, that farmers and others will do the best they can to protect soil and the rest of the environment.

Söyrinki

Referring further to tropical problems, in recent decades the coffee plantations in Brazil have proceeded about 300 kilometres inland from the Atlantic coast, and have devastated the nice forest vegetation so that now these lands are semi-cultivated, without any real primary vegetation; one can perhaps use them as pasture but one cannot cultivate coffee on them any more. As a result the coffee hegemony in Brazil has gone from São Paulo to another state, leaving an example of how the forest vegetation has been devastated during recent decades.

We know that Europe was covered with forest at the beginning of the present millennium, virtually the whole of it, so that a squirrel could spring from tree to tree from the Ural Mountains in Russia over the whole continent to the Atlantic coast without putting its feet on the earth. Now we have devastated our forests in Europe, too, but far more slowly than in those tropical countries; nor has the result been so disastrous. We must also refer to the temperate rain-forests in the southern Andes, in Chile and Argentina, which have been devastated but where moves are afoot to institute schemes for reforestation.

Professor Kassas has referred to the expanding desert of northern Africa, and this has its counterparts in Southern Africa. When the white man came there several centuries ago, there was fine subtropical rain-forest and other forest vegetation, most of which has now been devastated, the desert and semi-desert vegetation having extended very rapidly. South African botanical publications indicate that if matters continue as at present, by the year 2000 a greater part of the land will have become desert.

Dr Fosberg has spoken about the need for more protected areas in tropical rain-forests. Last September there was a symposium in Brussels, for the centenary celebration of the founding of the Botanic Garden there, at which I pointed out just this same thing—the widespread lack of large national parks in the world's tropical rain-forest areas. We cannot be sure that plant species can be saved there, and already many have disappeared. And now we are speaking of the landscape and of the soils which we need—really need in large protected areas in tropical rain-forests. So I will support Dr Fosberg most ardently in his plea, and suggest that this Conference put into its resolutions this point particularly.

Munch-Petersen

Though I expect to have more to say when we come to discuss global responsibilities, I'd just like to make a brief comment in connection with the one of the distinguished speaker from Egypt in which he referred to the lack of a coordinated and integrated approach from the United Nations system. I would be among the first to admit that maybe more could be done in this respect. Nevertheless, I would like to point out that to a larger and larger extent in the UN family—and by the UN family I mean not only the United Nations Development Programme but also the United Nations itself and all the so-called specialized agencies such as FAO, UNESCO, WHO, WMO, etc.—we have tried to develop precisely this integrated approach to urban problems and also to regional rural problems. Admittedly, it is a very difficult thing to accomplish; but it is essential, even in the face of certain difficulties resulting particularly from the fact that the agencies have their own specialized fields. Indeed that is exactly one of the reasons why the United Nations Development Programme, which I have the honour to represent, has been established as a coordinating force. And that is why now under the new system our representatives in the developing countries, our so-called United Nations' resident representatives, have been designated as the leaders of the teams of the UN organizations.

We support to an increasing extent, through our resident representatives in the developing countries, regional and integrated activities in which all these organizations participate actively, and we hope that these activities will go on and expand. At the moment we are involving twenty nations in country programming, and we are planning to increase this by the same number in the near future. We are also, in the United Nations Development Programme, assisting in many cases in the integrated rural development and regional planning of governments in dealing with a root problem of over-crowded cities, namely the depopulation of the countryside. We have recently approved the project in Afghanistan for the integrated development of a province which aims to restore the environment by controlling overgrazing and increasing arable production with its more intensive labour utilization. But, as I say, I think I would like to come back to such topics later in this Conference.

Haapanen

It was interesting to hear what Professor Cain thought about the financing of mining and soil preservation. In Finland we are draining about 300,000 hectares of peatland every year, and a vast amount of money is invested in this draining. It is taking place on state-owned lands but, I would say, perhaps mostly on land that is owned by private people.

The plans for draining are often made by persons without sufficient knowledge of peatland ecosystems and their possible productivity to raise forest. We have a lot of examples of peatlands being drained without the capacity to raise forests, their nature being destroyed in a few years through lack of proper planning. We still have some ten million or more hectares of peatland in this country, but most of it is situated in the northern parts. There are also peatlands remaining in the southern parts of the country—perhaps you have seen some of them—but these are mostly destined to be drained within the next ten years or sooner.

Polunin

Would Professor Kunin please inform us of the outcome of any recent studies on the effects of widespread irrigation and other major man-made changes in the Soviet Union on climate and/or soils? Especially would it be interesting to hear of any predicted effects on the soils of surrounding areas of major river diversion and damming schemes and other ecological 'face-lifting'. The Russians, as you will know, have always been leaders in soil science, and so it is fully to be expected that they will have studied these aspects just as deeply as may have proved practicable.

Kunin

As regards climate, if the irrigation is intensive and the area of the 'oasis' is not less than 1,000 kilometres in diameter, there may be some effects, such as a reduction of about 1°C in the average summer temperature of the air and, of course, a raising of its relative humidity. But that is all: on the basis of many investigations we have observed no other effects.

When we come to the effect on soils, this question has very many sides. If the reservoir is in a mountain situation, there is no marked effect on soils—apart, of course, from their loss under water and perhaps some very local effects from seepage. But the outcome may be very different around lowland lakes and rivers, being connected with the character of the depression concerned and with the underground water situation. The results may be either beneficial or undesirable, and extend over a wide belt around the reservoir, often affecting its inhabitants considerably in various ways. The problems of soil salinity as affected by irrigation are too large to discuss here; to speak about them would take whole hours.

As for major water-diversion schemes, there are several variations of those for transmittal of waters from the north slope to far south. What is needed is about 30 cubic kilometres or at most 40 cubic kilometres per year. These proposals are now being investigated. Meanwhile the great River Volga and some other sources are being invoked to help maintain a reasonable level of water in the Caspian Sea. Because many sides of the economy are connected with this level, it is necessary first to choose the optimal level, and then in order to maintain this, realize the effective project. The total run-off to the Arctic Basin from all the Siberian and European rivers of the USSR is more than 3,000 cubic kilometres per year, the total stream-flow of the USSR exceeding 4,000 cubic kilometres. If we take a very few tens of cubic kilometres from this, it is not expected that any serious effect will result. But to answer the question in detail would be very difficult, and could probably only be done step by step as development took place.

12

SUSTAINED BIOLOGICAL PRODUCTIVITY

Keynote Paper

Sustained Biological Productivity

by

E. BARTON WORTHINGTON

Formerly *Secretary-General, Scientific Council for Africa South of the Sahara;*
sometime *Deputy Director-General of the British Nature Conservancy;*
Scientific Director, International Biological Programme,
7 Marylebone Road,
London NW1,
England

Introduction

When the organizers of this Conference asked me to contribute a paper on sustained biological productivity, I presumed they had in mind the International Biological Programme (IBP) which runs for the decade of 1964–74, with more than sixty countries participating. Its purpose is the world study of 'biological productivity and human welfare', and it seemed that the Conference organizers were thinking in terms of sustained biological productivity linked to man's use thereof. Other speakers were billed to deal with conservation for its own sake, but my first point is that there is no real scientific difference between the two. Whether one considers a biological system of very high productivity (say, a field of cane-sugar or a carp pond), or of very low productivity (say, the arctic tundra or the Dead Sea), the flow of energy through the biological system is sustained, somewhere near the maximum, within the limits imposed by environmental factors. However, when it comes to management to meet human needs, we have to define our objectives carefully, because manipulation of a particular ecosystem is often possible in two quite different and even opposing directions.

I think, for example, of an area in Uganda, near the northern shore of Lake Victoria, with a climate influenced by the evaporation from that 67,000 km² of water. The area is remarkable for its sugar estates, but these were carved out of tall forest, of which I am glad to say there are a few remnants left and managed as forest nature reserves. The objective of the sugar fields is maximum productivity with minimum diversity, whereas the objective of the nature reserve is maximum diversity of plant and animal life without bothering about productivity. In the process of converting the forest to the sugar field, there must have been some kind of biological degradation which has to be made up for by regular additions of fertilizer and irrigation water. It is easy to change the ecosystem in that direction; but it is very difficult to do the reverse, namely, to create high forest from sugar land. The main reasons for this, doubtless, are physical factors of the environment—including the ecoclimate of the forest which, when once lost, is not at all easily recreated.

About a dozen years ago, speaking at a discussion on the elements of conservation, I found that Aristotle's 'elements' of 'earth, air, fire, and water' brought into a modern setting, provided appropriate headings under which to consider the main factors of conservation practices. Then my purpose was to emphasize that, if the environment is right, the organisms can generally look after themselves. This applies regardless of whether the object is the preservation of particular species of rare plants or animals or the continuance of the whole community. Aristotle's sequence of 'elements' applies equally well to the activities of nature or of mankind in the regular cropping of plant or animal life to obtain a maximum sustained yield. Thus, today the objective of sustained biological productivity echoes Theodore Roosevelt's dictum of nearly seventy years ago: 'Conservation through wise use'; and this is what my present paper is largely about.

No excuse is needed for harping back a dozen years to a discussion on conservation, or seventy years to Theodore Roosevelt, or two thousand years to Aristotle. For the basic subject of this Conference—the environment of man, even though we are looking into the future—has no beginning this side of half-a-million years; and provided we can apply scientific and technological knowledge, together with common sense, it should have no end.

Let us now look at some of the physical factors which underlie biological productivity, taking them in Aristotle's sequence.

EARTH

Earth comes first, because man is a terrestrial animal; but, in terms of the world's total biological production, the soil is not the greatest medium. If we take away the oceans, which account for about 70 per cent of the world's surface area, we are left with some 155 million km^2 of land surface. If from this we take away one-fifth which is too cold to support much life, another fifth which is too dry, and another fifth which is too high or infertile for other reasons, we are left with not much more than 60 million km^2—only about 12 per cent of the earth's surface—which is available for really active biological production. But, of course, this 12 per cent provides the greater part of man's food and other needs, and almost all of his living space.

In the IBP we divide the terrestrial world into its major vegetation formations or habitat types, referred to as 'biomes',* each of which embraces a series of ecosystems,† and we recognize four major biomes, namely woodlands, tundras, grasslands, and deserts. Each of these encompasses the primary producers (consisting mainly of green plants), the secondary producers (consisting of animals great and small which consume these plants), the tertiary producers which eat these animals, and then the innumerable organisms, plant and animal, which help towards the breakdown of what has been built up. Thus the products can be recycled through the soil, water, and air, thereby keeping the flow of energy through the system always on the move.

Within each biome, multidisciplinary teams of scientists in the IBP are seeking to analyse the driving force that makes ecosystems operate, to assess the processes which cause the interaction or linkage of the various components, and to develop procedures for predicting the consequences of environmental stress, both natural and man-made.

Since man has colonized nearly all ecosystems of the world, he has naturally had enormous influence upon them, taking off for his own purpose a proportion of the energy-flow at each cycle. Man as a hunter relies largely on the natural processes and takes off a relatively small proportion of the total product, though this may be increased significantly by the management of wild lands. Man as a pastoralist likewise relies largely on the natural energy-flow but, through intensive grazing and browsing by his domestic

* *biome* is defined in Webster's Third New International Dictionary as 'an ecological formation considered in terms of both plants and animals of the area concerned and usually identified in terms of characteristic vegetation forms'.

† *ecosystem* is defined in Webster as 'an ecological community considered together with the non-living factors of its environment as a unit'.

stock and his management of the environment, he may have a profound influence—even to the extent of converting one biome into another, as for example woodland into grassland, or grassland into desert. Man as a cultivator has even greater influence, though more locally, and he may succeed in removing for his own purpose something like half the total biological productivity of each cycle—amounting to almost the total shoot, or root, of domesticated plants grown in pure stand.

Woodlands

Each of the four major biomes has many subdivisions which greatly complicate the picture and make comparisons difficult. Take, for example, the woodlands biome: it can be divided into the great coniferous belt of northern latitudes, the deciduous and evergreen temperate forests, the tropical rain-forests and mountain forests, and the huge areas of savanna woodlands. But this is by no means the end, because one must consider the different species-composition of the forests in the major biogeographical regions of the world. There are some six to seven hundred woody plants to be found in the tropical rain-forests of Africa, which are almost wholly different in species-composition from those of the corresponding biomes in South America, Asia, and Australasia. By contrast the forests of Finland contain hardly a score of woody species.

Tundras

Tundra is commonly simpler than woodland in its basic composition and so may be taken as an example of how IBP operates in revealing the processes of biological productivity. Among major features of the tundra biome are shortness of the growing-season, accumulation of nutrients in decaying plant material, and periodic population explosions of the consumer animals. Much of the tundra, moreover, lies within the area of permafrost and so is easily damaged. It is a brittle biome which, when once damaged, is very slow to mend.

IBP projects on the productivity of tundras and related communities are now under way in Canada, USA, and Greenland (in the Nearctic region), and in Ireland, UK, Norway, Sweden, Finland, and the USSR (in the Palearctic). Cooperating projects in the southern hemisphere include those at Macquarie Island and South Georgia.

Even within this relatively simple biome there is a wide range of situations and of emphasis in the research. For instance, at Kevo in Finnish Lapland the Reindeer (*Rangifer tarandus*) is the main herbivore, and a major problem is the relationship and interaction between reindeer populations and their main winter food-source which is various species of lichens, particularly of the genus *Cladonia*. On the other hand, at Point Barrow in Alaska and at the USSR project in the northern Urals, attention is being given to the influence of populations of small rodents on the availability of nutrients to plants. At Hardangervidda in Norway and the Moorhouse site in the Pennines of England, the influence of herbivores appears to be rather small, and the major part of primary production goes directly into the detritus food-chain of leaves, etc., which fall and decay. At all these sites, the factors and components affecting the decay of dead organic matter is of great importance in analysing the ecosystem's functioning.

In the IBP we set much store by the interdisciplinary approach to problems of productivity, and among the disciplines invoked are mathematics and computer science—an object being to develop and refine for each biome a framework of functional modes as a basis for analysing and synthesizing the data obtained from field observation and experiment concerning all stages of the energy cycle. For the tundra biome it cannot be claimed that effective mathematical models are yet available, but what may be described as 'word models' for each active project have been developed, and to bring these together into an inter-project synthesis of results is an objective of the international tundra biome group.

Grasslands

In the case of the grassland biome, the complexities are greater than for tundra owing to the great range of grassland types and the large number of species which compose them in the different climatic and biogeographical zones of the world. However, the task of bringing large quantities of data into meaningful shape through 'systems analysis' is more advanced for grasslands, the focus being on certain large projects, each employing numerous research workers in many disciplines. These, situated in Canada and the USA, are linked to other grassland investigations in other parts of the world, for example in Poland and India. The possibilities of bringing the IBP approach on fundamental productivity into close liaison with the practical approach of the effective utilization and management of range-lands, particularly in developing countries, is currently being explored in depth in association with FAO and UNESCO.

Because of the preponderance of grasslands of one kind or another on the earth's land surfaces, the problems of their sustained productivity are of enormous importance to the future of mankind. Promising results are now emerging from a branch of IBP concerned with the production of edible protein directly from grass and other leaves; but within the foreseeable future it seems inevitable that the primary production of protein by most forms of vegetation will continue to pass through the animal food-link before becoming consumable by mankind, and in that process will be reduced in quantity to about one-tenth.

Domestication and Gene-pools

In this connection it is a matter of surprise that the domestic animals of the world are so limited in their species, and that modern man has never bothered to take advantage of the attributes of adaptation to hard conditions and lack of water, and resistance to diseases, which are so well illustrated by the great variety of wild mammals—particularly in Africa, but also in parts of the Americas and Australasia. In spite of the fact that archaeologists now inform us that man has lived longer in Africa than in any other continent, the origins of domestic animals, with a few minor exceptions, seem to be limited to Asia—presumably for the reason that that is where the main early civilizations developed. Since the domesticated Asian animals proved so successful, they have been taken to every continent and almost every size-able island in the world, and nobody has bothered much with the local fauna.

But now at last there is some awakening, for there is a herd of semi-domesticated Eland (*Taurotragus oryx*) in Rhodesia and another in Russia, with a project for another in Argentina. There is a project also for experimental domestication of Red Deer (*Cervus elaphus*) in Scotland. It has been well established by recent studies of their physiology and ecology that such animals are better attuned to their natural tough environments and so are capable of greater sustained biological production than are their domestic counterparts. On the Scottish island of Rhum—an experimental nature reserve since 1958—the Red Deer, for example, have been found to produce more venison than the former black-faced sheep could produce of mutton per unit area of ground. If Red Deer were not so wild, and were covered with wool instead of hair, there might have been no need for sheep in the highlands of Scotland, and the biological productivity of the vegetation, as also of the herbivores, would probably have been higher as a result.

The situation of domesticated plants is somewhat similar to that of ani-mals: mankind subsists on surprisingly few main species which have been intensively cultivated, bred, and adapted. In addition there are, of course, a large number of wild plants, as of wild animals, which are made use of by mankind as food, timber, fibre, medicines, etc. Some isolated groups of humans who live close to nature, mainly in tropical climates, know more about some of these useful plants than we do. Consider, for example, a 'pharmaceutical' such as curare, derived from a plant in the South American jungle, well known to the Indians as a powerful nerve-poison, and now of im-portance to modern medicine in treating some nervous disorders. This was 'discovered' by modern science not so many years ago; but my friends who work among the Amerindians tell me that there are many other plant products with particular uses and values known to these people, yet quite unknown to science in their biochemical effects or even in their botanical identity.

Such considerations raise the question of plant and animal gene-pools which are coming into ever-growing importance as a means of ensuring future needs of breeding material. There is no question that many species and varieties which are likely to be of value to future breeders are today in serious danger of extinction. Yet the present state of our knowledge about their properties and genetic make-up is so fragmentary that the only practical measure in many cases is to ensure adequate areas of conserved habitat where such species and varieties have a good chance to survive—to buy time for future research, so to speak. In other cases, as with the wild relatives of grain-crops, pulses, and fibre plants, a much more organized and sophisticated ap-proach is possible through plant exploration and breeding, together with the establishment of 'banks' of viable seed or other materials. This is another sub-ject in which IBP has been active in cooperation with FAO, and on which we have recently published a substantial volume concerned mainly with methods of research (Frankel & Bennett, 1970). Animal gene-pools are more difficult to form and maintain than plant ones, and little progress can yet be claimed in the research which must precede their establishment—except in the case of domestic species.

We must not move on from the earth without noting that one of the seven sections of IBP is devoted to terrestrial conservation (CT). Its basic purpose is to put the conservation of areas such as nature reserves and national parks on to a more scientific footing—both in their selection as being representative of the range of ecosystems existing in the world, and in their management. To this end the section has organized a world survey of areas and their environmental factors with the aid of check-sheets arranged so that the data can be fed into computers. In this and other respects section CT is in close association with IUCN.

AIR

Air comes second in Aristotle's list. As land mammals, we need it to breathe, and without its oxygen our whole metabolism quickly grinds to a halt. However, in its influence on total biological productivity, the air is far more important as the supplier of carbon dioxide to plants—this supply being the basis of plant biomass and hence of the animal food-chains. The quantity of CO_2 in the atmosphere, we are told, has increased steadily at the rate of 0·2 per cent annually since 1958—mainly from the combustion of fossil fuels (MIT, 1970). But only half the amount that man puts into the atmosphere stays there and produces this rise; the other half goes into the oceans or into living organisms. By the year 2000, it is projected that there will have been a total 18 per cent increase of CO_2 in the atmosphere (from 320 in 1958 to 379 parts per million), and that this might increase the surface temperature of the earth by 0.5°C from the same baseline of 1958. But as far as I am aware, biologists are not agreed as to whether this would be a good thing or a bad thing for plant life—whether it would increase or decrease biological production.

Atmospheric Change

Perhaps more important for our present thinking may be changes in the quantity of particles in the atmosphere—particularly in the trophosphere up to about 12,000 metres—as these both absorb and reflect radiation from the sun and the earth, alter the heat-balance, and by nucleation affect cloud formation. Recent studies suggest that man introduces fewer particles into the atmosphere than come from natural sources such as sea spray, wind-blown dust, and, especially, volcanoes, but he does introduce significant quantities of sulphates, nitrates, and hydrocarbons, the largest single source being of gaseous sulphur dioxide from burning fossil fuels.

Incidentally, in the many discussions and statements about air pollution and particularly smoke pollution which have been made in recent years, there appears to have been rather little reference to the annual burning of surplus natural grass and other vegetation which is so very widespread in tropical and subtropical lands, and locally also in temperate latitudes. To those of us who travel about the world by air at different seasons, the atmospheric effect of the seasonal firing in Africa and South America is very obvious up to heights of 8,000–10,000 metres. How far, I wonder, does this method of consuming sustained biological production affect solar radiation reaching the earth's surface, and is the quantity of CO_2 and other gases produced from grass fires of significance in relation to that from burning fossil fuels?

Amid these rather frightening man-made changes, which some people believe could reach ecocatastrophic proportions within the lifetime of people already living, it is a relief to learn that change in atmospheric oxygen is a non-problem, for oxygen has continued at 20.946 per cent of the air since 1910, having varied neither temporally nor regionally (MIT, 1970).

Apart from global changes which may be occurring, regional variations in the atmosphere from place to place, and hence in climate, obviously have the most profound bearing on biological productivity. In a crude sense, climate can be defined from the measurements of standard meteorological instruments such as raingauges, thermometers, anemometers, sunshine and light recorders, hygrometers, and evaporimeters. Not so, however, the ecoclimates and microclimates which are often of even greater importance to the survival, growth, and multiplication, of living organisms. For the measurement of these, the biologist, having decided what variables are likely to be important, often sets about inventing or adapting his own instruments. The standardization of such instruments is not yet achieved, but a useful listing, illustration, and description, of those now available has been prepared under IBP and will shortly be published in our handbook series (Monteith, in press). Some organisms, including very big ones such as forest trees and elephants, create their own atmospheric environment. Compare, for instance, the ecoclimate inside a tropical rain-forest with that of the savanna land at its fringes; or compare the microclimate inside and outside the 'earth' of an Arctic Fox or the clothes of a polar explorer.

Aerobiology

For a long time, biologists paid little attention to the air as a medium for life, except for the movement of birds and flying insects. Now, however, notice is being taken of new aspects of aerobiology, and IBP has a special theme devoted to this subject in which we are starting to coordinate observations made and methods employed in different parts of the world. It has been found that there is a considerable amount of aerial 'plankton' virtually everywhere, and although the productivity of this is quite insignificant in the atmosphere, it can have great effects on terrestrial production. This is because pollen, spores—including pathogens—some seeds, and the resting stages of small soil and aquatic organisms can, in certain circumstances, be distributed in the atmosphere right around the world.

FIRE

The term is used in this context to include the heat- and light-energy from the sun as well as the destruction and recycling of organic materials by burning.

Use of the Sun's Energy

In round figures 80 per cent of the total heat-balance of the earth's surface is consumed by evaporation, namely by the energy demand of the global water-cycle (*see* the section below on water). A small, indeed a very small, proportion of this energy is expended on maintaining the transpiration stream of plants. Since so high a proportion of the sun's energy goes on evaporation, it is well to remember that any change in the long-term global evaporation—even, say, of 5 per cent—would cause a relatively large change—say, of 20 to 30 per cent—in the other components of the heat-balance of the earth's surface.

In terms of biological productivity, much more important than the utilization of the sun's energy in maintaining the transpiration stream of plants and than sweating and panting in mammals, is carbon assimilation through photosynthesis; for this is by far the largest biological activity in building up organic material from inorganic sources. Sometimes we tend to think of photosynthesis as almost the only process of primary production, but recent research, particularly by Russian and Japanese scientists, has shown that in some lakes chemosynthesis through bacterial action can be of equal importance (*cf.* Sorokin & Kadota, in press).

The proportion of the sun's energy which is used in photosynthesis in those plant associations whose ecosystem physiology has been studied, is very small. In an area of perennial grassland vegetation in Michigan, for instance, of the total solar energy that was incident upon the vegetation, nearly 99 per cent was lost in reflection or used in evaporation, and of the remainder, which through photosynthesis and carbon assimilation was turned into gross production, there was some further loss of energy through plant respiration—leaving only about one per cent of the incident energy as being converted into net production (Golley, 1960). Although different types of terrestrial ecosystems will clearly produce differences in the equation, it does not seem that many of them will prove to be much more efficient than this.

Trophic Levels

Passing from the primary producer to the secondary producer, there is further loss of energy, for herbivores do not assimilate anything like all of the food which they consume. As much as 90 per cent of food intake may pass out of the body as faeces, and not all of the balance goes into building animal tissue, because there are further energy losses through movement, respiration, and reproduction. In carnivores, as tertiary producers, a higher proportion of the food eaten is assimilated—probably between 30 and 75 per cent—but the losses through energy consumption in searching for food are generally higher than in herbivores.

We should not forget that the apparent great loss of energy through faeces of both herbivores and carnivores is not lost to the ecosystem, for the faeces, together with the body tissues of the plants and animals, serve as food material for other animals and for Bacteria and Fungi before being recycled through the soil. At each transfer of energy, heat is evolved, the end point being such that solar energy entering the ecosystem equals the heat-energy leaving it; thus there is conformity with the laws of thermodynamics.

In attempting to assess sustained biological productivity, we are concerned with the energy after it has entered the system and before it leaves. An ecological system depends upon the transfer of energy from one organism to another, and such transfer of energy constitutes the food-chain or, as it may be more appropriately termed, the food-web.

Returning to the subject of direct energy from the sun, experiments in measuring photosynthesis of plant communities in relation to their structure, physiology, and environment, form an important theme of IBP, being looked after by its section on Production Processes (PP). Although such experiments, which are being made with a wide distribution through the climates of the world, have been applied so far mainly to certain crop plants such as maize, the relative efficiency of photosynthesis by different types of natural vegetation obviously has high importance as well.

In 1970, technical meetings organized in Trebon, Czechoslovakia, and Moscow, examined initial results from many parts of the world, and showed that the IBP research projects are geared towards collecting information which lends itself to the construction of operative mathematical models for photosynthetic production. Such models describe plant growth in its dependence on both the environment and the internal condition of the plant. They can be used for predicting production under various sets of situations, as well as for better management with the object of attaining higher yields. Clearly this is a long-term task which cannot be completed by the IBP, but the programme has already brought together the leading specialists and schools investigating this fundamental problem in different parts of the world, and there is every reason to believe that the pioneer work of IBP will be followed by other programmes which may be in a position to organize pertinent cooperative research in a more comprehensive manner.

Fire and Land-use

Something must be said about the cruder influences of fire on biological production. Some bush, grass, and forest, fires are natural in the sense that they are started by lightning or volcanic activity; but the great majority of all brush, etc., fires are man-made, so this 'element' brings in, even more than Aristotle's other three of earth, air, and water, the influences of man on nature. Except in very wet climates, fire has always been one of the simplest means of disposing of surplus vegetation. The hunter burns in order to get about in thick country, sometimes to drive his quarry, or more often to 'improve' the environment (as with the rotational burning of grouse moors in Scotland). The pastoralist burns to prevent the encroachment of bush over pasture, to stimulate the young shoots, and to reduce parasites and vectors of disease among his stock. Scientific study, particularly in Africa, has proved without doubt that all these three results are achieved with considerable success.

The cultivator burns vegetation to clear land and add mineral elements to the soil, and many are the varieties of 'slash and burn' shifting agriculture that are adapted to local conditions. It has proved a useful form of land management, provided the human population is small and there is plenty of land to go round. After a few years of cultivation, the area must be left to lie fallow and regenerate for, say, ten to twenty years, thereby resulting in a system of shifting cultivation which creates a man-made cyclical ecosystem. But if once that ecosystem is disturbed, as happens when the human species multiplies in excess of the natural capacity of the soil to support it, disaster comes quickly. The period of fallow is reduced, soil erosion sets in, the crops diminish, diseases take charge, and the rural people are driven to the towns.

In the tropics, fires probably dispose of more plant productivity than do animals, and fire is therefore wasteful and justly frowned on by conservationists. But there are environments in which it is quite impossible to stock the land with sufficient animals to consume more than a small proportion of its natural primary production. Such habitats may be of first-class importance in terms of biological productivity; many of them in the savanna zones have been created by fire and have to be maintained by periodic burning. Until systems of land-use are drastically altered, fire must continue as an essential tool of management to ensure the flow of energy through the system.

WATER

Water is the medium that supports the greatest biomass and the greatest number though not perhaps the greatest variety of living organisms. It is also the vehicle through which most forms of nutrient reach living organisms on land.

Distribution

To appreciate the overall relationship of water to biological productivity, we should look at the total distribution of water on this planet. In doing so I acknowledge assistance from Dr K. Szesztay (1970), a fellow member of ICSU's Committee on Water Research, who recently put the information together following a symposium on the world water balance which was held during 1970 at Reading.

The hydrosphere consists of four principal parts—the terrestrial, atmospheric, polar, and oceanic, subsystems—which are interrelated by movements and transfer processes that are governed primarily by solar energy. Dr Brower has noted in these proceedings that if the world were compressed to the size of a hen's egg, the entire hydrosphere would represent no more than one drop of water on its surface. But that drop, according to Szesztay (1970), contains $1,456 \times 10^6$ cubic kilometres. Of this, some 97 per cent is in the oceans, 2 per cent in polar ice, 0.5 per cent in terrestrial water*, 0.001 per cent in atmospheric water, and 0.0001 per cent in biological water. In mentioning these figures, however, it should be noted that those for the oceans, for the ice-caps, and for atmospheric water, are based on measurements which assure reasonable accuracy. The same applies to that part of the terrestrial waters which is contributed by lakes and rivers. But nearly all the terrestrial water is underground, being so hard to measure directly that even the order of magnitude may be questionable, and this accounts for different estimates being made by different specialists*.

Now the distribution of water in the hydrosphere is, of course, subject to change. For example, towards the end of the last glacial period, say 18,000 years ago, the sea-level was some 105 to 120 metres below what it is at present. If all the volume of water represented by this change in level was then stored as ice, the total water equivalent of the polar ice-caps and glaciers would have been about three times as great as it is at present. During the

* Different figures are apt to be given by others—including Dr Vallentyne on page 186.—Ed.

current period the total amount of ice-mass is increasing, from which we might deduce that the sea-level should now be dropping. In fact, however, the reverse is occurring, which implies an addition of water to the oceans from somewhere else—perhaps from the underground aquifers.

Man himself may have had some part in causing such change, but if so, it is only one of his many effects on the hydrological system. For example, some increase in the total evaporation is being caused by irrigation schemes in dry areas and the increase of water surface in man-made lakes, and this leads to a decrease in run-off. However, what most affects biological productivity from year to year and from season to season is not these global changes but the local variations from time to time and place to place—whether cyclical or secular—in the quality of water on land when related to the other major 'elements' of the environment.

Quality

For biological purposes the quality of water is often more important than the quantity. Many people think of only two kinds of water, salt and fresh, to which a third—polluted water—has been added only recently. In fact, of course, there is a complete range from almost the equivalent of distilled water, precipitated as rain in some places (which are becoming fewer as a result of atmospheric pollution), to saturated solutions in which sodium salts are generally dominant, either as chlorides or as carbonates. Natural waters, whether fresh or salt, have a wide range also of nutrients—from pure or depleted water which will grow almost nothing, to rich water which, with adequate sunlight, will grow Algae continuously to the consistency of pea soup. In terms of pollution, there is a range from the mild form of sewage effluent which increases productivity but may overdo it to cause troublesome eutrophication, to extreme forms of organic effluent with a huge oxygen demand. There are also various forms of toxic industrial effluent, and thermal pollution especially from atomic energy plants.

Regarding that part of the hydrosphere which influences terrestrial productivity, we may say that at least a partial solution of the hydrological equation (Precipitation = Evaporation + Percolation + Run-off) is essential to understanding any ecosystem and to estimating its productivity. There are, however, situations in which solution of the equation is simplified by one or other of the variables being reduced to insignificant dimensions, examples being: precipitation in extreme deserts, evaporation in the localized sites of perpetual spray from waterfalls, percolation on some rock and heavy clay sites, and run-off in areas of extremely pervious soils.

It is rather surprising how little is known about the hydrological situation of rivers. With few exceptions—such as the River Nile, where nilometers were established during the pharaonic period and river levels have been recorded, with some lapses, ever since—little effort has been made to measure any one of the components of the hydrological equation, until the last century when a start was made on rainfall. In many countries, including the United Kingdom, the few available records of water-flow in streams and rivers were largely the work of interested amateurs until the second world war. Serious study and measurement of evaporation is as yet by no means widely organized, and the same applies to percolation. Fortunately, however, a framework for coordinated data-collection and research has been established in many countries during the last few years, stimulated by the International Hydrological Decade.

Biological Water

Although water is a major component of all ecosystems and of all living organisms, only a very tiny proportion of the world's water-supply is actually used by plants and animals. The total biomass of the world's land surface is calculated at between 3,000 and 10,000 thousand million tons, of which more than 99 per cent is vegetation (UNESCO, 1970). Between 70 and 90 per cent of the biomass consists of water; so it would be reasonable to put the total amount of water in the biomass at any one time at around 5,000 cubic km. This is a negligible part of the global freshwater resources—about 0.015 per cent. Biological water is, however, a highly dynamic part of the hydrosphere: the total transpiration of the vegetation cover is calculated at about 40,000 cubic kilometres per year. Put in another way, the transpiration stream through plants causes their water content to be renewed about eight times a year on the average. The passage of water through animals is of the same order; domestic animals and human beings consume about ten times their own weight of water in a year.

When it comes to assessing the potential of biological production outside the oceans, the natural distribution of freshwater resources in the world is very far from being favourable. More than 99 per cent of all fresh water is concentrated in regions which, for reasons of light, temperature, or lack (or sometimes excess) of nutrients, have a very low productivity—examples include polar ice-caps, glaciers, and underground aquifers—whereas in large areas where the sun's energy and temperature are optimal, lack of available water keeps biological productivity at a low level. Thus, if an objective is sustained biological productivity over a large part of the terrestrial regions of the globe, the switching of rivers from areas of water surplus to areas of water deficit—such as has been discussed in an earlier session of this Conference—could help a lot.

CONCLUSION

While I have mentioned the activities of mankind from time to time as having an influence on biological productivity, nothing has been said about a large and well-organized section of IBP concerned with human adaptability (HA), nor about the biggest problem which has ever faced mankind—that of achieving a balance between the world's human population, its standard of living, and the biological resources on which it depends.

Already this Conference has considered this last, overriding problem from various angles. In relation to biological productivity, the ever-increasing pressure of human needs appears to have two somewhat contradictory effects. On one hand, quite significant areas of productive land are being taken out of production owing to urbanization, organized recreation, and the rapidly-growing communications system, while over much larger areas the biological productivity is being depressed through over-use—leading to desertification, soil erosion, over-fishing, and other land and water uses which downgrade the cycle of energy-flow.

On the other hand, on that part of the land surface, estimated at about 10 per cent of the whole, which is fully tamed—in the sense that it is profitably cultivated on a sustained-yield basis—the total biological productivity has been increased by making the resources of the soil more available to plants through tillage, and by adding fertilizers. Optimistic agriculturists have estimated that the total area of land that could be profitably cultivated might be increased under pressure of population as much as threefold. An even greater increase might, in the long term, be expected from the human take-off from the resources of the sea and of fresh waters through fish-farming, although it is a little depressing to learn from FAO that 1969 was the first year in the history of that organization in which the world's total yield of fisheries has shown a slight decrease instead of the usual substantial increase.

However optimistic or pessimistic one may be about the future of the world's resources, and however firmly one may pin faith on new kinds of foods which are beginning to become available through the aid particularly of micro-biology, there can be no question that the biological resources of the world are finite. Therefore, on present trends the human population and the available resources of the world are on a collision course. Under these circumstances I would reiterate a question that we here have already asked: is it wise for the world to continue, as it is still told to do by the majority of economists, to worship that brazen image, the Gross National Product—with all that this implies in increasing population, increasing take-off from biological produc-tion, increasing consumer goods, and increasing finance? As a biologist, I think not.

References

FRANKEL, O. H. & BENNETT, E. (1970). *Genetic Resources in Plants—Their Exploration and Conservation.* IBP Handbook No. 11, Blackwell Scientific Publications, Oxford & Edinburgh: xxi + 555 pp., illustr.

GOLLEY, F. B. (1960). Energy dynamics of a food chain of an old-field community. *Ecological Monographs,* **30**, pp. 187–206, illustr.

MASSACHUSETTS INSTITUTE OF TECHNOLOGY [as MIT] (1970). *Man's Impact on the Global Environment: Report of the Study of Critical Environmental Problems.* MIT Press, Cambridge, Mass., & London, England: xxii + 319 pp., illustr.

MONTEITH, J. L. (Ed.) (in press). *Instruments for Micro-Meteorology.* IBP Handbook No. 22, Blackwell Scientific Publications, Oxford & Edinburgh: illustr.

SOROKIN, Y. I. & KADOTA, H. (Eds) (in press). *Assessment of Microbial Production and Decomposition in Fresh Water.* IBP Handbook No. 23, Blackwell Scientific Publi-cations, Oxford & Edinburgh: illustr.

SZESZTAY, K. (1970). *The Hydrosphere and the Human Environment.* MS. 15 pp. + illustr. & tables.

UNESCO (1970). *Use and Conservation of the Biosphere.* United Nations Educational, Scientific and Cultural Organization, Paris (Natural Resources Research X): 272 pp.

POSTSCRIPT*

Listening to the papers and discussions at this Conference so far, I have noticed a good deal of repetition in both categories, indicating a common approach to many of our environmental problems and also a considerable consensus of opinion. Nevertheless, I have also noticed some division into two camps: on one side are those who are looking at the messes man is making in many parts of the globe and who call rather languidly for the world to stop, while on the other side are those who shout vigorously something like 'Catch the world by its tail, turn it around, and set it off in another direction'. I am on the latter side, for I like a positive, vigorous approach rather than 'let's stop what we are doing'. I believe in technical progress, at least in all ecologically desirable fields, but I also believe that in the present time our technical progress very sadly lacks intelligent scientific, economic, and political guidance.

Professor Kovda, in his excellent paper which was discussed this morning, reached—and indeed he reached this many years ago—the concept of a total biosphere, approaching this from the study of soils. Much the same is true of Professor Polunin from his discovery of viable 'botanical particles' over the North Pole back in the 1940s. I have reached the same conclusion from a study especially of inland waters. But to achieve that integrated approach we must first tear the situation apart and analyse it into its component parts. So far as this Conference is concerned, it reminds me a bit of a group of people, dare I say children, who are wanting to do a jigsaw puzzle. We have got past the stage of pouring all the pieces out of the box, finding some of them still stuck together from too-hasty breaking up last time, and separating these into bits and spreading all the pieces separately on the table. Now we have managed to put a few of the little bits of the puzzle together, so that some of the faces or roof-tops are emerging again. But we have gone only a very short distance as yet, in our integrated approach to the whole of the many situations of the environment, and this should be, as somebody remarked in the discussion this morning, a major task for our remaining days.

Now I have been asked to speak on Sustained Biological Productivity, and in so doing to introduce some aspects of the International Biological Programme, of which I have been Scientific Director from its inception. I should explain that although this was started as a five-year programme, it has now become a ten-year programme, lasting to the end of 1974. It is non-governmental, has some sixty participating countries, and is devoted to the study of biological productivity on the land and in the fresh waters and salt seas, with special reference to human welfare.

In our deliberations we should remember that sustained biological productivity depends on the continued interaction of the environmental factors prevailing locally, which can be coupled with management if the natural or semi-natural ecosystem does not suit human needs.

* As an addendum to the above keynote paper and to complete the background for the continuing discussion, it is considered desirable to publish the following excerpts from the recorded script of Dr Worthington's verbal presentation.—Ed.

DISCUSSION

Fosberg (Chairman)

We have just heard a masterly summary of the natural processes of primary and secondary production, with a characterization of the milieux or 'biomes' in which these processes take place, and of the circumstances under which they attain their maximum efficiencies. But I might point out parenthetically that there are various interpretations of the subdivisions of the world into its biomes, and that you will find there are a number of other biomes than the four Dr Worthington has mentioned, while even these four might be rearranged a bit. I myself wonder, considering the great variability recognized in the woodland biome, why we regard the tundra as a separate one from the grasslands.

Dr Worthington, with his vast experience and background with both natural and modified occurrences of these phenomena and their adaptation to human purposes, is eminently qualified for the task of presenting us with a thorough assessment of the long-term prospects for dependence of the human race on the sustained productivity of its environment. So his paper merits very careful reading.

I think one of the most critical matters for this Conference to consider is the necessity for man to make any required adjustments in his pattern of living to whatever limitations are imposed by the productive capacity of his environment. It would have been my impression that the task of this session of the Conference was to tell us what this carrying capacity is and whether it can be sustained indefinitely in the future. Unfortunately I do not think that Dr Worthington's interpretation of his assignment accomplishes this.

We are all too familiar with the manifold effect of man's use or misuse of his environment in degrading it and in exhausting its capacity to produce the organic matter, store solar energy, and retain the essential chemical elements that are required to support him. We have had repeated references in previous sessions to the irresponsible behaviour of man in his uncontrolled, heedless multiplication of his numbers with no regard to whether or not they can be supported by his environment. I have seen few if any at all convincing estimates of the possible sustained productive capacity of our environment, such as I would think Dr Worthington may be in a unique position to give. Indeed the fact that he has not done it for us here may well mean that it cannot yet be done. But the widespread prevalence of exhaustion, degradation, and impoverishment, of human habitats is ample justification for asking the question of whether or not there is indeed a possibility of the sustained productivity of the human environment that is necessary for continued habitation of the earth by man, at least in anything like his present numbers.

There are reasons to be afraid that man is fundamentally a pioneer type of organism, destined by his own ecological behaviour to vast and catastrophic fluctuations in numbers—attendant, as in the cases of certain other animals and plants, on his rendering his habitat unfit for his continued existence in it. We must, I think, ask ourselves two questions, neither of which is within my own capacity to answer satisfactorily. The first is: can there be sustained productivity of a sort that is suitable to support a large human population? To such ends, do we have examples of what might be termed a permanently productive form of agriculture? Looking for these, we might examine several which at least give such an appearance. I do not know enough about any of them to assess them in our context, but I can at least point them out and direct attention to and discussion of them. The Japanese wetland rice culture, rotated with vegetables, the fertility replenished with night soil and vegetable trash, seems to have some of the characteristics required. I do not know what the constraints on this system are, except that in Japan the area of suitable land for it is limited. Marsh taro cultures as practised in certain Pacific islands has some of the same features, but does not involve use of night soil, so its permanence may be questioned. However, it has been said that it is capable of sustaining a larger human population per unit area than any other style of agriculture. It is, however, only practicable within easy access of coral reefs, fish-ponds, or other sources of sufficient usable protein.

Other possible examples include sugar-cane plantations on low flat lands in the tropics, maize fields in temperate grassland areas, and intensively handled orchards or tree plantations in both these climatic zones when provided with continuing heavy applications of chemical fertilizers. But whereas these may continue to be productive for long periods, at least until effective diseases and pests appear, I do not know how long they can continue without soil degradation—especially in the tropics where humus accumulation is very low or impossible.

The diversified farms of the Pennsylvania Dutch country in the valleys of southern Pennsylvania, USA, have been cited as ideal examples of permanent agriculture. It is certain that under the loving care of their owners, whose great respect for their land is traditional, these farms become increasingly productive rather than exhausted. But I think the question of permanence here may depend basically on the continuing cultural tradition of the farmers and on the duration of a favourable economic climate. If the children grow tired of the hard labour and cultural restrictions imposed by the life-style of their parents, or if the government-enforced educational policies to wean them away from the ways of their culture—and this is not an imaginary contingency—then such a pattern may in the end prove to be relatively short-lived. There may well be other available examples or even better ones: I have by no means seen all of the world.

My other basic question has had many answers, most of them pure speculation: it is, what is the maximum human population that the world can continuously support while still maintaining a quality of life that is sufficiently rewarding and satisfying to be worth while? The most convincing answer to this that I have seen was contained in an unpublished manuscript which I saw a few years ago by an American named Alexander. I know nothing more about him or even whether the paper has ever been published. His answer was five hundred million people. He gave no suggestion of how this reduction was to be accomplished, but the implication was that either we would find the way or that nature would find one for us.

Dasmann

I wish to follow up Dr Worthington's remarks about the possible development and use of new domestic species as a source of animal protein. The definition of domestication may be debated, but I think it is true that more and more wild species are coming under some degree of semi-domestication. In addition to those which Dr Worthington mentioned, one could cite several in South Africa which are now used quite extensively. A recent example elsewhere is the American bison which, on an island in California, is now being raised in place of cattle, because it is more profitable to raise and market bison meat than ordinary beef.

Dr Worthington was one of the first, and perhaps the first of all, to point out the value of African game animals as protein producers on the so-called marginal lands of Africa, and their possible use in place of cattle which were damaging those same lands. I was one of the lucky ones who was able to put his principles into practice in a pilot project some years ago in Rhodesia. The project was quite successful, and there is no doubt in my mind that currently wild game could produce much more meat than cattle in that habitat.

Also, there was little difficulty in cropping and marketing this protein. Game ranching as a practice is now spread widely in Southern Africa, in Rhodesia as well as farther south, and last year I believe there were 120 separate game-ranching permits issued. Unfortunately, Rhodesia has been scratched off the list of acceptable nations these days and so the information that comes from there is not generally available.

The idea of game ranching is both biologically sound and practically— or should I say technologically—possible, but it has certain problems which limit it. Thus it requires a high degree of expertise and a kind of expertise that is very rare in the world—of people trained in the biology and management of the wild animals concerned. Secondly, if mismanaged and not closely controlled, it can be a factor leading to species decimation or even extermination. Now these two qualifications unfortunately mean that it would be quite successful in the areas where it is least needed, namely the developed countries, whereas it is an extremely dangerous technique to turn loose in many of the underdeveloped countries where they simply cannot control the activities of their own people, and where, if you open a market for wildlife, you run the risk that the wildlife will be over-cropped instead of cropped on a sustained-yield basis.

Finally, to return to the point which Dr Worthington made last of all in his paper—the fact that the resources of the world are limited—applies perforce to many schemes of protein production and also I fear to the green revolution in some countries. Clearly there are limits beyond which we cannot go, and so it is sad to see the increased yield often going to the wrong people. The people who can best afford it are the people who don't need it, and the people who really need it cannot afford it.

Kuenen

We have been asked whether we would estimate the maximum human population with which the necessary sustained yield is possible. It matters very little how we estimate this level, because the current growth of human population will overshoot this mark quite soon anyway, and we had much better aim a little too low than a little too high. For if once we attained a too-high figure, there would not be much hope for the future, whereas if we aimed too low the result would always be capable of adaptation.

Regarding terminology, I venture to suggest the following. It seems to me that pollution implies upsetting the biological cycle, whereas putting something into the environment does not matter so long as the environment can recycle it. But as at the moment we are putting in too much or the wrong kind, and so causing poisoning, the biological cycles cannot cope with it and so we speak of pollution: it is largely a matter of degree.

One more question of semantics concerns gene-pools and domestication. Whenever you ask somebody what he means by preservation of gene-pools for future generations, you get answers about species conservation. Dr Worthington has lightly touched upon the difference, but I want to emphasize the fact that most of the conservation of biological taxa is aimed at the conservation of species, and only very little is aimed at the conservation of gene-pools of lower taxa. Thus a great many people who talk about gene-pools in fact mean species reserves.

Fosberg (Chairman)

I would like to emphasize this point of the need for conservation of the variability within species as well as simply conserving species themselves. Species sometimes have enormous numbers of subspecies or lower taxa, and it may be the loss of only one of these variants that will cause trouble in the future—rather than the loss of entire species, though of course, if you lose the entire species you lose the particular biotype concerned. Very little attention is given to this except in the already domesticated species, and I wonder whether Dr Worthington has some response to propose to this?

Worthington

I am glad to have this opportunity to comment on some points that have been raised. The first is the Chairman's own in which he made a very justifiable comment about the use of the term 'biome' for the primary division of the terrestrial world. I would mention that this is entirely for convenience within our International Biological Programme, and does not imply scientific classification *per se*. We do, however, have a scientific or more or less scientific classification of vegetational types which is used widely in the IBP, particularly in the section of terrestrial conservation, and that is the one devised by the American scientist, Dr F. Raymond Fosberg.

The other multiple point which I would like to make is on the looseness of the terminology that is currently creeping into environmental studies. In addition to Professor Kuenen's instances, I was shocked recently to note how the word 'ecology' tends to be interpreted today. I happened to be in Tennessee, actually at the University of Tennessee, and noticed a label on a door indicating that there would be a meeting about the ecology of newspapers. As I am extremely interested in human ecology as well as in plant and animal 'ecology', I thought this could be interesting and so I went to the meeting, only to find that it consisted of a gathering of students who, admirably enough, were organizing themselves merely to collect the thrown-away newspapers all over the university campus and get them to where they might be used. But that was their interpretation of the word ecology!

Likewise the term gene-pools is becoming all too loosely used. It was originally employed in the narrow sense for storage of genes of domesticated plants or the races of domesticated plants and their wild relatives in the form in which they could be easily stored in 'pools', namely as seeds. Consequently the main existing gene-pools *sensu stricto* are collections of seeds or grains which are established in various parts of the world. But then the term came to be used for potatoes, which you cannot store as seeds but have to regrow at pretty frequent intervals, and it is now used in a very much wider sense to include really the entire gene-content of all wild plants and animals as well as domesticated ones. I think this terminology needs looking at, with perhaps a precise definition of terms and possibly the invention of one or two new ones.

Fosberg (Chairman)

On this subject of degradation of terminology I am going to steal a little bit of your time. I think that it is a most unfortunate thing and that any effort we can make towards retarding it will be all for the good. But we should not be too optimistic! I can remember a very amusing thing that happened at the International Botanical Congress in Stockholm in 1950. They had a whole session on the definition of the term 'ecotype'—a term that had been proposed some years earlier by Professor Göte Turesson to remedy some of the sloppy usage of the terms 'variety', 'subspecies', and so forth, by being precise about experimentally demonstrated subspecific populations. Professor Turesson was there and he heard a most diverse lot of interpretations of this word 'ecotype'. Finally, he could stand it no longer, so got up and said, 'When I coined this term twenty years ago, I did not mean what any of you are talking about.'

Polunin

[That Stockholm Botanical Congress, the first after the war and for about fifteen years, I also remember from the circumstance that we spent a long and hotly-debated period on no greater topic than whether or not to capitalize the initial letters of specific epithets or names in certain cases—but without coming to a final decision in the end, except to *recommend* the abolition of such capitals in conformity with zoological usage. This was despite much battling by the present chairman and myself against what we thought to be a nuisance anomaly, and under the chairmanship of the late and great E. D. Merrill—not for nothing dubbed 'the American Linnaeus'. That was before the world seemed to be becoming overcrowded, and petty strife so rife as a result. Merrill's message was that we must always strive for meticulousness, and this is the one I steal a bit more of your time to pass on to you. As an erstwhile plant taxonomist *pro parte* myself, it beats me to conceive how we can ever expect any science to advance solidly without precise, world-agreed-upon terminology. We must strive always to avoid meaning different things when we use a particular term, or different terms for a particular object or phenomenon.]

Johnson

[It should be pointed out that, if the developed world were to attain a net reproduction rate of unity by the year 2000, and the developing world were to achieve this by the year 2040—I mean, with each couple having two children—the global population would still not stabilize until the end of the following century. Moreover, the legacy of past population growth is such that, at this point of time, we would have some 15.5 thousand million people on the earth. So although I have a lot of sympathy with the idea of a carrying capacity of 500,000,000, we already have several times that number of people and are finding it quite difficult to cope.

Now I'll tell you a horror story. In 1963–64, Dr Norman Borlaug visited India and decided that the growing situtaion there looked quite like that in Mexico. So he sent 250 kilograms of his best lines of wheat to India and the following year India purchased 250 tons of seed from Mexico. It survived riots and the war between India and Pakistan, and the next year a larger order of 20,000 tons was dispatched and seeded. Meanwhile the Indian scientists were testing and trying out the other lines which Borlaug had sent earlier on, and from one cross, known as No. 8196, they developed two wheats which today are grown on almost the whole of the irrigated area which they have under wheat. This amounts to about 13,000,000 hectares, and probably accounts for 80 per cent of the area under new varieties which are currently being used in India. Thus you have 80 per cent of production in a sense deriving from a single plant.

As you well know, there could be very many dangers in this. Thus there are two main sorts of wheat rusts in India, one coming from the south and following the heat as it progresses northward, while the other comes from the Himalayas and follows the cold. They converge on reaching the plains. There is a very real danger that some pathogen will develop to which the new varieties would prove susceptible, whereupon you could lose 20,000,000 tons of food grain—a disaster beside which the Bengal one would seem of minor significance. The question is: what is the practical procedure there?

Meanwhile you have the FAO and the UNDP supporting genetic collection and maintenance of gene-pools around the world. One such is in Ismir in Turkey, and it is a particularly important station because in Turkistan for a variety of reasons you have had people crossing and recrossing from Europe and Asia for generations—plus enormously diverse ecological habitats, so that there is a great wealth of plant material. In Ismir they have built up a systematic collection over the years, but when I visited them recently they did not have enough money to run the cold storage plant which is important for storing germ-plasm, with the result that this immensely valuable material was kept in a butcher's shop downtown. Yet it could perfectly conceivably have a unique potential of germ-plasm which would enable the plant breeders to keep ahead of any devastating pathogen indefinitely.

If the international community cannot produce this sort of money for an exercise of such obvious value, yet goes on wasting in the manners we have heard about and often seen, one cannot but be very depressed concerning the long-term prospects of achieving anything like the increased agricultural productivity that is going to be more and more desperately needed in the future.]

Mäde

Dr Worthington has mentioned how prudently some ecosystems have to be handled if they are not to break down, but I submit that the problem of sustained biological productivity is also a problem of *optimizing* biological productivity and not merely saving it from deteriorating. This optimum should be considered as a term in the equation of the budget of the landscape, and this budget has its economic aspects. Allow me to describe to you the methods we have employed for the last several years in the German Democratic Republic.

On a regional level we try to find a model describing the production of biomass, because we wish to understand the efficiency of a landscape. This model should cover the entire budget from the scientific basis to the economic consequences. Such a first step gives us the relationships between local plant growth and the yields of agricultural plants under the influence of such environmental factors as weather. These relations are today the basis for our agrometeorological landscape classification.

Further research work is proceeding on agricultural ecosystems (as manmade ecosystems) and on natural ecosystems, in order to obtain a basis for computing economic expectations. The natural ecosystems are situated in our nature reserves, which in this way are used for the solution of practical problems. They thus have a concrete economic value, being no longer considered as relatively undisturbed areas, but areas necessary for the optimal development of the local landscape.

We hope that the results of all this work will enable our planning authorities to develop our landscape in the best possible way for multipurpose use, with at the same time high economic efficiency to improve the living standards of our people.

Fosberg (Chairman)

Dr Miller has asked for some discussion on the question of animal pollution, which he defines as such things as the introduction of goats on oceanic islands, rabbits into Australia, starlings in eastern North America, and so forth. I would be delighted to have a discussion on this subject but would like Dr Miller to start it.

Miller

I don't think there is need to say more than that the world exhibits, very widely over its surface, various evidences of pollutions resulting from the introduction of species. These turn out to be at best of questionable value when we are trying to improve the habitat of man, so that in this respect man has really worked against himself. Realizing this does not help us very much when these species have in many cases run wild and taken hold to the extent of being beyond logical control. I think that we should have more concern for endemic species, habitat protection, and improving the lot of man by wiser utilization of species. This is a matter of great potentiality which the world still does not care much about, but which should be opened up by a lot of investigation towards the necessary planning to provide for future populations of humans, other animals, and plants.

Fosberg (Chairman)

I may say that I have had considerable contact with this subject, especially in connection with my work on islands, and it seems that many people have an almost religious fanaticism or missionary zeal about introducing things. They are very seldom qualified to decide whether what they introduce should be introduced. We have ample horrible examples, of which New Zealand and Australia provide a striking array. Yet not even some of the scientifically trained people seem to be able to refrain from this sort of thing. A very charming female New Zealand scientist entertained me some years ago on the occasion of the Seventh Pacific Science Congress, taking me around and showing me New Zealand plants and animals, and also the effects of the introduction of rabbits and deer and various other exotic animals and plants. After I got home I wrote to her, thanking her for her hospitality and asking if there was anything I could send her, thinking she might want some books from the United States or something like that. But she wrote back and said, 'If you find any seeds of plants that would be interesting to introduce into New Zealand, please send them.' Naturally I was appalled.

Kassas

Now we have two ideas. The other day somebody told us: let us kill all the goats because they are sources of trouble. But when we look at goats we see that they are the animals which are most efficient in utilizing arid, austere habitats. Now it has been suggested that we try to introduce or domesticate more wild animals than at present because they are most efficient in utilizing areas that are described as marginal. But I think there is a certain danger in this: if we introduce a kind of deer, it may become the goat of the next century. We must be careful; it is not simply a matter of introducing or domesticating an animal merely because it is more efficient. The goat is a highly efficient animal under desert conditions, where now I regret to hear people advocating its extermination.

Worthington

I am afraid I must come back on that one because what I intended to put across was the fact that the goat, in common with the sheep, the cow, and all other domestic animals in Africa, was evolved in Asia, to which they were all extremely well adapted and where they were domesticated to take part in an optimal sustained yield of the habitats in which they lived. The objective of attempting to domesticate African, Australian, and American, animals and birds in relation to the ecosystems of those continents, is to remedy the mistake which in my view was originally made by early man in taking Asian animals away from the habitats to which they were adapted and in introducing them to other habitats all over the world to which they were ill-adapted and many of which they have greatly damaged.

Miller

Regarding the example of goats, I think we should mention also the context of oceanic islands. In the Galápagos Islands, which as you know are remarkable for their unique flora and fauna and the light which these features, resulting from long isolation, throw on how evolution has taken place, the goats, introduced by well-meaning mariners, have caused widespread damage —to the extent of endangering endemic species which they deprive of food.

Here I would say that there is yet another thing which we don't know: the future value of species and races. It would not be surprising to me if somehow we adapted some of those rare species to new uses. If you have ever studied the biology of the heart of a turtle, you will know that it is a very difficult thing to kill. Maybe my heart transplant turn will come when I would like to have the heart of one of the Galápagos tortoises which live for several hundred years!

Lähdeoja

I presume we all agree that the most important thing to be studied is the effect of environmental changes on living things, including man. In other words, it is pointless to monitor environmental changes without knowing their effects on biological systems. Biological production is, I believe, the most important phenomenon which takes place on the earth, and it should be the object of the best scientific research which can be established. As Dr Worthington has pointed out, research on whole ecosystems is one of the methods which is used when we want to monitor the changes taking place in biological productivity. Unfortunately, as many of us very well know, ecosystem studies are enormously laborious and very expensive.

There have been discussions for a long time about so-called biological monitoring. The idea is to find out research subjects which give reliable pictures of environmental changes and of their effects on biological productivity. This kind of monitoring should, of course, be based on ecosystem studies. So far we are not sure whether there are any such parameters available. Whether there are or not should be very carefully and critically studied. It is not a weekend job for some scientists but a very difficult task to find out these parameters.

Some preparatory work has been done in some countries, and more will be planned at a Scandinavian meeting to be held during the autumn. But still I am afraid that far too little attention has been paid to this matter, and I suggest that this Conference include in its forthcoming declaration a resolution calling on some organization, for example IBP or UNESCO, to take the responsibility of arranging a critical study of the methods and tools of biological monitoring. This kind of study might lead to measures which could be extremely valuable when mankind tries to understand what he is really doing in circumstances which often precondition his own future.

Worthington

May I just add that last Saturday and Sunday in Unesco House in Paris they held an international meeting on this very subject of trying to define the biological parameters which would be suitable for monitoring in relation to chemical and physical parameters.

Adlercreutz

Although the human population explosion has not been a formal topic here in this Conference, many people have mentioned it and most seem agreed that it is the greatest of all threats. I think that the human being is what really pollutes the world, and therefore I would like to say something about the prognosis for the inhibition by chemical means of the human population explosion. As you know, animals have a self-control system: if their population grows too much, there is always a limiting factor which makes the population decrease. I cannot give you examples here because of lack of time, but I am confident that you will all have some in mind, through food shortage or disease. We could also think of an automatic regulation of the population explosion of man. Already we know some means: we know that people may throw atomic bombs at one another, which is a very efficient means but the worst that can be thought of. We also know that by increasing the number of motor-cars, we can cause road accidents in developed countries to such a degree that a significant proportion of the young people are killed. This is also not a very good solution to the problem. Further, the use of certain drugs decreases the fertility of young people—which again is a means of self-limitation of population growth, but unfortunately only in the developed countries. This is a very pessimistic view, and is not at all my choice, but it has been discussed in international journals.

Now we have better means of keeping down human population by controlling birth through chemical and other devices and so on. I cannot go into details, though abortion is one means; but it would be a very complex set of procedures to develop scientifically a chemical means which would really be effective. Thus under the new rules of the United States Food and Drug Administration, you have to test a new substance for at least eight years before you can put it on the market. This means that if you have the substance today, you cannot put it on the market until about 1980. The pioneer work can practically be done only by scientists in highly developed countries in which the population increase is the lowest, while the time-scale of side-effects is such that we do not know much for about twenty years, or more than a generation in the case of transmittable effects that may need adult development to show up. Yet we cannot wait all this time before putting a new product on the market. What we need is a pill that would be acceptable to all as causing sterility indefinitely but reversibly, so that the general state of the adult human population would be one of infertility which could be changed only by a conscious act. But I do not think that within this century such a pill will be developed and come into widespread use.

13

GLOBAL RESPONSIBILITY: WHAT GOVERNMENTS AND INDIVIDUALS SHOULD DO

1. A 'Western' Viewpoint

by

STEWART L. UDALL

Formerly *Secretary, United States Department of the Interior;*
Chairman of the Board of Overview,
1700 Pennsylvania Avenue,
Washington,
DC 20006, USA.

'Man lacks the capacity to foresee and forestall; he will end by destroying the earth.'—Albert Schweitzer.

As this may well prove to be an historic event—the first international conference to discuss the environmental crisis and future in a planetary context—we should express thanks to the highest governmental and other authorities of Finland for sponsoring such an ambitious and auspicious conclave.

Our hosts have been wise to make this an informal, unofficial conference, for this circumstance enables us to ignore the stifling constraints of diplomacy,

detach ourselves from the narrow ambitions of nations, and think as cosmo-
politan members of the human family who are opting for a humanistic
environment for man.

We may disagree on some details, but I would like to believe that the
experts and authorities assembled here are close to a consensus on at least
the following eight basic propositions:

(1) We are in the early stages of a planetary ecological crisis which stems
from man's disregard for the finitude of the earth and the fragile
nature of its ecosystems.

(2) The explosive growth of human population is a major obstacle to
economic development and a factor which exacerbates all environmental problems; and many of the world's social, economic, political,
and environmental, problems would be more manageable if population growth-rates slackened.

(3) There is grave doubt that food supplies to sustain another doubling in
world population can be produced and distributed.

(4) The interplay of machine technology and expanding populations is
rapidly escalating demands on the resources of the planet.

(5) The industrialized nations are responsible for the most serious
environmental damage that has already occurred, and further
exponential increases in their demands for resources will inevitably
foreclose many economic options for the undeveloped countries.

(6) There is no technological panacea which can, by itself, resolve the
long-term environmental crisis.

(7) Global ecological erosion of various kinds is increasing at an alarming
rate, and each increment enlarges the risk of more devastation, while
diminishing opportunities for corrective action.

(8) Now that the habitability of the planet is the overall issue confronting
mankind, there must be aggressive, ecologically sound, regional,
continental, and planetary, cooperation if man is to survive.

And finally, I hope we are agreed that truth is ecological as well as
logical.

THE PLANETARY PROSPECT, 1971

Despite this consensus, the degrees of alarm among scientists and environmentalists who have studied the ecological crisis vary considerably.

It is significant, I think, that those who are least troubled are usually
engineers or aerospace scientists, while ecologists, biologists, and men and
women of the other life sciences, are most often filled with trepidation and
pessimism about the overall outlook. These point-of-vantage differences are
understandable; but they are not reassuring when one considers the urgency
of decisions on remedial action, and the latter's proper place on the
international agenda.

If there is a reasonable chance that the life-support system of this planet
is at stake—and if a new wisdom is needed to redirect human affairs—we are

ill-served by scientists and others who are uncritical of the growth patterns of the past. Maybe it is too soon to be certain how dire our predicament is. However, it is the whole course of events—and the momentum of the old engines of 'progress'—that engenders and bolsters the fears of ecological thinkers. Would it not be wiser, one asks, to assume the worst and take preventive steps now, than to tie ourselves to glib assumptions about the future?

My conviction on this point is, I admit, buttressed by the belief that our surging technology outruns our ability to monitor its side-effects, and our efforts to gather data about the 'unknowns' (the effects of SSTs on our ozone shield, for example) are inadequate.

Perhaps the most probing attempt by an international team of scientists to gauge modern man's impact on the global environment was the recent Report of the Study of Critical Environmental Problems (SCEP), an investigation supported by the Massachusetts Institute of Technology (MIT, 1970). I believe the following conclusions of this report (outlined in the cautious prose of troubled scientists) deserve particularly sober evaluation by the conferees at this Conference:

> Man does not yet threaten to annihilate natural life on this planet. Nevertheless, his present actions have a considerable impact on ecosystems, and his future actions and numbers will certainly have even more. The critical issue is the danger that we may curtail an environmental service without being able to carry the loss, or that we may irreversibly lose a service that we cannot live comfortably without . . .
>
> An intractable crisis does not now seem to exist. Our growth-rate, however, is frightening . . . the risk is very great that we shall overshoot in our environmental demands (as some ecologists claim we have already done), leading to cumulative collapse of our civilization . . .
>
> It seems obvious that before the end of the century we must accomplish basic changes in our relations with ourselves and with nature. If this is to be done, we must begin now. A change system with a time-lag of ten years can be disastrously ineffectual in a growth system that doubles in less than fifteen years.

The 'time-lag' issue is indeed crucial, especially in the high-energy societies. The scenario of the industrial nations in the 1970s, for example, has already been written for the levels of production, while the numbers of autos, young adults, and electric power-plants, have been substantially decided by events that have already occurred.

This lag is exaggerated further by lethargic political institutions, by the sluggishness of many of our international organizations, and by the ever-present forecasts of futurologists which tend to persuade most political leaders, planners, and private citizens, that the future is a linear extension of the recent past and is largely outside the reach of human control.

We must recognize that, to the extent to which most men today passively accept either the facile year-2000 predictions of futurologists, or the dismal doomsday prophecies of a few environmentalists, the capacity of the community to forestall crises is crippled.

In a very real sense the planetary ecological crisis is a crisis of human will. Unless men believe that innovative saving institutions can be created, and a missing element of restraint can be built into technology, industrial practices, and individual life-styles, the prospect for the future is bleak indeed.

However, we must not err by being so global in our thinking that we fail to recognize that the most urgent problems requiring corrective action now involve regional ecosystems managed (or mismanaged) by nations and groups of nations. It is the quiet, cumulative damage to these resources which undoubtedly constitutes the most serious immediate hazard. We must evaluate and counter the long-run perils to the oceans, the atmosphere, and the heat-balance of the earth; but at the same time we must realize that in the shorter run the food supplies of fish-eating populations are threatened by pollution, the lives of those who live and work in severely polluted industrial regions are shortened by many kinds of environmental contamination, and immense strains are being put on the limited resources of food-short regions.

Like skin eruptions that reveal serious internal disorders, people on all continents have watched quietly as mounting ecological breakdowns have warned them that their health is being diminished and precious symbols of their cultures are being destroyed or at least endangered. These warnings can no longer be ignored when:

—the pines of Rome are choking,
—the cherry trees of Tokyo are dying,
—the US national bird, the Bald Eagle, is endangered,
—air-pollution acids are eroding the Acropolis, the great cathedrals of western Europe, and master-works of sculptured stone everywhere,
—DDT has penetrated the food-chains of the Antarctic,
—the world's whaling industry is bent on a course of self-destruction,
—India's Tigers are headed toward extinction,
—the Peregrine Falcon is in trouble,
—and the pre-eminent artistic achievement that is Venice is sinking into the sea.

In addition, ecocatastrophes of larger scale are portended when such 'inland seas' as the Mediterranean, the Baltic, and Lake Erie, are badly polluted, and fingers of contamination have begun to invade the largest unsullied freshwater bodies on the face of the planet (Lake Superior in North America and Lake Baikal in the USSR).

Likewise, the overload put on the waste-carrying capacity of such great rivers of the world as the Rhine, the Danube, the Volga, and the Mississippi, forewarns of a similar fate for the other large and small waterways of the world—unless remedial regimens are enforced by the peoples who share these irreplaceable resources.

When one contemplates such massive ecological errors—and the thousands of smaller ones under way at this hour—one can only conclude that this *is* an endangered planet, and that it would be the ultimate folly for its inhabitants to assume that there are cheap, easy solutions to these problems.

Wherever one lives on this planet, whatever view nations or individuals take on the gravity of this crisis, it is clear that we face an enormous task in the next generation if we are to restrain or redirect the forces undermining the life-support system of the planet. If we lived in a world moving towards what has been called a 'stable state', most problems would be manageable. But the whole thrust of 'progress' is in the direction of instability, and it is certain that the crisis will widen as long as exploding populations, a vaunting technology, and dwindling resources of food and raw materials, exacerbate conditions of the 'unsteady state'.

Equally ominous is the possibility that life-giving amenities will be lost by a process of slow strangulation. In an incisive observation of this issue, the SCEP scientists (MIT, 1970) issued this warning:

> Once an ecosystem is severely damaged and becomes unattractive, its death is usually considered an improvement by the people who live with it.
>
> This general problem is labelled 'attrition' because it lacks discrete steps of change. Stability is lost more and more frequently, noxious organisms become more common, and the aesthetic aspects of waters and countryside become less pleasing. This process has already occurred many times in local areas. If it were to happen gradually on a global scale, it might be much less noticeable, since there would be no surrounding healthy ecosystems against which to measure such slow change. *Each succeeding generation would accept the* status quo *as 'natural'* (the italics are mine).

My own fear is that aspirations to sustain a quality-of-life milieu will slowly wither under a steady onslaught of imperceptible changes: such alterations will undermine ecosystems and gradually reduce and extinguish our expectations. In an over-populated and over-mechanized world there will be little fruit left with the taste of the sun still in it, few lovely beaches or marshes with the cries of wildlife overhead, and few places where the calls of wild geese still haunt the air. The eagle, the elk, the tiger, the impala —all the larger animals that require a spacious habitat to survive—will become mere memories embalmed in books. But weeds and noxious plants will thrive, and with them weedy birds and other animals such as starlings, rats, and cockroaches. But will not this same process of attrition slowly corrupt human life into a weed-like 'growth' as well? That is a question we must ask.

Events and Trends: Whither are we Tending?

Any environmentalist who attempts to evaluate current world trends holistically finds far more evidence to support a pessimistic, rather than a hopeful, outlook in 1971. Consider the following developments:

(a) The annual expenditures of monies by all governments on the world arms-race has accelerated from about 140 thousand million dollars in 1964 to an estimated 204 thousand millions in 1971. These investments in national security are, in a real sense, disinvestments in the struggle for survival.

(b) The widening economic gap between the have-not nations and the haves is propelling the world toward instability and conflict.

(c) The failure of many nations in Latin America and Asia to control galloping population growth is foreclosing their hopes for economic and social uplift.

(d) The 'resource machismo' of the developed countries—who are consuming and exploiting the great bulk of the world's available resources and raw materials—increasingly endangers world stability. In the words of Italy's Dr Aurelio Peccei (1970), '. . . it is inconceivable that the world's "underclass" will continue, year after year and decade after decade, to accept their fate as "marginal men" without revolting and tearing down the entire system'.

The wisest counsel the world community received in the past year surely came from the United Nations Secretary-General, U Thant, who warned that a social and environmental cataclysm was imminent unless nation states subordinated their narrow interests and antagonisms and began with this decade to work together to curb the arms race, check the population explosion, and achieve harmonious, equitable patterns of world development.

Fortunately we can see a few counter-trends which suggest that we may be coming to grips with the real issues. Some of these developments are, to be sure, ambiguous at this time, but their overall tenor is encouraging:

(1) The euphoria over the 'green revolution' that was so evident a year or two ago is fortunately abating. While this transformation of agriculture will help some developing countries to hold their own for a few years, it carried with it large ecological risks—and at best it can buy humankind only a brief period of grace. One of the distinguished 'architects' (in a sense) of the green revolution, Dr Norman Borlaug (1971), recently warned a US audience that the population explosion is a 'frightening monster'. Solving the food problem alone is no solution, Borlaug cautioned, 'It just buys a few years of time for people to come to their senses . . . The first thing lost in an over-populated country is democracy itself. Sooner or later these countries reach the point where they become ungovernable, and I'm afraid we may already be reaching it in our own country.' Such words are, I believe, a valuable antidote to the unwarranted elation over the short-term gains of 'miracle' crops.

(2) The costly, duplicating programmes of the USA and the USSR to explore outer space have rooted the invaluable concept of spaceship earth in our imaginations; but, by demonstrating with probability that the solar system, save for this fragile planet, is lifeless, they have given us the sobering message that there is no 'other place', to escape to if we mortgage life prospects on earth. This conceptual perspective, rather than the wasteful, duplicating 'race' of the technical teams of the two countries, is the most durable achievement of the space programmes.

(3) The United States, after an unprecedented national debate on technology assessment, has abandoned the development of commercial supersonic transport aircraft (though, regrettably, France, the United Kingdom, and the Soviet Union, have decided to produce fleets of SSTs which might destroy the ozone in the stratosphere that protects all living things from excessive solar radiation).*

* *See*, particularly, the discussions in Sections 4 and 5.—Ed.

(4) The Republic of China, Japan, and South Korea, are demonstrating the social and economic benefits of population control, while there are signs that India is belatedly awakening to the high economic stakes in its weak effort to slow population growth.

(5) The Strategic Arms Limitations Talks between the USA and USSR offer encouragement that the arms race may have reached a technological plateau, and that some resources, once allocated to weapons, may be channelled into development. The Nuclear Test Ban Treaty of 1962 was, in reality, an environmental truce for the whole earth. A successful outcome for SALT would also augur well for more balanced growth.

(6) The potential re-entry of the Republic of China into the Family of Nations is another encouraging development. The United Nations has been hobbled by its lack of universality, and should welcome China into its councils. Again, the environmental benefits of such a step could be considerable. In the long run the major environmental issues will not be solved unless all of the large influential countries participate in their resolution.

(7) Signs of an emerging economic nationalism in the undeveloped countries are also encouraging if they are to take shape as a counter-force to what I have called the 'resource machismo' of the developed countries. In the area of resources, a permanent seller's market seems to be emerging. The recent successful negotiations of the oil-producing countries, combined with the demands of other resource-rich new countries that raw materials be processed and converted to goods in the countries of origin, may raise commodity prices to the benefit of the have-not nations. If they also require the haves to pay a stiffer price to fulfill their ambitions of affluence, this could also be beneficient.

(8) I am convinced that there is also room for optimism in those international trends which are creating interdependence on common resources. Oil or gas lines linking Iran or Italy and the Soviet Union, for example, are bridges to international order. I am convinced that all canals, oil or natural-gas pipelines, common waterways, and electric transmission lines which cross national boundaries, not only create the need for a common approach to resource development but, more important, create shared lifelines that promote political stability. In the years ahead, the more such lifelines we build between East and West, North and South, the more will we synthesize attitudes towards resources and environmental values.

To summarize: if, as its citizens, we attempt to think of an imperilled spaceship earth, all of the great issues of our time will be seen as indissolubly intertwined. Environment, resources, population, economic development, and arms control, are interacting vectors that will either continue to foster—or extinguish—hopes for human betterment. 'Think holistically' is the command of ecology. It must also be the command of all environmental activities; compartmentalized, piecemeal efforts will invariably miss the mark unless we put upcoming decisions and proposed solutions into a focus that is rigorously humanistic.

We will not 'foresee and forestall' as long as men and nations ignore the overriding human predicament and pursue goals that are mindlessly nationalistic or expansionistic.

A recognition of the finiteness of the earth—and the interconnectedness of the works of man and the work of nature—is the environmental imperative of our time. We must be sceptical of panaceas and short cuts to ecological sanity, whether or not they present themselves in the appealing apparel of agricultural revolutions, political revolutions, technological extravaganzas, or medical miracles.

The minds of men and the orientation of human institutions must be enlarged and altered in the next generation if man is to maintain a climate of hope for the future and enhance his prospects of survival.

What can Governments and Individuals do?

The explicit assignment of this panel is to contribute ideas and proposals representing a strong response by the people and nations of the world to the environmental crisis.

It was, I believe, the French philosopher Montaigne (describing his education as a preparation for life) who wrote, 'The danger was not that I would do ill—but that I would do nothing.' As I watch the preparations for the United Nations Conference on the Human Environment which is to take place in Stockholm, Sweden, next year, Montaigne's epigram comes to mind. My worry is not that the United Nations Conference will do ill, but that it will be one more missed opportunity—an exercise in the eloquent rhetoric of concern.

What the world needs is not innocuous declarations, or vague agreements that ecological dangers should be monitored and analysed. Our cause will lose vital momentum next year unless bold action plans emerge from the Stockholm meeting and something is really done.

With this thought in mind I am submitting two concrete proposals for consideration at our present Conference, with the hope that they will both arouse intense discussion here and help to elevate the aims of those who are planning the UN Conference.

Proposal: a United Nations Institute for Planetary Survival

The Concept

The United Nations should create an *Institute for Planetary Survival*, to develop plans and programmes for a planetary strategy of survival. The Institute would concentrate in a single agency all facets of international action to cope with the ecological crisis. It would monitor environmental threats, whether global or subglobal; it would interpret and assess the data and disseminate its conclusions freely and regularly; and it would develop corrective action plans to meet such threats. The Institute's governing body would be expert and interdisciplinary, appointed by governments for a single fixed term but not accountable to them.

The Institute would be generously funded by assessment against the membership of the United Nations, and at least half of its budget would be allocated to research and the development of specific programmes of corrective action. It would be authorized to convene conferences of states for the consideration and adoption of its plans of action; these would be implemented either through the United Nations General Assembly or by the Institute on its own. And to give scope and appropriate status to the Institute's work, its recommendations would be placed on the regular agenda of the United Nations for debate and discussion—and be accorded a sense or urgency comparable with that given to the military and political crises that periodically constitute the central focus of concern for the UN.

In short, what I am proposing is something designed to be the world community's authoritative, independent interpreter and action-centre of the ecological crisis. May I add a few details?

The People

While academics would play a major role in the Institute, it would have little in common with the academic cloisters of the past. Its governing board would be made up of men and women of world stature who would elect to culminate their careers by serving the world community. At the same time it would emphasize youth. Its administrators and other staff would be drawn from a wide range of disciplines and from all regions, and they would be deliberately rotated every few years to avoid the well-known arteriosclerosis of sluggish bureaucracies. It would draw heavily from among the more brilliant and dedicated international civil servants in established organizations, as well as on other persons in private or public life in many countries.

Scientists and the best scientific tools would play central roles, but the institute would also rely strongly on social scientists, doctors, engineers, lawyers, and proponents of the other related disciplines which are needed to produce new problem-solving social and political 'inventions'. Its mission would be to innovate, and, for this, to develop the unprecedented team-work which it would need to produce new programmes within a short time-scale.

Funding

The Institute would be initially funded at an annual level of at least 100 million dollars—and its budgets would be doubled within five years thereafter. Until 1990 (as a realistic acknowledgement that the heavily industrialized, high-energy-using countries are responsible for the overwhelming preponderance of near-term impacts on the planet's ecosystem), only nations having an average *per caput* income of over 1,000 dollars annually would contribute to the fund under a formula that would gear payments to the overall energy-consuming industrial activities of nations. However, the developing countries would enjoy full participation in the work of the Institute.

Location and Relation to other UN Agencies

As most United Nations organizations are currently headquartered in 'western' countries, it might be logical for the Institute of Planetary Survival to be located somewhere in the Soviet Union or one of the developing countries. The Institute, once established, would not duplicate the work of existing agencies in the UN system or elsewhere. But I frankly say that the world community must not hesitate a moment to transfer any of those functions to the new body where the demands of effective action required it.

The Agenda

The Institute might logically begin its work with an aggressive research programme to determine the environmental impacts of SST aircraft on the lower stratosphere. As these aircraft may imperil all life by destroying the atmospheric ozone that filters the lethal rays from solar radiation, this research should have a paramount priority.

Most ecological problems are now so complex that a massive application of systematic knowledge is needed for their solution. The priorities of the Institute would be determined by existing dangers and anticipated threats: the assessment of technological developments in advance of their implementation, the effects of air and water pollution on the earth's ecosystems, the adequacy of the world's non-renewable resources, atmospheric perturbations or other circumstances constituting a threat to climates, food production, or deteriorating soils, and the heat-balance of the planet—these are only a few of the subjects that would require authoritative inquiries.

The Institute might decide, for example, to investigate the ecological and human health impacts of the Aswan Dam, or to advance environmental impact studies of the vast dams that are proposed for the lower regions of the Mekong River or, say, the sea-level canal proposed for the Isthmus of Panama. Its work would be preventive as well as corrective—and its warnings and findings would have a decisive effect on the decision-making process.

The Institute would also do advanced research on simple, humane methods of controlling human fertility. It would also issue incisive annual reports on the status of populations and related resources. It would be deeply concerned with the environmental consequences of the arms race, and its officials might wish to formalize some of the vital exchange activities performed so brilliantly heretofore by the scientists of the Pugwash Conferences.

In short, the exciting mission of this Institute for Planetary Survival would be to guard the health of the planet's entire ecosystem in the widest sense and preserve the fullness of the earth for generations yet unborn. Its outspoken findings and recommendations would strengthen the life-forces of the globe and counter the most dangerous habits of mind associated with the concept of national sovereignty.

PROPOSAL: A LARGER ROLE FOR THE PROCEDURES OF INTERNATIONAL LAW

Closely related to my proposal for a UN Institute for Planetary Survival is the suggestion that immediate attention be given (both within and without the UN) to the much larger role which international law might play in forestalling and resolving international disputes growing out of actual or threatened environmental injuries, and thus in preventing, abating, or providing other remedies for, such injuries.

A number of treaties or proposals for treaties have dealt with specific kinds of polluting activities—such as ocean oil-spills or dumping—and remedies therefor. I propose that we move towards a treaty which would develop and codify the general international law of remedies for environmental injury, which should be available for resolving disputes arising out of any such injury, and which would be designed to engage the real parties in interest to the maximum extent possible. Such a treaty could, for example, set up a legal framework that would

(a) allow injured nations, companies, or citizens of one country, to pursue legal remedies against major polluting industries in the courts of the country where the pollution originates;

(b) confer explicit jurisdiction on the World Court or an arbitral tribunal to provide appropriate relief expeditiously in cases involving multinational pollution both in legal proceedings brought by one nation against another (in the form of a 'class action') or otherwise; and

(c) provide an analogous forum for adjudicating the claims of aggrieved citizens of one nation against polluting activities, injurious to them, that were being carried on in another state.

The law is the most rational and least abrasive institution devised by civilized societies. It has great potential for resolving disputes and abating injuries that involve the health and welfare of people who share the environments and resources of whole regions of the globe. Such disputes are becoming a major aggravator to international amity, and legal adjustment is clearly the most promising way to resolve many of these issues.

I have been in public life long enough to know how many toes I tread upon in making proposals such as these—particularly that of suing in the courts of *other* countries! Governments are fearful of setting in train any international processes of perceptible vigour which they cannot count on being able to control. International bureaucracies, like all bureaucracies, feel they must guard their own fiefdoms. Nations which may be deeply concerned about what *other* people are doing to the common planetary heritage may be passionately opposed even to have questions raised about what *they* are doing inside their own borders. Men of undoubted goodwill have already marshalled a dozen arguments why, at Stockholm or even thereafter, we must proceed only step by tiny step in setting up new institutions. Yet an air of urgency surrounds the whole ecological crisis, and I am one who is fearful of what the future holds unless bold steps are taken, and taken with dispatch.

But to return to my earlier proposal: what kind of commitment would the establishment of an Institute for Planetary Survival require from national governments? Certainly not a willingness to give up vast pieces of sovereignty to a supranational legislative authority. Certainly not enormous commitments of national treasure. It would require only that all of us be unafraid to gather the best resources of intellect, scientific knowledge, and political wisdom that our species can muster, and turn them loose with a measure of freedom to tell us what we need to do to preserve the habitability of our planet. What reason, consistent with the native commonsense of our kind, for not taking so obvious a step, could possibly be adduced? What is required of us is only the courage to make the first modest moves towards proving Schweitzer wrong when he said what I quoted in opening.

REGIONAL ACTION AT THE MULTINATIONAL LEVEL

The most logical place to begin immediate corrective action to alleviate environmental ills is in the management of regional resources. Those nations which 'own' and therefore share common responsibility for such inland areas as the Baltic, the Mediterranean, the Great Lakes, and such huge river systems as the Rhine and the Danube, should lead the way by establishing multinational political institutions with power to set common standards of behaviour and compel pollution abatement by even-handed enforcement.

Such action could not only reverse the inroads of pollution, but it could create new patterns of cooperation between nations that will enlarge human control. I am convinced that events will ultimately compel such a management of common resources. But are we so tied to absurd and crippling concepts of national sovereignty that it will take a series of ecocatastrophes to produce joint action? Clearly, individual governments working alone cannot cope with the mounting pressures on regional ecosystems and resources which need to be shared.

To be sure, treaties and other arrangements will be needed to make regionalism work. But if nations can adapt to a regional common market, with all its different forfeitures of economic sovereignty, they can hopefully also pioneer transnational institutions to manage common environmental resources. (The recently announced executive agreement between the USA and Canada for a $2 thousand million, five-year joint programme to combat the pollution of the Great Lakes is a prime example of the kind of international cooperation that is needed. Let us hope that other nations with problems of similar magnitude will be emboldened to take equivalent action in the near future.)

Action in this arena is urgent; it need not await a global consensus or the development of a larger framework for action. Ecosystems do not obey national commands. It is the beginning of wisdom for nations to accept and act on this truism.

IMPERATIVES FOR THE INDIVIDUAL

It is easy to be either cynical or pessimistic when one turns to the efficacy of individual action. Yet, wherever we live, we must act on the faith that the process of individual osmosis—if it is persistent and pervasive—*can* change history.

Some assert that it is futile for individuals and groups of individuals to challenge the juggernaut of social forces and outdated political structures which impede change. Yet there is always hope that concerted action by determined individuals can redirect the powerful forces of the *status quo*.

This spring, for example, a loosely-organized coalition of environmentalists persuaded the United States Congress to stop appropriations for SST research. Our opponents in this case were the President, leading labour organizations, and the powerful lobbies of the aerospace industry. This quality-of-life coalition prevailed against that political Goliath not merely by pointing out the environmental risks, but by the cold logic of economics and an appeal for a more life-centred system of national priorities. This was a case where a few hundred aroused individuals themselves aroused the country and asserted new values that carried the day against tremendous odds.

The environmental movement today is essentially a counter-force for life. I would like to believe that this movement is still in the early stages of a ground-swell. If I am right, who knows what victories for common-sense lie ahead if we educate and organize effectively?

Of necessity, the fledgling world-wide environmental movement must play the 'negative' role of opposing conventional 'progress' in the short run. However, if we are wise we will devote equal energy to widening the circle of environmental awareness and developing life-giving new goals for our nations and mankind as a whole. And at the person-to-person level all of us can preach less, and bear witness more by acts of restraint that reject the fruits of technological hubris and set examples of more humane life-styles.

Whether individuals use their energies to improve food production, to slacken the population explosion, to save Lake Baikal, to sidetract SSTs, to preserve species of wildlife, or to fight for governmental reforms, they are expressing a personal faith that *Homo sapiens* is sapient enough to adapt in order to survive. For better or for worse, this must be our belief as we attempt to create the concepts of human stewardship that alone can save the planet and improve the quality of life everywhere.

REFERENCES

BORLAUG, NORMAN (1971). Speech delivered in Phoenix, Arizona, early June 1971.
MASSACHUSETTS INSTITUTE OF TECHNOLOGY [as MIT]. *Man's Impact on the Global Environment: Report of the Study of Critical Environmental Problems (SCEP)*. MIT Press, Cambridge, Massachusetts and London, England: xxii + 519 pp., illustr.
PECCEI, Aurelio (1970). Where are we? Where are we going? *Special SUCCESSO Report*, Rome, February, pp. 119–22, 124, 126, illustr.

2. An 'Eastern' Viewpoint

by

VLADIMIR NIKOLAIVICH KUNIN

Scientific Adviser, United Nations Conference on the Human Environment;
formerly *Vice-Chairman of the Scientific Council on Environment of the
Academy of Sciences of the USSR and of the Soviet State Committee on
Science and Technology; Professor and
Corresponding Member, Academy of Sciences of the USSR,
Leninsky Prospekt 14,
Moscow B-71, USSR*

and

SVENELD ALEKSANDROVICH EVTEEV*

*Executive Secretary, Earth Sciences Section,
Presidium of the Academy of Sciences of the USSR,
Leninsky Prospekt 14, Moscow B-71, USSR.*

INTRODUCTION

We would like to present our thoughts on problems of global responsibility, emphasizing that what we say does not necessarily represent the official point of view of the Soviet Union.

This frank and open Conference has now reached the second half of its work, and so we can say that we think it is proving an important occasion for which we would like to express our warm gratitude to the host country and to the tireless members of the International Steering Committee and

* Read by Dr Evteev, formerly of UNESCO, Paris.

of the Finnish Organizing Committee and its secretariat for making it all possible and successful.

Concerning the situation in the world, not everything was quite new to many of us, and so we do not think that it is necessary before such an audience —thoroughly familiar with the overall picture—to stress again the alarming aspects. What is much more important is to concentrate on practical measures that seem feasible to us and that can be proposed for action at different levels. In this connection we would like to cite the interventions of Professor Bryson and some others which, in our opinion, are good examples of the pin-pointing of areas in which we should concentrate our efforts.

We believe that the global aspects of the most important problems are commonly the most difficult of all to tackle. By global aspects we understand the world-wide treatment of individual problems rather than global responsibility in the sense of responsibility for everything. This could more properly be called responsibility for integrated approach to problems—which in itself is of great importance, but is not implemented in many areas, as all of us well know. But besides responsibilities, we would like to discuss also possibilities, in order to be practical and to be able to propose some plan of action on the global scale.

POLLUTION PROBLEMS PARAMOUNT

We are of the opinion that the main problem is the different kinds of pollution of the environment produced by man, not taking into account the natural pollutions from such sources as volcanic eruptions, which are not the responsibility of man. We know that man-produced pollution always has its 'owner' country, or in some cases two or more countries, that is or are responsible for it. But in order to detect and evaluate the effect of this pollution on ecosystems, we need in many cases to have a fully global approach to the problem—especially when the pollution occurs on a great scale.

Our Soviet scientists, and not only we two ourselves, commonly believe that there are three main levels at which we have to deal with the problem of pollution and eradication of its harmful effects: *local or national, bilateral or regional,* and *international or global.* It is of great importance that the whole spectrum of activities be undertaken, at all of these three levels, along the same lines and with the same scientific basis, and even using the same or comparable methods and equipment. Then in reality the activities should represent joint action, in which everyone knows what to do and how to do it.

The regional approach to the problems of pollution is of great importance. For example, the problems of the Black Sea can be studied, and preventive measures undertaken properly, only when the four countries of the region— Bulgaria, Romania, Turkey, and the USSR—work together on their solution. The same applies to the Baltic Sea where there are eight countries: Finland, USSR, Poland, German Democratic Republic, Federal Republic of Germany, Denmark, Norway, and Sweden. If any one of these countries will not participate in joint measures, the whole effort may fail. Therefore, we have to assure the participation of all the countries of a region when we are dealing with regional problems.

The same applies, of course, to global aspects—especially those involving the atmosphere and ocean, which are particularly susceptible to the global approach. Of great importance for the proper utilization and protection of the atmosphere and oceans are such aspects as: maintaining a common approach to a problem, undertaking systematic research and analysis, obtaining comparable data, exchanging information, using the same standards, etc., etc.

NEED FOR GLOBAL PROGRAMME

It is the task of scientists to pin-point the most urgent and far-reaching problems of our environment and to construct a real global programme of action, which should be backed up by the governments of the world. We agree with Mr Udall that for the moment we do not have such a programme; but we do not think that his proposals for action are very practical, and will tell you briefly why.

Very often—maybe we should say too often—we try to solve problems by the creation of something new, according to the size of the problem: a working group, an *ad hoc* committee, a special scientific committee, etc., etc., and finally an international organization. Between us we have been long enough in the international service to see numerous examples of the appearance of such new bodies and to be a little sceptical about such an approach.

One of us recalls the experience of his student days when his professor of petrography, a famous academician, informed his students that in order to simplify their tasks of going through the most complicated petrographical classification he had prepared a new one. But what was the result? The students were obliged not only to study and to remember the previous complicated classifications but now, in addition, to deal with a new one, which was no less complicated and difficult to memorize!

We have clearly to be very careful about *inventing* something new in the present, extremely complicated picture of the international governmental and non-governmental organizations. We should not try to do this before we are entirely sure that we cannot go further without creation of some new body at the international level, even if it should be established in our country, as proposed by Mr Udall. Nor at present do we think it would be practicable to expect countries to give up responsibilities imposed by their sovereignty, at least in the existing circumstances.

WHAT SHOULD WE DO?

Firstly, we have to outline a global programme to take care of different levels of orientation in the fight against the unwise use of the biosphere and its resulting pollution. Secondly, we have to evaluate the efforts of the existing organizations on the basis of their responsibilities, further possibilities, and actual efficiency.

With the exception of the monitoring programme of WMO, we have not discussed in any detail the activities of the international organizations, and perhaps this is not the job for such a free and largely informal body as we constitute here. But before proposing the creation of a new organization, we should first evaluate the activity of existing ones in and near the field involved. In this case they do not only exist but are engaged in extremely important programmes at the international level. We have mentioned already WMO, but should add at least WHO, FAO and, last but not least, UNESCO, which right now is discussing the new global programme entitled 'Man and the Biosphere', with its thirty-one projects any of which is a substantial programme in itself. We can mention also such projects of UNESCO as the Arid Zone Programme, from which a number of institutions emerged in developing countries, and there are others of both UNESCO and FAO.

Among non-governmental organizations we should mention ICSU, IBP, and IUCN, of which the first has its Scientific Committee on Problems of the Environment (SCOPE) which is now discussing in Stockholm a programme of global monitoring in a meeting that our experts went to with constructive proposals.

Having outlined a global programme and evaluated existing organizations, we have to underline the remaining gaps and modify the activities of the existing organizations in order to try to cover these gaps. We know this is difficult, but at the same time it is absolutely essential: only then can we see whether new organizations are needed and do something about establishing them.

INTERGOVERNMENTAL AND NON-GOVERNMENTAL ORGANIZATIONS

One thing should be kept in mind in our efforts to increase the efficiency of different organizations. We often speak about differences between developed and developing countries. Here we feel it is important to mention the differences between governmental and non-governmental international organizations. In our opinion, any global programme will consist of two different parts: the methodological and the operational. For the first part the international non-governmental organizations have the responsibility and best possibility, as no one can assemble in any international governmental organization such specialists as non-governmental organizations can and do. But the operational aspects of the global programmes can be properly dealt with only by the intergovernmental organizations. We think that experience proves our opinion to be correct.

Only after thoughtful and careful analysis and action within the orbit of the existing organizations should we have the right to propose and to insist on any innovations as far as structural and organizational changes are concerned. We sincerely hope and believe that our present Conference has thrown light on this task and will be a valuable contribution to the UN Conference on the Human Environment to be held next year in Stockholm, where our own considerations outlined above will be discussed.

CONTINUING TECHNOLOGY

Leaving aside individual involvement, which after all becomes corporate sooner or later, we would like in conclusion to add something which is not connected directly with the topic under discussion, but which seems to us highly important in a slightly wider context. One may speak about slowing down social progress, about going back to nature, or one may frighten developing countries with devilish consequences of industrialization; but all this will lead nowhere. The question that really matters is: do we or do we not like living in this time of scientific and technological revolution? If, as seems to be the case, the answer is in the affirmative, there is no way back, and in our opinion there should not be any way back.

Advanced technology, in the real sense of proper management of the renewable resources of the biosphere, is surely the only way for us to go. We have good examples of this proper management, including many here in Finland, and would like to hear of more during this Conference. We should collect the examples of appropriate measures leading to balanced and productive ecosystems and, through our published proceedings, show them to the world with the strongest possible recommendation that they be noted and followed as widely as circumstances allow.

3. A Viewpoint from a Developing Country

by

FATESINGH GAEKWAD

Maharaja of Baroda; Member of Parliament (India);
formerly *Minister of Health in Charge of Family Planning, Gujurat State;*
Laxmi Vilas Palace,
Baroda,
India

PREAMBLE

I trust I have not been called last because I am underdeveloped—or, rather, my country is—but I feel I should start on a note which may not be very palatable but which I think ought to be kept in view if success is to be achieved and there are to be any really fruitful results from this Conference or the United Nations one which is to take place in Stockholm next June.

Although I know many attempts were made to get more representation here from the Far East, and we have had some more until very recently, I appear now to be the only representative of the Orient remaining here, and yet we account for the preponderance of human population. It is said that every third person you come across in this world is a Chinaman, and I think it is about every seventh you meet on this basis should actually be an Indian. Therefore, I feel very strongly that, although we in India disagree with China on many issues as you well know, unless an important country like

mainland China and other countries in that region participate in such conferences, not much is going to be achieved. This is purely a personal opinion
which I hope does not leave a distaste in anybody's mind, for I am grateful to
the organizers of this Conference for giving me a rather belated, almost
posthumous, chance to speak before this distinguished assembly. I am something like what the theatrical world calls a 'stand in'—for an African who has
not turned up in the end. All the same, I am glad to have this opportunity to
say a few words.

For the last three-and-a-half days we have had extremely useful discussions
on a variety of subjects pertaining to our environmental future. While we
have talked about 'The Biosphere Today', 'Monitoring the Atmospheric
Environment', 'Effects of Pesticides', and so on, there is one subject which we
have not yet discussed formally in detail but which has been looming large in
the background all the time and which I feel we must come to grips with
before we arrive at the end of this Conference. Why are we all here? What is
the reason for this Conference? Who called it? The answer to all three
questions is a three-letter word, MAN. It is because of man's thoughtless
actions over the centuries that this Conference has been called to see if he can,
even now, be prevented from destroying all life on earth—including himself.
If you agree with this, the obvious answer is that our first and foremost task
is to control man's numbers, for he and he alone can be held responsible for
endangering the future of our environment. He is the 'root of all evil'. I shall
therefore restrict my remarks mainly to population control in general—with
no particular reference to its progress, its problems, etc., in underdeveloped
and developing nations, but with suggestions of what I feel governments
could and should do in that direction. This, of course, covers the ultimate
reactions—and, above all, actions—of individuals.

POPULATION THE KEY PROBLEM

At different times in the history of the human race, some problems have
always dominated the minds of men more than any others. The basic problem
that confronts the world community today is the problem of rapidly rising
population. It calls attention to the race between population growth and the
expansion of resources based largely upon the situation existing today. It
therefore evokes a global responsibility, for it affects the prospects of global
development and, because of this, it is bound to be or should be the concern of
every member of the world community. It is an issue that is intimately private
and yet inescapably public: an issue intolerant of government pressure and
yet endangered by government procrastination. During the past decade the
world population has grown at an unprecedented rate. The increasing rate of
population growth has been so acute that many responsible people now
acknowledge the population explosion as the greatest threat to world peace
and prosperity. In the words of Harry Emerson Fosdick, 'The population
question is the basic problem in the world today, and, unless we can solve it,
no other major problem of world society can be solved at all.'

It took more than a million years to about 1830 for the population to reach
the first thousand million mark, but subsequent increase has been swift: in

another hundred years the population doubled to the second thousand million. In 1950 the increase in world population was estimated at little more than 1 per cent annually. By 1960 the increase exceeded 2.8 per cent, and it is currently placed even higher. Predictions are made that the world population will probably reach 4 thousand millions by the year 1975, nearly 5 thousand millions by 1985, 5.5 thousand millions by 1990, and 6 thousand millions by 1995, hitting 6.5 thousand millions in the year 2000. Some estimates for the latter year are considerably higher.

The present world rate of growth is far from the maximum. In many countries populations are growing at the annual rate of 3 per cent or more—a rate that would double the population in less than twenty-five years. For example, India, my country, is adding over one million people a month to its population—that is almost one Australia or a seventh of a Brazil each year— and this in spite of the oldest family planning programme in south-east Asia! Clearly if the present growth-rate is not dealt with reasonably, in the words of Mr Robert McNamara, the crusading chairman of the so-called World Bank, 'One thing is certain, that the population will, in fact, explode. Explode in what? Explode in suffering. Explode in violence. Explode in inhumanity.'

Food the Great Need

The most tragic aspect of the population explosion is that it is particularly in Asia, Africa, and Latin America, where most of the people are already living at or near bare subsistance levels, with inadequate food, housing, education, and medical care, that the rates of growth are so alarmingly high. Even in the underdeveloped countries which have adequate potential resources, excessive population growth is swamping agricultural and economic development. Asia, with far less *per caput* resources, faces an even more dismal future in supporting its 4 thousand million inhabitants expected by the end of this century. The need for more food is the most urgent problem facing the world today. More than half of the world's people do not get enough to eat, or at least not enough of suitable quality. Hunger is, of course, an old story in human history. It is reflected in the Lord's Prayer where the appeal for food takes priority over the appeal for the forgiveness of sins. In more recent times Gandhi observed that 'To the millions who have to go without two meals a day, the only acceptable form in which God dare appear is food.'

It is estimated that about one-third of mankind today lives in an environment of relative abundance whereas the remaining two-thirds remain entrapped in a cruel web of circumstances that severely limits their rights to the necessities of life. They have not been able to achieve the transition to self-sustaining economic growth. They are caught in the grip of hunger and malnutrition, high illiteracy, inadequate education, shrinking opportunity, and corrosive poverty. These are the people belonging to the poorer, mainly underdeveloped eastern countries. The gap between the rich and poor nations is no longer merely a gap—it is a chasm. The misery of the underdeveloped world is today a dynamic misery, continuously broadened and deepened by a population growth that is totally unprecedented in history. This is why the problem of population is an inseparable part of the larger overall problem of development and environmental maintenance.

DEMOGRAPHIC DYNAMICS

The population crisis for any given nation reflects the capacity of that nation to respond to its own social problems. This capacity is like a feedback adjustment; it rests in the national institutions—political, economic, and so on—and in household decision-units as well. Thus the nature of the crisis varies according to the technological capacity of the nation concerned, according to the politically dominant values of the nation, and according to the aspirations of its people. Roughly, the argument goes that many nations have moved from a situation characterized by a low level of technology, political dominance by a traditional elite opposed to social change, and low aspirations of the people, to a situation characterized by high levels of technology, political dominance by a progressive elite within democratic institutions, and a high level of aspirations. Many other nations now show evidence of having similar transitions under way.

Vast demographic changes occur in the process of modernization. The first is a fantastic population growth that occurs especially when mortality-reducing technology takes effect more rapidly than fertility-rate-reducing technology. It is this change that dominates our fears today. Most of the nations that are undergoing such rapid population growth are at a relatively low level of technical development, have a relatively low capacity for political adjustment to social change, and have relatively low individual aspirations. The first two points suggest that such nations have a low capacity to respond to domestic problems. The last point, however, is a storm signal: for if aspirations rise and *per caput* resources fall, then the widening gap could well generate novel political pressures.

In the past, migration could relieve the crisis of growth-migration within countries and of migration between countries. Thinly-populated frontiers could absorb migrant peoples, and open political borders made this option available to all who could afford transport. Both possibilities have today disappeared. Only the urban areas remain open to displaced rural migrants; the capacity of these to absorb new population again turns on economic development and political leadership.

CHANGING POLITICS AND LEADERSHIP

How might the political institutions emerge that would provide progressive leadership? As aspirations and demands increase while technological and political response lags, revolutionary pressures may appear. Fatalism, formally sanctioned by traditional religion, now may be abandoned, and ideological activities may emerge. The various communist revolutions have fed on emerging activism. Recently, even the Buddhist monks of south-east Asia have acknowledged the significance of activist ideology and sought to reorientate their religious movements accordingly.

International politics and international economics enter here: the former shows in the rivalries between the communist nations and the NATO powers, while the latter is an essential instrument of this rivalry. It was Lenin who turned the class system of Marx into a relation between nations, rich and poor. With this instrument, international communism could identify the bourgeois with imperialism, imperialism with colonialism, and colonialism with exploitation of the producers of the raw materials. In the last twenty years there have been two responses to this challenge—one being military, and the other in the form of aid for economic development. The latter could relieve the population crisis if large-scale introduction of birth control could be appropriately combined with economic and social development.

Demographic problems can occur even when the transition to modern society is proceeding well. Changing age-distributions put new stresses on the economy—especially in the form of services for dependent populations, young and old. Migration and urbanization also produce pressures for new public service configurations: occupational skills, housing, and transportation, must all meet new demands.

Traditional and Political Differences

The resolution of these problems may lie partly in the different traditions and cultures of these nations, but it will lie also in the specific mechanism for planning and adjustment—the way in which foresight is built into the political process. A country with a communist or socialistic tradition may proceed quite differently from one with an ideology of decentralization. The way in which a country with a cultural tradition disposed to high-density living adjusts to increased urbanization may be quite different from the adjustment of a country with strong rural cultural themes. The population problem, I feel, must be resolved within a broader problem-solving effort. Absorption of increased population must take place within urban areas, and this must be done with a comprehensive programme involving a developing economy and expanding social services. Resources of capital and of management must be marshalled to meet a complex of social problems, and the tactics of resolving democratic aspects of decision must be devised within this larger framework.

In this respect, what should governments and individuals do? It is obvious that current birth-rates in many parts of the world are seriously crippling development efforts—especially in eastern countries. The intractable reason is that the governments of these countries have to divert an inordinately high proportion of their limited national savings away from productive investment simply in order to maintain the current low level of existence.

Birth Control Prospects

It appears that the prospect of spreading birth control in less-developed societies today are very much better than they were in the western countries in the late nineteenth century. In some developing countries there is now active government participation in, and financial support of, birth control movements. Research sponsored by countries and foundations may help to throw light upon the ways in which acceptance of birth control can be facilitated. Various forms of communication devices are being prepared and tested, and new, easily acceptable and more effective contraceptives are now at least in sight. Yet, though we may agree with much that is being done to spread birth control in the high-birth-rate countries, it is difficult to share the optimism of some of the sponsors. Much more needs to be done than is being done, and not solely within the field of population control. For example, the improvement in employment opportunities for, and in the social/legal aspects of, women; the provision of compulsory primary and expanded secondary education; the reform of the professions and the tying together of education, employment, and social status; the provision of community alternatives to kinship for support and social control; the expansion of the means of physical and intellectual communication, etc., are the areas that need to be taken up. At present none can be singled out as crucial; but together they help to raise not only levels of living but, also, aspirations; and they help to break the earlier social norms and customs, to increase the degree of rational self-interest in individual decision processes, and to make couples realize that limiting the family size is a rational way of achieving a desirable and attainable end.

These changes have been only partially effected in underdeveloped societies today. In some eastern countries, even programmes aimed at modernization—community development programmes, for example—contain powerful traditionalist elements. In other countries new techniques for reducing mortality have been largely external to the individual, and have thus not constituted an essential part in the overall process of social change—as the much more crude means of reduction did in the nineteenth century. What is needed is not just short cuts to better communication on birth control or more acceptable contraceptives, but short cuts also to the wider cumulative social changes which will help to create new pressures on reproductive behaviour.

This may require a fresh examination of priorities in economic and social planning on the part of governments. It may be useful to focus far more heavily on urban centres than has so far been done, to use 'self-help' and community development to clear slums and rehouse the urban working class—thus providing visible 'shop windows' of concrete change. More may need to be spent on compulsory education and adult literacy campaigns than would appear justified by a strictly economic calculation, in order to provide the basis for other phases of social change more rapidly. Closer links between central government and local community may help to intensify the sense of total investment of the society in development. More forcible efforts to replace the influence of kinship with less nepotistic forms of social support may help to convince the average man that there really are new opportunities for him and his children. Campaigns and legal action to raise the age of consent may, in some societies, extend the period during which young people can be exposed to less traditional influences. In some societies, national service of a non-military type might offer a very valuable means of counteracting traditionalism as well as providing direct assistance for needed projects.

So far as birth control projects are concerned, it may be relevant during the next few years to increase the concentration on the middle classes or on such other limited groups as have begun to show breaks with traditionalism and which might most likely respond fairly soon. Equally, community projects might be more immediately useful if addressed particularly to couples who have had two or three children rather than to the generality of married couples. Certainly, each society needs a demonstration project which can incite emulation, and action programmes should be organized with this in mind.

FURTHER REQUISITES

Controlled campaigns for family planning and their sponsors should be linked more closely with other measures designed to promote economic and social developments. Greater involvement in general social action might add realism to birth control campaigns and help to convince the prospective clientele that efforts to persuade them to control their fertility are neither eccentric nor authoritarian but that, in the long run, they form an essential part of a programme to raise individual levels of liberty. What is required to accomplish this is not so much a psychologically comforting optimism as an energetic, creative realism. By adequate and properly administered technical and financial assistance to the developing countries, the predicted population explosion can be substantially averted. There is a normal responsibility of the wealthier nations with low birth-rates to help the people of underdeveloped lands to exercise responsible parenthood.

It is in this context that the developed nations should give every measure of support to those countries which have already established family planning programmes. The governments of India, Pakistan, Korea, Taiwan, Hong Kong, and Singapore, have established both policies and specific targets for reducing population growth-rates that have shown some measurable success. Similarly Ceylon, Malaysia, Turkey, Tunisia, the UAR, Morocco, Kenya, Mauritius, Chile, Honduras, Barbados, and Jamaica, are giving governmental support to family planning programmes, but still need substantial technical and financial assistance before any significant reduction in birth rates is likely to be effected. Moreover, some twenty further governments are also considering family planning programmes. In other countries, where governments are only dimly aware of the dangers of the population problem, but would like, nevertheless, to ponder the matter, the developed nations can quietly assist by helping with the demographic and social studies that will reveal the facts and thus point to the urgency of the issue, and to the disadvantage and even danger of delay.

COUNTERING LOBBIES

And yet, I feel that it is my duty to warn you that there exists today, in some developed nations, a lobby or a school of thought which contends that the monies which are being spent in the developing countries on family planning programmes are an utter waste and therefore such aid should be stopped forthwith! This view was in fact expressed at a population control meeting I attended in the United States last November. Unfortunately, too, this was expressed in a condescending manner as if these monies were being 'doled out' to underdeveloped countries! Such a narrow-minded attitude will do great harm to the cause we have all gathered here to further. While I am fully aware of the responsibility of a country like mine to strive hard to check the population explosion, let the most important fact of all not be lost sight of— that this is a global responsibility.

This is indeed the responsibility that we all have to bear, and there is little time left to make any other decision. It would be tragic if primitive religious taboos, irrational political dogmas, biological illiteracy, and political expediency, should conspire to prevent or delay a rational solution to this problem. Population growth must be controlled either by high death-rates or low birth-rates. The world must soon choose whether future population growth is to be controlled by enlightened and artificial birth control, accompanied by economic and social advancement, or by the ancient destroyers—pestilence, famine, and war.

As we all know, on the political surface of this earth there are governments belonging to various ideologies and systems ranging from absolute monarchies to complete anarchies. No government, whatever its size, shape, or colour, will take the slightest risk when it comes to introducing measures which may become unpopular; for, speaking as a politician, after all, is not temporary and fleeting political power far more rewarding than working for an undefined, non-lucrative cause such as the environmental future? And yet, although a greater effort will be needed by the underdeveloped and the developing nations in the direction of population control, this need does not minimize the broader responsibility of the developed, progressive, and affluent nations.

There are some heads of nations whose attitude I find rather difficult to understand, but I gather reliably that the old attitude of the head of a geographically small but influentially powerful state may be changing. Up to now his attitude has been, and I quote, 'Fecundity is a gift to a nation. A numerous people is the greatest treasure. And if a country is in danger, it does not need to go begging for humiliating alliances with other people to defend its frontiers . . . . A large family is a gift to the nation because it encourages emigration which insures that the name of the "Fatherland" is carried to other countries, and with the name that heritage of glory which has accumulated over the centuries. It is a gift because it stimulates native ingenuity and makes people multiply their energies against spurring need in order that the land gives nourishment to its inhabitants.' In a stern warning against the use of artificial methods of birth control and abortion he has gone on record as saying: 'Confound those who place themselves against Divine will in this matter. The curse of God will descend on those families where matrimony is profaned by abominable usages and the breaking of its foundations.'

GET UP AND FIGHT

It is all too obvious that there is not much we can do to change an attitude— an almost primitive attitude—such as this. But this being so, are we to give up trying? We will be failing in our duty if we accept defeat. The battle *does* appear one-sided, the task steeply uphill, but press on, regardless, we must.

We seek the active cooperation of all—governments and individuals. We are all gathered here with one objective—to make the environmental future rosier. But if we are all going to leave here just satisfied by having given vent to our feelings, this Conference will bear the stamp of failure. Why cannot we act as an advisory body to governments and individuals? There are many governments, I can assure you, who, in spite of their great desire to lend active cooperation, are just groping in the dark, not knowing where to start. Why can we not make out a list of things to be done on a priority basis for their guidance? This is my humble suggestion for the consideration of the Conference.

Friends, we are fighting against time. What have we to lose? I shall conclude with this quotation from the Gita, the Bible of the Hindus: says the Gita, 'If you are slain on the battlefield, you shall indeed go to heaven; if you live through the battle, you shall continue to enjoy the earth; therefore, get up and decide to fight'.

DISCUSSION

[The Chairman, having introduced each speaker in turn, evidently felt that there was sufficient build-up for discussion to leave it open from the beginning.]

Udall

I just want to make two brief comments in response to the observations of Dr Evteev on my own paper. The first is that it is obvious—I can't avoid that conclusion—that there is an important difference in our sensing of the urgency of the environmental crisis, indeed whether there is a crisis at all. I do not believe, in my own country or elsewhere, that the problem is one of better management or better monitoring or anything of the kind. I think radical departures, radical measures, are needed; and if this puts me in the position of being a revolutionary and leaves him in the position of defending the *status quo*, we just have to accept that as the situation, and I do so without any embarrassment.

My other point—and I have not made this proposal for a new institution in the UN at all lightly, having probably had as much experience in bureaucratic in-fighting as anybody in this hall—is that I believe something of the magnitude of this problem is best approached through a new *ad hoc* organization. This is the way in which my own country has approached such problems in the last two years, so that we have created two new organizations which brought some existing activities together. I'm not sure whether we yet have the solution that we need; but I am convinced, from everything I've heard at this Conference, that with regard to the larger-looming problems which concern the planet and the biosphere as a whole, there is no one who has the responsibility of focus for action. So we'll just have to decide what is the best way to get it: my own feeling is that a new organization with a new action focus, with a new mission, would be the best approach. That's simply one man's opinion.

Thacher

I think it's clear that governments have already decided that the UN Stockholm Conference less than one year from now is to be an action-orientated conference. But I think it's also clear that there is not enough information to know what actions to take with regard to all the problems of the environment. It is equally clear that there is sufficient information—and more is accumulating very rapidly—on which to base discrete practical actions that governments, and only governments, can take in the near-term future.

The agenda for Stockholm have been set: there are to be six major topics. The first topic is to be: The Planning and Management of Human Settlements for Environmental Quality, which is to say population, but principally densities of population. The second topic will be: The Environmental Aspects of Natural Resources Management, and will be concerned with the impacts on the environment of various practices, of exploitation of resources, and the reverse impacts of the environment on those resources. The third topic will be: Identification and Control of Pollutants and Nuisances of Broad International Significance. The fourth topic will be concerned with: Educational, Informational, Social, and Cultural, Aspects of Environmental

Issues. The fifth topic will be: Development and Environment, and will consider the relationship between these two. The sixth and final topic will be: The International Organizational Implications of Action Proposals and will be concerned with the decisions that governments take at the Stockholm Conference.

Our approach to the Conference involves two levels of action, the first concerning those actions for which the need already exists, for which there is adequate scientific and other information to know what to do, and for which there is a compelling urgency, while the necessary political, economic, and legal, bases have already been satisfactorily prepared. The second level comprises those actions which can be started at Stockholm with plans for activities that will follow in the years after the actual Conference, which itself will then be but one step in the process.

Governments at the Preparatory Committee for the Stockholm Conference, which advises the Secretary-General of that Conference, have already identified five discrete areas which require preparation now, in order to be ready for decisions to be taken at Stockholm; and since the decisions, if they are to be meaningful, will require political, legal, and economic support, and also commitments of resources from governments, it has been recommended that governments put together working groups—intergovernmental working groups—in each of these five areas. The five areas are: *The Declaration*, concerning principles—and here I would remark that we opened this afternoon's meeting with a telegram of condolence to Academician Keldysh, as President of the Academy of Sciences of the USSR, concerning the death of the Soviet cosmonauts. It is well to recall that in outer space, for the first time in the history of man, law was created ahead of man's activities, and it arose as a result of action in the political committee of the General Assembly of the UN, beginning in the late 1950s, developing a statement of principles which in the mid-1960s were codified, put into treaty form, agreed, signed, and put through the constitutional processes of some sixty-odd states—so that they now constitute a portion of the law of the land in many parts of the world. And one of these principles was that astronauts and cosmonauts should be regarded as the envoys of mankind.

Another principle, and one which we put into this space treaty, was that whenever a state has reason to fear that the activities of another state may interfere with its peaceful usage of outer space, it has the right to consult. This is a principle which is today being considered for incorporation in a declaration of principles with regard to the environment. Then whenever a state fears, or thinks it has reason to fear, that the activities of another state may impair or interfere with the quality of its environment, it should have something it does not now have, which is the right to consult. So I think principles can have teeth, and I think the UN has a good track record of putting teeth into principles. Very recently, in December 1970, another declaration of principles was adopted with regard to the sea-bed area beyond national jurisdiction, and it is now a matter of principle that resources and activities in this area are regarded as a common heritage of mankind. Moreover, there is a principle which flows from this, namely that states should cooperate to protect this area from serious damage.

Another separate area for which an intergovernmental working group has been set up, and has already been active, is *Marine Pollution*. This gives us good examples of the two different levels of action which I referred to earlier. The first is a possible convention; the other is a comprehensive plan to preserve the marine environment. Two weeks ago the initial session of the Intergovernmental Working Group on Marine Pollution completed its week's work in London; they will next meet in November in Canada. They have already decided that by the time of the Stockholm Conference there should be made ready for signature by governments a treaty on the dumping of garbage in the oceans. There is a draft treaty, now under negotiation, which will call for a ban on all except licensed dumping, and which would start the process of identifying those criteria—those guidelines that should be followed by states in their issuance of licences for dumping. There is disagreement on this: some states feel that there should be a total ban, with only certain exceptions after the material that is being dumped has been proven to be harmless, whereas those who put the treaty forward call for a licensing system.

Another specific proposal, which developed during that week in London, is the recognition of the important role that regional bodies have to play—particularly with regard to the more acute problems of marine pollution in enclosed and semi-enclosed bodies of water, such as the North Sea, the Baltic, and the Mediterranean. Already the Mediterranean states that were represented at this meeting have agreed to give to the next session of this intergovernmental working group in November a progress report on special steps that they will have taken between now and then to develop specific arrangements with regard to the Mediterranean; these should parallel what is happening in the North Sea and elsewhere.

In the longer term, what is needed is a comprehensive plan. This emerges as a more difficult task when one considers that most of the pollutants of major significance in the marine environment get there as a result of man's activities on land, not on the seas. It is a fact that more petroleum pollution in the ocean reaches it as a result of exhausts going out of automobiles than as a result of the totality of man's activities on the seas, in the seas, or even off-shore in sea-bed or sea-floor drilling and other operations. Accordingly, the task of any comprehensive plan is to begin a process by which governments can come to grips at the source, which is the only place at which any really effective preventive action can be taken. If we had realized this when mercury started showing up as a problem five years ago, it could have made quite a difference—quite a difference in terms of health, and incidentally quite a difference in terms of the economies of developing countries which find suddenly, for reasons which to them are inexplicable and arbitrary, that the swordfish market, for example, has collapsed.

Another working group has just completed its first session in Rome, namely the working group on *Soils*—an obvious example of an irreversible environmental impact about which more urgent, precise actions are necessary—and recommendations have been made with considerable precision in that area.

In August there will be an Intergovernmental Working Group on *Monitoring or Surveillance*. It will meet at the World Meteorological Organization's headquarters in Geneva; and I should say that in preparation and as an example of the inputs to that meeting there was two weeks ago the beginning of the working group on monitoring under SCOPE—the Scientific Committee on Problems of the Environment—set up by ISCU (the International Council of Scientific Unions). Last week there was the beginning, in Stockholm, of a meeting called SMIC, which is the Study of Man's Impact on Climate. This is a multinational sequel to the study which Mr Udall referred to of SCEP, last year's primarily American Study of Critical Environmental Problems.

In addition to all these, it is well known that the entire UN system has been involved in the processes of collecting data, assuring compatibility of techniques of data-collection, compilation of data together with their assessment and evaluation, and rendering the results in an informative fashion back to where the consumers, usually governments, can make use of them. This should mean that for the first time the entire UN system will present a completely unified view of what it is already doing, what it is planning to do, and what it is capable of doing with regard to the entire agenda at the Stockholm Conference—and, before that, in time to be taken into account in the August intergovernmental working group, indicating specifically what they are doing with regard to monitoring environmental considerations.

Another Intergovernmental Working Group will meet in New York in the middle of September on *Conservation*. They will have before them treaties that have now already been advanced by such organizations as UNESCO and IUCN setting up natural heritage funds, islands for science, and a wetlands convention—specific discrete actions that governments can take if they want to do anything about not only cleaning up the mistakes, but preventing further mistakes, with costly environmental impacts.

On the subject of development, I think it is clear that this could be, and may already be, a divisive issue. There is no question that there can be different value-systems involved: a man who is facing starvation is not going to be very worried about the quality of life if it is taken to mean the preservation of edible species. Our tactic, frankly, to assure that this issue does not divide the Stockholm Conference, is to force the issue to the surface wherever and as fast as we can—to get it debated, fully involving the developing countries in this debate—and I think we are enjoying some success in this. Just as development, until very recently, in almost every country in the world, has been measured purely in terms of economic growth, usually indicated by the Gross National Product, similarly it is now uniformly viewed as embracing the achievement of specific non-economic social goals. Thus I think the developing countries, as well as the developed countries, now recognize that development without quality of life within an environmental as well as social context is simply not development at all. Environment, among other things, means clean water and air.

I should conclude simply by thanking you for this opportunity to address you at some length. The challenge to governments is a very strong one. Our experience in preparing for the UN Stockholm Conference is that the governments do mean business. There has been a very rewarding inflow of specific proposals from governments and from throughout the United Nations system, as well as from organizations lying far outside governmental or intergovernmental organizations—such as this particular gathering. We shall look forward with great expectations to your report, and will want to take it into account in our preparations. What we particularly want are indications of where the priorities are, of what are the specific steps to be taken. Though it is important to clarify the situation expertly, it's not enough merely to argue about DDT: if DDT is bad, somebody is going to come up with an alternative, and if this will cost more, somebody will have to supply the money for people who cannot afford it to make up the difference. What we want most is specific proposals and priorities to the utmost limit that this most remarkable and encouraging Conference can produce them.

Vallentyne

My questions are few and very simple. The first one is to Dr Evteev. It was rather notable that in his talk he did not make any reference to the population component of environmental problems, and so I wonder if he would care to comment on this topic now.

My second question is to the Maharaja of Baroda, in relation to his very natural comment that one of our most pressing problems is that of providing food. Here we certainly have a conflict, which I feel is really the most Faustian conflict of which I know, in that by providing food we create more problems for ourselves in the future, as one of our earlier speakers said with reference to Egypt. Yet if we don't provide food, it's really not humane. So I wonder if we might have some further comment on this.

My other question along similar lines concerns a possible conflict that might come from attempts to create a control of the growth of human population on a localized or continental scale and not a global scale. If one country succeeds in this and another does not, what can be foreseen in the way of conflicts of invasion of national privacy? Such questions make one wonder whether a piece-by-piece approach to the problem can give us a solution.

Evteev

First of all, I feel that the question of population has already been covered sufficiently in the discussions. Secondly, I should explain that I have tried to speak about the things with which I am familiar, and about which Professor Kunin and I can propose something concrete. I am just not personally familiar enough with this topic of human population to talk about it in front of people who know much more than I do about it.

Baroda

I don't think there is any contradication as to the priority in problems or to finding food. I was not suggesting, and I don't think anybody would suggest, low-feeding a population; but I think it is our responsibility, global responsibility, at least to try to give each human being two square meals a day. This is what I was referring to when I mentioned the food problem.

The second matter I should think would be more a job for the United Nations. However, I am glad it was raised because it gives me an opportunity to emphasize what I said at the beginning, namely that unless we have all major chunks of population represented at such conferences, and commit them, there is no hope of getting appropriate action on a global scale; but if we have them attending and commit them to all our programmes, then I do not expect any obstacles. Certainly we must bear this aspect in mind if, as is much to be hoped for, we have further such International Conferences on Environmental Future.

Mellanby

One day last autumn a helicopter flew over my garden in the countryside of Huntingdon in England and sprayed it with herbicide. This was reported in *The Times* newspaper, which said that a 'leading conservationist'—no doubt a flattering description—had been sprayed in this way, but that I did not attribute this to sabotage but to a mistake. Had I been in the USA, however, I would have realized that industry was getting its own back on the conservationists! The sequel to this, in the British context, was that the company concerned immediately got in touch with me, and instructions were given that the particular chemical which had been blamed was not to be sprayed from the air any more.

This illustrates the situation, I think, that if we are to get success in such matters we must somehow or other get a dialogue between conservationists and industry. Unfortunately, this is something that does not occur in all countries, and yet if we don't get it we are going to fail. I think those people, particularly in the United States, who seem to rush to the law courts at every possible opportunity, often with extremely bad cases which are presented by lawyers rather than conservationists, are not serving their cause but in fact fostering a divergence which will make things even worse. As I said yesterday*, I would like to commend to people of other countries a British compromise, the Pesticides Safety Precaution Scheme, as something which has enjoyed success in our country, and is something which, I think, could be beneficially exported. The scheme is voluntary at the moment, but it could be as effective if it were compulsory, though many of us would regret this, as it has been loyally adopted in its voluntary form by industry.

It has been pointed out by people from international organizations that we sometimes ask why they can't do this or that for the whole world, whereas actually in many cases to be effective we must start with a scheme which works within a nation, and then let the pressure develop from the national level to the international sphere. The necessary cooperation may not be easy to achieve, but I think that if it can be achieved it will have a much greater possibility of success than will other methods. So I think we should try to adopt a resolution or recommendation that other nations be invited to look at the scheme as we have devised it in Britain, to see whether it could not have far wider application.

Another thing which I would like to see recommended is that we look into the possibility of far wider application of a proposal that is being put forward to the Government by all the professional scientific institutions in Britain, namely that there should be a system of introducing an audit for all firms: just as we have an audit of their financial stability, so should we have an audit *inter alia* of all the pollution which they produce†. If this can be developed on

* *See* page 343.—Ed.
† *See also* the United States situation described on pages 467 *et seq.*—Ed.

a national scale, then I think other nations could adopt it, and again it might be widened into an international scheme. Then we would know what really was being produced. In the pesticide field we have always had tremendous difficulty, because in the past people have complained that they can't tell how much is being produced—how much is going out into the environment. Even less do we know how much of any of the other pollutants is going out. If we knew what is going out, and we knew what is important, then we could take the necessary action to deal with the things that really matter, instead of wasting our time, as we do in many of these meetings, in dealing with things that are not at all important.

The third thing we seem to need is a new type of system which would fit very well into Mr Udall's proposal. One of the things that his Institute for Planetary Survival, or perhaps some other organization of a similar nature, could do would be to have an authoritative body keeping a close eye on all industrial development, so that it could foretell, before a new industry developed, whether this industry was likely to be a polluting one; then this could be stopped before any damage was done. We have the example of what has happened with the polychlorinated biphenyls: we have probably been saved from widespread damage from these because of their being detected. But how much better it would have been if—and it would not have been difficult—scientists and industrialists had met together beforehand and recognized that here was an industry that was likely to produce a pollutant which might be seriously damaging, and had stopped these substances from being produced on a global scale.

So I think we have here three more proposals that might come out of this Conference, and although they would not solve anything like all of our remaining problems, they might make some contribution to the control of global pollution.

Udall

I quite agree with Dr Mellanby that, within the context of the present jurisdictional setting, some of the most effective things that are being done and will be done in the future will be by national governments, and oftentimes under the pressure of citizens and environmental action groups. And I think we should look at the applicability of experiences in Britain. I wanted to explain, however, because I'm very familiar with it, the rather extraordinary success we've had in the last two or three years in the United States with the legal approach. This has been led by the Environmental Defense Fund, of which Dr Wurster is Chairman of the Scientists' Advisory Committee. These are young activist scientists—or some of them not so young, I guess: I don't know what 'young' is—while the rest of us forming this team are lawyers, and the lawyers and scientists have to learn to work together.

Quite frankly we are going to court most of the time, not against industry, although this is being done on a local level, but mostly we're suing the US Government. We're trying to force the Government in its programmes to observe the law, and in its policies to carry out the Environmental Policy Act that was declared by the Congress a year-and-a-half ago. We try to make the bureaucrats, and the various Government bureaux, do their jobs, which they don't do all the time; we're trying to compel the various agencies of Government to observe the law, to enforce pollution controls, and so on. So this is another method that might—depending upon the nation, depending upon its own laws, and its own background—be successful in other countries as well.

Butler

I would like to comment on the proposal for a UN Institute for Planetary Survival. As Mr Thacher implied but did not say explicitly, one of the proposals for action at the Stockholm Conference will concern future institutional arrangements for the environment, and some recommendations along these lines will undoubtedly be made at that Conference. Because I have been present at a number of national and international meetings which have discussed this kind of proposition, and because of what I've heard, I feel that the proposal which is contained in Mr Udall's paper is likely to encounter the following criticisms or obstacles. First of all, from the great powers will come the objection that it would be too expensive; as you know, they are dedicated to keeping under control the operating expenses of the United Nations, since they are the ones that have to pay the bill. Secondly, from the less-developed countries will come the objection that it would divert money from economic development into channels which they don't wish to use. Thirdly, the specialized agencies will undoubtedly say that it would duplicate many of their programmes both present and future; this would introduce an element of competition and rivalry which doesn't work very well in the United Nations. And fourthly, from national authorities will come the objection that it would compete with them for qualified manpower, and perhaps water down their own national programmes.

I agree with Mr Udall on the necessity of the UN providing some kind of machinery for an environmental watch. And so that I can end on a constructive theme, I'd like to tell you a little more about the UN Scientific Committee on the Effects of Atomic Radiation, because I think this is a kind of machinery which could really do the job that we need to have done. This Committee was set up in 1955 in response to international hysteria about fallout. It consists of fifteen governments, represented by experts. It has a small secretariat of one man and two girls. It hires experts and consultants as it needs them to write reports and to prepare documents. It publishes reports every two years or so on the average. Its reports go to the General Assembly and are then published by the UN, giving a completely authoritative picture of fallout on a world-wide basis.

Among its activities the Committee also advises on suitable methods of analysis and sampling; it estimates the doses to man resulting from fallout; it estimates the biological risks to man from these levels; and it makes recommendations for research in areas where there are felt to be needs. It operates on a budget which averages about a quarter-of-a-million dollars a year, and, as I emphasize, with a secretariat of one man and two girls. I think this is a model of what could be done for other aspects of the environment, and that it could provide not only a model but a nucleus for some future committee activity by the UN.

Udall

I want to make a brief comment because I have no false pride about my proposal, and, in putting it forward, was already aware of most of the objections that Dr Butler mentioned with regard to any changes in the UN. I think we must all recognize that it is a world scandal, really, regarding the UN itself, that we invest so little in it, and spend so little on its agencies. Thinking globally as we do, it is nothing less than a full-scale global scandal. And if the great powers, including the rich countries, and particularly my own, don't see this, we've got to make them see it. In terms of priorities I might mention that my country is spending in the neighbourhood of 75 thousand million dollars on a military weapon system this year, while the Atomic Energy Commission has just finished spending 200 million dollars on digging a hole a mile deep to conduct a nuclear test that apparently is not necessary, so we are fighting this in court. Really, to say that we are so poor or so politically disorganized that we can't create new agencies or adequately finance existing agencies to do the scientific job that must be done for survival, is simply scandalous—that's all. That's my opinion. My own feeling, and my own experience in government—which I would like to pass on to the UN people here— is that sometimes, if you can persuade those concerned that there is a new problem, and that it is urgent, this is a way, and sometimes a vehicle, of creating a new organization to carry out a mission—a way of getting new funds. This is just a political judgment which I pass along.

Evteev

Mr Udall says that I am a conservative and he is a revolutionary: I like his approach very much! But I would say that to change the existing system of intergovernmental and non-governmental organizations in a good working picture, it would be a real revolution—even without the creation of any new institution at all. And if you try, you will see. This would be a real revolution to reorientate existing intergovernmental and non-governmental organizations. I don't think the most important thing is the problem of money in the UN system, but rather the diversity and duplication of effort. I'm sure that in the Stockholm Conference next year you will see this clearly from the reports of the different organizations. Maybe it is not practical, but as far as I can see it, it should be possible to establish some body—maybe not a committee like the one just mentioned by Dr Butler, but some kind of council of the Directors-General of the different organizations under the chairmanship of the Secretary-General of the United Nations—to discuss exactly environmental problems and the responsibilities of different organizations in remedying them. This would put more responsibility on the different organizations than they have now.

Polunin

If Mr Udall is a revolutionary I, for almost the first time in my life, have become a violent one on his behalf. I think we should spend—with your permission, Mr Chairman—a little more time looking at this plan, which, when it came to me to do what I call pre-edit, some days ago, struck me as something very important and urgent, and I've thought about it a good deal since, and I still think it is very important and urgent. Moreover it is—as one might expect, coming from that source—already well thought out.

Now I am not worried too much about Dr Butler's friendly warnings when it comes to matters of such enormous importance, though I must confess to being favourably impressed by Dr Evteev's counter-suggestion—but only for matters of less vital moment. Although as an outside and largely informal body, this Conference should, I feel, bear in mind the warnings we have been given not to get involved in intra-UN arguments and inter-agency rivalries, I cannot accept that they should be considered as beyond our ken or even moral responsibility where the world's future is at stake. So, as I indicated before, I feel and I recommend that we should carefully consider and debate such plans for the future as are put before us—particularly when they are advanced by seasoned campaigners and eminent participants—even if their implementation might risk treading on some toes or stifling some ambitions in the United Nations, and then put forward our considered views uninhibitedly and indeed quite boldly. For that is what we are really here to do, and have been repeatedly asked by the Stockholm Conference people and many other well-wishers to do.

On another theme I was delighted to hear, living as I do in the midst of what must be the greatest-ever concentration of UN agencies, that *any* of them could ever be allowed to function at such an insignificant 'level' as was given out—namely, one man and two girls, and at the rate of a quarter-of-a-million dollars annually. [My younger brother once had a colleague in Singapore, whose antibureaucracy satire is now well known. He is Professor C. Northcote Parkinson, and some wags say that he dare not come to Geneva for fear of being assassinated by employees of the UN, while other wags say that he dare not come there for fear of bursting with pride at witnessing such classic verification of his laws and fulfilment of his prophecies! The biggest of all such agencies is now in very serious financial straits, yet it is having a superb new set of buildings constructed to house all its thousands of employees together—who in some cases I can tell you in all seriousness simply do not know what the agency does! And if you think they are fooling me when saying so, just ask them! So we locals are not too keen to go on paying their taxes and having other costly arrangements made for them, such as a special access road through the middle of the grazed parkland on whose margin I live.

Dare I advance the very naughty *pace*-Parkinson suggestion that the reason behind the evidently successful functioning of the one United Nations outfit which was lauded just now by Dr Butler may well be that its secretariat consists of no more than a man and two girls! If, as is to be presumed, they are full-time and salaried, then we have largely run this present conference on far less—a part-time, unpaid man, namely myself, and a game septuagenarian secretary who has worked for me during the past few months for a few hours every other day. Yet I hope you would not deny us, Mr Chairman, the incipient satisfaction of feeling that, with the help of your Government and the Arts Festival, it has turned out to be not too much of a shambles, and that the 100-odd official participants found that normally they got replies from me to letters and cables more or less 'by return'. It merely meant working practically day and night, as dedicated people should always be prepared to do. But please forgive me, I did not rise to talk about this Conference, which others can judge far better than I, but to voice my grave misgivings concerning the proposed wide dependence on the United Nations. They perform many important functions with reasonable effectiveness if not dispatch, but I cannot see them carrying out urgent actions to save the biosphere *any more than they prove effective on the world's battle-fronts*; so I wonder, could we not have something in close touch but actually independent? Enough of my reasons for advocating this have, I believe, already been given in the form of suggested* remedies which, however, do not seem very likely to be effected: hence the need to look elsewhere.]

Siikala (Chairman)

If I may permit myself a comment here, I think that definitely the Resolutions Committee should take all of the ideas presented here into account, and—just to continue a bit on these bureaucratic UN wars—I think that ideas like yours would in any case compel the UN agencies to take a really hard look at their own operations. This is something I'm involved in from my Government's side, and I think we are not in such disagreement as it might appear to the audience here.

Fosberg

I am going to propose what may seem to be a repetition of what we have ust been hearing, and to some extent is. Certainly it will embody the ideas of Mr Udall and several others whom we have heard during the course of the day. I venture to make this suggestion only because it is the logical outgrowth of one which I published about thirteen years ago on a much more local and reduced scale, but which has been received very well by a great many people, although I must say it has been carried out rather sparingly if at all. Before I read this suggestion to the Resolutions Committee I would also like to comment on Dr Evteev's suggestion that we utilize the existing agencies. I would say, well and good—if we can; but I would put it as a matter of burden of proof on these agencies to show that either they are performing the function which I am going to suggest, or are capable and willing to do so. If they are capable and willing, then there is no point in creating a new body; but I have had quite a bit of experience with these organizations, and I'm wondering if they are really willing or capable.

The suggestion which I am going to make to the Resolutions Committee— and I have no objection whatever if they combine this with one, two, or a dozen other similar suggestions and come out with something better—is very simple and will need little elaboration if ever carried out. It is as follows: The Conference on Environmental Future requests the UN and ICSU cooperatively—or, I may add, in connection with Professor Polunin's last remarks, any other appropriate body, though I don't know of any unless it be an outcome of this Conference—to bring into being, and to assure the support of, a body of independent scientists, comprising members of all the major disciplines involved in the basis of ecology taken in the broadest

* *See*, for example, pp. 207-8.—Ed.

sense, whose purpose and assignment would be to anticipate and make known, to the best of their collective abilities, the probable consequences of large-scale on-going and proposed projects and activities, especially those which involve mega-manipulations of the environment.

Udall

I want to make, supporting Dr Fosberg, a brief comment. My own experience in government—and I hope the UN people will give this very serious thought—is that a sense of mission is quite crucial. What I really mean is that I want to see a group of people who get up in the morning and go to work with a sense that their mission is to protect the environment, to protect ecosystems and so uphold the environment: this is their task. My concern and my own experience in government is that if someone gets up in the morning and his mission is to protect the health of people, or to provide food, or whatever it might happen to be, environmental protection is naturally left in the background—it is going to get lost. And this is exactly what the US Government has now done something to counter, by setting up a law and an agency whose job it is every day to examine and evaluate the environmental impacts of on-going and proposed activities of the US Government.

Siikala (Chairman)

A final word here about the UN agencies' coordination problems. I must remind you that there has been for the past year a Functional Group on Human Environment of the Administrative Committee on Coordination of the United Nations, which is at the level of the heads of UN agencies. But now, how many inter-agency committees are there, and what will be their collective effect? This, of course, remains to be seen, but in any case we can rest assured that this problem is by no means unknown to the UN and its various agencies; in fact, it is one of the key issues.

Dasmann

I am sorry to change the subject, because this is one that fascinates me as well as I'm sure most of the others here present; yet I feel that there is something we have not given enough attention to in this Conference, and I would like to bring it up as part of the proposals for action by nations and individuals. As I see it, the environmental crisis is made up primarily of the interaction of three factors:

(1) population growth;
(2) the growth and expansion of technology, with its companion by-product of pollution; and
(3) land-use.

We've given much attention, and much-needed attention, to the questions of population and the joint technology-pollution problem. But we have given relatively little attention to the land-use problem. Earlier today we did have some references to some major ecocatastrophes that are building up—not because of pollution or population as such, but because of the widespread failure to control land-use. Examples include the desertification that is going on all around the edges of the Sahara and Arabian Deserts, and the destruction of the major tropical forests of the Amazon in South America, of Africa, and of south-east Asia.

The attitude we have toward land is reprehensible, to say the least. The attitude that you can own land, and have the right to do what you please with it, is to my mind one of the most unfortunate attitudes that has ever been foisted upon the human race. In actual fact, nobody really owns land. Rather does each person who occupies land hold it in trust for future generations, while each nation holds land in trust for the future of mankind; for who knows how the boundaries will change tomorrow? If this can be recognized, and if it can be made a statement of principle at the Stockholm Conference, or of our Conference here this week, I think we shall at least have stated an ideal towards which we should strive. But it is not enough just to state this ideal, because in the countries where land-use is the greatest problem, namely the developing countries of the world, they simply do not know how to control land-use. Chad does not know how to control its nomads, Brazil does not know how to control its peasants, Peru does not know how to control the squatters who build up around the edge of Lima: everything that these people are doing is illegal, but what can the countries concerned do about it? So I would like to suggest, as a major programme for the UN, a study by the best-qualified anthropologists, sociologists, economists, and political scientists, of new and better and more effective ways to reach these people, to control their activities, and to stop this massive destruction of land that is going on all around the world.

Adlercreutz

I promised to say something about what measures we have to take to control population growth. In fact, the Maharaja of Baroda has now given this out in such a nice way that I don't need to say very much, and can be quite short, while Miss Henderson will surely tomorrow give further views about this. Being a biochemist, I perhaps could give only the view of a biochemist trying to develop new contraceptives. We are reliably informed that the development of one contraceptive drug costs at least 3 million dollars. If you compare this with the amount of money which the Finnish Government gives for medical research for a whole year, which is 200,000 dollars, it means that if the whole of this money were given to one group in Finland, theoretically it would take them 15 years to develop one contraceptive. So you see that this is primarily an economic problem.

In the world there are perhaps about ten laboratories that are able to do the pioneer work to make, synthesize, and develop such drugs, then to test them, and finally have the clinical experience to evaluate the results and the capacity to do all the work which is needed concerning one contraceptive. Therefore, I think we have to support these groups because they are so few, and in the United States they are just now suffering from a lack of money which is quite terrifying, because of the Vietnam war. I heard so many comments on this the last time I was there that I am really worried about it. Also, governments in countries which are not increasing their population should take the responsibility of supporting this type of work, because one dollar put into it is at least ten times more effective than one dollar given to the support of already-born babies. I don't know whether it is ten times: it might be even higher. [A voice from the audience: 'Ninety'.] Oh yes, ninety, or something like that.

In America the rules governing clinical trials of such substances are so very hard to satisfy that one of the largest concerns producing them, having some very good research coming on, has now stopped such development, claiming that it is no longer possible. The rules of the United States Food and Drug Administration also militate against small groups doing such work. So it is suggested that there should be created a body—an international body—representing scientific and also moral and other considerations, which could be consulted by the US Food and Drug Administration and other comparable bodies in other countries, and by the scientists themselves, and which could make decisions as to whether a new contraceptive drug should be tried, whether it is worth trying, and, if so, where and how it should be tried. I think we could find from ten to twenty suitable people in the world who really could be given this responsibility, and who could constitute an international body.

Stenius

The main purpose of this Conference is to gain facts and information to be given to those who are responsible for our future, and especially for the future of our environment. But first we have to agree among ourselves as to what we really want the governments of the different countries to know. This seems to be a more difficult task than we might have expected, for even if we know exactly what to say, and know the people to whom to say it, I am not very optimistic about our message really 'getting home' with those who have the power to act nowadays in the urgent ways that we can see are often so important. For firstly, not all of them can have the basic ecological knowledge, and secondly, they may not have the right attitude to the environment. Unfortunately they do not even, many of them, care about our future, and especially not about long-term programmes.

I think we have to start with the education of the children. This in turn requires that appropriate information be given already to the teachers at the primary schools. These teachers should be able not only to give the children all the basic knowledge required, but they should also be able to educate the children to love nature and to enjoy its diversity and its interesting details as well. We therefore need special teachers and textbooks for them, and for all these purposes we need money. This is surely something that all governments should take into consideration as soon as possible.

Goldman

Several speakers have been advocating a pollution control measure that has already been introduced in the United States. Since no one has mentioned it, let me tell you about it.

As of 1 July 1971, actually today, every industrial manufacturer in the US must prepare an inventory of all the effluent that he or she discharges into any river or other body of water that his or her plant is connected to. This actually comes under an ancient law of 1899—by our standards that's ancient—which some of the environmentalists and some Congressmen have managed to pull out of the law books. As a result, as of today, six major items must be indicated. This involves something over 40,000 enterprises, and all such dumping must be reported and then must be approved by the state concerned, by the Federal Government, and by the US Army Corps of Engineers. Later on it is hoped to expand the number of indices that will be accounted for. Meanwhile every firm must obtain a permit from the US Army Corps of Engineers and the Environmental Protection Agency to continue dumping their discharge into the water, and if any one of the agencies involved should find that the discharges are in excess of what they should be, then the company must propose and show that it is undertaking a programme of corrective action. Failure to do so can result in fines of 2,500 dollars a day and imprisonment. As I say, this goes back to a law of 1899 but is being carried out as of today, and I think it's something which the rest of you might find worth looking into and possibly importing.

Just as biologists are apt to assume that economists understand their problems, so should we perhaps plead guilty for not explaining more of our own in the field of economics. We've been talking a good deal about economic growth, and one of the things that is developing now among some economists is the idea that the quality of life should be included as one of the ingredients which go into making up what traditionally we have called the gross national product (GNP). That's not completely impossible, which is saying that it is going to be difficult to do but it can be done. For example, we do now have other calculations, besides GNP, of individual national products, and we have calculations of national income and of net national product, all of which are different. We even have a calculation for gross domestic product. Some of these involve calculations of depreciation, some of them involve calculations of investment, and some of them involve all kinds of complicated calculations; but it can be done. What we are now proposing is something which we could call a variety of things, but one good title might be 'Net National Wellbeing'. If countries were judged by this, it might help to eliminate some of the environmental excesses that are now going on.

Let me give you an illustration of how this Net National Wellbeing might work: at the present time the paper plant in Jyväskylä is judged according to how much paper it produces in the course of a day or year or whatever period of time you want to calculate for. This amount is then entered into the gross national product of Finland. Now it happens, as I've been told but I hope is the case no longer, that this paper plant also discharges into the water quantities of sulphite and mercury which destroy the lake in a variety of ways. At present the deterioration which this plant causes is not entered into the calculation of its productivity, so that in a sense the firm appears to be doing only good, and nobody calculates on a national basis that it is also doing harm, though we may divine from the filthy stench that all is not well. Now I don't mean to say, of course, that this is only true of Jyväskylä; it is true all over the world, be it in the Soviet Union, in Japan, in the United States, in China—wherever we might be. What such a more refined calculation would involve would therefore be an attempt to say: OK, you produce so much paper in the course of the day, but you also produce so much destruction in the course of the day. Let's make a net calculation and see whether or not in fact you are doing more good than harm, and if you are, then we'll say there is something to be added to the Net National Wellbeing, and if you are not, we'll make a net subtraction.

Now I admit this would require a good deal of estimation, and it would also require a good deal of work by biologists and other scientists, because one of the things we would have to know is how much destruction of life and amenities is being caused by the dumping of sulphite and mercury into the lake. What is the result on balance? We know how much a ton of paper is worth, but we don't know what would be the value, for example, of not dumping these effluents in the lake. We also ought to anticipate the environmental damage of discharging, or the pecuniary cost of burning or otherwise disposing of, PCBs and other pollutants. Though such considerations and calculations would obviously be very difficult, this is the direction in which we are trying to move. This is the kind of calculation that we require for a country as a whole, and should then be done on a global basis.

Now what about the firm itself? Well, the price of the paper produced by that factory from this point on should also reflect these costs of environmental protection. In other words, if the price of a roll of toilet paper is now two marks, we would have to say that we should add to this cost due consideration of the fact that there is environmental destruction going on, and that's a social cost. That is something we all have to bear; but instead of all of us bearing this social cost without any money coming directly out of our pocket, but just by smelling the lake and not being able to enjoy it otherwise, what we could do then is to inflict this cost on the factory, so that instead of costing two marks maybe that toilet paper would cost three marks. Now what would this do? If it were done on a national basis again, for all kinds of commodities, it would make some commodities more expensive than they are now. Economists say that this would involve some manipulation of the supply and demand factors because if prices go up, we move up the demand curve, which means in effect that fewer people will buy the goods. Instead, they may buy other goods which do not cause such damage to the environment and therefore do not go up in price, and so we would tend to switch to those goods. Therefore we would cut back on the consumption of the goods which inflict damage to the environment and move to other goods. Also, firms would cut back on damage costs to reduce prices.

Let me give you an example of how in fact this might work out. Specifically, an example of this kind of thing would be the automobile. The automobile generates a large expense which is not borne directly by the driver: highways, parking lots, smog—we all bear these costs. If somehow or other these extra costs could be imposed on the private automobile driver, prices of automobiles would go up, which from society's point of view might not be such a bad thing. But then what would happen to society? There would presumably be more utilization of public transportation, and the embodiment in automobiles of these external costs would be one step in doing this.

Such things can be done. Already this kind of system is used in the Ruhr Valley in West Germany, where steel factories have to pay for the dirty water which they discharge as well as for the clean water which they use. As a result, the cost of water is very high in the Ruhr Valley. This is reflected in the cost of the goods, and so in the Ruhr Valley, instead of requiring somewhere over 100 cubic yards [76.5 cubic metres] of water per ton of steel, the West Germans manage to do with something less than 5 cubic yards of water. This system is also being utilized in parts of the United States, and I was told this morning that it is also being utilized in parts of Finland. But it's this kind of process which I think we should recognize and be aware of, because while there are many laws that we can pass, we also have to get the participation of individuals and people, and this is a way of making everybody pay who creates or bears the burden.

Reiner

[Concerning proposals for creating new international institutional arrangements for dealing with environment, such as an Institute for Planetary Survival, I would like to make some remarks which I feel should be borne in mind during this discussion. First I would like to make it clear, however, that I do not intend to argue at this stage for or against any particular solution to this problem. Yet I would like to caution you that the creation of a new international agency, by and of itself, is no guarantee that substantial and effective international action will henceforth systematically be undertaken. Governments would need to make effective use of such a new international institutional arrangement, they would need to be willing to accept the conclusions and recommendations from its work, they would need to allocate sufficient financial and other resources for the manifold activities envisaged, etc. We have heard from the representatives of various international organizations present here that much work is already in hand related to one or another aspect of environment. We may need, however, to make a greater effort to harmonize and coordinate our international efforts so as to maximize the results achieved. Moreover, there seem to be important gaps in international efforts for which no adequate arrangements have yet been made.

The second major point I would like to make is that the effectiveness of any new or existing international institutional arrangements for dealing with environmental problems must in the long run rely on the existence of adequate national machinery and facilities for dealing comprehensively and effectively with environmental problems. In a Pilot Study carried out a few months ago in the UN Economic Commission for Europe, we showed that only a few years back there was hardly a country in Europe—and in this connection it should be borne in mind that we are covering the most sophisticated region in the world—which had a high-level national focal point for dealing with environmental problems. Consequently, when economic development plans were being considered or decisions made about the location of new factories or the extension of some industry, there was no one at a cabinet level who could argue the case and say: No, this or that is 'wrong in terms of its adverse effect on the environment and quality of life', and who could then go on to show what the consequences might be over the next 5, 10, or even 50 years.

Many new national institutional arrangements have been initiated in the past year or so, but we could still characterize the present as a transitional period during which governments are seeking to set up the right kind of machinery. In some countries there is a new Ministry of the Environment or its equivalent; in the United Kingdom, for example, the new Department (as it is called) incorporates three old ministries which were dealing with housing, local government, and building and public works. In other countries, existing ministries such as the Ministry of Housing, the Ministry of Public Works, etc., is given additional environmental duties to carry out. I would strongly propose to the Resolutions Committee to include a plea for strengthening national facilities for dealing with environment, with suitable institutional arrangements at the federal level, at the sub-national level, and at the local level.

Now, since I have the floor, may I say a few words about the UN Economic Commission for Europe. As many of you will know, we had a forerunner of the UN Stockholm Environmental Conference—of course, on a much smaller regional scale—a month ago in Prague. Nearly 300 delegates from virtually all UN/ECE countries, six countries from other parts of the world, and about 40 international organizations, attended. The documentation comprised some 100 papers especially prepared for this purpose on a subject-by-subject as well as country-by-country basis. The ECE Prague Symposium surveyed the present environmental situation and discussed various means of environmental improvement at national and international levels; from its debate emerged a series of general and tentative conclusions. An innovation at the Symposium was a panel discussion led by specialists from different UN/ECE countries on major socio-economic questions related to environment. The proceedings of the ECE Symposium will shortly be published for wide circulation. It should also be recalled that the Economic Commission for Europe has made institutional arrangements for continuing intergovernmental cooperation in this field by setting up a new intergovernmental subsidiary body 'Senior Advisers to ECE Governments on Environmental Problems'. In addition, there already exist several other ECE subsidiary bodies dealing with: water management, including water pollution; housing and physical planning; air pollution, etc.]

Siikala (Chairman)

In concluding this session I would like to note that the discussion has been rather broad, and has not confined itself to the environmental issue proper. Other issues, which can be classified as the issues of peace, issues of development, and issues of population and environment, have been treated here. Nor have I tried to limit you, for in fact it seems that these things are bound up together. The environmental issue is one of the main problems now facing mankind, and all of these are inter-linked; in this sense I think there has been a degree of convergence exhibited at this session.

A number of interesting practical suggestions have been made during the debate, and there have also been healthy arguments for and against some proposals. It will be up to the Resolutions Committee to try to build a consensus of opinion on these various ideas, but not in their final form until tomorrow, when another very important aspect of this problem of Global Responsibility will be treated, namely, what organizations and industry should do.

[Finally, the Chairman suggested that speakers who wished to continue the discussion should seek the floor on the following day, after the next, allied paper.]

14

WHAT ORGANIZATIONS AND INDUSTRY SHOULD DO

Keynote Paper

What Organizations and Industry Should Do

by

DAVID R. BROWER

President, Friends of the Earth;
Director, John Muir Institute for Environmental Studies,
451 Pacific Avenue,
San Francisco,
California 94133, USA.

INTRODUCTION

Santayana tells us that those who cannot remember history are condemned to repeat it. Disraeli defined the practical man as one who can be

E.F.—16*

counted on to repeat the errors of his ancestors. But for this moment in time there is no history or precedent, and we have no handbooks, charts, or maps; nor have we any pharmacopoeia, or vaccine for the world epidemic of which we see the initial symptoms.

I believe we are headed for a technological epidemic, combined with a larcenous attack by this generation on the earth's biological capital that should serve many generations of mankind and of other living things. History cannot prepare us for it because there could be nothing like it in history. We need instead, I am convinced, to develop our anticipatory abilities as they were never developed before. We need to be informed by the four extremely powerful words which René Dubos combined:

'Trend is not destiny'.

To me the threat is now frighteningly obvious, but my alarm at its nearness does not approach my concern about those who refuse to be concerned. Experimenting with various ways to convince myself of the true situation, I came upon some aspects which I would like to share with you. Forgive me if they are already evident, but bear with me and pass them on to those in leadership in various parts of the world who do not seem to realize them at all.

Briefly, we need a perspective for mankind: where is he in the calibrations of scale and of time, and what had he better learn from this perspective? For the future, what bigger plans can he embark upon than those with which he has so far been content? How can he attach the importance which they demand to other forms of life than man himself? Kenneth Brower wrote (1969): 'A living planet is a rare thing, perhaps the rarest in the universe, and a very tenuous experiment at best. We need all the company we can get on our unlikely journey. One species' death diminishes us, for we are involved in life.'

This kind of consideration can be an integral part of our thinking at conferences like this, and, I am convinced, had better be. The more movingly the idea can be expressed, the likelier it is that our journey will end happily.

The Primal Alliance: Earth and Ocean

To begin with, let me quote in part from my foreword to a book which is to be published very shortly (copyright 1971 by Friends of the Earth). It is *The Primal Alliance: Earth and Ocean,* and the series to which it belongs, 'The Earth's Wild Places', is intended to be part of an unchauvinistic response to an American challenge in this way: The people of the United States use about half of the earth's natural resources and many of them seek a larger share still. The result is that the American Dream has almost been polluted out of a place to be dreamt in, and a better one, that can leave all people with a livable world, needs to be dreamed up. Those who make problems should propose solutions. In offering some here, I realize that it is bad to be didactic and worse to be presumptuous, and if you are about to be both, as I am, you had better admit it, explain, and hope for clemency.

Scenario for a President

Faced with the Now-or-Never Seventies, what course would you take if yours were one of the greatest burdens of all, that of being President of the United States of America? Whatever his achievements and failings, he must keep more than half the populace behind what he does lest he lose the opportunity to lead at all. If you were he, how would you address your directors, the public? How would you ameliorate the feeling of futility that is pervading America and the world? How would you encourage people to step on to the world's stage and play the role they must play, creatively, if we are to find the route to peace with the earth, with its life-support systems, with its peoples, and with ourselves?

This question is perplexing, and there is no oracle to consult. It is a good question, nevertheless, that each citizen who hopes to be responsible can help to answer. It is a question arising from man-made problems that men and women can solve. So what would you say, confronted with a threat to nature itself that is real, frightening, susceptible to treatment, and has never before been so severe?

If the job were mine, and happily this is unthinkable, I believe I would like the cameras and microphones set up on the Big Sur Coast somewhere near Garapata, late in a long summer afternoon. The camera would sweep the coast and zoom in on the podium. I think my speech would go something like this: 'Let me begin with concern for the whole earth, but focus first on a small detail of the natural world.' The colour camera would move in on the detail of a broken abalone shell, and I would read these lines from Robinson Jeffers:

> ... to equal a need is natural, animal, mineral;
> but to fling rainbows over the rain and beauty above the moon,
> and secret rainbows on the domes of deep-sea shells,
> not even the weeds to multiply without blossom
> nor the birds without music ...
> Look how beautiful are all the things that He does.
> His signature is the beauty of things.

Then I could continue: There will be no one to read His signature. There will be no America, nor will any other nation or people endure, on a dead planet. All nations, our own in the lead in an unhappy race, have been treating this planet as if we had a spare one, and as if nature were our enemy. Each of us, as a human being, arrived on this earth to find it a miracle and a treasure, to find it a source of all the beauty that we know, and we are in the midst of squandering it all.

We have glorified man's acquisitiveness, his aggressiveness, his search for convenience and comfort and security; we have not thought hard enough about his ability to love and to revere life. Because criticism of what we thought was good enough has made us uneasy, we have stifled the creativity and the new thinking which the world needs—without realizing that this was what we were doing. We thought that the formulas which have brought us to our present success—and to our present brink—were all we needed to sustain us and to rescue us.

There is need for change. There is still barely time for change. With fair application of the youth and imagination that should lie within each of us until we die, we can make this change and be delighted and pleased by it.

We need and, if we strive for it, we can have, a New Renaissance. Let it be informed by the insight of the late Adlai Stevenson in his last speech, given in Geneva in July 1965—a veritable universal pledge of allegiance to this planet and to its peoples:

> We travel together, passengers on a little space-ship, dependent upon its vulnerable reserves of air and soil, committed for our safety to its security and peace, preserved from annihilation only by the care, the work, and, I will say, the love we give our fragile craft. We cannot maintain it half-fortunate, half-miserable, half-confident, half-despairing, half-free in a liberation of resources undreamed of until this day, half-slave to the ancient enemies of man. No craft, no crew, can travel safely with such vast contradictions. On their resolution depends the survival of us all.

The peril to this planet—this fragile craft we share—and to ourselves, is a tremendous peril, one that we are only now beginning to perceive fully. Let me try to put the peril on an understandable scale—a scale something like that which was made available to the world through the Apollo missions. To the intrepid voyagers to the moon, the earth was an oasis in the vast desert of space. The French underwater explorer, Jacques-Yves Cousteau, who has plumbed another kind of space, has said that if we were to reduce the earth to the size of a hen's egg, the water of all the oceans would represent a single drop of water on that egg's shell. The drop would be about a fifth of an inch (one-half centimetre) in diameter, as the oceans average 1/2800th of the depth (i.e. radius) of the earth itself. The atmosphere, if concentrated to the density of water, would represent a sixth of the diameter of the drop of ocean. The crop-producing soil that life counts on would represent a sixth of the diameter of the droplet of air and be hardly noticeable to the naked eye. The drop, droplet, and speck, are what make our planet unique, and our very numbers and appetites threaten it as it has never begun to be threatened before.

Time and Man—A Perspective

Let me explain why I say that. If you let the earth's 25,000-mile (40,000 km) circumference represent the earth's computed age of 4.5 thousand million years, each mile (1.6 km) represents 180,000 years. Let's fly the great-circle route headed south-east from Dulles Airport, Washington, DC, and look at the time-perspective as we fly, to see clearly how long the earth got along without man, and how suddenly, in this most recent period, man and his technology are exploding.

We take off from Dulles on our 25,000-mile journey the day the earth begins. We travel 6,000 miles (representing a thousand million years) before there is any life on the planet. Half-way around, just west of Australia, life has become complex, diverse, reasonably stable, and would probably have seemed beautiful if we had been able to look at it two thousand million years ago. Two hundred miles (320 km) west of San Francisco, after 22,000 miles, we find that stone-crabs and cockroaches have been added to the life inventory—and they are still with us. As we touch Kansas air, the age of reptiles begins, and as we near Indianapolis it is over, but redwoods and pelicans have arrived. Just short of Cincinnati, whales and porpoises gather on shores and go back to sea. Our craft begins to let down, and we are 6 miles (9.6 km) from the runway before man appears. From touch-down almost to the end of the two-mile strip, man gets along with tools that are no more potent than a shaped stone, without enough energy behind it to interfere appreciably with the rest of the environment. With 400 feet (122 metres) of runway left, man discovers some simple agricultural techniques and applies them in south-east Asia. The Great Pyramid is being built and California's oldest bristlecone pine sprouts when we are 150 feet from the runway's far end, and Christinaity begins only 58 feet (17.7 m) from the end.

The purpose of this whole analogy comes next: *Not until the last six feet (1.8 m) of our 25,000-mile journey did the Industrial Revolution begin.* In 72 mere inches (1.8 m) man devised and used the tools that withdraw the biological capital of the earth and spend it. Before that he had lived on the earth's organic income without destroying or otherwise putting capital out of action.

Living Beyond the Earth's Income

Just a few more details: a foot (30.48 cm) from the end of our trip, man began using DDT and other chemical allies in his war against competing forms of life—a war which the world's life-support systems had managed very well without theretofore. In the last 15 inches (38 cm) the earth's population doubled and California's quadrupled. In the last 4 inches (10 cm) the world used half of all the oil that has ever been used. In the last inch (2.54 cm) enough people were born to populate a United States. Our own life-span gives us just two feet (61 cm) to stand on.

We are at this moment at the end of the runway and no one has proposed that we slow down. In fact, we have been asking for more speed. What kind of trip are we arrogant enough to think we can undertake next? Some of us are now planning to make demands that in the next ten years (a mere king-sized-cigarette length past the runway's end) will equal all the demands we have made thus far: the oil and power industries plan to double their output in less than a decade—to spend as much in the next ten years, and produce as much, as they have in all the world's history.

Too many people, in overdeveloped, underdeveloped, and normal nations, are counting on some kind of technological magic that will let us stretch a finite earth and keep doubling the demands we place upon it for things of all sorts and sizes. We will discover no such magic, no perpetual-motion machine—much less one that keeps accelerating! We must instead take a hard new look, in the coming years, into how we may live within the earth's income, and not continue to live beyond its means, and thus beyond our own.

The earth's income consists of the annual dividends that are available from the biological wealth which the sun lets the planet and life create and keep after various amounts have been debited. We have been spending capital furiously. We can no longer hope to be forgiven for not knowing what we do. We can now see what we are doing to the earth and can ask, with Thoreau, 'What is the use of a house if you haven't a tolerable planet to put it on?' The time has gone for undertaking vast projects without first asking: 'What does it cost the earth?'

Answers to this question must inform us as we study our energy-needs, our transportation, our development of food, our restoration of cities, farmlands, and forests, our renaissance of small towns and little crafts, our preservation of parks, wildlife, and wilderness, and also our approach to the population crisis, pollution, growth, and the yearning we have for more and more things. It must guide our use of international relations and natural laws that can lead to peace, including peace within our own land. We do not need departments of environment nearly so much as we need governments of, by, and for, people awakened to the need to preserve, restore, and respect, the life-support system. That system enabled the world to work before man came, and it can let him remain here.

The Need for New Perceptions

The ability to perceive is important, too. Thoreau had it when he looked anew at a resource available to all: 'The world has visibly been recreated in the night. Mornings of creation, I call them . . . . I look back for the era of this creation not into the night, but to a dawn for which no man ever rose early enough. A morning which carries us back where crystallizations are fresh and unmelted. It is the poet's hour. Mornings when men are new-born, men who have the seeds of life in them.'

Henry Beston developed the same theme. 'Creation is still going on', he said: 'creation is here and now'. He saw man as part of the endless and incredible experiment, to whom 'poetry is as necessary to comprehension as science. It is as impossible to live without reverence as it is without joy.'

Hay & Kauffman (1971) have taken this reverence and this joy to two different coasts, and have inquired into the forces of creation so beautifully manifested there. Where the shallows and salt winds are, where the land and the sea have most influence over each other, they watched the most important pageant, saw the sea breathing life into the land, the land nourishing the sea in return. But they saw that the primal alliance was flagging. The speed of the flagging should engage our attention.

'The wild sea, never the same,' I wrote in a narrative for a film, yet 'never to be changed by man.' That was in 1956, before I knew how quickly things like Lake Erie could be 'killed', or that even the ocean would not be a large enough sink to handle the radionuclides, chlorinated hydrocarbons, poison metals and gases, and oil-spills we have now tested it with. By 1970, one would think, the world would have learned that there is no 'away' any more in which to throw things, no great dispose-all on the ocean's floor or in its volume. Yet in the summer of that year, at the first *Pacem in Maribus* conference held on Malta, the alarm had apparently not been heard very clearly. The question asked there should have been whether man should continue to throw things into the ocean at an exponential rate and still hope to exploit the ocean for food and minerals at the same rate. But the question was not whether, or how fast. It was: should the ocean be exploited by the many instead of by the few? There is no quick salvation by this route. International conferences might better ask what limits man must impose upon his tendencies to usurp the earth—what limits will take landscapes, diversity, wildness, other species, and man himself, off the endangered list? And on the wild coasts, where the primal alliance has worked so well for so long, what should man's limits be there?

There is one ocean, with coves having many names;
a single sea of atmosphere, with no coves at all;
a thin miracle of soil, alive and giving life;
a last planet; and there is no spare.

Earth and the Great Weather—and Oil

Answers to the question: 'What does it cost the earth?' are implicit, I think, in my foreword to another book (copyright 1971 by Friends of the Earth) that is being published just now—one concerning the Brooks Range of Alaska, the Eskimo culture that has flourished there so long, and the exploitation of oil which threatens the best of both (Brower, 1971). The book title itself, used above, comes from a poem by the Eskimo Osarqaq, translated by the late Knud Rasmussen:

The great sea
Has set me adrift;
It moves me like the weed in a great river:
Earth and the great weather
Move me,
Have carried me away
And move my inward parts with joy.

The Brooks Range wilderness is one that I wish I knew well, but one that I shall never have time to know, and that may not exist long enough for any others to know, if we continue to let trend be our destiny. Perhaps no quest of mankind so threatens his chance to survive as does his almost irrational race for sources of energy with which to make his life more convenient, whatever else it may cost. One of the most dramatic confrontations of convenience *versus* cost is now taking place on the North Slope of Alaska, as my foreword explains.

Headed towards the Pole on the direct route from Copenhagen to Anchorage, we watched the sun set for the first time that day at four in the afternoon and flew north into night. The captain announced our estimated time of arrival and I divided the distance by the hours and wrote on the airline map the times when we would pass over principal points of interest. The map bore historical notes about the famous explorers and the successive dates on which their various expeditions got nearer and nearer to the point from which everything else on earth was south. Before the light was gone on the last bleak land passing seven miles below us, a strong feeling of admiration for the explorers welled within me. For a quickly passing moment I wished I could have been there with them then. Long before dinner it got quite dark, and as we sped above the land of arduous exploring long ago, I saw the lights of Spitsbergen far below.

But suddenly, far more diverting to me, was a bold white light arched broadly over us in the sky—the third time I had ever seen a display of the aurora borealis. There were not many passengers, so I could switch from port to starboard or back to port windows at will. I was fascinated by this phenomenon of nature. No one else seemed aware of it except a Japanese opposite me who kept his head to the window, a pillow alongside to exclude extraneous light. We exchanged glances of appreciation.

'Isn't the captain going to announce this display?' I asked the stewardess, still excited by what I had seen only twice before in fifty-eight years.

'No,' she said, 'the passengers would be annoyed to have the movie interrupted.'

Later she woke those who wished to know when we were directly over the North Pole and I looked out again. The aurora was gone. The clouds concealing the Arctic Ocean were lit only by starlight. As dawn broke in the south, the cloud cover thinned and strange patterns emerged—a lacework of new leads and old in the ice-pack. Ice patterns then changed to soil polygons; permafrost was under the snow, and our crossing of the Arctic Ocean was over. An airstrip showed faintly—Prudhoe Bay, I thought, but we passed too high and fast for me to spot landmarks that I had seen on the ground two months before, when the tundra world was green and the oil companies were showing conservationists their Prudhoe camp. We had learned then about drilling pads, berms, life below zero, the care and feeding of tundra, and the search for exotic grasses to heal scars. An Eskimo anti-litter crew was out on the near-by tundra with big plastic bags. We learned that the oil company's ecologist thought caribou liked the pads and berms, and would not be disturbed in their migration by the above-ground portions of the 800-mile (1260 km) proposed pipeline. We could marvel at the technology that allowed man to find oil in this icy desert and bring it to the surface. It was rather frightening to stand on a platform part-way up a rig and watch an expert team slap piping into the ground in a bit-changing operation. The rig, tower, platform, cables, winch drums, and engine, shuddered and shrieked in violent surges and smashing stops that seemed about to tear the place apart. I resolved not to use gasoline again if it took this much trouble to get it.

If the technology for getting at the oil and bringing it to the surface was impressive, the technology for getting it to market was not. Looking at the miles of four-foot (1.22 m) Japanese pipe piled on site, I worried about the rush to get it there before enough was known about whether it would work or whether, if it worked, the Alaskan environment could keep on working within range of it. I worried about the determination to get the oil out and used up quickly, and about the stubborn refusal to understand the long-term consequences of short-time exploitation.

Scenario for a Chairman

I began worrying all over again as our North Pole flight now sped us towards the Brooks Range. I conjured up disjointed paragraphs of a letter I would send, were I Chairman of the Board of Atlantic Richfield or of British Petroleum—chief developers of Arctic Slope oil—to my directors and stockholders. It would explain how the Company, out of corporate responsibility, must pause for breath in its dash for oil until a whole series of facts were in that were not yet available to anyone. The pause would cost everybody money; but if it were a pause that would help people to live longer, part of the cost ought to be recoverable. The Company was taking the lead in adopting a more rational approach to keeping our planet a tolerable one than corporations had previously thought necessary. The Company did not think that the environmental crisis was a figment. Would the stockholders therefore be helpful and patient with the corporation in its deliberate choice to forgo profits that might risk the environment excessively? And would stockholders who sincerely felt that costs to the corporation were more important than costs to the earth, please sell their stock to someone who felt differently?

A professional worrier could conceive the letter. But could a chairman send it, or a stockholder like it?

Twilight We Do Not Need

Alpenglow was now lighting the summits of the Brooks Range. Whether it was dawn or twilight, it would not reach the North Slope for months yet. Ahead, the sun broke the world's rim to the south of us and climbed feebly into a flaming sky as we flew over the tapestry of meanders of the Yukon River. Shortly, past Mount McKinley, we started letting down. Ten hours out of Copenhagen we landed in Anchorage at two in the afternoon, two hours 'before' we had departed from Denmark, and half-an-hour later the sun set in the south for the second time that day; night came again and stayed this time. The show was over.

Crossing several meridians at jet speed is always upsetting. Being benighted twice in one day was more than my sidereal clock could handle. Another kind of double twilight, however, was far more disturbing—the twilight for exploration and for wilderness. The speed and ease of my travel took the exploration out of it and off the planet. I could ask, as Aldo Leopold did, 'Of what avail are forty freedoms without a blank spot on the map?' The early explorers had earned a chance to see the blank spots of the Far North, but my fellow passengers and I had not. We could select from eight stereo channels as we looked down at where the blank spots had been.

The Last Chance for Wilderness

Concurrently, twilight was descending on wilderness. Just three years before my flights, Kenneth Brower, John Milton, and Steve Pearson, were soaking up the Brooks Range wilderness experience that *Earth and the Great Weather* has much to say about (Brower, 1971). Three people had only themselves to depend upon, no source of resupply, unknown mountains, nameless valleys, and seas of grass—the ultimate wilderness. In three short years the oil stampede had put a civilized stamp on an area the size of Massachusetts in the remotest part of the North Slope. The civilizing had only begun to run its course. There is tension in the fabric of wilderness, and when it is cut it withdraws fast and far. The 800-mile pipeline, cut across the ultimate wilderness, was to be the second civilizing step in a series of no-one-could-predict-how-many-more steps. Already, Ken, John, and Steve, were deprived of knowing again the wildness they had known. Their route had lost the beyondness that counted for very much. Where would their sons look for a chance to know wildness? 'To be precious, the heritage of wilderness must be open only to those who can earn it again for themselves', biologist Garrett Hardin has said.

Earn it where? Will any vestige of wilderness be left after this generation of brief tenants has glutted itself on conveniences, including a plethora of energy, and no matter what it costs all who are to follow? Do the oil seekers and users intend to leave anything unspoiled? The extractors, seemingly the most efficient international organization yet put together, plan to double their all-time drain in the next decade, and to do so come what may and from wherever it may—the Arctic, the western Pacific, the Continental Shelf off south-east Asia, the Near and Middle East, South America, Algeria, Santa Barbara. The possibility of slowing the mad race, of sparing a resource that was six hundred million years in the making and sixty years in the using, and of using if for purposes which oil alone can serve, seems not to have entered the mind of any system of government.

The oil people, finders and users, are the primary targets here because they are the best organized of all in the unintended war to eradicate wilderness from the earth. They have plenty of company. Surely they must be on the verge of sensing that a planet which is too-well oiled will, like a cormorant, die. Or do they? 'The connection between the ability of civilization to protect wildness and the ability of civilization to survive is not so tenuous as we might wish . . . . The kind of thinking that motivates the grab for what's left at the bottom of the barrel—the pitiful fragment of resources in the remaining wilderness—is the kind of thinking that has lost this country friends whom it cannot afford to lose.' I said this twelve years ago at the North American Wildlife Conference in New York City. Between then and now mankind has used up as much oil as in all the preceding years, and the United States has gone far towards losing every friend it had. Yet in March 1971 another North American Wildlife Conference, in Portland, Oregon, was hearing an industry-dominated panel argue long and loud, oblivious of alternative routes and schedules for development, that oil should be hurried to market across the last great wilderness within US borders and also across some of the most seismically active terrain within those borders or anyone else's. The oil-company representatives on the panel echoed the view of the Department of the Interior in its draft statement about the impact of North Slope oil development upon the environment: yes, there would probably be some damage, but demands for energy required forging ahead. National security would somehow be served. How depletion would serve national security was not explained; one who would strengthen the nation by using up its oil, a Friends of the Earth advertisement suggested, would probably burn his firewood before winter.

When the final depletion comes, what kind of ghosts do we want in the Arctic or North-west Passage ecosystems—still one of the greatest wildernesses on our planet? Voicing the concern of fellow Eskimos, 'spirited pure lovers of that land who depend upon that land for a living,' Willy Willoya puts a more cogent question: 'When will the Caucasians let us rest and live peacefully? Where is the god they worship, when they destroy all our human rights and privileges? Where is the liberty and justice they proclaim to the entire world? Where are the wise, the strong, and the brave, amongst the Americans who would be good to their brothers and their lands—and to the creatures and the islands and the waters and the meadows and the tundra and the caves and the mountains that are our home?'

Wilderness, in the days of popular concern about total environment and degradation, has had too quiet a voice speaking on its behalf. Pollution has been easier to herald because its impact is in nostrils, eyes, and genes—everywhere. If what wilderness we have left is to serve its highest purpose—being there for itself and its indigenous life-forms, being there as the 'outside' to a world that is otherwise a cage, and being there for its wholeness, its beauty, and its truth—then those who understand it must speak again as lucidly and as persuasively as did Aldo Leopold, Robert Marshall, and Howard Zahnizer. Nancy Newhall put it beautifully thirteen years ago: 'Wilderness holds answers to questions man has not yet learned how to ask.' Physicists are peculiarly mindful of natural law, and one of them, H. H. Rush, made the point just as tellingly: 'When man obliterates wilderness, he repudiates the evolutionary force that put him on this planet. In a deeply terrifying sense, man is on his own'—with no answers to the questions he might one day be wise enough to pose.

With no further effort at all, by merely letting our present momentum sweep us on with it, we can grind through the world's last wilderness by 1984 at the latest. Just the undisciplined dash for energy can by itself obliterate wilderness. So dash on then, find the energy, and spend it! But what are we to do for an encore? The recoverable fossil fuels will be gone. The feasible dam-sites will all have been built upon and will before too long be silted in. We will have run out of ways—once we find any—to dilute atomic waste from fission and will realize that fusion is better left in Pandora's box, remembering what came out the last time we opened it. We will have endangered the oxygen sink of the atmosphere by probing the earth's fossil fires in geothermal experimentation. So we will use less energy, not more. We will return to ways of getting by with the energy which the sun gives us each day instead of exploding and spilling our way through the energy capital which the earth took thousands of millions of years to acquire.

Do we return to those ways while the world still has wilderness in it, or do we postpone the inevitable turning until we have severed outright and irrevocably those unbroken living connections to the beginning of life that the wilderness has so far preserved? Do we really want to repudiate the evolutionary force? These are questions a rational man should not have much trouble in answering if he paused to think them through.

A Thousand-years Plan

Charles Burnham warned against making little plans; they lack the power, he said, to inspire men's admiration or support. So why not concoct a big plan? Blessed as we are with more data than were ever collected before, and confronted with an improving technology that might better serve us than direct us, we should prepare a plan not for a decade or a century, but a bolder plan to last a millennium, with option to renew.

A big, long-ranging plan of that order could lead to self-fulfilling predictions that are agreeable instead of the kind we have been getting lately. At a time when we see too many things wrong on the land and going wrong in the sea, why not contemplate a thousand good years instead of concocting sedatives for 1984?

Unconventional though the thought may be, the United States could make it clear that we would like to see international leadership rotate peacefully a few times in the course of this thousand years. Such a relaxed attitude might give mankind, and the other mutually dependent creatures in the biosphere which man is part of, a better chance at the succeeding thousand-years period.

Why have a plan of this magnitude? In part, it is because of the nuclear dilemma, that strange, self-centred behaviour allowing us to deposit high-level radioactive waste in the global ecosystem—waste that some one hundred thousand million future men must take meticulous care of in order that a multitude of us today may enjoy our own brief pass at the planet with all the conveniences we are accustomed to. *This waste is the dirtiest garbage of all.* Forgetting its thermal pollution for the moment, we know it is matugenic, teratogenic, and damnably long-lived. We have already produced a great deal of it, and this productivity is proliferating while we watch—or, rather, while we read advertisements calling it clean and then just look the other way. Our children must know where we left it and keep away. So must theirs, *and theirs*—by oral tradition if all other means fail. All this is destined to last for at least a thousand years, with no safe technique yet devised for the warehousing, no one putting up bond, no one prepared to write the insurance, no long-lasting Directions for Survivors chiselled in stone tablets, but with plenty of people willing to sell and install the machinery and merchandise the electrical power, and with all hands in the first, second, and third, worlds eager to buy without limit and without asking what it really costs.

The least we can do, if morality and ethics are still in our fibre, is to plan a thousand years of amenities for our progeny while they mind our nuclear garbage.

So let us have a thousand good years, and an aim. Mere survival is not enough in the world we seek. Our institutions need to accommodate an optimistic vision of man's future, to believe that if the golden rule of moderation is all right in religions, it should not be avoided in life.

A thousand-years plan for oil, with particular reference to the immediate foreground in Alaska, would recognize the contribution of those who discovered the North Slope oil resource, appropriately cover the costs they cannot cover, reward them, pay the state for storage underground, and then record the oil reserve as part of the inventory to be budgeted to last a thousand years. The plan would contemplate that oil may one day serve a more important purpose than fuelling automobiles and supersonic transports. Precipitate exploitation would be discouraged and extravagant use would be prohibited. Studies of potential dangers of removing and transporting the oil in and across fragile ecosystems would be exhaustive and not an exercise in salvage ecology. The costs of perfecting spill-proof transportation would be met, and development would await the meeting. Whatever the costs were, they would be passed on to the user, who has always paid the costs anyway—although he has not always known it. If this materially raises the price, that increase in itself would make economically feasible the development of more efficient oil-using devices. We would pollute far less because pollution would be too wasteful and too expensive. This would be a residual advantage and a welcome one, as the plan would not only anticipate the oil being available for a millennium, but would also lead us to expect the air to remain breathable for the duration.

Applied to people, the plan would celebrate and hold hard to the diversity that makes them strong, beautiful, and interesting. Applied to land-use, it would obliterate *laissez-faire*. In forestry, it would eradicate monoculture. In agriculture, it would stop decimating organic diversity which has been three thousand million years in the making. Moreover, the plan should recognize that population must decline.

Applied to pace, the plan would encourage people to slow down and live—to make time to look for the real show, heeding Robinson Jeffers:

> But look how noble the world is.
> The lonely-flowing waters, the secret-keeping stones,
> The flowing sky.

No one ought to have too little courage to try, for what is the alternative? Begun soon, the thousand-years plan should have rewards along the way. It should keep alive an orchestration of living things more beautiful than we now know, and perhaps even more beautiful than any of us remembers.

We are grateful that the world still has most of the potentialities of this ultimate wilderness still living, and that there lies within man the power to let it stay that way.

The Question Remains: What Should Organizations and Industry Do?

An attenuated preamble should by now lead to a things-to-do list for conservation organizations and for industry. The list should urge organizations and industry to step forward, in mutual support, to persuade the various publics and their governments to initiate crash programmes towards tenable, sustainable goals that would allow the various cultures to survive. This kind of effort is required around the world, to turn mankind's course in time, and to prevent the population crash and the culture crash that seem otherwise to be inevitable. The United States, with its superlative appetite for exploiting natural resources, has been the primary contributor to the threat to the planet's life-support systems. Yet the US has an important role to play in leading a vigorous turnabout, for within its bounds the environmental attack has been so swift that we can still see the dust swirling from beneath the feet of those who launched it. In other nations, many of them eager to follow the US mistake, the attack has not been swift enough to make the source of the stimulus for it unmistakably clear.

This is not an effort to denigrate my own country, but rather an attempt to explain some of the events of the last few decades. It is not an attempt to assess guilt. Let us instead realize that no leading system of government on earth has yet realized the full intensity of the environmental threat which it poses. None has realized the ultimate tragedy that will come if we insist on throwing a geometric curve at the earth in our demands upon its capital or organic and inorganic resources, and in dissipating them beyond all hope of recovery. There was once enough of the world and of time. There isn't enough of either any more for the numbers of us, multiplied by our desires.

General Amnesty Needed

We can, to begin with, declare an amnesty for all of us to desist from what we have done heretofore. We might as well do so, for we cannot undo our doings. But we can, so to speak, redo our intentions: we can begin to agree that guilt must really attend those who insist on carrying on with old, indefensible habits which a finite planet cannot sustain. We are stranded together on a ship that is drifting through space, and there is no possibility of rescue except through that which we ourselves discern, define, and deliver.

Let that be a summary of my own view from the United States, assisted by the travels I have enjoyed in Europe. But let a man of authority speak on the same subject—Sir Frank Fraser Darling in his foreword to the British edition of Paul R. Ehrlich's *The Population Bomb* (Fraser Darling, 1971):

> The one side of us, our heart, subscribes to the doctrine that a world-wide raising of the standard of living to something near that which we enjoy ourselves is necessary on grounds of common humanity. But the other side, our head, should realize this is impossible, and that if it did take place by some immediate miracle we should be in a condition of disaster. The resources are not there and we have not achieved the means of circulating what is needed. Furthermore, it is quite ridiculous to assume that the western standard of living is the most desirable. I say this, having known and enjoyed much simpler days. Our hope is in reducing world population (our own very much included) and maintaining reduction until we can evolve a new economics—one not based on a constant growth-rate of that figment, gross national product. Man as a species is capable of a joyous flowering, but until population is in control, the species as a whole is going to be continually degraded. We are using the planet's finite resources prodigally and asking more from its rehabilitative power than its somewhat debilitated condition can provide.

Sir Frank's appraisal thus modifies the one made by Adlai Stevenson barely six years earlier. When Stevenson alluded to 'a liberation of resources undreamed of until this day,' he hoped that this liberation could be extended to all. But in the following two thousand days almost four hundred million people were added to the number on the earth, all of them with growing appetites, few of these assuaged, and an ever-decreasing proportion of them likely to be in future. We knew the old dream could not be extended. We could sense that an earlier formula,

$$\text{Standard of living} = \text{resources times technology divided by population,}$$

was not quite working out. We could perceive that not only was population thinning out the standard, but that technology was thinning it, too. Technology was accelerating the liberation of resources, yes, but also accelerating their decimation and their scattering. It was not creating: it was finding,

moving, using up, then looking for the energy to repeat the process with progressively poorer materials, moving them faster, making them into smaller,
less recoverable fragments for a diminishing proportion of the earth's growing masses of people. The formulae had changed:

Standard of life = *resources* divided by *technology*, all divided by *population*.

Technology itself was not doing this, of course—its managers were. They
had never needed to learn otherwise. Now they need to.

I do not think that many conservation organizations have been aware of
this change; certainly, awareness has come only recently to those I have
worked with for thirty years. Nor do I think many industries are aware of the
change. At this moment, I cannot name any that are. Nor, to judge from
what we have been hearing, are the United Nations agencies really in the
picture.

What we need to do is to seek out and endow with leadership those organizations, non-profit or industrial, that are flexible enough to get us through
this decade and on into the next with a fair chance of surviving for still
another. We may then be on the way towards reshaping man's perspective
enough to cool the unconscionable drain on resources. If the overdeveloped
countries can renounce, the normal countries will have less to catch up with,
and may in due course conclude from their own observations that catching
up is not all that desirable.

If human pressures begin so to alter, there is a fair chance that humanity
can contemplate its span in thousand-year periods—rather than merely hope
that it can survive for the next thousand days or so.

Thirteen Tenable Predictions

To sum up, I would hope that we can agree to look on the following ends
as desirable and, having agreed, bring them to pass:

(1) The first thing to ask concerning any proposed new development,
public or private, in our own country or abroad, is the question: what would
it cost the earth, organically as well as inorganically?

(2) The next question should be a searching out of the least-studied
alternative—suppose we simply did not undertake the development, would
not the array of ultimate benefits be impressive?

(3) We must realize that an expanding population is a threat and a diminishing population a boon—diminished ultimately, and by willingly accepted means, to the carrying capacity of the earth.

(4) Population limitation should begin in the affluent countries, where
numbers multiplied by desire cost the earth most; to halve the numbers and
double the desire will get us nowhere.

(5) The search for new places to exploit must ultimately cease; we should
increasingly occupy ourselves, our science, our technology, and our good sense,
in going back over where we have been, restoring and healing the injuries
caused by our own depredations.

(6) We must realize that wildness, and large areas of wildness which we call

wilderness, indeed holds answers to questions that man has not yet learned how to ask—answers about the life-force that worked quite well before man arrived, the force that man can and should work with instead of against.

(7) High on our list of priorities should be ways to use our genius so as to diminish our requirements for energy, realizing how great has been the harm to the environment resulting from man's inability to manage energy wisely enough.

(8) We should understand that the so-called green revolution is fraught with danger: that it is indeed using up in a flash of time the organic wealth, energy, and diversity, which only aeons could assemble, and that it builds a hope which can be dashed in the cruellest of ways by predictable genetic or other disasters.

(9) We must agree that the poisons which make the chemicals of life unavailable to life are not to be disposed of by being buried or broadcast on land, in sea, in air, or in space. Instead, they are to be kept under man's control until he can disassemble them and recycle them usefully.

(10) We must discover that war and pollution are now outmoded, even though they have produced jobs and profits in the past. Satisfaction will come from abating the untenable, not from continuing it. Personal, corporate, or national, profit should ensue from a recycling revolution.

(11) We must conclude that the way to change course is not to construct a wall that is crashed into head-on, but to fashion a curve that can absorb safely the momentum which our cultures have developed and redirect that momentum on a safe course.

(12) We shall not require unanimity, because that gives too much power to the veto and takes too much from the essential human diversity which makes us interesting. We will learn to walk with each other and agree with each other as far as we can; otherwise there can be no real conversation and no understanding.

(13) It will become clear in all man's activities that a finite earth imposes limits—and is likely to impose them harshly if man does not himself impose them rationally first. We must be rational enough to impose limits ourselves, and to impose them before our numbers and desires have obliterated the heritage of organic wealth that made us possible and that is essential to keep us from being impossible.

There is an idealism about the above list which suggests that it could only prevail in a world of dreamers. But then, man does dream; each one has a poet in him, and music—and love for people near and far that he has been rather too embarrassed to display. His idealism will prevail, if only because the alternatives are prohibitively grim. The idealism will be driven into focus and into use by the most important driving power man has—self-interest—and by his comprehension, in this time of unprecedented crisis, that *self* cannot exist alone. There must be the *other* forms of living things, inhabiting the ecosphere, with which we were always interrelated and upon which we were always dependent, but which were never before in such short supply as to frighten us into reason.

REFERENCES

BROWER, Kenneth (Ed.) (1969). *Galápagos: The Flow of Wildness.* Sierra Club, San Francisco, California: 2 vols, 320 pp., 140 coloured plates.
BROWER, Kenneth (1971). *Earth and the Great Weather: The Brooks Range.* Friends of the Earth, San Francisco, etc., and McCall, New York: 188 pp., illustr.
FRASER DARLING, Sir Frank (1971). Pp. xiii–xiv in *The Population Bomb,* by Paul R. Ehrlich Friends of the Earth/Ballantine, London: xiv + 141.
HAY, John & KAUFFMAN, Richard (1971). *The Primal Alliance: Earth and Ocean.* Friends of the Earth, San Francisco, etc., and McCall, New York: 144 pp., illustr.

DISCUSSION

Palmstierna (Chairman)

After this excellent and in some respects rather poetic review, I would like to make a few remarks, which I hope will be constructive, to start the discussion. First of all, how would any government survive implementation of the kind of recommendations we have been hearing about? This is a very practical question. If we could find a way in which national governments could survive the often drastic actions involved, I think we would avoid quite a lot of the troubles.

Secondly, I would like to call your attention to the title of this session which I would have preferred to have been 'What Organizations and Industry *Could* Do' (instead of '*Should* Do'). This would give us more latitude, although some of you may think we have enough already, as the category of 'organizations' alone will embrace a vast range from the United Nations and its agencies to non-profit organizations and even trade unions, while of industries there seems to be no end either. Nor are matters as they used to be in olden times, when an ancestor of mine had as his motto, 'Take what you can and keep it'. He was a very efficient general! Fortunately things are not that way any more, and humanity has travelled far towards better understanding, one of the expressions of this being the international organizations which we have now.

Thirdly, I would like you to discuss how we could reform or rearrange the national, multinational, and—more widely—the international organizations in order to be able to implement the recommendations made by Dr Brower. It would also be very useful in this discussion if somebody would offer suggestions as to how we might fill gaps in monitoring the environment, introducing control measures, and legislation—not only nationally where we have to start, but also internationally. The opinion in my country is that this is no time for setting up new organizations, and that it is also unnecessary and will only bring fresh difficulties. A new organization will work for its own power, and so what we need to do is to recombine and reorganize what we have, going as far as proves feasible along that road. If necessary we can reconstruct organizations both nationally and internationally, and although this may seem too reformistic for some people, I think it is the only realistic way to proceed.

Polunin

Mr Chairman, I hate raising a point of order on such a friendly and constructive occasion as this, but if you have suggested changing the theme of this session to 'What Organizations and Industry *Could* Do,' I must intervene, as Chairman of the International Steering Committee, to say that we debated this matter rather carefully before deciding on the stronger '*Should*'. I therefore submit, Sir, that if you really wish to propose such a change, the matter should be put to the meeting. Subject only to the Chairman's approval, we may speak of whatever we desire; but we must be more careful about the announced and published programme.

Palmstierna (Chairman)

I withdraw any such suggestion; it was just to try to steer the discussion a little, because the basis of this is what we *could* do, and the next step is what we *should* do. We must know the basis first and then we can go on; but, of course, the title as printed is very much better, and I know it is very carefully phrased.

Munch-Petersen

I have listened with great interest to the statements made yesterday afternoon and this morning, dealing with global responsibility and future actions. I noted the different proposals for the establishment of new international institutions, and particularly the very eloquent speech of the Maharaja of Baroda regarding developing countries. I am sure that the question of the developing countries and the importance of our association, our collaboration, and our agreement, with them will be duly noted also by the scientists and others this afternoon when we talk about the means of action. But the fact remains that little can be done unless the less-developed and developing countries join forces and understand that environmental problems are not just a function of affluence. To some extent they are bound up with affluence; but they are also an outcome of poverty, just as the question of population is not only a question for poor countries but also for rich industrialized countries. We must learn to be on speaking terms between the rich and the poor. We must also be on speaking terms between individuals dealing with these questions, learning to converse with one another and thus including in our deliberations the scientists, the technicians, the economists, the national assemblies and various other organizations concerned, and also the international civil servants.

I was a little worried yesterday when, I believe, the chairman of the afternoon session mentioned that he was not quite sure that he understood the functions of some of the international organizations. Surely we must all learn to some extent one another's jargons. We must try to understand the scientists and their points of view, and they must try to understand the economists and the civil servants. If something is going to be done, then it has to be done jointly by all of us. For the future, the matter of environment is international; it isn't regional, but inter-regional and largely global. Therefore, as many speakers have already emphasized, it is a subject for discussions and actions by international covenants.

I would like to enter the discussion regarding the establishment of new institutions, and emphasize again that you already have an international system—the UN system consisting of the UN Organization and its specialized agencies in various fields. You have the United Nations Development Programme with nearly a hundred offices in developing countries, which should be used effectively. If it is not so used, it is the fault of the member states; if it does not work, if it is cumbersome or bureaucratic you should criticize it and if you don't do so it is your fault—the fault of your representatives who are sitting and representing you in different organizations. Maybe they are not making their points of view clear when they speak at meetings or wherever they are, or maybe they are not presenting consistent points of view in the

different organizations; maybe they do not speak with the same voice in the
UNDP, in the FAO, etc. If so, this should be changed. It is not enough to say
that the organizations are only concerned with their own specialities; this may
be true, but if it is it can be changed and improved upon.

Returning to the developing countries, their viewpoint cannot be emphasized enough. But I agree with the Maharaja that the representation at
this assembly is slanted on the side of rich countries, in spite of all the efforts
of the organizers. So I feel inclined to act now as a spokesman for developing
countries, because they must be, as I said before, in on this; consequently,
I want to refer to the UN General Assembly resolution on the international
strategy for the second UN development decade, adopted on the day of the
UN twenty-fifth anniversary last year. It stated—and this is what the world
has agreed to in that most global assembly of all—'the governments will intensify national and international efforts to arrest the deterioration of the
human environment and to take measures towards its improvement and to
promote activities that will help to maintain the ecological balance on which
human survival depends.' This is a part of the resolution that should cover the
next ten years. Maybe it is not a very specific resolution, but a general one.
Yet it is one that both industrialized and developing countries have agreed
upon. I mention this, because you have a system and the system has agreed
to do something efficiently about this matter, so before you establish new
institutions you should see whether the present system works in the way you
want it to work.

Gootjes

I appreciated what Dr Brower said about the dangers to the future of
human life. He related it in a way that few others can. But I was somewhat
disappointed about the few words that were spoken about what organizations
and industry already do. I do not accept his contention that only a few industries are aware of the change in the formula for the standard of life. At
least in the Netherlands there are plentiful examples indicating that they
really do. Thus the Dutch metallurgical industry closed three of its main
production units already two years before the end of their technical lifetime,
substituting new ones that are far less dangerous in the matters of air pollution and the general environment. Secondly, a nationally-integrated
automatic air pollution monitoring system is under construction, based on a
contract between the Government and Philips Industries in Eindhoven.
About three hundred monitoring units are involved, with changes in the SO_2
content of the air causing changes in the chemical composition of a fluid, the
result being transmitted by electrical current. I don't need to go into details,
but the system has been tried out in the delta of the Rhine, the measuring
results being computerized in a central chamber in such a way that under
unfavourable meteorological conditions, such as may lead to pollution, all
the industries in the delta are warned automatically. After such a warning the
industries, according to their promises made on a voluntary basis, minimize
their emissions by the interruption of preparation and other such measures.

So far this system has worked well, and we have just started the same kind
of development to combat water pollution; in this a lot of industries are

investing a lot of their resources. It is easy to speak about voluntary systems, but they are unaccountable if not automatically integreted in the matter of input and output quality. So there are positive sides to the subject, and I hope more speakers will strengthen our optimism on this. Organizations such as OECD and ECE are already doing a lot to encourage recycling projects. Let us support them as best we can.

Apollonov

It is gratifying to have this opportunity to say a few words more about the activities of the International Atomic Energy Agency (IAEA). The text of the statement which I was going to make has already been distributed,* so it is not necessary for me to repeat it but only to emphasize the part concerning the Agency's activities in promoting measures for protection of the environment. This can serve as an illustration of what organizations are doing already, and I speak of the organizations of the UN family.

Since 1958, the Agency has issued thirty-six guidebooks giving standards designed to ensure safety, in environmental connections, for every kind of activity in which nuclear energy is used for peaceful purposes. This work has been carried out in collaboration with the World Health Organization, and the standards and guides, based on the most authoritative advice available, were compiled jointly by the Agency and WHO, and addressed to the member states under the joint sponsorship of these two organizations. A number of these standards have also been sponsored by other specialized agencies, such as the International Labour Organization and the Intergovernmental Maritime Consultative Organization. All questions relating to the impact of radiation on man's food resources are dealt with internationally by the joint FAO/IAEA Division of Atomic Energy in Food and Agriculture. The decision in 1970 of the UN Scientific Committee on the Effects of Atomic Radiation† to devote more attention in future to the peaceful uses of atomic energy, is leading to a further strengthening of the excellent working cooperation that has already existed for more than a decade between the Agency and UNSCEAR.

The Agency has long been actively promoting research through coordinated programmes of contracts, and through the Monaco Laboratory of Marine Radioactivity since 1961. It has also promoted the exchange of information in the course of twenty-three symposia and about four times that number of smaller meetings on radiation and environmental questions during the last ten years.

A substantial part of the Agency's technical assistance programme is designed to help developing countries to introduce nuclear energy safely and with minimum environmental impact. Altogether, the Agency's environmental and related activities represent an expenditure each year of more than one million dollars, or about 7 per cent of our current budget. To this total must be added the complementary activities of other organizations of the UN family.

* *See* pp. 354-5.—Ed.
† The effective mini-agency that had been described so approvingly by Dr Butler of Canada (*see* page 461).—Ed.

What I have just said or put in my longer statement gives me the ground to disagree with Dr Brower about the impossibility of finding a solution to the problem of disposal of radioactive wastes of even the highest level of activity. The International Atomic Energy Agency and its staff members know this problem very well and are devoting their efforts to solving it, and in this you can find hope and, I believe, rest assured that a solution will be found.

Vadász

Let me first thank the authorities concerned for inviting the Council for Mutual Economic Assistance to participate in such an important conference. The problems of the environment, their effects on the community in such aspects as human health and standard of living, on agriculture and industry, as well as on economic life in general, are now objects of intensive study by the socialistic member countries of the Council. The Secretariat of the Council participated last month in the Symposium of the UN Economic Commission for Europe on environmental problems and is now taking measures to intensify the cooperation between the member-countries of the Council on this matter. At the moment there are fourteen permanent branch committees within the Council working to some extent on problems of water conservation. The Council regards the problems of water and atmospheric pollution as being of primary importance.

The organization and management of the cooperation among the member countries of the Council for Mutual Economic Assistance upon water conservation matters is carried out by a conference of leaders of the water conservation bodies, which in its turn organizes, on the basis of joint studies, the working out of the projects that are discussed. Thus we have an exchange of information and experience about water management, with a due stressing of the methods and principles of protection of the water resources against pollution. By joint efforts of the scientific institutes in the member countries of the Council, many important studies have been carried out in recent times. Within the framework of the Council, a long-term programme concerning water management up to the year 1980 has been discussed and organized. Its main purpose is to create and to produce new and elaborated modern methods and equipment for the purification of the waste waters.

Regarding air pollution, the member countries of the Council have for some years been coordinating their scientific and technological achievements in the protection of the atmosphere from pollution. A very important aspect of this is afforded by the projects to prevent air pollution by waste gases originating from different forms of industry—mainly from the chemical, metallurgical, and heavy, industries, as well as from road transport. Thus efforts are concentrated on working out the limits of tolerance to toxic compounds of the waste gases, and towards taking measures to diminish their concentration to satisfy the above-mentioned limits. Another important task is to prevent dust pollution of the air from different industries. This involves working out methods of decreasing the concentration of dust in the air in mines and quarries, and in the emanations from metallurgical and allied industries. It is regarded as very important to collect dust from the waste gases coming from these industries, and to have special technical methods to monitor the concentration of dust in the polluted air. In most of the coal-using factories in the member countries of the Council, a smokeless method of oven-charging has been introduced.

Within the framework of the Council, work is being carried out to eliminate the radioactivity of waste consisting of solid or liquid radioactive compounds as well as gases. It is also worth mentioning that technically-based economic and financial pre-calculations are made within the framework of the Council in order to facilitate the acceptance of the recommendations of its member countries and the signing of agreements between them concerning conservation of the environment as realized by each member country in accordance with its own national laws and the specific circumstances involved.

Experience has proved that integrated efforts of the member countries of the Council to protect nature and to struggle against pollution, as well as taking precautions with state plans concerning the development of the people's economy in socialistic countries, altogether can provide favourable conditions for the life and activity of man—even under circumstances of intensive development of an industrial capacity.

Butler

I'd like to return to the remarks which the Chairman made in opening this discussion. He gave us two challenges, and I'd like to deal with the first, in which he asked us to consider what would happen to some national governments if they tried to institute what Dr Brower recommends. This brings me to tell you that I have been listening to these speeches with more and more concern, because I feel we have been talking about symptomatic cures and are not getting to the heart of the problem. As biologists and environmentalists we are preaching to the converted. We all agree that the rate of exploitation of the earth's resources and technical innovation must slow down or even in some cases stop. Most of us would in fact, I think, accept a reduction in our standard of living if everyone else in our country were willing to reduce his or her standards. But the difficulty as I see it is economic and political—aspects which these days seem to be irrevocably committed to the economic system of expansion and inflation. As soon as we try to impose the levelling-off which various speakers have advocated, we induce economic recession and even depression.

I live in a country which for the last few years has tried to have a constant federal budget. Following this policy there has been widespread unemployment, especially among the young and particularly among the more highly educated. This introduces widespread disillusion and despair among these young people, which is, I think, in some ways even more important than environmental pollution. What is the answer to this dilemma? It is one of the most important problems that we have to solve today.

Palo

As a doctor of forestry working as a research specialist in forest economics at the Government Forest Research Institute in Helsinki, I would like to say something about what we could and should do in the light of elementary economic theory, and a little bit about linear and circular technology.

The classical theories of a firm and a consumer have until recently formed the basis for economics: the goal of the firm was to maximize its profits, whereas the goal of the consumer was to maximize his or her derived utility. We assumed a given income and that the consumer had the freedom of choosing his preferences in two respects—first, as to how much to consume now and how much later, and secondly, the mix of goods and services to be consumed. In making these decisions the consumer was guided to a great extent by the prevailing price-system; on the other hand, when maximizing its profits, the firm had at its disposal the choice of what kind of production technology to use. In the competitive market, a production technology was chosen which gave the lowest production costs, and production was carried to the point where marginal costs were covered by the price of the product. In this competitive market the demand for and supply of a product largely determined its price.

An interesting question now is: what kind of items were included in the costs? The answer to this is: those production factors having market prices—such as raw materials, labour, capital, and land. Other factors, such as water and air, were generally free; furthermore, costs of polluting the environment were not included. Consequently a firm could make its choice of a production technology by considering only the production factors having market prices—without paying too much attention to the pollution effects. Including also the costs of pollution in the prices of products could strongly affect the choice of technology and turn it in an ecologically more favourable direction. The transition which in many cases is already going on, from old-fashioned linear technology to what is called circular technology, will generally provide some hope for the survival of mankind.

[Adjournment to evening]

RESUMED DISCUSSION

[in a smaller hall making direct dialogue possible]

Malmi

The XXIIIrd Congress of the International Chamber of Commerce, held in Vienna in April of this year, took as a principal theme for debate, 'Technology and Society: a Challenge to Private Enterprise'. I have here the statement of the conclusions of this Congress, and would like to cite, up to the limit of my five-minutes' time-allowance, points in it which seem pertinent to the present discussion.

The choice of this theme by the International Chamber of Commerce reflects the growing concern that is being felt within the world of industry and commerce about the deterioration in many aspects of the human environment. This deterioration is often the indirect consequence of the utilization of modern technology, which has as a main *raison d'être* the provision of the goods and services that individuals need and demand; in other cases it results from the incorrect choice of technological options. It is significant that the ICC, which represents leaders of business and industry not only in industrialized but also in developing countries, has decided to pursue these questions—not only at its Vienna Congress, but also through continuing work in cooperation with other organizations, and on a wide range of environmental problems.

We feel that industry can claim a large share of the credit for the improved living standards and other advantages that have derived from the ever-widening application of scientific technology and technological development. More systematic efforts than in the past must, however, be made to balance the unquantifiable risks of technological progress against the more immediate and tangible advantages. With increasing public awareness of the problems, with better knowledge on the part of industrialists and especially of smaller firms, with more systematic research done in a non-political atmosphere permitting an unemotional evaluation of the facts, it should be possible to find this balance. The problems to be examined are not only those of the physical pollution of the environment; the possible long-term effects on human beings of biological and chemical changes in the environment are also important. Ever-increased efforts are needed on the part of businesses to foresee and prevent undesirable side-effects of their economic activities.

It is too frequently overlooked that the problems of resources availability are as acute as those of environment protection. Technology at the service of mankind makes heavy demands on mineral and energy resources. Indeed, there is a final limit to the world's natural resources, including unpolluted air, uncontaminated water, and cultivable land. The pressure on supplies of resources available at economic cost is constantly growing as a result of population increase, improved living standards, and the resources cost of improving the environment. Resource availability may be increased by new discoveries, substitutions, conservation, and recycling of wastes. Recycling can also achieve the additional objective of environmental conservation. In dealing with such problems, an orderly and sustained programme of research will be essential.

To strike a proper balance between economic advance and the social cost of economic and technical progress, it is necessary to assess the value to the community at large of factors which are often not comparable. Causes of pollution are many and should be analysed, while for each it is necessary to balance the cost of prevention against the negative value of the nuisance. Political choices have to be made when costs cannot be assessed in monetary terms, and the criteria for such choices will have to be agreed on increasingly in the future. Certain pollution limits should be agreed upon internationally, though governments will often find it desirable to impose more exacting standards at the national level.

The present trend of thinking, at least in the industrialized countries, seems to be leading to a shift of the balance, in that increasing weight is being given in some circles to the intangible benefits of a clean environment in relation to the importance attached to economic growth measured in quantitative terms. International cooperation may often be needed in this context. There are great advantages to be gained in many cases if the price to the consumer can reflect as closely as possible the total cost, including the cost of preventing harmful side-effects. In developing countries, however, needs and practices may be very different.

Government, business, and the scientific community, have specific—yet complementary and interdependent—responsibilities for safeguarding the environment. These require coordinated measures to protect and improve the environment and to repair past damage. Stronger links between these three factions need to be formed. After appropriate consultation of industry and scientists, governments should lay down the framework of regulations and environmental standards within which industry can effectively operate. Inside this framework, and in accordance with sound economic principles, private enterprise recognizes its responsibility to produce goods and to use production processes which have the least harmful effect on environment.

Cooperation is required between companies in the same branch of industry, and between the various industries established in a particular region. Different branches of industry which face common problems should come together to examine ways of tackling these problems, and should exchange know-how. Government should support such cooperation whenever necessary, and in particular should ensure that their anti-trust legislation does not hamper positive action by industry. Research must also be prosecuted very widely and supported 'up to the hilt'.

Developing countries need modern technology if they are to make satisfactory economic progress, and if they are to fight illness and improve agriculture. Each developing country already has its own pattern of pollution, but imported technology should as far as possible be 'clean' technology that will not sow the seeds of new pollution from which later generations will suffer.

Because of their economic and social situation, developing countries tend to see the problems of environment in a different light from industrialized nations, and their priorities are apt to be very different. They may not always regard pollution as their priority problem. It follows that products and processes which can no longer be considered acceptable in industrialized countries may still be used in developing countries if the consequences of their non-use would produce or leave worse problems.

Much thought needs to be given to the kinds of technology that developing countries need, and to the order of priorities in accordance with which they will tackle economic problems. Theirs should be a technology which will encourage economic development and avoid harmful social consequences from which so many industrialized countries have suffered in the aftermath of the industrial revolutions. Developing countries have the chance to avoid the past mistakes of others. Nonetheless, these countries have the right to decide what levels of new pollution they are prepared to tolerate in return for economic growth and alternative advantages for their peoples, although of course it is highly desirable that they respect the interests of neighbouring countries and of their own future generations.

In the decisions upon the steps to be taken to improve the environment and to protect the health and safety of individuals, the implications of these steps for trade and for international economic relations in general must be taken fully into account. Those individual enterprises or those countries which adopt strict standards in the common interest are entitled to expect that they will not lose national or international markets to irresponsible competitors. International cooperation can often help by pointing out to governments appropriate economic solutions to problems of environmental protection. The ICC believes there to be need for intergovernmental action, agreed upon under international convention, to bring about improved standards while at the same time avoiding undue distortion of international competition.

The United Nations Conference on the Human Environment can be expected to make an important contribution to the solution of many problems, for example by identifying the most urgent areas for research and for action, as sensible decisions cannot be taken without the basic scientific facts and a balanced view of the longer-term dangers facing the environment. Governments will need to accept obligations under international convention in respect of pollution having international consequences. It is also to be hoped that the Stockholm Conference will ensure better international access to research carried out nationally.

It is in the interest of countries with common problems to cooperate. Regional cooperation, within the framework of international organizations such as the Organization for Economic Cooperation and Development and the Council of Europe, or on an *ad hoc* basis, thus has an important role to play; for many of the worst problems of the environment can effectively be settled on a regional basis between neighbouring countries who share, for example, an international river or lake or inland sea.

The general objective to be pursued by governments, industry, and the scientific community, is a forward-looking and harmonized utilization—throughout the world and over time—of human and material resources. This implies the prevention of future deterioration and the rehabilitation of past damage to people and to the environment. It requires also the preservation and development of resources for the future. The ICC accepts the challenge to industry arising out of the impact of technology on society, and is examining the possibility of establishing a body, including scientists as well as businessmen, which would be capable of guiding its future work on environmental problems.

Many of these points apply to Finland, where for ten or more years it has been evident that the pulp and paper industry is the main polluter of the country's inland waters. But now the industry is attempting to reduce the pollution load, and some important improvements have already been achieved as a consequence of recycling measures. Also, when three years ago the question of mercury pollution became acute, and the dangers connected with it became obvious, the Finnish pulp and paper mills using chemicals containing mercury voluntarily abandoned the use of such chemicals.

Palmstierna (Chairman)

We all know that Finland is on the forefront in many of these respects and will probably remain so. But if I may allow myself one slight remark about research, of course much more must be done but there is a lot that has already been done without being used. So I would sometimes substitute for research the development of methods already known, citing as an example many of the recycling methods that have been known for a long time but have not been used.

Tunkelo

Technicians and engineers are often blamed for their eagerness to improve technical devices and methods without taking into account the full ecosystems of nature. I am sure that in many engineering associations and other circles this basic feature of technology has often been discussed, and that plans have been made to improve the situation. Here I just want to report that the Engineering Association of Finland, Suomen Teknillinen Seura, has taken action in the Federation of European Engineering Associations, to provoke discussion of methods in terms of the much-needed new technology. This new technology emphasizes recycling and other economies in the use of resources in the manner that has been called for so many times during this Conference. We need to cycle natural resources through production, utilization, and then the rejection process back into nature—without making them useless to man and without destroying nature through pollution.

The ideas behind the proposals were taken from a talk given last year to a meeting of the Finnish Technical Association by Professor Pentti Malaska, and since published in English as a pamphlet entitled 'Prospects of Future of Technical Man'.* The matter was discussed by the board of the Federation of European Engineering Associations, who appointed a team which proposed the following among other measures:

1. The Federation agrees in principle to support the inclusion of the new technology [corresponding to the natural cycle] development project in the programme of national engineering organizations and to appoint from among its members a team to be called 'The Committee on Environmental Engineering'.

2. The Federation will contact corresponding international organizations to make the theory known. It must be emphasized here that the balance of nature will be upset, due to the present use of matter and the population rise, unless we begin to use new alternatives.

3. The Federation recommends that engineering associations in the member countries continue to consider the idea of setting up national technology committees which will note that scientific testing of the ecological cycle theory and developing new technologies constitute an extremely demanding and interesting challenge for engineers, providing them with extensive research and development projects.

4. The Federation recommends that the following be made the task of the national technology committees: (a) making known the idea of the ecological cycle, and scientific feasibility testing; (b) searching for the technical means of finding solutions based on the cycle idea; and (c) drawing up pilot plans and studying the economic and practical aspects of these technical solutions.

*Insinöörilehdet Oy Ingenjörsförlaget Ab (The Engineering Publications), Helsinki: 8 pp., 4 figs, 1971. —Ed.

5. The Federation recommends that engineers be given instruction in eco-engineering and that courses in this be introduced in colleges and universities. Its Committee on Environmental Engineering will follow the work of the national technology committees, maintain contact with them, and act as a link between them by meeting at least once a year.

The Engineering Association of Finland expects this proposal to lead to a critical reconsideration of the ethics of engineers and technicians, and hopes that all the foreign participants of this Conference will try to get their appropriate national organizations to support this proposal.

Palmstierna (Chairman)

That was a very interesting contribution. How soon do you expect your engineering cooperation to start?

Tunkelo

Well, the team has just started its work, so I don't expect anything to happen before, let's say, a year from now.

Miller

My views on the educational aspects have, I think, been sufficiently expressed already in this Conference, but as there is no specific place in the programme for discussion of education, I would like to bring it in as a very important topic, and to say that in our work in the IUCN Commission on Education we have been concerned with developing a suitable curriculum. For this, we brought people from various parts of the world to a conference to discuss what they might wish to do—what might be appropriate for a curriculum in environmental education. I won't go into details, which are available from IUCN, but one of the main features of our deliberations was our unanimity in feeling that there is a need for an across-the-board, multi-disciplinary approach to environmental education. This means that, for example, in cities where you have all kinds of life and services, education should touch on all of these and either prepare people for full understanding as citizens or give them specific training for careers in environmental fields. At least there should be some environmental input into the education and training of the citizens.

As for what industry should do, our Foresta Institute in Nevada has lately been called upon to make some appraisals of land values. In the United States, this is ordinarily the function of a small segment of the real-estate people who are concerned to establish what is the value of a piece of property. Normally, this is done by finding out what the market value would be if the property were being sold, and in that way a court can determine what is proper compensation—for example, if the property is needed for government purposes such as putting through a highway. That kind of consideration has now been found to be inadequate for a comprehensive evaluation in some cases, and so we have been called upon by the owner and the state to make an ecological appraisal before the case was given to the court which would determine the proper value for compensation. This we did by taking the readings from existing analyses of the soil (which had been done by the Soil Conservation Service), from an analysis of the quality of the forest (which had already been done by the forest service), and from the figures for precipitation in that particular area (which had been done already by the government meteorological services). We also used available maps for physiographic features. From all of these we were able to draw on existing information, but this information had never before been integrated to the satisfaction of any land-user or in any plan for land-use. Our function was to integrate this information and arrive at a true valuation based on what the land could, or properly should, be used for, and the likely consequences of such use.

We have been called again into such a pattern of study for an American Indian reservation where the Indians need to know for their own decisions in the future what kinds of values to expect from the land they have. This type of study is still in its early stages, and we are trying to work things out so that it will become a suitable service in any kind of land exchange in the future. It is not exactly an industrial application of ecology, but it could certainly be an important phase in the proper development of the economy. It could also be valuable in regulating the requirements of communities that are subject to zoning, so that no person can do entirely what he wishes with his land even though he has the ownership of it. This kind of thing is becoming more and more widespread and important nowadays, and so we feel we can contribute something which, if perfected, could be useful in the future.

Palmstierna (Chairman)

In Sweden we have introduced courses on the environment, having one-year courses now in three universities and ten-weeks courses for the students in all our universities. The ten-weeks courses are open also to experienced administrators and sanitary engineers, etc., and we have found that they are useful though still in the experimental stage. I would be glad to supply details and written reports from Stockholm. [A comment from the floor: 'It seems that once again Fennoscandia is leading the way, and we hope others will take note!']

Palmstierna (Chairman)

We don't like to boast but it could be worth while at least looking at our mistakes: let's put it that way.

Polunin

[As I have been prevailed upon to rise and explain, on behalf of the International Steering Committee, why we have not wider representation of organizations and industry here, I must first apologize for the latest interjection from the floor; I had hoped to be less obtrusive! Of our attempts to get industry here and, when here, to voice their views, I have already said enough—except, perhaps, to stress adequately that we really did not give those busy men much time to arrange to come, and are getting in useful comments from some of them who seemed genuinely sorry not to be able to.*

* *See*, for example, those from Sir Harold Mitchell, Mr Augustine Marusi, and Mr Henry Ford II, published in the Addenda to this Section (pp. 510–15).—Ed.

Such international organizations as were invited to do so mostly sent delegates—even if we do not hear them—but a grave disappointment is the apparent absence of the Church and of international trade unions. It does not seem that either is particularly interested, though both have wonderful opportunities to do things for the world's good where the environmental future is concerned. The World Council of Churches certainly expected to send their maximum allowance of two delegates, and even mentioned likely names,* and of trade unions we invited the three main 'world' organizations. When these efforts appeared to be failing, I tried to get one or two outstanding and widely respected trade unionists to come as individuals— particularly the Right Honourable George Woodcock,† for many years the leading spirit for understanding and patience in the British Trade Union Congress, and latterly Chairman of the Commission on Industrial Relations— and now we do have Finnish representation, including their Central Trade Union, though it still seems to be voiceless.

To use what might facetiously be referred to in our midst as a Butlerian gambit, let me tell you why environmentalists should have close intercourse with trade unionists, whether they like it or not. With the influence of the pulpit no longer what it was, and government insistence widely anathema in 'western' countries, trade unions have a possibly unique opportunity to act powerfully for the environmental good by refusing to have their members and adherents work on projects which they consider inimical to the best environmental—and hence general public—interest. This has already happened with great effect—for instance in Australia, where in 1970 the action of the trade unions was decisive, even against local governmental pressure, in stopping drilling for oil which could have threatened the Great Barrier Reef.

There have been other instances of such enlightened trade-union action, and could surely be very many more—if only such organizations could be given, and would take, appropriate advice, and learn to place the general good before their immediate concern about employment and remuneration. I once tried to put this across in the Guildhall in London, on the occasion of the Countryside in 1970 Conference, but though the Chairman called for comments from trade unionists present, he got none at all. So I wondered whether I had made the proposal clear, until somebody told me that such people did not as yet want to understand such things, or see beyond their immediate noses. However, I feel strongly that we should go on trying to open up this promising avenue to action.]

Palmstierna (Chairman)

In my country, Sweden, the political movement is at such a stage that the trade unions are growing interested in environmental matters, and the reason is that they are finding out that such poisons as PCBs and mercury are first hitting the worker on the workshop floor, as I explained on the

* As is indicated on page 641, the World Council of Churches did send a suitably senior delegate, while the comments of the Executive Secretary of their Department on Church and Society are published in the Addenda to this Section (pp. 513–15).—Ed.
† See his comments published in the Addenda to this Section (p. 513).—Ed.

television today here in Finland. You can tell many fine stories illustrating this kind of thing, such as how the Mad Hatter in Alice's Wonderland was mercury-poisoned, and now I am finding a growing discontent inside the trade unions in my country, at least, on realizing that they are not on the bandwagon of the environmental movement. But when once these mighty bodies—and I think it will be very soon, within the next year or two—are on that bandwagon, matters will be changing in Sweden, and we could help to steer things in the right direction, so as to get action through honest and enlightened trade unions.

This matter of environment has, in the eyes of many trade unions, for a long time looked like the entertainment of the upper classes of the world, which in reality it shouldn't be and isn't. Indeed it would be tragic if such a thought should prevail for long and I certainly hope it will not; we must get it out of people's minds by propaganda and by different kinds of courses, for example on TV and radio, etc., to which most of us have good access. So I feel we could help to change the situation rapidly in the desirable direction in our various countries and ultimately throughout the civilized world.

Finally I would like to say on behalf of Dr Sten Renborg, who represents the Council of Europe but is not in this hall at present, that he has experience of this kind of worker/employer cooperation internationally in Europe, and his feeling is that we should start by educating the politicians. When they have become sufficiently indoctrinated—for example, by having recycling procedures firmly in their minds—then things will start to happen. Though he would have put it in more diplomatic terms than I do now, I think that is approximately what he wanted to have said to you.

Miller

This reaching of the politicians can be fatal if you don't also reach the industrial managers, because the latter are very persuasive in the politics of their local districts. So I'm wondering if you have advice or examples of persuading industry from the executive level to make a turn-around in procedures or in the activities of management in such a way as to benefit the environment?

Palmstierna (Chairman)

Let me speak of my own country which I know best; we haven't solved this problem, but one way of trying to do so has been to put some of the high-level industrial people for instance on my council, and this has had an effect upon one of these people, at least, as his plastics industry is no longer dumping PCBs into the sea, which could have caused an international scandal if it had continued.

Brower

In Sweden recently I have had a feeling almost of despair, that there is not enough participation in environmental matters. Thus a key biologist told me that it would be easier to get 40,000 dollars to develop equipment for spreading detergents than a smaller sum to conduct research on what happens when you put detergents on spilt oil—which makes one wonder whether it may not be similar to the situation in the United States. There, if you point to a cause of pollution, the first thing you get is a denial, followed by a cover-up story and then a diversionary public-relations campaign which we have come to refer to as eco-pornography. Under pressure, perpetrators and their allies will claim that, like war, pollution makes jobs, while if necessary it can be moved away. Meanwhile we are told that the United States should build SSTs to maintain its air leadership and improve its balance-of-payments!

On a happier note, there is a promising case of an international firm of management consultants who are training new executives to be ecologically responsible in their work for and advice to corporations, which I hope will help.

Referring to my paper, I feel I must have failed to put over the fact that we are embroiled in something which lacks rules to go by, as this has not been taken up in the discussion. In this attack on the environment which we are witnessing, the speed of degradation is so fast and it advances on a front so wide that we do not know how to avoid it, much less to combat it; but combat it we must, and surely will. Already, reading these papers and listening to the discussions, I am very impressed and even reassured, though I certainly want to hear more of the activities of those ecological engineering groups described by Professor Tunkelo. The Stockholm Conference should be getting plentiful inputs and be a real hope.

Finally, I would like to say that I think the conservation organizations have often failed in their human relations, worrying unduly about negative things and not recognizing their real friends. It is always easy to criticize but far preferable to praise when we can: 'You did a fine job; with an extra bit of effort put in together next time, let's see whether we couldn't even . . .' But here one worries a bit about the balance between information and action, the need for which balance has been illustrated repeatedly through this Conference: we need more research and yet it takes time, money, and real effort; meanwhile we may need action, though it should be based on the best and fullest information. Where do we find the balance, and when do we act? To answer will require ecological judgment of the highest order, which can only be based on sound training and experience—a combination which few at present possess, as was pointed out by Professor Polunin at the end of our last evening session.

Palmstierna (Chairman)

Concerning the Stockholm conference, it is indeed a hope but I do feel we ought not to expect too much: it is not to be a free conference of leading thinkers and scientific specialists speaking their minds as this one is, but a formal meeting of rulers and the like at ministerial level, and if we do little more than indoctrinate them in environmental matters and make them think ecologically, we shall have achieved a lot.

I would like to stress a wise thing that Dr Brower implied: don't necessarily wait for research. Of course, this doesn't mean don't do research, and don't spend money on research, but that we cannot always wait for all the details. Too often I have been in a situation in which industry has said:

please tell us all the facts, and we have to say, 'We don't have all the facts, but we have enough indications.' Already the new law on toxic products in my country will make it much easier for the government to act on indications, while the burden of proof will be on the one who wants to use a new chemical that may be dangerous. So the former situation is reversed, though we shall have a big job of cleaning up to do with the old chemicals.

Kerminen

As a comment on how Finnish authorities deal with oil-spills, especially when people use emulsifiers to dispel them, I may say that in the Finnish National Board of Waters we have given out recommendations to our own district organizations, the so-called water districts, as to how they should react. These recommendations are based on research that has been done all over the world—in the United States, in the United Kingdom, in Sweden, and also here in Finland—and have been approved by our courts, including the highest in Finland. The Finnish National Board of Waters has decided to recommend against the use of emulsifiers on all inland waters, and to place the sea waters in four categories.

The first category of sea waters is in harbour areas where we say that if mechanical means are not successful or adequate, then people can use emulsifiers just to clean up the vessels and harbour devices. On the other hand, the interior waters of archipelagos, etc., should be treated just like inland waters, and so should some of the outer archipelago waters, though in these latter areas the responsible authorities are the Finnish National Board of Shipping. If that Board allowed people to use emulsifiers there, they would have to be ones which have been tested and found to be not so very harmful. The same applies to the open seas, though we always recommend that technical advice should first be sought if possible. Concerning rocky and sandy shores which had become polluted by oil-spills, we decided to allow, on those that were in active use for recreational purposes or summer cottages, employment of certain non-toxic emulsifiers, of which we gave a list. This list we compiled from our own experience, from the literature resulting from research in other countries, and from the recommendation of water pollution control authorities elsewhere.

We went ahead with these recommendations because the situation was quite confusing here in Finland, and we decided we could not wait for further research or experience of what other countries might do.

Brower

It should, I feel, be noted not only that mankind is planning to use very much more oil in the coming years, so that more and more oil pollution is to be expected, but also that studies on the east coast of the United States have indicated that some of the oil which has been put down by emulsifiers has proved to be really very lethal. It just goes on being very deadly at the bottom of the sea where they are measuring its effects. The figure I got from a member of the Senator Hart's investigating committee in the United States Senate is that the indications are that the oil which has been so treated has a half-life in its lethal capability of about one hundred years, which is a very frightening thing to contemplate. So I think we need to insist upon smaller and safer tankers that will sacrifice something like one-quarter of their capacity in order not to be tempted to pump out their ballast. Also, to judge from the horror stories we've read, the training of the personnel involved is not very good, the control is not very good, and this really challenges industry to stop looking for straight-line, low-cost solutions and seek those that are now emerging as clearly right.

Palmstierna (Chairman)

Those sentiments seem very sound and proper, but the problem is to sell them to the authorities, to the ruling peoples; how do we convince governments? That is the basic difficulty; but we *must* find a way, and it would seem to lie with the other topic of our discussion, namely organizations, though admittedly one way is to sue. But it would be better to get the functional world behind us, and that should surely be our aim.

ADDENDA*

From Sir HAROLD MITCHELL, *Bt, international industrialist and student
of the Americas,*
Château de Bourdigny, 1242 Geneva, Switzerland

Of the many frightening problems which face our world of today, by far the most menacing in its implications is the doubling of the world's population by around the end of the century. We live and work in an age of change which is far more rapid than it was in the industrial revolution of the nineteenth century. Then, the demand was for people to man the mills and coal-mines: a need for manpower and womanpower. Today the successful management of an industrial company concentrates on the reduction of labour by ever-increasing mechanization. More and more new capital tends to be spent on machinery and equipment which will result in a reduction of labour.

Trained as I was in the coal-mines of industrial Scotland, I recall that 75 per cent of our cost of production was represented by wages. Today, in Canada, my company there has a comparable labour cost of around 30 per cent. Of course, the methods of production and equipment used have changed dramatically.

To take a different but major industry in a number of underdeveloped countries, in the growing of sugar-cane and the manufacture of sugar one can see a similar pattern. Despite Government reluctance to the introduction of mechanized cultivation in some countries such as Jamaica which have heavy unemployment, the pattern of change appears to be inevitable.

Another aspect is that countries with a high standard of living increasingly resent unemployment. If they accept immigrants, they are in a position to impose relatively high educational tests. In fact, the intake which they seek is the cream of the underdeveloped countries—the very people who should stay in their homeland to help in its development. My personal belief is that we are nearing a point at which large-scale emigration will end.

A significant side-effect of all this is the increasing reluctance of people to work on the land, not least in cutting sugar-cane, and the concomitant surge from the country into the towns—witness the *favelas* of Rio, the *barrios* of Caracas, and the *barriadas* of Lima. Nothing could be grimmer than the portrait of the poor area of São Paulo in Carolina de Jesus's *Quarto de Despejo*.

The late Ross Thatcher, when Premier of Saskatchewan, Canada, and himself a farmer, told me in May 1971 that in his Province people were moving off the land. Farms were becoming larger, employing fewer people. The same tendency may be observed in parts of the United States and, of course, Europe.

We are in a world in which the developed one-quarter faces an underdeveloped three-quarters, with the gap quite probably widening. Meanwhile everywhere the world's now slender resources of oil, coal, and natural gas, face accelerating exhaustion with the uncertain and unattractive alternatives which nuclear power presents.

* Further written contributions from invited participants who expressed regret at being unable to attend the Conference in person; for others, *see* pp. 58–64.—Ed.

Even when capital is introduced into the underdeveloped countries, it tends to be non-labour intensive. A striking example may be seen in the streamlining of the oil refineries in Curaçao and Aruba.

The India–Pakistan crisis, with its torrent of nearly eight million refugees, remains as a grim reminder of what may lie ahead—and the sands are running out.

It is hard to see the building up of a generally contented world population. Already guerrilla outbreaks and other forms of violence suggest the storm-signals of what may lie ahead for a world that pays too little heed to the pace of its population expansion and breeds accelerating discontent.

From Mr AUGUSTINE R. MARUSI, *Chairman and President of Borden, Inc.,*
277 Park Avenue, New York, NY 10017, USA.

Meetings such as the International Conference on Environmental Future afford outstanding platforms for business leaders throughout the world to tell the public what industry is doing to help solve the critical environmental problems which we all face. The emotionalism that has accompanied the rising level of international environmental awareness is gradually giving way to an understanding that all sectors are responsible for our environmental ills.

Certainly, industry must take part of the blame for pollution; for obviously, any manufacturing facility will produce some forms of waste by-products, and many of these by-products are environmental contaminants. But it is also true that municipalities, government agencies, and individuals, share responsibility for pollution, and all sectors must work together pragmatically and cooperatively to eliminate the problem.

In the United States, business has shown increasing recognition of the dimensions of the problem, and has set about putting its environmental house in order. Corporate leaders are no longer using the imperfect nature of our national standards, our limited knowledge, or the relative disorder of our enforcement machinery, as a pretext for stalling action on the problem. Instead, there is strong evidence that business and government are doing the best they can, as fast as they can, with the knowledge and the machinery available.

For its part, Borden, Inc., has developed a company-wide pollution control programme incorporating Environmental Quality Coordinators who are constantly on the watch for pollution problems at each operation and plant. Management at all levels is thoroughly informed on progress toward eliminating and avoiding environment problems. Furthermore, Borden uses a corps of roving 'environmental auditors' to make unannounced visits to company operations. As every manager within the company knows, the auditors have full authority to close down any operation which they determine is in violation of pollution control regulations.

Many other companies in the United States and throughout the world are also pursuing vigorous pollution abatement and control programmes. Meetings such as the International Conference on Environmental Future and the United Nations 1972 Conference in Stockholm offer a splendid opportunity for their management to tell their story and to offer the hand of cooperation to everyone who is concerned with solving such a vital problem. It would be most unfortunate if the business community were to discount prematurely the importance of these conferences and, in a sense, assure their futility by abandoning the field to governments and non-business environmentalists.

From Mr HENRY FORD II, *Chairman of the Board of Ford Motor Company, The American Road, Dearborn, Michigan 48121, USA (including excerpts from his book,* The Human Environment and Business, *published by Weybright & Talley, New York, 1970)*

Modern industrial society is based on the assumption that it is both possible and desirable to go on for ever providing more and more goods for more and more people. Today, that assumption is being seriously challenged. The industrial nations have come far enough down the road to affluence to recognize that more goods do not necessarily mean more happiness. They are also recognizing that more goods eventually mean more junk, and the junk in the air, in the water, and on the land could make the earth unfit for human habitation before we reach the twenty-first century.

In short, the terms of the contract between industry and society are changing. Industry has succeeded, by specializing, in serving one narrow segment of society's needs. We have bought labor and material and sold goods, and we have assumed that our obligations were limited to the terms of the bargain. Now we are being asked to serve a wider range of human values and to accept an obligation to members of the public with whom we have no commercial transactions. We are being asked to contribute more to the quality of life than mere quantities of goods.

Now that public expectations are exploding in all directions, we can no longer regard profit and service to society as separate and competing goals. Instead, we should start thinking about changes in public values as opportunities to profit by serving new demands. We have to ask ourselves: what do people want that they didn't want before, and how can we get a competitive edge by offering them more of what they really want?

It is clear that people want clean air, and want it very much. Before too many years have gone by, the only market left for motor vehicles will be the market for vehicles that are virtually emission-free. As a motor vehicle manufacturer, Ford's responsibility throughout the world is to enhance its stockholders' investment by developing vehicles that provide the best possible combination of minimum emissions with all the other qualities people want in their cars.

With regard to the International Conference on Environmental Future, I much regret that prior commitments prevent me from attending what seems destined to be a most important meeting. But I shall await its outcome with much interest, and hope to be free to participate on some future occasion of the kind.

From the Rt Hon. GEORGE WOODCOCK, *P.C., C.B.E.,*
24 Lower Hill Road, Epsom, Surrey, England

Although unfortunately unable to attend the International Conference on Environmental Future owing to being otherwise very heavily committed for the same period, I'd nevertheless like to help but I doubt if it is possible to say anything about the attitude of trade unions towards pollution that would be encouraging to environmentalists.

In most situations a trade union—and most of its members—would be more concerned about opportunities for employment than environmental considerations. Thus it is most unlikely that any trade union would declare a proposed development 'black' on those grounds.

Moreover—and apart from their reluctance to diminish employment prospects—trade unions are inclined to resent suggestions that they should take particular responsibility for, and suffer the main consequences of, decisions on general issues of concern to the public as a whole.

There is, of course, one area where trade unions and environmentalists ought to be on common ground—namely, the use of materials and substances in manufacture that are dangerous to the employee as well as injurious to the environment.

From the Rev. PAUL R. ABRECHT, *Executive Secretary,*
Department on Church and Society, World Council of Churches,
150 route de Ferney, 1211 Geneva 20, Switzerland

The religions of the world, with few exceptions, have not concerned themselves with the impact of the scientific and technological revolution on man's environment, though some Christian churches have been active participants in the movements which today call attention to the urgency of the problem. Recently, however, certain religious groups have begun to sense the fundamental, spiritual, and ethical issues posed. In 1969 the World Council of Churches* started an enquiry on 'The Future of Man and Society in a World of Science-based Technology', with special attention to the issues of Science and the Quality of Life, including the threat to the environment. Subsequently a group of environmental scientists, social scientists, and men of public affairs, as well as theologians and church leaders, convened in June 1971, issued a statement on the *Global Environment, Responsible Choice, and Social Justice.* This was approved by the Executive Committee of the World Council in September 1971 and was issued forthwith as 'A call to the

---

* The World Council of Churches is an organization of some 250 independent Christian denominations. As yet the other religions of the world lack similar organizations to enable them to focus attention throughout their domains on the religious dimension of such problems as those of the environment; consequently no single concerted effort is likely to be forthcoming from them in the manner of this movement of the WCC to activate matters from their pulpits all over the world. For religions as a whole, however, it seems that much might be done to further joint action on such matters of common concern as the human environment through such organizations as The Temple of Understanding, with headquarters at 1346 Connecticut Avenue N.W., Washington, DC 20036, USA (Finley P. Dunne, Jr, Executive Director) and the World Conference on Religion and Peace, with headquarters at 2-7 Motoyoyogi-machi, Shibuya-ku, Tokyo 151, Japan (c/o Rev. Shuten Oishi).—Ed.

churches for study, comment, and action'. It is hoped that it will be widely circulated in the churches and encourage a process of reflection and action.

The statement recognizes that the churches must be self-critical concerning their own interpretation of the idea of man's dominion over the earth and the abuse of this in contemporary thought: 'For too long Christians have thought of creation as having to do with the beginning of things instead of understanding it in terms of God's continuing work and man's continuing responsibility.' The statement stresses the need for a new, responsible understanding of dominion in the light of modern technological power:

> Technology and science have vastly increased man's dominion over the earth, not only enriching life but also by contrast creating problems of pollution, of exhaustion of resources, of the subordination of man to machine, and above all of injustice. Nations and groups within nations use technology and science to dominate and exploit other nations and groups, thus increasing the gap between rich and poor peoples. However, man's dominion over the earth cannot be abandoned now, as some would argue, but must be exercised with greater wisdom and skill to ensure social justice to all peoples. Christians must re-examine the biblical concept of dominion, as a basis for intelligent, responsible choice in environmental issues.

The statement calls attention to three critical points for the concern of the churches:

1. *The consequences of the approaching exhaustion of non-renewable resources.* The claims of future generations must be considered in determining present consumption, and in view of the approaching exhaustion of some valuable resources this raises fundamental questions about further economic growth in some countries. At the same time 'the challenge of international social justice confronts us at the outset of any inquiry into the environment question.' The statement to the churches emphasizes the need for a global approach to environment:

> The lesson for the future is plain. What is needed is a radical change in attitude towards the natural resources of the world and their distribution and use. They were created by God, and particular countries are stewards and trustees for their world-wide use by present and future generations; all people have the right of access to them, not through condescending grants from the affluent but as a common human inheritance.

2. *The continued massive increases in population and the pressure this puts on limited resources.* The churches have always defended the right of parents to decide how many children they might have. But today it is noted that 'this right should not be exercised apart from the right of children to physical, social, and psychological, health [and] to an environment which gives scope to the fulfilment of their human potentialities'. Hence, 'Population control puts the emphasis on parents having the number of children that can be adequately cared for in the world, rather than on the number of children parents may want to have'. While stressing the need for control 'achieved voluntarily', the statement nevertheless recognizes the increasing demands for some form of compulsory control and points to the issues which the churches must examine:

Many believe that some form of compulsory population control will be necessary. What degree of state coercion is appropriate and what means may be employed in bringing about the necessary changes in population trends? Here there are complex questions of social ethics and personal conscience which are becoming increasingly urgent, and which call for serious discussion in the churches.

3. *The ever-increasing industrial expansion and the rising danger of pollution* through the deposit of chemical and physical materials in the environment which nature can no longer correct or absorb. The statement to the churches emphasizes the immense long-run economic, political, and social, consequences of the discoveries which have been made concerning ecological balance and the need to check those tendencies which threaten man from his pollution of his air, water, and soil. The challenge to undertake a new, responsible use of nature is clear:

> Man who causes pollution has also the technical capacity to put an end to almost all these destructive practices. The accumulation of pollutants in the environment is tied closely to styles of production, industrial and agricultural, which are not easily or quickly changed, since they form parts of entire patterns of living. Nevertheless, correction is possible when once public attention has been drawn to the dangers and the political will has been created to bear the considerable costs involved.

The statement recognizes that the Christian churches have no distinctive answer to the many technical problems posed by the state of the environment, but recommends that 'Christians should play their part in initiating and supporting creative action in cooperation with people of various faiths, disciplines, and cultures.' It is in this spirit that the World Council of Churches has launched its inquiry into these issues, and its drive towards widespread action.

15
URBAN SPACE AND AMENITIES

URBAN SPACE AND STRUCTURE

Keynote Paper

The Future of Urban Environments

by

VÁCLAV KASALICKÝ*

*Secretary, Czechoslovak Organizing Committee, UN/ECE Symposium on
Problems Relating to Environment;
Deputy-Director, Research Institute for Building and Architecture,
Letenská 3, Malá Strana,
Praha 1,
Czechoslovakia*

INTRODUCTION

Environmental studies are nowadays coming more and more to the fore
and emerging as a highly complex interdisciplinary science. In this paper,
however, I shall confine myself to that part of the environment which is

* Read by Professor Emil Hadač, Director, Institute of Landscape Ecology, Czechoslovak
Academy of Sciences, Průhonice near Praha, Czechoslovakia, in the absence of his fellow-
countryman.—Ed.

created by human activities, dealing particularly with the urban environment. The disciplines which are concerned with this field include architecture, town planning, the sociology of housing and of cities, communal hygiene, various aspects of engineering, and some more modern fields such as ekistics or the science of human settlements (Doxiadis, 1970).

In order to look into the future, our basic prerequisite is to outline an ideal model of life for human society—a model of its style of living, its needs, its materials, and its production—on the basis of the development for which it will be possible to satisfy future demands, etc. This is not new; but what constitutes a novel approach to future development of the life of society is the set of new relationships between man and the material environment surrounding him.

Although this paper is concerned primarily with knowledge gained in Czechoslovakia, it naturally uses also the generalized world achievements in such work as are most pertinent. Particularly does it draw on the numerous papers submitted by countries and international organizations to the Economic Commission for Europe's Symposium on Problems Relating to Environment (ECE, 1971). It also draws on publications of the International Committee on Housing, Building and Planning (UN/ECE, 1970, etc.)

At this stage it is necessary to elucidate the criteria of the definition of the environment in the meaning in which it is considered in this paper. The essence of this definition was submitted by the Czechoslovak Delegation to the Secretariat of the United Nations Conference on the Human Environment at its Preparatory Committee's second meeting which took place in February 1971 in Geneva, Switzerland (UN General Assembly, 1971). It follows generally from the realization that the basis of all life on earth is the biosphere, which includes all forms of life. The environment for us is a certain part of the biosphere in which man lives permanently—not only as an individual, but also, and indeed in particular, in a highly-developed, organized society which undertakes the most varied activities. The environment of man consists of both natural and man-made substances and conditions in which, and by means of which, human society satisfies its most varied material as well as cultural needs.

Man (in the sense of human society) is connected with his environment by constant interaction. The environment affects man both physically and psychically, forming him and determining some of his characteristics, reactions, etc. On the other hand, man constantly affects the materials surrounding him, changing them (in ways both good and bad, from his own viewpoint and that of nature), and thus becoming, to a considerable extent, the creator of the living conditions and style of the generations to come.

It should be noted that we do not include in the sphere of environment, i.e. the environment in which human life in all of its complexity takes place, the manifestations of life itself. Nor do we include in this term the relationships among people themselves. For these relationships present part of human life itself, and we do not wish to degrade any person, much less whole groups of strata of society, to the role of merely forming part of some environment, while the term 'social environment' belongs rather to sociology, which is entirely apart from the framework of this paper.

The City as an Environment

It follows from the preceding paragraphs that the place or situation, as an important component of the living environment, can satisfy a number of material as well as cultural (or spiritual) needs of man and society. In other words, it fulfils certain functions and, logically speaking, will be the better environment the better it fulfils these functions. It is not necessary to examine this theme in detail, for it is obvious. What we must, however, consider is the question of what functions the city should fulfil particularly in the future, and in what mutual relationships or proportions.

Analyses of cities which we have inherited from our ancestors, and which our generation is now developing with not too much success, have shown primarily what is not good in them—what defects we have in different countries in the structure of our cities and in their relative positions. However, even the best analysis does not, and surely cannot, yield the answer to the question of what the city of the future will be like. Nevertheless, some experience from analyses of existing cities can form a sound basis for our consideration of the future, so let us begin with them.

Dissatisfaction in Existing Towns

A common characteristic of all analyses of towns and cities is the statement by the population of some degree of dissatisfaction with the environment in which they live and are forced to go on living by circumstances commonly beyond their control. Therefore it is only natural that the inhabitants of cities want their cities to satisfy—apart from the basic need of supplying the wherewithal of life—also as many of their other needs as possible. The interests of administrative authorities of cities, as well as of major territorial units or even of whole states, are much the same, as dissatisfaction with a general social feature is politically negative and can lead to results that are undesirable for the whole social structure. The general consequences of the achievement of these analyses of contemporary cities are, therefore, the seeking of the roots of dissatisfaction of the population, the curing of its causes, and the formulation of measures to attain permanent improvement if possible.

Yet the very discovery of the actual roots and causes of manifestations of dissatisfaction is apt to bring to an end the progress of the involved political authorities in various parts of the world, to say nothing of the differences that can be observed between the measures that are proposed and those that are actually taken! For us who deal systematically with the problems of the environment, it is very interesting to note that, if the inhabitants spontaneously formulate the causes of their dissatisfaction with their city, their comments concern *primarily* the material aspects of their environment. Indeed some sociological surveys from the most varied parts of the world even state this to be their invariable experience in this field.

As a general rule, the first problem is the housing environment—the housing itself and its various relationships to the city such as the position of the abode, its standards, the technical and hygienic amenities, the local services, the rent, etc. The problems of housing and of housing environment are the problems which have found general understanding already, and are being included even in election programmes of the political administration of cities and major territorial units. However, there is another—in our opinion very important though little understood—aspect of the environment, particularly in new towns, namely the proportion of public structures which are built as civic amenities but which must fulfil other important functions in the complicated organization of the life of a modern society.

It has been ascertained from a number of sociological investigations of new parts of various towns inhabited by people who had formerly lived in bad conditions, that their initial feeling of satisfaction was mostly replaced in time by a feeling of dissatisfaction with defects in civic amenities, transport facilities, services, etc. The effect of this secondary feeling, which need not be very strong individually, is enhanced by the fact that it is participated in by a great number of people concentrated in a relatively small territory. This can be best testified to by the deputies of various electoral authorities who canvass the votes of their constituents.

The controversial amenities include the facilities that satisfy the basic needs of the population, such as crèches, nursery schools, elementary schools, medical institutions, local administrative institutions, etc.; they also include the facilities for which the demand depends on the general style of living, examples being cultural institutions, clubs, cinemas, civic centres, museums, art galleries, etc. These last several facilities are the ones for which the need is generally felt spontaneously only after people have got used to their new existence and want to introduce variety into the regime of their everyday life.

On the other hand, the people who feel this need are socially constituted quite differently from the people who are orientated on the satisfaction of basic needs only, and it is of no consequence to which social stratum they belong. Yet for the population as a whole it is important that there be well-established facilities for education of the adults. Thus can a government, as well as local governmental authorities, by means of purposeful investments in civic amenities in the present times, lay the foundations for future success of their general policy.

Towards Forecasting Future Needs

It is accordingly possible to forecast, on the basis of the assumed future structure of civic amenities, the likely material as well as cultural and political standards of living of the population, the general characteristics of the administration and its policy, and the attitude towards the environment. If we want to make this assessment correctly and justify it scientifically, we must know the proposed structure of the civic amenities in considerable detail, although even in the framework of the higher groups of civic amenities there are nuances which influence the development of the life of the future society. There are certain mutually replaceable amenities and even whole groups of mutually replaceable amenities whose social importance, however, differs greatly. This statement requires some elucidation.

In the framework of, for example, sports facilities intended as one of the means of the population spending spare time, there are two extreme possibilities—either of investing in the construction of big stadia for a large number of spectators but relatively few active sportsmen, or of building a great number of small sports-grounds and gymnasia with relatively small spectator capacity but, in their totality, catering to a large number of active sportsmen. The ratio of these two extreme categories indicates a number of important criteria of the future life of society, as well as the needs of the contemporary administration of the city and major territorial units.

Analogous examples could be quoted from the field of cultural amenities, e.g. preference given to cinemas or theatres, a small number of major theatres or a large number of small theatres, a uniform network of cultural establishments intended for amateurs or a network of exclusively professional institutions, etc. These preferences represent important characteristic indices of the general trend of the cultural policy of the state, region, city, etc. It is probably not necessary to quote further illustrative examples, although it would be quite possible.

Apart from the social interest, the investment policy, even when considered from a long-term viewpoint, is influenced also by economic criteria which, however, are very often unsatisfactory. Unfortunately, contemporary economists and others seem incapable of furnishing generally persuasive reasons which explain the social effect of this or that investment. Consequently the final and decisive criteria are, in the majority of cases, economic estimates of costs and benefits on the level of the direct, i.e. private (individual or private company), or group (cooperative, public company, etc.), investor. For this very reason the number of types of so-called civic amenities is apt to be very limited even in recently built towns, and these amenities are usually of a very stereotyped character. Standard department stores of big business firms are becoming typical characteristics of new towns, as were the Gothic or baroque cathedrals which characterized the old cities.

A number of towns, particularly in Europe, are characterized on one hand by having a historical core with a number of civic amenities which have outlived their usefulness both technically and functionally, and are difficult to incorporate into the life of contemporary society, while on the other hand they have modern boundary quarters with incomplete civic amenities—particularly in respect of cultural, sports, and other facilities. They create the kind of environment that is imperfect in its basic concept, suffering, moreover, from the general defects of contemporary environments—particularly atmospheric pollution, a great volume of solid wastes, noise, polluted water, shortage of natural components of the environment, etc. In our forecasting of future trends and needs we must remember these mistakes and look ahead to what is really desirable.

THE CITY AS COMPONENT OF A WIDER ENVIRONMENT

When analysing the urban environment, particularly from the viewpoint of its civic amenities, it is impossible to neglect the fact that within the city, especially in its centre, the satisfaction of its needs is sought not only by the population of the city proper, but also by that of its wider surroundings—particularly by the population of the rural suburban zone. The size of this zone depends on the function played by the city in the whole system of the settlement pattern. Some basic function has been fulfilled by towns and cities from the very beginning of their origin. At present their role has usually become greatly multiplied by the diversity of functions of contemporary life and, naturally, by the overlapping of the radii of action of the individual settlement formations. The majority of current theories of urban origin recognize the so-called stepped-up settlement system, in which the individual settlement formations (villages, towns, metropolises, etc.) differentiate their functions or mutually compete in their fulfilment, thus influencing the style of living in the settlement formations situated in their so-called convergence territories.

More detailed investigations have shown that the differentiation of functions is facilitated by, above all, the standard of the civic amenities in the individual towns, at least if we consider the production potential of the city as a characteristic determining its economic rather than its functional potential. The production potential of a city is also of great importance in connection with the determination of its function, as it is the source of wealth and widely determines the standard of living of its population—high productivity naturally increasing the attractiveness of the settlement or town both for its own population and for investments, including those in all types of civic amenities.

Payment of deference to this fact enables the contemporary town planners and others to rationalize the designs of cities with regard to their wider functions; simultaneously the respective ministries, responsible today in the majority of countries for much of the development in public sectors, can rationalize the territorial networks of the individual types of facilities and avoid excessive errors and economic losses connected with them. The peak rationalization is thus based on the qualitative synthesis of the projects of the ministries with territorial projects, supported by the projects of national economic development, and accompanied by a satisfactory standard and style of living, etc.

Three-tier System

A number of theories are based on the three-tier system of settlement pattern; however, there are also systems with more than three levels. In Czechoslovakia, for example, a system is under consideration at present comprising:

(a) Settlements with no function in the settlement pattern, i.e. mostly small communities without any outstanding economic basis, and without historical or cultural importance;

(b) Settlements as centres of rural areas (centres of the first category), within accessible distance of all the communities of their convergence territories, with civic amenities capable of satisfying the everyday needs of their population;

(c) Settlements as centres of urban character (centres of the second category) ensuring the satisfaction of needs of a higher order than (b) and including administrative functions, whose convergence territory comprises, as a rule, several convergence territories of several centres of lower functional importance;

(d) Big regional centres (centres of the third category) comprising, in some cases, civic amenities of national or even international importance, with convergence territories comprising a number of those of centres of lower categories;

(e) Capitals of nations and of states as well as other cities of national or international importance.

There is a danger, however, that such a theory which should aid towards better knowledge and practice, will become a dead formula that diverges from the wishes of the living population and the objective reality of life itself. Therefore, all such theories must be regarded very soberly.

Beyond the Confines

It is indisputable that the city as an environment has its functions not only internally but also beyond the boundaries of its territory, and *vice versa*, while it requires, for the satisfaction of the needs of its population, living environments outside of its own framework. The relatively large background areas of major industrial or regional and super-regional cities, therefore, fall into the category of the so-called 'zone of interest' of the city, i.e. the territory which is of interest to the population of the city in their spare time, and which comprises the material base of the recreation of the population of the city, the source of cheaper purchase of agricultural products, etc. The interest shown by the urban population can be very advantageous for the surrounding territory also from the economic point of view; however, proximity to the city is usually a more or less devastating factor from the viewpoint of the quality of the environment. Thus all too commonly the territories which are particularly attractive for recreation are devastated by the unrestrained construction of holiday houses (e.g. Grindelwald in Switzerland, the surroundings of Frankfurt-am-Main, etc.).

The increasing mobility of urban populations, due to the ever-increasing degrees of motorization, extends the radius of action of the territory of interest of the cities and also the density of the secondary settlements in the regions where those territories that are of interest to two or more cities mutually overlap. So the territories adjoining heavily industrialized agglomerations necessarily suffer grievously. The original rural settlements situated in these territories—formerly agricultural communities in the majority of cases—lose their original character and dissolve into amorphous, in no way characteristic, formations of secondary settlements, in which the number of the 'weekend' population markedly exceeds the number of the sedentary population. This also has considerable consequences, naturally, for the functioning of civic amenities, technical facilities, etc.

Creating Environments

Thus the inhabitants of the cities pass, within a very short period, through the effect of various forms of environments (of housing, working, recreation, etc.). At the same time, in accordance with what has already been said, very often none of these environments is really of sufficiently good quality—a circumstance that may reflect adversely in the demeanour of people and become the source of various individual as well as collective ailments. Very often these ailments are called 'civilization ailments' and, more unfortunately, very often this term just camouflages either reluctance or impotence to cure them by dispensing with the very roots of their origin.

While on the subject of curing ailments, we should also recall the well-known medical truth that the illness should be prevented rather than cured. In the case of the environment this means that on one hand we should protect it from the negative influence of various social activities, and on the other hand we should remedy the errors of past 'development'. However, every organized society is interested in seeing progress, and both the prevention of future harm and the making good of past mistakes mean the attainment and the conservation of the highest standard possible. Yet from the viewpoint of long-term development, this is still only a very passive approach. An active approach means a very difficult task of purposeful creation of environments for the future life of both the contemporary and coming generations, and not only of human beings but also of wildlife. A good deal is being done in some countries through creative conservation (Benthem, 1968) and land consolidation (Benthem, 1969), and far more is to be hoped for elsewhere in the future. These are, however, problems rather for our biological colleagues, who rightly say that man and nature should live in harmony and that development need not be incompatible with conservation. But we must now analyse in great detail the creation of desirable urban environments for the present and in the future.

Future Cities as Environments

Whenever we consider the future arrangement of any artificial organism—including, in our particular context, the city—we run the realistic danger of falling into irrational phantasies, visions, and illusions. This is particularly the case when we consider future social formations regardless of realistic possibilities and the purposiveness of the development of material resources. It is indisputable that due consideration of the environment will be needed for future rationalization, as it clearly comprises also various thresholds and critical situations of desirable development.

The contemporary technical literature offers numerous considerations as well as realistic projects of cities of the future—cities characterized often by surprising elements of predestination of the living conditions of future society, including predestination of its environment. Every prognosticating author is entitled to think as he sees fit, but although I would like to add my name to their number, it is my intention rather to make an analysis of the defects and shortcomings of these visions from the viewpoint of the environment as we understand it, and to suggest what should be taken into account more than has been done hitherto to avoid the repetition of such errors. Unfortunately it is by no means easy to offer such a picture to experts; nor is it attractive to the uninitiated, lay public.

In the first place it is necessary to realize the possible pace at which qualitative change of the existing cities into what we generally call 'the cities of the future' may proceed. We have barely thirty years before this century will be ended. If we consider the average age of buildings as one hundred years, we shall be able to change barely one-third of our cities by the end of the century. Even if the whole of human society were sufficiently affluent at present to afford building for a shorter period of life-expectancy, and even if the problems of the materials originating from the demolition of obsolete buildings were solved, we could say with relative certainty that the cities at the end of this century would not differ over much from the cities in which we are living now. When the age of the 'cities of the future' will come is a question whose asking has no practical sense at the moment.

On the other hand, we can speak about the environment of the future much more realistically. For its parameters are determined with relative accuracy, and it is possible for human society to attain these parameters successively to the desired extent at least very widely among the population of the world. When speaking about the cities, we must include particular consideration of those parameters of their environment that are purposively created by humans for the most varied functions and activities necessary for the preservation of man as the most highly developed and organized biological species on earth.

Needs of Man

We are basing our considerations on the fact that man as a biological creature, after developing for hundreds of thousands of years, has a number of characteristics and, consequently, also requirements which are generally constant or at least non-variable over such a short historical period as we are capable of forecasting. At the same time, in the climatic zones in which his majority lives, man cannot get along without protection against the natural conditions, and the environment which he is purposively creating represents the necessary prerequisite for his existence.

The basic methods of measurement and ascertainment of the qualitative parameters of man-made environment are continuously being improved. Man has also mastered many aspects of the contemporary scene through relatively high-standard techniques by means of which he can, for example, ensure clean air, heat, and lighting, even in hermetically closed spaces that are separated from the outer environment. Technology can, moreover, settle the problems of exhaust fumes from motor vehicles, industrial exhalates and effluents, etc. We may conclude, therefore, that we can expect satisfaction of the physical parameters of the future environment probably to a better standard than we have them at present.

What remains a great problem of the future of cities, however, is the style of life of the future society. Although we can count on certain constants even in this field, the problem will involve a number of variants of structural character, whose forecasting will require at least a partially fixed and logical, often scientific, basis. The numerous constants can include, for example, the fact that, even in the relatively distant future, things will have to be bought; consequently there will be need for shops, department stores, exhibitions, trade fairs, etc. The possible forms of doing business may be entirely different, but the general character will remain. Analogous situations can be imagined also in other fields, and already there are relatively detailed and well-elaborated considerations of the likely development of education, medical care, etc.

Catering for Leisure

Whereas the functions last considered are irreplaceable and consequently essential, there is a wide field of mutually exchangeable and replaceable functions and activities concerning particularly the spheres of leisure, culture, entertainment, sports, and general recreation. The style of life of the future society will have a determining influence in this respect on both the quantity and the quality of the public facilities required. This statement could be illustrated by a whole range of examples, but two will suffice.

Although it seems beyond question that, for example, music will rank— even in the very distant future—among the foremost cultural media as well as means of popular entertainment, the construction of the facilities intended for the performance of music will depend greatly on such considerations as whether, for example,

(a) the relationship of society to music will be predominantly passive (i.e. listening to music performed by large professional bodies) or active (widespread amateur performance of music in small or large groups); in the second variant the two approaches (amateur and professional) do not exclude, but suitably supplement, each other;

(b) the interest in serious or light music will prevail;

(c) the technique of recorded music will attain such perfection that it will replace, to a really large extent, direct attendance at concerts.

On the basis of the answers to these questions, the needs for the construction of concert halls, theatres, and music clubs, are deduced, and the indices of their allocation in the settlement pattern and system are determined.

Analogous is the case of an entirely different field—sport. Here, too, the future provision of sports facilities for cities and other settlements depends on whether

(a) physical training and sports will be performed regularly as an important activity that is intended for the upkeep of physical as well as spiritual strength (e.g. at least for 2 hours weekly by one-third of all the adult population, and by all young people less than 24 years of age);

(b) either the relationships of society will continue to be passive—at least in respect of some sports and peak outputs—and will take on the form of sports shows, or else amateurism and mass sport performance will return and prevail;

(c) the techniques of transmission of sporting events will improve to such an extent that it will replace, even more than at present, the direct attendance of spectators at the actual events.

On the basis of these circumstances—analogously with the aforementioned case of cultural facilities—directions will originate either for the construction of a dense network of small gymnasia and sports-grounds, or for a sparse network of large sports stadia (arenas) or, perhaps more likely, for a suitable combination of both.

Linking of Past, Present, and Future

It would certainly be possible to continue such illustrative examples with others of an analogous character. However, I believe that the examples quoted are sufficient to illustrate the problems under consideration, though mention must be made of one very important fact which is usually neglected. The roots of future changes lie in the present. Every organized human society which wants to utilize the achievements of science and influence with them the development of not only contemporary, but also future, generations, necessarily admits the objective validity of a number of 'laws' which must be taken into account in every realistic consideration of the future development of human society and of human settlements. The three of these which are connected most closely with the construction and future development of cities include particularly:

1. The development of society, as well as the development of cities, is continuous. Thus even the new buildings and organizations are encountered by people with ideas dating from previous institutions and organizations. A new facility, if it is to be fully attractive and effective, cannot, therefore, entirely overlook what we might call short-term tradition: it must build on it, develop it in a novel way, and modify it in relation to new needs. On the other hand, a society undergoing a phase of purposeful preparation for new development must (though still in the framework of its contemporary life) begin to develop relations and customs for which it intends to create complete material prerequisites in the future.

2. The life of society is always more diverse and variegated in its requirements than are even the boldest efforts of the town planners, architects, sociologists, etc. Therefore, what contemporary society hands over to future generations as its firm heritage, such as the buildings of public amenities, must be considerably flexible and adjustable to cater to defined future requirements. Otherwise there will result undesirable waste of social resources and wealth; and even the most favoured nations have no right to waste their wealth, while there is poverty and even hunger in the world.

3. The life of future society will be in big cities to a considerable and probably increasing extent. The prerequisite of preservation of a highly developed and numerous human society in general is that its life will be highly organized and disciplined, with a minimum of negative consequences for the urban environment and for the environment in the surrounding vicinity. Urban life should (and under the development of science and technology perfectly well can) have assured adequate hygienic, cultural, and social, parameters for the life of the whole population; it must also reduce the dependence on short-term recreation in the immediate vicinity of the city to a purposeful minimum.

The relations of the city to its surroundings must necessarily acquire the character of purposively controlled relations, ensuring the optimum effectiveness of functions of both urban and rural areas with reference to the contemporary needs and interests of the entire society. The allocation and distribution of the facilities that have been built by society to ensure the performance of these functions will, therefore, be based on scientific principles, using mathematical methods of optimization as a basis for the making of decisions.

It may be noted that I have made no attempt to deal with a number of topics which lie outside my own field of specialist interest and, indeed, competence—such as the iniquities of excessive noise and the psychological effects on children of being brought up in high buildings from which they always look down. It is accordingly to be hoped that these and many other topics— including urban parks and other open spaces and the significance of 'green belts'—within the wider conference title of 'Urban Space and Amenities' will be dealt with in the discussion.

Although this paper is mainly concerned with the ideas and principles that have been advanced and evaluated by Czechoslovak research as fundamental and decisive for the prognosis of the further development of urban settlement, it embraces also the often parallel experiences and achievements of scientific work carried out in a number of other countries. Whereas it is obvious that not all these principles will have a much wider application, and still fewer will be of entirely general value, the author is of the opinion that they should prove useful as information to those who are concerned with the future of human population—from which the pressures seem destined to increase greatly in the foreseeable future.

References

BENTHEM, Roelof J. (1968). Creative conservation. *Biological Conservation*, **1**(1), pp. 11–12.

BENTHEM, Roelof J. (1969). Changing the countryside by land consolidation. *Biological Conservation*, **1**(3), pp. 209–12, 2 figs.

DOXIADIS, Constantinos A. (1970). Ekistics, the science of human settlements. *Science*, **170**, pp. 393–404, 21 figs.

ECONOMIC COMMISSION FOR EUROPE [as ECE] (1971). Numerous (*ca* 100) papers submitted in mimeographed form for the Conference (subsequently styled 'Symposium') on Problems Relating to Environment, 2–15 May 1971, held mainly in Prague, Czechoslovakia. To be published (apart from 'country monographs') by the UN *Economic Commission for Europe*, Palais des Nations, Geneva.

UN/ECE (1970, etc.). UN/ECE Committee (international) on Housing, Building, and Planning. Numerous publications in recent years of the *Economic Commission for Europe*, Palais des Nations, Geneva, Switzerland.

UN GENERAL ASSEMBLY (1971). *Preparatory Committee for the United Nations Conference on the Human Environment*. Second Session, Geneva, 8–19 February 1971, 86 pp. (mimeographed).

DISCUSSION

Mansikka (Chairman)

I would like to thank Professor Hadač for his opening statement and rendering, and to claim the privilege of contributing some remarks on Ing.arch. Kasalický's excellent paper before opening the discussion.

I fully agree with the author that the city and its social amenities must be seen as one component of a wider environmental system, that is, as one part of the settlement and service-centre organization of a particular area. However, I would like to point out some further possible trends—or are they laws—of the future development of society. Our experience in this field indicates that the strongest force underlying changes in settlement structure—at least in Europe—is the development of the service sector. It seems to me that, if we consider that one of the most important human objectives is to facilitate contact between members of society, the most urgent objective in the development of the service network is to optimize the contact pattern. This can be done by creating the system of collective services that will be best fitted to satisfy the increasing need for mutual exchange of information between the members of society on the one hand, and between public institutions and private organizations on the other hand.

The recent discussion concerning the most desirable future settlement network has been very lively here in Finland. The viewpoints both for economic efficiency and for an equal distribution of social welfare have been stressed. It seems to me that, according to our experience, two problems in particular deserve special attention. These problems may also have a wider interest in other countries. The first concerns the feasibility and potential of centres on the regional level, serving as principal growth-points in the future. By regional centres I mean in this connection centres which serve a region with from 100,000 to 300,000 inhabitants. This question, I feel, has not yet been subjected to sufficient analysis. The other question has to do with the creation of a sufficient service standard on the micro-level, especially in rural areas. The further urbanization of the countryside has many effects on the natural components, and on the landscape and recreation values of the environment.

I would also agree with Ing.arch. Kasalický as to the difficulties involved in sociological forecasting and in evaluating the life-style of future society. I should add only one more example in this connection. The functional changes in the role of the family are of fundamental importance for the future style of life. There are some indications that some of the functions of the family will come under the scope of public and private institutions and organizations. The family as such, however, will not disappear; indeed its development will surely have a considerable effect on the contact pattern of future society. It will probably be easier to create contacts with the expected dependence between various social groupings in the future. Consequently, the development of the service network by means of intimately integrated social, economic, and physical, planning will be one of the most important tasks of environmental policy.

After these comments from the Finnish viewpoint I have pleasure in declaring the general discussion open, and in first giving the floor back to Professor Hadač.

Hadač

The paper of my distinguished compatriot Kasalický is interesting not only for what it contains but also for what it does not contain. I am neither architect nor urbanist, but as I live in a city I sometimes feel I am a victim of architects or urbanists. So if I may be allowed to offer some remarks, I would start by saying that many modern urbanists treat towns and cities as something quite independent from their local setting. Yet for me a town or a city is a densely-inhabited part of the landscape.

Why were many of the medieval towns so beautiful? Why, for example, are Finnish towns beautiful and simultaneously functional? Because they are built as an integrated part of the landscape! Contrast the cities that have grown in recent decades as mushrooms so widely in the world, without any respect for the landscape, and you will see at once what I mean.

Going further I would emphasize that, in my opinion, the surroundings are a part of the habitation, or at least of the habitat in the ecologists' sense. In former days you had to pay more if you wished to have a beautiful view from your window. I don't actually suggest that pretty surroundings can compensate for many of the amenities mentioned by Ing.arch. Kasalický as relatively essential, but they can be important to many people. It also matters what amenities you have around your leisure-time cottages or cabins to which every weekend hundreds of thousands of people stream out of towns because they feel themselves better there than in cities lacking these amenities.

Speaking of the definition of environment, I feel that we should always say whose environment we have in mind; otherwise the term as such has little sense. Every dog and every daisy has its environment, so I think the term we have in mind just now should be called man's environment.

Ing.arch. Kasalický says rightly that the environment affects man, and so we have to influence our local, regional, or state, governments to get them to create healthier environments; the governments should, moreover, educate people to lead a healthier life. He also says that the town's amenities should be interchangeable, but I do not say this. With wise government, some of them should not be interchangeable at all: I mean, for example, gymnastics and sports grounds for active physical training, and a big stadium for more or less passive sporting shows. Both are necessary, but I think we should invest more in catering for more active sports than for passive sporting shows, even if the latter bring in more money. The same can be said about active and passive musical performances.

Some of the prophets of the future of our biosphere are of the opinion that, during the next fifty years or so, most of the oxygen in the atmosphere will be exhausted by the population explosion and its promotion of industry, SSTs, etc., etc. Now the only reasonable method of producing free oxygen in sufficient amounts is through the photosynthetic activity of green plants. As herbs and grasses have shallow roots and are more vulnerable to periodic or more or less permanent droughts, trees are more useful in this respect. But trees grow only slowly, so that it takes at least thirty to forty years under most conditions to produce middle-sized trees. So we must start at once if we want them to contribute to the oxygen supplies of our children and their children, and to that extent be less alarmed at the threats to the oceans which at present return to the atmosphere nearly three-quarters of the oxygen in it. If every owner of a piece of land, if every village and town, will plant as many trees in their surroundings as possible, then our planet will be more beautiful, more healthy, and we shall give to our children and grandchildren something they will sorely need and highly appreciate.

Considerable parts of the world's continents are now covered by deserts and semi-deserts, scarcely contributing to the common oxygen and food supplies. It is important for the lives of our children that we make them green. Many of these areas are desertic not because they have no water, but because their water is situated too deep in the ground for use by plants. To take an example from the southern desert in Iraq, near Basra there is an extensive area of vegetation where the water level lies at a depth of about eleven metres beneath the surface. Some acacias were planted in this desert, watered for about five years until their roots reached the ground-water table, and now a nice acacia forest stands where there was only desert not so many years ago.

This example shows that to make our globe more green is not as 'impossible' as it might seem to be. Some countries are trying to do this, and we should encourage them to double their efforts. Developing countries should get more support from more developed and overdeveloped ones, as this would be in the interest of all mankind. Indeed, I suggest that some such passage should be incorporated in our resolutions.

Reiner

What may be termed 'urban environmental disfunctions' are more than an arithmetic totality of individual nuisances. Together they represent a special environmental climate resulting from the mutual and rather lasting interaction of numerous individual pollutants, noises, hygienic shortcomings, misuses of land, aesthetic offences, and psychological stresses—all concentrated in a single area.

Mr Kasalický, the author of this session's keynote paper, rightly draws our attention to desiderata for new settlements that are being built, whether in the form of new towns or as extensions of existing towns. We have heard the expression 'new-town blues', referring to the restlessness of new immigrant populations in settlements where adequate amenities are not provided at the start. And we have often also observed that, in the process of urban renewal, what we produce which is new may sometimes be worse than what is replaced. Thus, sometimes old and well-established neighbourhoods are replaced by high-rise and generally expensive flats or by office buildings which further strain the city's creeping transport paralysis. We have unfortunately not yet fully understood—and certainly not mastered—the urban renewal process as part of an ever-continuing, and above all guided, urban development.

A point which might be emphasized with regard to urban renewal is the importance of preserving our cultural heritage by protecting buildings and areas of historical or architectural interest and value, and doing this by trying to preserve them not just as museums, but as living components of the contemporary environment. Incidentally, motor traffic during the last few decades is said to have done more damage to them than centuries of ageing.

Turning now to specific amenities—sports facilities, for example—Mr Kasalický indicates the range of choices to be made. I would wish to emphasize with regard to recreational amenities, however, that while much has been done to provide for the longer annual holidays enjoyed by so many workers nowadays, we still have far to go in the matter of providing proper facilities for daily recreation. Now that the daily working hours tend to get shorter and shorter, a range of such facilities should be provided in close proximity to the homes of the participants.

As this Conference is in substance future-orientated, I would like to see the discussion under this topic turn a bit more towards *future* human settlements. As we have heard, demographic factors—that is, the rise in population, perhaps doubled by the end of this century, and continuing urbanization whereby in most countries the overwhelming proportion of the population will be living in urban areas—pose a grave responsibility on us for a planned use of urban space and for a more rational distribution of population and activities. In the next thirty or so years we shall have to build as much housing and as many schools, hospitals, administrative buildings, factories, power plants, etc., as man has built so far throughout all his history. What should, then, be the form and pattern of our future human settlements?

People are becoming increasingly discontented at the way in which industry and commerce determine the shape and functions of our cities. However, the factors which provide satisfaction or dissatisfaction are still largely unknown, as is also the matter of the optimum balance between alternative land-uses in cities. Systems of transportation modes which are environmentally satisfactory, and types of housing which meet the needs of different population groups, should, more than in the past, determine the urbanization process.

Among the urban development processes which are likely to continue in the future are the trends towards large urbanized areas, rapidly expanding suburban peripheries to the growth-centres, increasing communication within and between the large urban areas, decentralization of many activities from the old urban cores, and increasing proportions of areas with recreational and leisure facilities. Some cities in their narrow geographical sense are actually losing population, while the wider city region may be gaining population: this probably means that some better-off families in search of a better quality of urban life are moving to the outskirts of the city. A consequence of this might be that the poorer people, who are sometimes in the minority and have been 'disinherited', would inherit the city proper.

But what should be our future urban development? Should we encourage a more balanced regional development, or should we accept trends towards more concentrated urban agglomerations? There is much to be said on both sides of this issue. Do we know people's preferences in living in small or medium-sized or large cities? What are the economics, that is the cost/benefit, in maintaining efficiently these different-sized cities?

Here I would like to make a plea with the Resolutions Committee to include in the overall statement of the Conference the need for comprehensive physical planning both on the national and local levels, and integrated with economic and social planning. We need a 'space inventory' of current land-uses, and a forecast of future land demands—in other words, a sort of balance sheet. We need planning legislation with 'teeth' in it to ensure future urban development in the right direction. If we do not get these things and act on them, we shall find available space rapidly disappearing when it comes to the community's needs—we shall find land wrongly used from society's point of view. Then the result will be an irrational urban development which is costly to maintain and often functionally breaking down—in other words, a poor quality of urban environment.

Benthem

The relationship of urban structure and the surrounding countryside deserves, I feel, far more of our consideration than has yet been accorded to it in this paper and the discussion. With respect to the reservation and management of rural open spaces, at least in Europe, changes in human society and increases in population have resulted in ever-increasing interdependence of different countries and, within them, of regions and even districts. This has been fostered by modern transport facilities, general mobility, and increased prosperity, which have resulted in more and more exchanging of men, materials, and ideas. A number of the problems that arise from these changed social conditions cannot be properly solved by the respective national governments. Such matters as air and water pollution, the protection of birds, and the mass migrations of tourists, do not stop at national boundaries. Other phenomena such as the growing population densities, the urbanization processes, the expansion of industry, and the structural changes in agriculture, lead to more and more changes in land-use patterns. Especially in the densely-populated countries is an alarming reduction and deterioration of the open spaces to be observed. Open areas which formerly seemed unlimited are being reduced by new or expanding settlements and intersected or otherwise disturbed or destroyed by highway systems, airline runways, and overhead power lines. Hedgerows and coppices are disappearing and so are many other aspects of formerly attractive countrysides. In most countries, major forests are already a thing of the past.

In the absence of an effective policy for conservation, these developments will inevitably cause irreparable losses to the flora and fauna, to the landscape, and to the recreation potentialities, at least of the small continent of Europe. In order to avoid as far as possible such a continuous desecration of environment, in my opinion international coordination of effort and cooperation in the fields of physical planning and landscape planning are badly needed. In my capacity as Rapporteur for Theme One on Urbanization at the opening conference of European Conservation Year at the Council of Europe's headquarters in Strasbourg in 1970, I advocated the establishment of a system of planning for the preservation and management of Europe's open spaces. The planning of national parks and recreation areas should be developed within such a greater framework of a European open-space system, as should also nature reserves, valuable cultural landscapes, scenic mountain areas, and lands of essential importance for forestry and agriculture—all should be included in this continental open-space system.

A skilfully designed network of international parkways closed to commercial traffic could be developed to connect these main centres of interest for recreation. In any adequate common policy for our environmental future, high priority should be given to the upkeep and use of open spaces, which surely to a great extent will determine the real habitability of Europe in the years to come. Therefore a permanent cooperation should be promoted to design the blueprint for the physical planning of this continent. A general framework will be needed for particular regions to develop a suitable international policy, and thereafter the necessary legislative, financial, scientific, and management, measures can be worked out to create an international status for the most important areas of 'European space' involved.

Mellanby

As has been pointed out, this is a tremendously important subject because more and more people are going to be living under urban conditions in the future. It is also very important because it is something people can do something about—that is to say, by proper planning. There is the possibility of making the cities better, and this has been stressed. But to me it is depressing to realize how little attention has been given to this part of our Conference by the eminent members in the front rows; indeed I think we have shown ourselves as a body of people to be essentially frivolous, or at least not interested in this really important thing that we can do something about. On the other hand, I congratulate those who have come forward and taken part, and I feel sure there will be others.

Much of the development of new housing and so on that has been done has been very unsatisfactory, what with its one-class development, etc.; even with the introduction of new amenities, it has remained unsatisfactory. Great improvements have been made latterly, with much better architectural standards; the new buildings have won prizes for the architects and have formed very beautiful pictures when photographed and put in the architectural press. This has been very nice. Much better facilities for recreation and so on have been provided in all our new towns and in many other places, but the practical result has been most depressing and even distressing. For the thing we find is that even in many of what appear from modern standards to be the best-designed towns, there tend to be higher and growing degrees of vandalism, and apparently increasing delinquency. This does not seem to be controlled by the developments that we have been making: in fact, we have sometimes worse conditions of this kind, and worse crime-records, in a well-designed newly-planned town than we have in an old slum! I feel that this is something we really need to learn about—on which a great deal more work needs to be done.

It has already been stressed that we are going to be building as many new houses in approximately the remainder of this century as we have built up to now in the world as a whole. Maybe this is the case, but do we know at all what people want? As you said, Mr Chairman, the ideas of the family may be changing: but are the architects really preparing for this, are the planners preparing for this, and do they know what to do? I think these matters are very important. Professor Hadač said we must plant more trees, and I am glad to say that I have planted several thousands of trees myself in the last few years. But when we plant trees in our new towns, vandals often cut them down.

This is very depressing, but I think it is altogether one of the most important subjects that we have to consider. It is a subject, moreover, that we can do something about; yet it is one concerning which we really know awfully little.

Miller

I am personally privileged to live in an uncongested area, but we are getting the impact of migration from urban areas to rural areas in the United States because of the political policies and unfortunate evolution of the attitude that any migrations from poor districts will be to the cities where there is a better opportunity for people without resources to get government help. This has made for bad conditions in many towns; but my point here is that for conservationists and environmentalists everywhere, there is the real problem that we do not have a communication with such people either in undeveloped situations or in family situations where they do not have adequate resources for livelihood. In my own community we are put down when we try to enlist these people or to get them to hear what we are trying to say about the needs for the future environment, because they are unhappy about the currently existing environment that is their lot. They believe and say very clearly that when we talk about the environment we are doing this in order not to look at the present situation that they are in, and they believe we should correct the social condition now before we try to go on and do something about the future. I think this is a very important aspect for us all to consider.

We have somewhat the same problem of lack of credibility with youth. Education is really the thing we should be concerned with in this connection, I feel, and I look towards it as the solution for the future in getting mankind to see better what is his relationship as an integral part of the environment. Much of our difficulty with youth stems from the fact, I think, that we pay too little attention to it. I am greatly impressed with the young people of Finland, and of the whole of Europe as far as I have seen them. I think, though, that we have a lack of contact with them. We are rather like the older members of the family who, practically speaking, come together only at the time of a funeral, and do not see each other until the next funeral. Meanwhile we wonder whose it will be. The young people do not have time for such waiting—they are trying to do their 'thing' and get somewhere with their ideals, yet we keep putting them down. I feel that part of our lack of contact, part of our lack of *rapport*, is that we are always telling them: 'Wait for a couple of years and you'll know better.' Yet they do not want to hear this— they have been hearing it all the time throughout their lives. I feel that this is cutting the contact rather than encouraging them. We should remember how we once had such ideals, as many of us still do, coupled with much sensitivity of the other person's point of view. We should listen to what they have to say, what they are fighting for—particularly when they really know, which unfortunately is not always the case. Even then we should not act as city fathers, designing all their work and keeping them down. When they try and really have something to tell us, we must listen and faithfully exchange ideas. This is the time to put our case.

I feel strongly that we are not going to get far in the future with what we believe or even know should be done unless we can hear youth and spare a little time and latitude for constructive exchange with young people who, after all, have their own ideals and ideas—and sensitivity. Last year my Institute in the western United States had a working meeting, participated in by UNESCO and IUCN, on 'Environmental Education in the School Curriculum', particularly for curriculum designers from the Ministries of Education of whatever countries we could get sufficiently interested. Though we had difficulties of organization and a shortage of money for tickets for these people, we brought together twenty from fourteen countries of Africa. Asia, Europe, and North and South America. Owing to some lack of sensitivity as to what was needed, we did not get our three-weeks' course put over very well; but one of the things that emerged was that our work in education in the future, in the designs for curricula for environmental education, must be interdisciplinary, and this realization has since been strengthened. We also learned that we have to be sensitive to social demands and to the feelings of minorities.

Kassas

My comment concerns the development of cities as a whole and in particular those in underdeveloped countries. One feels very sorry that so much traditional architecture, befitting the local environment, is giving way in so many places to an imported type which does not suit the climate. I am thinking particularly of all the big cities in Africa or in the Near and Middle East, which have the same type of blocks of flats as are built in Paris or Rome or London, while Professor Hadač and Professor Polunin have lived in Iraq for some time and will have noted that some of the old buildings there have devices for air cooling in the windows and cool basement parts of the house for people to live in during the summer.

For architecture, people in underdeveloped countries of tropical climate should desist from copying what people in regions of temperate climate are doing. This brings me to a second point, namely that I understand the continent of Africa imported from Europe and America in the year 1969 building materials to the value of two thousand million pounds sterling. Instead, these industries with such a great need of a market should spend some money doing research and development studies towards producing building materials that fit the environmental conditions in those tropical countries.

Fosberg

Again I am going to say something which may not be popular, at least judging from what has been said earlier. It has to do with urbanization only in a negative way, being concerned with deserts. Everybody seems to be recommending the reclamation of deserts by planting trees all over them, and things like that. Personally I like trees very much and am all in favour of having trees planted in the places where they belong; but I would hope that we could keep at least some of the natural deserts, though not perhaps the man-made ones that are all too extensive. Doubtless in company with many others, I can look back and see that I have not only learned a great deal from the considerable amount of time I have spent in deserts, but I have also benefited emotionally—spiritually, if you like—from being able to get away from urbanization and enjoy solitude while being inspired by what I saw of nature's remarkable success in overcoming some of the most extreme stresses of the environment.

Personally, I feel that we ought in our planning to provide people with a chance to get away by leaving a few of the deserts intact: I do not mean little ten-acre pieces of deserts, but thousands of square miles in which one can really be on one's own. I think we have been doing ourselves a great disservice by reclaiming too many desert and semi-desert areas in America. In California such areas are being urbanized, which is an indication that people like them, and in flying over some of those that I had walked and driven over as a youngster I see everywhere little or not so little urbanization projects going on. I just hope we can be a bit restrained about this and keep something of what I see as one aspect of our human environment.

Bryson

[Regarding the lack of voice of students who were here in much larger numbers earlier on, they may be a bit overawed by some of us, and hesitant to rise before their fellows; on the other hand, with the sanction of the commonly lenient chairmen of our sessions, we have been discussing a mountain of often seemingly little-related topics. We now have somehow to bring these things together, I feel, and to say what they all mean on a global basis. Towards this I understand the Resolutions Committee is working very hard, practically day and night; but I feel we should make a start more publicly this afternoon. We have been hearing about conditions for building and the necessity of having internationally agreed-upon land-use laws in Europe, but what does this mean to Africa, to Asia, and to Latin America? We keep on being told that life in the future will be more and more concentrated in big cities; unfortunately this is probably true, and, still more unfortunately, it will involve more and more organization and regulation. Yet I for one, and surely many of the students also, want more freedom—which can only come from dispersion, and surely not from concentration.]

Polunin

Mr Chairman, our doughty friends of many parts, Dr Miller and Professor Bryson, have said among other things practically what I wanted to say when I requested the floor for one minute. Now I am afraid I need nearer three minutes to tie up some loose ends. I'm sorry, but am grateful to you for your nod of approval.

First, to plead that education is surely the key to ending such atrocious vandalism as breaking planted trees and so on, which my colleague Dr Mellanby referred to: we've all seen this kind of thing, or even worse, and surely education from an early age is the answer—the hope for the future. It is indeed a pity that, as in the case of human population, we could not have had a special session on environmental education at this Conference; but we have not neglected either of these topics, having had some useful interventions and written contributions on both. To the extent that suitable education is of fundamental importance but may not have been adequately covered as an underlying theme in our formal sessions, we hope to give it due consideration in an additional section of our published account. Much the same applies to legislation, on which we had a useful 'rump session' the other evening under the *de facto* chairmanship of Mr Udall.

Towards far more widespread environmental education, much is being done in many quarters, some of which was indicated just now by Dr Miller, and already there are encouraging signs and improving portents for the future. In our village in Switzerland we used to dig up primroses in early spring to fill bowls for our homes. But then a few years ago we came to an understanding that we would only do this if we replanted them religiously after they had flowered, and just recently in my family we made a rule that we must not disturb them even to pick the blossoms. Now we have moved practically into Geneva, to an area where there is much building going on but where a profusion of often interesting wildlife persists. The other day our undergraduate daughter came home delighted. She had seen some small children playing with frogs. At first she had thought they were harming them and so started remonstrating: but no, they were collecting them to take them to a safe place because they knew that the area concerned was about to be cleared and built on. This is in marked contrast to the experience of my own childhood when, brought up on farms in England, the 'village' children used to do all sorts of awful things to frogs and other wild creatures which commonly ended in their agonized death. Perhaps children still do; but I am convinced that they can be taught better ways, and that in such respects the prospects are far more encouraging than they used to be. For we surely have a great awakening as to what our environment is and means to us, and a concomitant conservation movement that we hope is gathering momentum all the time.

[Regarding population, as the basis of most of our worries and even of this current session (from whose subject I must apologize for wandering rather far), I cannot for the life of me see why, even in the United Nations, there could not be some tacit 'agreement to disagree' with those nations which want to go on increasing their population, meanwhile allowing the rest to act within an overall, global strategy of population control. For at present in an ever-increasing number of quarters the symptoms seem to me as a biologist to be of an almost classic case of 'species swarming' which, if not checked, can have only the usual devastating outcome of mass mortality. Thus we have the necessary environmental conditions of the wherewithal of life coupled with relative impotence of the usual kinds of controls such as predators and pestilence, together with increased crowding and strife and now ominous indications that this stage of human population dynamics may be short-lived for reasons that are already emerging.]

As for the paucity of active participation of youth in this Conference, we did try to get more, indeed wanting far more, and I have just been trying to persuade the offspring of one or two of our most effective participants to come forward. The Arts Festival Secretary-General Hannu Halinen, himself a young man to whom I would like to pay warm tribute, has also tried on our behalf. But young people find it difficult to step onto platforms when we oldsters are around, often including their parents, though we have had a few exceptions, I am glad to say, and I hope we will still hear others. For the future is theirs more than ours—or so we hope—and towards it the entire biosphere is changing, as we have observed almost *ad nauseam* in this Conference. They should be encouraged to watch and do all they can in ecologically-sound directions.

Finally here I would resurrect a wise thought I believe from Dr Brower: we must not henceforth try to throw things away, for really there is no longer any 'away' to throw things to. Truly the world is changing, and, as he also said so pungently, *there is no spare*. Yet this may not matter so much to us humans in the long run, for what affects and strikes us is largely relative to what we know or have recently experienced ourselves, and if future generations do not know or experience our pampered circumstances they will not miss them—all of which presupposes that our species will survive, as I believe it will. But such survival may be a 'near thing', and certainly cannot be counted on.

16

THE MEANS OF ACTION

Keynote Paper

The Means of Action: Managing the Planetary Life-support Systems

by

LYNTON K. CALDWELL

Chairman of IUCN Commission on Environmental Policy, Law and Administration;
Arthur F. Bentley Professor of Political Science,
Indiana University,
Bloomington,
Indiana 47401, USA.

INTRODUCTION

The price of survival for modern man in a finite world is restraint of his insatiable demands upon the natural environment and due treatment of that environment with the respect and care which he would accord to the life-support system of a space-ship upon which he was a passenger. Self-control has now become the quality that is perhaps most essential to the individual and to society alike. Collective self-control became essential when man found himself the greatest threat to his own survival and development.

This point in time was reached when human ingenuity created the accelerating process of technological development that historians call the Industrial Revolution. The explosions of human populations, of economic productivity, of technologies for resource exploitation, and of information, are manifestations of this revolution which continues to accelerate. This state of affairs, which Ellul (1954) describes as a technological society and Brzezinski (1970) describes as the 'technetronic era', continues an accelerating course of development and growth through a kind of positive feedback in which innovation triggers innovation, and growth induces growth. The energies of peoples, of collective enterprises, and of governments, are largely absorbed in maintaining the imperfectly articulated components of the technoeconomic system which, at times, appears to be about to fly apart under the stress of unremitting accelerating change.

This preoccupation with maintaining the momentum of an accelerating system, if projected indefinitely, appears to lead toward self-defeat. No phenomenon known to man, unless it be perhaps the universe itself, appears to be capable of infinite growth. Eventually, the technoeconomic system must slow down or drop back to a steady state, which we might hope would be dynamic but would no longer be expansive. Yet whether modern society can operate indefinitely in a dynamically steady state remains to be discovered. It is certain, however, that it cannot indefinitely continue to expand. And so a time must come when human society will face the alternative of effectively managing its relationship to the planetary life-support system or acquiescing in the decline and fall of the human species—accompanied, perhaps, by the destruction of the planetary biosphere itself. The means to safeguard the viability of the planet are already within the reach of man, but the will to use these means and the purposes towards which they should be directed have not yet been clearly established. No collective effort of mankind has, as yet, been mobilized in defence of the earth, but movements towards this mobilization are now under way and should become crystallized in prospect at the United Nations Conference on the Human Environment to be held in Stockholm in 1972.

THE TASKS REQUIRED

The tasks of managing man's relationships with his environment may be separated sequentially into four logical divisions. They are:

(1) recognizing social and personal responsibility,
(2) formulating the public intent,

(3) translating goals into programmes, and
(4) devising goal-achieving strategies.

We will now examine these tasks and describe a course of action, together with feasible alternatives, that will illustrate how modern society might organize and direct these activities to protect and maintain the planetary life-support system.

Recognizing Social and Personal Responsibility

The first task is recognition of collective and individual responsibility for the continuing viability of the earth. This responsibility is both social and individual. The circumstances of modern society render the individual increasingly ineffectual unless his efforts are joined and reinforced by those of other individuals. There is little that the isolated individual can do to cope with the massive problems or environmental pollution that are the products of the technoeconomic system as it has evolved to the present. But although the individual is dependent upon society, society is fundamentally dependent upon the individual. No society, nor any part of one, is able to act with full effectiveness unless appropriate behaviours are internalized in (i.e. become an integral part of the life-styles and reaction patterns of) the individuals of which it is constituted. The task of developing collective and individual responsibility implies a task for education in the broadest sense— including the public communications media. It especially implies a task for public leaders whose influence and example are believed to be expressive of the goals and values of society.

Formulating the Public Intent

The second task towards satisfactory environmental management is to establish the protection of the biosphere as a public goal or collective purpose. A formal statement of public intent is especially necessary because of the lack of historical precedent for comprehensive public responsibility for the quality of the environment. The action necessary to protect the biosphere is at variance with many patterns of behaviour that are traditional among most peoples and nations. In many instances, public laws and statutes are inimical to ecologically-based policies and so, before an effective programme and corrective action can be undertaken, it will be necessary to establish, as fundamental law and policy, the goals and purposes of environmental protection. In order to imprint these goals and purposes on the public consciousness and to assist the internalization of ecologically-sound behavioural patterns, a clear and succinct *declaration of intent* is necessary. Upon the basis of such a declaration, criteria and standards for action can be developed, though the declaration would be the more effective if it specified the nature and the purpose of such criteria and standards.

Translating Goals into Programmes

The third task that must be accomplished before effective environmental protection can be approached is the translation of qualitative goals into specific programmes of operation. Without definite programmes of action, declarations of intent are likely to be mere exhortations. Action-forcing or at least facilitating provisions should, therefore, accompany or be built into declarations of intent wherever possible. In the translation of goals into operating programmes, the structure through which action takes place must be considered. The traditional hierarchical structures of national and international organizations have not hitherto been well adapted to interlocking plans and programmes to achieve a forceful and coherent execution of the public intent. The problems of the environment, moreover, are inherently multiplex. Man-made systems to observe, to modify, or to protect, the systems of the natural world must be designed to cope with this complexity.

Devising Goal-achieving Strategies

From the third task of translating goals into programmes, a fourth task, namely the development of a strategy for putting plans into action, logically follows. By these elements of a strategy, we do not simply imply the substance of the plans and programmes themselves, but rather the means by which the specific intentions can be realized. Included in any effective strategy must be consideration of the personnel or manpower necessary to do the work, of the budget which will provide the material means, and of the planning required to reach the goal from whatever point one begins. Formalized systems of planning, of programming, and of budgeting and the drawing up of budget statements by programme rather than by a 'line-item' of a specific category such as supplies, afford a means to a more rational and results-directed allocation of public resources than was possible by traditional budgetary methods, which were largely designed for purposes of fiscal control. For global programmes, the logic of these results-directed budgetary methods would be some articulation of national budgets with the budgets of international organizations—and within nations, a similar articulation is particularly important in federal systems such as, for example, those of Australia, Canada, the German Federal Republic, the Soviet Union, and the United States of America. Political concepts of sovereignty and autonomy might be advantageously modified to the extent that the resource allocations of all human society towards the protection of the biosphere might be optimized. Such optimization, however, is not likely to be effected in anticipation of coordinative global and national efforts towards environmental protection. Instead, a rationalization and articulation of international, national, regional, and local, budgets is likely to be the outcome of combined attacks upon specified problems of the environment, and could have the best chance of success.

If the earth is to be effectively protected, responsibility must be universal—all society must be involved, transcending all contrary traditions, institutional arrangements, and geographical jurisdictions. A system of international-national-regional-local interaction is required to enable men to cope with ecological problems through what may often be largely unecological sociopolitical arrangements. As we shall presently contend, some significant restructuring of institutional arrangements will be necessary to cope with problems of the global environment. Systematic intergovernmental interaction is an essential aspect of protective action, because the role played by each level of government will in some measure be contingent upon stimulation, support, and assistance, from other levels. Just as the individual cannot act effectively unless the collectivity of individuals comprising society also acts, similar reciprocal dependencies exist among governmental organizations—local, regional, national, and international. There are few matters upon which action can be taken at one political level without regard to the others. International action can seldom be effective in the absence of national readiness for effective cooperation and collaboration, while local action is almost universally contingent upon some form of national authorization or leadership.

Whether modern societies can bring their development under control is at present conjectural. They may destroy themselves through error-accentuating positive feedback that accelerates the rate and magnitude of change until, at last, outstripping human control capabilities, modern technoeconomic systems founder upon some unforeseen economic or ecological reef. The salvation of modern societies may require a transition strategy through which they can be gradually guided into states of dynamic stability, with economic growth selectively controlled and with populations stabilized at levels that may be indefinitely sustained by a self-renewing natural resource base. Whereas this is the larger dimension of the specific tasks of environmental management and protection with which we are primarily concerned, the courses of action towards environmental quality and self-renewal can succeed only if they are undertaken with due recognition of this larger context of evolving concepts, laws, and institutional arrangements.

Courses of Action

We have now identified the tasks that must be performed if there is to be effective protection of the biosphere. Regardless of the courses of action which governments or peoples might elect to follow towards environmental protection, it is difficult to be confident that any could succeed in which one or more of these tasks were omitted. Nations vary in many ways and it is, therefore, plausible that the courses of action towards environmental protection might vary considerably from country to country, even though the critical tasks to be performed were the same in each case. For the world as a whole, the challenge of environmental protection has only recently been posed, and there are not an endless number of ways in which the world can organize itself to meet this challenge. Our concern, therefore, will not be with the various means towards protective action that may be found among countries with widely contrasting ecological and economic conditions, but rather with those things that governments everywhere, in some measure, must do if they are to deal effectively with man/environment relationships. Most particularly, we should concern ourselves with the courses of action that must be taken at international or transnational* political levels in order to safeguard the viability of the earth itself.

* For example, programmes that operate across national boundaries but under a unified administration and personnel, who are responsible to the 'transnational' authority rather than to specific national administrations.

Developing Popular Acceptance

As we have already stressed, action to accomplish the task of establishing recognition of social and personal responsibility for the state of the environment must involve the development of popular acceptance of this responsibility. Efforts towards this end have already been made to some extent by national governments and, more recently, by several international organizations. But mainly this activity has been the work of non-governmental voluntary societies and associations. At the present time there are under way many concurrent efforts to develop a public awareness, understanding, and acceptance, of responsibilities for the protection of the biosphere. For the most part, however, these efforts are not concerted, and almost every one appears to be the result of special, and sometimes localized, initiative.

Far-sighted and highly motivated individuals have contributed to public awareness of an environmental crisis. Individual efforts to instill this sense of public responsibility go back at least a century to the publication of a book by George Perkins Marsh entitled *Man and Nature; or, Physical Geography as Modified by Human Action* (1864). Corrective efforts to protect nature and conserve natural resources were begun in the latter years of the nineteenth century; but although they won some victories, they have only recently begun to gain real power at national and international levels. Throughout the intervening years there has been an interaction between the articulate leaders in environmental protection movements and organized voluntary social efforts. In America, John Muir was not only a highly articulate defender of wilderness in the natural environment but also founder of the Sierra Club. Men such as Max Nicholson in the United Kingdom and Jean Dorst in France have played multiple roles as educators, organizers, and administrators, in their respective countries. But the task of protecting the biosphere must eventually enlist governmental action. To the extent that formal public education helps to shape popular acceptance, the role of governments is indispensable, since they alone can act in a sufficiently all-embracing manner to be really effective.

Voluntary action is usually organized along national lines, as in the case of the appeals of the World Wildlife Fund, and persons prominent in national governmental affairs are often influential in bringing public needs to public attention. For example, the activities of Philip, Duke of Edinburgh, of Bernhard, Prince of the Netherlands, of President Julius K. Nyerere of Tanzania, and of Presidents Johnson and Nixon in the United States, have helped to focus public attention upon environmental issues. Organized efforts involving both governments and voluntary groups, such as the European Conservation Year of 1970, have similarly sought to develop public awareness of environmental issues and, hopefully, have helped to gain acceptance of the dire need for public action on behalf of the environment. One could develop an imposing record of official and voluntary activities that have been orientated towards stimulating public awareness of an impending environmental crisis. Public opinion polls in Sweden, Norway, and the United States, have indicated a high degree of popular receptivity of environmental protective measures. And yet, if one may judge by events that actually occur, much more is needed before the full weight of public opinion is brought to bear on behalf of biospheric protection.

What more is needed? What problems or obstacles to receptivity must be overcome in order that measures which are truly protective of the biosphere may be undertaken on a global scale? First, it is clear that the ecological orientation which is now widely evident in Europe and North America must be extended throughout the world. Currently, in most parts of the world, even the most elementary principles of resource conservation or environmental protection are understood by only the smallest fraction of the population. Moreover, receptivity to ecologically-based policies is only a very recent development even in advanced countries, and is only understood by an undetermined but small faction that is normally limited to the better-educated members of the population. Throughout the greater part of the world, the prevailing ideologies—political, social, and theological—are thoroughly unecological and must in this respect be corrected, amended, or displaced, if effective action to protect the biosphere is to be forthcoming.

Among these unecological ideologies are natural-rights doctrines that are inconsistent with biological and ecological realities. A second group of unecological ideologies are those of economic determinism: thus both a Marxism that neglects nature and the unrestricted growthmanship of the traditional American free enterpriser are equally inconsistent with ecological reality. Yet another is the potentially disastrous fallacy that human beings can, and should, go on breeding unrestrictedly. A final example is the myth of unrestricted national sovereignty—the doctrine that political entities, such as national governments, can somehow 'own' a piece of the ocean or the lives of wild plants and animals. For the most part, these unecological ideologies obstruct rather than facilitate the solution to real social problems; they are inconsistent with the realities of the world as revealed by scientific inquiry, and the cause of environmental protection on a global scale would be much advanced if they were replaced by more valid and reliable propositions.

At least in northern Europe and North America, there are movements under way in education, in government, in science, and in the mass-communications media, that should substantially change public attitudes towards man/environment relationships within the present generation. The change may not be universal, but it has already been substantial. The vastly larger and more difficult challenge to popular acceptance is presented by the less-developed countries, including most of Asia, Africa, and Latin America. For several decades, governments in these countries have largely pursued unqualified economic development. Although there are wide differences among them, the so-called developing countries have in common certain major characteristics that are highly prejudicial to the biosphere. In relation to their present life-support capabilities, nearly all are overpopulated; nearly all have been massively acculturated by economic, social, religious, and political concepts, and by science-based technologies that originated in the 'western world'; and the overwhelming masses of their peoples are poor and under-educated, at least by 'western' standards. Finally, in most of them, some sense of national consciousness has been created and with it resentment towards real or imagined exploitation from the more advanced nations.

It follows that there has been widespread resistance among the leadership in the less-developed countries to the idea of environmental protection, at least to the extent that economic development might thereby be retarded or curtailed. And, even in the more developed states, this leadership is apt to be driven by impoverished, unstable, and dissatisfied masses of people to preserve its own position whatever the ecological costs. This apparent practical necessity is unfortunately reinforced by widespread acceptance of political and economic doctrines which are rapidly becoming outmoded in the more advanced countries. Thus, there is not only a lag in technical and economic performance in the less-developed countries, but also a lag behind the more advanced industrial nations in concepts and ideas. Concepts of economic growth and resource development that are now viewed sceptically or, indeed, have been discarded, in the more advanced countries, are still considered to be the essence of modernity in the less-developed societies.

There is little reason to believe that the majority of development programmes now in effect in the less-developed countries can do more than buy time for the leadership and power structures that now prevail. All of the economic and ecological problems of the less-developed countries are greatly exacerbated by continued population growth. Unecological trends in the less-developed countries have too often been reinforced by the influence of international technical assistance and international business, both of which have tended to emphasize resource development and exploitation, and which, although creating jobs and raising standards of living, have tended to facilitate an ever-increasing, counter-productive, growth of population.

This destructive and ultimately self-defeating cycle can be arrested by rational means only if those means are acceptable to the national and ethnic sensibilities of nations and peoples. The need is urgent for insights, propositions, and ideologies, that are ecologically valid and transnational in character. The less-developed nations are resistant to being told what they ought to do, however tactfully it may be expressed, by the more advanced states, and particularly by the United States and the Soviet Union—both of which are for various reasons held suspect of ulterior motives whatever position they may take. One hopeful aspect of this situation is, however, that the new concepts and actions that are required are needed equally by the more- and the less-developed nations. There is, for example, a most urgent need for more valid measurements and indices of the wealth of nations, and for more realistic and sophisticated interpretations of such vague popular concepts as the 'standard of living.'

A major obstacle to the popular acceptance of ecological reality has been the highly abstract character of economic thought that has largely prevailed for the greater part of the past century. But there is nothing inherent in the study of economics that requires its detachment from physical and ecological reality. As Boulding (1966), among others, has repeatedly observed, economics and ecology are in certain respects very closely related. They are, one might say, both sciences of the household in its widest sense, and the human household is now hardly less than the biosphere itself.

To save the biosphere, a transnational body of concept and doctrine should be developed as rapidly as possible. And although other efforts for national and international environmental protection should move ahead as rapidly as proves practicable, this effort to reform human perceptions and understandings is the most fundamental course of action that could be taken. Without massive world-wide change of popular attitude, it is difficult to foresee how far and how fast operational measures to protect the environment can be instituted, let alone be effective. The momentum of ecologically-harmful development policies and programmes is sustained by popular acceptance of social and economic doctrines that, however erroneous, nevertheless provide rationale and seeming justification for the development measures that are now being undertaken.

If these trends are to be checked and human efforts redirected, a new basis for belief and behaviour must be provided. The basis must be the outcome of a truly international effort, which means that it must include contributions from all parts of the world—developed and undeveloped, eastern and western, northern and southern. The UNESCO Biosphere Conference, the United Nations Conference on the Human Environment, a growing number of regional efforts, and the activities of non-governmental international bodies such as the International Union for Conservation of Nature and Natural Resources, have already provided major inputs to this task; but the effort must continue and must be extended throughout all parts of the world where the human impact upon the environment has been reinforced by a science-based technology—which now means practically everywhere!

Declaring a Policy

An international declaration of the need for protection of the biosphere could be a powerful instrument on behalf of public awareness and responsibility, if it were made at the highest political levels and were reinforced by scientific evidence and the endorsement of credible representatives of peoples in all parts of the world and in all stages of economic and technical development. International declarations on the environment have already been issued by a conference convened in Stockholm, 15–17 December 1969 (by the United Nations Associations of Denmark, Finland, Norway, and Sweden), and by the European Conservation Conference, convened in Strasbourg, 9–12 February 1970, by the Council of Europe. A general declaration is expected to be an outcome of the 1972 United Nations Conference on the Human Environment. But it may, of course, transpire that the nations of the world are not yet ready for a declaration that is sufficiently comprehensive, positive, and operational, to capture the imagination of men and women or to influence their conduct.

For all its diversity and contradiction, the earth is a unity; and because from our point of view the most fundamental part of that unity, the biosphere itself, is now being threatened by human actions, some means must be found to cope with the danger on a planetary basis. Regardless of what is possible for man, nothing less than a universal policy for the biosphere will provide an adequate conceptual foundation for its protection. Without this foundation, there is no real basis for the kind of transnational institution-building and international cooperation that must be established if the practical problems of environmental protection in the oceans, in the atmosphere, in the polar regions, and indeed in the respective nations themselves, are to be resolved. If *ad hoc* and incremental measures should, through some good fortune, succeed in arresting the ecological deterioration of the earth, it would be because a convergent consensus among people and nations had been reached; but the nature of the tasks to be done make it dubious and dangerous to rely upon unspoken agreements and unspecified understandings.

The political and social experience of mankind affords the kind of evidence that makes an official international declaration of environmental policy a practical necessity. Such an international declaration would no doubt generate many comparable declarations at the national level. There are fashions among nations as among men, and international action could reinforce these groups and potential groups—particularly in the less-developed nations that could see the need for national policies for environmental protection but lacked the strength of an articulate public opinion in their own countries to achieve such an objective unaided.

We have identified a formulation of intent as the second major task of environmental protection. The means of action in performing this task is to declare a policy; and because the ultimate task is one of action, the declaration must lead from principle to action. An illustration of the kind of declaration that leads to action has now become available in the American National Environmental Policy Act of 1969, signed into law by the President of the United States on 1 January 1970. Although each nation must necessarily develop its own environmental policies in a manner consistent with its circumstances, the declaratory sections of the American Act are worth citing in full—not to suggest them as necessarily a model for other nations, but to illustrate the characteristics of an instrument of public policy that is at once both comprehensive and operational:

PURPOSE

Sec. 2. The purposes of this Act are: To declare a national policy which will encourage productive and enjoyable harmony between man and his environment; to promote efforts which will prevent or eliminate damage to the environment and biosphere and stimulate the health and welfare of man; to enrich the understanding of the ecological systems and natural resources important to the Nation; and to establish a Council on Environmental Quality.

TITLE I

DECLARATION OF NATIONAL ENVIRONMENTAL POLICY

Sec. 101. (a) The Congress, recognizing the profound impact of man's activity on the interrelations of all components of the natural environment, particularly the profound influences of population growth, high-density urbanization, industrial expansion, resource exploitation, and new and expanding technological advances, and recognizing further the critical importance of restoring and maintaining environmental quality to the overall welfare and development of man, declares that it is the continuing policy of the Federal Government, in cooperation with State and local governments, and other concerned public and private organizations, to use all practicable means and measures, including financial and technical assistance, in a manner calculated to foster and promote the general welfare, to create and maintain conditions under which man and nature can exist in productive harmony, and fulfil the social, economic, and other requirements of present and future generations of Americans.

(b) In order to carry out the policy set forth in this Act, it is the continuing responsibility of the Federal Government to use all practicable means, consistent with other essential considerations of national policy, to improve and coordinate Federal plans, functions, programs, and resources to the end that the Nation may–

(1) fulfil the responsibilities of each generation as trustee of the environment for succeeding generations;

(2) assure for all Americans safe, healthful, productive, and esthetically and culturally pleasing surroundings;

(3) attain the widest range of beneficial uses of the environment without degradation, risk to health or safety, or other undesirable and unintended consequences;

(4) preserve important historic, cultural, and natural aspects of our national heritage, and maintain, wherever possible, an environment which supports diversity and variety of individual choice;

(5) achieve a balance between population and resource use which will permit high standards of living and a wide sharing of life's amenities; and

(6) enhance the quality of renewable resources and approach the maximum attainable recycling of depletable resources.

(c) The Congress recognizes that each person should enjoy a healthful environment and that each person has a responsibility to contribute to the preservation and enhancement of the environment.

The sections of the Act following this declaratory statement provide for its implementation. The Act is primarily directed towards guiding and controlling the environment-affecting activities of the administrative agencies of the federal government of the United States. Section 102 of the Act requires that for all proposals on legislation and other major federal action significantly affecting the quality of the human environment, the agencies submit a detailed statement indicating:

(1) the environmental impact of the proposed action,

(2) any adverse environmental effects which cannot be avoided should the proposal be implemented,

(3) alternatives to the proposed action,

(4) the relationship between local short-term uses of man's environment and the maintenance and enhancement of long-term productivity, and

(5) any reversible and irretrievable commitments of resources which would be involved in the proposed action should it be implemented.

These proposals are reviewed by a Council on Environmental Quality created by Title II of the Act and, for the first time in the history of the United States, provide the President and the American people with means by which the environmental impact of proposed governmental activities can be questioned and reviewed. Section 103 of the Act requires all federal agencies to review their statutory authority, administrative regulations, and current policies and procedures, in order to determine whether there are deficiencies and inconsistencies therein which would prohibit full compliance with the purposes and provisions of the Act. Thus, the Congress of the United States did not only in this Act state a purpose and declare a policy with respect to the environment, but it also made this policy operational through specific action-forcing provisions joined to, and by implication interpreting, the Congressional intent.

The relationship of national to international policy was recognized in the above Act, and Paragraph E in Section 102 contains a concept that would be highly desirable in any national declaration of environmental policy. The American statute declares that all agencies of the federal government shall '... recognize the world-wide and long-range character of environmental problems and, where consistent with the policy of the United States, lend appropriate support to initiatives, resolutions, and programs designed to maximize international cooperation in anticipating and preventing a decline in the quality of mankind's world environment.'

Organizing for Action

Beyond declarations, the tasks of developing programmes and strategies for biospheric protection require the establishment of agencies to do the work. No suitable international instruments now exist for performance of all of the necessary tasks. An outcome of the United Nations Conference on the Human Environment should, therefore, be the establishment of some type of international structure that would be capable of developing the necessary programmes and strategies for action. This structure should so far as possible be fashioned out of existing agencies: it would not necessarily require additional specialized agencies (although it might entail the reorganization of existing agencies). It should be flexible and capable of adaptation. Elements of such a system have already been widely discussed. Although there are numerous variants among the proposals, most of them involve some reorganization of existing international agencies (or anyway of their environmentally orientated parts) and the creation of several new bodies constituted to perform specific tasks that no existing agency is designed to undertake, or could be expected to do well even though reorganized.

A practical difficulty in designing the structure for environmental protection is that the tasks required are both scientific and political, and although these tasks frequently interrelate, their actual performance requires differing kinds of authority and expertise. There appears to be some feeling, although far from universal agreement, that the United Nations configuration of agencies may afford the best *general framework* for the establishment of such a structure. But identification within the UN family of agencies should not imply the use of existing bodies or procedures as models for new institutions. We should learn from experience with UN programmes and specialized agencies, avoiding past errors and sources of weakness and indecision—to break new ground for improved performance and real action stemming not only from new efforts but also surely from some present commitments. Because it may be unwise to rely wholly on the politically vulnerable United Nations organizations for biospheric protection, and because of their inherent or inadvertent weaknesses, it is desirable that certain critical parts of an international system be separately constituted. Fortunately, the International Council of Scientific Unions (ICSU), and certain non-governmental organizations such as the International Union for Conservation of Nature and Natural Resources (IUCN), provide supplementary, although not fully alternative, systems for the development of environmental policy and control. Another, looking at the future as does this Conference, may grow out of it: a council of 'experts' on the environmental future.

Within or allied to the United Nations structure, the establishment of at least three new agencies seems necessary. These agencies would be required for purposes of (1) formulating and coordinating environmental policy, (2) settling international environmental disputes, and (3) monitoring and interpreting environmental change. Two other purposes might require new organizations, but might also be implemented through reorganization of structures now in existence. They are, in brief, a regime for the management of the oceans and a foundation for the further protection of the world's heritage in cultural monuments, endangered wildlife, and distinctive landscapes.

Formulating and Coordinating Environmental Policy

Most importantly and, indeed, indispensably, there needs to be created at the highest levels of the United Nations an Environmental Council or Commission that would be quite separate from the Economic and Social Council and from the Security Council. This body should be limited to a manageable size (perhaps not more than sixteen members) and should have certain qualifications specified for its membership. Upon it would fall the principal task of considering and where necessary activating, global strategies for protection of the biosphere. It should report annually on the state of the biosphere to national governments through the General Assembly of the United Nations. It could be created as an interim body by resolution of the General Assembly, although a permanent status within the UN system might eventually require amendment of the Charter of the United Nations. But while this difficult process was under way, the work of this body could go ahead on an *ad hoc* basis.

Settlement of Environmental Disputes

The second institutional need is only partially new: an Agency for Settlement of Environmental Disputes, that should probably be attached, or somehow related, to the International Court of Justice (World Court). Unlike the so-called Permanent Court of Arbitration, which is associated with the World Court but is really a panel from which arbitrators may be selected in particular cases, the Agency for Settlement of Environmental Disputes would have a permanent technical staff, and would have liaison arrangements with the Environmental Council as well as with the scientific and technical environmental agencies for global protection discussed below. Controversies that could not be resolved through the Agency, and those involving the interpretation of treaties, could be referred to the World Court. It may be anticipated, however, that serious efforts to protect the biosphere will require transnational regulatory measures and will give rise to questions of fact and interpretation which juridical bodies may not be well constituted to resolve. Thus, there is a need for an agency that can apply a large variety of methods, formal and informal, to obtain the objectives of international environmental protection with a minimum of friction and controversy among nations and international business interests. The Agency for Settlement of Environmental Disputes would perform the quasi-judicial functions of an international environmental ombudsman, finding the means most appropriate for the resolution of each individual dispute.

To rely upon the goodwill and good intentions of nations to conform to an environmental policy which they had merely accepted in principle would be naïve. The needs for a policy-formulating Environmental Council and for an Agency for Settlement of Environmental Disputes is already implied in the following observation of Falk (1969):

> Appeals to conscience have very little prospect of success. The only hopeful prospect is some kind of central framework of control to design comity interests and to impose them on a global basis. This kind of solution is essentially political and moral rather than technical.

A Global Environmental Monitoring Network

A third element of an international coordinative system for biospheric protection would be a global monitoring network related to a centre, or centres, for interpretation of the assembled data. The design and critical surveillance of the operation of such a network are tasks for scientists; its deployment and operation are largely tasks for engineers and administrators, although scientific workers in the fields concerned should also be involved. Because a diversity of monitoring systems is already in effect, and because important sectors of the global monitoring system are likely to be administered by national governments, the network as a whole would probably have to be established by some international organization with political competence, such as the United Nations.

Supervision of the effectiveness of the monitoring and the collation and interpretation of the collected data, however, should be undertaken by scientists who would be independent of political or other sectional affiliation. It therefore may be desirable to establish a supervisory responsibility for the network in an entity created by the International Council of Scientific Unions. Such an entity, the International Centre for the Environment, has already been proposed through the Council's Scientific Committee on Problems of the Environment (SCOPE).

Certain large portions of this task could be accomplished through existing organizations that are already performing important monitoring functions. For example, the World Meteorological Organization has already established an important atmospheric monitoring system in its World Weather Watch, which its own executive head told us about earlier in this Conference. Implementation of the planned extension of WMO's activities to the ocean surface would be a logical and, indeed, necessary complement to its original mission inasmuch as the ocean–atmosphere interface is a major locus in the generation of the world's weather. In the complex area of the periodical surveying of biological phenomena, the International Union for Conservation of Nature and Natural Resources has had considerable experience in observing and reporting on the status of endangered species of plants and animals. This function of the IUCN could be enlarged and regularized with adequate financial and physical support, and its information shared with a central data repository and research facility such as the proposed International Centre for the Environment (ICE).

An Ocean Regime

An especially troublesome environmental problem is the management of the oceans. There is now widespread if not general agreement that the traditional status of the seas as an international no-man's-land is no longer safe or feasible. Oceanic pollution and the depletion of marine life have reached truly alarming proportions (Cousteau, 1971; Heyerdahl, 1971). Disputes over territorial waters continue and could become more dangerous as nations seek to exploit the rapidly-diminishing living resources of the sea. On 17 December 1970, the United Nations General Assembly passed Resolution 2750 (XXV) calling for an International Conference on the Law of the Sea to be held in 1973; but meanwhile the hazards to the viability of the oceans continue to increase, although new international structures for governance of the oceans have been proposed.

There has been strong opposition, especially among the more powerful nations, to the establishment of additional United Nations specialized agencies. However, it might be practicable to enlarge and extend the jurisdiction and functions of existing agencies to meet the most immediate threats to the oceans. For example, the Intergovernmental Maritime Consultative Organization (IMCO) might very well be reconstituted to take jurisdiction over traffic on the seas and the exploitation of marine resources. The new structure, perhaps called the International Maritime Organization, could be given the authority to establish general regulations governing the types of craft and cargoes that could be permitted upon the seas, and to establish more comprehensive standards and controls to minimize or prevent pollution of the oceans. The activities of the Food and Agriculture Organization (FAO) with respect to food from the sea might still be left with that agency. And the scientific functions of monitoring the physical environment in and about the surface of the oceans could probably be left to an expanded World Meteorological Organization, which might perhaps be renamed in a manner indicative of this expanded activity (e.g. World Geophysical Organization).

World's Heritage in Culture and Nature

Although the effect of the foregoing institutional developments would help to safeguard the beauty, variety, and natural resources, of the earth, more specific measures are needed to protect those cultural monuments, plant and animal species, and cultural and natural landscapes, that lie within the political jurisdiction of national and other states. International protection of the world's heritage in culture and wildlife has hitherto been organized chiefly through the United Nations Educational, Scientific and Cultural Organization (UNESCO), and the International Union for Conservation of Nature and Natural Resources (IUCN). But the task requires greater resources in money and trained personnel than have heretofore been available. To reinforce the efforts of these agencies, which in any case should be supported by greatly increased national contributions, a Trust for the World Heritage has been proposed (Fisher, 1969). This agency could be established as a mixed governmental or non-governmental fund-raising philanthropic foundation to assist governments and international organizations in the preservation of those cultural and natural assets of which the loss would impoverish all mankind.

Laying out the Tasks

Once this structure, and particularly the Environmental Council, is created, a three-level strategy should be developed, through the initiative of the Council, for arresting the deterioration of the biosphere and beginning the tasks of effective protection and restoration. These levels of action might be described as immediate, intermediate, and ultimate. The level of immediate action pertains to present and accelerating threats from which irreversible damage may occur. It is a level at which information for action is largely available and action is long overdue. For example, an immediate moratorium of perhaps ten years should be placed upon the taking of endangered species of whales or members of other endangered marine groups. Similar restrictions should be established through treaties for a number of large terrestrial species, particularly among predators. Immediate action should be taken to stop the indiscriminate use of pesticides and other toxic substances that threaten food-chains and the reproduction of numerous species of birds and other animals. The proposed Environmental Council or Commission would seem to be the appropriate initiator of these measures, particularly when advised by the appropriate scientific authorities.

The intermediate level of action would, for the most part, require more information than is now available, though action may sometimes be necessary even though the information is incomplete. The organization and extension of monitoring systems for air and water, and of surveying vicissitudes of wildlife, necessarily belong at this level, inasmuch as the monitoring networks, etc., could not be activated or anyway completed immediately, even though their establishment should be pursued as expeditiously as possible.

The level of ultimate action will be dictated by the goals towards which social efforts are to be directed—towards the end of establishing and maintaining the biosphere in a dynamic, self-renewing state. It may, of course, be argued that all man need do to enjoy the advantages of self-renewing equilibration in the planetary ecosphere is to let it alone, and indeed, there are parts of it that surely should be left alone or used much more lightly than they are at present. But present-day life-styles and levels of population do not permit man the choice of affecting or not affecting the biosphere. His activities affect it profoundly, and it is for this reason that his own activities must be managed so as to maintain its life-support capabilities.

Making the Utopian Practical

In a small conceptualizing book entitled *Operating Manual for Spaceship Earth* (1969), Buckminster Fuller argues that the means towards managing man's relationships with this life-supporting planet are through the development of general systems and combined practices in the proper relating of specialization to comprehensive purposeful planning. He rightly observes that it was on the oceans that men first discovered the global nature of the earth and began to sense its unity. It may well be that in organizing and controlling man's relationship to the three-quarters of the surface of the earth that is water, the first truly global or at least transnational—in contradistinction to international—institutions will be developed. The means of action on behalf of the biosphere, if they are effective, will lead towards a coherent system for guiding and controlling man's interactions with his environment. If this is a Utopian concept, it is no contradiction to declare that it is also practical. The system that is needed does not now exist, and the deterioration of the biosphere is an indirect consequence of this fact. There has been no feasible way by which the many nations of the earth can unilaterally or concurrently concert their efforts towards biospheric protection. Were they seriously to attempt to do this, they would have to create a coherent system corresponding in principle to the one just described.

What would be the principal hazards to such a system? Even with the highest level of agreement and the greatest goodwill among nations, the magnitude and complexity of the task of biospheric protection would make it exceedingly difficult. Modern society has barely begun to apply science and technology to the protection of the environment and to the management of man's relationships to it. There is much to be learned before one can be assured that the results of human efforts will be successful and will be only those that are intended. But the socio-economic and psychological barriers to protection of the biosphere are even more obstructive than are the technical problems.

Among these obstructions are egos of prominent political personalities; for it often seems that the personal qualities that enable men to become leaders of other men make them unfit for tasks for cooperation and peace. The mass of humanity appears to react to leadership upon the basis of instincts that were practical in the Stone Age or in the era of medieval war-bands. But this instinctive attraction to the magnetic, aggressive leader appears to be counterproductive to the needs of a society in which atomic bombs and persistent biocides are available. And closely related to the ego demands of highly visible, popular and aggressive leaders is a touchy popular pride in national self-determination. This exaggerated patriotism was once widely believed to be a civic virtue. Today, it is virtuous only when modified by intelligent regard for the holistic character of the planetary life-support system and for the ultimate unity or at least interdependence of all living processes.

Economic opportunities and temptation present barriers to international cooperation on behalf of the environment that are probably more profound and pervasive than political dogmas and ideologies. Regardless of its internal socio-economic structure, almost every modern industrialized nation has behaved like an old-fashioned capitalist entrepreneur with respect to external economic affairs. Practical socialism ends at national frontiers, and a socialist state may drive as hard an international economic bargain, or be as rapacious in its exploitation of the common wealth of the world, as any self-seeking capitalist. Potentially more obstructive is the prospect of conflict between the goals of national development, when interpreted in narrow economic terms, and the objectives of environmental protection, when formulated with insufficient regard to accommodating genuine human requirements. There is need for a new theory of social action that would integrate the goals of national development and environmental quality in propositions that are ecologically valid and economically sound.

What is required of the peoples and nations of the earth is that they transcend their own histories. They must learn to be more far-sighted and more realistic (as well as more altruistic) than they have ever been. But there is no inexorable imperative compelling them towards this new and higher level of political development; the situation is simply that, if they do not or cannot move in this direction, they cannot avoid paying the costs of failure. These costs have by now been enumerated so frequently that it is hardly necessary to do more than state them here. They are:

(1) impoverishment and degradation of the human environment,
(2) adaptation to progressively lower qualities of life, accompanied by declining levels of public health and, perhaps, by increasing genetic deterioration, and
(3) ultimate ecological catastrophe.

Humanity need not survive, nor need it maintain or improve the present level of existence; but, if survival or improvement is the social choice, then hopes, desires, and intentions, will not be enough to preserve and protect the space-ship earth. If the viability of the earth were to be threatened by some inimical extra-terrestrial force, the peoples and nations of the world would surely make common cause to save themselves from disaster. To the extent necessary to safeguard the viability of the earth, governments would almost certainly subordinate those nationalistic and particularistic doctrines and behaviours that would obstruct defensive action. Yet the defence of the earth demands no less because the enemy is not from outer space but has grown out of the unecological behaviour of man himself!

If modern man is asked to see himself as his own worst enemy, he is also asked to see himself as his only possible salvation. If, in the language of traditional religions, divine grace is the source of man's salvation, it can only be operative through the acts of man himself. The eyes of men have been opened to the human predicament, and human knowledge and ingenuity have equipped man with the tools and the concepts necessary to preserve the earth—at least from his own undoing through terracide or war. How modern society responds to this challenge will surely be overwhelmingly the most important single event of the remaining decades of the twentieth century. For there seems little doubt that the battle to preserve our world will be won or lost in the years lying near ahead.

REFERENCES

BOULDING, Kenneth E. (1966). The economics of the coming spaceship earth. Pp. 3–14 in *Environmental Quality in a Growing Economy* (Ed. Henry Jarrett). Johns Hopkins Press, Baltimore, Maryland: xv + 173 pp.

BRZEZINSKI, Zbigniew K. (1970). *Between Two Ages: America's Role in the Technetronic Era.* Viking Press, New York: xvii + 334 pp.

COUSTEAU, Jacques-Yves (1971). Statement on global marine degradation. *Biological Conservation*, **4**(1), pp. 61–5.

ELLUL, Jacques (1954). *The Technological Society.* Translated from the French by John Wilkinson. Alfred A. Knopf, New York: xxxvi + 499 pp.

FALK, Richard A. (1969). Article in *The New York Times*, 7 April 1969, p. 10.

FISHER, Joseph L. (1969), New perspectives on conservation. *Biological Conservation*, **1**(2), pp. 121–6.

FULLER, Buckminster (1969). *Operating Manual for Spaceship Earth.* Southern Illinois University Press, Carbondale, Illinois: 143 pp.

HEYERDAHL, Thor (1971). Atlantic Ocean pollution and biota observed by the 'Ra' Expeditions. *Biological Conservation*, **3**(3), pp. 164–7, illustr.

MARSH, George Perkins (1864). *Man and Nature; or, Physical Geography as Modified by Human Action.* Charles Scribner, New York: xix + 577 pp. (Reprint edited by David Lowenthal. Harvard University Press, Cambridge, Massachusetts: xxix + 472 pp., 1965.)

DISCUSSION

Henderson (Chairman)

Understanding as I do from Professor Caldwell that the general parts of his paper, the very important ones, should stand open for discussion with the questions of institutional arrangements, I shall welcome due consideration this afternoon of the whole means of action, and call first on Professor Bryson, who said this morning that we had talked a lot about disparate things but had not pulled them together. So I hope he will take this occasion to help us on the road of integration.

Bryson

We have heard much about the trinity of population, development, and environment—a trinity that is indeed three-in-one. I would like to suggest a way of considering these three-items-in-one that may help to clarify our thinking about the situation as a whole. We'll write some equations, but they are very simple ones—the simple ones, you know, being the important ones; they usually happen to be trinities. In fact, important equations such as Newton's Laws of Motion are all about three variables. For example, the pollution per unit area and time is equal to the population density times *per caput* resource consumption rate times an efficiency factor: $P = pRt_1$. That's a simple enough equation, indeed a primitive one, and although these factors are not independent of one another, it can be expanded from this form. The competition between individuals, biological competition (I am told by biologists), is proportional to population density times resource consumption rate factor of proportionality: $C = pRt_2$. Energy consumption per unit area and time is equal to population density times resource consumption rate times the energy cost of using the resource: $E = pRt_3$. Gross national product can be expressed as a sum of similar equations.

The purpose of this is not to establish a set of equations which are operative but to demonstrate that there is indeed an interrelationship between human population, resources which are so vital to development through technology, and efficiency in the use of materials; and, of course, when we talk about population densities, about resources and the technology of their use, and about pollution and competition and energy, we are also talking about the environment. Technology enters widely, being concerned also with the efficiency with which we use resources, and the quantities that are utilized. Moreover, there are social arrangements and cultural factors to be considered and the fact that to a large extent population is related to cultural attitudes, which in turn reflect the efficiency with which we use resources. Thus, a person who says he has to have a new car every three years does so for cultural reasons, not because a car falls apart after three years. And in our discussion of these problems we should keep in mind that when a nation's population goes up, unless something is done about the efficiency with which it uses its resources, pollution will increase also. Thus there are ways in which we can attack these problems: for example, if, with an increasing population, we are not to increase the pollution levels, we must look very hard at the efficiency with which we use resources and deal with wastes, etc.

I hope we can agree that, with this close connection between technological development, human population, and resource consumption, we should be looking at all these three together rather than as separate elements. The one that we have paid the least attention to so far is the resource issue. Now, we can say some things about resource consumption that are related to what we have been talking about but have not yet said. For example, pollution of the air by internal combustion automobiles is a problem that in time will disappear by itself, as we can see if we study the literature on the reserves of petroleum that we have in the world. We are already nearing the half-way point; by the end of the century it is likely that, if these figures are correct, petroleum and petroleum products will be so expensive that the use of petroleum in aircraft and automobiles will be ruled out. Perhaps gasified coal will drive our transportation, and that's a much cleaner fuel. This takes us right back to one of the suggestions we have heard repeatedly before: we ought to make an inventory of our resources to see what we have on this space-ship with which we can survive. Then we shall be able to decide how best to use them to do it.

Udall

I wanted to have a little dialogue with Professor Caldwell because, as you should understand, he is an adviser of the President of the United States and one of the very creative authors of some important recent reports based on protracted experiments and observations in our country. Nor do I think he and I have any quarrel as to whether we have his Council or my Institute, provided there is an effective organization focused on the environment—in which tackling the urgent problems of the environment is not simply a new over-layer on what people are already doing, but is a very sharply focused and clearly established function to be performed as basic to all others. There are several different institutional ways in which this can be done, and possibly you could do it by a process of reorganization, though personally I do not think that is the proper solution.

My other feeling that I want to sharpen is this; as a former administrator I have seen some very good ideas put forward with very good rhetoric, and I have seen laws passed. But except in an area where you make policy merely by passing a law, or at least if you have to change many things, unless you have money to back up your new policy or institution, you're not going to get very far; you have to put up with the same people, for money is like fuel that drives the engine. Now I haven't worked within the United Nations and I may be wrong, but it seems to me that we ought to be able to get the UN people to see that if environment is really important, then something must be done, and that this will cost money. Then if it is really urgent they can get the nations of the world to realize that they've got to put more money into this whole effort.

If there is anything that distresses me about the UN as an organization, it is its lack of vision and real jurisdiction; and I'd like to see it take jurisdiction over the seas, as comprising more than 70 per cent of the surface of the earth. This would seem to me a very logical function, though I know something of the attendant problems. The more I think of what the UN could do if it had a budget of 2 or 3 or, preferably, 6 thousand million dollars a year from some sources or other, rather than only about one-tenth of that last amount, the more I can foresee their potentialities *inter alia* of retaining people of the highest calibre. Towards raising this kind of money, why not have tonnage tags on certain kinds of shipping, which the maritime powers could arrange so that it wouldn't cramp other activities. In any case I don't see why we could not be clever enough to come up with something that would provide a regular tax income for the United Nations, *inter alia* to enable them to provide this 60 million dollars or whatever it is that is needed to enable the countries which must have pesticides to use the least damaging ones for their own benefit and the world's.

Caldwell

I did not attempt to develop the idea of an international centre for environmental research along the lines of the institute for survival which Mr Udall has suggested, because he has already developed it. Personally I am convinced that such an institute is needed, and meanwhile would note that the International Council of Scientific Unions is considering something of the kind in the form of an International Centre for the Environment. Moreover in the United States, as an indication that not all national governments are unresponsive, there has been introduced into the Senate, by Senator Magnuson of the State of Washington, a resolution with half of the Senate as co-signers, supporting the idea of a world environment centre, and I think one will ultimately emerge. I would advocate its being intergovernmental, at least in part, although I must say that I do not think it feasible, as we look to the environmental future, to push too much the idea of what is governmental and what is non-governmental, etc.; this is an old-fashioned idea. Nowadays interrelationships are not as distinct as they used to be, and things are becoming more and more blurred. But I think we will, in some form, probably create such an institution.

On the question of the ability of the United Nations to work more effectively, I feel very strongly that we greatly underestimate the potential of the human animal for sensible behaviour. After all, it was men who created this very large and complex, world-wide system of governments, etc., and really it was a tremendous step; but now everyone complains about the ineffectuality of the United Nations as an operating body, and the great difficulty it has in coordinating its activities. Yet it is perfectly clear who the bosses of the United Nations really are: *they are the national governments*. It is the national governments that can coordinate the United Nations. When the UN specialized agencies need to be straightened out, it isn't the Administrative Committee on Coordination that can do it, though they can and do negotiate internal differences, but only the General Assembly where the nations of the world are represented. There you can get an effective expression.

What money we channel from our national governments into the United Nations is ridiculously low in amount. Here in this Conference we have had a debate about whether the less affluent nations of the world can afford to dispense with DDT. I think that fifty years from now people will laugh at this kind of proposition, and say: If we need a better pesticide than DDT, and it's merely a matter of cost, well, for heaven's sake let's get the money, let's not say to India or Ghana or Venezuela that you have to use this old stuff simply because somehow the world cannot afford anything better. In my own country we have spent thirty thousand million dollars to get to the moon, and immense sums on armaments or even on Olympic Games, and on all sorts of other things [a comment from the floor: 'Precisely'.], so I'm feeling impatient and fully share Mr Udall's feelings that we expect far too little of our collective agent here, the United Nations—basically because we don't support it adequately to be really functional.

Takanen

I wish to comment briefly on the spirit of this Conference, and at the same time to review the gap which exists between ecology and planning. The Conference is proving successful, at least to the extent that it has gathered together a group of the most eminent scientists and others in the fields concerned to speak freely in often highly enlightening ways. However, this is scarcely its main goal; if we do not manage to present value-estimates, we shall be curtailing the field of our future possibilities.

We have hardly heard anything of what really should be done, and under what conditions. Nor have we been able to penetrate into the wider sociostructural field, our thoughts having been mainly restricted by so-called neutral objectivity-pursuit—the ecology-strangled view which has largely restricted description to the present situation. The outcome of this has been that the intercourse has stuck to its old path, and we have not succeeded in realizing full freedom of discussion about the foreseeable future.

So far we have not been able to define a framework of reference to enable us to find the necessary measures to restore the ecological balance. We have ascribed especially little attention to the very concept of man's environment. When concerning ourselves with this environment, we should start from the possibilities offered by modern systems-analysis and cybernetics. Man's environment forms one entity, an entire system which is divided into sub-systems or sub-environments. These include the ecological, cultural, psychological, and political, environments of mankind. The target for man should be an undisturbed, self-adjusting, total global system of which the ecological system is an integral part.

Because the ecological system is only a part of a wider total system, and a part of man's environment, we should review—while striving for the undisturbed ecological environment—the structures of the different subsystems and the connections between them. At this juncture we have to put forward a question: What kind of sub-environment guarantees a self-adjusting ecological system, fit to live in, and at the same time a self-adjusting total system? Thus we have unavoidably to face the further questions: Under what kind of economic, cultural, psychological, and political, systems can we best safeguard an undisturbed, self-adjusting ecological system?

Regional exploitation of natural resources can bring considerable regional pollution, and it is only by eliminating strained conditions in the sub-systems at every instance of exploitation, that we are able to reach a world-wide, self-adjusting ecological system. Attention has been drawn in this Conference to the fact that decision-makers do not take ecological knowledge sufficiently into account, whereas actually they are not able to do this because the supply of ecological information is offered in a largely irrelevant form. We may catch glimpses of returning to nature and admiration of beauty, but then will be running away from our responsibility. What we really need is scientists and others who realize that man's ecological environment is dependent on the situation in the other sub-environments—on the factors of social structure and the stresses which control it. The future of mankind requires such people, but how and where are they to be trained and found?

Henderson (Chairman)

That is a very wide-ranging and pertinent question, and I think it's a pity it was not asked earlier in the session, because it gives us something to think about for quite some time. Perhaps it can be worked on by some of the younger scholars and students in this audience?

Now I have a question from Professor Adlercreutz which reads as follows: 'What are the prospects that the present approaches in population control will make a difference to the long-term environmental troubles?'

As, clearly, one of the main 'means of action' should be through population control, I'll take this occasion myself to say one or two things on the subject. Several times during this Conference we have heard the projections of human population coming from United Nations sources—mainly with different sets of assumptions but indicating in any case that there will be something between six-and-a-half and eight thousand million humans by the end of this century at the present rate of growth, and that, even if we stabilize the population growth by the year 2000 in the advanced countries and by 2040 in the developing countries, we will still have some 15·5 thousand million people on earth at the end of the twenty-first century. This does not look very favourable in terms of the equations which Professor Bryson made for us, and I must admit that, if I'm asked about the present approaches to population control, I have to say frankly that I do not think they will make enough difference to have a major impact on our ecological or environmental future in this century or the next.

In matters of population control we are proceeding at a very slow pace indeed, and can still count on the fingers of one hand the countries that have succeeded in effecting a significant reduction in their birth-rates after having announced a policy of reducing them. In my organization, the International Planned Parenthood Federation, we have seventy-five member associations with a voluntary family planning programme. This means that, even with expenditures of half-a-million to a million dollars in particular countries, we succeed in reaching perhaps 65,000 women in one country and 100,000 in another, and this indeed is not going to have a dramatic impact.

In this Conference we are talking about environment: we are not talking simply about the human right to plan and space one's children but about vital demographic pressures and their effects. There are a few experiments going on in the world which show that one can make a difference on the demographic side. The Japanese, of course, showed it in the decade of the 50s by rather strong methods, mainly depending on abortion. The information we have from China these days indicates that they are making a massive effort, bringing to bear all the forces of the state, to turn around on their growing population: they are using the para-medical 'barefoot doctors' throughout the country, not tying themselves to the medical profession as many of the other countries who are engaging in population policies are now doing, but making all methods available. They are also making massive propaganda efforts, and have changed their legislation on the minimum age of marriage so that it is now postponed to twenty-five for women and thirty for men. Altogether they are making what is turning out to be probably the most comprehensive effort in population control of any nation to date. There is a new publication of the Population Crisis Committee that will give you authoritative details on the situation in mainland China*'.

In India we know that, contrary to the often-repeated view that little is happening, there are three states which are making good progress in the matter of family planning. But it seems to me that there are parallels here again between what we have to do in population and what we have to do in environment. We need to have government policies, we need to turn around the pro-natalist legislation into a quite different legislation to support planned parenthood activity, just as we need to turn around the pro-exploitation legislation into different kinds of legislation. And we obviously have to be far more committed to population control than we are today, when most people are still talking about strictly voluntary methods—which I must say in my view will not answer the question of environmental future.

Siirilä

Representing as I do both the International Union of Students and the National Union of Finnish Students, I want first to make a brief remark about population control as a means of action. It has been calculated that every person in the United States uses as much in the way of natural resources as fifty persons in the underdeveloped countries. If you calculated the population of the United States on that basis, there would be 10,000 million persons in the United States, and besides that all manner of dogs and cats and other pets. So population control in the United States and other rich countries would seem more important than, or at least as important as, population control in the underdeveloped countries.

Another matter which I feel should be discussed further is that, whereas the population in the United States is only about 6 per cent of the population of the whole world, they are said to use annually more than 40 per cent of the resources that are used in the world. And to maintain this the United States does all sorts of things that may result in people dying from starvation and diseases, and I think that, when we are talking about environmental problems, one of the most important items to discuss is the inequality between different nations and between persons within the same nation. Nor do I think the proposals that have been made here about new international organizations and international law and things like that will help. For if a new international organization in the United Nations, for instance, does very good research or other work which the United States and all the other rich

* 'Population and Family Planning in the People's Republic of China', of which a résumé is given in the 'Addenda' to this section (pp. 575-7).—Ed.

countries think is dangerous for them, or at least for the big multinational companies, the new organization will not get any more money and so cannot do anything. And so it is with international law: even if I or the Finnish Government or the IUS or any other organization goes to court and accuses the United States and the leaders of big companies about the war in Vietnam, and the people concerned are jailed for the rest of their lives, there will still be other people who will take their places, and so the system goes on much as before. This is, of course, a very primitive analysis, but I want to say, on the basis of this example, that to my mind it is the system and structure which are to blame, and we should find some means of changing them.

There has been talk here of uniting forces between rich and poor countries, between developed and underdeveloped countries. When this kind of suggestion is made, one must always ask on whose terms do these people unite forces, and I'm afraid that it will be on the terms of the rich countries, and so will not provide an equitable answer to the problems. Yet environmental and social needs should surely be dealt with collectively as among the basic ones of all people.

Caldwell

Though one might have wished that Mr Siirilä had listened more carefully to what has been said, it's a very good question as to who are the exploited and who the exploiters in this world, particularly if projected over a long period of time. Mr Udall pointed out the other day that we in the United States are fully aware of the fact that we have made mistakes, but I would also recall that the United States has had the capacity to rise to some levels of generosity, and I hope that one of our characteristics—certainly not unique to us—is the capacity to take criticism for our own behaviour and to correct it as rapidly as we can.

As to the proposition that the United States has 6 per cent of the people of the earth but consumes more than 40 per cent of its resources, I must say I have searched most diligently for the basis for that contention, which Mr Udall referred to the other day, and have tried through the US Department of Agriculture, the US Geological Survey, the Petroleum Institute, and even the United Nations, without being able to corroborate it. It is a figure which I think is a generalization that may need a good deal of examination—the sum total of a lot of different things, so that I'm far from sure how meaningful it is. But I might also say that, were the United States to live upon its own resources, which technologically it ought to be able to do, this might be not at all welcome to peoples in developing countries who wish to acquire foreign exchange—who have minerals or agricultural products that they wish to export.

Now, what we have been attempting to do in these sessions today is almost precisely what has been suggested. Who can be satisfied with the structure that we have; its failures are visible, and were demonstrated in the excellent film that preceded this session. And I don't blame the younger people for being impatient. But what we are attempting to create is a kind of institution in which all of the peoples of the world, regardless of whether they are poor or rich, and all nations regardless of what their social or economic systems may be, can have confidence. This is not a situation in which there is a monopoly of virtue or wisdom in any particular country or bloc, and I would therefore simply enter a plea for some patience and some charity for good motives, and indeed perhaps for good deeds—even on the part of people from the highly industrialized nations. If we cannot find ways of working together in attacking these problems, most assuredly we shall not be passengers for very long on this space-ship earth.

Mikola

Professor Caldwell deals early in his paper with personal or individual responsibility, and I would like to add a few words on this subject. When listening to the papers and discussions of this week, I have had the impression that we do not always see various problems in their right proportions. Let me give you one example: A couple of days ago there was a heated discussion on whether DDT is carcinogenic or not, and whether it should be banned because of this property. If I understood correctly, we do not yet know whether DDT is carcinogenic to human beings. One thing, however, which we certainly do know, is that tabacco is carcinogenic to man. Dr Wurster mentioned that if a substance is carcinogenic in high concentrations, it is apt to have the same property in low concentrations. Accordingly, it seems quite likely that thousands of people, who do not smoke themselves, die of lung cancer every year because other people smoke and pollute their environment with this carcinogenic substance. Thus, if we are going to ban substances because of their carcinogenic properties, we should ban tobacco first and then perhaps also DDT.

The day before yesterday we were also discussing the wise and unwise use of chemicals. Dr Mellanby did not mention tobacco in his paper, but the only wise use of it is through application of nicotine as a pesticide in horticulture, whereas smoking tobacco is a most splendid example of an unwise use.

There are other aspects, too. One big global problem which has been mentioned several times during this Conference is world nutrition—how to produce enough food for the growing human population. Millions of hectares of the most fertile soils of the earth, however, are used today to grow tobacco and some other useless crops. Many food problems could be alleviated for a long time ahead by growing on this area food for people and domestic animals. It was also mentioned that there is something wrong with the circumstances that the fish catch of some developing countries where peope are short of proteins is mainly used to feed pet animals in rich countries. Isn't it then still more wrong that some of the best soils of those countries are used to grow a crop of which the principal use is pollution of the environment? So far, however, tobacco growing is actively promoted by FAO and many local governments.

Thus, when the question is raised as to what individuals should do, I can give just one concrete practical answer. If you wish to do something to protect the environment for humans, the simplest thing to begin with is to refrain from smoking. Here you have a good opportunity to show individual responsibility.

Estlander

Scientists may talk about their sciences and organizational people may talk about what their organizations are doing, but very few come out of their frameworks to see what actions should really be taken. Conferences and resolutions are not means of action, though they may sometimes lead to some action. Those of us who have been talking about our future environment have been very concerned and pessimistic, and seem to have ample reason to be. But real action means action on the political level, and to get to this level scientists have to become active science politicians, because science is only a material, and action depends on how this material is used. Scientists have to become aware of their responsibility to their fellow-citizens, try to inform them in an understandable manner, and likewise inform the politicians. The scientists should come down from their Eiffel Towers and participate in discussions in the newspapers, on the streets—everywhere that ordinary people are discussing problems.

Väisänen (Pentti)

Here it has become clear how important it is to turn ecological knowledge to political goals and political action. Our environment has been polluted and the global resourses are getting used up. Because natural resources are limited, it's not enough to think of how they are used now; it is of vital importance to study how they can best be used in the future to satisfy the needs of all mankind on equal bases, giving priority to the primary needs of the majority rather than to the luxury needs of a minority. If we accept this goal we could ask, what is the real situation now? The richest 25 per cent of the world's population utilizes two-thirds of world's resources, and we are told that the limited resources in all the world could give to all of mankind a United States living standard for only twenty years, or to the United States population their present living standard for 150 years.

When the primary needs of the richer countries have been satisfied, the market economy turns to their secondary or luxury needs, boosted by intensive advertising. All of this means wasting natural resources for irrational purposes rather than canalizing them to satisfy basic needs of food, housing, health, and education—and of course for protecting our environment and natural resources—on a world-wide scale. Transferring these natural resources often leads to over-exploitation and a heightening of the environmental crisis. So we find great differences between those who get benefits and those who suffer, and to solve these problems needs world cooperation as well as structural reforms in the manner indicated by Mr Siirilä.

Rayzacher

I work with an international institute which was founded by an industry that, according to many contentions, is a real devil of our time—the oil industry. I don't try to defend this industry, knowing that some errors have been committed by it in the more or less recent past. Nor will I discuss the reasons for these errors, because it would surely not bring us any nearer to our real goal which is the solution of environmental problems. The objective of our institution is to combat pollution of the environment by any form of activity of the oil industries or their products, and to solve cognate problems. I will not bother you here with detailed solutions, because the problems that are solved are no longer problems at all, and we ought not to be concerned with them in the future. But I should tell you that if an oil refinery of, say, fifteen or twenty years ago could be a real and heavy polluter of waters, a modern one pollutes water much less than a speed-boat with an outboard engine of 50 horsepower.

Concerning problems that are not yet solved, our experience indicates that even if the technology for pollution prevention already exists, not everything can be done by industry itself; there is a strong need for action by governments, and even by intergovernmental bodies, to implement the use of this technology. Before I had read the extremely interesting paper of Professor Caldwell, I proposed that action should be undertaken quickly by the United Nations to solve one of the most urgent problems of our times, namely the pollution of sea waters. To my delight I found that a similar proposal is being made by Professor Caldwell. As many of you probably know, some years ago a system called 'load-on-top'* was adopted by many tanker fleets to avoid seawater pollution by oil. Today this system is used by about 80 per cent of the world's tankers and this avoids a calculated pollution of the seas and oceans by about 2 million tons of oil yearly. But here we have the problem that 20 per cent of the world's tanker fleet has not accepted this solution. Most of these remaining ships fly the flag of one of the biggest industrialized countries of the world that is, moreover, a heavy importer of oil. There is also a problem of other vessels crossing our seas and oceans and quietly discharging their bunker tanks of oily water into the sea.

It has been calculated that the remaining tanker fleet and other vessels discharge into sea water some 2 million tons of oil yearly, and that the voluntary acceptance of the load-on-top system by all oil companies and by most tanker companies has cut the sea pollution by half. But to abate this sea pollution by oil almost completely I feel we need to change the status of the so-called international waters from being nobody's property into being the property of all, and putting them under the United Nations' responsibility. Only in this way could working control and enforcement schemes be elaborated which would cover not only oil pollution but any other kind of pollution that is caused by dumping of waste into sea water.

Henderson (Chairman)

I think it's very clear from the discussion this afternoon that the majority of speakers are calling for bold political action on behalf of the environment, and I think there will be no disagreement in this Conference that bold political action is called for in view of the seriousness of the situation. The question of cooperation of the third world and the rest of the world has also been a basic tenet of other sessions in this Conference, and is, I think, one of the reasons why Professor Caldwell has stressed, in his paper concerning the institutional arrangements, the importance of using the United Nations system which has

* Essentially the avoidance of returning to the sea the oil-contaminated water from ballast and tank washings remaining in a tanker towards the end of her voyage back to a loading port.—Ed.

built into it the cooperation of the third world, the developing world, and the affluent world.

The question of the ways in which we will achieve our goals—and I think these coming goals have emerged most appropriately from this Conference—is one which we have not made entirely precise, because there are obviously differences of opinion about the exact formula to be recommended for achieving the goals we seek. But I think there is a fair degree of agreement among the speakers both this afternoon and this morning that the UN system is the one most likely to be used, and that we have to mobilize the energies of the institutions which already exist—even though we may have to add to that structure something which will be a focal point for the responsibility and will attract new resources, both human and material, to this most important undertaking. I believe there was also agreement that there does have to be a solid, organic kind of relationship between the work on environment, on population, and on development.

ADDENDA

Population Control in Mainland China*

'Two in the first generation means a thousand in ten generations', is a Chinese proverb with a definite truth in it—i.e. 2, 4, 8, 16, 32, 64, 128, 256, 512, 1024. It also indicates vital awareness in China that its population must reduce its birth-rates to be able to support itself. Chinese leaders, headed by Premier Chou En-lai, aiming at realizable short-term goals, have instigated powerful birth-control campaigns to lower the natural growth-rate of 2 per cent per annum to below 1 per cent. They are trying to get this result at latest by the end of this century—a goal that could well be adopted by all nations as the agreed world one for the next thirty years.

Having begun controlling its population about fifteen years ago, China has made dramatic advances particularly in the last two or three years. In widespread use now is the 22-days pill, in preference to uterine devices, but more recently the once-a-month pill has begun to be used, though it is not yet nationally approved. Research is being carried on with a once-in-three-months pill and even towards development of one pill to be effective for about a year.

In his travels in China, Edgar Snow, author of *Red Star Over China*, reported early in 1971 that 'my wife and I found family planning in practice among women in factories, institutes, neighbourhood communities in cities, and communes in the countryside down to the village level. Clinics in the communes supply propaganda and materials. At the brigade (village) level, medical workers [para-medical personnel known as 'barefoot doctors'] who have been trained at commune or country hospitals to carry out vaccination, first aid, and other treatments (including acupuncture), are qualified to distribute the pill . . . free of charge. Abortion is legal and given to the pregnant woman free of charge, if a worker, and for a small fee—two yen—if not. The method up to 2½ months is by vacuum removal.' This is practically painless, and the woman is observed for two hours afterwards and then sent home. No one should conclude from this, however, that abortion is encouraged in China as a substitute for contraceptive measures. It is a last resort for mothers of one or more children who have not received and succeeded with contraceptive devices. As there are no illegitimate children in China, abortion is not normally a means of avoiding unmarried motherhood.

Two children are the recommended limit—'two children just right, three too many, four a mistake', according to the slogan. During the mid-1960s, no ration ticket for clothing was issued to a third new-born baby and too-early marriages were not registered. This resulted in workers and employees with many children receiving fewer economic benefits, thus making people realize deeply that having too many children is 'not only a disadvantage to themselves but also an offense to the Government. It will be subject to criticism and considered as committing "an error". Therefore . . . practising birth control has become a social trend for everyone.'

* Based on *Population and Family Planning in the People's Republic of China*. The Victor-Bostrom Fund and The Population Crisis Committee, 1730 K Street, N.W., Washington, D.C. 20006, U.S.A.: 36 pp., illustr., Spring 1971.

The age of marriage used to be about fifteen or sixteen. During the 1950s the age was raised, until now, in the 1970s, twenty-five for women and thirty for men are the recommended minima. Although 'recommended' does not mean it is as yet a universal practice, still the fact that society now frowns on violations exerts pressure. There is less of a problem in influencing young couples than there still is with mothers-in-law and grandmothers-to-be who cling to the centuries-old traditions. By delaying marriage, and thus reproduction, a better balance can be established for the individual, who has more time to grow and mature, intellectually and physically.

Between 1948 and 1970, or a generation span, China's mainland population rose from an estimated 530 millions to some 800 millions. Balancing population and food creates a major problem in China that is far from being solved. 'About 11 per cent of the land is cropped, almost all in the habitable eastern third of the nation. The long history of population pressures and the nature of Chinese farming suggest that nearly all the land that can be cropped is in production. . . . Population projections for the 1970s indicate that China must increase its grain output by 50–60 million tons over the decade merely to maintain present *per capita* levels. Such an increase would require between 20 and 30 million tons of chemical fertilizer. More importantly, the increase would require major modernization efforts in various farm areas, including improved marketing facilities, transport, research, extension and cropping systems. Current policies clearly focus on the rural sector. There is promise of expanded rural education and some possibility of permitting migration to the cities, as well as of the development of rural industry and the introduction of urban amenities in the countryside.' As conditions become progressively tighter in China, there may be an acceleration of the social changes required to make birth control take massive hold more quickly.

According to the Chairman of the Victor-Bostrom Fund Committee in his letter terminating the pamphlet: 'World population increases by 2 per cent— or slightly more—each year. Seventy-five million people are added every twelve months. 200,000 more hungry mortals are pulling their chairs up for breakfast each and every day of the year. If nothing is done to slow this rate, the world will have more than seven [thousand million] people before the end of this century. Most of them will be living in abject poverty. But instead, if the world follows Premier Chou En-lai's example and sets a first goal at 1 per cent, to be reached by the year 2000, the world may indeed achieve this goal and insure better conditions for all. It certainly can be done, if, under inspired United Nations leadership, the whole world accepts this commitment. It requires a very simple, clear and understandable commitment by every country in the world—to cut its own rate of population growth in half before the year 2000. If on the average this is actually accomplished before century's end, we can all breathe easier, with a world growth-rate at 1 per cent. There would still be five to six [thousand millions] at century's end—and perhaps nine or ten [thousand millions] when the world hopefully would reach zero population growth thirty or forty or fifty years later. That should be enough for anyone, and should be the real long-term goal—not more than a ten [thousand million] world population. It still would stretch the world's resources to the very limit.

'Eventually, the earth and its resources being finite, the human race *must* limit its growth to zero, and adopt for the whole world Chairman Mao's concept for China of a stable replacement-only population. For the first step the world should aim at not over 1 per cent growth by the end of this century. If eventually, why not start now?'

From H. E. ESKANDAR FIROUZ, Undersecretary, Ministry of Agriculture and Natural Resources, and Director, Department of Environmental Conservation, 21 Shah Abbas Kabir Avenue, Tehran, Iran

COMBATING ENVIRONMENTAL DEGRADATION IN ARID ZONES

In relation to many environmental criteria, the increase in the populations of the nations of the Near East and of the rest of southwestern Asia is perhaps as critical as that of the more densely-populated countries of the world. Undoubtedly, one of the most destructive results of the burgeoning populations is the degradation of the arid zones and of their component ecosystems. In the past the alteration of a specific ecosystem might take millennia; today in certain areas the needs of a growing society produce radical transformations of the natural environment in a mere decade or less.

Arid by nature, enormous areas of the Near and Middle East progressively assume a more and more xeric appearance with the retrogression of plant life as a result of various human practices. Forest is transformed to steppe, steppe to semi-desert, and semi-desert ultimately to sterile wasteland that is virtually devoid of all vegetation. This tendency is not confined to the arid regions, but it is there that the problem is now assuming disastrous proportions: the prospect in the offing is an almost total loss of vegetation over wide areas. The question is not whether such a state, if matters are allowed to proceed unchecked, will come about, but merely how soon!

The mechanism of range-land destruction is well documented. As the range deteriorates, the herdsmen turn to more adaptable species of livestock; sheep are substituted for cattle, and then goats replace sheep more and more. The problem is often compounded by the persistent tendency to convert easily accessible parts of such areas to dry farming, notwithstanding the fact that these lands are invariably ill-suited or marginal for such purposes. Thus still less forage is left for the additional livestock now required to support a larger populace.

If the phenomenon were only dependent on livestock grazing, perhaps the law of diminishing returns would set a limit to the extent of retrogression: that is to say, at some point prior to complete vegetation destruction, grazing would prove uneconomic and thus be terminated. Unfortunately, this is generally not the case, for the desert is also mercilessly exploited as a source of fuel. Trees are cut, then shrubs, and finally perennial and annual forms of vegetation are also doomed. The death-knell is sounded with wind and water erosion, soil deflation, sandstorms, sand-dune accumulation, loss of wildlife, and climatic changes. It is only when villages are buried beneath the sands of the desert, when there is misery and suffering for man, that the phenomenon is understood and bewailed.

Any environmental degradation is undesirable, but the immediate and pressing issue here is to determine the minimum levels to which plant retro-gression could be allowed to proceed in arid zones, and to insure that such criteria of deterioration are not exceeded.

It is evident that the insufficiency of resource managers precludes the im-plementation of sound range-management practices throughout the region. Eventually, training programmes may provide personnel in adequate numbers to monitor these problems and to propose as well as enforce guide-lines. What is proposed in the meantime is that the respective governments undertake immediate and drastic action to halt, and hopefully reverse, these trends in the more endangered areas before the damage is irreversible.

Where forage production does not exceed certain levels, grazing or other exploitation of the vegetation is not economically productive and becomes, in fact, counter-productive. To disregard this fact will ultimately lead to national disaster. For once a given level of degradation is reached, attempts at restoration, if not wholly outside the realm of possibility, become prohibitively expensive.

Serious attention must evidently be given to demographic trends. The location of human settlements must be studied in depth and on a long-range basis with a view to limiting, if not relocating, villages and towns (particularly those with inadequate access to suitable fuel sources) in arid zones. Where plant production has fallen to unacceptable levels of denudation, or where climatic and edaphic factors support vegetation only on a marginal basis, governments should consider a total ban on vegetation exploitation. At the same time, the prospect of supplying desert residents with fuel sources, whether fossil fuels or hydroelectric power, should be seriously examined. Until alternative programmes are developed, various countries might con-sider the provision of energy sources at subsidized rates.

Such emergency measures should be enforced in order to buy time until comprehensive management plans can be implemented. If the action pro-posed appears drastic, failure to apply it might prove disastrous. Clearly there is no single solution to these grave and complex problems, and closing certain areas to population will increase the pressures elsewhere.

As an example of action, Iran has (by law) prohibited the cutting, etc., of all desert vegetation. However, enforcing this has, to date, been proble-matical in many areas. But in our 'Protected Regions' not only is this aspect rigorously enforced by strict wardening, but over large areas (totalling some-thing like four million hectares) of steppe and desert land in these regions grazing as well has been partially, and over some 70 per cent of the area totally, banned. As we have described and illustrated in *Biological Conservation* (Vol. **3**, No. 1, pp. 37–45, 1970), the resulting regeneration in these regions has been very encouraging. But in the long term it is most essential to tackle the problem of human population, which in Iran is increasing at the quite devastating rate of over 3 per cent per annum. Consequently, the Govern-ment has instituted a family planning service, which it is ardently hoped will in time lead to the rate of increase being reduced to 1 per cent.

17

THE BIOSPHERE TO COME

Keynote Paper

The Biosphere to Come

by

GERARDO BUDOWSKI

Of Caracas, Venezuela; formerly *Professor in the Inter-American Institute of Agricultural Sciences, Turrialba, Costa Rica, and Programme Specialist for Ecology and Conservation, UNESCO;* currently *Director-General, International Union for Conservation of Nature and Natural Resources, 1110 Morges, Switzerland*

PREAMBLE

Ecologists who have attempted in recent years to look into the crystal ball to find out what is likely to be the biosphere-to-come, will surely, sooner or later, have reached the conclusion that the future depends almost entirely on how man handles the biosphere within the coming decades. Such forecasting also involves a series of problems, such as the following:

(*a*) How can we circumscribe our vision to make it operational? Should a specific date be set, for instance the year 2000? Or should there be a continuous or periodic appraisal over a definite period of time, as obviously we cannot foresee indefinitely into the future?

(*b*) How far and how reliably can present trends be projected into the future? In this connection an evaluation should be made of the extent to which current trends will generate reactions by mankind, and thereby deflect some of the curves which we have drawn on the basis of past experiences. Some of these problems were admirably illustrated in a recent paper by Peccei (1971), who included part of the accompanying diagram (Fig. 1). This diagram, resulting from the use of computer simulation models, is one example of what has been obtained by the Massachusetts Institute of Technology team working under the direction of Professor Jay W. Forrester and aiming at studying the dynamic behaviour of interacting systems and how they would react to certain policy changes (C. L. Wilson, 1971).

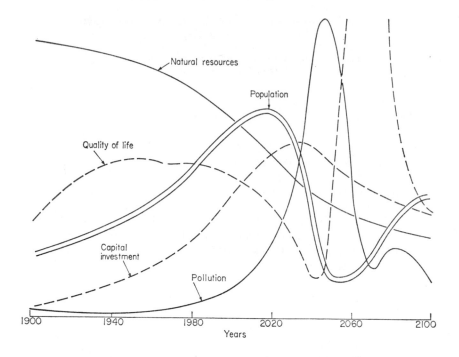

Fig. 1. Computer Simulation of Pollution Limit to World Growth.

Diagram showing trends during the period AD 1900 to 2100 of the world's natural resources, human population, quality of life, capital investment, and pollution. The simulation above shows what might happen if capital investment were increased now by 20 per cent in an effort to reverse a decline in the quality of life. The pollution crisis worsens when the upsurge of industrialization overtaxes the environment before a depletion of natural resources has a chance to depress industrialization. An apparently desirable change in policy has caused unexpected consequences. The quality of life continues to decline until rising pollution and other factors produce a drop in total population and a concomitant increase in the availability of goods and services. (After C. L. Wilson, 1971.)

For the present paper, the following criteria are used, though admittedly quite arbitrarily:

(1) The biosphere-to-come is set for our purposes as a relatively short period, up to around the year 2000, which has, among other advantages, the fact that it covers about one human generation. The biggest difficulty, it was felt, is to make predictions and even suggestions for attitudes whenever long-term bases are considered.

(2) The assumption is made that the present projections will necessarily be deflected, although no detailed attempt is made to prognosticate how much and in what direction they will be deflected, or to foretell in detail what new considerations are likely to become of primary importance in man's life.

Rather than quoting extensively from the literature and trying to analyse what others have said, particularly those who may consider that they qualify as prophets of the future, my purpose here is somehow to integrate the various thoughts that have been generated by the impact from reading—admittedly very incomplete—and by activities connected with my professional life. I am the first to admit that all this is necessarily subjective, biased, and possibly influenced by a heavy dose of conservation.*

THE BASIC PREMISE

It is assumed that man will always look for a 'better' life, although it is very much to be doubted that he will really achieve it, and at least it seems safe to conclude that a majority of his numbers will not. But working towards it is likely to remain the main motivation of individuals, families, and governments; it is a dominating factor in all human activities. The 'better' life is of course very difficult to define, as it means different things to different people. One may, however, venture to say that it corresponds to a definition based on relativity, such as: 'to have the feeling that one is better off today than yesterday, and the distinct hope of being still better off tomorrow.' This applies not only to individuals but equally to organizations, to governments, and even to the whole man–biosphere relationship.

The above criterion of a 'better' life may even serve as the basis for a definition of happiness for human beings; but however satisfying this may sound, it does not serve our purpose at all well when we think ahead of what is likely to be the biosphere-to-come. A definition more in accordance with ecological principles may be that a 'better life' for man involves a relationship between man and his environment which may be termed a dynamic balance—one that is mutually advantageous, and sufficiently flexible to allow progressive change. This would imply also keeping options open for the future, favouring diversity and, even more important, inducing in man the desire to enjoy and promote such diversity.

* At the 10th General Assembly of IUCN, held in New Delhi in November 1969, conservation was defined as 'management of the resources of the environment—air, water, soil, and living species including man—so as to achieve the highest sustainable quality of human life. Management in this context includes surveys, research, legislation, administration, preservation, and utilization, and implies education and training.'

Towards Establishing the Desirable Man–Biosphere Relationship

The above desiderata may be regarded as epitomizing some of the basic philosophical guidelines that have so often been advocated in recent publications. Indeed, I feel that man needs these guidelines very badly as a basis for his ethical conduct—rather than using precepts based on nationalistic, religious, or other beliefs derived at different times in history and which, with the passage of time and the development of new ways of life, need to be modified and adapted, often very painfully, in order to remain valid. But man's relation to the biosphere, we must admit, is not at present determined by an overall philosophy and desire to reach such a dynamic balance. Rather is it the outcome of successes and failures derived from past experiences and their related short-term projection into the future. The important difference, as many have pointed out, and notably Szent-Györgyi (1970), is that the past cannot be projected into the future, because the speed of change tends to accelerate exponentially, and critical thresholds are being reached and passed as the biosphere is finite. We see these thresholds in the daily manifestations of our life. If only the thresholds would behave like the bang of the sound barrier, their presence, whenever felt, would make the impact which we obviously need! Unfortunately, thresholds are insidious, and some of them are passed without much notice; or when we have become aware of their consequence, it may be too late. Let us not forget that the Torrey Canyon disaster did more to awaken environmental awareness than many much more important but less dramatic degradations of the environment. Yet, if valued objectively, the Torrey Canyon disaster was only a 'drop in the ocean'—sure enough, a big drop of oil, but still only a drop if weighed against the totality of degrading factors. Must we always wait until the water reaches our necks before we are so seriously alarmed that we take action?

There is no doubt that the whole present concern about environmental matters has its roots in a sudden awareness that growth and its manifestations cannot be projected *ad libitum*. Meanwhile it has become clear that, in order for civilization to continue progressively, growth must be carefully matched by the biosphere's capacity to support it.

The discovery of insidious changes and the impact of their speed, together with trespassings on critical thresholds and the consequent influence on man's life—these will be, I believe, the greatest modifying factors of the man–biosphere relationship in the years to come. Most significant and certainly most visible, will be the increased pressures of growing human populations, having ever-higher aspirations to the earth's resources; these are likely to produce catastrophic repercussions—the so-called ecocatastrophes. More than anything else, these considerations will influence decision-making in the future.

The Ideal and the 'Doom' Situations

Any analysis of the biosphere-to-come, based on some of the factors outlined above, implies considering two different approaches which we may label hopefully as extremes, and neither of which is at all likely to happen.

These are the 'ideal' and the 'doom' situations. The purpose of polarising towards these extremes is, of course, to help in facilitating some guesses as to what will seem most likely to be the future of the biosphere when projected along the line of reasoning that neither the ideal solution nor the worst doom is likely to take place. Man will certainly not meet correctly the challenge and reach the satisfying dynamic balance referred to above. On the other hand he will presumably—maybe it would be better to say 'hopefully'—avoid doom. For there need be no doubt that there will always be a reaction when the situation becomes unbearable, and attempts will be made to find some type of solution that will avoid the very worst outcome of any evident threat.

MAINTAINING A WELL-BALANCED BIOSPHERE
(Ideal Situation)

By realizing that the biosphere is a single super-ecosystem in which manipulation concerning one of the factors is apt to affect the whole system, we unavoidably reach the conclusion that global management, based on the best scientific evidence, emerges as a logical step. Most important as a basis of such management is knowledge of the thresholds which must not be crossed because of their having a point of no return.

These thresholds are best visualized today as physical factors, but they may well cover man's health in all its different implications. A simple example is afforded by the pollution of a lake through excessive organic matter. The lake has a certain capacity for absorption of increased organic matter, but beyond this capacity it may, and probably will, degrade more or less fatally. The whole biosphere can be viewed as a similar system but of course the processes in it are not often so simple. However, if the different interactions are well understood and a definite effort is made to keep the super-ecosystem in a healthy balance, an ideal situation may arise and be maintained. For this principle of health is not only true of the lake but also of the infinitely more complex biosphere. It can be reasoned that such an ideal situation will involve various premises.

The Need for Global Management on Scientific Bases

A concentrated approach by all people on earth to the problems of manipulation of the biosphere is agreed to as essential in our viewpoint of the biosphere. This implies, for instance, that beyond and above the approach that would favour each person or each country individually, there would be *global* or anyway *international* agreement as to how to handle the biosphere in all the manifold aspects—and needs for action—involved. It is important that the long-term basic ecological principles which govern natural interrelationships would be at the base of any type of management plan. Thus when it came to decision-making by a government, for example, as to how to handle or manage its part of the biosphere, and *before* thinking of short-term economic and social solutions—or, rather, compromises—for its people, the first consideration would be pursuit of those ecological relationships that would be the 'healthiest' for the biosphere itself, and, by implication, for all the biosphere's human inhabitants. On these bases would be elaborated secondarily the economic and social considerations that would benefit man directly. The obvious reasoning behind this distinction of levels is that it is impossible to achieve sustained and long-term benefits for man in any type of management of the biosphere unless such management is based on sound ecological principles.

Such reasoning obeys essentially Liebig's Law of the Minimum. For countless ages, as long as resources were plentiful and there was some 'new frontier' to conquer, it was particularly territorial ambitions, diseases, and social and economic factors, that dominated policies and decisions. These were the leading and often the limiting factors which, more than any others, determined the course of humanity.

In the ideal situation, the concept of an ecological balance, and the urgent need to consider ecological factors, has not only come to supersede but to influence decisively all other limiting factors.

Management of the biosphere to be successful needs to be based on thorough scientific knowledge—which at present is much too scanty and not universally available. Planning and the appropriate follow-up action are necessarily based on scientific facts, and this implies shunning those who spice their recommendations and plans with emotional overtones. In the ideal situation, it is inadmissible to allow 'eco-hysterics' to take over. It is therefore assumed that an intensive and global research programme regarding the functioning of the biosphere is undertaken, and that the main thresholds are already known. It can also be assumed that the broad aspects of harmonious relationships between people and resources are also known on the basis of both local and global studies, though priorities for further research will obviously need to be established.

One could describe a series of solutions that have been brought forward to reach this type of balance, and I know such have been illustrated in other papers. Among these, a change in technology implying recycling and better use—one which has aptly been called 'circular' as opposed to 'linear'—will undoubtedly be of paramount importance. The need to reach systems of utilization of natural resources that are as nearly 'closed' as possible, has been aptly described by many scientists including, notably, Dubos (1970) and Daly (1971). Such systems appear to be absolutely indispensable, and I for one have no doubt and agree with many outstanding economists and other speakers that the philosophy of continuous growth, which in some areas is really exponential, is not only outright dangerous, but will soon come to an end. It is incompatible with a well-balanced biosphere. In fact, there is no doubt that there can be no escape from a complete reorientation of our economic values as exemplified by such yardsticks as gross national income.

Altogether it appears to be essential that the use of scientific knowledge must become directed and applied in such ways that, more and more, considerations of global relationships will supersede regional and local ones. Global management, in order to be effective, demands that a sound policy be agreed upon by all countries, and that the proper legislation be enacted and enforced—which, obviously, in order to be successful, must be understood by a substantial majority of people.

Basic Ethics and Education for World Citizenship

Awareness of global relationship based on a combination of feelings such as the need for survival and the desire for a better life, will shape ethics involving a population number that will be in balance with resources throughout the world. The most salient feature of the ethics will be respect for, followed by admiration, enjoyment, and even promotion of, *diversity* throughout the world. A principle that is adopted universally will not necessarily make people similar wherever they live; rather will it have them enjoy the diversity that currently is found throughout the world. This concept should apply to the diversity found in the environment—particularly by preserving samples that are closest to its natural state—and should make it possible for all people to feel that they are the recipients of a world heritage which has been passed down through millions of years, and will continue to be passed down, in the form of landscapes, wild animals, and plants, for which man is merely the current, ephemeral guardian (Monod, 1970). Diversity here will not only act as a stabilizing ecological factor but it will also enrich the possibilities of human experience by providing the best possible choice of options for every individual.

Education programmes will have to achieve this impact and the population must become aware that a superior consideration to a strictly national aim is only reasonable—not merely for survival but also for achievement of the higher qualities of life. This last is a rather loose concept which has different meanings to different cultures, but to use one definition it implies 'the wants and desires as expressed by different human cultures for particular physical, chemical, and biological, features and arrangements within environments designed for work or play, for creative activities and leisurely repose . . .'. (UNESCO & FAO, 1968).

Global Administration and Politics

From a complex of national sovereignties of countries, as perhaps best illustrated by the functioning of our present United Nations system, there will be a healthy evolution—particularly within the UN system itself—of ever-closer coordination between governments towards the primary objective, namely, the sound management of the biosphere, including its improvement in some ways especially from man's viewpoint. This of course is not denying sovereignty but rather is placing superior interests above national considerations. It is almost like thinking that our planet is being invaded by extra-terrestial aggressive invaders and that all countries have rallied together to defend the world and themselves against the 'destroyer'. A situation very similar to this has indeed arisen, except of course that the destroyer is man himself—particularly that attitude of man which puts national rivalry and sectional interests above global considerations.

In this connection a new type of leader will doubtless emerge—one who will be imbued with an ecological point of view, appealing for global considerations and proposing solutions of environmental problems that are based on the best scientific information and foresight (T. W. Wilson, 1970).

The 'Doom' Situation

Man's present use and abuse of the biosphere, if projected into the future, will produce ever-increasing deterioration in the conditions of human life. Ever-increasing human populations and their technologies will proportionally strain the environment. Solutions, being mostly national or more locally based, will prove to be insufficient to cope with the situation. Countries which are better off will, for diverse reasons, tend to isolate themselves from the global need to manage the biosphere as one integral whole. Yet this will only generate resentment from the less-privileged countries whose aspirations have been rising. Nationalistic interests and policies will prevail over global appraisals of the situation, and endless disagreements will develop and expand. International cooperation will fail or will be slow to cope with the problems of managing the biosphere on a global basis, and indeed the very survival of human beings will ultimately be at stake. Chaos and conflicts resulting from widespread egoism and downright selfishness—the 'my life, my country first' attitude—will prevail. Insecurity, fear, and suspicion, will foster arms races, wars and, more than anything else, the overwhelming failure to think of long-term solutions as shown by a typical *'après moi le déluge'* attitude.

It is not really necessary to comment at length on the doom biosphere; it simply reflects man's inability to foresee and to forestall as has been so aptly noted by Dr Albert Schweitzer. It represents, really, the *pro tem.* triumph of the selfish man who puts his own interests or those of his limited supporters before those of humanity—before those of the biosphere as a whole.

One can only speculate that wars and the grimmest types of fighting for survival will result, and it is really impossible to foresee all the consequences. Several science-fiction books have dealt with this situation, and any one of them may prove perfectly right.

How to Influence the Likely Outcome

The greatest hope to find a path for the next thirty years that would bring us as close as possible to the ideal solution lies in the attitude of some present world leaders. With their basis of scientific facts and political courage—but also aware of the difficulties of changing the present world administrative patterns—they can suggest some of the ideal solutions and rally behind them the opinion of a substantial part of humanity. If only a sufficient number of decision-makers can shortly be persuaded to take necessary steps in this direction, then there will be definite hope.

But are we moving in this direction, and, if so, how swiftly? The question is wide open, and hopefully the United Nations Conference on the Human Environment, to be held in Stockholm in 1972, should provide sensible answers. While the gap to be crossed looks quite alarmingly wide, it is reassuring to note that, from among the many conferences and other meetings that are taking place throughout the world in preparation for this one in Stockholm in 1972, some enlightening declarations are being issued. One of the most powerful came in May 1971 from the then President of the UN

General Assembly, Ambassador Edvard Hambro of Norway, whose statement, here summarized, made it clear in what direction the UN is apparently moving (Hambro, 1971).

In his statement, Ambassador Hambro said that the adoption of the International Development Strategy by the UN General Assembly in the preceding October marked a new era in international cooperation. The objective of the strategy's measures was to promote sustained economic development in the third world. But, he added, the international community was now faced with another problem which must be speedily solved if efforts to promote development were not to be in vain: 'We must use all our strength and all our imagination to save the human environment.' There was no question of choosing between development and environment; the question was one of assuring progress and doing so in an improved environment. For this it would be necessary to retreat from the old concept of the necessity to 'conquer' nature and to replace it with the concept of 'harmonious collaboration' with the forces of nature. The problems of the environment were international and universal. For the environment ignores political sovereignty, while the effects of pollution respect no national frontiers. Mr Hambro also stated that the idea of absolute national independence was obsolete: 'Modern international law might be called a law of coexistence and must be transformed into a law of cooperation.'

CONCLUSION

In conclusion, it is clear that actions must be taken *now* in order to influence the shape of the biosphere in the year 2000, and especially to reverse some of the present unfavourable trends. Accordingly the following suggestions are made as to indispensable ingredients which need urgent consideration:

(1) A philosophy and a code of ethics as to the relation between man and his environment is urgently needed and must be 'sold' to all humanity. It should include such premises as looking at the biosphere as one unit, striving to preserve and enhance diversity, managing the biosphere for the very best long-term interests of humanity, and preserving all the possible options for future interventions. It is clear that the education and communication systems must be geared to get the message through.
(2) It is imperative to set up the necessary world-wide structures that would bring the philosophical concept of global management into practice.
(3) It is equally imperative to have an up-to-date research and appraisal system, so that the biosphere can at all times be diagnosed as to its state of health. Particularly important is to have the best possible knowledge of the thresholds which are points of no return, and to watch carefully, and to act expeditiously against, any at all close approach to any of them.

We all understand, of course, how difficult it is to get this message through.

Having myself worked almost all my life in the developing countries of Latin America, I am acutely aware how difficult it will be for this philosophy to be fully grasped by the large masses of hungry and illiterate rural populations; but we have no choice. Fortunately we can place many of our hopes in the amazing receptivity found in youth throughout the world. However, it is distressing to see that this idealism, as well as the energy displayed by youth, is not adapted or channeled towards the 'right kind of revolution'.

While it is quite clear that in many parts of the world there is certainly room for a social revolution to bring basic rights and dignity to large masses of populations, there is a need for a much more comprehensive revolution—one with everlasting consequences involving the reaching of a harmonious balance between man and his environment. Certainly, it implies social equality as far as we can have it; but it needs to bring much more than that. Theoretical principles and their code of ethics need to be quite different from anything we have had so far. The two revolutions should not be confused. Social equality can be, and already has been, achieved in many countries; but the balance between man and his environment should be global, and should become a permanent *raison d'être*, a *Leitmotif*, of our future activities. In fact there is no doubt that a sound conservation programme of the biosphere is perfectly compatible, even desirable, in promoting 'development' in pursuit of a better life.

It is remarkable that among those who have tried in recent years to attempt to foresee the likely shape of the biosphere-to-come, the appraisal of the present trends always made it clear how urgent it was to take action now. The biosphere-to-come will without doubt be decisively influenced by our attitudes and actions in the next ten years or so.

REFERENCES

DALY, Herman E. (1971). National Economy: how high is up? *Consulting Engineer* (March), pp. 107–11.

DUBOS, René, (1970). *Reason Awake; Science for Man*. Columbia University Press, New York & London: 280 pp.

HAMBRO, Edvard (1971). Statement to annual UN Conference of Non-Governmental Organizations, United Nations, New York: 26 May 1971. UN Press release PI/125, New York, 2 pp. (mimeographed).

MONOD, Th. (1970). Protection et conservation: pourquoi? *International Conference on Rational Utilizationand Conservation of Nature*, Tananarive, Madagascar, 8 pp. (mimeographed). (Proceedings to be published by IUCN, 1110 Morges, Switzerland.)

PECCEI, Aurelio (1971). How to survive on the planet earth. *Special SUCCESSO Report*, Rome, February, pp. 129–32, 134, 136–8, illustr.

SZENT-GYÖRGYI, Albert (1970). *The Crazy Ape*. Philosophical Library, New York: 93 pp.

WILSON, Carroll L. (1971). Environment: preparing for the crunch. *Saturday Review* (23 January), pp. 42–3, 93.

WILSON, Thomas W., Jr (1970). *The Environment: Too Small A View*. Occasional Paper, The Aspen Institute for Humanistic Studies, Aspen, Colorado: 32 pp.

UNESCO & FAO (1968). *Conservation and Rational Use of the Environment*. Report submitted by UNESCO and FAO to ECOSOC, E/4458, 12 March 1968, pp. 103–4 (mimeographed).

DISCUSSION

Cain (Chairman)

From Dr Budowski's former paper which was distributed, there were some conclusions which I think we might comment on before taking up questions that are direct. We do not, as Budowski did not, attempt to forecast for you in any detail. If one reads the newspapers, listens to radio and television, reads books, he knows that a great many data have been presented about the condition, and the rate of change of the component conditions, of the earth. You can make your own guess as to how long some of these changes can go forward, though that's really not the point. We can, however, be sure that next year will be less pleasing to man than this year with respect to what's wrong with our environment—unless certain new changes are made which will slow, stop, and deflect, the kinds of changes that we have experienced in recent history.

Dr Budowski's first concluding point was that we must have a philosophy and a code of ethics. We must have mores for our guidance, and I think it is implicit also that we must have regulations and laws. Let me suggest that we will be fortunate if the decade of the 1970s comes to be remembered as a decade of environmental law. It is beginning to show already. Law can be and must become operative at the municipal or other levels of local government, provincial or state levels, national levels, regional levels, and international levels, as fast as possible. I said both regulations and laws because there are possible regulations under administrative conditions which do not have the force of law but are nevertheless effective. In private as well as public enterprise, there are possibilities of managerial decisions which could be made today.

The speaker's second point was that we must have a system of appraisal. We now have one such system to which every nation, East or West, rich or poor, is devoted, and on which the United Nations Economic and Social Council reports annually for every country. This is the gross national product (GNP) divided on a *per caput* basis. Those of us who are not quite young probably realize that gross national product is a new concept: it was only developed about the time of World War II and yet we have become slaves of it. As nations, we look forward to quarterly and annual reports—just as private enterprises look forward to their reports to see what is happening to their economy. We have become quite used to aggregating the total goods and services—our transactions of this kind that can be so measured.

The gross national product is an entirely false and hopeless basis for the philosophy of operating a government for the people or by the people in regard to social and environmental conditions. What we need has been suggested before, a gross environmental product (GEP). We need the same diligency and assiduous approach to measuring the conditions of the environment as we use for business. We enter this new period of history without the necessary data, and so have no baseline. But we could start now doing a better job, so that next year we would know whether we are better off or worse off in all of the aspects of the environment that can be analysed.

More importantly than GNP and GEP, we need a gross social product (GSP). The US Public Health Service recently put forward a brochure describing a plan for measuring the gross social product in the United States—primarily with respect to health services, as one would expect. This is grand. Also, the Economic and Social Council adds up many of the physical features that are accountable about health services—how many hospital beds there are for 100,000 people, etc. The gross social product goes far back to the UN bill of human rights. Let us find out how to gather such data and how to keep track of the changes from year to year.

Dr Budowski had a concluding remark in which he referred to the urgency of environmental improvement. I would like to tie this sense of urgency together with what I said about administrative, regulatory, and legal, enforcements of environmental standards, because I believe it is necessary for the more informed people to act for the uninformed and for the less-informed: to act, if you will, to curb the selfish, the unconcerned, the venal. For those who do not understand evidence, scientific or otherwise, are in no position to do anything but mouth defences for their suppositions without substantiations. This may sound authoritarian, but there is no escape from law if society is to function. We know this because it permeates all of history. So put the mores together, draw our conclusions, and add law—which is tacit —and perhaps we can make a better world.

Allow me to conclude with an aside to the young people speaking at this Conference who are concerned and frightened and angered—they have every reason to be. Still, I don't know a single person from the United States or in any other country, now at this meeting, who couldn't do a better job at damning the United States or any capitalist country than you young people have done. We've got it coming to us, but there is no solution in grousing; we must find the means of action. I cannot expect you to be patient with the people who are older than you and who have left you a helluva problem to solve, but would note that you cannot solve it by polemics.

Caldwell

This is a plea for more realistic economics: we are in great need of it! I think there's nothing more misleading than the concept of gross national product which we've just had analysed for us unless it is the concept of standard of living. Now I would suggest that this latter term really ought to have more sophisticated treatment than it has had in the hands of social scientists; I feel that among other things we ought to distinguish between what I would call the public standard of living—based on the amenities in life such as parks, streets, forests, public transportation, health services, etc., which is one thing, and the private individual standard of living, which is quite another. In many ways I think the highest public standard of living in the world today, certainly on a *per caput* basis, is enjoyed in northwestern Europe—more specifically in the Scandinavian countries, including Finland. Here is the highest standard of living if you want to look at it from the point of view of public amenities; for I'm not sure that having three television sets necessarily adds to the quality of life or signifies a higher standard of living except in strictly materialistic terms.

Now the future meaning of this concept of standard of living, it seems to me, ought to be valid for the world as a whole, and I think that's what some of the younger people here in Finland have been suggesting to us in their apprehension that, in the development of international institutions and programmes for the environment, we shall get what has been foisted upon the world, namely a set of values and concepts that are peculiar to the technologically advanced countries. But I think it's important to realize that a standard of living is not just a standard of material wealth, but something which includes the kinds of knowledge, the kinds of services, the kinds of capabilities, that a society has. For no matter how effectively you distribute the world's resources, or the world's wealth, something else is required to give you adequate dental care, to provide good medical services, or to provide good mechanics.

So I believe we need to re-think this concept of standard of living—to look at the conditions which prevail and not merely at economic statistics—and that, as the developing countries come to a more highly developed and more adequate kind of economy than they have at present, the technologically more advanced countries should be able to give improved pointers with respect to the environmental future. This would be something far more rewarding in terms of satisfying human needs and values through *ad hoc* employment to clean up our habitat rather than to have the redundancies that we now get in many of the technologically advanced countries, or than the abstractions which we get in the measurements of the economists— which really describe economic processes and don't have a great deal to do with the real-life experience of people.

Cain (Chairman)

I think Professor Caldwell is correct; for most people, standard of living currently means levels of consumption.

Hadač

I would like to comment on this graph [a prototype of Fig. 1]. I think it's quite illogical to have the population going down but pollution going up; surely, if you diminish population, then from there on the pollution will start to diminish. So I think this part is somewhat suspect, shall we say?

As to the natural resources going slowly [in the prototype] down, I think they are often dependent on the technology of how we get them—isn't that right? So, if we improve our technology, at least some of our resources will be more available than they are now. So I think the last part of the graph [in the prototype going up to AD 2060 only], which is very pessimistic, may also not be right.

> [Thereafter a number of people were heard talking at once, with the speaker protesting from the platform, until the Chairman called for order.]

Udall

In government I remember my science people telling me that 'technology will open the door, we must process more and more.' But now we find, of course, that people take larger and larger amounts of energy to achieve this, and so go back to the sources that Dr Brower discussed, though often without due concern for the pollution effects that any energy-production system engenders.

Mellanby

Just very briefly: I think that this [graph] is stimulating and gives us ideas, but surely Dr Budowski doesn't really mean it to be any more than this! Yet there seems to be an assumption that, as this was done in a computer, we should be impressed that it really means something. Now this is simply nonsense for the data taken up over the year 1970, which we know—at least without clarification of what is meant for example by natural resources. Thus look at the line [in prototype of Fig. 1] representing natural resources; we have been talking of how the world has used as much petrol in recent years as ever before, so this curve should obviously be much steeper around the present time if it refers to such resources, as we are told it does, and if this one is wrong, then anything may have gone to the computer, and I suggest that it would really be much better to suppress the drawings altogether.

Budowski

I must answer this: the curve for natural resources is a general one, but probably should be steeper [*see* the final version of Fig. 1].

Goldman

[There was an article in *The Observer* last Sunday which explained this graph of Professor Forrester of MIT. Actually, several variations were plotted, of which *The Observer* gave two. The reason why pollution continues to go up in this graph even after population starts to go down drastically, is that the decision has been made to preserve natural resources and this means using more synthetics. Therefore we can see why pollution goes up without great difficulty. The question is, why should the population go down, and the explanation in *The Observer* was that the population would go down because they would be killed off by the pollution, whereas in the following stage population would go up again, as some of the Malthusian forces would be relaxed.]

Fosberg

I would like to support Professor Hadač's suggestion that the reason why natural resources go down as slowly as they do on the [prototype] chart is because of the increasing technology.

[Someone in the audience: 'That's the explanation.']

Budowski

That was part of the explanation, but I would like to comment that the graph is drawn exactly as it was published, with each one of those curves projected by the computer on changing different possibilities. This is only one of the many graphs which this computer produced by changing different projections. I would like to comment also regarding this projection of pollution that even when men pollute today, the effects of this pollution may go on for many years—which is why, even if man goes down in numbers, the amount of pollution still goes up for some time.

In fairness I should emphasize that this work was done as an exercise and has been included here to indicate how one centre with many workers having an input to it is dealing with this idea. I do not claim to back it, but merely bring it forward as an example of what is being done today in specialized centres which try to foresee what may happen to the biosphere. Actually, it is clear from this and other discussions that we don't know ourselves in what direction we are going.

Baer

Can I just add one point which is rather paradoxical? As capital investment goes up, the quality of life comes down. There is no common sense in this.

Goldman

I'd like to respond to some of the suggestions that have been posed about what should be done in the sense of what hasn't been done—specifically to some of the comments that were made earlier this afternoon. For the Americans, as has been indicated, the criticism we have been receiving is not new and nor is it necessarily wrong. But while I, too, lament the failure to find a solution, I think the explanation for this failure is not that it is due to some conspiracy by the exploiters, but because of the inherent difficulties of finding a solution no matter who looks for it. And I fear that the difficulty with the attempted solutions of the radicals here—and we have more extreme ones in the United States than you have in Finland—is that they don't do much to improve the situation. Indeed as one of the speakers said, some of the analyses he is making and solutions he is advocating are 'very primitive', and I would really urge that such people try to refine their solutions or suggested solutions, and if possible carry them through to a logical conclusion. Personally, I would try to do that if I could.

It's true that the American consumer imposes an undue burden on the world's resources and biosphere. We are all aware of that, and certainly haven't had to wait until today to hear it. Indeed that is why we in the United States are so firm in our advocacy of birth control, and were the ones who led in the discovery of the pill. Nor are we saying that it should only be used elsewhere: we are employing it very widely ourselves, despite some questions about its medical safety.

Now while it's true that we lead in consumption, we are trying to take some corrective steps, and that's one of the reasons why we rejected SSTs; it's also why we considered it so important to do so. But there are countries that are poorer than we are which haven't done that, so even if the United States should disappear from the earth, I'm not sure where that would leave the rest of the world. And even if capitalism should disappear from the face of the earth, we'd still have the SSTs, and consumption rates would presumably continue to go up annually by 5 or more per cent, as they are doing now in some countries of the world. The United States has not seen rates of growth of 5 per cent or more in its gross national product since the early 1960s, yet proportionately other countries are doing their best to catch up.

There is a tendency for us in the United States to blame industry, for industry to blame the state, for the state to blame the Federal Government, for the Federal Government to blame the cities, and for everybody to blame everybody else but nobody to accept responsibility. This includes the consumer who wants his two cars, his three television sets, and his two country homes. But just as there is this tendency to 'pass the buck' within a country, so is there a tendency to pass the buck to economic systems other than our own. I think what we have to recognize is that we are all in this together, radicals and conservatives, communists and capitalists, east and west, north and south.

To examine the radical proposals, let's assume that we have a revolution and turn over control of the resources of the exploited nations exclusively to the exploited nations themselves—which personally I think might be a very good idea. Now let's ask what would happen then? I'm seriously afraid that there would be even faster exploitation of the world's resources, not necessarily by the capitalists, but by the people of the developing countries. In fact one of the underlying currents in this Conference is the fear that next year in Stockholm the underdeveloped countries are going to view all the discussions on environmental control as nothing but a ploy to hold them in an impoverished state. And I'm worried that in fact they will respond that way.

It's important to recognize that the developing countries want to produce their ore, they want to exploit their oil (even if maybe they don't want it to be owned by the United States or other 'western' countries, though that's another issue). The important thing is that they want to become developed nations and develop their heavy industry. Any attempt to impose environmental control is likely to be rejected by them—if only because this, too, will be viewed as a ploy to make their goods more expensive. If they are forced to install pollution control equipment, they will lose the advantage which they currently have which comes from using cheap labour, and also from avoiding the expense of controls that we now impose in our own country. I'm not saying there is a solution to this dilemma, and I'm not saying that one should tell the exploited countries that they must buy such equipment; what I am saying is that if they do gain control over their own resources, we are going to see that this will be no solution to the problem of pollution. In fact, things will probably get worse.

The proletariat of my country, and I'm sure in your country, want their two cars, or anyway a car. This is happening now in the Soviet Union, where they want their television sets, and want to improve their standard of living, which is surely as it should be. But the question I ask is what is this going to do to the environment? Now let's assume that there is a redistribution of wealth, which again is one of the proposals we have heard. I don't see how this would solve the problem for the environment, because if you take my second car and give it to somebody who hasn't got a car, you are still going to produce as many cars as you are doing now, and will probably use them more. Presumably such a political revolution would solve some psychological need that many of us have, but it wouldn't do much for the environment, which after all is what we are talking about, and what is basically most important of all. Really what I'm saying is that if we apply such reasoning to its logical extreme, we will probably end up doing exactly what we were doing before.

The only way to solve many of our pollution problems before population control becomes effective will, I fear, be through reverting to some of the discussions we've been having about the gross national product, and to adopt some of the economic solutions which have been suggested, so that the prices of goods will reflect the damage that is done to the environment in their production. This would mean pricing them high. However, I'm not sure that under a socialist society it would be politically and ideologically possible to impose an added value on these goods. Yet not to do so would probably have the opposite effect to that desired, as in the case of free water. For when anything is free, we are apt to use it to excess and run the risk of exhaustion. So while I'd like to confess my own guilt for not finding a solution, I really fear that those who want to have structural changes will find that, if indeed they get their way, the environmental conditions will not improve but more likely worsen.

Siirilä

I want to make only a brief comment on the definitions of the concepts that were used earlier in this discussion, such as standard of living and gross national product. I think that it's very important to take into consideration how, for instance, income or housing or whatever you want to use is distributed: you have not allowed for how equally things are distributed among people, for instance in the United States and also in Finland, have you? When a few people have very large incomes and good housing but the majority live in very bad conditions, to average matters doesn't tell us very much— especially in comparison with socialist countries in which for instance we are assured there is decent housing for everybody, and also a more equitable distribution of income. So I feel these distribution factors are important in making comparisons between the standards of living in different countries.

Fosberg

I'm not an economist, God forbid, but I think perhaps I've discovered a use for this gross national product concept. We've been objecting to it because it includes bad activities as well as good: for even tearing something down increases the gross national product. Perhaps we could use this GNP as a measure of probable or potential environmental degradation. It would not be quantitatively exact, but then economic measurements and their interpretations seldom are. Clearly, countries will have to desist from worshipping this empty idol if we are to have a desirable biosphere in years to come.

> [The representatives of student organizations who spoke on this and earlier occasions did not appear to be actual students and when a chairman asked the youngest-looking how old he was, he replied 'thirty-five years'.]

18

EDUCATION, LEGISLATION, DECLARATION

The above seventeen sections corresponding to sessions of the Conference, headed by keynote papers and terminated by detailed discussions with or without contributed addenda, have covered, so far as proved practicable in the time and space allowed, most of what seemed to the Conference's International Steering Committee to be the really pertinent topics concerning Environmental Future. But there are others—particularly human population, environmental education, and suitable legislation together with its enforcement. The first of these, including the mounting effects of demographic pressures, seemed to be always with us, being referred to in almost all of the papers and coming out in the discussions, etc., on numerous occasions—particularly in sessions 1, 2 (Addenda), 3, 5, 12, 13, and 16 (including Addenda). Indeed it could be said with basic truth that 'human population is what it is all about'.

Concerning environmental education we had a contributed paper which was circulated (see 3, pp. 98–9) and, after extension, is published next below—followed by a paper on documentation, which is so necessary for effective research and will be so important to the consultative and advisory services that one can foresee developing in the future. The vital need of more and better education in ecological matters pertaining to the human environment was also an underlying theme that emerged on numerous occasions and was the subject of 'interventions' by Dr Stenius in session 13 (p. 467) and by Dr Miller in sessions 14 (p. 503) and 15 (pp. 537–8). Much the same could be said of research, though there seems less need to treat this topic separately, and indeed some question as to whether it is treatable separately.

On legislation and its necessary enforcement, we have two contributed papers which are published below. Around the second of these and some other submissions we held an evening 'rump session' under the *de facto* chairmanship of Mr Udall, who himself dealt with some international aspects of environmental law in his paper (*see*, especially, pp. 434–5), as did Professor Caldwell in his (pp. 557–8). A brief résumé of this 'rump session' is given on pp. 628–9, as an addendum to this second paper on legal aspects.

As regards a 'declaration' embodying the main feelings and conclusions of the Conference, the diverse but strong Resolutions Committee appointed at the initial session received numerous draft resolutions, etc. (some of which are mentioned in the published discussions), which they incorporated in a document that was considered in detail at the final plenary session on the morning of 3 July under the chairmanship of Professor Baer. On this occasion it was decided that, in deference particularly to the United Nations, this document would merely be called a 'Statement' and circulated after due amendment. The Statement is published near the end of this final section (pp. 631–6), followed only by some terminal notes and an 'Anti-pollution Ballad' which was sung lustily on a memorable night-time cruise on the main Jyväskylä lake's ancient S.S. *Suomi*.

Achieving Environmental Quality Through Education*

by

JAN ČEŘOVSKÝ

*Education Executive Officer,
International Union for Conservation of Nature
and Natural Resources (IUCN), 1110 Morges, Switzerland*

INTRODUCTION

It is beyond any doubt that concern for the quality of the environment, first voiced by scientists, is now really becoming a matter of interest to more and more people in all segments of society, and in more and more countries throughout the world. During the past few years a considerable degree of awareness of environmental problems has spread widely among the general public, awakening ever-increasing interest in the solution of these problems. This awareness and interest is, however, by no means sufficient, even though it is the basic prerequisite in the contemporary striving after environmental quality.

In many countries of the world, the developed ones particularly, groups of specialists of various professions, of ordinary citizens, and—which is the most encouraging feature of all—of young people, are being formed in order to get suitably involved in environmental issues. 'Environmental action' is their slogan in this recent period of ecological awakening which is to be observed in an increasing range and number of countries and also at the international level.

Another term has been introduced, namely 'environmental revolution', of which Nicholson (1970) wrote: 'The environmental revolution, amid which we live, has a double face. It can be seen as a man-made change, sudden and world-wide, in our natural environment. It can equally be regarded in the light of a transformation in our attitude to that environment.'

The 'first face' of Nicholson's environmental revolution is a fact. The 'second face'—a revolutionary change of attitude—is badly needed. Attitude is the key word: for the question can still be posed as to whether the very

* Based on an intervention paper circulated at the International Conference on Environmental Future, Finland, 29 June 1971, drafted after detailed discussions with the Chairman of IUCN's Commission on Education, Professor L. K. Shaposhnikov.

natural feature and tendency of man as a biological species is not just a mainly careless, hostile exploitative attitude towards his natural environment. This would mean in the end a very real danger that man could be destroyed by his own development of his 'civilization'. But when we talk thus about the environment (which must be someone's environment), we are already displaying a basically man-centred approach, because it is man who is both the biggest danger and himself in danger. As for man's relation to nature, we have tacitly assumed a special position for man as a human being.

The environmental revolution, which we need, is a revolution of attitudes. There exist conflicts between rational, ecological management of the environment, and the prevailing economic systems and structures. The natural environment functions according to natural laws, of which even man is extremely limited in his ability to change the basic substance. Thus man must study them and manage the environment in accordance with them, for he himself as a biological species is subservient to them. Economic and social laws were and are created by man and his society and, as such, reflect man's attitudes; but natural laws are otherwise. Our only hope is that the human element of the human being will become strong enough to overcome the spontaneous tendency towards self-destruction through wrong use and management of the environment that is regarded by some as a rather natural corollary of development.

EDUCATION THE KEY

The whole of human population—or at least its preponderance—has to become concerned about the environment in the sense of actively cooperating in its conservation and proper management. But constructive attitudes towards the environment, in both the philosophical and the pragmatic senses, have not yet become an ingredient of everybody's thinking and acting. Here we have to turn to education for solutions (Čeřovský, 1971a).

As Brennan (1970) pointed out, when writing about the US scale of operations, the existing educational systems and prevailing programmes do not offer much along environmental lines, and it seems that education is still not prepared to offer the real solution. This, unfortunately, may be said generally—indeed with global validity. On the other hand it can be stated unequivocally that considerable efforts have been developed in recent years in the field of environmental education, and may be confidently expected to expand.

The UNESCO–IUCN–Foresta Institute international working meeting on 'Environmental Education in the School Curriculum', held in Nevada in 1970, suggested and approved the following definition:

> *Environmental education* is the process of recognizing values and clarifying concepts in order to develop the skills and attitudes that are necessary to understand and appreciate the interrelations among man, his culture, and his biophysical surroundings. Environmental education also entails practice in decision-making, and the self-formulation of a code of behaviour about issues concerning environmental quality (IUCN, 1970).

The first phase of environmental education involves development of understanding: how the environment functions, how it is interrelated with man, how man affects his environment, and what the consequences of man's actions really are. The second phase is the development of attitudes—especially attitudes of responsibility for the environment—which are also often called conservation 'ethics' or 'morality' (e.g. Budowski, 1971). Whereas the first phase interprets knowledge, the second provides guidelines for action; furthermore, seeking after man's personal fulfilment in 'partnership with nature through and with natural forces' (UNESCO, 1969) is an important objective, as we do not want only to use the environment wisely, but also to enjoy it.

Returning to the matter of attitudes in teaching man how to behave, this is by no means an easy goal to achieve. It certainly imposes limits on uncontrolled actions affecting the environment, requires that man should show self-control, and presupposes recognition that everyone shares in responsibility for the quality of the environment—this share, of course, being by no means equal for everyone. To express the prevailing situation in rather trivial terms, it is still much more comfortable for too many people to believe that the solutions to environmental problems lie far beyond the sphere of their individual influence.

Different Levels Required

All citizens of space-ship earth should be exposed to a continuous and sustained programme and process of environmental education. In accordance with the different shares of responsibility of different groups of people concerning the quality of the environment, an interpretation in terms of possible levels and purposes is necessary.

Environmental education is an essential part of a well-integrated scientific and liberal education of children and young people. Everybody agrees with the importance of both physical and mental hygiene of people as individuals, and, surely, that this subject should be (as it actually is) given an important place in education. Environmental conservation is an environmental hygiene for society, and as such must surely have its place in education.

Specialists of different professions dealing with management of the environment must be given sound knowledge concerning the environmental impact of their special field of competence during their pre-service as well as inservice training.

Adults among the broad general public have to be fed with information, which of course must be scientifically based and correct, to enable them to develop criteria by which they can judge policies and practices affecting their environment and act accordingly. It should be stressed that this is also important for the proper and effective education of their children.

Young people themselves spontaneously desire to get actively involved in the study and in the solution of environmental issues. This must be encouraged and further developed. Through the direct involvement of young people in the political, social, and economic, aspects of environmental problems, the changes of human attitudes that are necessary to achieve a rapid improvement in the condition of the environment can be accelerated—particularly when taking into account the well-known enthusiasm of young people, and their readiness to strive for improvement of human life on the earth.

Changed Approach Important

When observing the increasing interest in environmental matters in many countries, we notice that the background is very often a strongly emotional one. The emotional approach is largely good and has to be used, but surely is not enough without the background of solid knowledge! In most countries of the world, people working in education—particularly in formal school education—oppose the introduction of new materials into the existing programmes, curricula, and syllabi, pointing out, quite correctly, the general overloading that exists already. But environmental education does not mean so much a real overburdening with completely new material as a revision of approach in presenting the material that is already included in educational programmes.

The kind of presentation should be an ecological approach in following the problems of change in the human environment and the techniques for its design and management. This chiefly involves changing the manner of application of the knowledge available concerning matters already included in educational programmes, which at present is not dealt with sufficiently from the point of view of the relationship between man and his environment. For the present inadequate application of the available knowledge to the promotion of environmental education, so that the given education is brought closer and closer to real life and its actual needs, is one of the striking inadequacies in our present system (*cf.* Pritchard, 1968).

Environmental education is needed as something to be properly integrated within general educational systems—perhaps not so much as a subject of direct instruction, at least in the lower grades, as in the form of an environmentally orientated approach in interpreting the materials and knowledge involved, and so providing education in the wider sense of the word.

The above-mentioned principle nowadays leads the specialist dealing with environmental education to one of two extreme positions regarding formal, obligatory education in particular. One, especially developing in North America, finds the coverage of environmental education so broad that it comes to the thesis expressed by Terry (1971) 'that all education is environmental education'. The other requires, and in some places actually effects, the introduction of environmental education (eventually under different names) as a special, separate subject. The argument mostly used for the second trend is that the integrated and multi- and interdisciplinary approach is finally becoming such a general and even vague one that environmental education along those lines is not effective enough or, even, at all.

My opinion is that, in the lower grades of obligatory schools, environmental education should be elaborated throughout the whole curriculum and in as many subjects as possible. It should not be a matter of one subject only, nor should it be separated as a special subject of instruction. Nevertheless, it is fully appropriate that science (particularly biology and geography) teaching, to which still in many countries of the world a fragmentary environmental (or, rather, conservational) education remains limited, should keep a key position in this respect (Čeřovský, 1970).

Introducing Comprehensive Programmes

According to its various levels and purposes, introducing environmental education involves particularly (*cf.* Čeřovský, 1971*b*):

(*a*) Appropriate education at pre-school level, i.e. at a child's most formative age; this includes kindergartens as potentially very effective establishments, education by parents (in close relation with out-of-school education and information for adults), and, eventually, very special mass-media—particularly in highly-developed countries;

(*b*) Teaching environmental conservation in primary and secondary schools, which involves in this context a profound revision and innovation of school curricula, textbooks, teacher-guides, teaching aides, study facilities (outdoor areas), and adequate teacher training —the last being one of the key components of environmental education in general, requiring special environmental courses and programmes of studies in both pre- and in-service teacher training;

(*c*) Teaching and training professionals in high schools and at the university level, where special subjects and courses are to be introduced, and special chairs, departments, and institutes, are to be established; here we can distinguish two, or eventually three, main types of studies: (i) highly specialized training of environmental specialists ('generalists'), (ii) informative synthetic courses for all other professionals prepared through higher education, with a special emphasis on the specific relations between the respective profession and environment, and (iii) the latter aspect eventually being elaborated in special courses, if necessary; these could involve postgraduate long- and also short-term programmes of studies that had already proved to be effective particularly in solving the need for appropriate education as urgently as possible;

(*d*) Education through interesting programmes within the activities of out-of-school organizations and establishments for children and young people, both specialized (conservation and nature-study groups and centres) and general (tourists, boy-scouts, young pioneers, students, etc.). We see actually that notable, effective programmes were started in this sector of education before formal education even became interested in getting involved, while through their unique position (interesting activities in leisure time, better opportunities for outdoor work and studies, etc.) they always will be a very important component in a manner that should be complementary to school education;

(*e*) Creation of new, and development of existing, voluntary organizations and citizens' groups, with spreading of solid, scientifically correct information and its translation into direct action—which

E.F.—20**

should involve all good citizens and not merely those whose scope is primarily concerned with environment, conservation, nature study, etc.;

(*f*) Full environmental use of various cultural, social, sports, and other establishments (clubs, museums, houses of children and youth, outdoor centres, etc.), providing opportunities for both youngsters and adults, and helping them, while being educated, to spend their leisure time efficiently and constructively;

(*g*) Use and further development of special methods and forms of environmental education—such as competitions, nature trails, visitors' centres in national parks and other protected areas, etc.; and

(*h*) Dissemination of information widely among the general public— particularly through the use of mass-media.

A remaining problem of environmental education is the question of local, national, regional, and global, scopes and approaches. It is, in my view, not a question of choosing an alternative but of finding the right proportions. A conscious and constructive patriotism, emphasizing not vague symbols but a concrete appreciation of environment—the natural environment in the first place—is a very important basis in environmental education. On this should be built nowadays a necessary awareness of the global environment and its problems—the problems of our one biosphere with its intricate, subtle, and highly complex, interrelations. In this context environmental education is an international matter. On the other hand, regional, national, and even local, approaches are very important in the application of the generally globally valid principles, because of the relevant diversity of cultural and socio-economic backgrounds.

Fortunately, in the past few years, many of the efforts that are briefly outlined above have already been launched or prepared. But the size of the movement and the speed at which it is happening are still quite alarmingly limited.

Environmental education is an urgent challenge to all educators who wish seriously to execute this mission under the scientific guidance of environmental and conservation specialists. Proper understanding of, and conscious cooperation in, environmental issues, which in fact require really revolutionary changes in people's thinking and behaviour, are essential for the quality of the environment in which we all are, and future generations always will be, forced to live. This is what environmental education is aiming at as its supreme goal.

References

Brennan, Matthew J. (1970). Making tomorrow now: Building a qualitative environment for all children. Reprint from *Childhood Education*, pp. 2–5, October 1970 (Association for Childhood Education International, Washington, DC).

Budowski, Gerardo (1971). *Ecology and Conservation in a Changing World* (with particular emphasis on forestry curricula). Lecture delivered at the Meeting on Problems and Tasks of Reforms in Higher Education in Forestry and Biotechnological Studies at the University of Liubliana in January 1971. 13 pp. (mimeographed).

ČeřOVSKÝ, Jan (1970). Environmental education—An urgent challenge to mankind. Pp. 34–42 in *Environmental Conservation Education Problems in India*. IUCN Publications New Series, Supplementary Paper No. 25. IUCN, Morges, Switzerland: 74 pp.

ČeřOVSKÝ, Jan (1971*a*). *Environmental Education (A Step Towards the Solution of Environmental Problems by Changing People's Attitudes)*. Economic Commission for Europe: Symposium on Problems Relating to Environment, 2–15 May 1971, held mainly in Prague, Czechoslovakia, Discussion paper ENV/CONF. F.15, 10 pp. (mimeographed).

ČeřOVSKÝ, Jan (1971*b*). Environmental education: Yes—but how? *Your Environment* (London), **2**(1), pp. 15–19.

IUCN (1970). *Final Report—International Working Meeting on Environmental Education in the School Curriculum*. IUCN, Morges, Switzerland, 33 pp. + Appendix.

NICHOLSON, Max (1970). *The Environmental Revolution. A guide for the New Masters of the World*. Hodder & Stoughton, London: xiii + 366 pp., illustr.

PRITCHARD, Tom (1968). Environmental education. *Biological Conservation*, **1**(1), pp. 27–31.

TERRY, Mark (1971). *Teaching for Survival. A Handbook for Environmental Education*. A Friends of the Earth/Ballantine Book, New York: 213 pp.

UNESCO (1969). Education. Pp. 21–5 in *Final Report—Intergovernmental Conference of Experts on the Scientific Basis for Rational Use and Conservation of the Biosphere*. UNESCO, Paris: 35 pp., 5 Annexes.

Problems and Requirements in Environmental Documentation

by

TOMISLAV MUNETIC

Sometime *Librarian, Museum of Comparative Zoology, Harvard University;*
Formerly *Chief Classifier, FAO; Documentation Officer, IUCN,*
1110 Morges, Switzerland

PROBLEMS

Recent years have witnessed a veritable 'environmental revolution' accompanied by an enormous increase in environmental conservation activities in all parts of the world. These activities have, in turn, been accompanied by a corresponding explosion in the literature of the subject.

Brown (1971), discussing the exponential growth of world science literature, which is giving rise to a chaotic situation that might soon be disastrous for the healthy development of science, pointed out that today we are confronted world-wide by a total of some 35,000 journals which publish about 2,000,000 articles each year, written by some 750,000 scientists in about fifty languages. The scientist of fifty years from now will have some 8,000,000 colleagues world-wide with whom he can try to communicate, and some 350,000 scientific and technical journals from which to make selections for his reading.

The problem of bibliographic control of the vast amount of published and unpublished information in the field of environmental conservation arises with particular acuity as a natural consequence of the enormous number of subjects, areas, aspects, and approaches, that have to be covered. This greatly reduces the possibility of effective specialization.

A continuous flow of information on various environmental conditions is essential for a viable environmental information system. But even though, at this time as at no other in history, there are numerous and diverse studies, programmes, and projects, generating data on the environment, exchange and widespread diffusion of environmental information is hampered by the inadequacies in the flow of information especially in developing countries. This results more often from shortages of bibliographic control, of trained librarians, of abstractors, and of other personnel, than from deficiencies in the primary sources of material. Thus, a great store of information lies buried in formal and informal reports and documents, and in computer systems that are available to few.

US Congressman Dingell (1970), testifying in support of a bill to provide for a national environmental data system, emphasized that governmental agencies at all levels, industrial and agricultural officials, and others whose decisions affect the environment, are expected by the public to manage the natural resources of their country for maximum productivity with minimum environmental degradation. But too often these decision-makers do not have available to them adequate information and knowledge of consequences.

Effective conservation decisions require up-to-date information. Not only are facts on environmental matters required, but regional and even world-wide patterns must be considered for proper assessment of some problems. Similarly, information on past and present conservation actions must be known, and sources of expert information made immediately available.

The potential for optimum environmental management would be greatly enhanced if a method could be found to improve the flow, analysis, and utilization, of the enormous information base which exists. However, 'on the whole, little or virtually no coordination seems to exist in most countries as regards the production and flow of information, the coverage of subjects, and/or areas, etc.' (Economic Commission for Europe, 1971).

The lack of coordination is particularly due to the fact that much in-formation is released through governmental channels and generally not made at all readily available—often because of the confidential nature of the data. Mechanisms for exchange of this type of information must be simplified and improved.

Lack of standardization in environmental terminology is another factor which hampers the effective flow of information. Compilation of multi-lingual glossaries of environmental terms would be an important first step towards a solution.

In sum, the greatest problems in environmental conservation docu-mentation are those inherent in the nature of the information in the field of environmental conservation, such as the great volume of data to be handled, the interdisciplinary character of the subject, the enormously numerous sources of information, and the fact that there is a very broad spectrum of consumers of environmental information—ranging from the general lay public on one hand to specialists in widely diverse scientific disciplines on the other. Serious problems are created also by inadequacies in data-processing, and by a lack of standardization and coordination.

REQUIREMENTS

Documentation activities in environmental conservation involve collection and dissemination of information on environmental action ranging from basic research up to long-term strategies, operational policies, and appropriate measures. These include legislation, standards, conventions, agreements, methods of environmental improvement, and also educational and related activities.

Particular attention needs to be given to selection and bibliographic control of environmental literature (e.g. indexing of titles and compilation of bibliographies, abstracts, digests, and monographs), and to the storage and circulation of selected documents ('hard' copies or micro-reproductions). Translations of individual documents are often required.

The above work, in order to be effective, requires that information be collected and transferred rapidly, and that data be kept up-to-date and complete. Moreover, the quantity of data processed by any particular centre must be kept within manageable limits by careful selection of the information and by cooperating with other data-processing agencies in the field.

The cost of collecting and supplying scientific information is bound to continue escalating. It is therefore essential to avoid needless duplication of effort and expense, through cooperation and coordination of the systems used by other, related agencies.

This need for cooperation in scientific and technical documentation in general was the basic idea that had led UNESCO and the International Council of Scientific Unions to undertake a joint study on the communication of scientific information, called UNISIST (Wysocki & Tocatlian, 1971). UNISIST was conceived as a flexible international network integrating, on a voluntary basis, existing scientific information services, and, eventually, those to be created. Initially the system will be limited to the natural sciences, but later it will be extended to technology and other fields of knowledge (UNISIST, 1971).

Cooperation of this type is enormously important and should win support from all concerned with scientific and technical documentation. As a prerequisite for successful cooperation, it is essential to know who is doing what and with what results. In this respect, a world directory of environmental agencies and the scope of their activities should be compiled with the least possible delay.

Standardization of bibliographies, of key words, of classification schemes, and of thesauri, is another prerequisite for cooperation and more economical processing of data. The exchange of publications (inter-library loans and free international exchange of publications, including government documents) should be promoted and simplified.

Bibliographic control of the available audio-visual material represents another difficult area. An international clearing-house for the exchange of information on the sources of such materials is greatly needed.

Another important area in which cooperation is greatly needed is that of helping developing countries in building up and expanding their documentation and library resources and in training personnel for employment in documentation.

In all this work, it is necessary to take into account the activities of organizations other than one's own in the field of environmental conservation. For there are at present many institutes and agencies whose activities relate directly or indirectly to the collection and exchange of information in the general field of environment.

Any listing of such organizations should include the United Nations Specialized Agencies, e.g. WMO, WHO, ILO, UNESCO (especially the 'Man and the Biosphere' programme, set up by UNESCO, will require facilities in the form of data banks, information systems, communication networks, etc.), UNIDO, UNITAR, IMCO, IAEA, FAO, and ECE. Also, intergovernmental organizations such as OECD, the Council of Europe, and NATO, and non-governmental international organizations such as ICSU and IUCN, should be mentioned. All these organizations are important sources, as well as consumers, of information in various areas of environmental interest.

Documentation techniques are rapidly evolving, and attention must therefore be paid to finding the most effective tools. The actual form of a centre of environmental information would depend on local conditions and scales of operation, ranging from a simple card-filing system to sophisticated electronic data-processing equipment substituting magnetic tapes for the cards. The tapes produce printouts for distribution and individual use.

CONCLUSION

Documentation centres, libraries, and similar institutions throughout the world, are facing the increasingly difficult task of collecting, processing, and transferring, information in the field of environmental conservation. They are required to gather, from all sources, information and intelligence that is relevant to the environment, and to disseminate the accumulated information to their consumers. Satisfaction of some of the problems discussed above would go a long way towards facilitating documentation work in the environmental fields, at least in the immediate future.

Long-range solutions, however, must be sought along different lines. Either within some kind of world-wide organization for environmental intelligence which might perhaps be set up as an outcome of the United Nations Conference on the Human Environment in Stockholm in 1972, or linked to UNISIST (which is currently being established and put into operation), the future trend will inevitably be towards an ever-greater interdependence of all agencies concerned with environmental documentation. The success of environmental documentation, as well as of environmental protection itself, will largely depend on our willingness to acknowledge this interdependence.

REFERENCES

BROWN, H. (1971). Toward an effective world science information system. *ICSU Bulletin*, **23**, pp. 3–12.

DINGELL, J. D. (1970). National environmental data system. *U.S. Congressional Record—House*, 7 Dec. 1970, 11259–62.

ECONOMIC COMMISSION FOR EUROPE (1971). *First Stage of a Feasibility Study and a Draft Plan of Action on Suitable International Arrangements Aimed at Facilitating and Coordinating the Exchange of Environmental Information Among the Countries of the ECE Region.* Symposium on Problems Relating to Environment, Prague, 2–15 May 1971, 26 pp. + annexes (mimeographed).

UNISIST (1971). *Study Report on the Feasibility of a World Science Information System by the United Nations Educational, Scientific and Cultural Organization and the International Council of Scientific Unions.* UNESCO, Paris: 161 pp.

WYSOCKI, A. & TOCATLIAN, J. (1971). A world science information system. *UNESCO Bulletin*, **25**(2), pp. 62–6.

The Need for Strengthening Legal Systems for Protection of the Environment

by

HOMER G. ANGELO

Professeur, Institut d'Études Européennes, Université libre de Bruxelles;
Founder-Governor, International Council of Environmental Law;
Vice-Chairman, Environmental Law Committee, IUCN;
Consulting Editor of Biological Conservation;
Member, Board of Governors, Foresta Institute for Ocean and Mountain Studies;
Professor, School of Law, University of California,
Davis, California 95616, USA

INTRODUCTION

Nowhere in the environmental movement is the need for improved education greater than in the development and use of law at most levels of human society. Indeed the need is paramount internationally, nationally, and locally. Mankind's current ecological plight is due in large measure to the failure of public institutions to provide either substantive norms or legal procedures for dealing with environmental issues. Ignorance and false conceptions underlie these basic legal shortcomings.

Many examples are illustrative. On the larger scale, they are epitomized by the non-existence or gross inadequacy of national rules to regulate what has become a rampant wastage of the earth's natural resources. Similarly, the uncurbed power of individuals, of governments, and of economic organizations, to pollute air, water, and earth, illustrates the failure of law systems of earlier centuries to establish a duty requiring potential polluters to respect the interests of (1) society as a whole, and (2) the welfare of neighbours and other citizens affected by pollution.

The gaps in the law are also manifested by the continued existence of vast areas of the planet's land, oceans, and other elements of the biosphere, which hitherto have been considered to be *terra nullius*—or, at the best, *res communis*—and hence under no legal system that would place restraints upon exploitation by nations or their subjects. The amalgam of mankind's legal systems has not yet given adequate recognition to the vital mutual interests of all societies in the preservation of these common territories and resources through effective rules and legal procedures.

As the environmental crisis has developed largely since World War II, popular demands for corrective measures have characteristically and inescapably called for modern human actions that can only be put into effect and enforced through measures which may be described as basically legal in character. Scientists insist that diverse ecological steps be taken. But commonly these can be implemented only through parliamentary or executive action of governments. Conferences such as this one on Environmental Future and the forthcoming Stockholm one on the Human Environment will suggest numerous far-reaching scientific, economic, and social, changes whose achievement will often depend upon legal innovations.

In these brief introductory comments* it is possible to touch on only the barest elements of what legal changes may be required for environmental protection on an international scale. But the prospective impact of such developments on existing concepts of law should be anticipated. Many proposals for environmental protection call for fundamental and drastic reexamination of relations between man and man, man and nature, man and society, and societies *vis-à-vis* societies. The results of their adoption would bear an inevitable impact upon, and could possibly demand a drastic reshaping of, the content and use of countless existing laws and of men's expectations about the role of law and its application throughout the world. Moreover, as will be discussed later, the substance and scope of existing laws and men's expectations about their enforcement will, in turn, affect the possibility of change to meet environmental needs.

Need for Environmental Awareness in Legal Systems at Various Levels

It is not only from a lack of ecological awareness that past failings to anticipate the legal dimensions of environmental requirements have arisen. They have resulted also from the proclivity of people and bodies concerned with the law (legislators, administrators, courts, private lawyers, and—possibly most important—'interested groups' whose rights and expectations are based upon existing legal norms) to resist new developments to meet resource-depletion and ecological challenges. This problem is manifested at local, national, regional, and international levels, with frequent interconnections.

Law in National Systems
Environmental law awareness at the local and national levels has grown enormously in the last decade. National reports presented at the Symposium on the Environment held in May 1971 by the Economic Commission for Europe showed that numerous nations, including many of those that are most responsible for current environmental degradation, have developed a new understanding of the need to change legal structures and standards to meet environmental requirements.

* Produced, we would like to explain, by their generous author working under considerable pressure of circumstances (including time).—Ed.

The Stockholm Conference should delineate more comprehensively both the achievements of, and the needs for, national law measures.

Until now, most national legal steps have been responsive dominantly to indigenous ecological needs—as, for example, Canada's Arctic Waters Pollution Prevention Act of 1970. But, increasingly, a tendency can be discerned in national legislation to respond to a concern for the environmental positions of other nations, of regions, or of the general international community.* Yet despite this awareness it must be recognized that most nations remain parochial in their national approach to environmental problems possessing an international dimension. Differences between industrial and developing nations' legal positions in preparations for the Stockholm Conference are illustrative. A key problem lies in the perception of vital national self-interest: the practice remains for virtually all nations that, where in the view of a country's leadership a crucial national interest is at stake, deference will be accorded to outside interests only out of obeisance to a stronger power or as a part of reciprocal concessions.

The difficulty of attaining harmonized reciprocal national laws on environmental problems is aggravated by the sheer difficulty of obtaining accurate facts—and then of adjusting national action to achieve environmentally sound and economically fair results. Mention of but two current national problems should suffice to illustrate this point.

The first is the effort to establish just and workable standards on automobile exhaust emissions. In many cases the nations principally concerned have stakes as consumers, manufacturers, exporters, importers, and victims of exhaust-caused air pollution. Standards set by the United States in its criteria of increasing strictness concerning exhaust emissions have already affected planning for automobile production in Japan and in Europe. West Germany's 1970 action in applying standards for its own motor vehicle traffic has created an as yet unresolved difficulty for automobile manufacturers in that country's partner nations in the European Common Market. This task of finding and achieving proper emission standards for Europe promises to carry drastic economic side-effects to the petroleum refining industry in the European communities. An independent study of this problem would provide an exemplary demonstration of the complexity of achieving just and effective legal regulation of a cross-frontier environmental problem requiring diverse national and possible international action.

The second example arises from the manufacture and use of products that were originally considered to be a matter of purely local concern—pesticides. Should the controlling standards and legal norms be laid down by producing or by consuming nations? And should the mounting evidence that the massive and prolonged use of pesticides can create a more general international impact far beyond the place of consumption, lead to programmes for internationally prescribed limits on pesticide use? If so, how can proper standards

---

* An example is provided by the US National Environmental Policy Act of 1970. It is to be regretted, however, that the US Government has not, at the date of submission of these comments, voluntarily contributed to the United Nations any reports on the estimated environmental effects of federal agency action in a fashion that is required (by Section 102, C, of the Act) to be filed within the US for domestic effects.

be formulated to accommodate the interest of diverse consuming groups in developing nations as well as in producing, industrial ones?

Beyond such intensely practical contemporary issues, some long-range philosophical problems involve possible changes in national attitudes, as well as in the law, on basic relationships in human society. Some of these factors have been touched on in earlier presentations in this Conference. They and others will require volumes of analysis and countless hours of discussion for achievement of a rational adjustment of individual rights and national actions with international environmental needs.

One example of such fundamental jurisprudential issues stems from the cluster of problems relating to the private ownership and use of property. Such concepts and legal rules widely affect both the depletion of resources and pollution of the planet. Never in fact immutable (though often described as such), the concept of private ownership of earth resources has in past centuries been consecrated in contemporary western (civil or common) law* and, to a lesser degree, in other legal systems. In contradistinction, some earlier social systems—such as native North American tribes and indeed some Biblical societies—did not consider private ownership to be a natural or unalterable right belonging to any individual or user-group within that society. Under the law systems of such societies, these property users were considered to be something like 'trustees' during the period of their possession. The basic rights to the objects (property in the form of land or movables) were considered to belong to the community as a whole, and in any event not to be susceptible to total consumption or to private transmission as individual property by the users to successors (whether by sale or inheritance).

Contemporary pressures of population growth and accelerated use of resources within this finite globe appear to foreshadow inevitable limitations upon freedom to use and transfer property, which have hitherto been considered as inalienable rights in many systems. The resolution of such issues may bring titanic pressures to bear on basic concepts of individual rights embodied in national law systems. But international solution of problems arising from private use of property cannot be achieved unless the local and national jurisprudential issues are recognized and faced.

Even less tractable under prevailing social and religious precepts as consecrated in modern legal systems, is the question of population control which also illustrates how the parameters of basic social, economic, and environmental, problems are marked by legal dimensions set forth by national law systems. The population explosion of course causes at the same time international and numerous national dilemmas. But if more than temporarily expedient and hortatory solutions are to be sought, biological, sociological, and economic, movements cannot advance without the use of legal techniques. From this point in time and in world social organization, population limitation programmes appear to be required in both international and national dimensions, with the latter dominant.

In this glimpse of national law problems, we thus come again to look at some of the most fundamental relationships between man and society in any

* A scientist's forecast of future changes in legal rights and attitudes towards property is set forth by Spilhaus (1971).

legal system. Many of the most intimate and deeply-imbedded personal and religious beliefs of the world's people are brought into scrutiny by proposals for birth control and other methods of regulation of population. As national laws and policies are involved, they cannot be changed without indigenous state action. To what extent should such national systems be amenable to international pressures? The answers will be critically difficult to find. But they cannot even be approached meaningfully—or with pragmatic chances for success—without honest and searching studies of the national, social, religious, and legal, systems involved. More and better education is paramount to this task.

Regional Environmental Action

Between geographically limited local or national action and global measures for environmental protection, much scope may be accorded in the future to regional measures to achieve action which a consensus holds should be regional in range. Even in these preliminary stages of biospheric concern, a clear need appears for some intermediate measures. But the legal framework for such regional action has hardly begun to emerge.

Europe's multiple and proliferating efforts towards joint ecological protection have already achieved substantial intergovernmental and some private cooperation. But again, Europe's first steps in this direction (Angelo, 1971) illustrate the governmental dilemmas and political shortcomings as well as scientific, functional, and economic, needs for regional cooperation. Among the numerous European institutions that are actively concerned with environmental protection, only one—the European Communities, comprising ECE, the European Coal and Steel Community (ECSC), and EURATOM—possesses even an embryonic structure for binding supra-national control. The other laudable regional programmes rest upon hortatory powers of persuasion which have not yet been utilized effectively to promote governmental agreements or harmonized national legislation to limit pollution and protect resources within Europe.

Other regions in the world also face ecological problems which can, in principle, be resolved by legal steps stemming from regional initiative and leading to coextensive control. But in those areas, even such beginnings as Europe's tentative steps remain to be initiated. Nor will such regional measures spring full-blown from any Medusa-like structure: preliminary institutional (including legal) measures must be weighed, planned, and instituted. Until this is done, it is both futile and misleading to speak of regional efforts as presenting viable prospects for environmental protection.

International Measures to Meet Global Needs

The current environmental crisis is, in many dimensions, planetary in scope. Scientific and functional solutions must accordingly be found that can be applied where appropriate through general international (or so-called universal) rather than regional or local systems.

In this task mankind confronts a cruel irony in its societal oganization: no world legal system or institutions exist which possess the capacity to establish ecological standards, ensure compliance, provide for peaceful change, and settle transnational environmental differences.

Despite pretentious rhetoric, the classic public international law of 'western' origin provides in most areas no rational guidelines for solution of biospheric issues. Thus Falk (1971) gives a cogent description of the short-comings of pre-existing doctrines of international law*. Worse still, by con-secrating state sovereignty, the traditional international law has created expectations of right and duty in successive national governments which per-mit unbridled national action to despoil the globe—to which only the dim-mest general duty has been acceded. Moreover, customary international law has not purported to preserve the international 'commons' territory (earth, water, or air) which exists outside national jurisdiction: on the contrary, it has fostered the idea that such areas are free for exploitation.

Similarly, general international law has not in any meaningful way sought to protect through law processes the people and resources of one nation from ecological degradation by others. The seeds of such protective principles are present in broad concepts such as 'sic utere tuo' which, generalized inter-nationally, could lead in time to protection of neighbours' rights under con-cepts that would be common to many national law systems.

In man's search for survival he faces, therefore, a legal jungle. In this jungle there exist vast areas of 'no-law', in which much human conduct brings wide-spread biospheric consequences without subjection to legal standards or societal regulations. In addition, there are many thickets of national laws and practices which are widely disparate in character and often conflicting in scope and impact.

No international institutions as yet possess the capacity to create system out of this disorder. The United Nations and its subsidiary organs and affiliated agencies have not been vested by their member states with either substantive authority or administrative power to act effectively; nor do they seem to have the capacity at present, though Gardner (1971) gives a description of changes in their structure which, if implemented, might help. Moreover, as world power-structures now exist, no single nation or contemporary grouping of states possesses the political strength and organization to impose functional ecological solutions on a generalized transnational pattern.

Processes of international agreement, despite some promising achieve-ments such as the 1969 Conventions sponsored by the Intergovernmental Maritime Consultative Organization (Busha, 1971) on (1) oil pollution casualties, and (2) civil liability for oil pollution damage, have so far been only fragmentary at best and basically insufficient to meet contemporary needs.

CONCLUSIONS

In company with other responsible disciplines, the legal profession must not turn away but instead redouble its efforts in face of the multiplicity and mag-nitude of these problems with which it will have to cope in remedying the present highly unsatisfactory situation. Development of an international con-sensus about necessary measures, and concrete professional action to provide

* A more sanguine view is expressed by M. S. McDougal: 'Legal bases for securing the integrity of the earth–space environment', *Annals of the New York Academy of Science*, 1971.

legal changes and innovation, should go hand-in-hand. Especially needed are continuing comprehensive revaluations of the diverse and frequently inter-connected local, national, regional, and international, law requirements to match emerging ecological programmes.

From within the general United Nations and other international organizations systems and the storehouses of national and international law and allied techniques, sufficient legal processes could surely be conceived and marshalled to carry out whatever measures may be determined as necessary for the world's environmental future. To this end, current proposals for separate international conventions on such subjects as ocean pollution, population control, sea-bed use, and resource allocation, are creditable (Sand, 1971). But the calls for their adoption should not be so couched as to create the impression that agreements will be easy to attain or that piecemeal legal steps will by themselves be enough.

For the creation of adequate legal norms and procedures to meet the needs considered by this Conference, nothing less than a massive continuing programme of research, education, and innovation, by the world's law-trained disciplines, will suffice. No lesser effort can provide the necessary juridical tools for the 'revolutionary' biospheric measures which ecological and other scientific activists prescribe. If provided in sufficient depth and competence, such legal contributions can share in the building of new institutions, in the developments of new national laws and international agreements, and in the growth of a long-overdue and now critically needed 'common law for the earth and mankind'.

REFERENCES

ANGELO, Homer G. (1971). Protection of the human environment—first steps toward regional cooperation in Europe. *The International Lawyer*, 5(3), pp. 511–26.

BUSHA, Thomas S. (1971). *Statement of the IMCO Representative* to Sub-Committee III of the Committee on the Peaceful Uses of the Sea-bed and Ocean Floor beyond the Limits of National Jurisdiction. The United Nations, Geneva, 9 August 1971, 3 pp. (mimeographed).

FALK, Richard A. (1971). *This Endangered Planet—Proposals for Human Survival*. Random House, New York: 495 pp.

GARDNER, Richard N. (1971). Global pollution. III: UN as policeman. *The Saturday Review*, 7 August 1971, pp. 47–50.

SAND, Peter H. (1971). *Methods to Expedite the Adoption and Implementation of International Rules and Standards for Environmental Protection*. Legal Office, Food and Agriculture Organization of the United Nations, Rome: 14 pp.

SPILHAUS, Athelstan (1971). The next industrial revolution. *Commercial Letter, Canadian Bank of Commerce*, No. 1/71, pp. 2–8.

Our Earth's Future:
What International Law Could Do

by

EDWIN SPENCER MATTHEWS, Jr

Member of the Bar of the State of New York;
Director and European Representative, Friends of the Earth;
Partner, Coudert Frères, 52 Avenue des Champs-Elysées, Paris 8ᵉ, France

A NEW ECOLOGICAL CONSCIENCE FOR THE LAW

Man has, we hope, begun to realize what his brief visit to this planet has cost, and what awful limits his current habits place on his continued stay. He has begun to understand just how incredibly fragile his unique life-supporting ecosystem is. With this may come a renewed sense of humility, which is something he may also have lost 'along the way'. Man, we hope, is relearning his part. If he can be kind, if he can now use his genius to understand how he and his fellow creatures have been able to travel this far and stay this long, and if he can for the first time in his existence move as one species with unprecedented speed to apply his new knowledge, he might stay a while longer. If not, man will assuredly leave this planet and he will take along many life-forms that share it with him and do not deserve to leave it; in that event one hopes evolution will do a better job next time around.

What we now sense is the beginning of the ecological revolution which is needed to give man a new conscience that is based upon a renewed humility and a new perception of the limits of his house. Acceptance of these limits will offer us a chance to enjoy a longer and finer visit than has latterly appeared likely, and also the hope that comes with belief in the future. It is this hope which brings us to Jyväskylä.

International law and lawyers must be a part of this revolution, as all disciplines and all men must be. Ecology is showing us that much of human thinking has failed to consider man's house, and has misconceived the place of man by forgetting that he must share this small planet with other life-forms on which he absolutely depends for survival. As contrasted with so-called 'primitive' cultures, we have forgotten that survival must be our first priority. The law has also failed to include this overview of man. With proper education of lawyers and their clients, this view could come—in time, one hopes, for the law to make its contribution. But it must happen very soon.

We must not be afraid to admit that much of current legal thinking has become obsolete. An ecological conscience demands drastically new and imaginative legal education, with broader curricula to inject essential new premises and values. It demands that new principles must be admitted by courts and other decision-making authorities in interpretations that are right for the planet and that can make man's future probable. It demands writing what we already know about our house into the codes of nations, and indeed much more.

But an ecological conscience must not only motivate our laws and our lawyers. It must also motivate their constituency: governments, corporations of all kinds, groups, and individuals. Laws, including international laws, are formed and enforced by men. Their scope and effectiveness do not exceed the consensus and resolve of those who, through one political process or another, consent to be governed by them. A law of broad scope can only flow from a wide consensus. Only a resolve to see a law effective will produce adequate enforcement.

Laymen and lawyers from many countries have expressed their belief or hope that the law, especially international law, can be a force to bring us back into balance with the earth. They see the law as if it had a life of its own and could tell us where to go—as if international law might hold the secret solution. Personally, I do not share this view, for the law is only what men will make it. It is a powerful tool when used well; but when not used, it is pointless verbiage.

An international order to restore, protect, and require rational use of, the earth must be based upon an earth-wide consensus. Those trained to interpret that order, the lawyers, must have clients. These clients must include individuals, groups of individuals, institutions, corporations and, especially, governments. The obvious failure of international law to establish such an order is not due to a missing part of the tool, a missing legal theory, but to a missing consensus. International lawyers have no clients, and international courts have no cases. Therefore, it is tragic that our fascination with the law, with its complex internal logic and its effectiveness as a tool when used well, has created a myth of its power and blinded us to its limitations. We must use international law as a tool for all that it is worth, and far more than ever before. But if we delegate responsibility for our future to international law before we have that consensus, we won't have a future.

What We Have Not Done: An Example from the Law of the Sea

The pollution of the earth's oceans—our last wilderness—is another version of the 'tragedy of the commons' (Hardin, 1970): the few seeking and achieving their own personal gain and thereby depriving the whole society of an essential resource. The history of the failure of international law to prevent marine oil pollution shows that what is needed most is not a series of innovations in the law of the sea, but an agreement among the earth's peoples that action is necessary. Given the resolve to take action, the law will follow.

In analysing the current international law of the sea, Professor Myres

McDougal of Yale University (*see* McDougal & Burke, 1962) distinguishes between 'exclusive' and 'inclusive' interests of states. 'Exclusive' interests are those which are particular to one country or to countries alone, being reflected in such concepts as internal waters, territorial sea, and continental shelf. 'Exclusive' interests are selfish interests, and international law of the sea has done a good job of protecting them. 'Inclusive' interests are those of all countries, expressed by concepts such as the freedom of the high seas, the freedom to fish, and the right of innocent passage. International law has not protected the inclusive or common interests very well; they have been left to take care of themselves, relying on the tremendous expanse and seemingly inexhaustible richness of the oceans.

One of the most vital inclusive rights is the right to enjoy an uncontaminated sea, to eat food from it, and to breathe the oxygen which it produces. Our oceans are contaminated, yet this common interest goes unprotected. Attempts to protect this interest through international law have withered in the face of tenacious traditional concepts protecting less important exclusive interests. The chronicle of such attempts includes short-sighted, inadequate solutions of woefully limited scope with 'killing' enforcement problems. The failure to control oil pollution is an example.

Apart from some historical items (Bowett, 1967; Ray, 1970), the first attempt came only in 1926, when thirteen maritime nations met in London to consider the causes of and solutions for ocean pollution—already an apparent problem. The United States advocated a complete ban on the discharge of oil, for example, but it was only agreed that discharge of substances of which the oil content was greater than 0.5 per cent would not be allowed. Incidentally, we must note that although oil pollution of the oceans has grown much worse since 1926, the United States has softened its view. The London agreement did not go very far, but even this modest effort failed to secure the necessary five votes for ratification. The nations thereupon returned to more familiar pursuits, including ocean exploitation and war, and their concern with ocean saving ended. There were a few attempts to persuade the League of Nations to deal with the problem, but they did not succeed.

By 1954, ocean oil pollution had obviously reached alarming proportions, and a second conference was called in London. Thirty-nine countries now adhere to the resulting agreement, which is inadequate to meet the problem of oil pollution. The scope of the 1954 agreement is too narrow, discharge of oil being prohibited only within an arbitrary one hundred miles (160 kilometres) from shore. There is still no evidence that oil discharged at sea (beyond 100 miles) is less of a threat. Evidence has been presented recently to an investigating group in the United States Senate, indicating that oil dispersed and sunk with detergents has a toxic half-life on the sea's bottom of one hundred years. Thus oil that is out of sight cannot safely be forgotten. It goes on damaging the primal life-support system, even as it does on coasts where ameliorative steps cannot be taken—such as almost all the coasts of Africa, if we heed the evidence presented at the *Pacem in Maribus* meeting in Malta in 1970.

It is obvious that a total ban on oil discharge into the sea is the only safe approach. Moreover, the 1954 agreement deals only with the *deliberate* discharge of oil and does not even set up standards of negligence for accidental discharge. The agreement does not even mention off-shore drilling. Nor has it any effective enforcement mechanisms. Because leading nations insisted on total inviolability of the freedom of the seas concept—remember, an exclusive interest—the agreement provides that enforcement can only be carried out by the flagship state. The flagship nations, as everyone knows, have important economic and political disincentives to investigate and prosecute violations. Other member states and injured coastal states have no right to prosecute. An attempt in 1969 to cure some of these serious defects accomplished nothing, and the Canadian Government called the 1954 agreement no more than a 'licence to pollute'.

In 1958 there were adopted in Geneva four conventions (*cf.* Ray, 1970), including some general provisions on the prevention of ocean pollution, but so far they have had negligible impact. These conventions are also prisoners of exclusive interests.

More recent developments offer only a faint hope for international co-operation so far as we can see. In 1967, Malta proposed to the United Nations General Assembly that the ocean floor be declared 'the common heritage of mankind', and that an international agency be created to govern the deep sea-bed. In response, a United Nations Permanent Committee to Study the Peaceful Uses of the Sea-bed and Ocean Floor Beyond the Limits of National Jurisdiction was set up. So far, however, the Committee has made no recommendations concerning marine pollution control. The first *Pacem in Maribus* meeting was convened in Malta in 1970 to search for a solution, and the second coincides with our present Conference. It has far to go.

In May 1970, President Nixon of the United States proposed that the deep sea-bed beyond 200 metres depth be placed under an international regime which would have responsibility for administering marine pollution controls. But so far there have not been any serious multilateral negotiations over this proposal. In the existing vacuum, in April 1970, the Canadian Parliament unanimously enacted the Arctic Waters Pollution Prevention Act, which institutes the most far-reaching marine pollution controls yet devised. Yet such controls are essential to protect some of Nature's simplest and most fragile ecosystems, which are particularly vulnerable to oil pollution.

The Canadian Act neatly side-steps the problems of scope and enforcement which we have perceived thus far. It simply prohibits deposit of any waste in Arctic waters, and thus controls all forms of marine pollution whether emanating from ships, shore installations, or off-shore mining and drilling rigs. The definition of waste is comprehensive; it includes all substances which would degrade or alter the arctic waters in a manner detrimental to their use by man, other mammals, fish, or plants that are useful to man. The Act empowers the Governor-General-in-Council to impose technical requirements of hull structure, navigation, personnel, and time and route of passage within one hundred nautical miles (180 km) of the nearest Canadian land.

Enforcement of the Act is by Pollution Prevention Officers with wide powers of inspection. Actual polluters are subject to absolute civil liability, and the Governor-General-in-Council may require proof of adequate resources to finance clean-up and liability for damage from potential polluters.

In short, the Canadian Act is what the 1926 and 1954 treaties should have been.

But comprehensive as the Canadian Act is, it does present a grave problem—the precedent of unilateral action. Canada now asserts exclusive control of pollution for one hundred miles from its shore-line, refusing to submit its action to the International Court of Justice. Some day, perhaps, after substantial royalties from arctic oil exploitation begin flowing into Ottawa, Canada will no longer be so interested in pollution control in the Arctic. Moreover, pollution control is salutary; but Canada's initiative may be a precedent for unilateral action to extend sovereignty to exploit the oceans, rather than to preserve them. Unilateral action provides no assurance that the inclusive interests of all states will be considered, and the preoccupation of states with their exclusive interests has been the problem with effective pollution control all along. The Canadian Act should have been a multilateral treaty!

WHAT WE COULD ACHIEVE THROUGH INTERNATIONAL LAW

This brief summary of our feeble efforts to protect our seas from threatened oil pollution should suffice to disabuse us of any hope that international law will be a motive force to help man bring himself back into balance with his fragile planet. The law of the sea is no exception. International law has nowhere adequately expressed the *inclusive* interest of all peoples for a living earth. This failure, however, has not been the failure of the law, but the failure of us all, and, in particular, of the major powers, who have not yet placed a high priority on survival.

Let us now look briefly at what international law could do if given the chance, which simply has to come.

International law must begin soon to define the inclusive interest of all peoples in the protection, restoration, and rational use, of our earth, for which *there is no spare* (Brower, 1971). International law must begin to provide for the regulatory mechanism of an ecological conscience. This appears Utopian, but is an absolute imperative. We need right now, and it may already be too late:

(a) A planetary population control agreement, providing for an international authority with power to impose population controls on all countries—especially those with high gross national product *per caput*—so that some day there will be no more of us than the earth can carry;

(b) A planetary resource agreement, providing for an international authority to allocate consumption of our finite resources in all countries—we know where to start—so that all our children may have an equal chance at what is now left; and

(c) A planetary energy agreement, providing for an authority to impose limits on our energy consumption—to stop sooner rather than later our exponentially increasing consumption of energy at exponentially increasing cost to the earth and man—and we know here again with which countries to start.

This should only begin the list of multilateral agreements defining the real and paramount inclusive interest of all peoples for survival on a finite planet. But let us start as a child learns to walk. Our first steps should be manageable acts, each quite possible, but they should be many. Let us start with multi-lateral agreements limited to a single threatened area, such as the Baltic, the Arctic, the Grand Banks of Newfoundland, or the Alps; or they might be limited to a single threatened resource, such as the air, nickel, oil, timber, or whales. We can call such agreements regional or resource-protective treaties; they should honeycomb the planet earth. They must define the inclusive interest of their signatories in the region or resource protected. They must be multilateral and include the representatives of as many peoples as possible, to guarantee that the agreement will reflect the inclusive interests of all. Their essential components must include:

(1) *Research.* Each agreement must provide for a competent research body, adequately staffed and financed, to study the region or resource covered by the treaty, in order to understand its history and present state and the threats to it. This same body should be required to provide technical advice and independent opinions to an executive authority established by the agreement, and also to any party that shows interest, including private groups. It should periodically and publicly report on the state of the region or resource, on the present and future threats, on the effectiveness of all protective action taken, and on the prognosis—both short- and long-term.

(2) *Execution.* Agreements must provide for a directive-issuing agency with the power delegated to it by signing states to order things to happen or not to happen. This will mean asking the traditional political authorities on our planet to transfer some of their exclusive competence over the region or resource to an international agency, and is crucial. The executive agency will need the exclusive power to license, direct, or prohibit, activity within a member state which can be shown to affect the region or resource. It should be required to follow the opinions of the research arm, and to consult with representatives of member states, though of these it should not be dependent upon the approval of any more than a simple majority.

(3) *Money.* The treaty agencies should be guaranteed subsistence by a small, fixed percentage of the national budget of the member states, set in advance. This could be supplemented by licence fees and fines, although ideally not at all.

(4) *Enforcement.* The courts of the member states should be open to enforcement, by the executive authority, of its orders, independently of member-state support. Penalties should be set in the treaty. International courts and arbitration could be entrusted only if all member states agreed in advance to submit themselves to their jurisdiction and to enforce their judgements through their local court machinery without review on the merits. Our imperilled life-raft cannot afford voluntary compliance.

(5) *Duration.* In order to give such a new order a fair chance to be effective, member states should specifically renounce their right to withdraw—for a specified period which should be long enough to make apparent to all the benefits accruing from the protected region or resource. Ten years might be sufficient.

(6) *Scope.* The scope of any such treaty should be the restoration, preservation, and rational use, of the region or resource concerned. Treaty authorities should be competent to deal with anything that affects the region or resource. Proper balance with other exclusive and inclusive interests of member states can be assured, not by narrowly defining the scope of the agreement as we have done before, but by establishing a procedure for that purpose under the treaty. I have suggested above a representative committee of the member states acting by simple majority. The place for the manageable beginning step can be in the definition of the region or resource covered by the agreement. We can modestly begin with endangered species, bits of wilderness, or antiquities that are integral parts of a world heritage, concentrating at first on single examples.

If man is to have a future at all equal—in quality or time—to his brief past, we must begin right now to bring the earth's peoples back together. What we must all have in common is an ecological conscience. International law can help to define this common interest which those of us who want to are now at last perceiving. It may be asking too much of man—a pitifully blind creature most of the time—to achieve with one bold document a new international order that would be responsible for the future of life on this planet. But it cannot be too much to ask him to begin with some responsible act now. International law is a powerful tool if we want to use it.

REFERENCES

BOWETT, D. W. (1967). *The Law of the Sea.* University Press, Manchester: 117 pp.

BROWER, David R. (1971). Forward. Pp. 14–18 in *The Primal Alliance: Earth and Ocean* (Ed. Kenneth Brower). Friends of the Earth, San Francisco, etc., and McCall, New York: 144 pp., illustr.

HARDIN, Garrett (1970). The tragedy of the commons. Pp. 31–50 in *The Environmental Handbook* (Ed. Garrett De Bell). Ballatine/Friends of the Earth, New York: xv + 367 pp. (Reprinted from *Science,* **162**, pp. 1234–8, 1968.)

McDOUGAL, Myres S. & BURKE, William T. (1962). *The Public Order of the Oceans.* Yale University Press, New Haven, Conn.: xxv + 1226 pp.

RAY, Carleton (1970). Ecology, law, and the 'marine revolution.' *Biological Conservation,* **3**(1), 7–17.

ADDENDA

On the evening of Tuesday 29 June 1971, a 'rump session' was held around the last paper (which had been circulated earlier) and some additional submissions—particularly on behalf of the Interparliamentary Union by Mr Wolfgang E. Burhenne, Secretary-General of the Interparliamentary Working Centre, Adenauerallee 214, Bundeshaus, 53 Bonn, West Germany, who is also a Governor of the International Council of Environmental Law. Those taking an active part in this discussion were (in order of first speaking): Udall, Matthews, Goldman, Caldwell, Rayzacher, Brower, Polunin, and Panikkar, and the main points which emerged can be summarized as follows:

(1) Law is crucial for the solution of many environmental problems and an ecological conscience should be basic to it.

(2) That international law has not yet come to control man's treatment of the earth for the general good is due to man's failure to make and enforce suitable laws based on unselfish understanding; now that this last is coming with widespread ecological awakening, mankind must act and establish the necessary legal framework. [An encouraging start seems to have been made with the recent agreement on the use of outer space.]

(3) The main difficulty is, all too often, natural sovereignty, and the consequent inability to get a forum that can be sufficiently widely respected to enforce laws in lagging countries.

(4) Enlightened regulations in one country can often be usefully imposed on others through international trade or other regulations, examples being the exhaust-control requirements of cars imported into the United States which have to conform to local standards, and the possibility of banning all SST landing or flights over that country.

(5) Whereas it is to be hoped that nations will vie with one another to pass and enforce harsh laws to uphold environmental standards, there is a danger that some will lag in this and so encourage unscrupulous developers from countries where the laws are strict—hence again the need for full international cooperation. Some feeling was expressed, however, concerning the possible desirability of 'spreading around' pollution for the time being by encouraging more processing and manufacturing in undeveloped countries.

(6) There is need for more knowledge of the possibility and means of getting nations—especially leading ones—to agree to accept limitations on their sovereignty and to recognize the authority of an overall legal body such as the International Court of Justice which should probably have a special agency for the expeditious settlement of environmental disputes.

(7) Although there are difficulties in getting unanimity or even a strong consensus among nations, the growing realization that sheer survival is at stake should help to convince the selfish ones to conform, e.g. with regard to oil pollution of the seas, which should be controlled through aggressive policy of the United Nations.

(8) It is necessary to define man's common interests and the world's as a whole, regardless of all national and sectional bias.

(9) We seem to be at or nearing the end of what has long been considered the modern age, and to be coming into a new kind of civilization. So we are not in a good position to advocate values which by no means all the world shares. Our common enemy is widespread environmental degradation and pollution, largely stemming from ignorance or apathy but latterly getting widely out-of-hand, and we should develop its abatement by creating suitable jobs throughout the world. In this, the United States is showing fine leadership which it is to be hoped will be maintained.

(10) More difficult than passing laws is, often, their enforcement, and here again recent experience in the United States is proving very enlightening although international circumstances would often be quite different. Actually, the mere passing of laws can be a danger, as people then sit back and think the problem is solved, whereas nothing results without proper enforcement. Apart from suing in the law courts, a way to get action is through pressure-groups whipping up public opinion and getting governments to respond, or, when they do not do so, stimulating international forums to embarrass the governments.

From Professor CARL AUGUST FLEISCHER, *Institute of Public and International Law, University of Oslo, Oslo 1, Norway*

First of all I shall state that I look forward to seeing the results of the Conference, which it seems to me has every possibility of [making] an extremely valuable contribution to the protection of man's environment. Second, I wish to avail myself of this opportunity to call to the attention of the Conference that, although in the future one must envisage a more or less total system of surveillance and control of environment changing and the exploitation of resources (eco-management, as it has been called), one must in the meantime not refrain from supporting and even pressing [for] special action with respect to more partial solutions, in cases where certain forms of activity present serious danger of harmful effects to the environment.

Third, I should like to direct the attention of the Conference to one certain case which calls for special action at the present stage of development, namely the dumping of persistent and toxic materials into the sea. I should in this connection refer to Article XXXV of the Draft Convention on Environment Cooperation among Nations, presented by me to the World Peace Through Law Center in the beginning of this year,* on the prohibition of dumping of harmful substances and on the licensing by a state of, in principle, all dumping.

Reference is further made to the conclusions of the meeting of the International Working Group on Marine Pollution of the United Nations Preparatory Committee for the 1972 Stockholm Conference, held at the head-

* *Draft Convention on Environment Cooperation Among Nations*, prepared for the World Peace Through Law Center by Carl August Fleischer. World Peace Through Law Center, 75 rue de Lyon, 1211 Geneva 13, Switzerland: Pamphlet Series Number 16, 72 pp. [1971].

quarters of IMCO in London from 14 to 18 June of this year. This meeting registered general agreement that the dumping of certain substances which may have harmful consequences to the marine environment should be prohibited, and that all ocean dumping, in particular of industrial waste, should be brought under control by the issue of permits from national authorities— also that no dumping should be allowed unless proved harmless and therefore authorized by a responsible authority.

It would greatly advance this work if the Conference would express its view in support of the above conclusions, and underline the necessity of reaching formal international agreement as soon as possible on the above principles.

STATEMENT*

International activity in the sphere of environmental conservation has become one of the major concerns of the United Nations and its agencies, of many other organizations, and of individual citizens throughout the world. It is recognized that the protection of the environment is essential for human life. For such purposes as the successful functioning of the United Nations Conference on the Human Environment, to be held in 1972 in Stockholm, exchange of opinions and discussions are important. Therefore the Government of Finland, the Finnish National Commission for UNESCO, and the Jyväskylä Arts Festival, convened an International Conference on Environmental Future which was held mainly in Jyväskylä during 27 June to 3 July 1971.

The Conference's aim was to bring together a number of leading experts, and qualified observers from chosen international and Finnish organizations, to speak freely as private individuals in outlining the global situations in their own fields and in forecasting what, in their opinion, might happen in the future. They were to suggest what can and should be done to alleviate environmental degradation and to avoid its dangerous consequences for man and nature. The following statement is a contribution to the discussion going on all over the world, *inter alia* in preparation for the United Nations Conference already mentioned. Because there could not possibly be enough time to come to a complete consensus, the contents of this document do not necessarily commit the international and national bodies represented, or their observers who took part in the discussions.

Our meeting was of a scientific and technical character. We can only indicate the most urgent problems, and we request that the United Nations Conference make the appropriate political decisions.

In an attempt to provide guidelines for governments, national bodies, and interested citizens everywhere, as well as for the United Nations Conference on the Human Environment to be held in Stockholm in June 1972, the International Conference on Environmental Future, 1971, submits the following conclusions and recommendations.

CONCLUSIONS

We believe that recent developments in the global environment can bring mankind to a dangerous period. We are convinced that the people of this planet and their governments must take immediate measures to halt further deterioration of the environment. The success or failure of this enterprise

---

* Drafted by the Conference's Resolutions Committee consisting of Prof. Jean G. Baer (Switzerland), Prof. Mohamed Kassas (Egypt), Prof. Donald J. Kuenen (The Netherlands), Prof. Vladimir N. Kunin (USSR), Prof. Hans Luther (Finland), Dr Norman W. Moore (UK), Prof. Kauko Sipponen (Finland, Chairman) and the Hon. Stewart L. Udall (USA). Approved in principle at the Final Plenary Session of the Conference on Saturday 3 July 1971, under the chairmanship of Professor Baer, with amendments incorporated here and some additional editing sanctioned by the chairman of that occasion. Proposed as a 'Declaration', but use of this term was objected to on behalf of the United Nations, on the basis that the Conference was a free one convened by invitation and without official status.—Ed.

will determine the quality of life, and perhaps even the prospect of life, of future generations.

The combined effects of misdirected technology, short-sighted and inequitable exploitation of resources, lack of population planning in many parts of the world, emphasis on military constructions and weapons at the expense of human welfare, and the excessive production of the affluent societies, are the most important causes of the present state of the environment.

Our conclusions concerning the nature and dimensions of the problems facing mankind are as follows:

  I If present trends continue, progressive environmental deterioration may lead to the extinction of the human species, or will at least condemn future generations to survive under inhuman conditions, as already two-thirds of the world's population is apparently doing at the present time.

 II Most of the serious disruptions of the earth's ecosystems are caused by misuse of the soil and other natural resources or by misguided technology. Man is a victim of his own technological arrogance. Life is endangered by a technology that is steadily destroying and impairing the vitality of ecosystems through destruction and pollution.

III Man is also the victim of the excessive multiplication of his own species: unbridled population increases are causing social, political, and environmental, problems over an increasingly large part of the world, and defeating the legitimate aspirations of mankind. Therefore, the need for population control is urgent in most parts of the world. Since developed countries consume a large proportion of the world's resources, population control is necessary in nearly all of them in order to reduce pressure on natural resources throughout the world. Equally, population control is necessary in most of the less-developed lands where population pressures impede economic advance. It is unlikely that enough food can be produced and distributed to sustain the world population in the next thirty years, after which time the present number will have doubled—unless vigorous programmes of population control are systematically pursued.

 IV It is evident that present patterns of environmental exploitation, and the distribution of the profits therefrom, are undermining the political stability of the world. We believe that the widening economic gap between the rich and the poor nations poses a formidable hazard to world order and deprives vast millions in the poor nations of human dignity and social justice; wiser use of renewable and expendable resources will help to solve this problem.

  V The application of science and technology without restraint—related to over-consumption—cannot alleviate the major ills and errors that are at the roots of the alarming global situation. The benefits of modern technology have brought the peoples of the world nearer to each other, making them more interdependent. For these reasons, common plans and cooperative action to conserve regional resources must be extended to the whole biosphere; this is the new imperative of our age.

RECOMMENDATIONS FOR THE STOCKHOLM CONFERENCE 1972

We do not think the collapse of civilization is imminent; there is time to avoid the abyss. This is a solemn call for world-wide action and for collective self-restraint. Now is the time for decisive action for the conservation and amelioration of the human environment. Delayed action may result in irreversible damage and may bring the biosphere to the brink of ecological disaster.

In this spirit, we submit the following recommendations to those who will assemble in Stockholm next June, and to the citizens and leaders of the nations of the world who must make many critical decisions.

1. General

(A) Added momentum to the global movement for environmental reform must be one of the principal objectives of the Stockholm Conference. The need for a world-wide programme of population planning is urgent. The dangers of double standards are obvious: further widening of the gap between the rich and the poor must be halted, and efforts should be made to abolish this gap. The problems of man and his environment have a great potential for bringing all the nations together. The leaders of the Stockholm Conference must fearlessly confront these difficult but decisive issues. Consequently, we appeal to governments and the United Nations to give the delegates to the Stockholm Conference the widest latitude to develop creative plans for vigorous national and international action by governments and by the United Nations and its agencies.

(B) The conservation of the biosphere requires the establishment of an international structure, capable of developing the necessary programmes and strategies for action. The principal functions of this structure should be:

 i. Formulating and coordinating global environmental policies;
 ii. Settling international environmental disputes;
iii. Monitoring and coordinating of environmental parameters, and interpreting environmental data collected by national and other specialized bodies;
iv. Mobilizing and stimulating existing national and international bodies, both governmental and non-governmental, already engaged in various aspects of the environmental and population problems.

This may involve the reorganization of existing international agencies or their environmentally orientated parts and/or the creation of new institutions, e.g. within the framework of the United Nations family. It is recognized that this new focal point of environmental organization at the international level must be closely associated with agencies for development and for population programmes if the cooperation of all countries is to be achieved and if environmental programmes are to be effective.

(*C*) Misuse and deterioration of regional resources will continue unless there is coordination of research and management between the countries involved. We urge the United Nations to support and assist the establishment of the necessary regional organizations.

(*D*) The people of the earth should enact into law, nationally and internationally, the inalienable right of societies to freedom from ecological assault. We urge adoption of international treaties and agreements that would allow the process of law to adjudicate and resolve international disputes involving environmental damage.

2. *Natural Resources*

(*A*) Exploitation of natural resources has often been short-sighted and has led to an increasingly rapid depletion of the non-renewable and even of some of the renewable resources of the world. Long-term planning for the use of the non-renewable resources and the maintenance of the sustained yield of renewable resources are part of our obligation to future generations. Therefore, conservation principles that call for adopting methods and processes close to natural cycling of materials must be taken into account before projects for the development of natural resources are supported or executed.

(*B*) All efforts should be made to maintain the natural wealth of plants and animals as they provide valuable genetic sources for the future development of crops, domestic animals, and forests.

(*C*) The maintenance and enhancement of the existing world-wide network of national parks and natural reserves, and the creation of more such reserves wherever necessary, are important for the future of man and for their scientific and educational values.

(*D*) It is also important that means should be made available to authoritative organizations concerned with the conservation of nature, and to provide avenues for expression of their findings.

3. *Monitoring*

Monitoring is essential to any programme for environmental conservation and for studying climatic and biological changes affecting productivity of biological systems and of man's environment. Our present knowledge about biological parameters, especially with regard to relationships to the chemical and physical composition of water and the atmosphere such as result from changes coming from natural or man-made causes, is insufficient. It is urgent that international agencies within their specific fields of competence continue critically to evaluate all relevant parameters, take further steps to standardize methods, and exchange information pertaining to the monitoring of the environment.

4. *Pollution*

(*A*) Pollution has become a serious threat to man's environment. It was recognized that dusts, particularly from soil erosion and burning in connection with agriculture and forestry activities, may become (along with other atmospheric pollutants) a major cause of detrimental changes in climate.

The Conference noted that in some nations successful anti-pollution measures have been implemented already without impeding economic development.

(B) At the present stage of knowledge, pesticides are often necessary to protect human health and for the control of insect populations in agriculture, although the use of some of them may often be counter-productive in the long run. Certain persistent pesticides become environmental pollutants and are hazardous to many species other than pests. The use of these materials should be discontinued. It is recognized that unless the richer nations can develop and finance the use of safer compounds, the persistent compounds used today cannot be phased out immediately in some lands. Research in agriculture and biology towards integrated control of pests and disease vectors must be greatly accelerated, and implementation of the results of this research is essential. All pesticides must be thoroughly tested and shown to involve a minimum of risk before they are released for general use. New pesticides should not be introduced for general use unless exceptionally rigorous testing has shown that they do not provide hazards to the environment. We also disapprove of the use of defoliants in warfare.

(C) It is requested that the status of all extraterritorial waters of the seas and oceans of the world be no longer called 'res nullius' but only termed and considered as 'res communis', being submitted to the direct jurisdiction of the United Nations. It is urged that the dumping of pollutants in the seas and oceans be prohibited unless special permission is given by an appropriate UN or other agency, and that measures be taken for establishing an effective control system.

(D) The immediate and long-term effects of supersonic transport at high altitudes can only be surmised. However, many countries have collected data that are at present unavailable to the scientific community. It is therefore urged that all such data be published and scientifically evaluated before any large-scale productional use of such forms of transport is continued. International organizations should initiate research to complete our knowledge about any long-term climatic effect.

5. Cultural Heritage and Natural Monuments

The Conference noted that man-made lakes in several parts of the world have inundated valuable cultural and archaeological sites. Money is often not available for carrying on the required programmes of research. It is suggested that an international fund be raised for financing such studies. It may be feasible to allocate for such archaeological research a proportion of the money made available for the construction of dams.

6. Human Settlements

(A) Urban environmental disfunctions are more than an arithmetic totality of individual nuisances. Together they represent an environmental climate resulting from the mutual and lasting interaction of innumerable individual pollutants, noises, hygienic shortcomings, transport paralyses, misuses of land, aesthetic offences, and psychological stresses.

(*B*) In view of demographic developments, especially those resulting in by far the greater part of a population living in urban centres, there is a need for guided urban development which will improve the quality of urban life. During the coming decades we shall have to provide as much housing and as many schools, hospitals, administrative buildings, factories, power plants, etc., as man has built throughout all his history. Consequently, long-term physical planning integrated with economic and social planning must ensure land-uses for society's greater benefit.

The objective should be a rational distribution of population and activities giving a network of human settlements which would maximize the quality of urban life.

7. *Public Standard of Living*

The Conference recognized that too much emphasis has been put on Gross National Product (GNP) and quantitative economic growth. It was suggested that nations should now develop the concept of a Public Standard of Living (PSL) to measure the quality of life.

8. *Our Heritage of Natural Beauty*

The Conference urges that natural beauty be ranked along with food, shelter, and health protection, as one of the basic necessities for human well-being.*

After detailed consideration of the draft declaration which was amended as the above Statement, the proposal was made and unanimously approved by the assembled Conference at its final plenary session that there should be further such international conferences on environmental future at intervals of from two to four years henceforth in other countries, the outgoing chairman of the disbanding International Steering Committee, although he had just undergone metamorphosis to Editor of the Proceedings, being appointed to continue—first by exploring suitable possibilities of interested countries and also the setting up of an umbrella body to look after such occasions and perhaps have a wider watchdog function.

Finally, at the following 'state' luncheon in Jyväskylä and an after-dinner party (of 'Finnish champagne' made principally from white currants) given by the Editor of the Proceedings for about sixty remaining participants in Helsinki, various speeches of gratitude and exhortation were made and telegrams were sent to the Prime Minister, the Scientific Patron, and others, while cables were read from various organizations and persons who had been unable to attend the Conference. These included Bernhard Prince of the Netherlands, Dr J. C. de Melo Carvalho, the Academia Sinica of Mainland

* Although it did not appear in the version sent to us a few weeks later, we have the distinct recollection (confirmed by the Chairman) of acceptance of our suggestion, made at the Final Plenary Session, of a terminal paragraph to the effect that '*If some such proposals as those made above are not implemented very widely, we shall continue to have the gravest possible fears for the future of the biosphere and all its inhabitants, human and otherwise.*'—Ed.

China, Miss Sylvia Crowe, Mr O. V. Wells (the Deputy Director-General of FAO, in the absence of Dr A. H. Boerma), Dr Henry Field, Lord Hayter, Professor V. A. Kovda, and Mr C. H. Mace (the UN Deputy High Commissioner for Refugees, in the absence of Prince Sadruddin Aga Khan).

ANTI-POLLUTION BALLAD*

By George Ledyard Stebbins, Davis, California,

&

Nicholas Polunin, Geneva, Switzerland

(Published in embryonic form in *Biological Conservation*, Vol. 2, No. 2, p. 155, 1970. Copyright by Elsevier Publishing Company Ltd, Barking, Essex, England)

To be sung to the tune of 'John Brown's Body'—staccatoed where necessary

Mary-Ann MacCarthy was a young and bright co-ed.
She asked if she might study Algae brown and green and red.
Her botany professor said 'Yes, Mary, go ahead—
But pollution is doing all life in.'

CHORUS:

> All that we can find is oil slicks
> Horrible and filthy dirty oil slicks—
> All that we can find is oil slicks
> 'Cause pollution has done the Algae in.

She put on rubber booties and went down to Skagit Bay.
She climbed on rocks and dug in mud throughout the livelong day.
But Algae brown and green and red, they all had gone away
'Cause pollution had done the whole lot in.

CHORUS:

> All that she could find was oil slicks
> Horrible and filthy dirty oil slicks—
> All that she could find was oil slicks
> 'Cause pollution had done the Algae in.

So Mary-Ann decided she had something big to do.
She called on her professor and on all her boy friends too.
She raised a mighty army and she shouts at me and you
'Let's fight to do pollution in!'

* *See* page 600.

CHORUS:

Let's all put an end to oil slicks
And all the other nasty things that give to nature kicks;
If we do not the world will end from man's unworthy tricks
So we'll all fight to do pollution in.

Appendix 1

LIST OF PARTICIPANTS

(including invited Principal Speakers, Chairmen of Sessions, and 'Roving Eminents'*, also Delegates of invited International Organizations [c/o] and Observers from Nations [†]; Official Representatives of Finnish Organizations and Institutions etc. are listed separately on pp. 644–6)

ADLERCREUTZ*, Professor Herman: University Institute of Clinical Chemistry, Meilahden sairaala, Helsinki 29, Finland.

APOLLONOV, Mr Guerman I.: c/o International Atomic Energy Agency, Kaerntner-ring 11, A-1010 Wien 1, Austria.

BAER, Professor Jean G.: Directeur, Institut de Zoologie, Université de Neuchâtel, 2000 Neuchâtel 7, Switzerland (also representing as its Vice-President the International Union of Biological Sciences, 106 Lange Nieuwstraat, Utrecht, Netherlands).

BARANESCU, Professor George: Président de la Commission pour la Préservation de l'Environnement de l'Académie de la R.S. de Roumanie, Rue Victoriei 125, Bucharest, Romania.†

BARODA, H. H. The Maharaja of, Lt.Col., M.P. (India): Laxmi Vilas Palace, Baroda, India (also representing as a Trustee the World Wildlife Fund, 1110 Morges, Switzerland).

BARTSCH*, Dr Alfred F.: Director, Pacific Northwest Water Laboratory, United States Environmental Protection Agency, 200 SW 35th Street, Corvallis, Oregon 97330, USA.

BENTHEM*, Mr Roelof Jan: Chief of Staff, Department of Landscape Planning, State Forest Service, Museumlaan 2, Utrecht, Netherlands.

BROWER, Dr David R.: President, Friends of the Earth, 30 East 42nd Street, New York City, NY 10017, USA, and Director, John Muir Institute for Environmental Studies, 451 Pacific Avenue, San Francisco, California 94133, USA.

BRYSON, Professor Reid A.: Director, Institute for Environmental Studies, University of Wisconsin, Meteorology and Space Science Building, 1225 West Drayton Street, Madison, Wisconsin 53706, USA.

* 'Roving Eminent' was a designation used in the early planning in Finland and somehow 'stuck' as signifying an eminent personage who would be invited and encouraged to enter discussions whenever so inclined rather than be responsible for any particular paper or session; 'c/o' before the address of an international organization indicates that the person concerned represented that organization officially when not its administrative head or invited in a personal capacity. A dagger [†] after the name of a country ending an address indicates that the person concerned was sent as a national observer. So far as is known, all individuals listed here were present for at least part of the conference in Jyväskylä except in the cases of three contributors of keynote papers who were unable to attend in the end and whose papers were presented *in absentia*. Other invited persons who were unable to attend the Conference but who generously contributed papers or comments which are incorporated in these (extended) proceedings may be identified through the Index. Principal speakers are indicated in the table of contents (pp. vii–ix); chairmen of sessions or discussion leaders are likewise named there and in the text.

BUDOWSKI, Dr Gerardo: Director-General, International Union for Conservation of Nature and Natural Resources, 1110 Morges, Switzerland.

BUTLER*, Dr Gordon C.: Director, Division of Biology, National Research Council of Canada, Ottawa KIA OR6, Ontario, Canada.

CAIN, Professor Stanley A.: Director, Institute for Environmental Quality, University of Michigan, 2200 North Campus Boulevard, Ann Arbor, Michigan 48105, USA.

CALDWELL, Professor Lynton K.: Department of Political Science, Woodburn Hall, Indiana University, Bloomington, Indiana 47401, USA.

CMEA: *see* Mata and Vadász.

COUNCIL OF EUROPE: *see* Renborg.

DARLING, Sir Frank Fraser: *see* Fraser Darling.

DASMANN, Dr Raymond F.: Senior Ecologist, International Union for Conservation of Nature and Natural Resources, 1110 Morges, Switzerland (also representing IUCN).

DAVIES, Dr David A.: Secretary-General, World Meteorological Organization, 41 Avenue Giuseppe Motta, 1211 Geneva, Switzerland.

DORST, Professor Jean: Directeur, Zoologie: Mammifères et Oiseaux, Muséum National d'Histoire Naturelle, 55 rue de Buffon, 75-Paris V , France.

ECE: *see* Reiner.

ERIKSSON, Mag. Ulf: c/o Nordforsk, Ainonkatu 10, Helsinki 10, Finland (alternate).

EVTEEV, Dr Sveneld Aleksandrovich: Executive Secretary, Earth Sciences Section, Presidium of the Academy of Sciences of the USSR, Leninsky Prospekt 14, Moscow B–71, USSR.

FAO: *see* Mahler.

FOSBERG, Dr F. Raymond: National Museum of Natural History, Smithsonian Institution, Washington, DC 20560, USA.

FRASER DARLING, Sir Frank, DSC, FRSE: Shefford-Woodlands House, Newbury, Berkshire, England (contributor of keynote paper read *in absentia*).

FRIENDS OF THE EARTH: *see* Brower and Matthews.

GAEKWAD, Fatesingh: *see* Baroda, Maharaja of.

GOLDMAN*, Professor Marshall I.: Harvard University Russian Research Center, 1737 Cambridge Street, Cambridge, Massachusetts 02138, USA; Professor of Economics, Wellesley College, Wellesley, Massachusetts 02181, USA.

GOOTJES*, Dr P.: Economist, Rijks Instituut voor de Volksgezondheid, Anthonie van Leeuwenhoeklaan 9, Postbus 1, Bilthoven, Netherlands.

GREVE, Dr P. A.: Laboratory of Toxicology, National Institute of Public Health, Utrecht, Netherlands.

HADAČ*, Professor Emil, DSc.: Director, Institute of Lanscape Ecology, Czechoslovak Academy of Sciences, Průhonice near Praha, Czechoslovakia.

HALINEN, Mr Hannu: Secretary-General, Jyväskylä Arts Festival, Kauppakatu 9 C 36, Jyväskylä, and Munkkisaarenkatu 10 B 10, Helsinki 15, Finland.

HANSEN, Miss Karen: c/o Nordiskt Kontaktorgan för Miljövårdsfrågor, Forureningsrådet sekretariatet, Holmbergsgade 14, DK-1057 København K, Denmark (alternate).

HASHIMOTO, Dr Michio, MD, MPH: c/o Organization for Economic Cooperation and Development, 2 rue André-Pascal, Paris 16°, France; Environmental Pollution Control Section, Welfare Ministry, 1-2 Kasumigazeki, Chiyoda-ku, Tokyo, Japan.

HEINØ, Mr John: Procter & Gamble Ltd, Newcastle Technical Centre, Newcastle upon Tyne, England.

HELA, Professor Ilmo: Director, Merentutkimuslaitos (Institute of Marine Re-

* 'Roving Eminent'—*see* footnote on page 639.

search), Tähtitorninkatu 2, Helsinki 14, Finland (also representing the International Council of Scientific Unions, 7 Via Cornelio Celso, 00161 Rome, Italy).

HELANDER, Dr Elisabeth: c/o Nordforsk, Ainonkatu 10, Helsinki 10, Finland.

HENDERSON, Miss Julia: Secretary-General, International Planned Parenthood Federation, 18-20 Lower Regent Street, London S.W.1, England.

HOLMSTEDT, Mr Sven: c/o Nordiskt Kontaktorgan för Miljövårdsfrågor, Jordbruksministeriet, S-103 10 Stockholm 2, Sweden.

HOLOPAINEN*, Dr Eero: University Institute of Meteorology, Fabianinkatu 33, Helsinki 10, Finland.

HONKARANTA, H. E. Reino: Minister in the Finnish Foreign Ministry, Maasälväntie 16 A, Helsinki 71, Finland.

HOOTON*, H. E. Dr Frank G.: Canadian Ambassador to Finland, Canadian Embassy, P. Esplanadinkatu 25 B, Helsinki 10, Finland.

HOPTHROW*, Brigadier Harry Ewart, CBE: Surrey House, Cowes, Isle of Wight, England.

IAEA: see Apollonov.

ICC: see Paavolainen and Malmi.

ICRC: see Sandberg.

ICSU: see Hela and Mikola.

ILA: see Manner.

IPPF: see Henderson and Johnson.

IUBS: see Baer.

IUCN: see Budowski and Dasmann.

IUS: see Siirilä, and Pentti Väisänen.

JOHNSON*, Mr Stanley: Liaison Officer with International Organizations, International Planned Parenthood Federation, 18-20 Lower Regent Street, London S.W.1, England (also representing IPPF).

KALLIOLA, Professor Reino: Government Councillor for Nature Conservation, Nature Conservation Office, Unioninkatu 40 A, Helsinki 17, Finland (also representing Nordiskt Kontaktorgan för Miljövårdsfrågor).

KAPRIO, Dr Leo, M.D.: Regional Director in Europe, World Health Organization, 8 Scherfigsvej, 2100 København Ø, Denmark; c/o WHO, Avenue Appia, 1211 Geneva 27, Switzerland.

KASALICKÝ, Ing. arch. Václav: Deputy-Director, Research Institute for Building and Architecture, Letenská 3, Malá Strana, Praha 1, Czechoslovakia (contributor of keynote paper presented in absentia).

KASSAS, Professor M.: Professor of Applied Botany, Faculty of Science, University of Cairo, Giza, Egypt, UAR.

KØIE, Professor Mogens: Institute of Ecological Botany, University of Copenhagen, Gothersgade 140, 1123 København K, Denmark.

KOLBIG*, Dr J.: Meteorological Service of the German Democratic Republic, Luckenwalderstrasse 42–46, Potsdam 2, GDR 15, East Germany.

KORTEKANGAS, Professor Paavo: c/o World Council of Churches, 150 route de Ferney, 1211 Geneva 20, Switzerland.

KOVDA, Professor Viktor Abrahamovitch: Subfaculty of Pedology, Moscow State University, Moscow V-234; Director, Institute of Agrochemistry and Soil Science, and corresponding Member, Academy of Sciences of the USSR (contributor of keynote paper presented in absentia).

KRUISINGA, Dr R. J. H.: Ministry of Social Affairs and Public Health, Zeestraat 73, The Hague, Netherlands.†

KUENEN*, Professor Donald J.: Director-General, Rijksinstituut voor Natuurbeheer, Kemperbergerweg 11, Arnhem, Netherlands.

* 'Roving Eminent'—see footnote on page 639.

KUNIN, Professor Vladimir Nikolaivich: Vice-Chairman of the Scientific Council on Environment of the Academy of Sciences of the USSR and of the Soviet State Committee on Science and Technology; Professor and Corresponding Member, Academy of Sciences of the USSR, Leninsky Prospekt 14, Moscow B-71, USSR. Scientific Adviser, United Nations Conference on the Human Environment, Palais des Nations, 1211 Geneva 10, Switzerland (which he also represented).

LAIRD*, Professor Marshall, DSC: Head, Department of Biology, Memorial University of Newfoundland, St John's, Newfoundland, Canada.

LIEVENS, Dr F.: Directeur Général de l'Administration de la Recherche Agronomique, Ministère de l'Agriculture, Tour Madou 20ᵉᵐᵉ étage, 1030 Bruxelles, Belgium.†

LRCS: see Sandberg.

LUTHER, Professor Hans: Helsingin Yliopiston Kasvitieteen Laitos, Unioninkatu 44, Helsinki 17, and Djurgårdsvillan 8, Helsinki 53, Finland.

MÄDE*, Professor Alfred: Agricultural Meteorologist, Sektion Pflanzenproduktion, Martin-Luther-Universität, Halle-Wittenberg, Grosse Steinstrasse 81, 401 Halle (Saale), East Germany.

MAHLER, Mr P. J.: c/o Food and Agriculture Organization, United Nations, Via delle Terme di Caracalla, 00100 Rome, Italy (Senior Officer, Natural Resources and Human Environment, FAO).

MALMI, Mr Ensio: c/o International Chamber of Commerce, 38 Cours Albert 1ᵉʳ, 75-Paris 8ᵉ, France.

MANNER*, Dr Eero: Supreme Court, P. Esplanadinkatu 3, Helsinki 17, Finland (also representing International Law Association, 3 Paper Buildings, Temple, London E.C.4, England).

MANSHARD, Professor Walter: c/o United Nations Educational, Scientific and Cultural Organization, Place de Fontenoy, 75-Paris 7ᵉ, France (Director, Department of Environmental Sciences and Natural Resources Research, UNESCO).

MANSIKKA, Mr Mikko: Division for Planning and Building, Ministry of the Interior, Et. Esplanaadi 10, Helsinki 13, Finland.

MATA, Dr Béla: c/o Council for Mutual Economic Assistance (CEV), Prospekt Kalinina 56, Moscow K-31, USSR.

MATTHEWS*, Mr Edwin Spencer, Jr: Coudert Frères, 52 Avenue des Champs-Elysées, Paris 8ᵉ, France (also representing Friends of the Earth).

MELLANBY, Dr Kenneth, SCD, CBE: Director, Monks Wood Experimental Station (The Nature Conservancy), Abbots Ripton, Huntingdon, England.

MIKOLA, Professor Peitsa: Professor of Forest Biology, University Department of Silviculture, Unioninkatu 40 B, Helsinki 17, Finland (also representing the International Council of Scientific Unions, 7 Via Cornelio Celso, 00161 Rome, Italy).

MILLER*, Dr Richard Gordon: Director, Foresta Institute for Ocean and Mountain Studies, Route 1, Box 620, Carson City, Nevada 89701, USA.

MOORE, Dr Norman W.: Head, Toxic Chemicals and Wildlife Section, Monks Wood Experimental Station (The Nature Conservancy), Abbots Ripton, Huntingdon, England.

MUNCH-PETERSEN, Mr Finn: c/o United Nations Development Programme, 8 Sankt Annae Plads, 1250 København K, Denmark, and 866 United Nations Plaza, New York, NY 10017, USA.

MUSTELIN, Dr Nils: c/o Nordforsk, Head, Secretariat for Environmental Sciences, Lonnrotsgatan 37, Helsinki 18, Finland.

NICULAC, Dipl. Ing. Teodosic V.: Secrétaire de la Commission pour la Préservation de l'Environnement de l'Académie de R. S. de Roumanie, Rue Victoriei 125, Bucharest, Romania.†

* 'Roving Eminent'—see footnote on page 639.

NORDFORSK: *see* Helander, Mustelin, and Eriksson (alternate).

NORDISKT KONTAKTORGAN FÖR MILJÖVÅRDSFRÅGOR: *see* Kalliola and Holmstedt; also Hansen and Saether (alternates).

NUORTEVA*, Dr Pekka: Division of Entomology, Zoological Museum of the University, P. Rautatiekatu 19, Helsinki 10, Finland.

NYBERG, Dr Alf: Director-General, Swedish Meteorological and Hydrological Institute, Fridhemsgatan 9, Stockholm 12, Sweden (President of World Meteorological Organization until 1971, and also representing WMO).

OECD: *see* Hashimoto and Roderick.

PAAVOLAINEN, Mr Eero-Pekka: c/o International Chamber of Commerce, Cours Albert 1ᵉʳ, 75-Paris 8ᵉ, France.

PALMSTIERNA, Professor Hans: Environment Advisory Committee, Department of Agriculture, S-103 10 Stockholm 2, Sweden.

PANIKKAR, Professor N. K. DSC: Director, National Institute of Oceanography, Miramar, Panaji-Goa, India.

PAVANELLO, Dr Renato: World Health Organization, Avenue Appia, 1211 Geneva 27, Switzerland (also representing WHO).

PEKKANEN*, Dr Raimo: Supreme Administrative Court, P. Esplanadinkatu 3, Helsinki 17, Finland.

PERIÄINEN, Dr Tapio: Mannerheimin Lastensuojeluliitto, 2 linja 17, Helsinki 53, Finland.

POLUNIN, Professor Nicholas, DSC: Editor of *Biological Conservation* and of *Plant Science Monographs*, etc., 15 chemin F.-Lehmann, 1218 Grand-Saconnex, Geneva, Switzerland.

POLUNIN, Mr Nicholas V.C.: Christ Church, Oxford, England.

RAYZACHER, Dr B.: Stichting Concawe, President Kennedylaan 21, The Hague 2012, Netherlands.

REINER, Mr B. F.: c/o Economic Commission for Europe, Palais des Nations, 1211 Geneva 10, Switzerland (Deputy-Director, Division of Environment and Housing, ECE.).

RENBORG, Dr Sten: c/o Council of Europe, Maison de l'Europe, 67 Strasbourg, France.

RODERICK, Dr Hilliard: c/o Organization for Economic Cooperation and Development, 2 rue André-Pascal, Paris 16ᵉ, France.

SAETHER, Mr Leif: c/o Nordiskt Kontaktorgan för Miljövårdsfrågor, Industridepartement, Akersgatan 42, Oslo-Dep., Oslo 1, Norway (alternate).

SANDBERG, Miss Eila: c/o International Committee of the Red Cross, 7 Avenue de la Paix, 1202 Geneva, Switzerland, and c/o League of Red Cross Societies, 17 chemin des Crêts, 1211 Petit-Saconnex, Geneva, Switzerland.

SEIDENFADEN*, H. E. Dr Gunnar: Ministry of Foreign Affairs, 1218 København K, Denmark.

SIIKALA, Department Chief Kalervo: Director, Department of International Relations, Ministry of Education, Rauhankatu 4, Helsinki 17, Finland.

SIIRILÄ, Mr Tapio: c/o International Union of Students, 3 Voclova, Praha 2, Czechoslovakia.

SILLANTAUS, Member of Parliament Pentti: Käsälä 6, Jyväskylä, Finland (Chairman of Jyväskylä Arts Festival).

SIPPONEN, Professor Kauko: Niemenmäentie 3 G 53, Helsinki 35, Finland.

SKULBERG, Cand.real. Olav M.: Norwegian Institute for Water Research, Gaustadalléen 25, 260 Blindern, Oslo 3, Norway.

SÖYRINKI*, Professor Niilo: Visuvesi; also Topelinksenkatu 10 A, Helsinki 25, Finland.

STENIUS*, Dr Sten: Box 33, Kotka, Finland.

* 'Roving Eminent'—*see* footnote on page 639.

THACHER, Mr Peter S.: c/o United Nations Conference on the Human Environment, Palais des Nations, 1211 Geneva 10, Switzerland (Senior Programme Director, U.N. Conference on the Human Environment).

UDALL, The Hon. Stewart L.: Chairman of the Board of Overview, 1700 Pennsylvania Avenue, Washington, DC 20006, USA.

UNDP: *see* Munch-Petersen.

UNESCO: *see* Manshard.

UN CONFERENCE ON THE HUMAN ENVIRONMENT: *see* Kunin and Thacher.

VADÁSZ, Dr Zoltan: c/o Council for Mutual Economic Assistance (CEV), Prospekt Kalinina 56, Moscow K-31, USSR.

VÄISÄNEN, Mr Pentti: c/o International Union of Students, 3 Voclova, Praha 2, Czechoslovakia.

VALLENTYNE, Dr John R.: Scientific Leader, Eutrophication Section, Freshwater Institute, 501 University Crescent, Winnipeg 19, Manitoba, and Environmental Quality Directorate, Sir Charles Tupper Building, Ottawa, Ontario, Canada.

VERKOREN, Ir J.: Director of Nature Conservation and Landscape Planning, State Forest Service, Museumlaan 2, Utrecht, Netherlands.†

VRECKEM, Mr A. van: Adviser to Ministry of Economic Affairs, 23 Square de Mecus, Bruxelles, Belgium.†

WARIS*, Chancellor Klaus: Helsinki School of Economics and Business Administration, Runeberginkatu 14-16, Helsinki 10, Finland.

WHO; *see* Kaprio and Pavanello.

WMO: *see* Davies and Nyberg.

WORLD COUNCIL OF CHURCHES: *see* Kortekangas.

WORTHINGTON, Dr E. Barton: Scientific Director, International Biological Programme, 7 Marylebone Road, London NW1, England.

WURSTER, Dr Charles F., Jr: Associate Professor of Environmental Sciences, Marine Sciences Research Center, State University of New York, Stony Brook, New York, 11790, USA.

WWF: *see* Baroda.

WYNNE-EDWARDS*, Professor Vero C., DSC, FRS: Department of Zoology, University of Aberdeen, Tillydrone Avenue, Aberdeen, Scotland (Chairman, U.K. Natural Environment Research Council and Member, Royal Commission on Environmental Pollution).

REPRESENTATIVES OF FINNISH ORGANIZATIONS AND INSTITUTIONS

Academy of Finland: Professor Helge GYLLENBERG, Lic. Matti LÄHDEOJA; Bulevardi 28, Helsinki 12.

Association of Finnish Architects: Techn. lic. Jere MAULA; Unioninkatu 30 A, Helsinki 10.

Board for Farming: Maist. Niilo HINTIKKA; Mariankatu 23, Helsinki 17.

Board of Forestry: Maist. J. PIIRONEN, Maist. T. LEHVÄSLAIHO; Erottajankatu 2, Helsinki 12.

Board for Roads and Water Building: Mr Ario REINOLA, Mr Ora PATOHARJU; Et. Esplanadinkatu 4, Helsinki 13.

Central Association of Finnish Woodworking Industries: Mr. Eero-Pekka PAAVOLAINEN, Dipl. Ins. Ensio MALMI; Et. Esplanadinkatu 2, Helsinki 13.

Central Forestry Board: Mr Toivo MATILAINEN; Salomonkatu 17 B, Helsinki 10.

Central Union for Regional Planning: Architect Timo MATTELMÄKI; Aurorankatu 19 A, Helsinki 10.

Centre for Economic Planning: Director Erkki LAATTO; Erotajankatu 15–17, Helsinki 13.

* 'Roving Eminent'—*see* footnote on page 639.

Environmental Committee 2000: Mag. Olli PAASIVIRTA; c/o Aro, Laajasalontie 69, Helsinki 84.

Finnish Association for Nature Protection: President Dr Olli OJALA, Dr Sten STENIUS; Fredrikinkatu 77 A 11, Helsinki 10.

Finnish Egyptological Society: Maist. Rostislav HOLTHOER, Chairman; Snellmaninkatu 9–11, Helsinki 17, Finland.

Finnish Central Trade Union: Dipl. Ins. Heikki LOPPI; Paasivuorenkatu 5 B, Helsinki 53.

Finnish Environmental Council: Secretary-General Ilppo KANGAS, Maist Harri DAHLSTRÖM, Maist. Olavi MARTIKAINEN, Dr Olli OJALA, Dr Pertti SEISKARI, Dr Weijo WAINIO, Miss Irma KARIO, Ekon Kati KEMILÄINEN; Prime Minister's Office, Aleksanterinkatu 3 I, Helsinki 17.

Finnish Forest Research Institute: Dr Matti PALO; Unioninkatu 40 A, Helsinki 17.

Finnish Union for Industry: General Director Oiva LEHMUS; Eteläranta 10, Helsinki 13.

Forest Research Institute Nature Conservation Office: Professor Reino KALLIOLA, Dr Antti HAAPANEN; Unioninkatu 40 A, Helsinki 17.

Game and Fisheries Research Institute: Dr Matti HELMINEN; Unioninkatu 45 B 42, Helsinki 17.

Helsinki City: Mr Ora PATOHARJU; P. Esplanadinkatu 11-13, Helsinki 17.

Institute of Occupational Health: Mr Alec ESTLANDER; Haartmaninkatu 1, Helsinki 25.

Institute of Marine Research: Professor Ilmo HELA, Director: Tähtitorninkatu 2, Helsinki 14.

League for Domicile Associations: Mr Martti LINKOLA; Kluuvikatu 8, Helsinki 10.

Meteorological Institute: Dr Veikko ROSSI, Dr Antti KULMALA, Lic. Daniel SÖDERMAN; Vuorikatu 24, Helsinki 10.

Ministry of Agriculture and Forestry: Administrative Councellor Paavo VÄISÄNEN, Ritarikatu 2 B, Helsinki 17.

Ministry of Commerce and Industry: Dr Pekka LINKO; Aleksanterinkatu 10, Helsinki 17.

Ministry of Justice: Legislative Counsellor Kalervo AIRAKSINEN; Ritarikatu 2, Helsinki 17.

National Board of Waters: Dipl. Ins. Seppo J. SAARI, Maist. Sakari KERMINEN, Maist. Pirkko LINNILÄ, Maist. Emelie ENCKELL, Maist. Marja-Liisa POIKOLAINEN, Maist. Kimmo KARIMO; Pohj. Esplanadikatu 37, Helsinki 10.

National Union of Finnish Students: Mr Pentti VÄISÄNEN, Mr Tapio SIIRILÄ, Mannerheimintie 5 C, Helsinki 10.

Natur- och Miljövård: Member of Parliament Per STENBÄCK, Managerial Director Lars BLOMBERG; Lappviksgatan 13 A, Helsinki 18.

Nordforsk (Scandinavian Council for Applied Research): Dr Nils MUSTELIN, Dr Elisabeth HELANDER, Mag. Ulf ERIKSSON; Lönnrotsgatan 3y, Helsinki 18.

Prime Minister's Office: Research Fellow Irmeli MUSTONEN, Research Fellow Ilpo TAKENEN; Aleksanterinkatu 3 D, Helsinki 17.

Regional Planning Association of South-West Finland; Mr Osmo KONTTURI; Kristiinankatu 1, SF-20100 Turku 10.

SITRA (Finnish National Fund for Research and Development): Chancellor Klaus WARIS, Professor Eino TUNKELO, Dipl. Ins. Jali M. RUUSKANEN; Uudenmaankatu 16–20, Helsinki 12.

State Institute for Technical Research: Lic. Veikko T. RAUHALA; Lönnrotinkatu 37, Helsinki 18.

Suomenlahti-toimikunta (Gulf of Finland Committee): Dr R. LAAKSONEN; P. Esplanadinkatu 37, Helsinki 10.

Union of Finnish Engineers: Engineer Kari IMMONEN, Engineer Paavo RISTOLA; Yrjönkatu 30, Helsinki 10.

University of Oulu: Dr J. HAVAS; Pakkahuoneenkatu 12, Oulu.

University of Technology (Helsinki): Mr Markku NURMI; Otaniemi.

University of Turku: Professor K. K. SIEVERS; Yliopistonmäki, Turku 2.

University of Turku, Department of Zoology: Dr Rauno TENOVUO; Yliopistonmäki, Turku 2.

In addition there were about fifty members of the Finnish press, radio, and television services present, while a few foreign journalists attended. With simultaneous interpretation provided into and from Finnish and Russian, the meetings were open to the general public, who were present in fair numbers—particularly on the initial and final days, when the back hall was opened and the accommodation extended to something approaching 1,000.

Appendix 11

MEMBERS OF COMMITTEES

1. INTERNATIONAL STEERING COMMITTEE

Professor Nicholas POLUNIN, 15 Chemin F.-Lehmann, 1218 Grand-Saconnex, Geneva, Switzerland (Chairman).

Sir Julian HUXLEY, 31 Pond Street, Hampstead, London NW3, England (Scientific Patron and Consultant).

Dr Raymond F. DASMANN, Senior Ecologist, IUCN, 1110 Morges, Switzerland.

Dr David A. DAVIES, Secretary-General, World Meteorological Organization, 41 Avenue Giuseppe Motta, 1211 Geneva, Switzerland.

Professor Reino KALLIOLA, Government Councillor for Nature Conservation, Unioninkatu 40 A, Helsinki 17, Finland.

Professor V. A. KOVDA, Subfaculty of Pedology, Moscow State University, Moscow, V-234, USSR.

Professor Hans LUTHER, Djurgårdsvillan 8, Helsinki 53, Finland.

Professor Anna MEDWECKA-KORNAŚ, Nature Conservation Research Centre, Ul. Lublicz 46, Kraków, Poland.

Dr Tapio PERIÄINEN, Mannerheimin Lastensuojeluliitto, 2 linja 17, Helsinki 53, Finland.

Professor Kauko SIPPONEN, Niemenmäenti 3 G 53, Helsinki 35, Finland.

2. FINNISH ORGANIZING COMMITTEE

H. E. Dr Ahti KARJALAINEN, Prime Minister, Prime Minister's Office, Aleksanterinkatu 3 D, Helsinki 17 (Chairman).

Professor Kauko SIPPONEN, Niemenmäentie 3 G 53, Helsinki 35 (Vice-Chairman).

H. E. Reino HONKARANTA, Maasälväntie 16 A, Helsinki 71.

Dr Pertti SEISKARI, University Faculty of Agriculture and Forestry, Fabianinkatu 35, Helsinki 17.

Department Chief Kalervo SIIKALA, Rauhankatu 4, Helsinki 17.

M. P. Pentti SILLANTAUS, Käsälä 6, Jyväskylä.

Secretary-General Hannu HALINEN, Jyväskylä Arts Festival, Kauppakatu 9 C 36, Jyväskylä, and Munkkisaarenkatu 10 B 10, Helsinki 15.

3. RESOLUTIONS COMMITTEE

Professor Kauko SIPPONEN, Niemenmäentie 3 G 53, Helsinki 35 (Chairman).

Professor Jean G. BAER, Directeur, Institut de Zoologie, Université de Neuchâtel, 2000 Neuchâtel 7, Switzerland.

Professor M. KASSAS, Department of Botany, Faculty of Science, University of Cairo, Giza, Egypt, UAR.

Professor Donald J. Kuenen, Director-General, Rijksinstituut voor Natuurbeheer, Kemperbergerweg 11, Arnhem, Netherlands.

Professor V. N. Kunin, Academy of Sciences of the USSR, Leninsky Prospekt 14, Moscow B-71, USSR, and Scientific Adviser, United Nations Conference on The Human Environment, Palais des Nations, 1211 Geneva 10, Switzerland.

Professor Hans Luther, Djurgårdsvillan 8, Helsinki 53, Finland.

Dr Norman W. Moore, Head, Toxic Chemicals and Wildlife Section, Monks Wood Experimental Station (The Nature Conservancy), Abbots Ripton, Huntingdon, England.

The Hon. Stewart L. Udall, Chairman of the Board of Overview, 1700 Pennsylvania Avenue, Washington, DC 20006, USA.

Index

54, 55, 56, 70, 86, 97, 98, 99, 118, 156, 162, 168–71, 205–7, 324–5, 327, 328, 330–1, 351, 353, 393, 411, 416, 462, 464, 492, 504–5, 507, 538, 539–41, 620, 637
Polunin, N. V. C., Jr, 284–5, 321, 349, 352
Ponnamperuma, C., 29
Population: see under Human Population
Population explosion, 205, 285, 420–1, 426, 429, 430, 447, 456, 616
Porter, R. D., 299, 310
Porterfield, W. A., 221, 235
Poverty, 7, 8
Powers, T. F., 192
Precipitation total, 187
Prestt, I., 337, 344
Prigogine, I., 25, 29
'Primordial soup', 24
Pritchard, T., 604, 607
Probionts, 25
Property and laws, 616
Proteins, 23, 24, 46
Protobionts, 25
Prouty, R. M., 309
Prudhoe, Bay, Alaska, 482
Psychosomatic depression, 13
Public health pesticides, 94
Public transport, 469
Publicity, 91–2, 169
Pugwash Conferences, 434
Pullman, B., 29
Purines, 23–4
Pyramidines, synthesis of, 24

Quality of life, 194, 203, 631–2
Quarantine, 20, 39, 98

Ra and Ra II (rafts), 288
Rabies, 238
Radiation, from fallout, 461
Radiation, natural, 34
Radioactive pollution, 72, 119, 124, 161, 162, 262, 279
Radioactivity, sources of, 161–2
Radl, S. L., 47, 52
Radomski, J. L., 304, 309
Rajputana Desert, 139, 140, 141, 142, 143
Randtke, A., 272, 309
Rasmussen, K., 481
Ratcliffe, D. A., 299, 300, 309
Ray, C., 77, 86, 251, 255, 264, 266, 272, 623, 624, 627
Rayzacher, B., 572–3, 628
Recreation, 225, 534
Recycling, 48, 190, 211, 490, 501–2, 586
Reed, J. C., 83, 86
Regression (ecological), 36
Reichel, W. L., 309
Reiner, B. F., 470–1, 533–5

Relic species, 61
Renborg, S., 506
Resources of world, use of, 15, 16, 81, 414
Revelle, R., 61–2
Rhine, 315, 340, 404
Rice, T. R., 254, 272
Ricker, W. E., 279
Ripper, W. E., 301, 306, 309
Risebrough, R. W., 296, 300, 310
River Thames, 5, 11, 48
Rivers, total water in, 186
Road accidents, 281
Robinson, G. A., 271
Rockefeller, J. D., 97
Roden, G. I., 230, 235
Roderick, H., 318
Rodier, J., 219, 235
Rodin, L. E., 46, 50
Roosevelt, T., 10, 398
Rosenau, D. G., 308
Rubey, W. W., 186, 199
Rudd, R. L., 298, 310
Rudolph, E. D., 40, 52
Run-off following rains, 71, 367–8
Rush, H. H., 485
Russell, R. S., 34, 52, 72, 86, 265, 272

Sahara, 48, 389
Said, R., 217, 235
Salinization of soil, 82, 190, 242, 374–5
Sand, P. H., 619
Sankaranarayanan, K., 72, 85
Santa Barbara, 76
Schild, R., 235
Schistosomiasis, 245
Schlueter, R. S., 50
Schweitzer, A., 425, 436, 588
Science as remedy, 8
Scientific integrity, 11
Scientists and politics, 202, 426, 572
Scudder, T., 223, 235
Seabirds and oil, 73, 255–6
Sea-level changes, 407–8
Seaman, D. E., 221, 235
Sears, P., 11, 13, 71, 86
Sediments, 35
Seed dressings of organomercury, 340
'Seeding' of clouds, 336
Seidenfaden, G., 164, 166, 172
Serebrovskaya, K., 29
Seventer, H. A. van, 339, 344
Sewage treatment, 190
Shaler, N., 10, 13
Shaposhniker, L. K., 98
Shellfish production, 254
Shiff, C. J., 224, 235
Siberian rivers, 241, 246
Siikala, K., ix, 463, 464, 471